# ISLAM

## AN ILLUSTRATED HISTORY

by
G.S.P. Freeman-Grenville
and
Stuart Christopher Munro-Hay

continuum

NEW YORK • LONDON

2006

The Continuum International Publishing Group Inc
80 Maiden Lane, New York, NY 10038

The Continuum International Publishing Group Ltd
The Tower Building, 11 York Road, London SE1 7NX

www.continuumbooks.com

Revised and Expanded edition of
*Historical Atlas of Islam*

Portions of this volume have been published previously as
*Historical Atlas of the Middle East*
*The New Atlas of African History*

Copyright © 1991, 1993, 2002 by Carta, the Israel Map and Publishing Company, Ltd.

All rights reserved. No part of this book may be reproduced, stored in a retrieval system, or transmitted, in any form or by any means, electronic, mechanical, photocopying, recording, or otherwise, without the written permission of the publishers.

Printed in the United States of America

Library of Congress Cataloging-in-Publication Data
Freeman-Grenville, G.S.P. (Greville Stewart Parker)
Historical atlas of Islam / by G.S.P. Freeman-Grenville and Stuart Christopher Munro-Hay.
p. cm.
Includes bibliographical references and index.
ISBN 0-8264-1417-6
Islam : an illustrated history ISBN 0-8264-1837-6 (paperback : alk. paper)
1. Islamic countries—Historical geography—Maps. 2. Islamic countries—Civilization—Maps. I. Munro-Hay, S.C. (Stuart C.), 1947- II. Title.
G1786.S1 F7 2002
911`.17671–dc21

2002031019

Printed in Israel

# TABLE OF CONTENTS

Preface ..................................................................................................xi
Glossary .............................................................................................xiii

I. **Introduction: Before the Hijra of the Prophet Muhammad** ...............1
   Middle East — Physical ..................................................................1
   Middle East — Mean Annual Rainfall............................................3
   Middle East — Vegetation...............................................................3
   Middle East — Agriculture and Livestock ....................................4
   The Ancient Middle East, c. 2050–1000 BC .................................5
   Ancient Egypt ..................................................................................8
   The Seaborne Phoenician Empire ................................................10
   Ancient Israel and Its Neighbors, 10th to 6th centuries BC.......12
   The Empire of Persia ....................................................................15
   Alexander the Great's Empire and Its Division
      Amongst His Successors ........................................................17
   Rome in the Middle East...............................................................19
   Middle Eastern Commerce c. AD 50 ...........................................21
   Commerce with the Middle East c. AD 50..................................22
   The Expansion of Christianity, 1st to 6th centuries ...................23
   Arabia at the Time of the Birth of Muhammad
      c.570 until the Caliphate of Abu Bakr...................................25
   Claudius Ptolemy's Map of Arabia ..............................................26
   The Middle East at the Time of the Birth of Muhammad..........27
   Semitic Languages and the Development of the Art of Writing....28
   History of the Alphabet ................................................................30

II. **From the Hijra (AD 622) until the End of
   the Umayyad Dynasty (750)**.........................................................32
   The Arab Conquest of Syria, Iraq and Persia .............................32
   The Arab Conquest of Egypt........................................................35
   The Arab Conquest of North Africa and Spain..........................37
   The Umayyad Caliphate ...............................................................40

III. **From the Abbasid Dynasty until the Crusades (750–1087)** ............42
   The Abbasid Caliphate .................................................................42
   Arabs in the Mediterranean in the 9th century .........................44
   The Spanish Umayyads and the Emirate....................................46
   Islamic Dynasties in the East, 9th to 11th centuries..................49
   The City of Baghdad, 9th century ...............................................51
   The City of Samarra, 9th century ................................................54

Dynasties in North-West Africa...54
Tulunids (820–872) and Ikshidids (935–969) in Egypt...57
Tahirids (868–905), Saffarids (867–908), and Samanids (874–909)...59
Qarmatian, Shi'ite and Other Dynasties (800–1281)...61
The World as Known to al-Masoudi (d. 956)...64
The World as Depicted by Ibn Hawqal, c. 988...65
The Umayyads in Spain (950–1050)...67
The Fatimids in North Africa and in Egypt, 904–1171...69
North-West Africa after the Fatimids, 11th and 12th centuries...72
Conquests and Dominions of Mahmud of Ghazna (997–1030) and His Successors...74
Los Reyes de Taifas, or Party Kings, of Spain, c. 1009–1286...76
The Almoravid Domains...79
The Almoravids in North Africa and Spain, 1056–1147...80

## IV. Latin Kingdoms and Muslims...81
Christianity and Islam at the Close of the 11th century...81
The Crusades, 1095–1291...84
Crusader Principalities, 1096–1291...86
The Latin Kingdom of Jerusalem and Principalities...87
The Seljuq Turks, 1077–1307...88
The Almohads in North Africa and Spain, 1130–1269...91
Saladin and the Ayyubid Domains, 1169–1250...94
The World as depicted by al-Idrisi...94
The City of Cairo, from the beginning until 1517...96
The Ghurids in Afghanistan and North India, 1175–1206...98
Successor States of the Almohads in North Africa, 1200–1560...100
The Mamluks in Egypt, 1250–1517...102
The City of Jerusalem...105
The City of Mecca...108
The City of Medina...110
The Spanish Reconquista, 13th to 15th centuries...112

## V. The Further Spread of Islam...115

### (i) India...115
The Indian Sub-Continent — Physical...115
The Indian Sub-Continent — Annual Rainfall...117
The Indian Sub-Continent — Vegetation...118
The Indian Sub-Continent — Agriculture and Livestock...119
The Sultanate of Delhi, 13th century to 1525...120
Travels of Ibn Battuta in Sind, India, Maldives and Ceylon...123
The Mughul Emperors of India, 1526–1858...126
The British in India and Partition, 1947...131

Portuguese Possessions in India and the
Far East to the 20th century ................................................................. 134

**(ii) Central Asia and the Middle East** ................................................. 137
Central Asia — Physical ........................................................................ 137
Central Asia — Annual Rainfall ............................................................ 139
Central Asia — Vegetation .................................................................... 140
Central Asia — Agriculture and Livestock ........................................... 141
Campaigns of Hulagu Khan and His Generals, 1253–1260 ................. 142
Commerce in the Middle Ages .............................................................. 144
Travels of Ibn Battuta 1324–1348 ......................................................... 147
Travels of Ibn Battuta in North Africa .................................................. 148
Travels of Ibn Battuta in Hejaz and Iraq .............................................. 150
Travels of Ibn Battuta in Southern Persia and the Gulf ...................... 151
Travels of Ibn Battuta in Egypt and Syria ............................................ 152
Travels of Ibn Battuta in Anatolia,
the Black Sea and Constantinople ................................................... 152
The Spread of the Black Death, 1331–1368 ........................................ 153
The Dominions of Timur-Leng (Tamerlane), 1360–1405 ................... 156
The Expansion of the Ottoman Dominions, c. 1300–1520 ................. 159
The Il-Khanids of Persia, 1236–1353 ................................................... 161
The Timurids, 1369–1506, and Shaybanids, 1506–1570 .................... 163
The Safavids in Persia, 1501–1737 ....................................................... 165

**(iii) Eastern Africa** ................................................................................ 168
Eastern Africa — Physical ..................................................................... 168
Eastern Africa — Annual Rainfall ......................................................... 170
Eastern Africa — Vegetation ................................................................. 171
Eastern Africa — Agriculture and Livestock ........................................ 172
Nubia and Ethiopia, c. 600 .................................................................... 174
Ethiopia and Eastern Africa, c. 1200–c. 1500 ...................................... 176
Travels of Ibn Battuta in Yemen and East Africa ................................ 177
Nubia and Ethiopia, c. 1200–c. 1500 .................................................... 178
Ethiopia, c. 1200–c. 1500 ...................................................................... 180
East Africa, 13th to 16th centuries ....................................................... 182
The Lamu Archipelago and Ancient Sites ............................................ 184
Zanzibar and Pemba ............................................................................... 186
Eastern African Trade in the Indian Ocean, c. 1500 ........................... 188
Ethiopia, 16th to 19th centuries ........................................................... 190
The Portuguese off Eastern Africa, 1498–1698, South Arabia,
and the Route to the Indies .............................................................. 193
The Dominions of Oman in East Africa, 1698-1913 ........................... 196

- (iv) **Western Africa** ............ 198
  - Western Africa — Physical ............ 198
  - Western Africa — Annual Rainfall ............ 200
  - Western Africa — Vegetation ............ 201
  - Western Africa — Agriculture and Livestock ............ 202
  - The Western Sudan in the 11th century ............ 203
  - The Western Sudan in the 12th to 14th centuries ............ 205
  - Northern African Trade with the Western Sudan, 13th–14th centuries ............ 207
  - The Moroccan Conquest of Songhai, 1591–1753 ............ 210
  - The Western Sudan, 16th and 17th centuries ............ 212
  - The Western Sudan, 18th and 19th centuries ............ 214

- (v) **South-East Asia** ............ 216
  - South-East Asia — Physical ............ 216
  - South-East Asia — Annual Rainfall ............ 218
  - South-East Asia — Vegetation ............ 220
  - South-East Asia — Agriculture and Livestock ............ 221
  - Early Seaborne Contacts, 7th to 15th centuries ............ 223
  - Early Islam in China, 7th to 14th centuries ............ 224
  - Islam in China, 15th to 20th centuries ............ 228
  - Islamic Communities in Arakan, Myanmar (Burma) and Tibet, 9th–20th centuries ............ 232
  - Islamic Inscriptions in Malaysia and Indonesia, 11th to 15th centuries ............ 233
  - Marco Polo's Sumatra, 1292 ............ 235
  - Marco Polo's Travels, Late 13th century ............ 236
  - Early Islam in Sumatra, Ibn Battuta's Visit, 1345–1346 ............ 237
  - The Malaccan Sultanate at its Greatest Extent, 15th century to 1511 ............ 239
  - The Spread of Islam in Sumatra and Java, 15th to 17th centuries ............ 241
  - The Spread of Islam in Borneo, Sulawesi and the Moluccas, 15th to 17th centuries ............ 244
  - Siam, the Malay States and Britain, 15th to 20th centuries ............ 247
  - Travels of Ibn Battuta in China, Assam and South-East Asia ............ 249
  - Tomé Pires' Account of Trade, c. 1515 ............ 250
  - Islam in Southern Thailand, 17th to 19th centuries ............ 250
  - Islam in Cambodia and among the Chams, 17th to 20th centuries ............ 253
  - South-East Asia and Britain, 17th to 20th centuries ............ 255
  - Islam in the Philippines, 15th to 20th centuries ............ 257

## VI. The Ottoman World and European Imperialism .......... 260
    The Ottoman Empire at its Greatest Extent,
        16th to 17th centuries .......... 260
    Ottoman Territories in Europe, 16th to 17th centuries .......... 264
    The Filali Sharifs of Morocco, from 1631 .......... 265
    The Ottoman Empire in Decline, 1699–1913 .......... 267
    The French in Egypt and Syria, 1798–1804 .......... 270
    The Barbary States, 17th and 18th centuries .......... 271
    The United States War with Tripoli, 1801–1815 .......... 274
    The Egyptian Campaign in the Hejaz, 1812–1818 .......... 276
    The Egyptian Campaign in the Sudan, 1820–1880 .......... 279
    Ibrahim Pasha's Campaign in Greece, 1824–1833 .......... 281
    The Egyptian Campaign in Syria, 1831–1841 .......... 282
    The Suez Canal, 1869, and World Trade .......... 284
    Islam in Africa, 7th to 20th centuries .......... 288
    Notable European Travelers in the East,
        14th to 16th centuries .......... 291
    Notable European Travelers in the Middle East,
        18th to 20th centuries .......... 293
    Russian Expansion into Central Asia .......... 296
    European Penetration of Africa, up to 1830 .......... 299
    European Penetration of Africa, up to 1890 .......... 301
    Dutch Possessions in Indonesia, 17th century .......... 302
    Dutch Possessions in Indonesia, from the 18th century .......... 305
    Portuguese Possessions in Africa, 20th century .......... 308
    Former Spanish Possessions in West Africa .......... 310
    Egypt and Other Powers, 20th century .......... 312
    The Sudan, 19th and 20th centuries .......... 313

## VII. The Twentieth Century .......... 316
    The Expansion of Saudi Arabia, 20th century .......... 316
    World War I: The Turkish Fronts in the Caucasus, Syria,
        Mesopotamia and Arabia .......... 318
    The Hejaz Railway .......... 320
    The Arab Revolt .......... 321
    World War I: Gallipoli, 1915–1916 .......... 323
    The Middle East Following the Treaty of Versailles, 1919 .......... 325
    The Jewish Diaspora, 1920s–1930s .......... 327
    Palestine, from the Peel Commission to the
        War of Independence .......... 331
    World War II: Egypt and North Africa, 1940–1941 .......... 334
    World War II: Sudan, Ethiopia and Somalia, 1941 .......... 336
    World War II: Iraq and Iran, 1941 .......... 338

Decolonization of the Middle East, 1946–1967 ............................................. 340
The First Arab-Israeli War, 1948 ..................................................................... 342
Immigration to Israel, from 15 May 1948 ...................................................... 344
The Suez War, 1956 .......................................................................................... 346
The Second Arab-Israeli War, 1967 ................................................................ 348
The Third Arab-Israeli War, 1973 ................................................................... 350
The United Arab Emirates and the Gulf States ............................................ 352
Israel, Lebanon and Syria ................................................................................ 354
The Iraq-Iran War, 1980-1988 ........................................................................ 356
The Russo-Afghan War, 1979–1988 ............................................................... 358
Former Russian Islamic Countries in Asia,
    from the 20th century ................................................................................. 360
The Union of North and South Yemen, 1990 ............................................... 362
Minorities in the Middle East ......................................................................... 364
Kuwait, 1991 ..................................................................................................... 367

**VIII. Islam in 2002** ........................................................................................... 370
Political and Population .................................................................................. 370
Natural Resources ............................................................................................ 372
Higher and Religious Education, Literacy .................................................... 374
Islam in the Balkans ........................................................................................ 376
The Palestinian Diaspora ................................................................................ 379
Israel and Palestinian Areas and Settlements .............................................. 381
The Pilgrimage to Mecca ................................................................................ 384
Afghanistan in 2002 ......................................................................................... 387
Islam in the World Today ............................................................................... 389
Islam and the West, 2002 ................................................................................ 392

INDEX ................................................................................................................ 397

# PREFACE

THE birth of Islam in Arabia in the seventh century was to entail geopolitical changes of the first magnitude. In the first surge of the Muslim armies out of Arabia they wrested the eastern lands of the Roman empire from the polity that had ruled them for almost seven hundred years; by destroying the Persian empire they ended the centuries-long rivalry of the Christian Roman and Zoroastrian Persian "superpowers." In the west the Muslims took over the whole of North Africa and occupied part of Spain; they even crossed over the Pyrenees and pushed deep into France and Switzerland, while in the east they penetrated as far as the outlying fringes of the defunct Persian empire and to Afghanistan.

Even if the monolithic structure of the early Islamic state was soon to fragment, the religion was still destined to spread vigorously. There were two main methods of propagation. One was the result of outright military conquest. Even if the Qur'an explicitly forbade the imposition of Islam by force, social and financial pressures, combined with the prestige of the conquerors, were highly effective. Christians, Jews and Zoroastrians, commonly called "people of the book," were required to pay a tax that Muslims did not pay. The second method was by the slow penetration of Muslim merchants, who would set up trade and market centres, sometimes resulting in the conversion of the local inhabitants to Islam. In religion, Islam claimed to constitute a restoration of the simple faith of Abraham, a strict monotheism, an element that may have assisted its adoption in some of the vast Christian regions taken in the early conquests.

Later phases of the penetration of Islam involved very substantial areas of the world. A good part of the Indian subcontinent was conquered by Muslim armies, as was the rest of the Eastern Roman Empire, and substantial regions of eastern Europe to the borders of Hungary. In Africa, slower penetration deep into West Africa founded powerful Muslim empires. In eastern Africa mosques already existed on the Swahili coast by the eighth century A.D. The ancient Christian state of Nubia became Muslim in the fourteenth century, and parts of Ethiopia too came under Muslim control. Islam in Central Asia is evoked by the names of some great cities beautified by Muslim rulers: Bukhara, Khiva, Samarqand. It also spread in Kashgar and Chinese Turkestan, and communities were established in China as well. Seaborne penetration into the East Indies established yet more distant outposts of the faith in Sumatra, Malaya and Indonesia, a process that has continued until the present day.

The Atlas depicts the course of this expansion in pictorial form all over the world, from the initial conquests to the present day. The drama of the events that brought a religion born in the Arabian desert, and its vehicle, the Arabic language and script, into far-flung regions of the world, is illustrated and described by these maps and texts. The historical processes active in each separate theatre of action are indicated, from the outset to the present day. Islam has experienced checks and reversals, as in Spain and Eastern Europe, temporarily during the Crusades, and in aspects of European colonial rule. Yet it remains an active and still-spreading phenomenon whose influence in different parts of the world is profound, and, to many non-Muslims, mysterious and little understood.

As the illustrations show, the growth of Islam in the different regions of the world was both a religious and a cultural phenomenon, entailing at times an extraordinary flowering of literature and the arts, and some superb architectural achievements. Cairo and Baghdad, Isfahan and the cities of India are among the indices of the level attained.

There are numerous differing conventions for transliterating Arabic, and no less for the many regional tongues. For geographical names the *Times Atlas of the World* has been followed. For other words the practice of the *Encyclopaedia of Islam*, revised edition, has been used, but without diacritical marks, and likewise j and q in place of dj and ḳ.

There is no bibliography. There are already ample bibliographies in G.S.P. Freeman-Grenville, *Historical Atlas of the Middle East*, 1993; *The New Atlas of African History*, 1991; *The Oxford Encyclopaedia of the Modern Islamic World*, O.U.P. 1995; and C.E. Bosworth, *The New Islamic Dynasties*, Edinburgh U.P. 1996.

1 May 2002.                    G.S.P.F.-G.                    S.C.J.M.-H.

# ACKNOWLEDGEMENTS

IN preparing and illustrating this atlas we wish to express our gratitude to Ralph Pinder-Wilson, for twenty-eight years in the Department of Islamic Art in the British Museum; for advice from Professor D. O. Morgan, former editor of the *Journal of the Royal Asiatic Society of Great Britain and Ireland*, and much valuable criticism; to Professor William Glanzmann for unpublished material on his excavations at Marib, Yemen; together with Miss Leila Ingrams for her photograph of the ruined city of Marib; to Dr. Mark Horton for photographs of his excavations in the Lamu Archipelago, Kenya, and Pemba Island, Zanzibar; to Andrew Forbes on China and the Far East; to Dr. Peter Garlake and the British Institute in East Africa for permission to reproduce his isometric reconstruction of the Sultan's Palace of Husuni Kubwa at Kilwa; to Michael Pollock, Librarian of the Royal Asiatic Society; to Ahmed R. Bullock, of Oxford; to Margaret Dillon and Kate Evans of the University Library, York, and the librarians of the Society of Antiquaries of London, and School of Oriental & African Studies, University of London; and not least to Barbara Ball and Lorraine Kessel, and all the patient and painstaking staff of Carta. Jerusalem.

If we have inadvertently omitted the name of a copyright holder, please contact Carta, P.O.B. 2500, Jerusalem 91024; E-mail: cartaben@netvision.net.il.

# GLOSSARY

*Abbasid* —
name of the caliphal dynasty in Baghdad 750–1517, and thereafter as a shadow dynasty in Cairo, to 1913.

*Aliyot* —
Hebrew, migration; used specifically for the return of Jews to Israel in the twentieth century.

*Almohad* —
dynasty in N. Africa and Spain (Ar. *al-Muwahhidun*), 1130–1269.

*Almoravid* —
dynasty in N. Africa and Spain (Ar. *al-Murabitun*), 1062–1147.

*Amir* (and commonly *emir*) —
originally military, a common title; the ruler in Kuwait.

*Amir al-Muminim* —
Commander of the Faithful; title of certain rulers.

*al-Andalus* —
Ar., name, initially Spain as a whole; later restricted to Córdoba.

*al-Aqsa* —
see *Haram al-Sharif*

*Askia* —
title of rulers of Songhay, 1493–1591/2.

*Assassins* —
Ar., *Hashashun*, a movement based on Alamut and Syria, derived from the Ismaili, which practiced assassination for political ends, inaugurated by al-Hasan al-Sabbah (d. 1124).

*Awqaf* —
see *waqf* (s.), a charitable bequest, generally for a mosque or school, or for some persons specially nominated.

*bagt* —
a treaty established between Muslim Egypt and Christian Nubia.

*Bahri* —
Ar., literally, riverain; the title of the Mamluk regiment, from which Mamluk sultans of Egypt were drawn, 1250–1390, from the name of their barracks on the Nile (*Bahr al-Nil*).

*Bektashi* —
Turk., the name of an order or fraternity of dervishes.

*blad* —
Morocco, for Ar. *bilad*, country.

*bunga mas* —
gold and silver flowers offered as tribute in Malaya.

*Burgi (Burji)* —
the name of the Mamluk regiment, from which the sultans of Egypt were drawn, 1382–1517, from the name of their barracks in the citadel (*burg, burj*) in Cairo.

*Caliph* —
Ar. *khalifa*, literally successor, deputy title used for the civil headship only after the death of the Prophet Muhammad; used for the first four of his successors, for the Umayyads of Damascus (661–750) and for the Abbasids (*q.v.*).

*calligraphy* —
ornamental Arabic or other script.

*changwat* —
provinces in modern Thailand.

*citadel* —
a fortress, as at Aleppo, Cairo and elsewhere.

*city-state* —
a form of government by cities, with little external claim to outside territory.

*colony* —
in the ancient world, a foreign trading settlement, not to be confused with later European and other domination over national or tribal territories.

*Companion(s) of the Prophet* —
Ar., *ansar*, literally helpers; those who joined him after the *Hijra* (*q.v.*) to Medina.

*consul* —
in the middle ages, a residential commercial agent.

*Copt* —
the name of the ancient inhabitants of Egypt, from Greek, and later restricted in use for Christians.

*Dia* —
the title of the rulers of Kukia.

*dikka* —
a raised platform in a large mosque in front of the *mihrab* (q.v.) for cantors, to enable the congregation to keep in time with the *imam* (q.v.) in prayer.

*dinar* —
Ar., Islamic issue of gold or silver coinage, in imitation of the Byzantine gold *denarius*.

*emir* —
see *amir*.

*factory* —
(Portuguese, *feitoria*) a trading agency in Africa or in the east, often fortified.

*Fatimid* —
the name of a Shi'ite dynasty claiming title of Caliph, in N. Africa, and then Egypt and part of Syria, 909–1171, in Cairo from 969.

*Ghazi* —
Ar., Turk., originally one who took part in a *ghazzu*, or tribal raid; later one who fought in Holy War against unbelievers; a title for a war leader.

*Great Mosque* —
a mosque of the largest size in a major city, used for Friday prayers, and having a pulpit (*minbar*) and often a *dikka* (q.v.).

*hadith* —
the name for a tradition of an action, decision or other utterance of the Prophet, and regarded as a source of law.

*hajj* —
pilgrimage, esp. the pilgrimage to Mecca; a pilgrim.

*haram* —
Ar., forbidden, sacrosanct; thus the holy places of Mecca, Medina and Jerusalem; and for Shi'ites Karbala, Najaf and others; likewise women's quarters in a dwelling; in Aden, a drinking saloon.

*al-Haram al-Sharif* —
Ar., the noble sanctuary, the shrine of the rock from which the Prophet is believed to have ascended on his mystical journey to heaven, consisting of the Dome of the Rock and the Aqsa Mosque.

*hatti-sharif* —
Turk., a decree of the Ottoman sultan.

*Hijra* —
literally, migration; the migration of the Prophet and of the Companions (q.v.) from Mecca to Medina in AD 615.

*holy war* —
see *jihad*.

*Id al-Adha* —
Ar., the Feast of Sacrifice, commemorating Abraham's sacrifice of a ram as a substitute for his son Isaac, by divine command, the culminating point of the pilgrimage to Mecca.

*Id al-Fitr* —
Ar., the celebration of the Breaking of the Fast at the end of fasting in Ramadhan.

*ihram* —
Ar., the (sacred) dress of a pilgrim (*hajj*, q.v.), consisting of two lengths of white cotton, one round the waist, the other round the shoulders.

*Imam* —
Ar., literally, a leader, and so the leader in prayer in a mosque; sometimes, a ruler.

*Infante* —
Portuguese, infant, and so a royal prince of Portugal.

*intifada* —
Palestinian armed struggle against Israel.

*Iran* —
official name of the former Persia, since 1935.

*Ismaili* —
Shi'ites who believe that only a divinely inspired Imam descended from Ali, son-in-law of the Prophet, could be the true restorer of Islam, and conquer the entire world as Mahdi, and usher in a millennium before the end of all things.

*Ithna'ashari* —
believers similar to the Ismaili, but counting twelve visible Imams, as opposed to the original believers, who believe in seven only.

*Jihad* —
Ar., Holy War against unbelievers as the collective duty of the Muslim community when it is assailed.

*jizya* —
a poll tax payable by non-Muslims in an Islamic state as prescribed by the law.

*Ka'aba* —
Ar., the cube-like structure containing the

Black Stone, at the center of the Great Mosque of Mecca.

**Kashee** —
Tibetan Muslims (from origin in Kashmir).

**Khalifa** —
Ar., see Caliph.

**Khan** —
(i) a hostelry for merchants; (ii) a ruler, correctly *khaqan,* a Turkish title with no relation to (i).

**Kharijites** —
early Muslim sectaries who believed in a wholly elective Caliphate, and rejected the doctrine of justification without works.

**Khedive** —
Turkish title, viceroy, esp. of Egypt until 1913.

**Khojas** —
a division of the Ismailis (*q.v.*).

**Knights Hospitaller** —
order of knights founded to care for poor pilgrims and the sick poor in Jerusalem; later denominated Knights of Rhodes, and subsequently Knights of Malta.

**Knights Templar** —
founded c.1119, military knights to protect pilgrims to Jerusalem from bandits.

**Koran (Qur'an)** —
the sacred book of Islam believed by Muslims to have been delivered to the Prophet from a copy laid up in Heaven.

**Kufic** —
a type of Arabic script evolved in al-Kufa, Iraq, and still used for calligraphic ornamentation.

**Latin** —
(i) language; (ii) a term used for Christians using the Latin liturgy, or a translation thereof, to distinguish them from other Christians using liturgies in other languages.

**madhhab** —
a school of religious doctrine, generally applied to one of the four orthodox schools of legal interpretation of Islamic law.

**madrasa** —
school, college, and esp. one of Islamic learning.

**Magi** —
from Persian, *magus,* pl. *magush,* a Zoroastrian priest; those who came to adore the infant Christ.

**Mahdi** —
the 'rightly guided one' who will inaugurate the millennium before the end of the world. *Cf.* Ismaili above.

**Mamluk** —
originally 'owned', a slave, white male only, esp. the Bahri and Burgi dynasties in Egypt.

**mandate** —
a legal commission to act; here a Mandate of the League of Nations to govern former German or Turkish possessions with a view to bring them to such political maturity as to be able to become self-governing.

**medrese** —
Turk., see *madrasa.*

**mihrab** —
the niche in a mosque set to indicate the direction of Mecca.

**millet** —
a religious domination recognized in Ottoman times for the purposes of its private and domestic law.

**mkanda** —
a unique Swahili word of unknown provenance, the name of the tidal channel between Lamu Island and the mainland.

**Monophysite** —
a Christian who believes that Christ had a single nature only, both God and man.

**mosque** —
any Islamic place of prayer, generally of stone or brick; a reed one is known.

**mud-brick** —
in many Middle Eastern countries, esp. Iraq, mud bricks made from mud hardened by sun-drying, and then plastered, making it very durable.

**mujahid, pl. mujahidin** —
a fighter in a holy war.

**musalla** —
the main congregational space in a mosque.

**Muslim** —
any adherent to Islam.

**Mutazilite** —
an extreme conservative sect in early Islam.

**al-Nakba** —
Ar., calamity, disaster; term used by Muslims

*xv*

to denote the date of the proclamation of the State of Israel, 15 May 1948.

*naksat* —
twelve animals representing months of the year.

*Orthodox* —
implying correctly believing; specifically, Christian adherents to the Greek Orthodox Patriarchate of Constantinople and associated bodies.

*Ottoman* —
name of Turkish dynasty descended from Othman, 1281–1924.

*Papal Legate* —
a personal representative of the Pope with ambassadorial rank.

*Patriarch* —
the title in the Christian hierarchy above Archbishop of the principal historic patriarchates of Rome, Jerusalem, Antioch, Alexandria and Constantinople, and, as an honor, to certain other sees.

*qadi* —
a judge of Islamic law.

*al-Qa'ida(h)* —
with definite article, literally, a base; title of the terrorist organisation led by Osama bin Laden.

*Qasba* —
Ar., a citadel, a walled town.

*raden* —
a Malay title.

*rais* —
Ar., leader, President, departmental head.

*rajah* —
title of Indian princes and some Far Eastern rulers.

*Reconquista* —
Sp., the recovery of Spanish territory, finally in 1491, by stages, following the Islamic conquest of 711.

*ribat* —
Ar., Morocco, a fortified monastery; a dervish convent.

*satraps* —
local governor(s) under the Persian empire.

*Sayyid* —
Ar., a title, in wide usage, from Prince to Mr.; esp. also for descendants of Husayn, grandson of the Prophet by his daughter Fatima.

*shahbandar* —
customs officer or harbor-master.

*Shahinshah* —
the ancient imperial Persian title.

*shamanist(s)* —
a priest or witch-doctor claiming direct contact with a divinity.

*Sharif* —
a descendant of the Prophet's grandson Hasan by his daughter Fatima; a nobleman.

*Shaykh al-Islam* —
a chief justice of Islamic law appointed by the state.

*Shi'a, Shi'ite* —
Ar., opposite of Sunni (*q.v.*), any Islamic sectarian.

*sufi* —
Ar., literally one who wears wool; a member of any dervish fraternity.

*sultan* —
Turk., Ar., originally he who has authority, a ruler subordinate to a caliph; later, independent ruler.

*Sunni* —
Ar., generally translated 'orthodox', as opposed to *shi'a*.

*Swahili* —
Ar., *sahil*, coast; any inhabitant of the Eastern African coast; not a tribesman.

*Taliban* —
Pushtu from Ar., literally 'pupils', an Afghan politico-religious group.

*Talmud(ic)* —
Jewish biblical commentaries.

*tariqa* —
literally, a way, road: the rule of a dervish fraternity.

*Teutonic Knights* —
a German division of the Knights Templar.

*Tijaniyya* —
A dervish fraternity of worldwide membership. *Tijaniyya* dervishes — a strict *tariqa* (*q.v.*) principally in Ghana, Guinea and Senegal.

*Ulama* —
Ar., literally, 'the knowledgeable persons'; scholars of Islamic religious subjects.

*Umayyad* —
see caliph.

*vizier* —
from Turk., Ar., *wazir*, a minister, officer of state, head of administration.

*Wahhabi(sm)* —
Ar., from Muhammad ibn al-Wahhab, conservative puritanical religious reformer, 13th/14th century, in Damascus. His austere code was revived in central Arabia in the 19th century, and led to the foundation of what is now the Saudi state.

*waqf* —
see *awqaf*.

*wilayet* —
Turkish administrative district.

*Zamorin* —
title of 15th century ruler of Malabar.

*ziggurat* —
tower of a Babylonian temple.

*Zoroastrian* —
a follower of the religious system taught by Zoroaster (Zarathustra) in the 6th century BC, in ancient Persia, and still surviving in minorities in Iran, India and elsewhere.

# I. Introduction: Before the *Hijra* of the Prophet Muhammad

## MIDDLE EAST — PHYSICAL

Rudyard Kipling was unobservant when he wrote:

> Oh, East is East, and West is West, and never the twain shall meet...

for the Middle East is a land bridge across which civilization after civilization has passed. Originally defined as scarcely more than Mesopotamia, its kingdoms spread ideas both eastward and westward. At one time the power of Persia stretched from the present Pakistan border to Libya, Egypt, and Nubia (Sudan); at another, Islam and the power of the Arabs stretched from the Atlantic to the Kyrghyz steppe and the Indus River.

Fire and tools were the first products of civilization. It was the people of Urartu in the Armenian mountains who first mined and manufactured metal, practices that rapidly became known in the Zagros Mountains and in Egypt, Nubia, and Ethiopia. The search for metal lured the Levantine Phoenicians to Spain and even Britain.

Commercial enterprise necessitated the keeping of records. Thus it was in Syria that the art of cursive writing was developed by Semitic-speaking peoples, whose alphabets are ancestral to numerous present-day writing systems.

It was in this same geographical area that four great religions evolved. If the Mosaic concept of the unity of God has priority, it was the Persian seer Zarathustra (Zoroaster) in the sixth century BC, who first taught the concepts of immortality, the Last Judgment, and the activity of God through the Holy Spirit — concepts that found their way into Judaism, and from Judaism into

*The Nile Valley, Egypt*

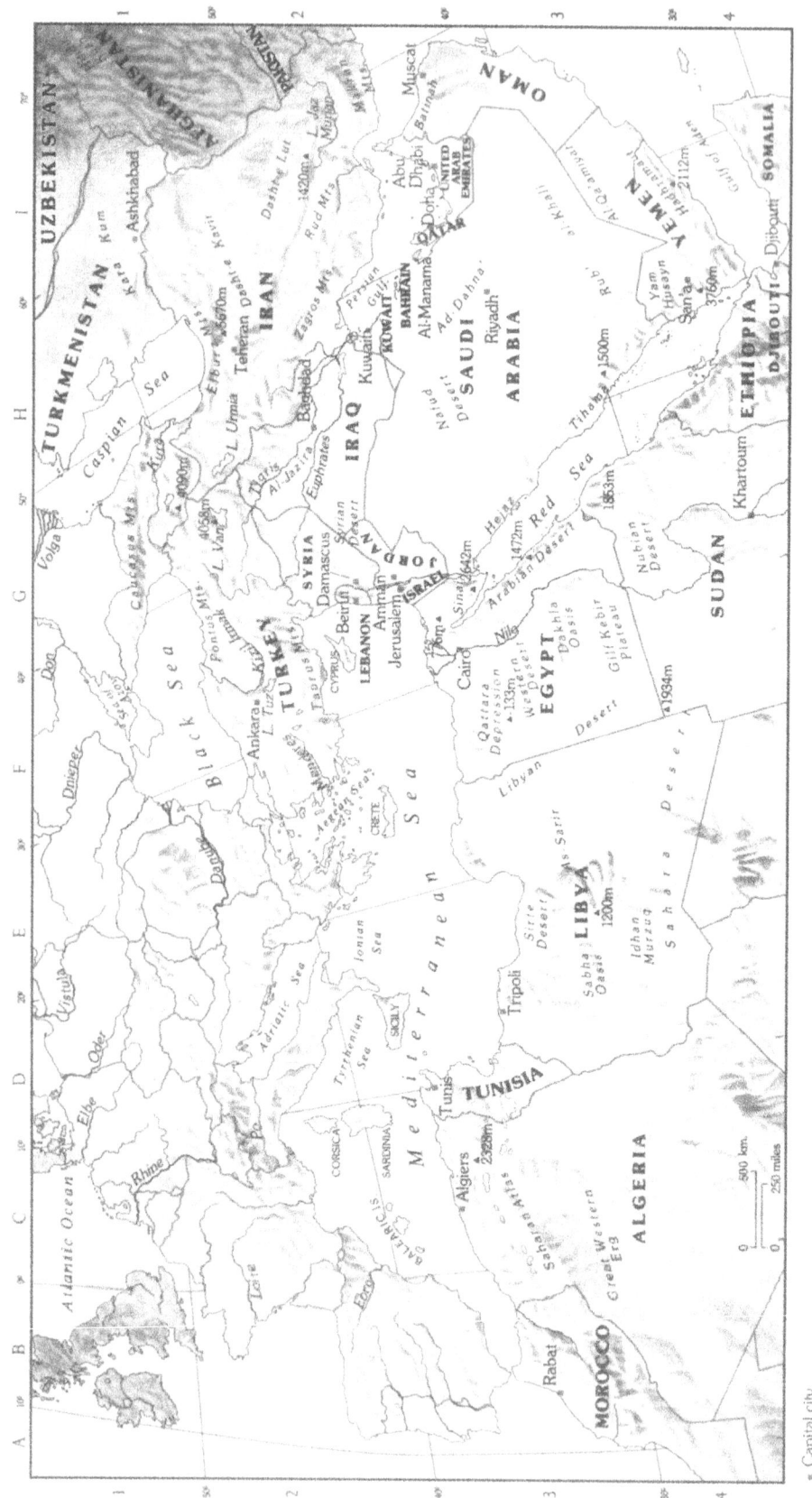

MIDDLE EAST — PHYSICAL

MEAN ANNUAL RAINFALL

Precipitation:
- 0-100mm. (0-4")
- 100-250mm. (4-10")
- 250-500mm. (10-20")
- 500-1000mm. (20-40")
- Over 1000mm. (40")

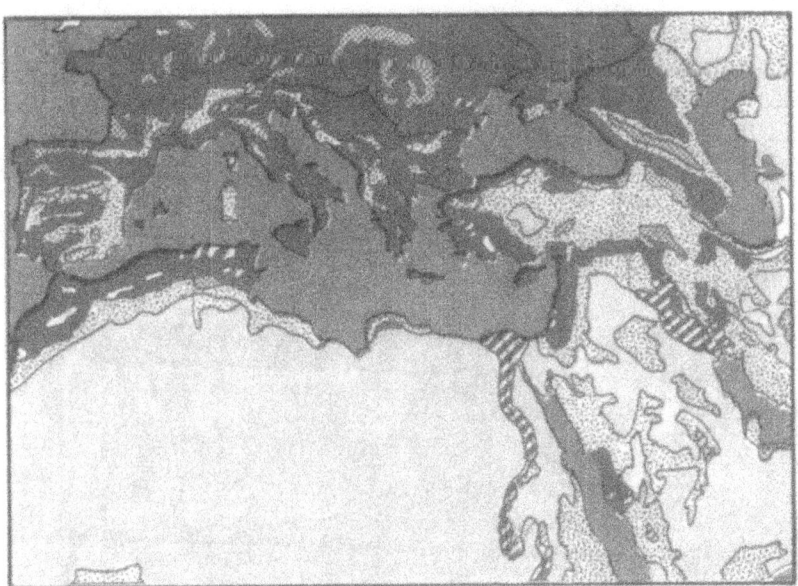

VEGETATION

- Arable land (intensive farming)
- Grazing land
- Other irrigated land
- Forest
- Tropical woodland and grassland
- Desert

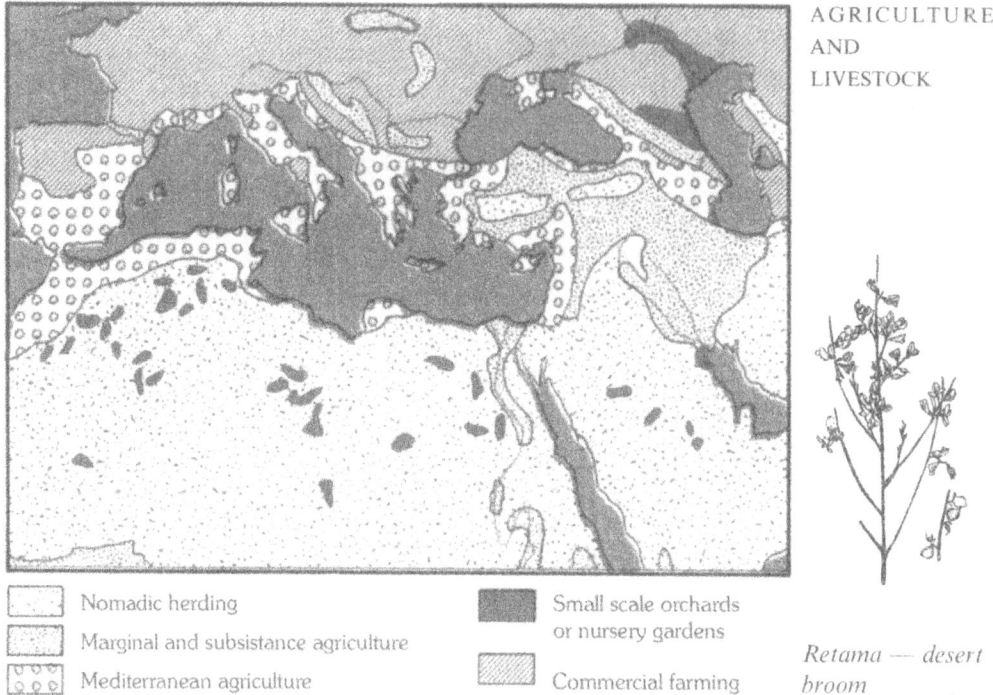

AGRICULTURE AND LIVESTOCK

*Retama — desert broom*

Christianity and Islam.

Herodotus claimed that it was Egypt that taught Greece religion. Be that as it may, it was in the following century that the Greeks under Alexander carried Hellenism as far east as India and established Alexandria on the northern shore of Africa as a world center, not merely of commerce but also of philosophy and learning.

The first kingdoms evolved around river systems. The gradual desiccation of the Sahara forced men into the Nile Valley. In Mesopotamia a similar effect was

*Camel herd – from an Arabian miniature; Al-Hariri (1054–1122), MS dated 1237*

produced; fertile soil was washed down each year from the northern mountains, as the Nile brought down soil from the mountains of Ethiopia.

Shortly before the beginning of the first millennium BC, the Arabian camel was domesticated and bred throughout the whole desert area, providing, with the horse, a primary means of land transport. By this time shipping had evolved in the Persian Gulf and the Red Sea as well as the Mediterranean. Land and sea transport were linked by the establishment of ports. Under the Persian ruler Darius, the utility of linking the Mediterranean to the Nile and the Red Sea was perceived, and the first canal begun.

With the discovery of the rich oil fields in the Zagros Mountains, Mesopotamia, the Persian Gulf, and Arabia, the region took on immense economic importance during the twentieth century, in addition to the commercial and cultural significance that it had had for four thousand years.

*Mount Ararat, Turkey*

## THE ANCIENT MIDDLE EAST, C. 2050–1000 BC

In ancient Mesopotamia, a series of city-states arose. Perpetually at war with each other, none achieved superiority for any great length of time, save Babylonia and Assyria. The earliest city-states in the Middle East had arisen long before, but, in the absence of written records, their history is largely closed to us. Although Jericho was fortified by 9000 BC we have only an archaeological record of artefacts.

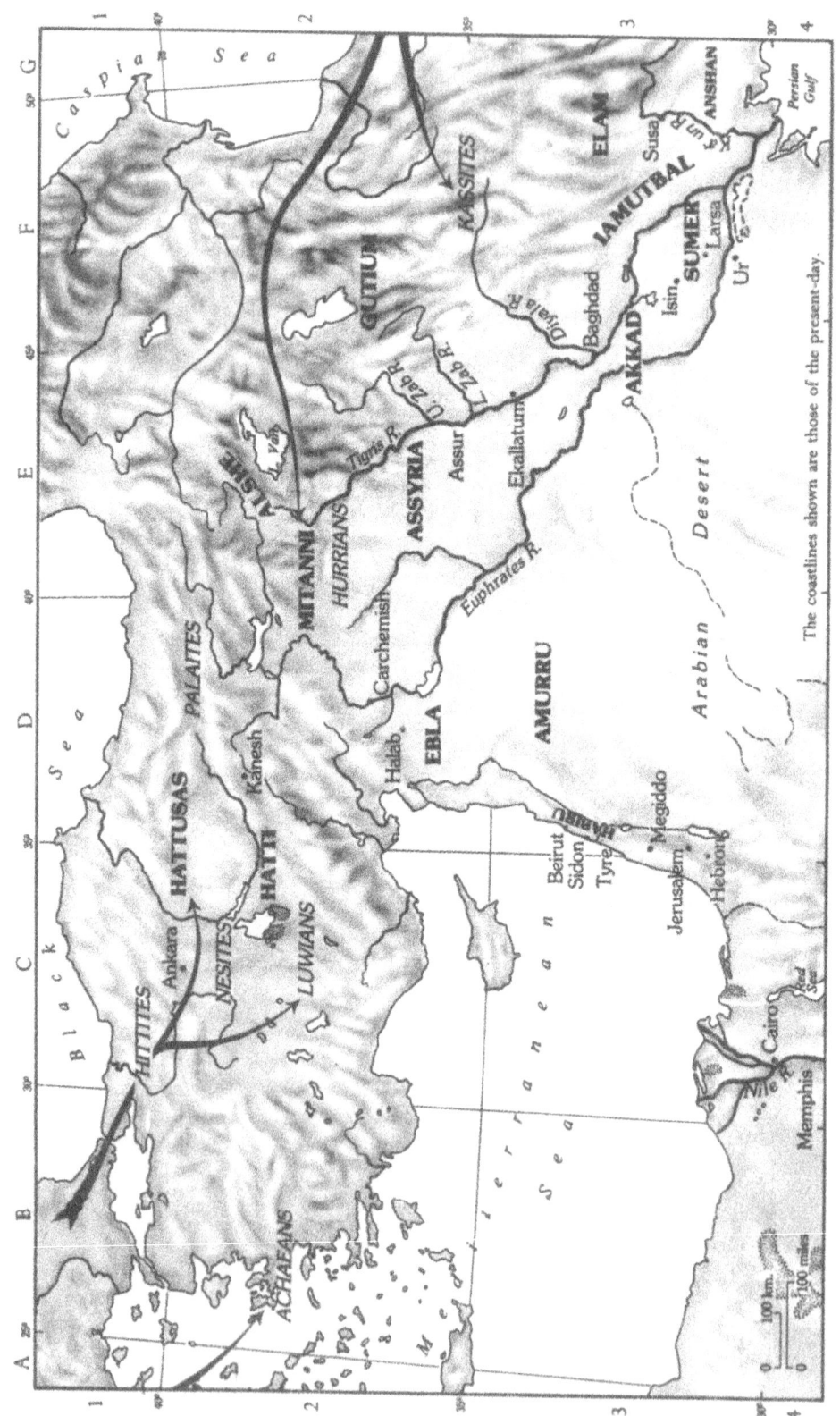

THE ANCIENT MIDDLE EAST, C. 2050–1000 BC

*Two deities depicted on a panel in the palace at Mari, Mesopotamia*

By 3000 BC a group of city-states had come into being in southern Iraq with a common Sumerian language that had been committed to writing; these are the first written records. It is to this group that we owe the beginning of Middle Eastern history, properly so called. Their religion was pantheistic; their system of government was theocratic, with a priest-king whose will was absolute. In architecture, their greatest achievement was the ziggurat, and in agriculture, the use of irrigation canals. It is this area that the Bible names the Garden of Eden.

By 2400 BC, these city-states were displaced by Akkadian rulers of Semitic

*Relief decoration on the walls of the palace of the Persian kings in Persepolis*

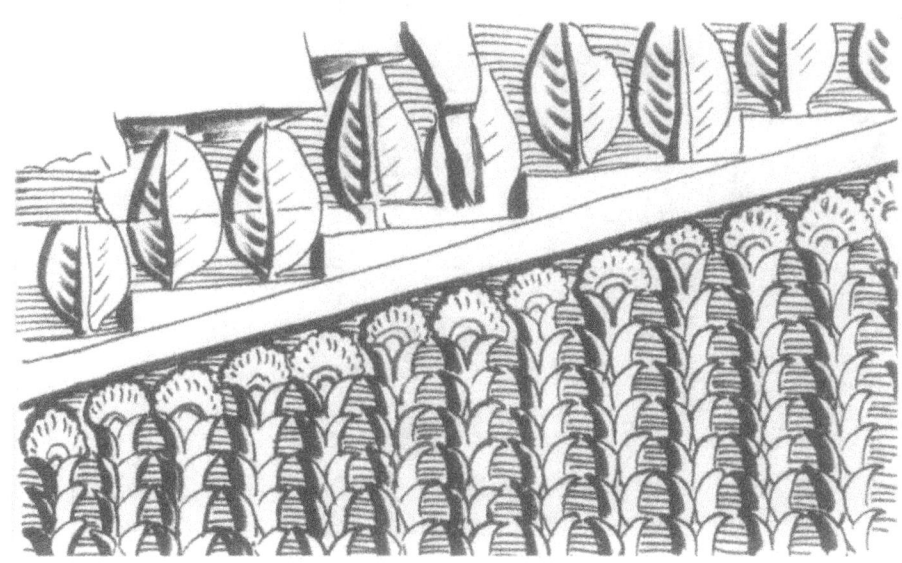

origin, who made Babylon their capital. Under these rulers a monotheistic form of religion developed, together with a coded legal system whose origins can be traced to the small kingdom of Ur. Under the great law-giver Hammurabi (1792–1750 BC) the tribal law of revenge was replaced by fines, a legal concept that persists to our day. This code of laws marked the beginning of modern Syria and Iraq. Between 1595 and 1300 BC, the Hittites of Aryan descent penetrated Syria as far as Damascus. A warlike people, they encountered a civilization more sophisticated than their own and were absorbed by it. Around 1300 BC the Semitic Babylonians, so long under a conquering heel, overthrew them, creating an empire that stretched as far as the Levant, but not into Egypt.

## ANCIENT EGYPT

By the fourth millennium BC the gradual desiccation of the Sahara had forced substantial populations into the relatively small cultivable lands on either side of the Nile. The annual flooding of the Nile, which brought down the rich silt on which their agriculture depended, compelled these populations to form strict administrative structures. Knowledge of this organization and the art of metallurgy had been brought from western Asia. Some time before 3100 BC two kingdoms developed, with a capital of Upper Egypt at Hierakonopolis, and at Buto in the Delta About 3100 BC Menes, founder of the First Dynasty, is said to have built Memphis, in the region of modern Cairo. Shortly before 3000 BC these kingdoms were united.

In the south the boundary reached the First Cataract, below which the whole river is navigable. Under the Old Kingdom (2700–2200 BC) the capital was shifted to Memphis, in the region of modern Cairo. Here the Pyramids bear mute witness to a highly sophisticated development of mathematics, engineering, medical science, and religion. None of this development would have been possible without a lively foreign trade with the Levant, and even the mysterious PWNT, the Sudan-Eritrean coasts and

*The funerary temple of Queen Hatshepsut at Dayr al-Bahri, near ancient Thebes*

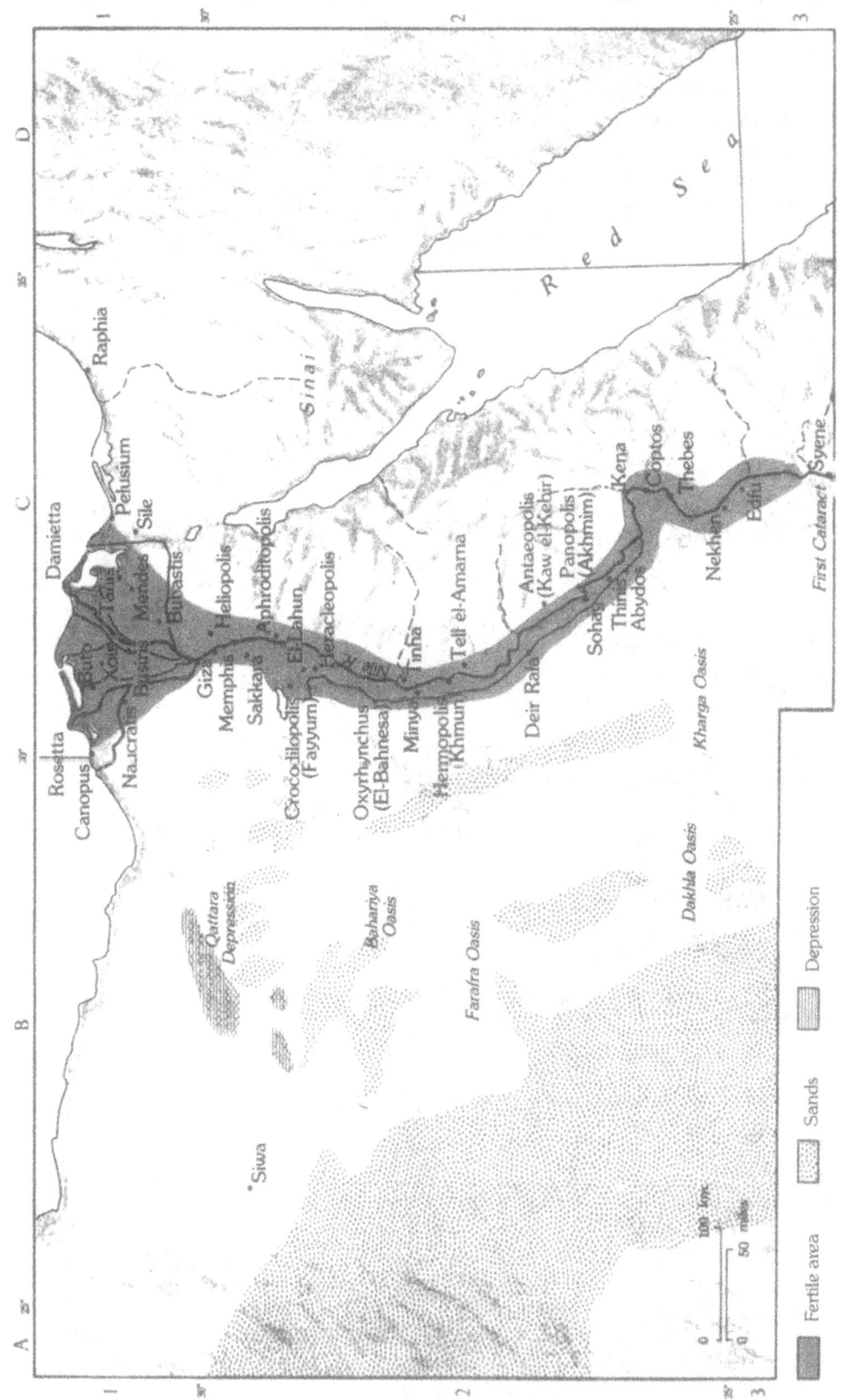

ANCIENT EGYPT

with the Levant, and even the mysterious PWNT, the Sudan-Eritrean coasts and possibly Somalia, from which — along with southern Arabia — came the immense quantities of frankincense used in temple worship.

Between around 2250 and 1750 BC, under the Middle Kingdom, there was some expansion into Palestine. There followed two centuries under the Hyksos. Under Akhenaton (c.1367–c.1350) religion was reformed and a new capital built at Thebes. During the twelfth century BC Egypt suffered raids by the Sea Peoples, but independence was preserved until Cambyses II of Persia seized the country in 525 BC Except for a brief interval, the Hyksos ruled until Alexander the Great swallowed Egypt up into his vast empire. To him Egypt owes the creation of Alexandria as a port, which was to become the pivot of trade between East and West.

## THE SEABORNE PHOENICIAN EMPIRE

The Phoenicians are also known as Canaanites and Sidonians in the Hebrew scriptures. In northern Africa, where they set up trading colonies, they are known by the name of their principal colony, as Carthaginians. Their language was

*Relief showing Phoenician vessels*

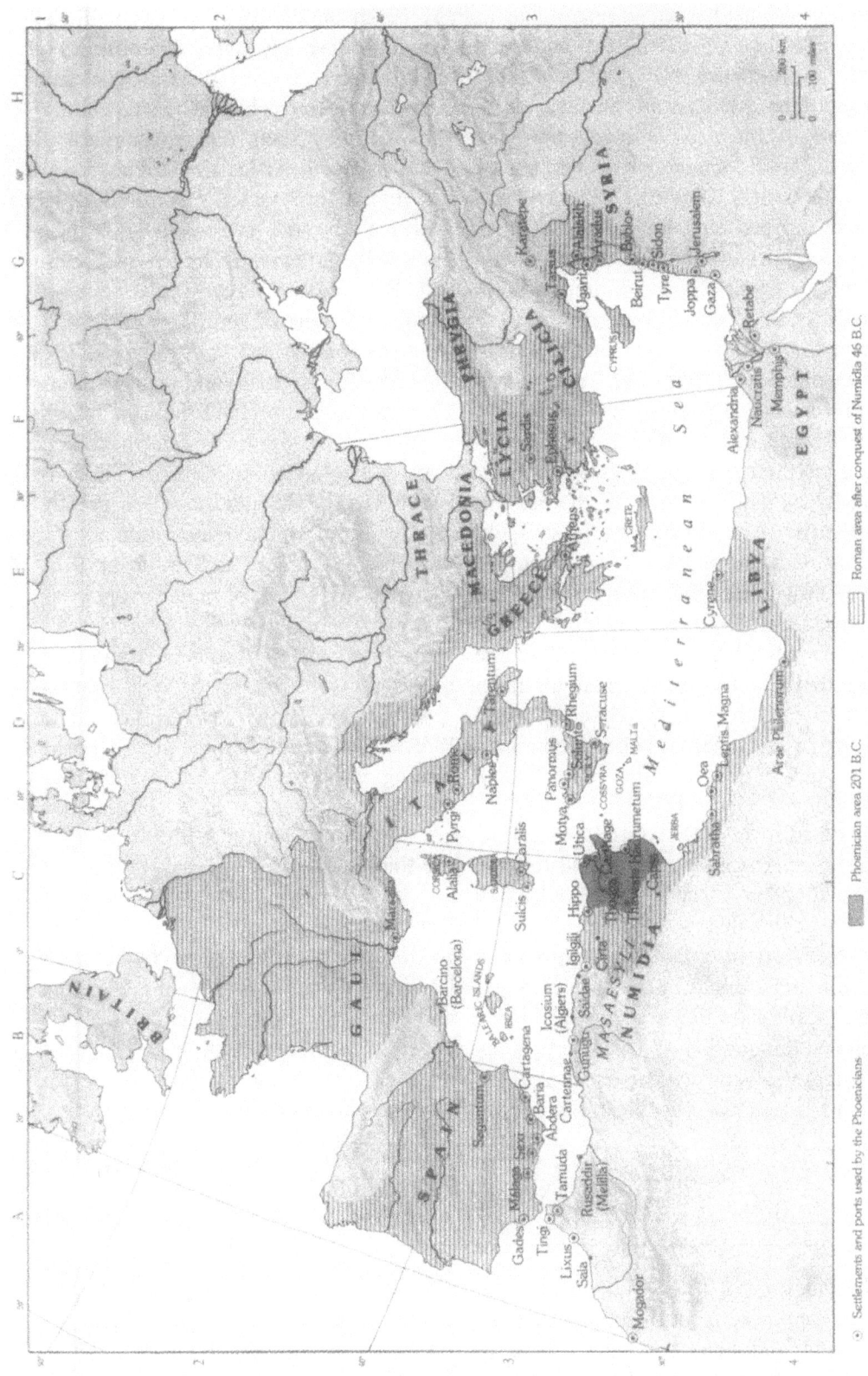

THE SEABORNE PHOENICIAN EMPIRE

unquestionably Semitic, as was that of their Levantine neighbors. Their distinctiveness was neither racial nor linguistic, but as dwellers on the Levant coastland with a preference for peninsulas and islands, they were distinct in their development of the arts of navigation and long-distance commerce. In their hinterland, present Lebanon, they were fortunate in possessing huge forests, which provided not only ships' timbers but also wood for export to, for example, Solomon's Israel. Timber was also sent to Assyria and Egypt, and supplied ships that traded in the Red Sea and perhaps with Yemen or Somalia. Through a series of entrepôts, merchandise from India was reaching the Levant by the tenth century BC. In the ninth century BC the Phoenician cities — each apparently self-governing — were under Assyrian control. Not until the eighth century did the Assyrians impose direct rule.

The Annals of Tyre record that in the seventh year of King Pygmalion's reign (814–813 BC) his sister fled and founded Carthage in Libya. Phoenician colonization long antedates this period. The founding of Gades (Cádiz) is traditionally dated to 1110 BC and Utica to 1101 BC; some African cities are said to have been founded earlier. These dates are highly debatable, as are those of alleged ninth century inscriptions in Cyprus and at Nora in Sardinia. By the term colony is here meant a trading settlement, not the political domination of a people by alien immigrants. The classical Greek authors maintain that the Phoenicians monopolized trade in the Mediterranean before the maritime expansion of Greek trade. Precise chronological evidence for Phoenician expansion is highly tenuous, but it is certain that by 509 BC Carthage and Rome had entered into a treaty relationship, defining their respective areas of trade. In north Africa the Carthaginian-Phoenicians increased in number, as evidenced by the necropolises in their numerous settlements. In the fifth century BC, because Greek traders cut off communications with northern Europe at Marsalia (Marseilles), long voyages were undertaken past Spain and Gaul as far as Cornwall in southwest Britain in search of tin. During this time a Carthaginian, Hanno, is claimed to have circumnavigated Africa. The tale has been greatly disputed, and he may have reached only the Gulf of Guinea, itself no mean feat. The principal object of these voyages was to obtain gold, silver, and tin, which were transported via the trans-Saharan trade routes as far as from the gold-bearing areas, later known as Guinea. The Phoenicians established the first seaborne trading empire, a loose-knit system that linked the prosperity of western Africa and the Mediterranean with the cities of the Euphrates and the Tigris.

When Rome dominated all Italy in 272 BC, it came into inevitable conflict with Carthage. Three wars (264–261; 209–206; and 201–146), known as the Punic Wars, ended with the destruction of Carthage and the absorption of northern Africa into the Roman orbit.

## ANCIENT ISRAEL AND ITS NEIGHBORS,
### 10TH TO 6TH CENTURIES BC

The Palestine of the Bible, which occupies the western horn of the Fertile Crescent and links the land masses of Africa and Asia, has been the scene of constant migration, struggle, and conquest. It was a collection of small city-states up to around 1800 BC, when, according to the Bible, a group of

# ANCIENT ISRAEL AND ITS NEIGHBORS,
10TH TO 6TH CENTURIES BC

nomadic herdsmen — 318 fighting men with their families, flocks, and herds — migrated under the leadership of Abraham from Ur in Chaldaea. They settled near Hebron. Around 1500 BC famine forced their descendants to migrate to Egypt, from which they returned around 1250 BC.

The returning Israelites were loosely organized under tribal leaders. These "Judges," as they were called, had been primarily settlers of tribal disputes; now they emerged as war leaders. Philistine immigrants and native Canaanites had a technological superiority in their knowledge of the use of iron and war chariots. The Israelites were thus forced to unite under a king, Saul (r. c.1020–1000 BC), and to learn the art of war from their enemies. Under David (r. c.1000–961) the kingdom was consolidated, and Jerusalem became the religious as well as civil capital. Under Solomon (r. c.961–922) a splendid temple, palaces, and other public buildings were erected. The expansion was the result of a great increase in foreign trade with Syria, Egypt, southern Arabia, and perhaps Somalia.

On Solomon's death, the kingdom split into northern and southern segments, possibly representing an ancient division among the tribes. In both kingdoms prophets arose, crying out against injustice and preaching a renewed moral system. In 721 BC Israel, the northern kingdom, was seized by Assyria; Judah became a vassal of Egypt at the end of the seventh century. In 605 BC Egypt was defeated by Babylon far away at Carchemish, and around 597 Jerusalem also surrendered. Some three thousand citizens were deported. Nevertheless, unabashed, the Jews revolted in around 595/4. The Babylonians again besieged the city. When it fell after eighteen months, it was sacked and Solomon's Temple destroyed. Numerous citizens were deported to Babylon in 587 BC and again in 582, taking their religion and culture with them.

*Relief cut into the rock face on Mount Hisutun (also called Behistun)*

# THE EMPIRE OF PERSIA

Early in the first millennium BC, Aryan peoples migrated from north of the Caspian Sea into the south-western part of modern Iran, which borders the Persian Gulf. These people were absorbed into an already existing civilization that dated back to around 4000 BC This area was later known to the Greeks as Persis, and to the Arabs as Fars. Here grew the great cities of Persepolis, Pasargadae, and Susa. In the north their kinsmen, the Medes, had settled south of the Caspian Sea in the region of modern Azerbaijan, with a capital at Ecbatana (Hamadan). They took Nineveh from the Assyrians in 612 BC and destroyed their empire.

Some sixty years later, in 550 BC, an obscure Persian, Cyrus II, succeeded in gaining a hegemony over the Medes, and then absorbing neighboring Assyria, Mesopotamia, Armenia, and Cappadocia. Finally, in 538 BC, he took Babylon, whence he allowed the Jews to return from exile. His successor, Cambyses II, extended the conquest to Egypt, but his successor failed to conquer the Greek states.

This huge and ramshackle empire was held together by satraps, or local governors, and by a constitution remarkable for the stability of its laws and the extent to which the "Great King" was constrained by convention "that altereth not." Thus in Babylon the "Great King" was a Babylonian monarch, in Egypt he was a pharaoh. The governors, virtual kings wielding both civil and military authority, were nevertheless subject to scrutiny by inspectors, who were known as the "king's eye" and the "king's ear." The governors were responsible for a comprehensive taxation system based on a survey of the whole empire, on lines similar to the Domesday Book. Perhaps the greatest binding force was language; Aramaic was the official language of record, displacing local languages, including Hebrew, except for religious purposes. The system of satraps gave way to the consolidated empire of Alexander the Great.

*Alexander the Great, from a mosaic at Pompeii*

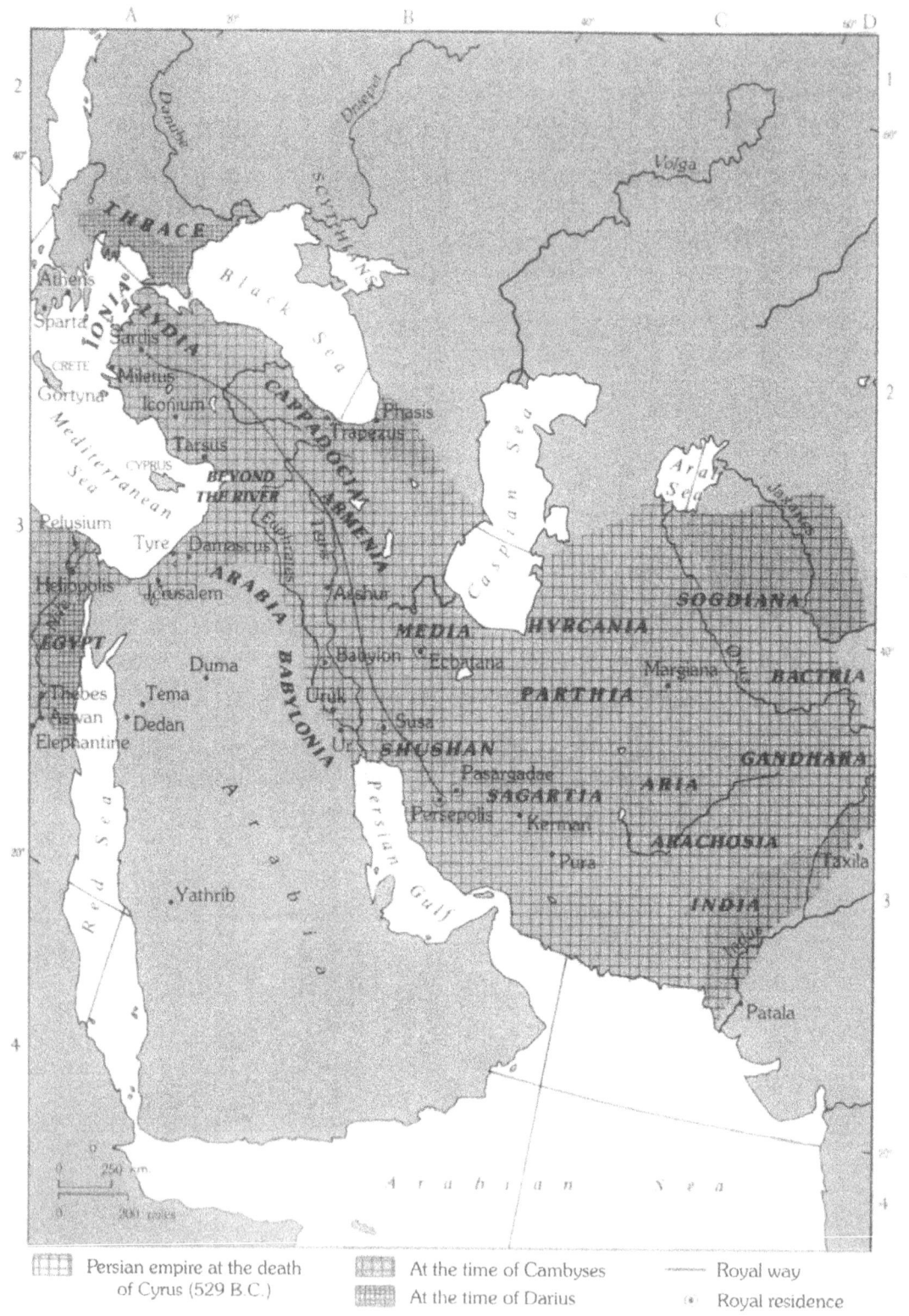

# THE EMPIRE OF PERSIA

# ALEXANDER THE GREAT'S EMPIRE
## AND ITS DIVISION AMONGST HIS SUCCESSORS

Alexander the Great's short life (353–323 BC) and reign (336–323 BC) mark a crossroads in European and Asiatic history. In a Mediterranean and Oriental world fragmented among many small powers, he moved the centers of Hellenic civilization from Greece and Macedonia as far as the Punjab, inaugurating a Hellenic cultural empire that was effective from Gibraltar to the Hindu Kush in Afghanistan. Alexander was the greatest general the world had yet seen, and few have ever equaled him. He initiated a new age that, in the form of Greek monarchies, was the precursor of the Roman Empire and of Christianity as a world religion. This achievement survived in different cultural forms in empires in both East and West, as Byzantium and the caliphate, Charlemagne and the Ottoman empire, in Imperial Russia and Austria, and the transitory empires of Britain and France.

The map displays his achievements in Greece and Asia Minor, and then in the Levant, Egypt, and northern Africa. The road to his real goal, the conquest of Persia, now lay open. The defeat of the Persians at Gaugamela was decisive, and, as an act of revenge for earlier Persian wars against Greece, Xerxes' palace at Persepolis was burnt. Media was occupied in 330 BC. Adopting the Persian title "Great King," he campaigned in central Asia and, in 327 BC, India.

His conquest was not one of destruction. Rather, it was of the foundation of cities and the organization of commerce. He had a special interest in geography, exploration, and natural history. Administration was conducted through satraps, governors on the Persian model. Strictly controlled, between 326 and 324 BC over a third of them were accused of corruption and superseded.

Alexander's final aims are not known. His untimely death at the age of thirty led to the breakup of the empire under his principal generals. The Seleucids failed to hold the East together. In Egypt the Ptolemies reigned as Pharaohs from Alexandria. In the West, the Roman star had yet to rise.

*Ruins at the Palace of Persepolis, from the time of Alexander the Great*

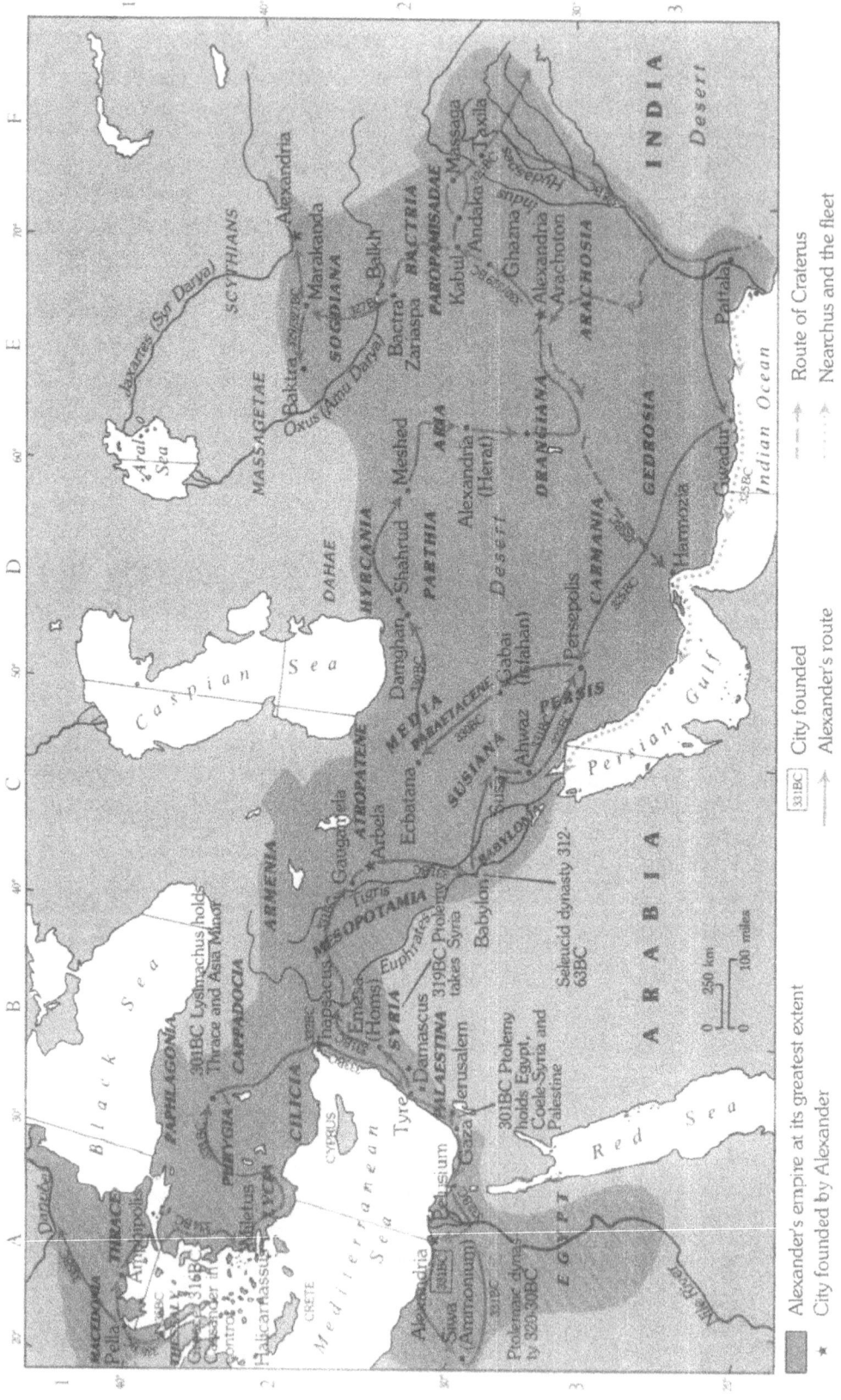

ALEXANDER THE GREAT'S EMPIRE AND ITS DIVISION AMONGST HIS SUCCESSORS

# ROME IN THE MIDDLE EAST

During the second century BC Rome slowly developed influence in Asia Minor. By around 90 BC, after various diplomatic and military setbacks, Mithradates, the king of Pontus, had created an empire on the Black Sea that stretched as far as India and challenged Roman commercial supremacy in western Asia Minor. Following several wars, in 70 BC, Pompey made Syria a Roman province, while Lucullus drove Mithradates out of Asia Minor into Armenia. Asia Minor was now Rome's chief source of revenue.

From 57 to 55 BC Judaea rebelled against Rome, which had come face to face with the Parthian empire. In 40 BC, in an attempt to reinforce indirect rule, Herod was made King of Judaea. After 30 BC, Rome became the direct ruler of Egypt. From 27 BC, when Octavian was proclaimed emperor as Augustus, until the Arab invasion in the seventh century AD, the whole area of the Levant was organized under a constitutional government. Arabia proper was never conquered, but the Roman frontier was to some extent secured by the client kingdoms of Ghassan and Nabataea. In the north, Armenia and Parthia presented continuous problems. The optimum frontier was the Euphrates. In an area that

*Roman soldiers, 1st–2nd centuries*

had become deeply Hellenized under Alexander's successors, the Jews stood alone in declining to acknowledge the state religion of the Pantheon and the deified Roman emperors. Their rebellion in AD 67 resulted in the devastation and ruin of Jerusalem, but not of the large Jewish community in the great trading city of Alexandria. By AD 72, the Euphrates was again Rome's frontier. In AD 73, Masada, the last Jewish stronghold, fell as the defenders committed mass suicide. After a further rebellion, Jerusalem was rebuilt as a Roman colony in AD 135.

In the following centuries, the long struggle between Rome and its successor, Byzantium, continued. Christianity, which was to change the character of world civilization, blossomed, with Alexandria as its intellectual center until it suffered partial eclipse at the hands of Islam.

*Coin of Mark Antony, issued in 39 BC*

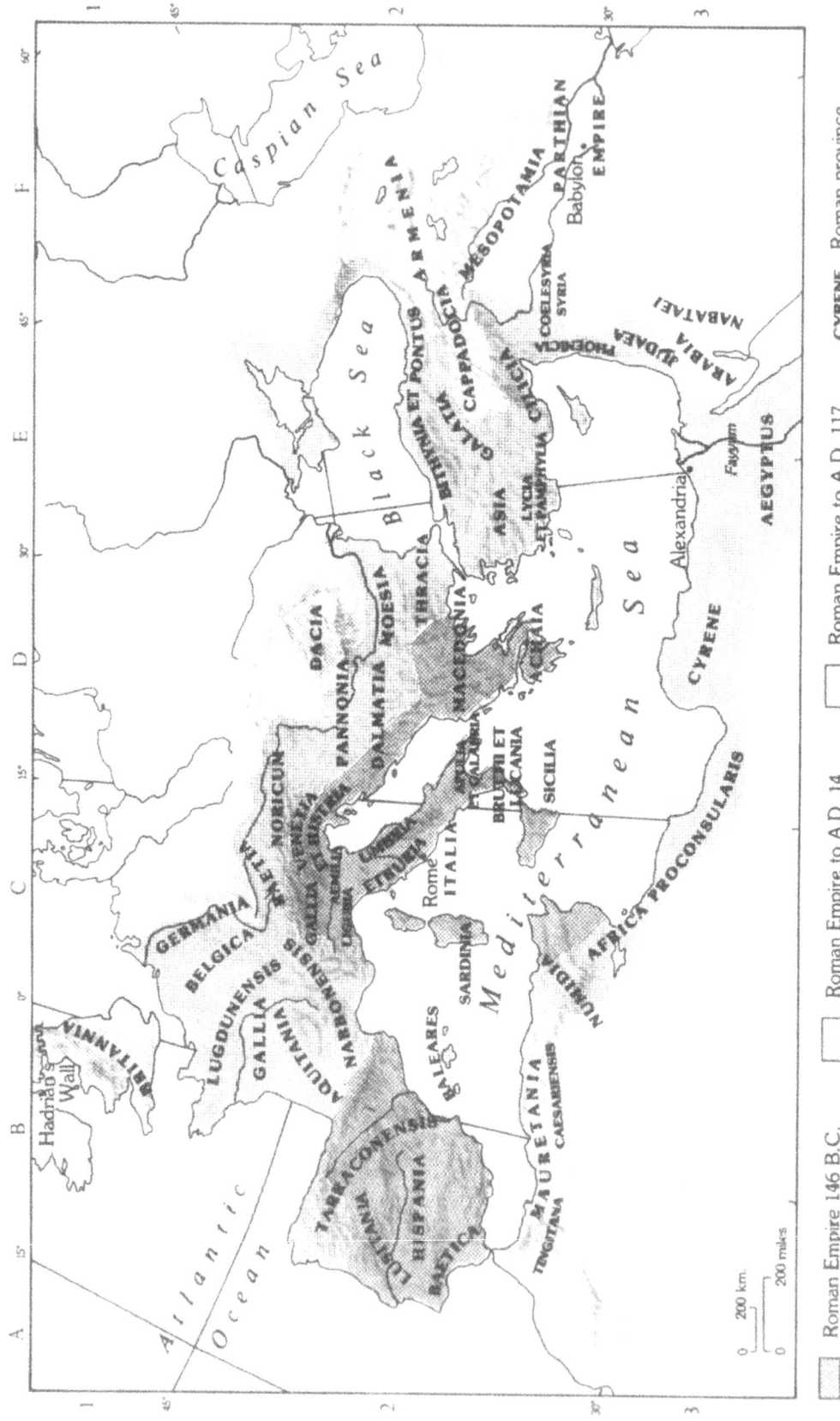

ROME IN THE MIDDLE EAST

# COMMERCE WITH THE MIDDLE EAST, C. AD 50

Already by 1000 BC ships sailed the Indian Ocean from ports in the Persian Gulf. They traded with southern Persia and western India, and with Indian vessels voyaging in reverse. Farther west Pharaohs had already traded down the coast of the Red Sea to Punt, Sudan-Eritrean coasts and possibly northern Somalia. By 116 BC, Eudoxus of Cyzicus had sailed to India and back — a practice that Strabo would regard as normal in AD 6.

Written around AD 50, the anonymous Periplus of the Erythraean Sea presents a report on Egyptian and Arab trade in the Indian Ocean, in which Aden was an important entrepôt. Finds of Roman coins and pottery in India attest to a greatly increased volume of trade, which under the emperor Augustus extended down the eastern coast of Africa, as well as to India and, possibly, China. These voyages were seasonal and regular and had access on arrival at Egyptian ports to organized land transport services using camels and donkeys. Similar services were found in the southern Arabian ports whence caravans set off for the Levant and Syria.

*Sidonian merchant ship, AD 2nd century*

Although records are in Greek, this was simply the lingua franca of the time; the operators were Egyptians and Arabs, who often settled abroad as agents, intermarried locally, and learned the local languages. The principal bases of this commerce were luxury goods — ivory, tortoise shell, rhinoceros horn, spices, frankincense, precious stones, fine cloth, silk and pepper — in demand in

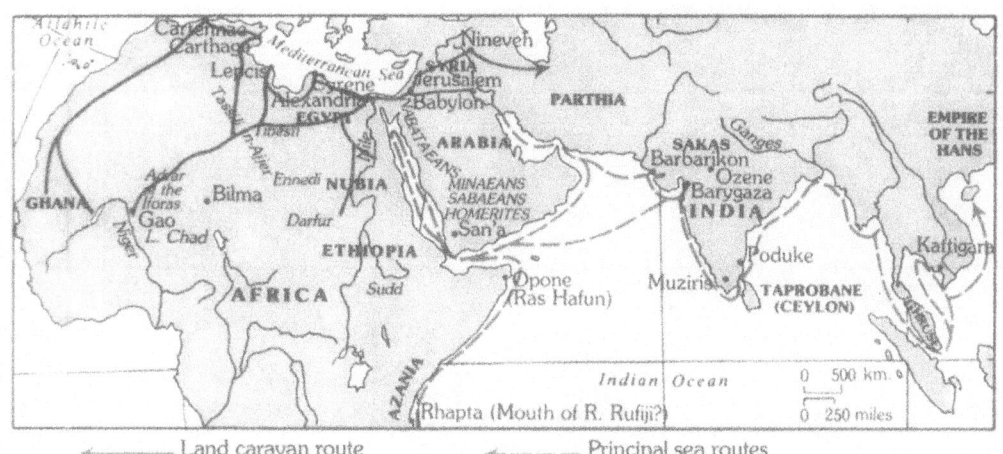

## COMMERCE WITH THE MIDDLE EAST C. AD 50

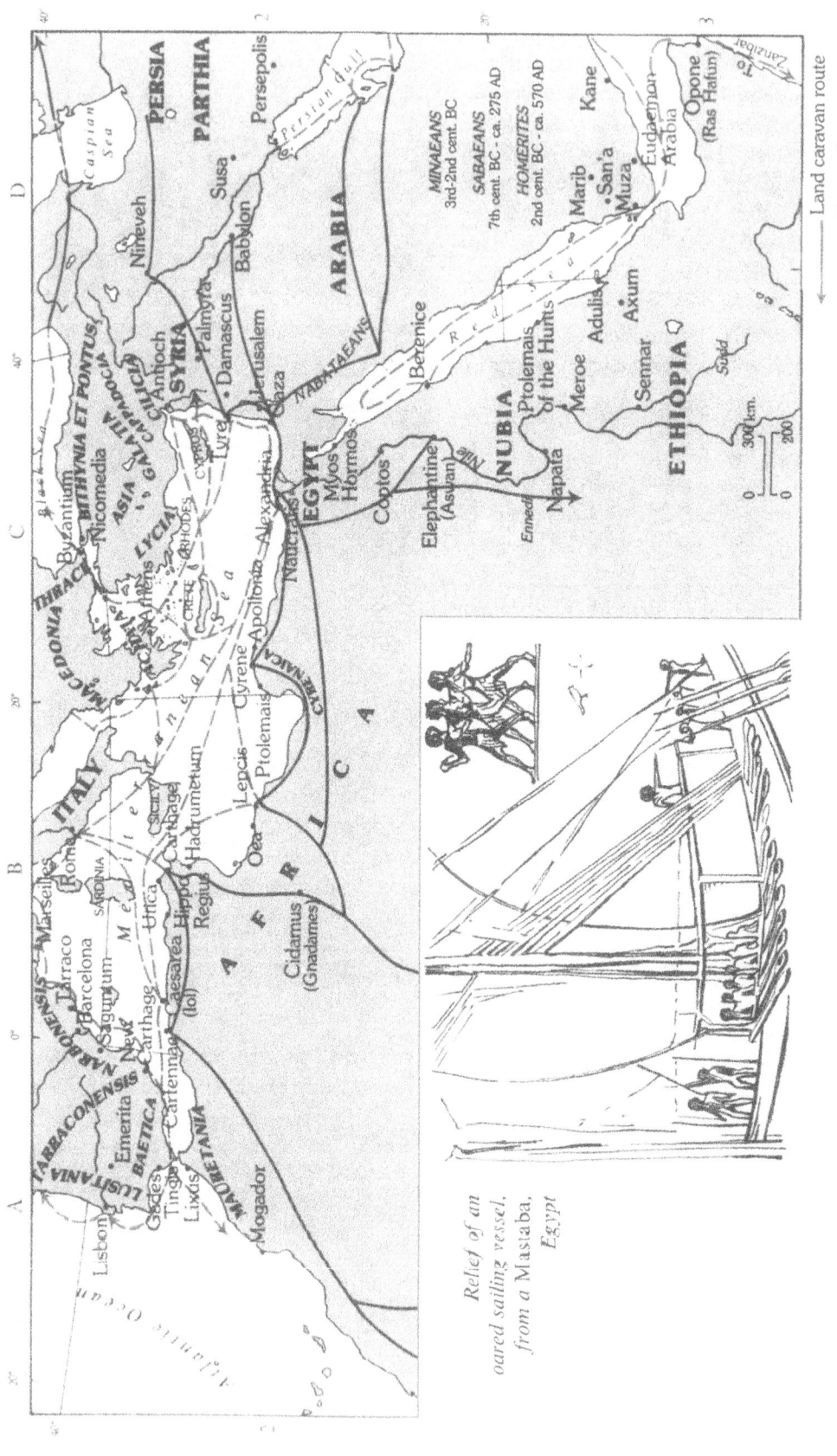

*Relief of an oared sailing vessel, from a Maštaba, Egypt*

COMMERCE WITH THE MIDDLE EAST c. AD 50

the Mediterranean region and distributed by long-established sea and land routes used for ordinary commerce. It was the Roman emperor Tiberius who complained that "the ladies and their baubles are transferring our money to foreigners." Nevertheless, to India went expensive manufactured cloth, glassware, copper, tin, lead, cosmetics, silver, wine, with slaves and slave girls.

## THE EXPANSION OF CHRISTIANITY, 1ST TO 6TH CENTURIES

Before the sudden emergence of Islam most of the Middle East was Christian. During its first two centuries relatively small areas had been converted, either from Judaism or from pagan cults. These areas were chiefly urban — potent areas of theological development where Jewish concepts of monotheism and Greek philosophy met and coalesced. Aside from these intellectual levels, the new religion offered all, without distinction of race or social status, a spiritual life in sacraments accessible to all and the promise of resurrection to eternal life.

Alexandria, in which a catechetical school had been founded before 155, was the leading center of advanced study by the early third century. Rome, Carthage, Lyons, and cities in Asia Minor had similar centers. In Palestine, Origen, the most brilliant and original thinker the church had yet seen, taught chiefly in the capital, Caesarea Maritima. Here, in the early fourth century Eusebius Pamphili, the first ecclesiastical historian, became bishop.

*Coin of Constantine the Great*

At a popular level, a monastic movement was born — first in Egypt, then Palestine, then throughout the Roman world — devoted to ascetical exercises, the psalms and the scriptures. Antony of Egypt gave inspiration to the first monasteries, to which Pachomius later gave order and discipline. To these monks, and their routine of prayer, manual work, and study, the contemporary world owes its schools, universities, and hospitals.

Under Constantine the Great (r. 306–337), Christianity became a state religion. His motives have been variously assessed, but his concern was genuine. The institution of church councils, an agreed canon,

*Philo of Alexandria, philosopher, d. AD 40*

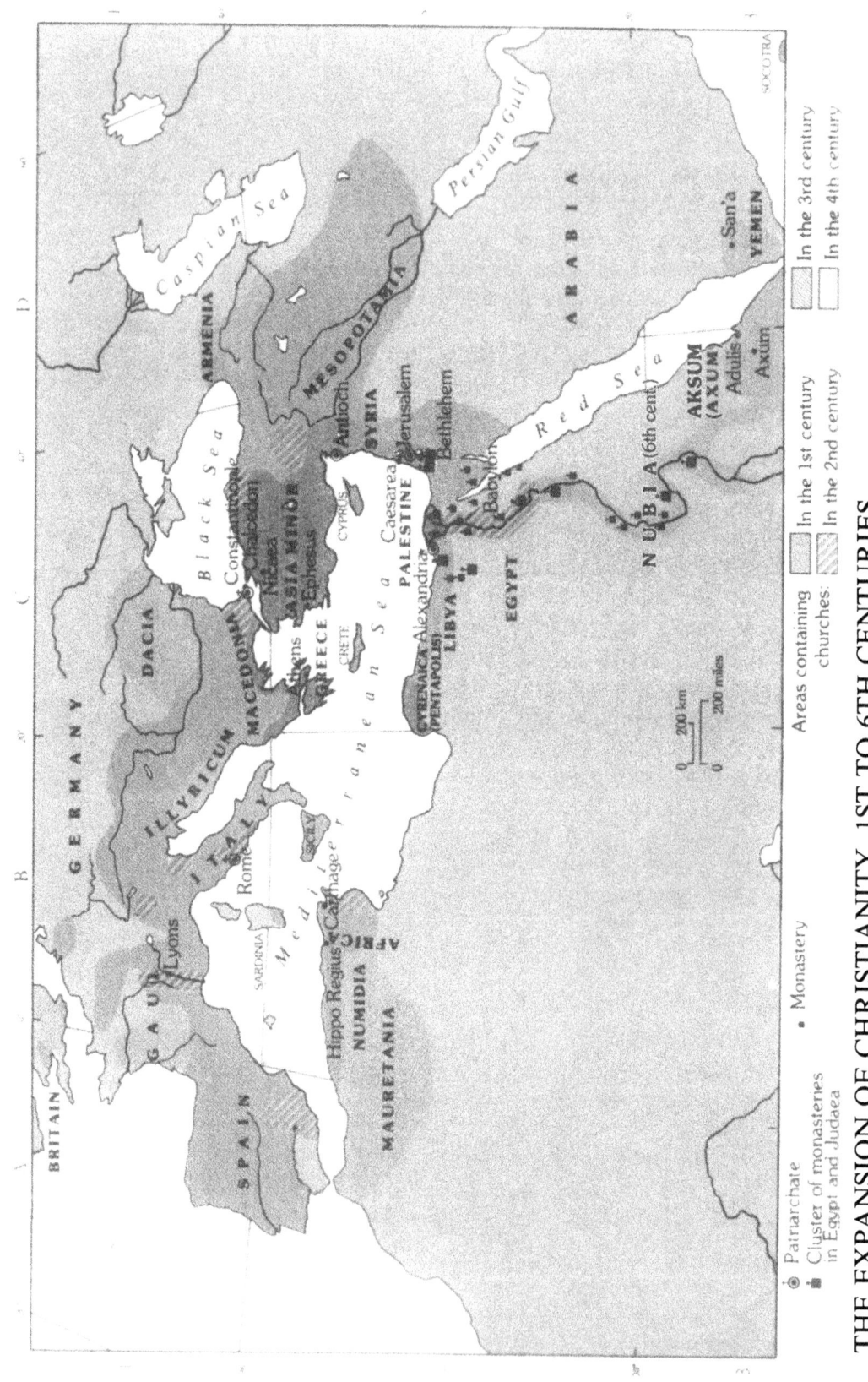

THE EXPANSION OF CHRISTIANITY, 1ST TO 6TH CENTURIES

or rule, of scripture, a recognized calendar, and systematic theology all spring from Alexandrian thought and teaching. Imperial involvement had its dangers, and local reactions emerged as separatist, heretical movements, weakening the entire body and providing an effective opening for Islam.

# ARABIA AT THE TIME OF THE BIRTH OF MUHAMMAD
## C. 570 UNTIL THE CALIPHATE OF ABU BAKR

The Prophet Muhammad's birth is commonly assigned to the *Year of the Elephant ('am al-fil)*, traditionally 570 or 571, but perhaps later. It was so called from an elephant which accompanied an Aksumite army, a sight never seen in Arabia before.

The Aksumites had usurped power in Yemen ca. 530, and held it until evicted by forces from Persia, who were to hold it until 632. It was incidental to the long struggle between Byzantium and Persia for control of the trade routes across the deserts. Under a peace treaty between the two great powers Byzantium was to pay an annuity to Persia, and this the Emperor Justin II refused in 572. In 574 Persia took the stronghold of Dara;

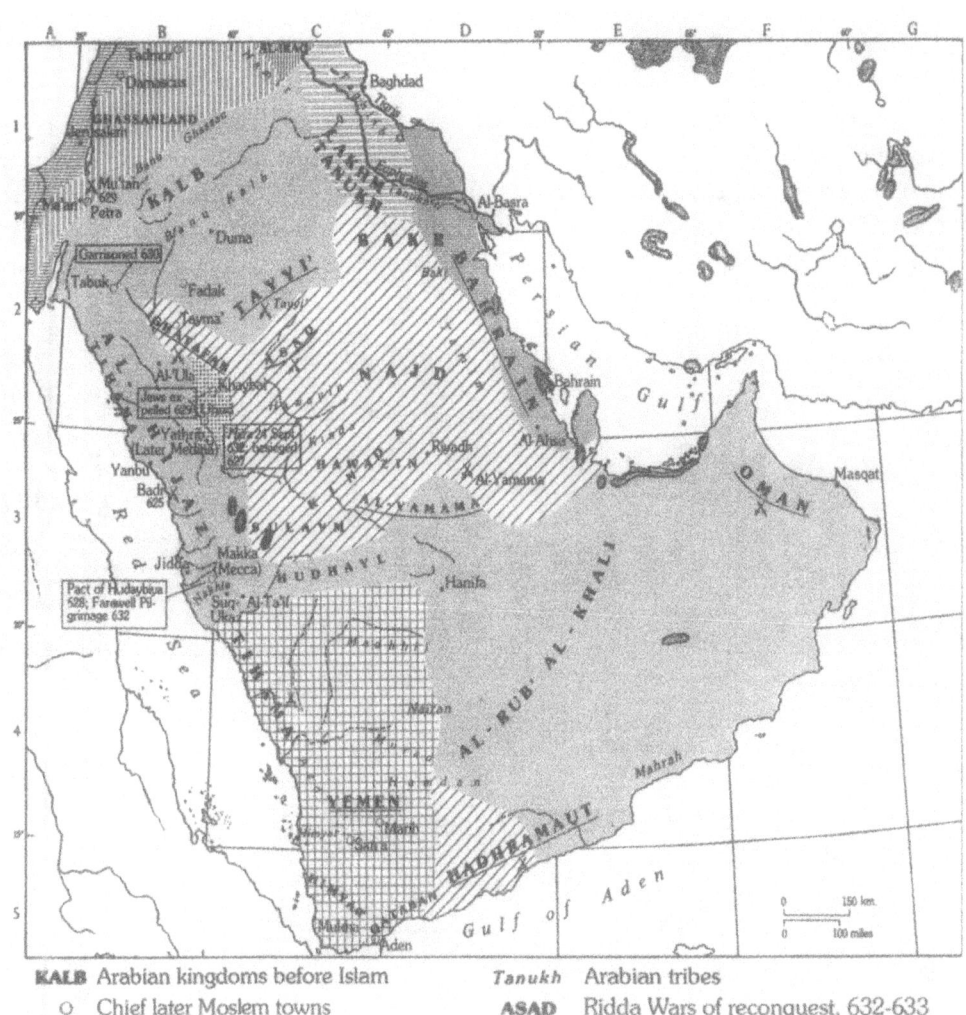

**KALB** Arabian kingdoms before Islam
○ Chief later Moslem towns
*Tanukh* Arabian tribes
**ASAD** Ridda Wars of reconquest, 632-633

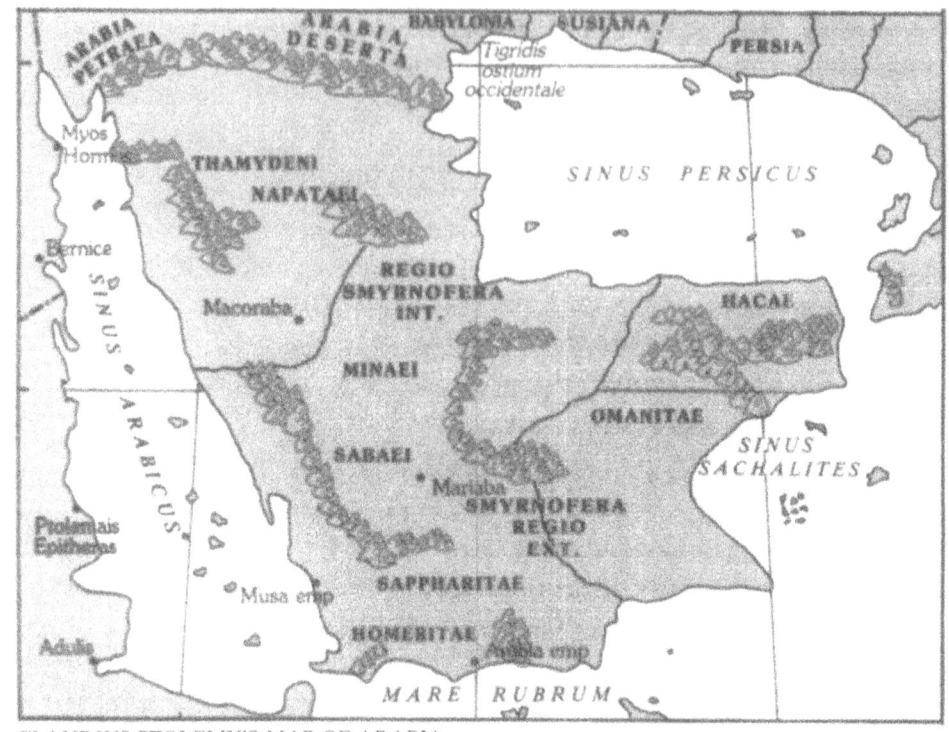
CLAUDIUS PTOLEMY'S MAP OF ARABIA

Byzantium secured a year's truce on payment of 45,000 gold pieces. In 575 the Aksumites were finally ejected — in spite of the elephant. Yemen now became a Persian viceroyalty, which held until the last satrap, Badhan, became a convert to Islam in 632. The rest of Arabia was divided among a number of petty kingdoms and nomadic tribes with shifting allegiances. Among the most prominent

*Old city of Marib
Photograph courtesy of
Leila Ingram*

*Aerial photo showing exposed masonry structures of the Mahram Bilqis, Marib Yemen.
Photo courtesy of Dr. Brian Moorman*

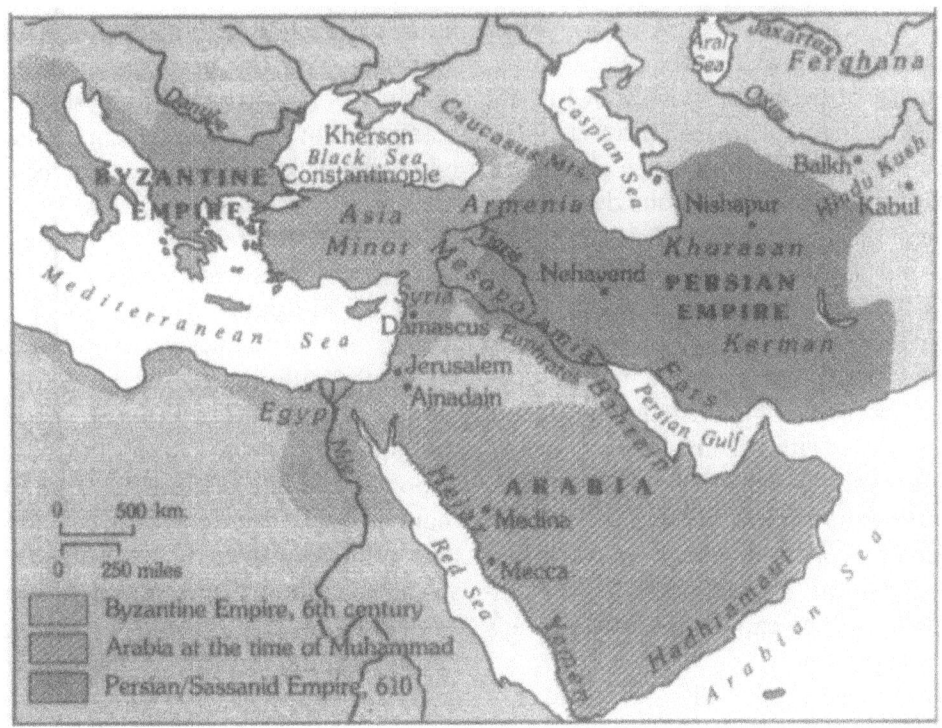

THE MIDDLE EAST AT THE TIME OF THE BIRTH OF MUHAMMAD

were Tadmor (Palmyra), Ghassan, Lakhm, Nabataea, and in the far south the ancient line of Himyar until its last king was deposed by an Aksumite army ca. 530. Many of these kingdoms and tribes were clients of Persia. In the Hejaz and Nejd the vast majority of the inhabitants were nomads, with poetry as their only expression of art. Mecca is located in the Hejaz, and Medina in an enclave between Hejaz and Nejd. Some idea of the historical situation is conveyed in Claudius Ptolemy's map of Arabia. Originally composed around AD 150, this map underwent numerous recensions until his *Geography* reached its present form in around 450. It is thus impossible to ascribe a precise date to it. Muslim historians refer to the time before the Prophet as *al-Jahiliyah*, the Days of Ignorance. If, as now, the Bedouins have little or no idea of religion, in southern Arabia there were elaborate cults with ornate temples. In Petra and Palmyra, and in Marib, the sun god and astral deities were popular. Natural objects, trees, wells, caves, and stones, were conceived as sacred. At Mecca, Arab authors believed that the well Zamzam had given water to Hagar and Ishmael,

*Ruins of the temple of Ilunquh, in the ancient kingdom of Saba, in Yemen*

and that in the Ka'aba there was a black meteorite, known as the Black Stone, which had been given to Ishmael by the angel Gabriel, who had instructed Ishmael in the ceremonies of the pilgrimage. In this sanctuary numerous deities were worshipped, of whom Allah, the principal but not the only god of the Meccans, was believed to be the creator and provider of all good. In addition to Jewish settlements in the north, there were colonies of Christian and Jewish merchants, with Medina as the principal settlement of Judaized clans of Arab and Aramaean origins. Among Christians, heterodox as well as orthodox beliefs were present, and parallels to Muhammad's teaching can be found in a variety of Christian sects.

Muhammad's adult life falls into two distinct periods. From AD 610 to 628 he taught in Mecca; in 628 until his death in 632, he resided in Medina. It was in this latter period that he emerged as a ruler and lawgiver. In 630, he made the pilgrimage to Mecca and smashed the many idols in the sanctuary, said to have numbered 360. In 631, his secular power had developed to the point that he was able to conclude treaties with Christian and Jewish tribes and to receive delegations of allegiance from almost all Arabia. In the following year, he again made the pilgrimage; he died three months later, in June 632. The suddenness of the Prophet's death was catastrophic, and the unification of Arabia that had begun had to be renewed under the caliph Abu Bakr (r. 632–634) in the so-called secession, or apostasy, wars. These had the effect not only of completing unification, but also of training and coordinating armies for the period of conquest that was to follow, even though this was hardly the primary intention.

# SEMITIC LANGUAGES AND THE DEVELOPMENT OF THE ART OF WRITING

Before 3000 BC, different forms of pictographic writing had evolved, chiefly in Egypt and Mesopotamia. In these forms, small pictures stood for objects and concepts. Around 1700 BC, there developed syllabic systems, in which each sign represented a syllable. Thus, in the cuneiform (Latin, cuneus, a wedge = form) system that developed in Mesopotamia, almost six hundred signs were used. Some of these signs had more than one sound value; some retained a pictographic type of function.

So large a repertoire of signs is obviously inconvenient, as the Chinese system seems to Westerners. It is unknown who first devised the first alphabetic script. There have been many different views, often held with tenacity, but no final conclusion. According to Greek legend, Kadmos, son of Agenor, king of Phoenicia, brought the use of letters to Greece from Phoenicia. Whoever it was, certainly this person was a Semite, for he isolated consonantal sounds and ignored vowels, although later, in Aramaic and Hebrew, and yet later in Arabic, signs to indicate vowels were occasionally used.

The term Semitic was introduced by the German philologist August Ludwig von Schlözer in 1781. It was chosen in the belief that those who spoke a particular group of languages were descended from Shem, son of Noah, as recorded in Genesis 10. This classification was made on a wholly geographical basis and included peoples who did not speak Semitic languages, Elamites and Lydians, and ignored others who did speak them. Among those excluded were Canaanites,

SEMITIC LANGUAGES AND THE DEVELOPMENT OF THE ART OF WRITING

who spoke a language closely akin to ancient Hebrew, and the peoples of Arabia and Ethiopia.

The ancient Semitic languages resemble one another as closely as do the Romance languages in Europe. They share easily definable characteristics: the predominance of triconsonantal roots, the similar formation of nominal and verbal stems, the use of personal pronouns to inflect verbs, and the use of two principal tenses — incomplete and completed time. These characteristics, with, of course, many local differences, persist to this day over a wide range of languages, all of them ultimately descended from Ur-Semitic (or primitive Semitic), now long extinct. The earliest of these languages, known as old Akkadian, was in use in Iraq between 2400 and 2200 BC Although derivatives of it survived long after, it eventually gave way to another Semitic language, Aramaic, the official language of the Persian empire of Cyrus II. Parallel to Aramaic were the languages of Canaanitic origin: Phoenician and Punic, the language of Carthage; Hebrew; and the speech of certain adjacent peoples, such as the Moabites and Edomites. These two branches are known as West Semitic (derivatives of Canaanite) and East Semitic (derivative of Aramaic), the latter being the first to disappear. From Canaanite, modern Hebrew is a descendant; and from Aramaic, a number of existing a languages and dialects descend. South Semitic forms a separate branch from which descend northern and southern pre-Islamic languages together with classical and modern Arabic in all its forms, the languages of Ethiopia, and small, archaic language groups in Yemen and Socotra.

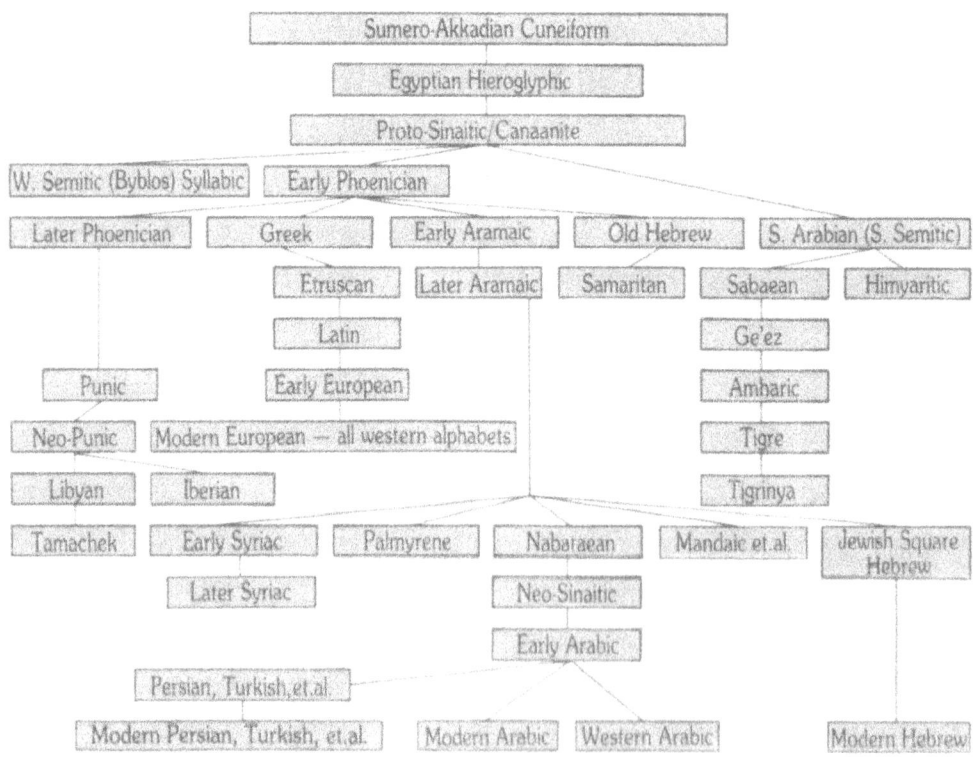

HISTORY OF THE ALPHABET

*Table showing the principal scripts in the development of the history of the alphabet*

# II. FROM THE HIJRA (AD 622) UNTIL THE END OF THE UMAYYAD DYNASTY (750)

*Mosaic in the bathhouse of the Umayyad Hisham's Palace at Jericho*

## THE ARAB CONQUEST OF SYRIA, IRAQ AND PERSIA

By AD 629 and 630, Arabs from the peninsula had raided Byzantine territory in southern Syria. In 633, regular operations began with as many as nine thousand men. This army was later expanded to 22,500. Amr ibn al-As led along the coastal route via Aylah. Yazid I ibn Abi-Sufyan attacked southern and southeast Syria. The generalissimo Abu Ubaydah ibn Jarrah proceeded along the ancient trade route to Damascus. On 4 February 639, the Byzantine troops facing Yazid I were almost annihilated; around the same time, Khalid ibn al-Walid led a raid into Iraq and seized al-Hira (Hira). He then turned northwest and, after a brilliant forced march, outflanked the Byzantine army. He defeated the Byzantines at Ajnadain on 30 July 634, laying almost all Palestine open. After a further Byzantine rout in January 635, Khalid laid siege to Damascus. After the city surrendered in September, all the great cities of Syria fell.

The emperor Heraclius's army of fifty thousand men was defeated decisively at the battle of the Yarmuk on 20 August 636. Only Jerusalem and Caesarea held out — the former until 638, the latter until 640. The superficiality of the Hellenization of Syria was now exposed: an Arab ruler was preferable to an alien.

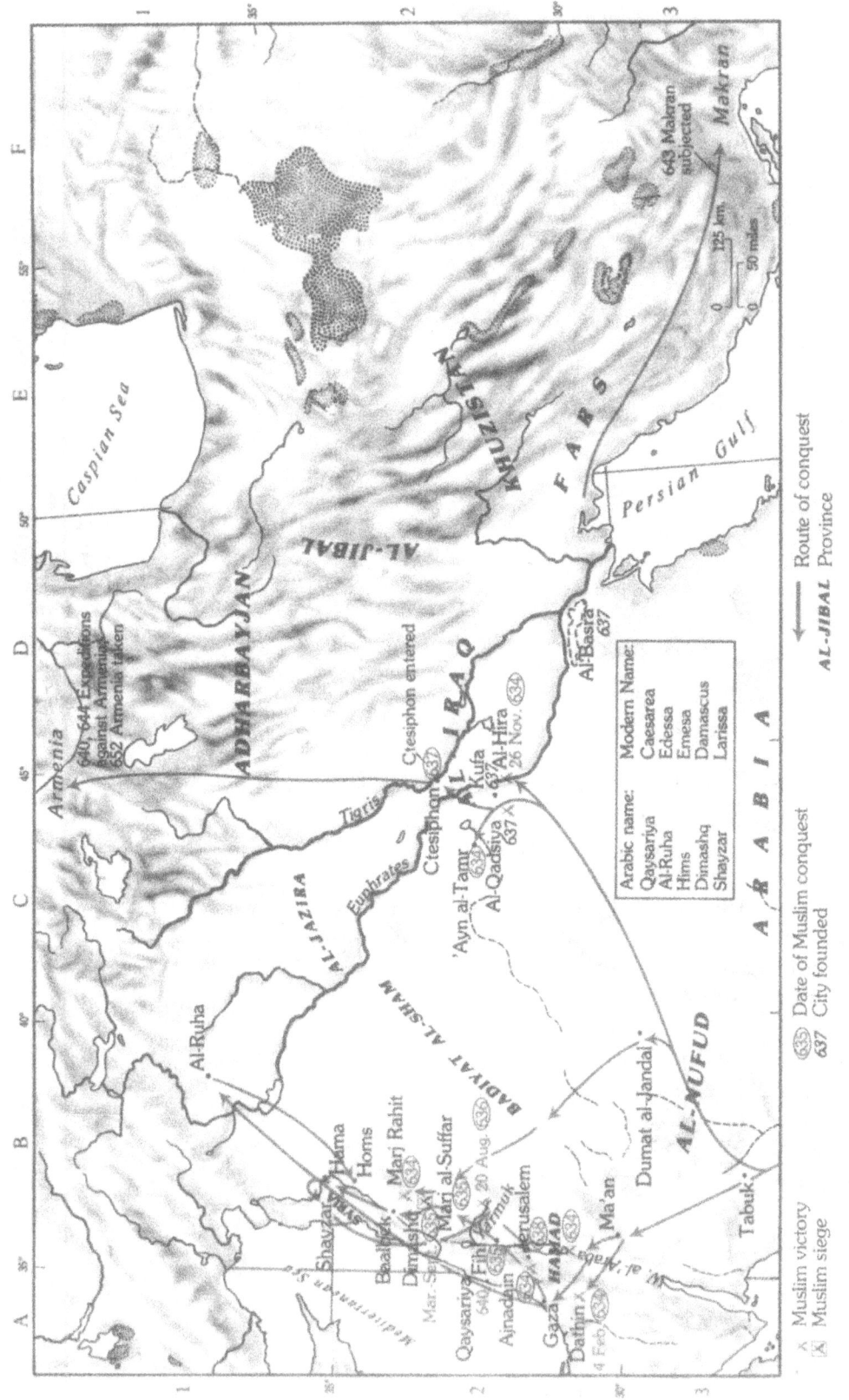

THE ARAB CONQUEST OF SYRIA, IRAQ AND PERSIA

*The Umayyad mosque in Damascus*

In Iraq the Arabs left behind by Khalid were almost annihilated by a Persian force near al-Hira on 26 November 634. On 31 May or 1 June 637, an enlarged Arab army defeated the Persian force in southern Iraq, whose inhabitants had sentiments similar to their Syrian fellow Semites. Later in June, the Arabs made a triumphal entry into Ctesiphon. They now possessed the most sophisticated capital in the east and endless booty. Garrisons were established at al-Kufa and Basra. In the Persian highlands, the Sassanian dynasty of Yazdagird III stood out, but all was over when, in 641, al-Mawsil (Mosul) was captured, and the Persian army was annihilated at Nehavand.

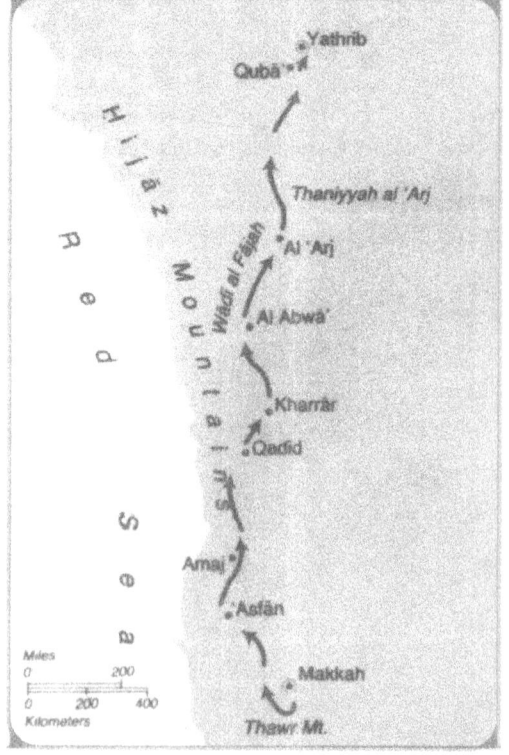

*Illustrative map of Muhammad's migration to Yathrib (Medina)*

# THE ARAB CONQUEST OF EGYPT

It was obvious to Amr ibn al-As that as long as the Arab left flank was exposed to Byzantine forces in Egypt, the conquests of Khalid ibn al-Walid in Syria and Persia were insecure. Amr had known Egypt well from caravan trading in his youth, and now he took advantage of the caliph Umar I's visit to Jerusalem to seek permission to cross to Egypt.

In December 639, Amr and four thousand cavalrymen reached al-Arish via the route that Abraham had taken and that later Cambyses II, Alexander, the Holy Family, and, finally, Allenby would take. Napoleon would take this route in reverse.

In January 640 al-Farama (Pelusium) fell after a month's siege. Amr at once marched on Babilyun (Babylon), where a Roman fort dominated the peak of the Nile Delta, the present-day Old Cairo. Shortly thereafter, he was reinforced by ten thousand men, thus bringing an army of fourteen thousand against the twenty-five thousand Byzantines. Amr attacked at 'Ayn Shams (Heliopolis) in July 640. Cyrus, Patriarch of Alexandria, who was also acting governor, tried to buy Amr off, but failed. The fortress capitulated on 6 April 641.

Amr still had to take the Delta. Nikiu fell on 13 May, but Alexandria, the commercial capital of the world, lay ahead.

*Mosque of Amr, Fustat, Cairo*

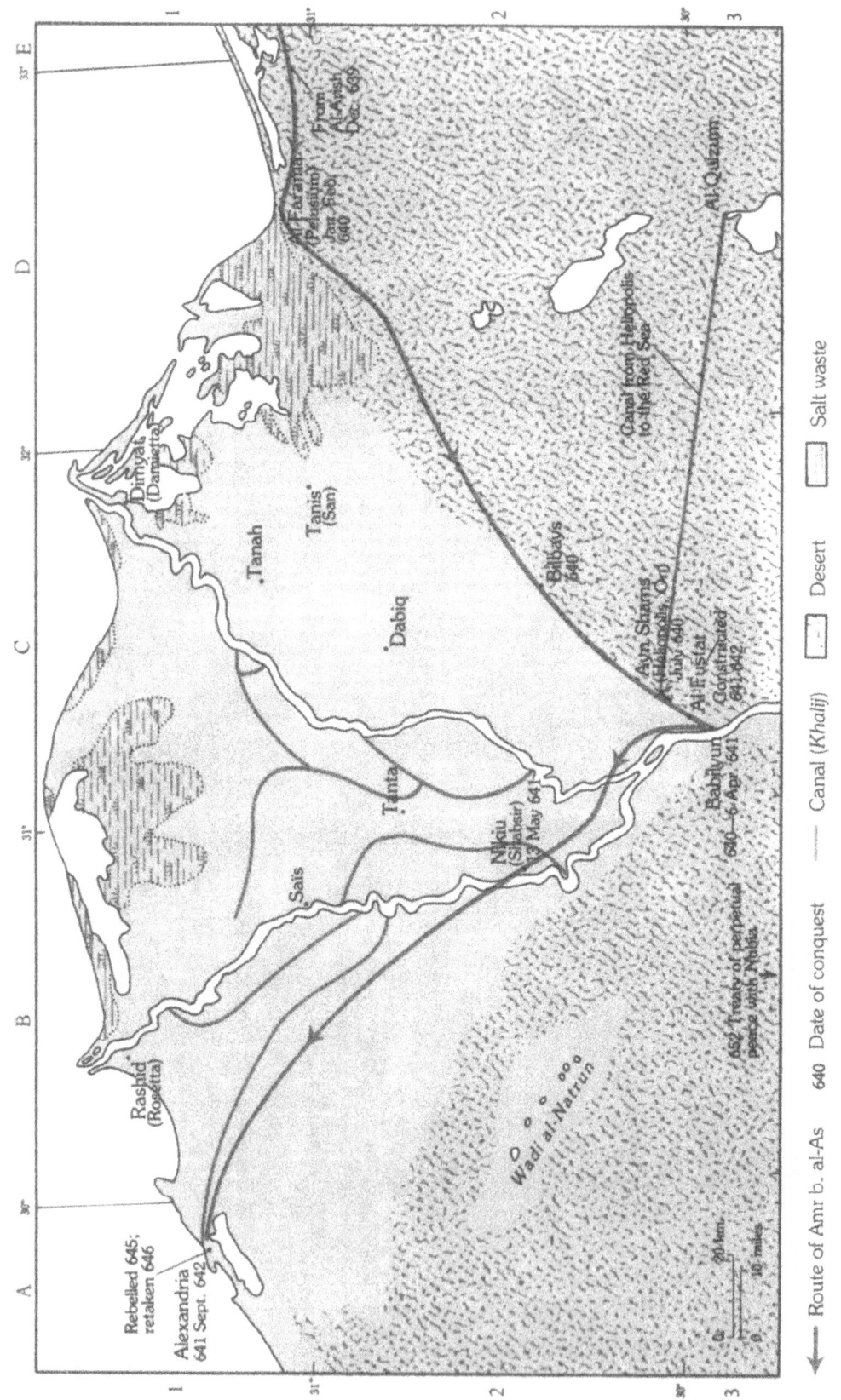

THE ARAB CONQUEST OF EGYPT

Alexandria was a splendid city, garrisoned by fifty thousand men and backed by the whole Byzantine navy. On 8 November the Byzantines capitulated. The Coptic population of native Egyptians had no love for the Byzantines, and the poll tax exacted by the Muslims was less onerous. In spite of their numbers the Byzantines had no stomach to fight an enemy that had so often defeated them. Amr had now to provide an administration. A camp was set up with a defensive ditch, whence its name al-Fustat, the fosse. The old Pharaonic canal connecting the Nile with the Red Sea was reopened, and trade could flow between the Red Sea and the Mediterranean. The Byzantine administrative system was maintained for the Coptic clerks could hardly be replaced by warriors from the desert.

*Great mosque of Sidi Uqbah in Kairouan, Tunisia*

## THE ARAB CONQUEST OF NORTH AFRICA AND SPAIN

Although Alexandria had been acquired, the Byzantine fleet presented a continual threat. In 649 a Muslim fleet was built for the Egyptian rulers in Alexandria, enabling the seizure of Cyprus. A struggle for mastery continued into the ninth century.

It remained to secure Egypt's western flank. In 642–643 Amr ibn al-As led his cavalry into the Libyan Pentapolis, or

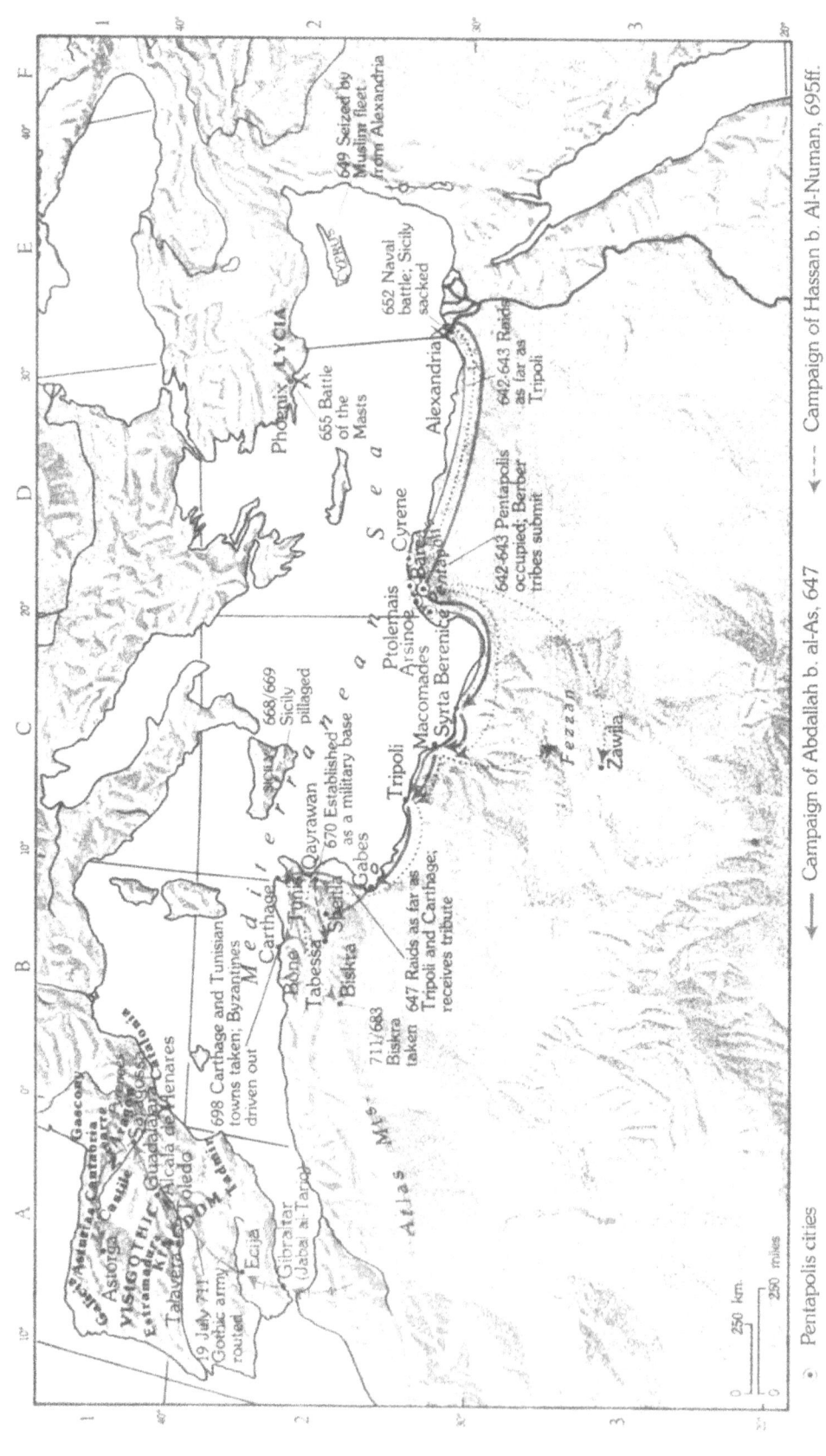

THE ARAB CONQUEST OF NORTH AFRICA AND SPAIN

Mihrab, mimbar *and* dikka *of the Great Mosque, Kairouan*

Cyrenaica. Barqa (Barca) was occupied without difficulty, and several Berber tribes submitted to him. Amr's brother Abdullah pushed further to Tripoli and then into the Byzantine province of Africa, receiving tribute from Carthage. In the south a treaty was made with the Nubian kingdom of Dongola, providing the Arabs with an annual tribute of slaves.

In the west no attempt at further conquest was made until 670, when Uqbah ibn Nafi founded Kairouan (Arabic, *Qayrawan*, from Persian, *karwan*, caravan) as a military base. The mosque he built has been rebuilt many times, finally in 836. According to tradition Uqbah advanced westward until the Atlantic stopped his horse. Under the governorship of Hassan ibn al-Numan al-Ghassani, the Byzantines were driven from Carthage in 698; Hassan now had to face Berber resistance, led by a prophetess (Arabic, *kahinah*) until she was defeated by treachery. His successor, Musa ibn Nusayr, subdued the north African coast. In 711 his lieutenant, Tariq ibn Ziyad, a Berber freedman, led a raid into Spain, crossing at Gibraltar, which carries his name (Arabic: *Jabal al-Tariq*, the mountain of Tariq).

A wholesale campaign of conquest began. On 19 July 711, Tariq's twelve thousand men defeated the Visigothic king Roderick's army of twenty-five thousand. Thereafter the conquest was virtually a ceremonial parade, and by the end of the summer Tariq held half of Spain. Acting out of jealousy, Musa put Tariq in chains, and recalled him. On the same grounds, the caliph recalled Musa to Damascus, which he entered in 715 with four hundred Visigothic princes and a huge retinue of slaves and prisoners bearing booty. The Arabs had seized the fairest of the Byzantine provinces.

# THE UMAYYAD CALIPHATE

Muhammad left no constitutional arrangements for a successor. As prophet he could have none. The first three caliphs succeeded simply as senior tribal elders. Ali, the fourth caliph, was acclaimed because he was Muhammad's first cousin and the husband of his daughter Fatima, introducing the prospect of hereditary legitimacy which led to a quarrel between the Sunnites and Shi'ites, the traditionalists and sectarians. The latter supported Ali, who was murdered on his way to a mosque by a Kharijite on 24 January 661. His successor was Mu'awiyah, leader of the Sunnites.

The new dynasty, proclaimed in Jerusalem, established Damascus as capital. Under this dynasty, north Africa was added to the caliphate, and Khorasan and Turkestan were raided. Mu'awiyah had substantial administrative abilities and gave order and discipline to the army. The civil service was reorganized on Byzantine lines, and a period of stability was inaugurated. An immense free-trade area was now open to commerce.

Under the reigns of his grandson, Abd al-Malik ibn Marwan (685–705), and his four sons (705–743) the Islamic empire reached its greatest extent, from the Atlas Mountains and the Pyrenees to the Indus River and even into China. This area far surpassed that of the Roman Empire and even the empire of Alexander the Great. Khorasan, Sughd (Sogdiana), Khwarizm, and Farghana were the crossroads of east-west trade. Trade with India after the conquest of Sind (711–712) enabled the magnificence of the Umayyad mosques and palaces. The Dome of the Rock in Jerusalem, among the most splendid of man's architectural achievements, belongs to this period.

The Umayyad state was now an Arab state; Arabic was the official language, and there was an Arab currency, postal service, chancery, and judiciary. An immense construction program included new irrigation canals. Though the desert austerity of the Muslim population now gave way in this period of prosperity to drunken debauchery and lechery, poetry, music, and other cultural values survived.

*Early Umayyad* dinar, *imitating a Byzantine gold piece, which was decorated with a gold cross; the Umayyads deleted the cross-bar, leaving the upright*

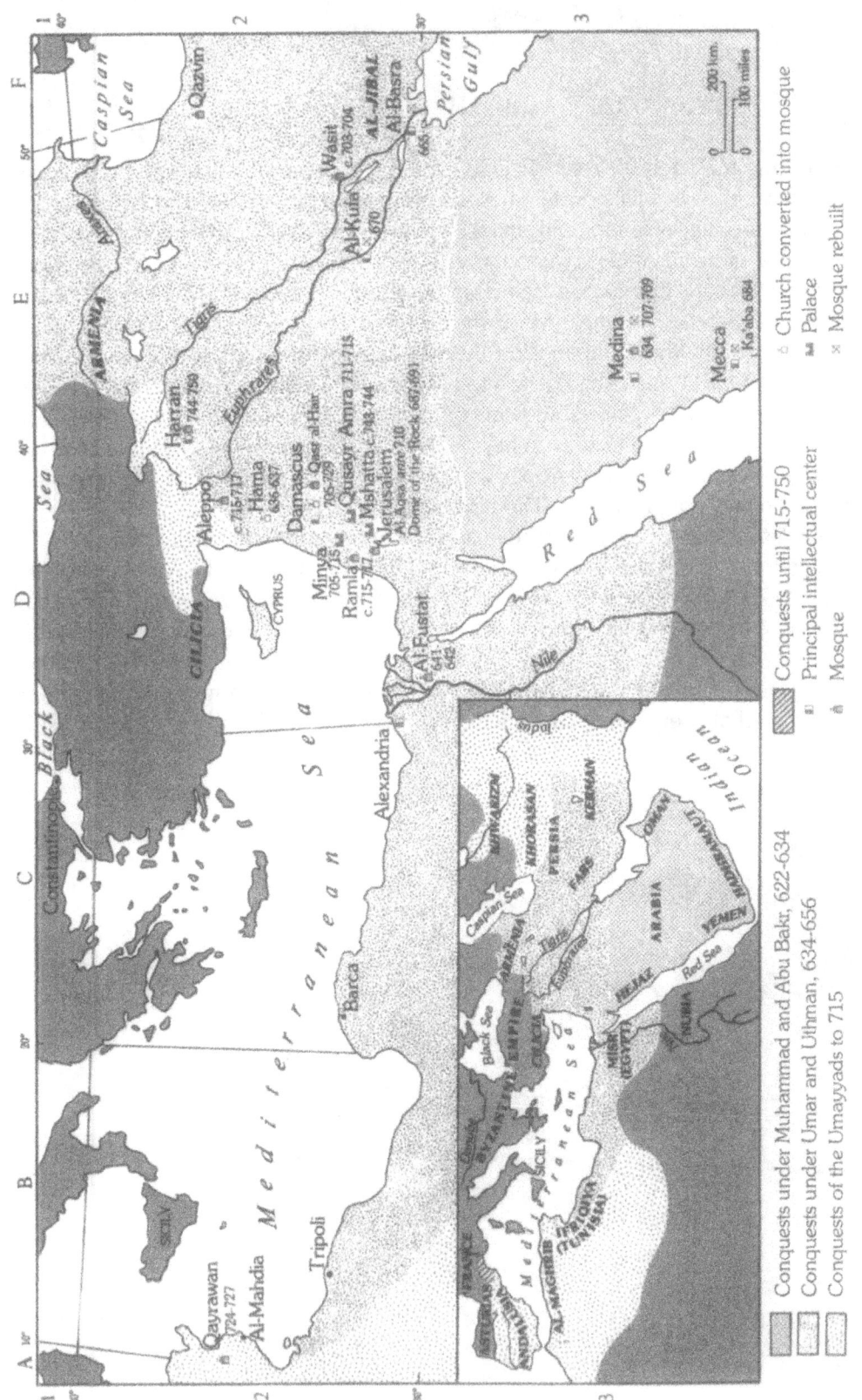

THE UMAYYAD CALIPHATE

# III. FROM THE ABBASID DYNASTY UNTIL THE CRUSADES (750–1087)

## THE ABBASID CALIPHATE

Even during the reign of Yazid II (720–724) the caliph was accustomed to pass his time hunting, wining, and in the harem. Poetry and music were more entertaining than the Koran (*Qur'an*) and affairs of state. Hence when the descendants of al-Abbas, an uncle of the Prophet, pressed their claim to the throne, they rapidly gained adherents, especially among the Persians. Thus it was in Khorasan that Abu al-Abbas was first proclaimed caliph in 750. The new dynasty lasted 508 years with Baghdad as its capital and in shadow form in Cairo until 1517. After the ninth century, however, caliphs reigned rather than ruled.

The Abbasid caliphate was a theocratic state. The caliph wore the *burdah* (cloak) of the Prophet at his accession and on state occasions. As in medieval Europe, the caliph was surrounded by canon lawyers, among whom were Persians and other non-Arabs. Though Spain slowly began to be lost, by 762, when Baghdad was founded, the empire was solidly established. As described in *One Thousand Nights and a Night*, the reign of Harun al-Rashid (786–809) launched an era of prosperity in which the arts and sciences blossomed.

The weakness of this highly bureaucratic state lay in its army. The Arabs had never had a standing army with discipline, training, and tradition. A caliphal bodyguard provided a nucleus of infantry, archers, cavalry, engineers, and naphtha-throwers. Persians from Khorasan

*Arab caravan, Hariri MS, dated 1237*

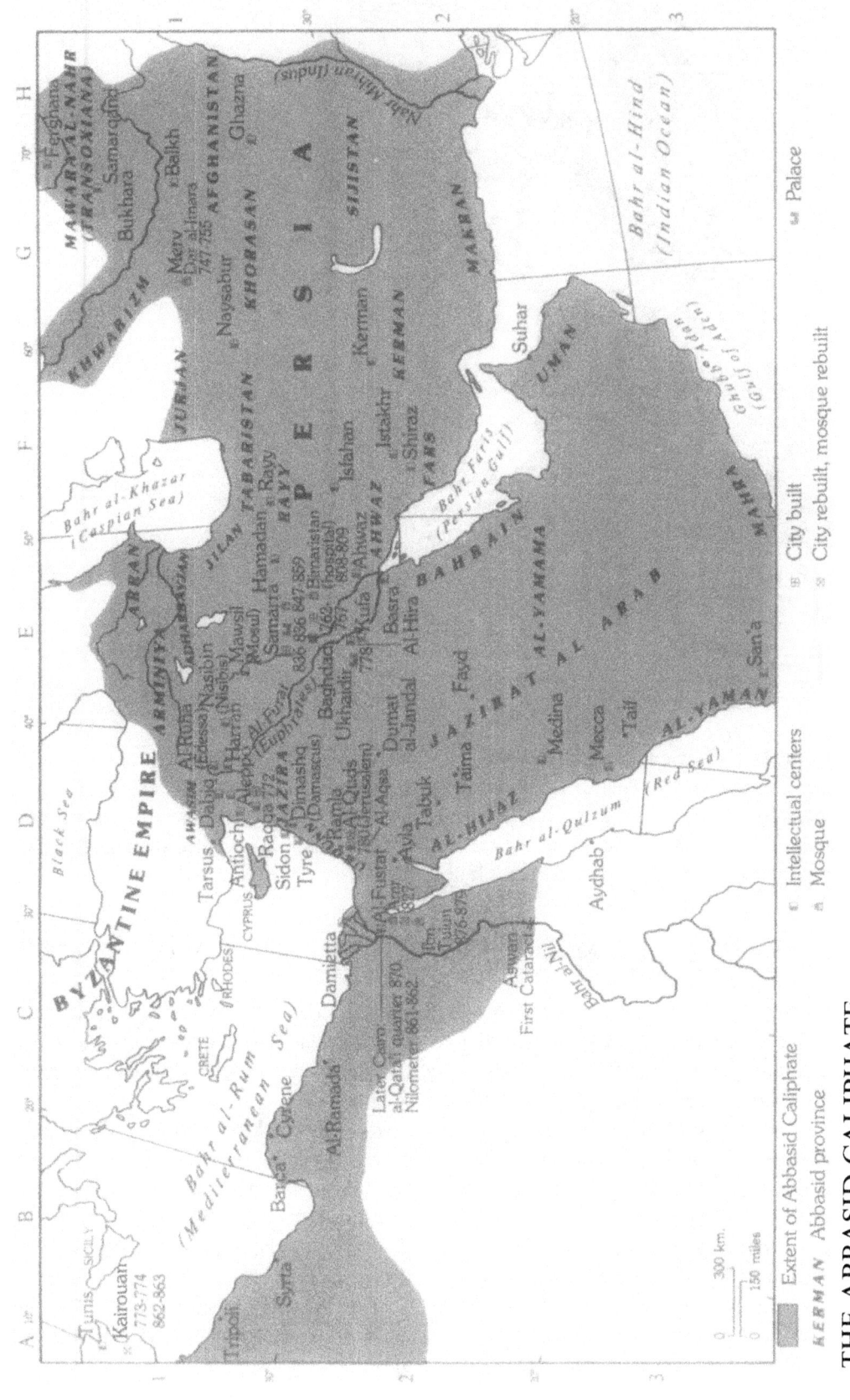

THE ABBASID CALIPHATE

*Arab rider - 10th century Arabian papyrus*

formed this nucleus until 833, when they were replaced by Turks. By 836 these were the terror of Baghdad. The caliph built a new capital at Samarra, where the habits of the Roman Praetorian Guard were speedily reproduced. The empire slowly dissolved into governorships, often with the hereditary title of sultan, with the caliph no more than a shadow.

## ARABS IN THE MEDITERRANEAN IN THE 9TH CENTURY

During the ninth century, two Muslim powers — in the east the Abbasid caliphate, in the west the Aghlabids from Ifriqiya (approximately modern Tunisia) — disputed Byzantine supremacy in the Mediterranean. In 797 the caliph Harun al-Rashid had campaigned in Asia Minor as far as Ephesus and Ankara; and this démarche against the Byzantines was undoubtedly related to the caliph's relationship with Charlemagne between 797 and 806. In the eastern Mediterranean pirates from Crete raided the Aegean Islands and in the tenth century the Greek coast. These operations were random and with merely temporary consequences.

In the western Mediterranean the Aghlabids prosecuted a war of quite different character. The founder of the dynasty, Ibrahim ibn al-Aghlab (r. 800–811) was the Abbasid governor of Ifriqiya, who declared himself independent within a year of his appointment. Thereafter no Abbasid authority was exercised in the area.

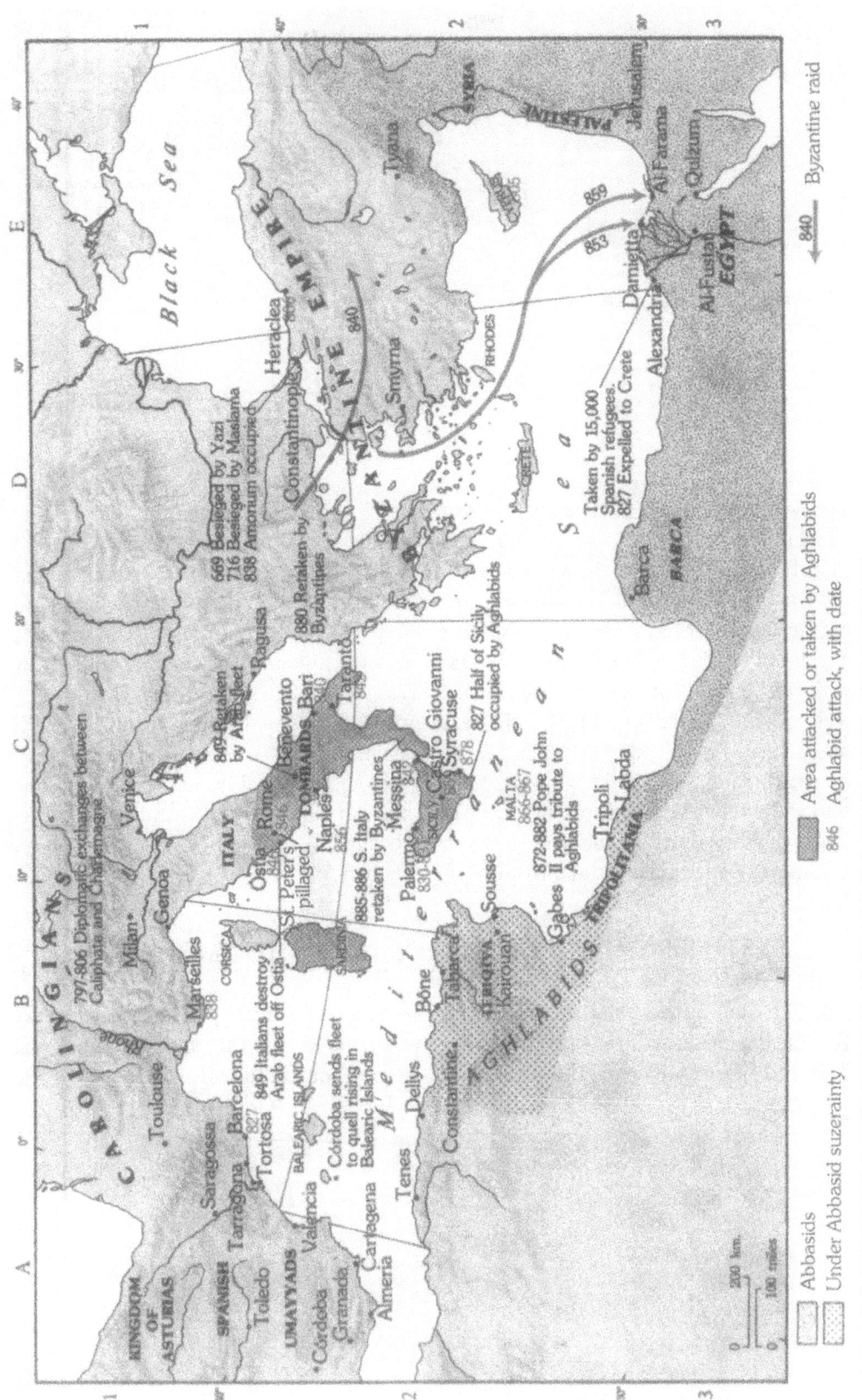

ARABS IN THE MEDITERRANEAN IN THE 9TH CENTURY

*Arabic tax receipt, from Egypt 812*

The Mediterranean was now surrounded by Islamic powers on the west, south, and east. It was logical that the successors to the Carthaginians would dispute control of the central Mediterranean, and this began under Ziyadat-Allah I (r. 817–838) with an expedition against Byzantine Sicily in 827. The conquest of Sicily was not achieved until 902. What began as piratical raids resulted in permanent settlements in Sicily, Sardinia, and in much of Italy south of Naples. In 846 a landing at Ostia failed to take Rome, but the basilicas of St. Peter and of St. Paul's outside the Walls were pillaged. In 849 the Arab fleet was destroyed off Ostia, but this was a temporary setback. In 866–867 Malta, the key to the central Mediterranean, was taken, and from 872 until 882 Pope John II found it prudent to pay tribute. In 882 John II was murdered by the Roman nobility. Two short papal reigns followed, and then in 885 to 886 the Byzantines reoccupied southern Italy under Pope Stephen V.

## THE SPANISH UMAYYADS AND THE EMIRATE

All but the northwest corner of the Iberian Peninsula was in Arab hands by 715 and answerable to the caliph in Damascus. About 717 or 718 France was raided as far as Narbonne; an attempt on Toulouse was defeated. In

*Enamelled mosque lamps*

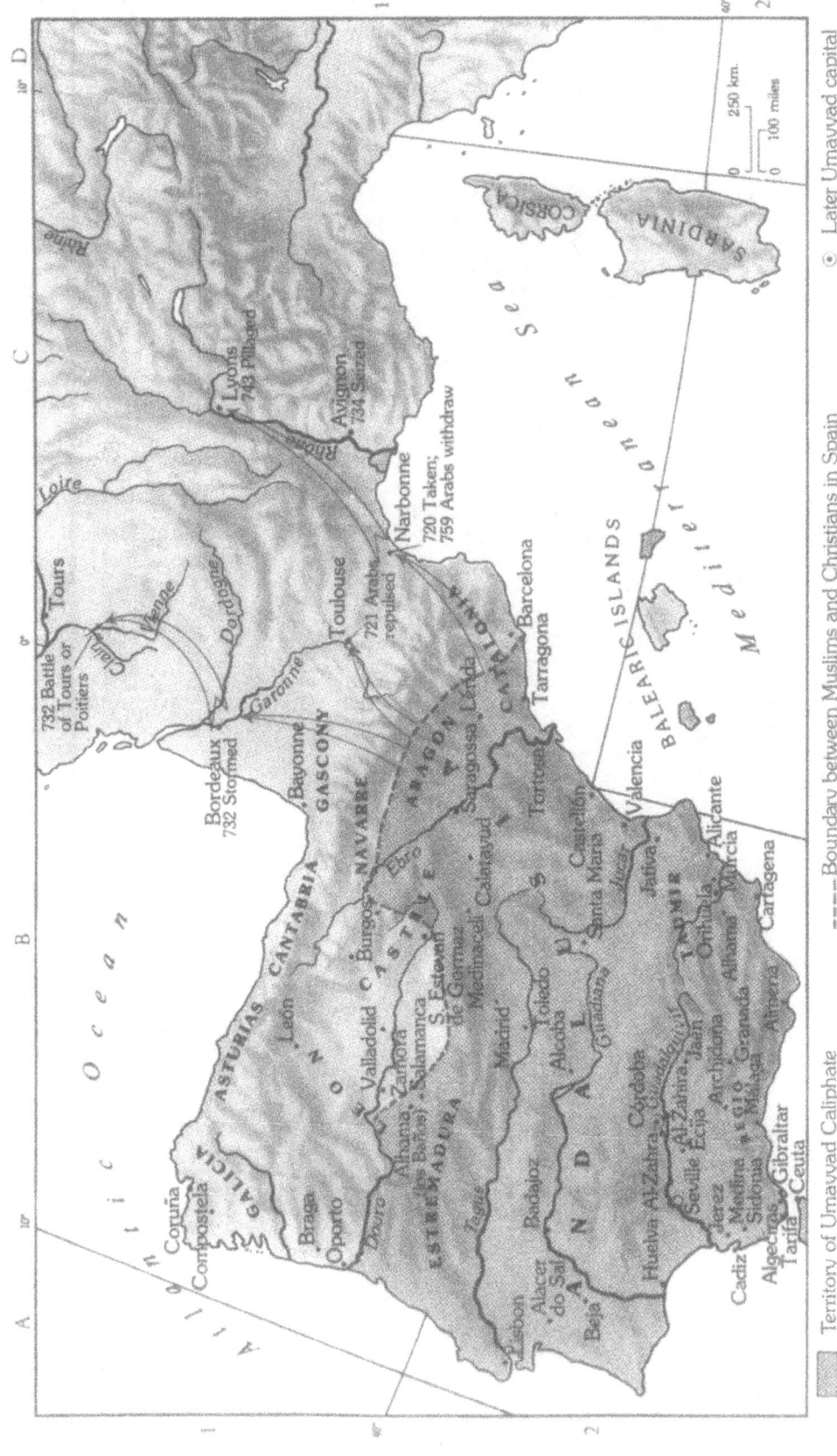

THE SPANISH UMAYYADS AND THE EMIRATE

732 Abd al-Rahman al-Ghafiqi stormed Bordeaux and advanced on Tours. After a day of battle with Frankish forces under Charles Martel, the Arabs slipped away during the night. It was not so much a victory as the beginning of an ebb tide. In 759 the Arabs relinquished Narbonne and finally withdrew from France.

The capital of the emir, or lieutenant-governor subject to the provincial governor at Kairouan, was at first in Seville and then in Córdoba. The emirate was torn between factions of Arabs from Syria and Yemen and the Berbers from North Africa. In 755, following the overthrow of the Umayyads in Damascus by the Abbasids, the Spanish Umayyad emirate declared its independence. Abd al-Rahman I, a survivor of the Umayyad massacre by the Abbasids, seized power in Córdoba. Many years of struggle

*Sanctuary of the Great Mosque of Córdoba, Spain*

*The* Musalla *of the Great Mosque*

among Arabs of different origins, Berbers, Goths, Hispano-Arabs, Numidians, Syrians, and the earlier mixed populations of the peninsula followed. The zenith of Moorish Spain was signified in 788 by the building of the Great Mosque of Córdoba, with its forest of columns and arches, splendid mosaics, and monumental outer court. Though transformed into a cathedral in 1236, it is still known as la Mezquita. Córdoba now rivaled Baghdad as a cultural center and mediated Eastern culture to barbaric Europe. Whereas the rulers were Muslims, the majority of the population remained Christian, affecting Arab culture. In 854 a Christian writer remarked: Our Christian young men with their elegant airs...are...intoxicated with Arab eloquence...knowing nothing of the beauty of the Church's literature, and looking down with contempt on the streams of the Church that flow forth from Paradise....Hardly a man in a thousand can write a letter to inquire after a friend's health intelligibly [in his native language] but can learnedly roll out grandiloquent periods in the Chaldaean tongue.

## ISLAMIC DYNASTIES IN THE EAST, 9TH TO 11TH CENTURIES

After the murder of the caliph al-Mutawakkil by his guard in December 861, the history of the caliphate presents a confused picture of disintegration and

*Vakil Mosque, Shiraz, Persia*

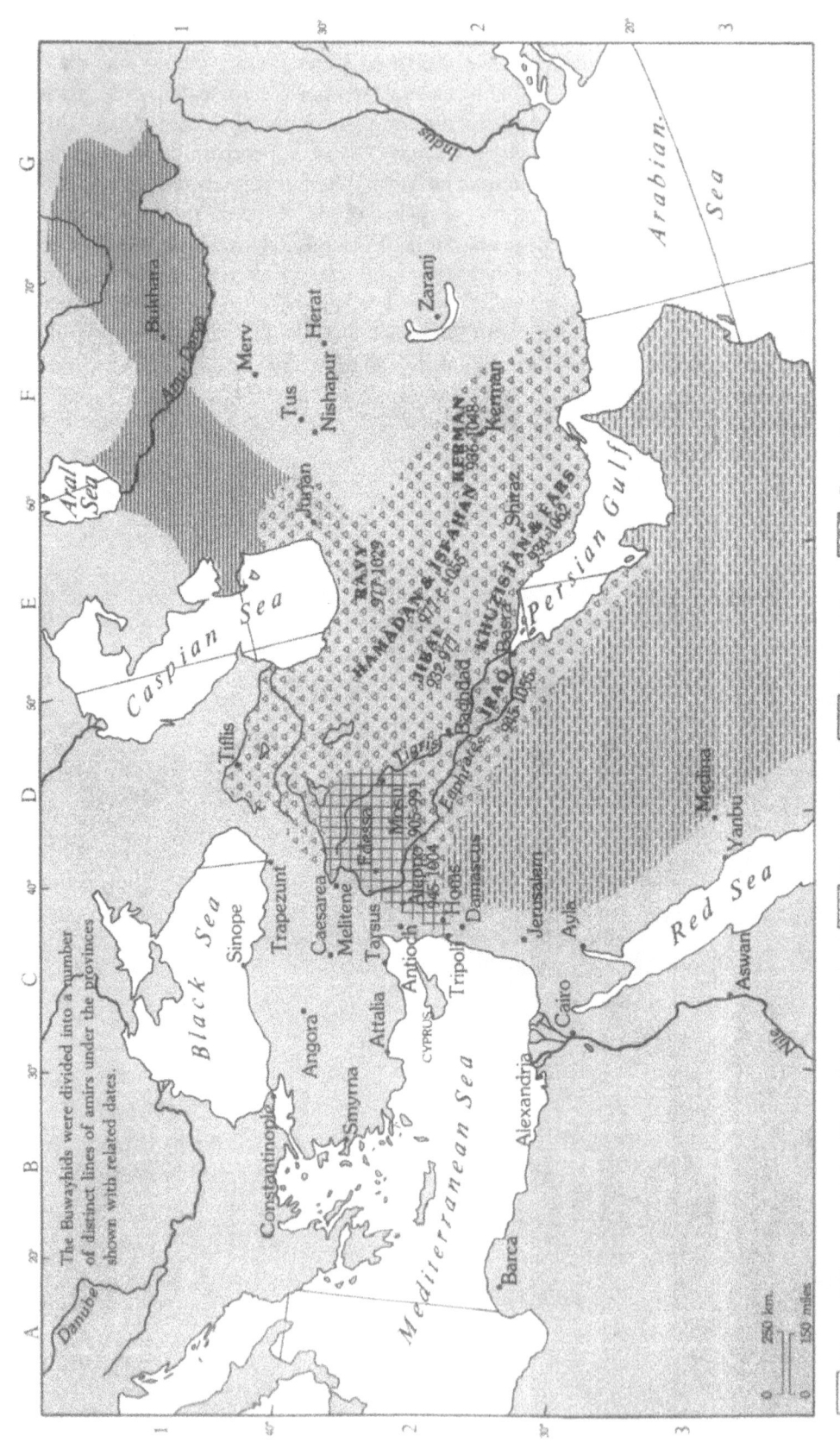

ISLAMIC DYNASTIES IN THE EAST, 9TH TO 11TH CENTURIES

unstable rule by a series of puppets of the Turkish troops. Spain, North Africa, Egypt, and the Levant had long been lost. At one time in the mid-tenth century, three former caliphs, all blinded, could be seen in Baghdad begging for bread.

From 945 until 1055 a succession of *amirs al-umara* (emirs above all emirs) ruled, making and unmaking caliphs. The Buwayhids had come from the southern shores of the Caspian Sea, and in the first half of the tenth century they had taken Persia and Iraq. They preferred Persia as a residence, and Baghdad was governed as a province from Shiraz. Under Adud al-Dawlah, Buwayhid power was at its zenith; he assumed the title of the ancient rulers of Persia, *shahanshah*, underlining the essentially Persian character of the Shi'ite dynasty. This character is also reflected in the building of mosques, shrines, hospitals, public buildings, and canals. The Bimaristan al-Adudi, a hospital in Baghdad with a teaching faculty, was the most sophisticated of its time. Tolerant to all, the Buwayhids repaired even churches and monasteries.

Buwayhid power was swept away by the advent of the Seljuq (Seljuk) Turks. Family quarrels were tearing apart the Buwayhids when the Seljuq Tughril Beg entered Baghdad in 1055. This family had originated in the Kyrghyz Steppe of Turkestan; it then settled near Bukhara and fought its way into Khorasan and finally through Persia to Isfahan. As the Turkomans entered Baghdad, the last Buwayhid governor fled. The caliph al-Qa'im hailed Tughril as "King of the East and West" and invested him with the title sultan ("he who has authority"), the first time that this title was used in Islam.

*Buwayhid* dinar *of Rukn al-Dawlah*

## THE CITY OF BAGHDAD, 9TH CENTURY

Khatib al-Baghdadi, described his native city as the "navel of the universe." It was indeed a commercial center and the capital of the Abbasid caliphate until it was overtaken by Fatimid Cairo and subsequently razed by the Mongols in 1258.

The caliph al-Mansur chose the site for his capital in 762 for military, economic, and agricultural reasons. Originally a small Persian settlement during the Achaemenid dynasty, it was at the crossroads of river and caravan routes to east and west and north to south. Situated on a fertile plain, it was traversed by irrigation canals that afforded rich cultivation and water supplies to a substantial human population and their cattle. With Basra as a port of transit, smaller vessels came up river. The Tigris similarly brought commerce from the north. It was healthy and free from mosquitoes.

Baghdad was planned initially as a round city, with a high defensive wall. Inside were empty spaces for maneuvers and then a second wall. The caliphal palace, located in the center, was surrounded by yet a third wall, which enclosed the great mosque and official buildings. High officials and officers lived between the third and second walls. Outside were suburbs, provided for different ethnic groups — Arabs, Khwarizmians, and Persians — and different vocations — soldiers, merchants, and craftsmen. Each had its own mosques, shops and markets. Altogether they formed on the west side of the Tigris a remarkable example of town planning, for which a team of architects with 100,000 craftsmen and laborers was employed.

On the east side of the Tigris a palace and mosques were provided for the caliph's heir, al-Mahdi, with houses for his officers and a commercial quarter. Poets celebrated the splendid palaces and houses, the wonderful furnishings, restful gardens, and green countryside.

After civil disorder in the early ninth century Turkish mercenaries were recruited as caliphal guards. The Turks soon fell foul of the Arabs in the army, and for this reason al-Mutasim and other caliphs resided at Samarra from 836 until 892. Baghdad, however, remained the center of commercial and cultural activity and continued to grow in extent outside the walls.

In 892 the caliph al-Mutamid returned to Baghdad. He and his son, al-Mutadid

*Slave-market in Baghdad, al-Hariri MS, dated 1237*

# THE CITY OF BAGHDAD, 9TH CENTURY

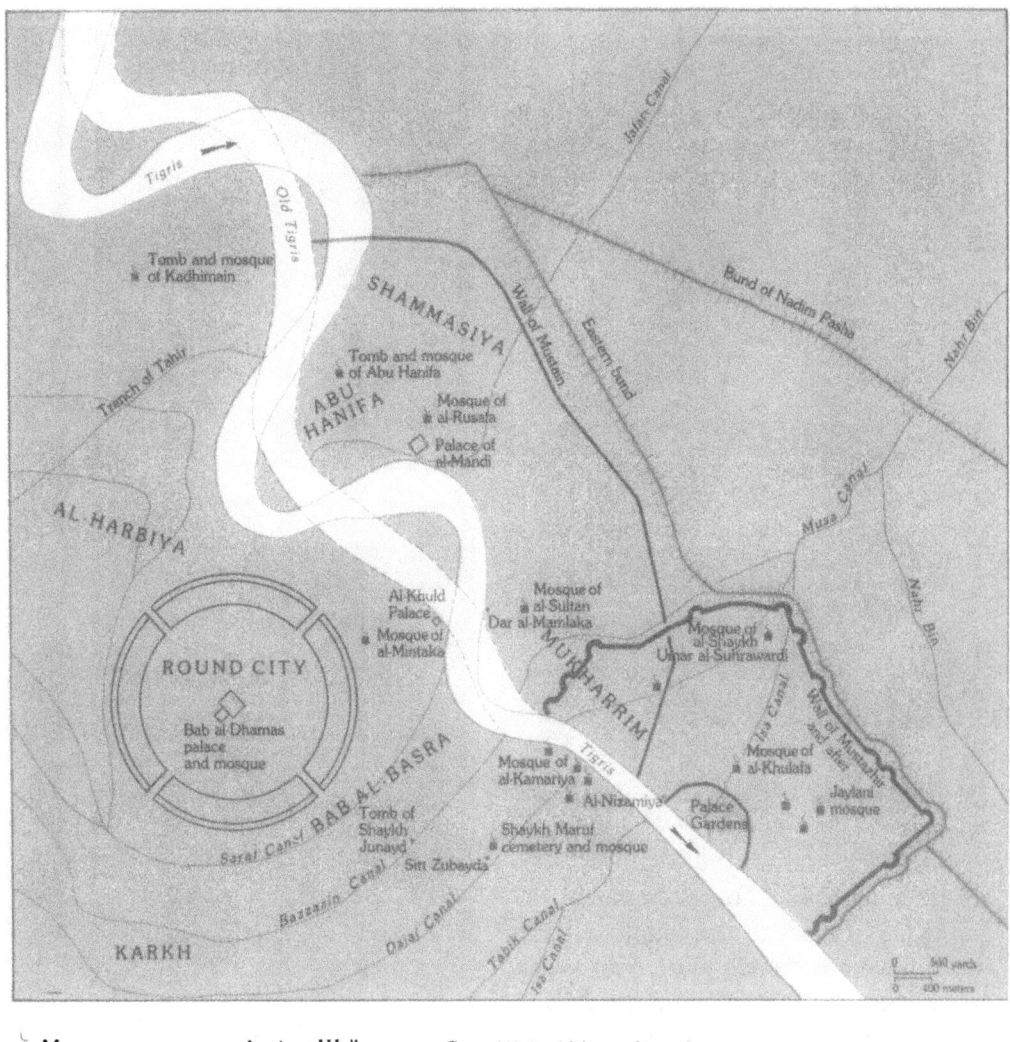

(892–902) rebuilt the palace and added other palaces, prisons, and a racecourse. Al-Muktafi's palace, built between 901 and 907, was an architectural curiosity for it had a high dome, on which he could ride a donkey. Al-Muqtadir added palaces, a zoo, and a silver tree with eighteen branches, on which silver and silver-gilt birds shrilled and sang. The lion house had a hundred beasts.

There were numerous markets — fruit, meat, cloth, flowers, goldsmiths, booksellers, with a special one for Chinese merchandise only. The volume and scope of trade necessitated a banking system. There were innumerable mosques and baths. Many mosques had madrasas (residential teaching colleges) attached. Culturally, the city was also important for its schools of law and translation, hospitals, and libraries. There were numerous *ribats*, built during the twelfth century as hostels for Sufi religious ascetics and mystics. The most outstanding of the mystics was al-Ghazzali, a Persian by birth, whose teaching had

# THE CITY OF SAMARRA, 9TH CENTURY

*The Al-Malwiyeh Tower of the Great Mosque at Samarra, 9th century*

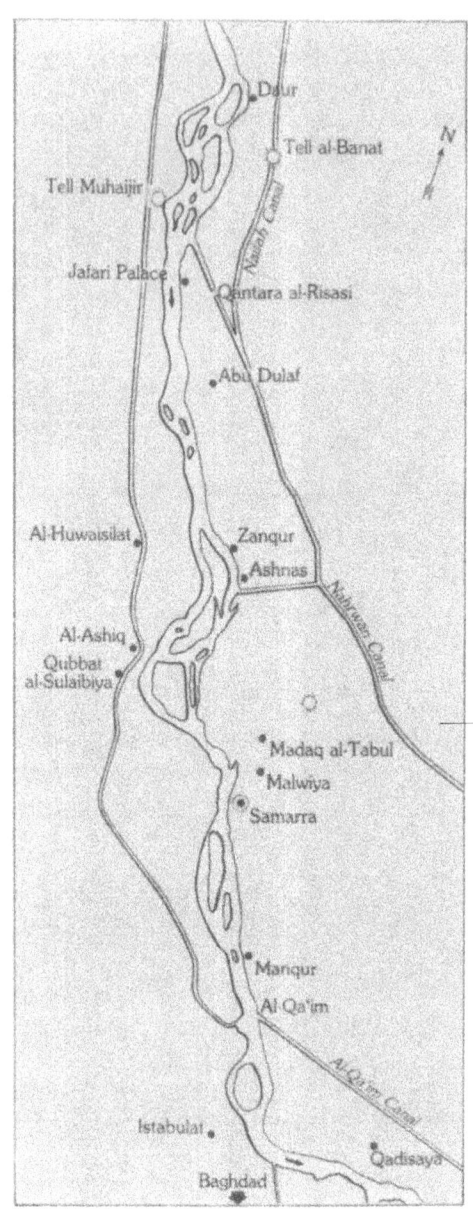

influence on Saint Thomas Aquinas.

In the last century of the caliphate there were numerous floods and fires. Weak government brought in its train riots and pillage, and irrigation was neglected. On 10 February 1258 the city fell an easy prey to the Mongol army of Hulagu Khan. Estimates of those killed vary from 800,000 to two million. In 1261 the last caliph of Baghdad was carried off to Cairo as a prisoner of the Mamluk Baybars, but the city lived on a half life under local, Turkoman, Persian, and finally Ottoman rulers.

# DYNASTIES IN NORTH-WEST AFRICA

As the Battle of Poitiers (732) marked the turn of the tide of Arab expansion in Spain and France, so Berber nationalism, latent even in Roman times, began to reassert itself in northwest Africa by the mid-eighth century. In the region of Sijilmasa the Midrarite dynasty dominated the region from 757 until 976, as did the Rustamids at Tahert from 776 until 906; in the region of Fez (Arabic,

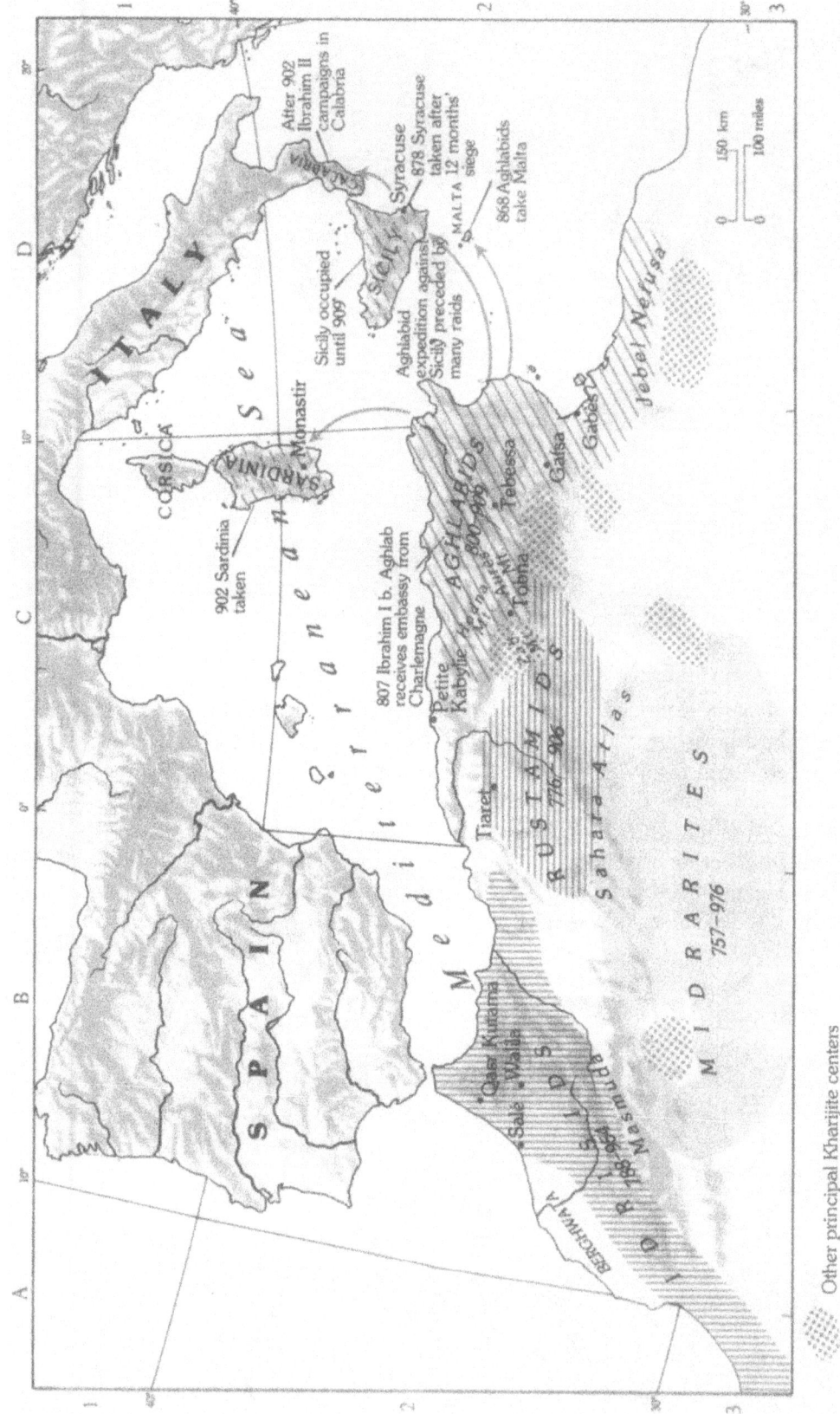

DYNASTIES IN NORTH-WEST AFRICA

*The port of Algiers*

Fas) a dynasty founded by Idris ibn Abdallah, a great-great-grandson of the caliph Ali, ruled from 788 until 974. In what is now Tunisia (with some of Algeria) Ibrahim ibn al-Aghlab was appointed governor by Harun al-Rashid in 800. He and his descendants ruled as virtually independent sovereigns from 800 until 909.

From their capital at Kairouan the Aghlabids dominated the western Mediterranean. Following raids that began around 827, Sicily was conquered in 902, followed by the fall of Malta and Sardinia. The Great Mosque of Kairouan, erected between 670 and 675, replaced an earlier, humbler building; completed in 836, the Qur'an has been

*The ancient city of Kairouan, Tunisia, with the Great Mosque within its walls*

recited continuously by day and by night ever since, and from it went out teachers, who now transformed an outwardly Christian, Latin-speaking province into an Islamic, Arabic-speaking province. Nominally the Aghlabids were subject to the Abbasid caliphs in Baghdad and used the title of emir only. This subjection was of trifling importance in practice, and for western Muslims Kairouan became a fourth holy city, ranking only after Mecca, Medina, and Jerusalem. At the same time the Tunisian cities provided a link with western Africa south of the Sahara — a region rich in gold and salt, essential to the prosperity of Cairo. In 909 the Aghlabids were swept aside by the Fatimid dynasty.

## TULUNIDS (820-872) AND IKSHIDIDS (935-969) IN EGYPT

*Mosque of Ibn Tulun, Cairo, 876–879, with Saladin's Citadel, built 1176–1207, with Muhammad Ali's Mosque, begun 1824, completed 1857*

The disintegration of the Abbasid caliphate that had occurred in the west eventually reached Egypt. Ahmad ibn Tulun, whose father was a Turkish slave from Farghana, had the advantage of an education in Baghdad. He was sent to Egypt in 868. Shortly after becoming governor he ignored the caliph in Baghdad and made himself independent. Egypt thus became an independent state for the first time under Islam and was able to enjoy its own revenues. Since the rule of Amr ibn al-As. Egypt had had more than a hundred governors for an

*Interior and* mihrab *of the Ibn Tulun Mosque, Cairo*

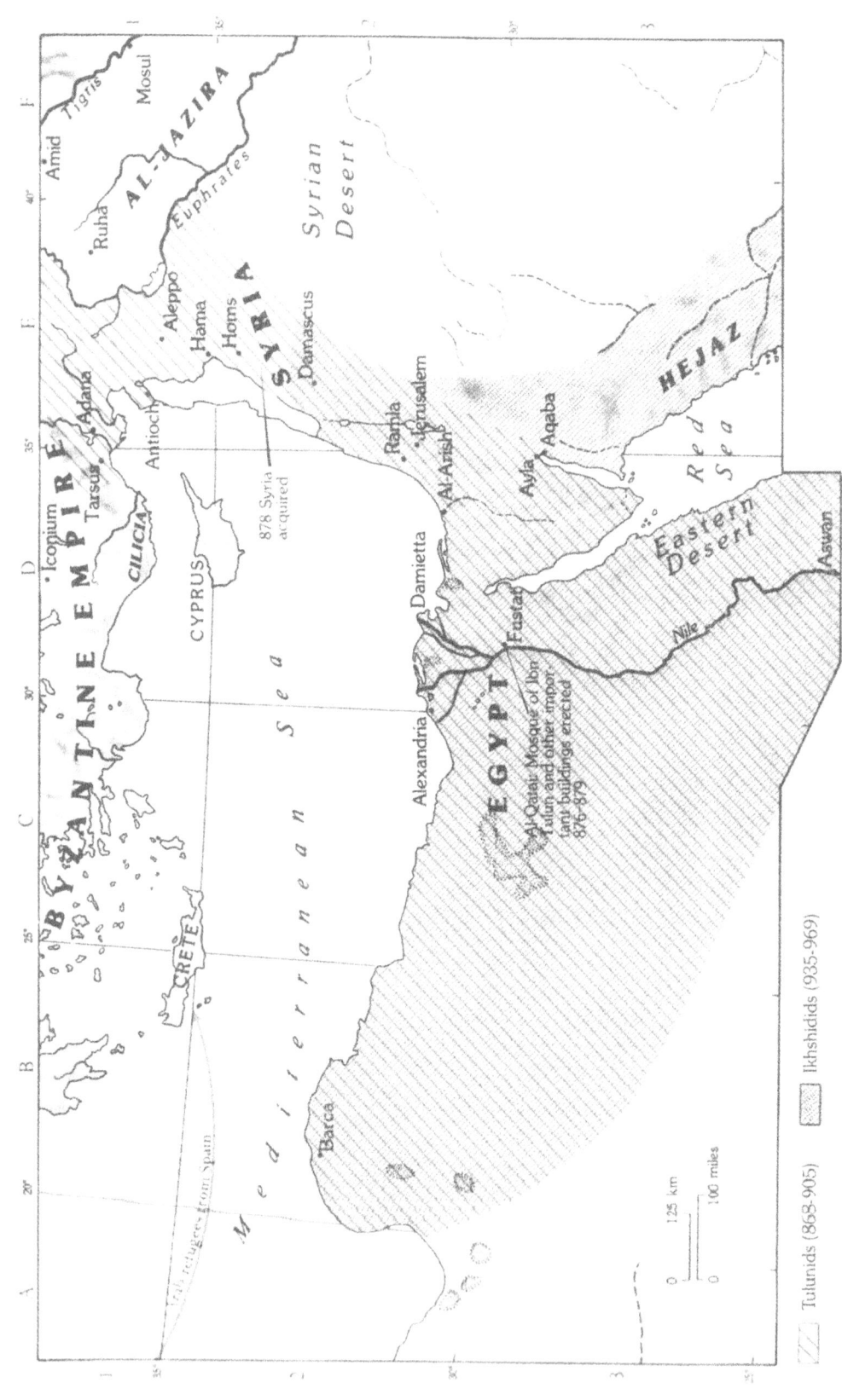

TULUNIDS (820-872) AND IKSHIDIDS (935-969) IN EGYPT

average of two and a half years each, lining their own pockets and transmitting the residue to the caliph. In 877 Ibn Tulun, as he is usually known, added Syria to his domains, with a naval base at Acre. A new capital was built beside al-Fustat, with a great mosque that still exists, together with other magnificent buildings, including a hospital.

Khumarawayh (r. 884–895), who succeeded Ibn Tulun, was a sybarite and an idler, whose wine-swilling habits earned him the contempt of the orthodox. On his death it was thought appropriate, when his body was being lowered into the grave, that it happened that quite by coincidence the Qur'an readers chorused: "Seize ye him and drag him into the midfire of hell." Under his feeble successors the Abbasid caliphs regained Egypt and Syria without difficulty in 905. Thirty years later another Turkish dynasty of Farghana origins, the Ikhshidids (r. 935–969), gained the throne. They speedily regained Syria, and then the province of Hejaz, and its chief towns of Medina and Mecca. Under the reigns of Muhammad al-Ikhshid's two sons, the real ruler was an Ethiopian eunuch and former slave soldier, Abu al-Misk Kufur. He took pleasure in his table, and the daily order for his kitchen, the Arab authors claim, included 100 sheep, 100 lambs, 250 geese, 500 chickens, 1,000 pigeons, and 100 jars of confectionery. A year after his death, the Fatimids seized Egypt.

## TAHIRIDS (868–905), SAFFARIDS (867–908), AND SAMANIDS (874–909)

In the same way that states split off and developed independently from the caliphate in Egypt and the Maghrib, other states grew up east of Baghdad. The first was the quasi-independent state of the Tahirids. Tahir ibn al-Husayn, the

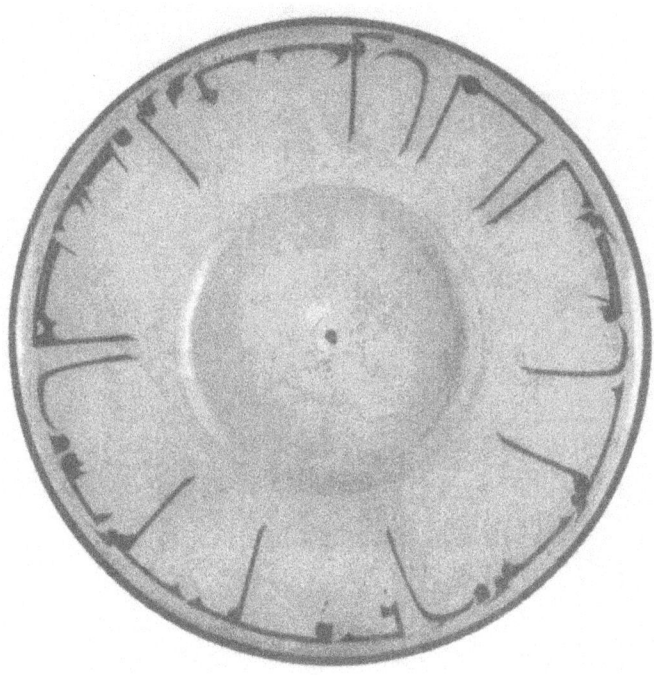

*Samanid dish with decorative calligraphy, Transoxiana, 10th century*

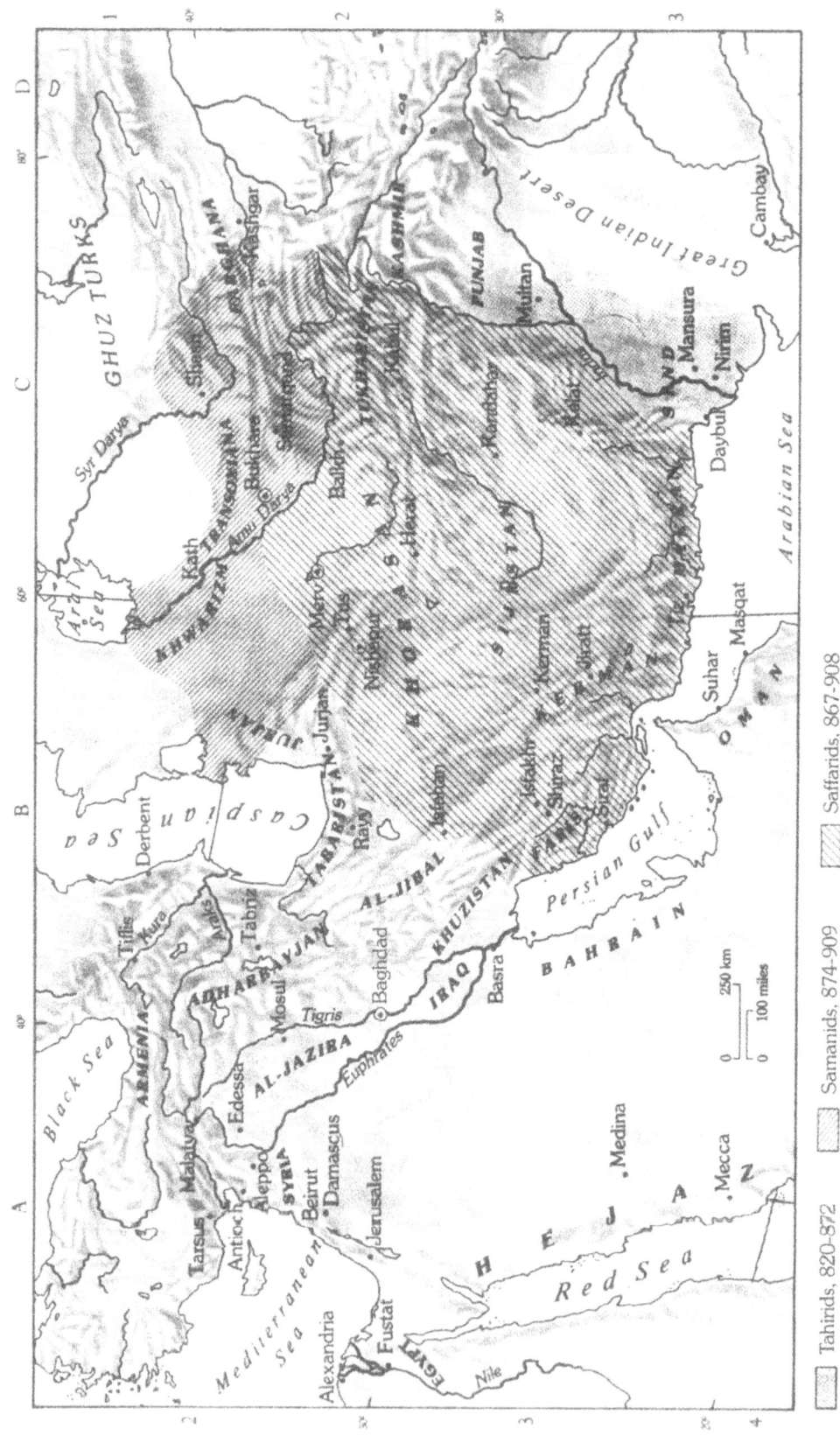

TAHIRIDS (868–905), SAFFARIDS (867–908), AND SAMANIDS (874–909)

descendant of a Persian slave, was made governor of all the lands east of Baghdad in 820. In 822 he omitted mention of the caliph's name in the Friday prayer, substituting his own. His capital was at Marw (Merv). His successors extended his kingdom as far as India, transferring the capital to Naysabur (Nishapur).

In 872 they were superseded by the Saffarids, who took their name from Ya'qub ibn al-Layth al-Saffar (r. 867–878), a coppersmith (Arabic, al-saffar) who had turned brigand. His abilities and chivalrous conduct attracted the attention of the governor of Sijistan, who made him his commander. Ya'qub succeeded his master and ruled almost all Persia and Afghanistan as far as India.

In Transoxiana and part of Persia, the Samanids, a family of Zoroastrian origin from Balkh, ruled from 874 to 909. The dynasty took its name from Saman, a Zoroastrian nobleman. His great-grandson Nasr (r. 874–892) was founder of the dynasty, but it was his brother Isma'il (r. 892–907) who seized Khorasan from the Saffarids in 900. Under Nasr II (r. 913–943) the kingdom was extended to include Sijistan, Kerman, Jurjan, al-Rayy, and Tabaristan, Transoxiana, and Khorasan. Outwardly the Samanids professed allegiance to the Abbasids, but in all other respects they were independent. Bukhara, their capital, together with their leading commercial city, Samarqand, became centers of learning and art, almost overshadowing Baghdad. Persian and Arabian scholarship was protected, and it was in Bukhara that the young Ibn Sina (known in the West as Avicenna) acquired the knowledge of medicine, philosophy, poetry, and philology that caused the Arabs to acclaim him "shaykh and prince of the learned." In 994 the Samanid territory was conquered by the Ghaznavids.

## QARMATIAN, SHI'ITE AND OTHER DYNASTIES (800–1281)

Tradition reports that the Prophet Muhammad said, "The Israelites have been divided into seventy-one or seventy-two sects, and so have the Christians, but my community shall be divided into seventy-three." True or false, by the ninth century opposing sects had formed, with the same fissiparous consequences that are observable in sixteenth century Europe, where also they took on a political form.

A basic division was between Sunni and Shi'ite, between traditionalists and believers in the prescriptive right of the descendants of Ali to the caliphate. A new major division appeared in 827 when a rigid puritanical Mu'tazilite judge asserted that the Qur'an had been created, as opposed to the orthodox belief that it is the identical representation of a celestial original. Shortly thereafter Baghdad proclaimed the former position

*Page from 11th century Qur'an, written in Eastern Kufi script*

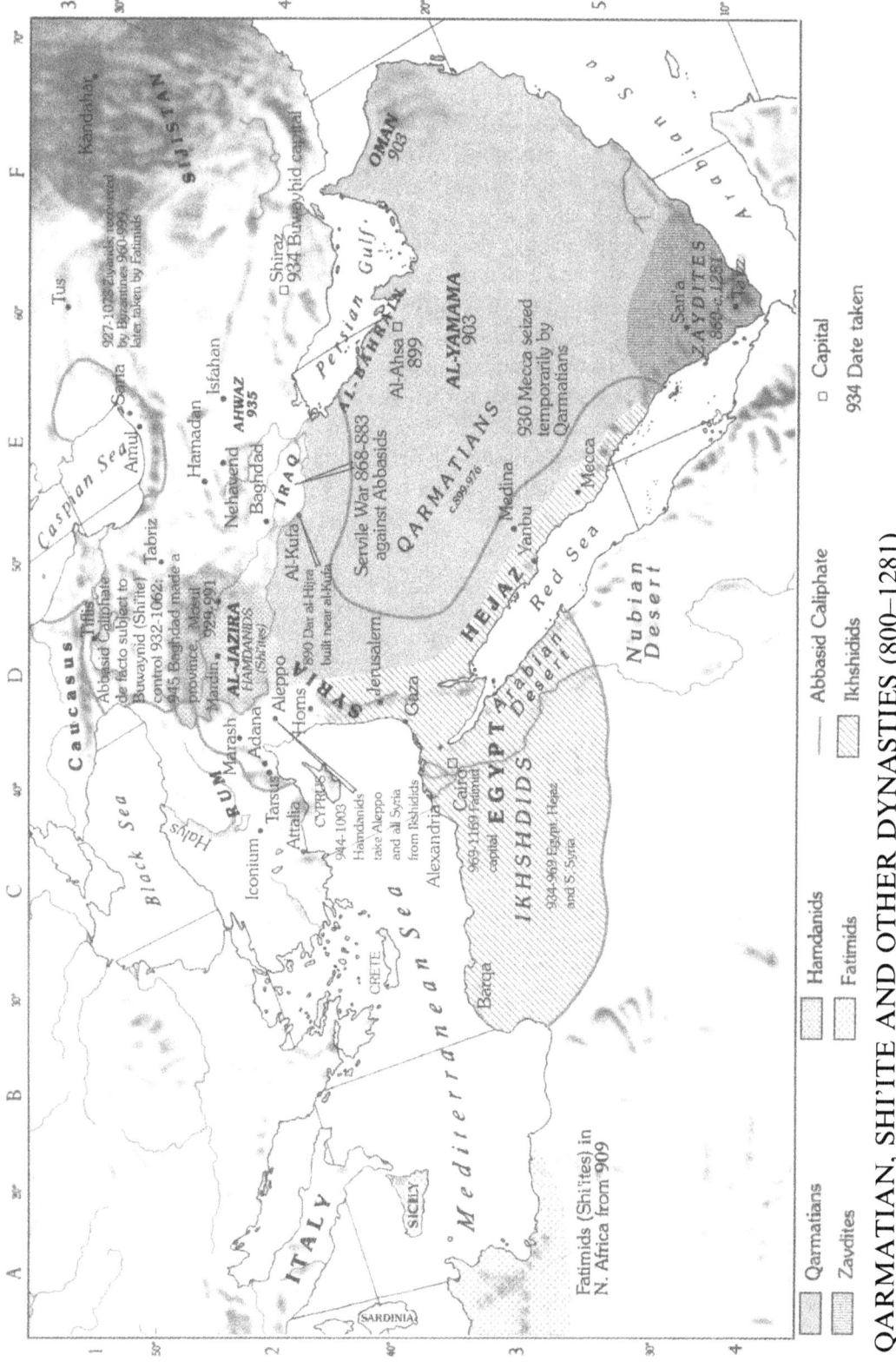

QARMATIAN, SHI'ITE AND OTHER DYNASTIES (800–1281)

to be law, and the caliph al-Ma'mun instituted an inquistion.

In the mid-tenth century the orthodox creed was reestablished in Baghdad, and scholastic theology developed. Its greatest exponent was Abu Hamid al-Ghazzali, a professor at Nizamiyah college. To him is owed the development of Sufism and the mystical practices of the Islamic fraternities, similar in many respects to Christian religious orders. These fraternities contributed significantly to the spread of Islam beyond its Middle Eastern home as far as the Atlantic and sub-Saharan Africa and to Malaysia and China.

In opposition to this orthodoxy the Ismailis, who today claim the Agha Khan as their leader, spread their esoteric doctrines by means of underground missionaries. From the Ismailis in the mid-ninth century Hamdan Qarmat, an Iraqi peasant, organized a secret society that preached a form of communism and set up an independent state in the Persian Gulf. From this society were derived the doctrines that formed the seed of the Fatimid movement in North Africa. In the eleventh century the Qarmatian movement engendered the Nusayris in northern Syria, while the Fatimids were the progenitors of the Druse in Lebanon and later the neo-Ismailis or Assassins, of Alamut and Syria, both borrowing greatly from Christianity. The Ithna'ashari Shi'ites in Persia and the Zaydites of Yemen and Tunisia represent a middle course, nearer to the Sunni doctrine, and more tolerant.

*Zoroastrian Temple of Fire, Naksh-e Rostam, Persia, Achaemenid period*

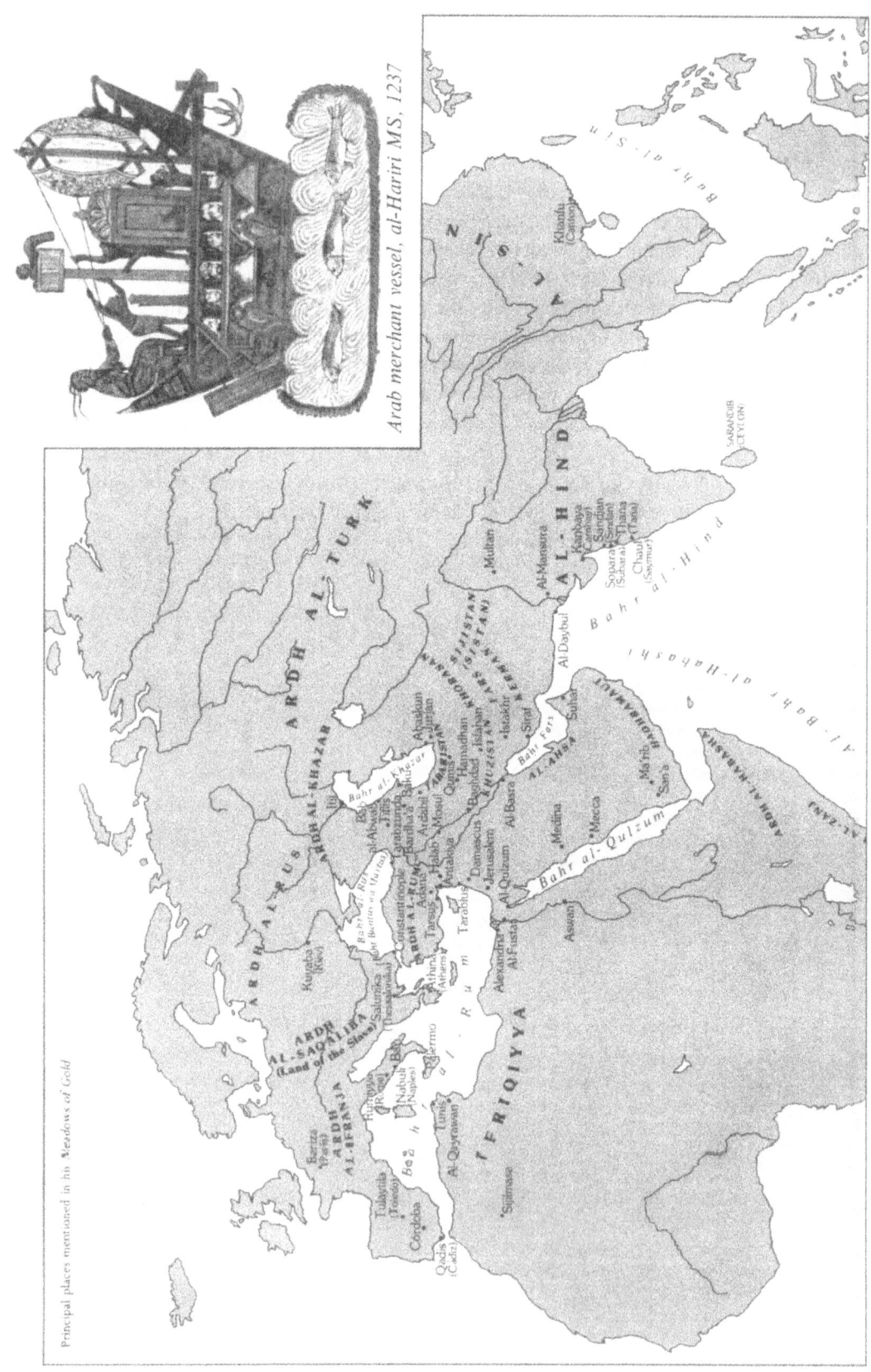

THE WORLD AS KNOWN TO AL-MASOUDI (D. 956)

## THE WORLD AS KNOWN TO AL-MASOUDI (D. 956)

Abu al-Hasan Ali ibn al-Husayn ibn Ali ibn Abdallah al-Masoudi, usually known as al-Masoudi, was the most remarkable traveler, historian, geographer, and writer of the tenth century. He is believed to be the descendant of an eminent Companion of the Prophet Muhammad. He was born in Baghdad around 893–898. Nothing is known of his immediate forbears, education, or means of livelihood, but his very extensive travels suggest that he was engaged in commerce. His surviving works show that he was a scholar. He was born at a time when it was considered meritorious among Muslims to travel in order to acquire religious knowledge. He was a Shi'ite, but nothing suggests that he engaged in missionary activity, nor, for that matter, in diplomacy. His interests were not confined to Islam. Unlike other Muslim scholars, he was interested in non-Muslim communities — Christians, Jews, Manichaeans, Sabaeans, and Zoroastrians. He was not less interested in heretical sects, and he recorded his debates and discussions with their learned adherents. He also took an interest in flora and fauna, in meteorology and dendrology, in tides, minerals, merchants, warriors, ordinary sailors,

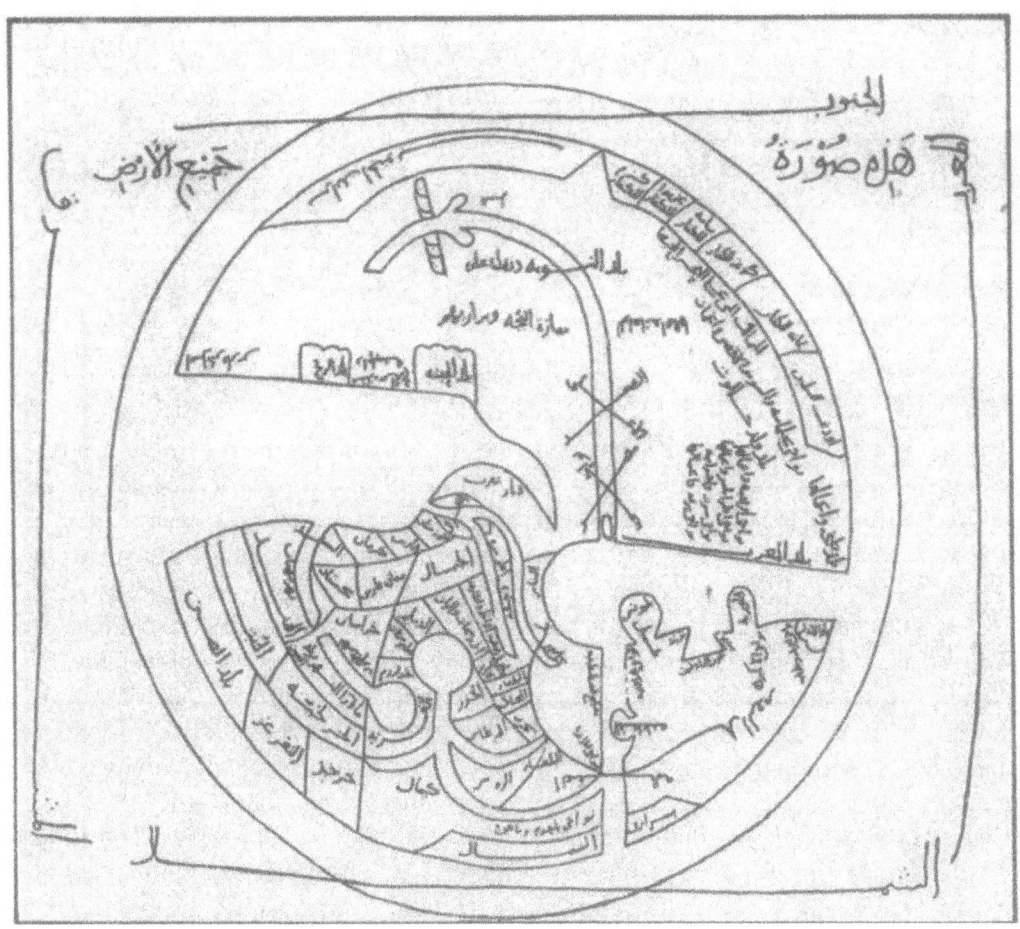

THE WORLD AS DEPICTED BY IBN HAWQAL, C. 988

ancient monuments, and tombs — all of which and more receive mention in his works in a random manner and without any appearance of planning. He made the pilgrimage to Mecca and took the opportunity to attend lectures on genealogy. In Cairo he attended the Coptic festival of the Epiphany, in which Muslims participated with Copts in celebrating not only the visit of the Magi but also the baptism of Christ.

sailed to Suhar, then the capital of Oman. He also describes Siraf and Basra, where he probably acquired his knowledge of China.

After further travels in Syria and on the Byzantine frontier, which included the Christian shrines in Jerusalem and Nazareth and Jewish scholarship in Tiberias, he traveled to Armenia and near the Caspian Sea, thus acquiring a knowledge of the Black Sea and southern Russia. In

*Muslims at prayer*

Though it is not possible to construct an itinerary of his journeys because many of his references are simply incidental and given without dates, it is known that in 914–915 he was in Persia and then India. In Persia he was particularly interested in Zoroastrians. In India he had extensive contacts with merchants in the Indus valley, many of them Arabs from Iraq and Oman. Although some of his remarks suggest that he visited Ceylon and even China, this is unlikely, for his accounts appear to be based on the work of others. In 916 he visited Qanbalu, which possibly refers, as recent archaeology and numismatics show, to Pemba Island off Mombasa. From there he

941 he was in southern Arabia, in the mountainous country of northern Yemen, Hadhramawt, and Oman. The last fifteen years of his life were spent in Egypt, where he died around 956.

The great age of systematic Arab geography, of which al-Masoudi was one of the forebears, began with Abu Zayd al-Balki (d. 934), whose work al-Istakri elaborated around 950. Al-Balki's work even had colored maps. At his request Ibn Hawqal (fl. 943–977), who had traveled in Spain, revised his maps and text, later rewriting the whole book. Other contemporaries were al-Maqdisi (also called al-Muqaddasi), whose name implies that he was born in Jerusalem, and al-Hamdani, who was also an archaeologist. These laid the foundation for the later work of twelfth-century geographer and cartographer al-Idrisi and the great geographical encyclopedia of Yaqut.

## THE UMAYYADS IN SPAIN (950–1050)

Abd al-Rahman III al-Nasir (r. 912–961) succeeded to the emirate in 912, and proclaimed himself caliph on 16 January 929. By then the Abbasid caliphs were virtually prisoners of their Turkish mercenary guards, and in North Africa the Fatimids had already laid claim to the caliphate. It was politically important reassert unity. There were also external enemies: in the south, the Fatimids; in the north, the Christian kings of the Asturias and of León; in the east, the ancient kingdoms of Aragon and Navarre.

Córdoba, which now had the most splendid court in Europe, had half a million inhabitants, seven hundred mos-

*The Alhambra at Granada*

that al-Andalus (Arabic name for the Arab possessions in Spain) should not give the appearance of acknowledging a superior. Moreover, the latter years of the reign of Abd al-Rahman's predecessor and grandfather, Abd Allah (r. 888–912), had been years of unrest and rebellion in many provinces, and it was imperative that he restore order and ques, three hundred public baths, and a palace with four hundred rooms and thousands of guards and slaves. Outside the city was the summer palace of al-Zahra. Partly destroyed in 1013, it still has a haunting beauty. An army of more than 100,000 recruits comprised eastern Europeans, so-called Slavs, from which comes the word "slave." The city's yearly

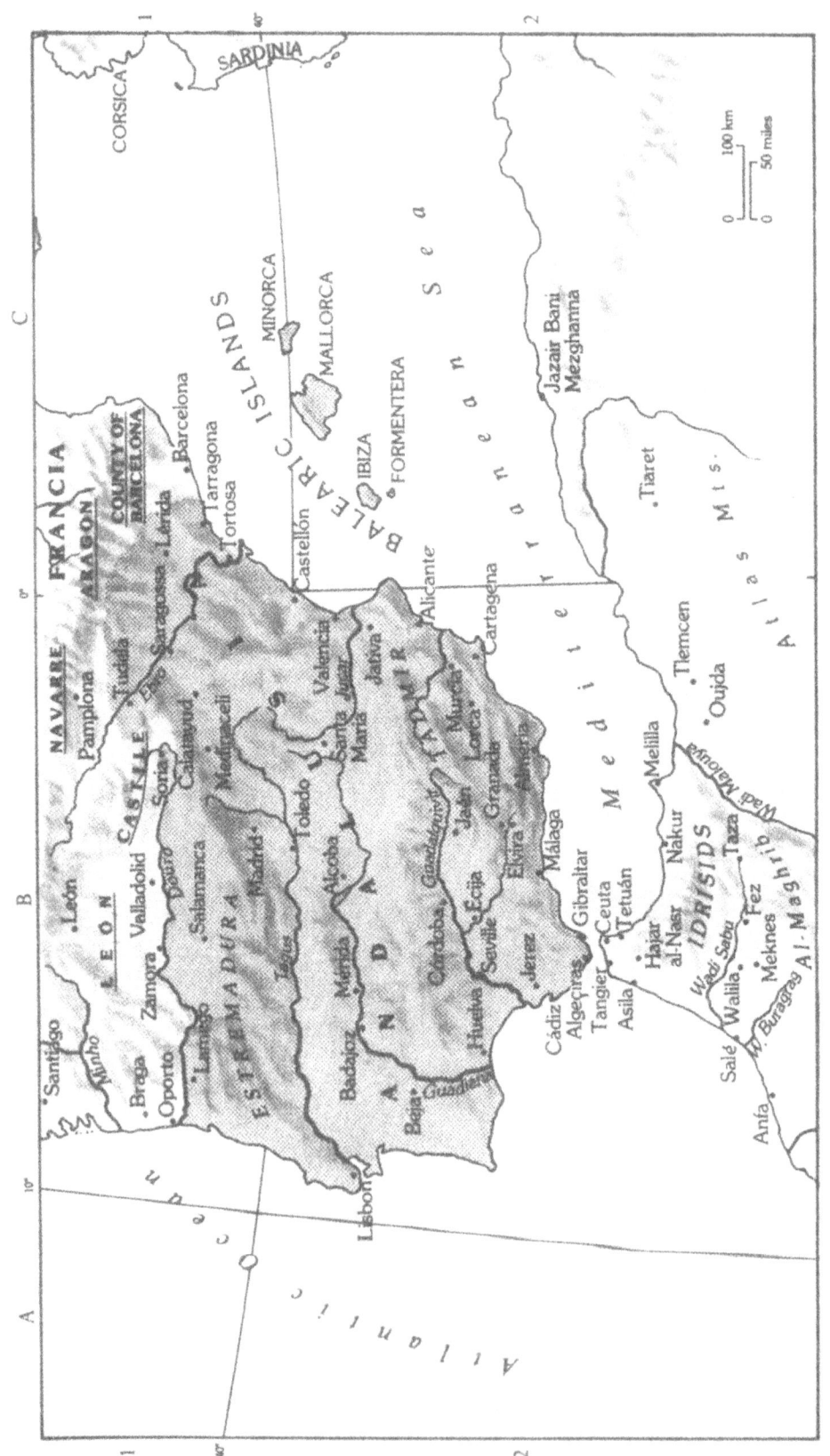

THE UMAYYADS IN SPAIN (950–1050)

revenue was 6,245,000 gold dinars. The army took a third; public works took another third, while a third was put in reserve. Despite the prosperity of his caliphate, al-Rahman, as he died amidst so much magnificence, remarked that he had had only fourteen days of happiness in his life.

His successor, Hakam II (r. 961–976), was a scholar and patron of learning. The Great Mosque of Córdoba housed a university that drew students even from al-Azhar in Cairo and the Nizamiyah in Baghdad. The library contained 400,000 books. Here, for a brief period, was the intellectual capital of the Islamic world. It was but a short moment of greatness. A son and six nephews followed Hakam II, under whom the caliphate foundered and dissolved into petty states.

*Spanish Umayyad* Dinar *of Abd al-Rahman III, 933*

## THE FATIMIDS IN NORTH AFRICA AND IN EGYPT, 904–1171

The Fatimid Caliphate was the only Shi'ite caliphate in Islam. Whereas orthodox Sunni Muslims hold that the first three caliphs were constitutionally elected, the Shi'ites hold that a divine right of succession to the caliphate rests

*Man's face on a potsherd, 11th century Fatimid period, Egypt*

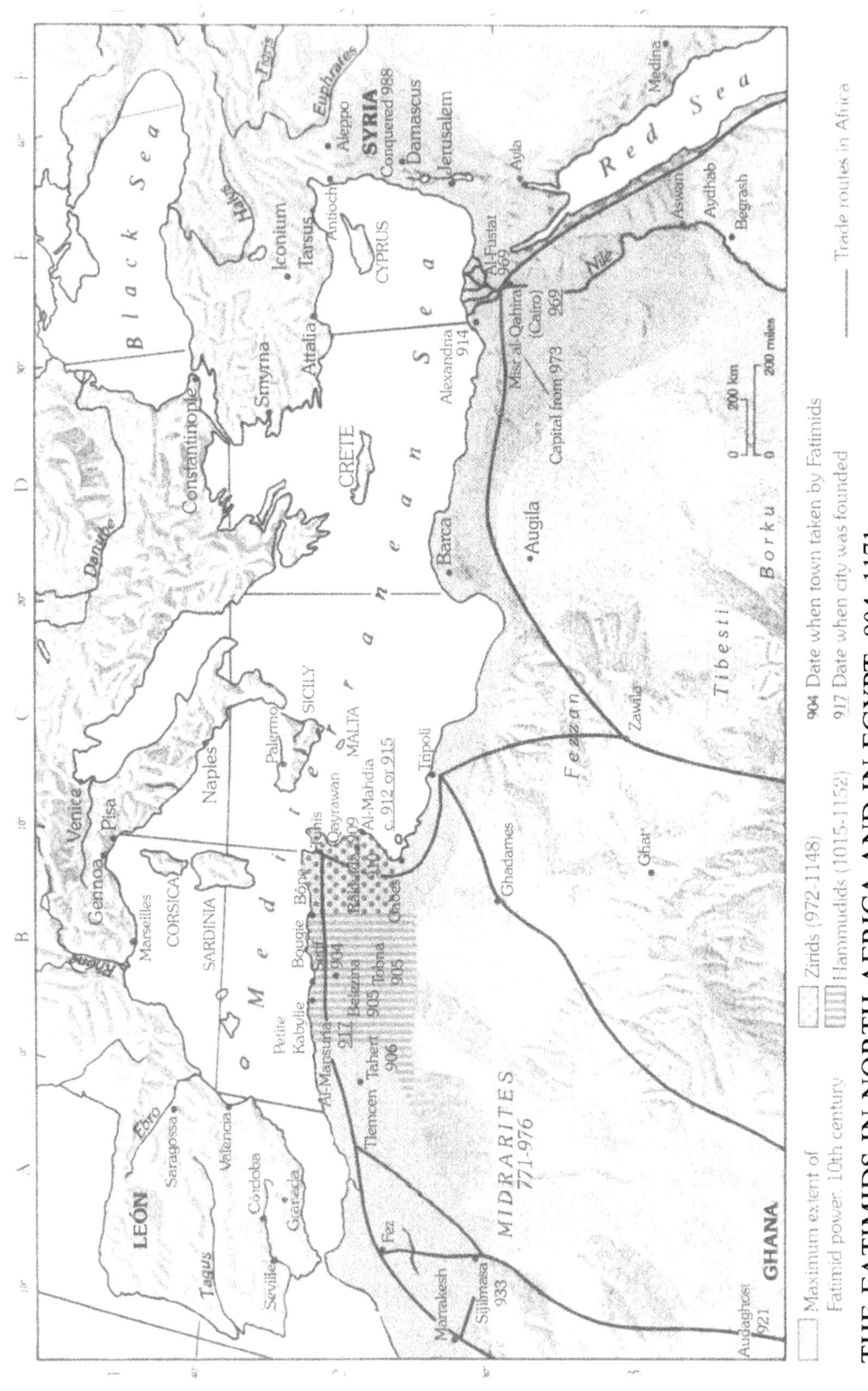

**THE FATIMIDS IN NORTH AFRICA AND IN EGYPT, 904–1171**

*The Great Mosque of Tlemcen, North Africa, built under the third Almoravid Ali Ibn Yusuf (1106–1143)*

in descent from the Prophet's daughter Fatima and her husband Ali. By the mid-ninth century the Shi'ites had elaborated an intricate theological system, in which God is always incarnate in a spiritual leader, or imam, who must be a descendant of Fatima and Ali. Accordingly, in Persia and Lebanon the Ismailis and the Assassins evolved, and in North Africa Ubayd Allah al-Mahdi declared himself imam.

Ubayd Allah seized Kairouan from the Aghlabids and Morocco from the Idrisids. In 914 he took Alexandria, and in 916 his troops devastated the Delta. Sicily, Malta, Corsica, Sardinia, and the Balearic Islands soon fell within his control. He established his capital at al-Mahdia, near Kairouan. Finally, in 969, a Fatimid general took al-Fustat, establishing the caliph al-Mu'izz in Egypt. Shortly thereafter, Mecca and Medina, and all Syria were added. Only Islamic Spain and the Abbasid territories near Baghdad were excepted.

Al-Mu'izz's successor, al-Aziz (r. 975–996), now controlled all the trade routes of the eastern Mediterranean, trading as far as India and eastern and western Africa. A luxurious building program in Cairo was financed by this commerce, of which the most lasting acheivement was the foundation of the university mosque of al-Azhar, later to become the intellectual center of orthodox Sunni Islam. Al-Aziz's son al-Hakim was an insane megalomaniac, and his caliphate was followed by a series of youths in the hands of viziers, who tried in vain to control a mercenary army of Turks, Berbers, and Sudanese. The regime was brought to an end in 1171 by Saladin (Arabic, *Salah al-Din*), a commander of Kurdish origin.

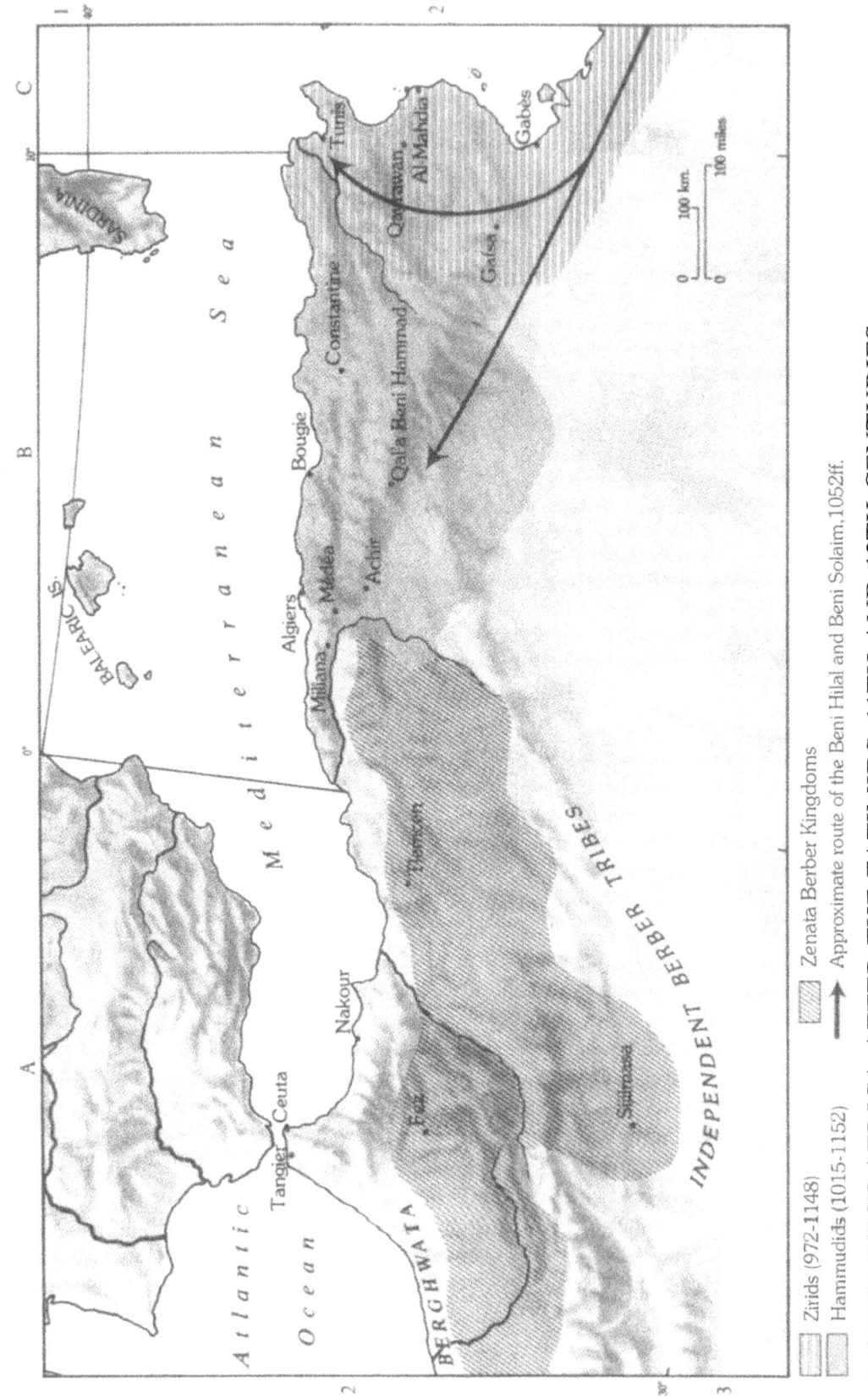

NORTH-WEST AFRICA AFTER THE FATIMIDS, 11TH AND 12TH CENTURIES

# NORTH-WEST AFRICA AFTER THE FATIMIDS,
## 11TH AND 12TH CENTURIES

After 1043 the Fatimid possessions showed obvious signs of disintegration. Fatimid power in Syria shrank before the Seljuqs, and in northwest Africa small principalities reverted to allegiance to the Abbasids in Baghdad. From 1050 to 1052, the Banu Hilal (Beni Hilal) and the Banu Sulaim (Beni Solaim) tribesmen from Najd and then from Upper Egypt, moved westward and ravaged Tripoli and Tunisia. During this period, Sicily was taken by the Normans, who likewise raided the African coast. In 1055–1056, the Almoravids (Arabic, *al-Murabitun*) from the Sahara seized Morocco, with its western trade routes, which led to the gold of Ghana and the salt of Taghaza. The Fatimid caliph al-Mu'izz made the Sanhaja Berber Bulugin ibn Zairi governor in Tunisia and Tripolitania. He and his son paid tribute to Cairo. Under Badis (r. 996–1016), the people became more anti-Shi'ite in sentiment, with the result that al-Mu'izz (1016–1062) threw off the Fatimids and proclaimed allegiance to the Abbasids. At the capital, Mansura, an important textile industry developed, while the seaports of Tunis, Sousse, al-Mahdiya and Gabès had an active trade with Egypt, Sicily, Italy, and Spain.

The Hammadid kingdom stretched from near Algiers to the foothills of the Aurès Mountains. It had been set up in 1014 when Hammad, brother of the Zirid emir al-Mansur, broke with his nephew, the emir Badis, and paid fealty to the Abbasid caliph. The capital, Qal'a Beni Hammad, had been founded in 1007, but it was no more than a citadel, for the warlike Beni Hammad, of Sanhaja Berber origin, were fully occupied in resisting the encroachments of the Zanata. These, which at one time had owed allegiance to the caliph in Córdoba, were but bands of rival tribesmen, thus bringing all Morocco into a state of anarchy.

*Qasba Gate, Rabat, Morocco*

# CONQUESTS AND DOMINIONS OF MAHMUD OF GHAZNA (997–1030) AND HIS SUCCESSORS

In 962, Alptigin, a Turkish slave who had risen to be governor of Khorasan, seized Ghazna (present-day Ghazni) from its native rulers and developed what became an empire that extended throughout Afghanistan and the Punjab. The founder of this dynasty was Subuktigin, a slave, who was Alptigin's son-in-law and successor (r. 976–997). His empire extended from Khorasan to Peshawar. His son Mahmud (r. 997–1030) became the most distinguished scion of this dynasty. Between 1001 and 1024 he conducted seventeen campaigns into India, annexing the Punjab, Multan, and part of Sind. This established Muslim influence in the Punjab and brought fabulous riches, the spoils of Hindu temples, to Ghazna. He was the first Muslim warrior to receive the title Ghazi for his leadership in war against unbelievers. In the west he took the Persian province of Iraq, including Rayy and Isfahan, from the Shi'ite Buwayhid dynasty. In the north and Khorasan, he held Tukharistan, with its capital Balkh, and parts of Transoxiana and Sijistan.

Ghazna now became a center of culture, with an academy and other magnificent buildings. Mahmud's wealth enabled him to become the patron of poets and men of learning, of whom the most distinguished were the scientist and historian al-Biruni, the historian al-Utbi, and the Persian poet Firdawsi, who had to flee for his life when, as a reward for his sixty thousand-verse epic Shahnameh, he received only 60,000 silver dirhems instead of the expected 60,000 gold dinars, and responded with a satirical poem.

*The Allah ed-Din gatehouse of the Kutub Mosque, Delhi, c. 1000*

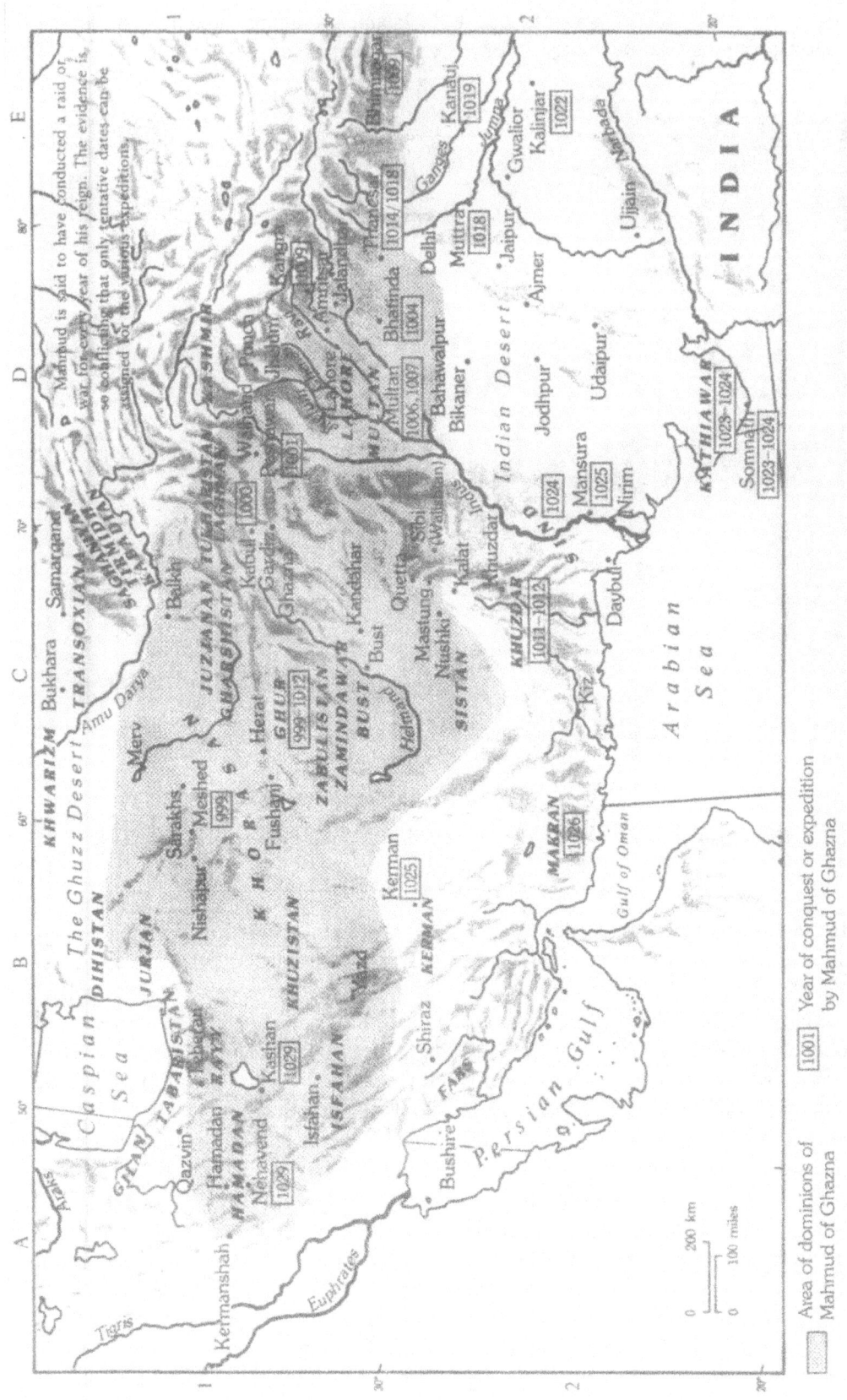

CONQUESTS AND DOMINIONS OF MAHMUD OF GHAZNA (997–1030) AND HIS SUCCESSORS

The Ghaznavid dynasty, which continued until 1186, marks an important turning point in Islamic history, for it was the beginning of Turkish dominance in Islam, presaging the Seljuq sultanates and the Ottomans.

*The Lion Court in the Alhambra, the zenith of Moorish architecture in Spain*

## LOS REYES DE TAIFAS, OR PARTY KINGS, OF SPAIN,
### C. 1009–1286

"In 1002," wrote a monk, "died Almanzor, and was buried in hell." During the rule of Hisham II (r. 976–1009), who succeeded the caliphate at age twelve, political power rested in his mother, Subh (Dawn), whose protégé, Muhammad ibn Abi-Amir, was royal chamberlain. He reduced the caliph to a nullity, shutting him up in the palace. For more than twenty years, up to his death in battle in 1002, he raided North Africa and the Christian kingdoms. In 997 he even raided Santiago de Compostela and robbed the church of its bells and doors. Fragment by fragment the caliphate dissolved, as local leaders arose. In fact, the caliphate suffered a weakness inherent in all medieval (and some modern) Arab states: it never developed a written constitution or even an unwritten one, buttressed by law and convention. Even at its zenith it never developed beyond the loose organization of an Arab tribe under a sheikh, chosen from a prominent family and ruling by skill, intrigue, and force.

Córdoba had rulers "whose interest in life," writes Ibn al-Idhari, "centered in sex and stomach, winebibbers, cowards and imposters." The Córdobans abolished the caliphate in 1027 in favor of a sort of republic, but they were absorbed

# LOS REYES DE TAIFAS, OR PARTY KINGS, OF SPAIN, C. 1009–1286

# PARTY KINGS: CAPITALS AND TRIBAL ORIGINS

| | | | |
|---|---|---|---|
| Málaga | Hammudites | Alpuente | Banu Qasim |
| Algeçiras | Hammudites | Córdoba | Banu Jahwar |
| Seville | Abbadites | Badajoz | Banu al-Aftas |
| Granada | Zairids | Toledo | Dhu al-Nun |
| Carmona | Bani Birzal | Valencia | Amirids |
| Runda | Bani Birzal | Almeria | Banu Sumadih |
| Murum | Bani Birzal | Murcia | Banu Sumadih |
| Arcos | Bani Birzal | Saragossa | Tujibites |
| Huelva & Saltes | Bakrids | Lérida | Tujibites |
| Niebla | Banu Yahya | Tortosa | Tujibites |
| Silves | Banu Muzayyin | Denia & Ibiza | Amirids |
| Sta. Maria de Al-garve | Banu Muzayyin | Mallorca | Amirids |
| Mertola | Banu Muzayyin | Minorca | Quraishi |
| Albarracin | Banu Razin | | |

by Seville in 1068. Berber families ruled Granada and Toledo; in Granada the real power rested in the hands of a Jewish vizier — a similar pattern obtained throughout the peninsula.

The petty states were not without culture. The arts flourished. The failure to produce strong rulers benefited the Christian kingdoms of the north. It was an age par excellence of Christian chivalry, of which El Cid's conquest of Valencia was an example. The Muslim princes now made the fatal error of inviting the Almoravids to assist them, for the Almoravids swallowed the whole peninsula into their North African empire in 1090–1091.

*Torre del Oro of the Alcazar Palace, Seville*

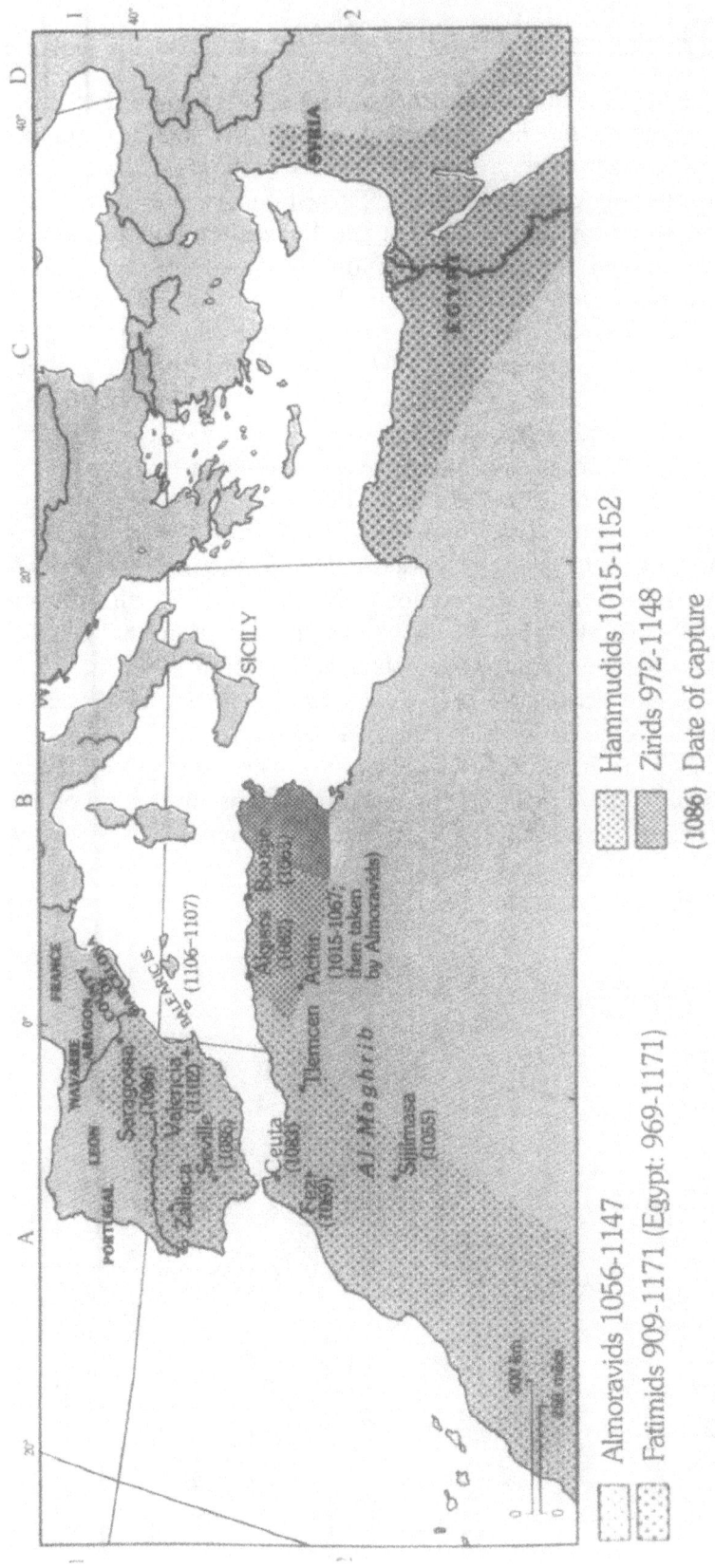

The Almoravids are also known as Al-Murabitun or Al-Mulaththamun (veil-wearers).
The men wore veils as do their present-day descendants the Tuareg (Tawariq).

# THE ALMORAVID DOMAINS

# THE ALMORAVIDS IN NORTH AFRICA AND SPAIN, 1056–1147

Like many of the petty dynasties that had called them into Spain, the Almoravids were Berbers. Originally they were a military religious brotherhood centered on a fortified monastery (Arabic, *ribat*) in lower Senegal. The founder of the dynasty in North Africa was Yusuf ibn Tashfin. In 1061 he assumed the title *amir al-Mu'minim* (commander of the Faithful), thus acknowledging the suzerainty of the Abbasid caliph in Baghdad. His reign was characterized by extreme zealotry and the persecution of liberal Muslims as well as Christians and Jews. Under the Umayyad caliphate, these minorities had enjoyed great toleration, and the Talmudic school of Córdoba was famous throughout the Mediterranean. In 1086 Yusuf crossed into Spain and defeated Alfonso VI so decisively at Zallaca that he is believed to have sent forty thousand heads back as a trophy. Casualties among Christians were estimated at 300,000.

The new regime in Spain was essentially militaristic and soon succumbed to idleness. With no further foes to fight or conquer, the Berbers gave way to the vices of civilization. As a religion Islam had not penetrated deep into Spain, but Arab culture was paramount. In the Christian kingdoms the coinage had Arabic legends, and Peter I of Aragon (d. 1104) could write only in Arabic script. The Berber Almoravids thus faced a people who had already accommodated themselves to their conquerors' culture.

Cultural influences, however, flowed both ways. The Great Mosque of Tlemcen was modeled on the Great Mosque of Córdoba; and in many North African cities architectural traditions that Islamic Spain had derived from Syria and the Yemen engendered a new and elegant variant of Islamic art.

As a state the Almoravid dynasty was weak, and after the rise of the Almohads in the Atlas Mountains, it speedily collapsed.

*The rulers of Granada, from the* Sala del Tribunal *in the Alhambra*

# IV. Latin Kingdoms and Muslims

## CHRISTIANITY AND ISLAM AT THE CLOSE OF THE 11TH CENTURY

As the eleventh century drew to a close, Christians from the West and Seljuq Turks from western Asia converged in Syria, which was divided among many different chieftains, Arabs as well as Turks. The Seljuqs controlled the north and were encroaching upon eastern Asia Minor and the Byzantine dominions. In Lebanon the Ismailis — later to engender the Assassins, the Nusayris, and the Druses — formed schismatic communities opposed to orthodox Islam. Christianity was no less divided among Armenians, Georgians, Greeks, and Maronites with a Syriac liturgy. In the south lay Shi'ite Fatimid Egypt, with important Coptic, Greek, and Jewish minorities. In the holy city of Jerusalem the Shi'ite Fatimids held the Haram al-Sharif, the Noble Sanctuary, where once the Jewish Temple had stood. Latin pilgrims had had a hostel and church adjacent to the Holy Sepulchre since the time of Charlemagne, and they, with Copts, Ethiopians, and others also celebrated at the Tomb of Christ.

A Seljuq sultanate had been established in Baghdad in 1055, and every city in Syria had either an Arab or a Seljuq ruler. The Byzantine frontier towns rapidly changed hands among the Seljuqs. In 1070 the Seljuq sultan Alp Arslan took Aleppo; at the same time his general Atziz entered Jerusalem. The Seljuqs soon took all Palestine from the Fatimids, conquering Damascus in 1075. In 1098 the Fatimids retook Jerusalem and the Levantine coastal towns, but this restoration of the former status quo had not been anticipated in the West.

*Seal of Baldwin III, King of Jerusalem, (1143–1162)*
*Obverse:* ( + Baldwin by the Grace of God King of Jerusalem) *The King, enthroned, invested with Crown, Sceptre and Orb*
*Reverse:* ( + City of the King of all Kings) *Holy Sepulchre, dome with Holy Fire; Gate and Tower of David, with flag; Dome of the Rock, with Cross*

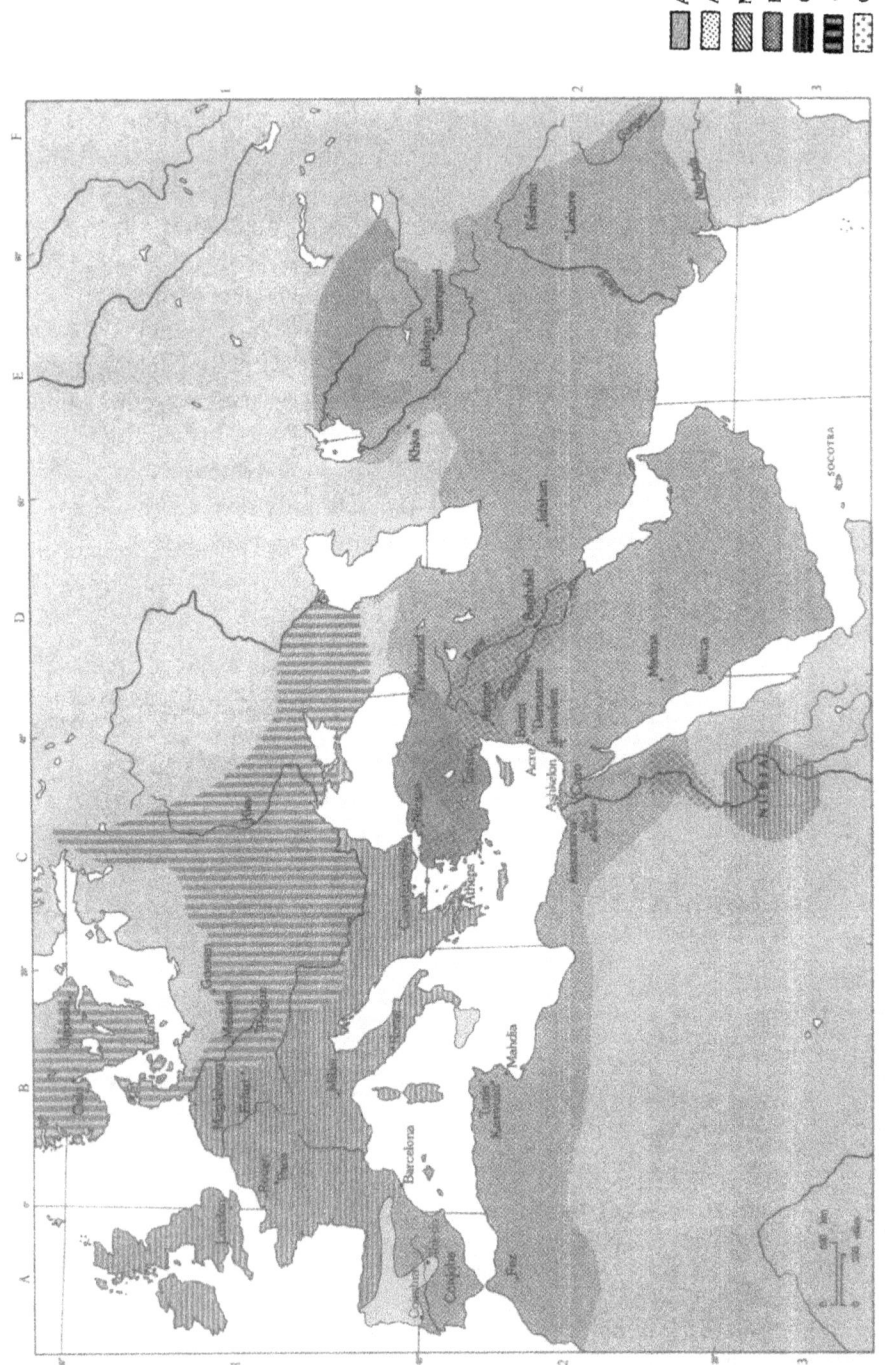

CHRISTIANITY AND ISLAM ON THE EVE OF THE FIRST CRUSADE, 1096

The Byzantine emperor Alexius I Comnenus (r. 1081–1118) was a statesman of distinguished stature. He was also an experienced general, and not less expert in diplomacy. His treasury was empty, and he lived on a financial tightrope. In Europe he held the Balkan Peninsula, albeit precariously in Serbia and Dalmatia. His Danube frontier was continuously threatened by the Turkish Pechenegs. The Normans threatened him in south Italy and Sicily and finally defeated his forces by treachery in 1082. In the east he still held Antioch, but the Seljuqs had the greatest part of Asia Minor.

When the Norman military leader Robert Guiscard died in 1085, the Italian Normans were no longer troublesome to Alexius. By 1092 the Seljuqs had taken to quarreling, so negating their power. In the West a Christian concept of holy war had developed in response to the Islamic doctrine of jihad, which claimed that war against the infidels was justified in the eyes of God. Moreover, in such wars, Christian knights could retain the lands they conquered, along with the spiritual rewards their actions merited. In 1064 Pope Alexander II offered indulgences to all Christian campaigners — a doctrine that would flourish.

The patriarchs of Alexandria, Antioch, and Jerusalem were politically under the Muslim heel. Though the patriarch of Constantinople had the prestige of the imperial capital, Rome claimed supremacy, for had not Christ committed the power of the keys to Peter and to him alone?

Pope Urban II was forty-six years old when he was elected and in full vigor. He had had diplomatic experience as papal legate in France and Germany from 1082 to 1085. Rome itself was governed by the antipope Clement III, and Urban could not assume office until 1093. Careful diplomacy made him spiritual leader of Western Christendom by 1095. He was greatly concerned for Christian unity, and friendly relations among Christians were realized by 1090, when he convoked the council at Piacenza. The attending representatives laid emphasis, it seems, on the duty of Western Christians to sustain those of the East. Another council was held at Clermont in 1095, and there, on 27 November, Urban II called on Western Christendom to a crusade to regain Jerusalem and rescue the East from the infidels.

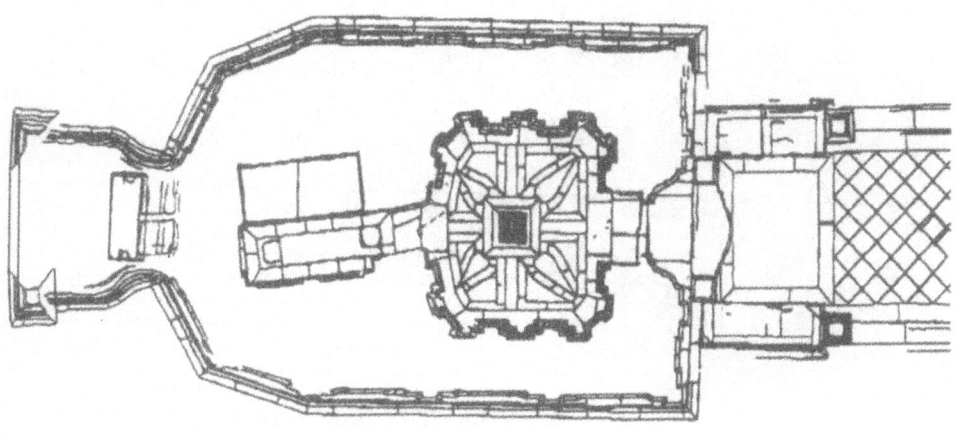

*Plan of the Edicule in the Tomb Chamber in the Church of the Holy Sepulchre, Jerusalem*

# THE CRUSADES, 1095–1291

The immediate occasion of Pope Urban II's call to a crusade was a request by Emperor Alexius I Comnenus for assistance to recover Anatolia from the Seljuqs. By way of inducement, he suggested that the employed forces should continue on to liberate Jerusalem from the infidels. Urban II's response was the proclamation of a "holy war" and plenary indulgences — "the remission, that is, of all the punishment due to sin after sacramental absolution" — for all who took part.

Four separate armies converged in Constantinople in the winter of 1096–1097 from Lorraine; the Norman kingdom of Apulia; Brittany, Normandy, and Flanders; and Provence in France. In spite of quarrels among the leaders, Nicaea was taken shortly thereafter in June 1097, and Dorylaeum on July 1. The armies then proceeded to Antioch, besieging it from 21 October 1097 until 3 June 1098. Al-Ruha (Edessa) was now conquered, and the first Latin state was founded as the County of Edessa. The Norman crusader Tancred, from Apulia, took Cilicia. While this was occurring, the Fatimids retook Jerusalem from the Seljuq Turks. Nevertheless the Crusaders, under the command of Raymond IV, continued down the Syrian coast. On 7 June 1099, Jerusalem was besieged, and Bethlehem was taken shortly thereafter. On 15 July Jerusalem fell to the Crusaders, who wept as they entered the Church of the Holy Sepulchre. Notwithstanding religious sentiment, they murdered every Muslim — men, women, and children alike — except for those who were fortunate enough to escape. The Jewish inhabitants had fled to their chief synagogue, where they were all burned alive.

The leaders now met and elected as king of Jerusalem Godfrey de Bouillon, the duke of Lower Lorraine. He declined the title, accepting only to be "Advocate of the Holy Sepulchre." Jerusalem was divided administratively into quarters, and the spoils of war were distributed among them. The Italian cities that had provided capital were now rewarded. A commercial agreement with Venice was concluded by Godfrey de Bouillon as he lay on his deathbed, and Pisa was given rights in Jaffa. In 1103 the Crusader Tancred was finally awarded the regency of Antioch. Any military danger from the Fatimids ended with Baldwin I's defeat of their army at Ramla.

The Crusaders seized territory that had formerly been within Byzantine provinces, to which Constantinople had juridical claim. Nevertheless, from 1104 until 1108 Bohémond I of Antioch campaigned against Byzantium. In 1109 Tripoli (Syria) was taken, and its territory made a county under Raymond I of Toulouse. Beirut and Sidon were added in 1110. In 1124 Tyre was taken, and in 1126 Baldwin II advanced as far as Damascus. The tide, however, was beginning to turn, and around 1140 the Assassins took the northern Syrian

*Crusader knights in battle with Muslim warriors; stained-glass window, S. Denis, Paris*

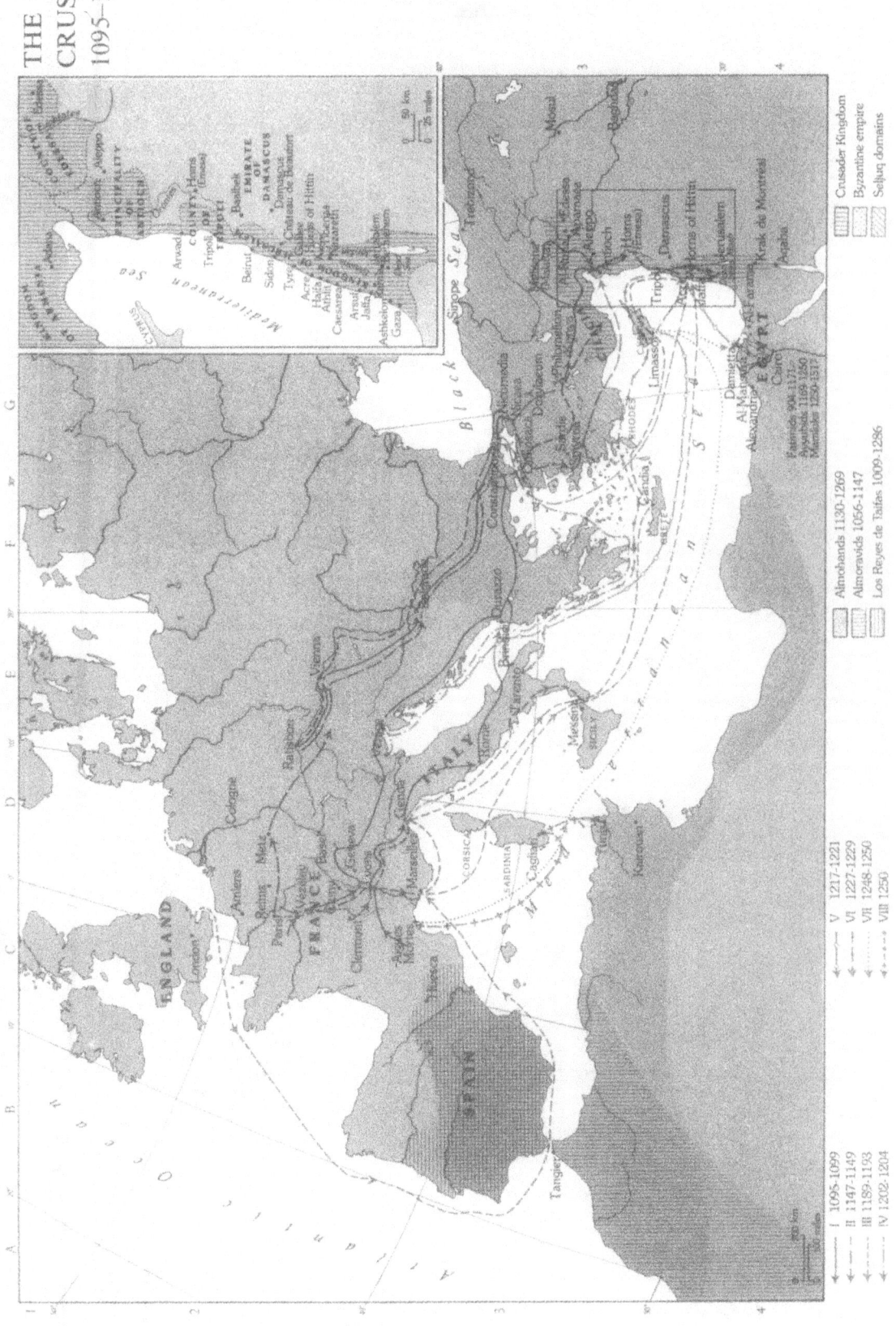

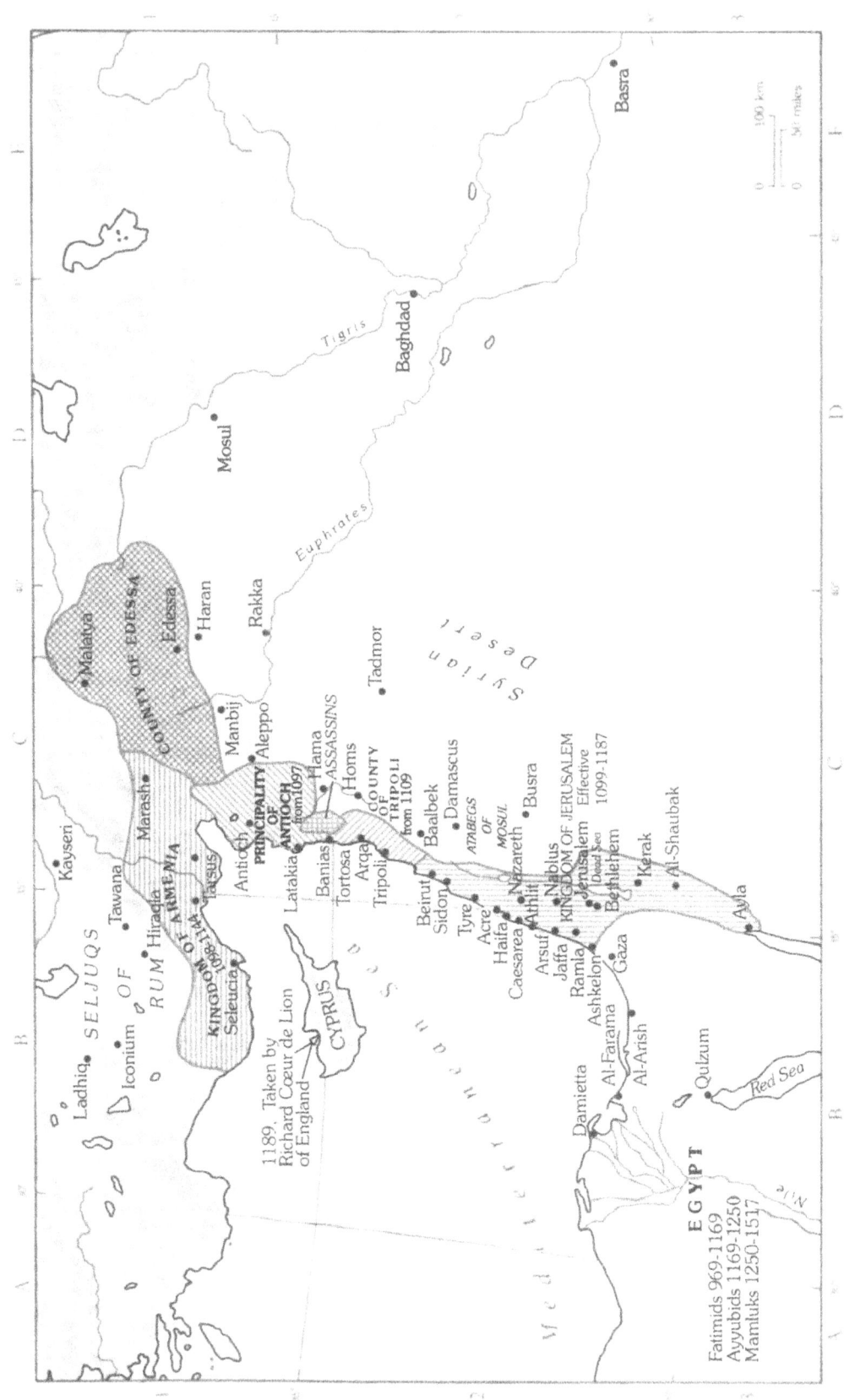

CRUSADES, PRINCIPALITIES 1096–1291

fortresses. Edessa fell in 1144, and it was this defeat that called forth the Second Crusade. Conrad III of Germany and Louis VII of France besieged Damascus inconclusively. Control of the frontier wavered among the Byzantines, Crusaders, and Muslims. Eventually the Muslim commander Saladin conquered Syria. There were no fresh attacks by the Seljuqs on Byzantine territory. On 3 to 4 July 1187, Saladin defeated Guy de Lusignan, king of Jerusalem, and took him prisoner.

In the Third Crusade (1189–1192), Barbarossa (Frederick I) of Germany, Philip Augustus of France, and Richard I of England responded. A peace was patched up in 1192 that left the Latins in possession of the coast. The Fourth Crusade (1202–1204) was diverted by the Venetians to Constantinople. They sacked the capital and established a Latin empire. Evicted in 1261, the Greeks have never forgotten — nor forgiven. During the Fifth Crusade (1218–1221) the Crusaders attacked Egypt. It proved abortive. The Sixth Crusade (1228–1229) was led by the emperor Frederick II, who obtained a ten-year truce, which restored Jerusalem, except the Muslim holy places, to the Franks. Internal quarrels between Knights Templar and Knights Hospitaler so weakened the kingdom that it fell to the Khwarizmian Turks in 1144. The Seventh Crusade (1248–1250), in which Louis IX of France attacked Cairo, cost him imprisonment. He ransomed himself, and later was able to regain some lost ground and to rebuild Acre, Jaffa, Haifa, Caesarea, and Sidon. In 1260 a Mamluk general, Baybars I, halted the Mongol invasion of Syria. Shortly thereafter he captured all Palestine. In 1263 he destroyed the church at Nazareth; in 1266, in spite of an amnesty, he executed two thousand Knights Templar. This slaughter marked the end of Latin rule, but not of Latin trade, for Venice, Pisa, Genoa, and other cities maintained a lucrative commerce. Trade, however, was hardly the original intention.

## THE LATIN KINGDOM OF JERUSALEM AND PRINCIPALITIES

The four Crusader principalities were the county of Edessa, founded in 1098; the Kingdom of Armenia, founded in the same year; the principality of Antioch, which had been founded in 1097; and the county of Tripoli, effective from 1109, of which the kingdom of Jerusalem was the overlord.

The county of Tripoli had an unexpected ally in the Assassins, a Shi'ite sect that maintained itself by terrorism. For two hundred years this unnatural alliance maintained a front against the Atabegs of Damascus, representing an extreme example of the process of social and economic adaptation that the Crusaders underwent. Their aristocracy intermarried freely with the Armenian royalty, the last of whom was to die in Paris. A series of castles guarded the flank of Tripoli and underwent twelve sieges between

*Crusader fortress, Krak des Chevaliers*

1142 and 1271. While there are unmistakably European features, such as the twelfth century citadel and walls of Cairo, which were built by Armenians from Edessa, the fundamental architectural concepts are to be found in the citadels of northern Syria.

The defense of these castles and the protection of pilgrims visiting Jerusalem were entrusted to the Knights: The Hospitalers originated as guardians of the hospice of St. John in Jerusalem; the Knights Templar were quartered in the Aqsa Mosque, and followed a military-cum-religious rule that had been composed by Bernard of Clairvaux in 1128; the Order of Teutonic Knights was confined to German citizens. All three had standing armies and were answerable to the pope as sovereign.

These Crusader principalities were feudal. During the twelfth century they steadily maintained and developed trading links with their countries of origin and with the East. For example, the Polo brothers made Acre the starting-off point for their journeys to China, but their connections extended to India and to eastern Africa. At Acre, too, Nicholas Tebaldi served as papal legate when he was summoned to Rome to be elected pope as Gregory X (1270–1276). From here also, it was possible to outflank the Fatimid and Mamluk trade with the East in silks and spices.

*Horns of Hittin, site of battle between Muslims and Crusaders*

## THE SELJUQ TURKS, 1077–1307

The period from Tughril Beg's entry into Baghdad in 1055 through the reigns of his nephew and successor, Alp Arslan (1063–1072), and his son Malik-Shah (1072–1092) is one of Seljuq ascendancy over the Muslim East. In 1065 Alp Arslan took Ani, capital of Armenia, and in 1071 he defeated the emperor Romanus IV Diogenes at Manzikert, taking him prisoner. The Seljuq nomads were thus the first Muslims to bring Turkish culture to Asia Minor. In 1077 Sulayman ibn Qutlumish, a cousin of Alp Arslan, was made governor of the new

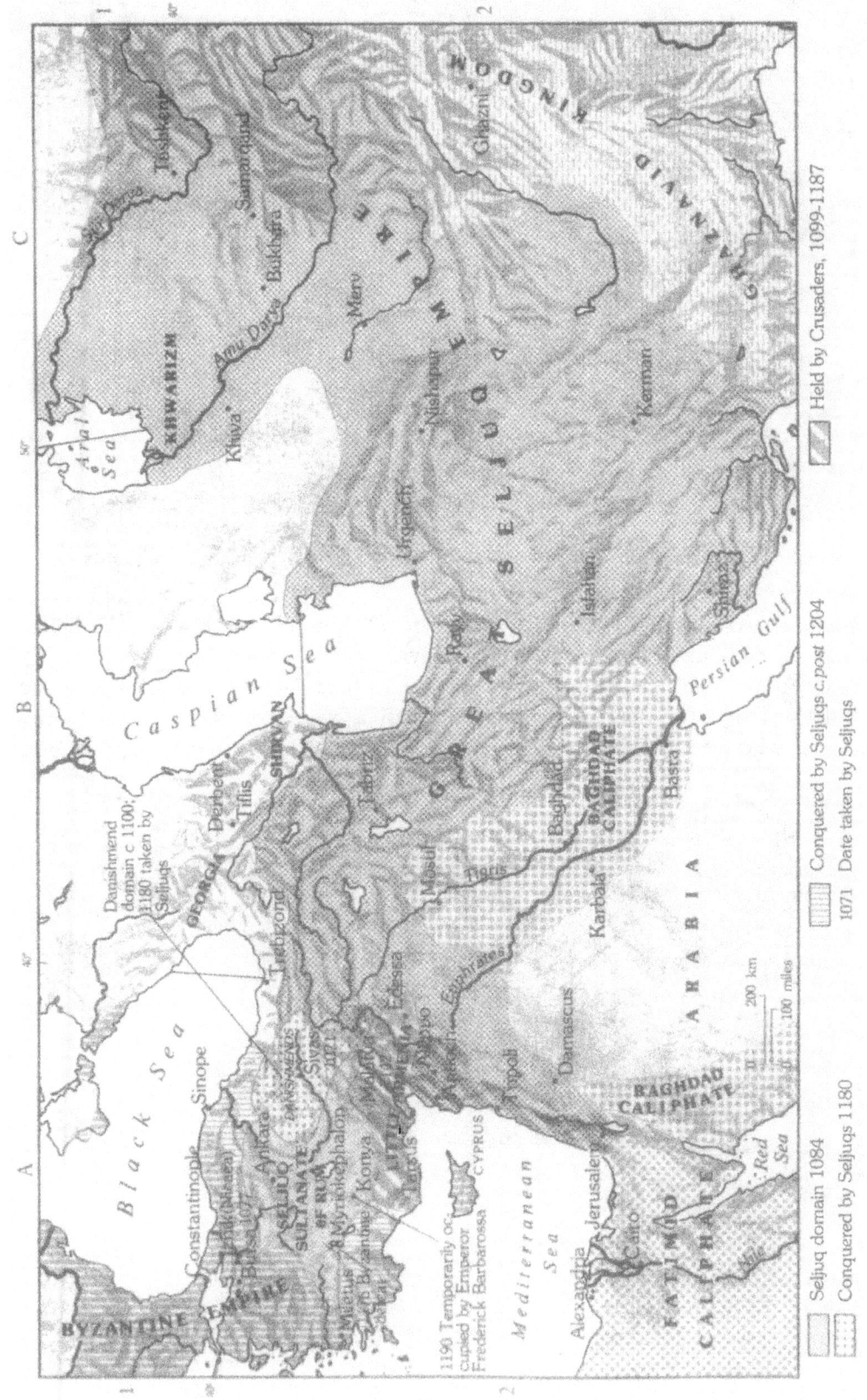

THE SELJUQ TURKS, 1077–1307

*Whirling dervishes, from Ignatius Mouradgea d'Ohsson's* Tableau Général de l'Empire

province, establishing a dynasty that came to be known as the Seljuqs of Rum (Rome). The new capital was at Iznik (Nicaea). After 1084 the capital was transferred to Konya. In Syria, Tutush, a son of Alp Arslan, founded the Seljuq dynasty of Syria at Aleppo (1094–1117), from where the holy cities of Mecca and Medina were controlled. These cities functioned as provincial capitals, for

*Central Mosque in Isfahan, Iran. Chief Seljuk Turk monument*

Alp Arslan resided in Isfahan; only after 1091 did the Seljuq sultan reside in Baghdad, thereby maintaining a puppet caliph.

These sultans were not simply rulers. Roads, walls, mosques, canals, caravanserais, and khans, covered an empire that stretched from Transoxiana to Syria and Asia Minor. From 1065 to 1092, the vizier was the gifted Nizam al-Mulk, a cultured scholar and author of a treatise on the art of government. The revision of the calendar was entrusted to the poet Umar Khayyam, celebrated in his day as an astronomer and mathematician. In Baghdad the Nizamiyah academy was founded in 1065–1067, long anticipating the universities of the West. Nizam al-Mulk was murdered by a Persian Ismaili Assassin in 1092. In the East the Seljuq dynasty of Persia survived until 1157.

Although the Crusaders dominated much of this period, the caliphs and their sultans stood by as indifferent spectators.

## THE ALMOHADS IN NORTH AFRICA AND SPAIN, 1130–1269

Like the Almoravids, the Almohads (Arabic, *al-Muwahhidun*) originated as a Berber politico-religious movement. Muhammad ibn Tumart proclaimed himself Mahdi, the expected one who would come to foretell the Day of Judgment and to recall Muslims to the original purity of belief in al-Wahid (One God). He and his followers held that they were the only community of true believers. In 1147 Ibn Tumart's successor, Abd al-Mumin ibn Ali, seized all Morocco and

*The bridge at Ronda, the Andalusian town in southern Spain*

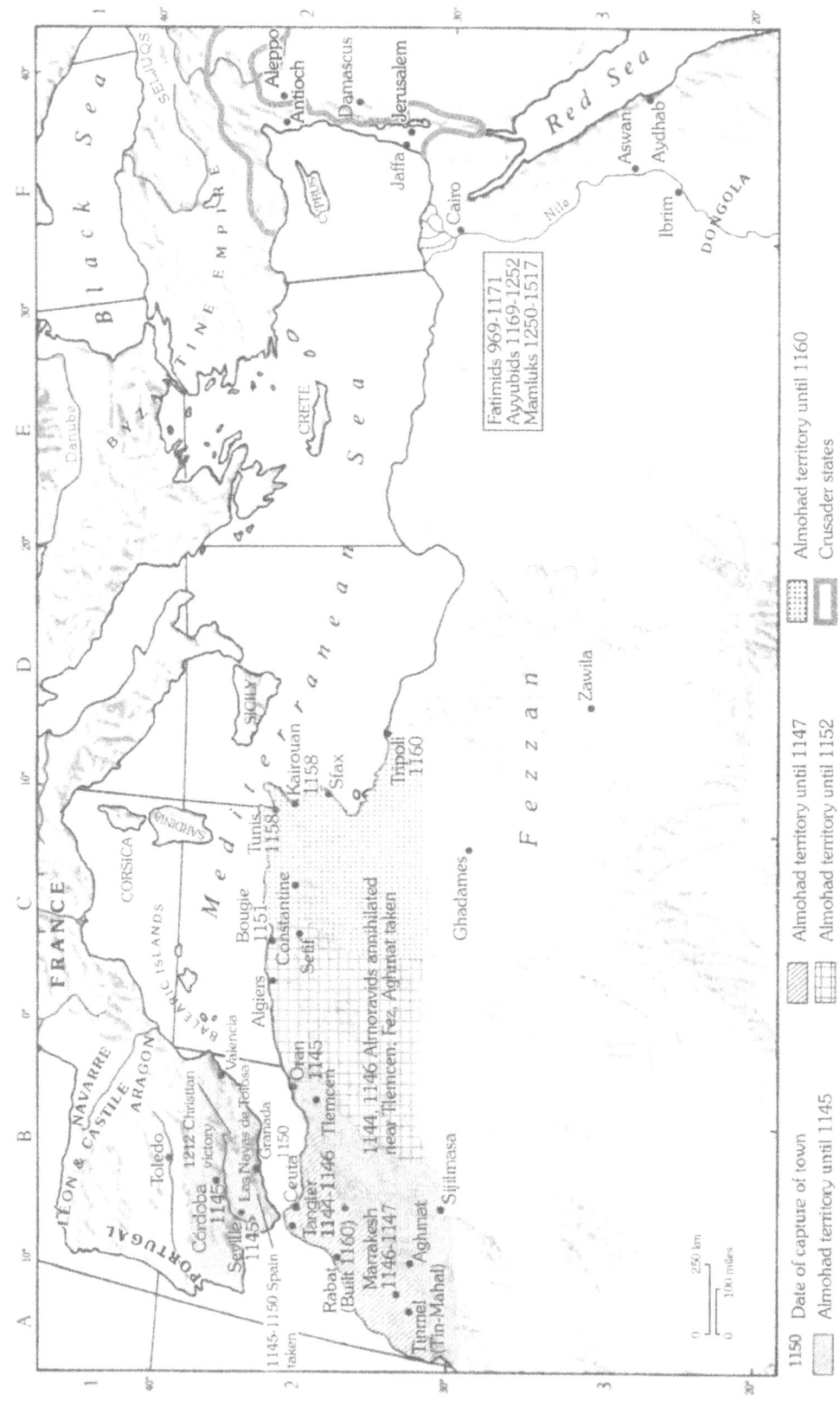

## THE ALMOHADS IN NORTH AFRICA AND SPAIN, 1130–1269

extinguished Almoravid rule. By 1150 he had taken Spain, and then he advanced through North Africa, taking Algeria in 1152, Tunisia in 1158, and Tripoli and as far as the Egyptian border in 1160.

The capital of this huge empire was transferred to Seville in 1170. Here, in 1172, a great mosque was begun, of which the minaret with an atrium survives and is known as the Giralda Tower. In Morocco he built the city of Rabat, and in the city of Marrakesh he founded a hospital that was boasted to be unequaled in all the world.

In 1170 Abd al-Mumin's grandson, Abu Yusuf Ya'qub al-Mansur, renewed the holy war against the Christians, but with little result. In 1184 his son Abu Yusuf succeeded. Crossing over to Andalusia, he made a five-year truce with the king of Castile and León. In 1195 he defeated Alfonso VIII of Castile at Alarcos.

Although it was a great military victory, al-Mansur did not follow it up. This failure created a political stalemate. In 1212 an alliance of Aragon and Navarre, the Templars from Portugal, and French Crusaders was led by Alfonso VIII. At Las Navas de Tolosa this force annihilated the Almohad army; of 600,000 men it was claimed that only one thousand escaped death.

The Almohad regime in Spain now collapsed. Christian kingdoms and Muslim dynasties parceled out Spain. In North Africa the descendants of Abd al-Mumin reigned in Marrakesh until 1269, when the Banu Marin took the city. Once again, the failure to organize a stable, constitutional form of government that did not depend on the emergence of strong personalities proved the undoing of a dynasty.

*One of the Alhambra Palace halls*

# SALADIN AND THE AYYUBID DOMAINS, 1169–1250

With the accession of Zangi as governor of Mosul (r. 1127–1146), the tide began to turn in favor of Islam against the Crusaders. In Syria Zangi's son Nur al-Din (r. 1146–1174) recovered Damascus in 1154 and Antioch in 1164. In his campaign against Fatimid Egypt in 1164, the Kurdish general Ayyub took his nephew Saladin (Salah al-Din Yusuf) with him. A serious young man, Saladin sought to replace Fatimid Shi'ism with Sunni Islam and to wage a holy war against the Crusaders.

In 1174, following Nur's death, Saladin declared himself independent in Egypt, and in 1175 he was invested as sultan by the caliph, with full power over Egypt, the Maghrib, western Arabia, Palestine, central Syria, and Nubia, which last, however, retained its independence. In 1176 he neutralized the Assassins, and then, on 1 July 1187, he defeated the Crusaders at the Horns of Hittin, near Megiddo. Jerusalem capitulated on 2 October, and only a small coastal fringe near Acre was left to the Crusaders. Shortly thereafter, Saladin died. It was a life of extraordinary accomplishment. In Cairo he had built walls, madrasas (colleges for theological education), mosques, schools, canals, dykes, and the Citadel. He had patronized scholars, such as the Córdoban philosopher Musa ibn Maymun (Hebrew, Mosheh ben Maimon; Greek, Maimonides), his secretary and personal physician, but also an astronomer, theologian, and philosopher.

On Saladin's death members of the Ayyubid dynasty divided his sultanate among themselves, resulting in internal discord but favorable commercial relations with the Crusader colonies, especially the merchants of Venice and Pisa, who had consulates at Alexandria. The principal branch of the Ayyubids resided at Cairo, but in Syria and Yemen other branches proclaimed themselves independent of Cairo. They were eventually overthrown by the Mongols and then by the Mamluks.

THE WORLD AS DEPICTED BY AL-IDRISI

*Karatay Madrasa, Konya, Turkey, 1251*

# THE AYYUBID DOMAINS, 1169–1250

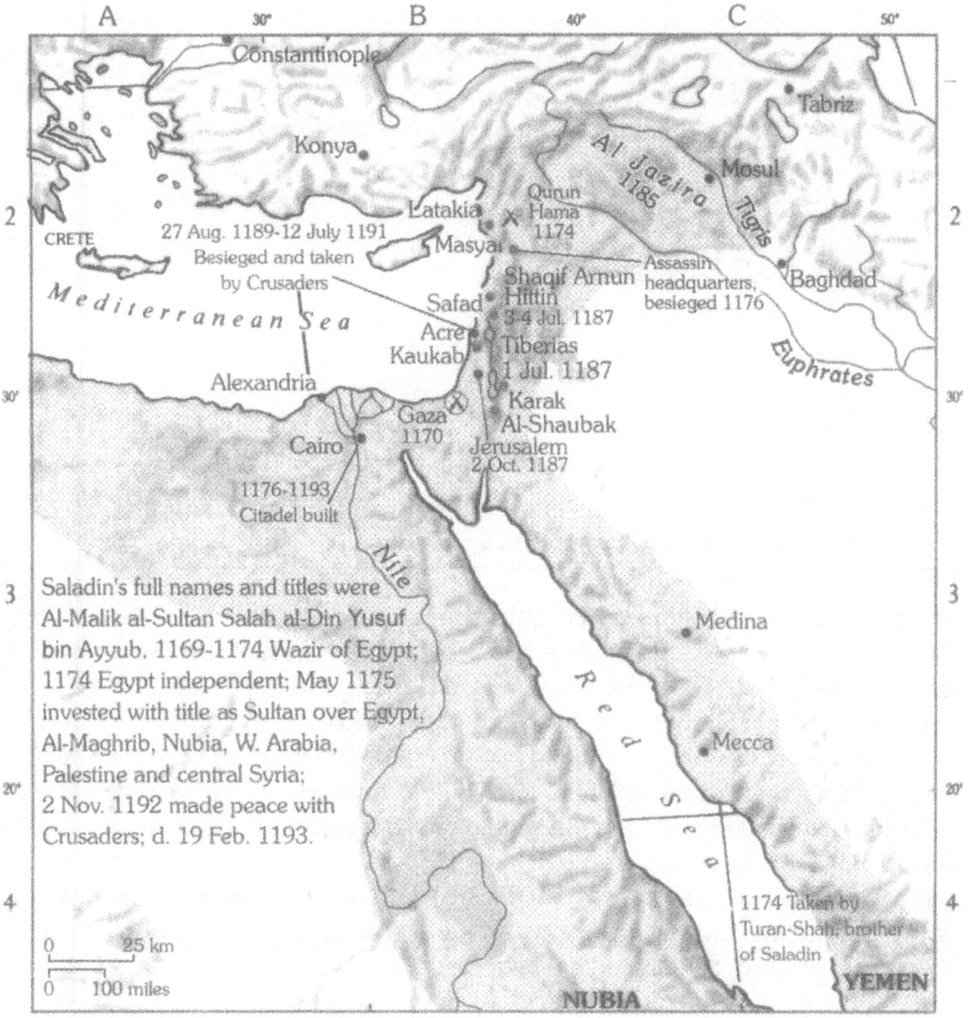

Saladin's full names and titles were Al-Malik al-Sultan Salah al-Din Yusuf bin Ayyub. 1169-1174 Wazir of Egypt; 1174 Egypt independent; May 1175 invested with title as Sultan over Egypt, Al-Maghrib, Nubia, W. Arabia, Palestine and central Syria; 2 Nov. 1192 made peace with Crusaders; d. 19 Feb. 1193.

- ⊗ 1170 Crusader victory, with date
- ✗ 1187 Battle, with date
- 2 Oct. 1187 Town or area taken by Saladin, with date
- • Town taken by Saladin between 1187 and 1189
- ▭ Empire of Saladin 1169-1250

*The El-Aqsa Mosque, Jerusalem*

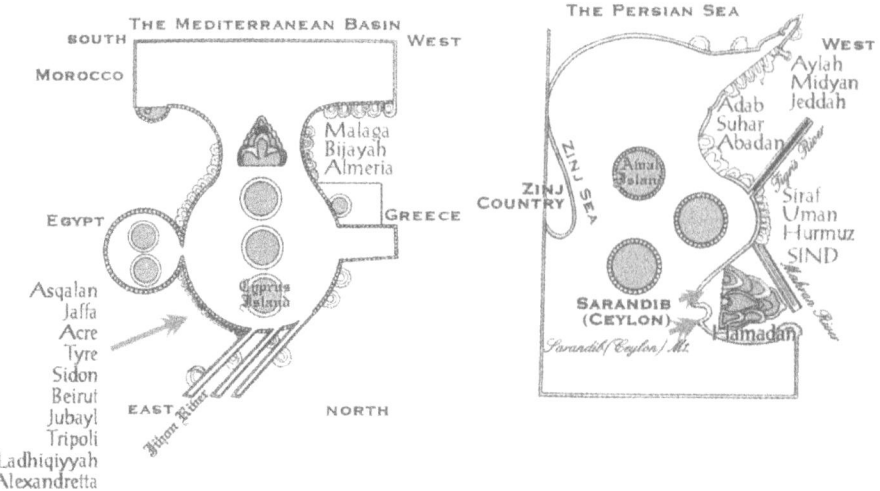

*The Mediterranean and Persian Seas, according to Istakri, c. 950*

## THE CITY OF CAIRO, FROM THE BEGINNING UNTIL 1517

The historian Ibn Khaldun called Cairo the mother of cities. No city in the world, save perhaps Rome, contains so many monuments. By 1951 some five hundred monuments were listed, but these did not include the Coptic churches nor some three hundred buildings of the Ottoman period (1517–1804).

Cairo is located on the east bank of the Nile, opposite Memphis, which stretched between Giza and Saqqara. The pyramids and the Sphinx are all that remains of the pharaonic city. Modern Cairo — it was given the name al-Qahira in 969 — originated as a Roman fort, built in 27 BC, that accommodated a legion stationed at the apex of the Delta. Beside the fort grew up the Greco-Coptic town of Babilyun (Babylon), where a Persian fort had been located in 500 BC. The Holy Family is believed to have sought refuge from Herod in its Jewish quarter, and the apostle Peter and Mark the Evangelist are reported to have preached here in AD 42. A synagogue and early churches still survive in what is known as Old Cairo.

When Amr ibn al-As took Egypt in 641 he built his garrison headquarters north and east of this site. A Friday mosque known by his name still stands, though it has been enlarged and rebuilt many times. This was the center of his buildings, around which other public buildings — a treasury, administrative offices, a post office for rapid communication with Medina, and courts — were built. The city of al-Fustat was divided into quarters, each with its own mosque and administration.

In 751 the Abbasids built a new headquarters at al-Askar, but this has wholly disappeared. In 868 the Egyptian governor, Ahmad ibn Tulun, knowing the weakness of the caliphate, declared Egypt independent. He seized all Syria as far as the Euphrates and Libya as far as Barca. In what is now the al-Qata'i quarter he built a splendid mosque that still survives; the palace, barracks, offices, hospital, baths, markets, racecourse, and polo ground have long since disappeared. After they conquered Egypt in 969, the Fatimids built a new palace city. On 5 August astrologers stood by to determine when the first sod should be turned. The city's boundaries had been marked with

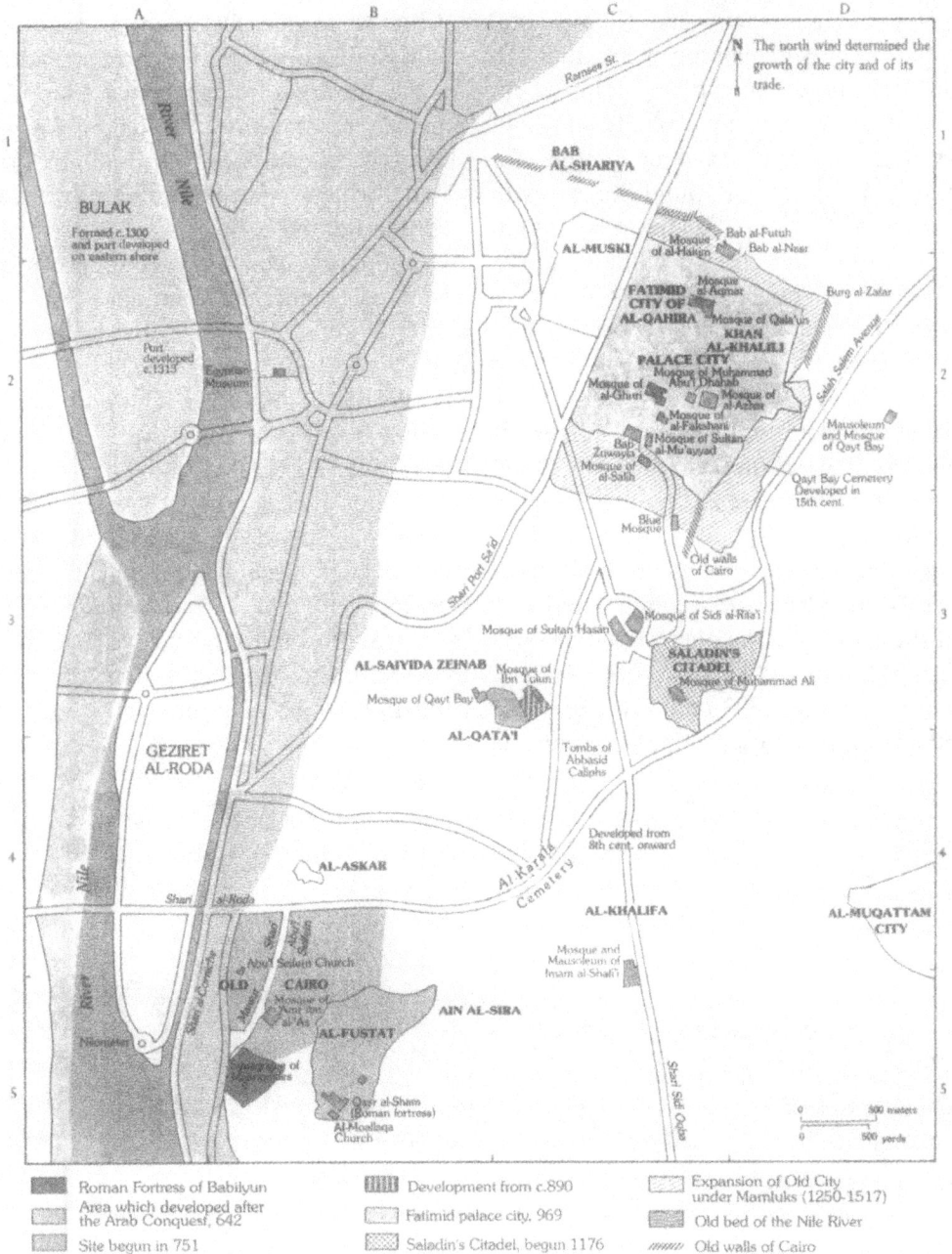

# THE CITY OF CAIRO, FROM THE BEGINNING UNTIL 1517

ropes, on which bells had been hung to give the signal to commence. A raven anticipated the astrologers by alighting on a rope. The moment was unlucky, for Mars (Arabic, *al-Qahira*) was in the ascendant, thus giving the city its name.

Elaborate buildings now arose, of which the palace mosque, al-Azhar, was destined to become the intellectual center of the Islamic world.

The Fatimid dynasty collapsed in 1168. The next year Saladin became governor.

His great monument, the Citadel, still stands. The surrounding walls, built by his Armenian commander, Badr al-Jamali, were never completed. He also built twenty madrasas (teaching colleges for religion), replacing Fatimid Shi'ism with Sunnite orthodoxy. Saladin also sought to organize an orderly administration. For this he trained Mamluks — slaves who received a full Islamic education and training in the arts of government and war. The early Mamluks, of largely Turkish origin until 1382 and thereafter chiefly of Circassian origin, dominated Egypt until it was seized by the Ottoman Turks in 1517.

On 8 August 1303, a massive earthquake devastated Cairo, destroying a majority of the buildings. The older part of central Cairo belongs chiefly to the Mamluk period between 1303 and 1517, for little other than domestic building can be attributed to the Ottoman Turks. To the Mamluks are owed the most splendid of the mosques, mausoleums, dervish monasteries, and hospitals, one of which still survives as an eye hospital. In the Citadel a new mosque and palace were built on a grand scale as were the rest of the buildings. Nor was it merely on a grand scale: under the Mamluks it was an age of taste and elegance for the whole city, which reached its apogee in the reign of Qayt Bay (1468–1495). This was made possible by the Mamluks' continuance of the trade policies that had been developed under the Fatimids. As the city slowly developed northward to take advantage of the prevailing north wind, the same wind inhibited sea traffic up the Red Sea. For most of the year, Cairo thus became a trading center for the caravan trade between east and west.

*The Citadel of Cairo, built by Saladin*

## THE GHURIDS IN AFGHANISTAN AND NORTH INDIA,
### 1175–1206

Although Islam reached the Indus valley early, it did not begin to expand across the subcontinent until the last quarter of the twelfth century. This expansion occurred almost accidentally. A successor of the sultan Mahmud of Ghazna had executed two princelings of Ghur, an obscure principality southeast of Herat. In response, the Ghurid Ala al-Din Husayn sacked Ghazna and laid it waste. Ghuzz Turkmans then attempted to seize the city, and it was from them that the

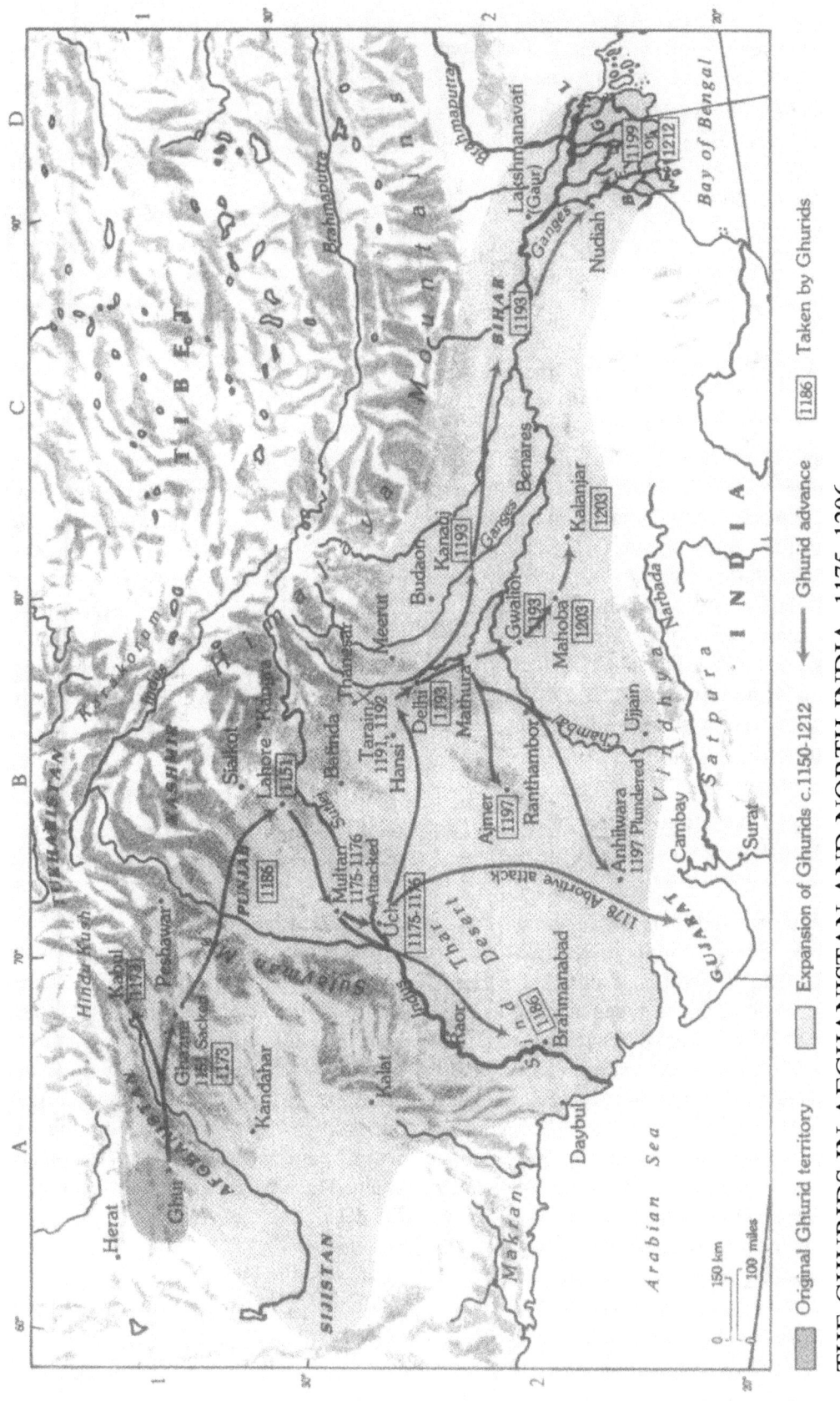

THE GHURIDS IN AFGHANISTAN AND NORTH INDIA, 1175–1206

Ghurids wrested it in 1173, when Muhammad Ghuri (Arabic, *Muizz al-Din Muhammad al-Ghuri*) emerged as a conqueror, moving steadily eastward. Following an unsuccessful attack on Gujarat in 1178, Muhammad Ghuri occupied the Punjab in addition to Sind.

Such aggression roused the Hindu rulers of northern India, who formed a confederacy under the ruler of Delhi, Rai Pithaura. At Tarain, which commands Delhi and the Ganges basin, Muhammad Ghuri was defeated. Once again, however, he was undeterred. In the following year, 1192, ten thousand mounted archers utterly routed the Hindu confederacy — a defeat due largely to the troops' own immobility. Now the cities of India lay open to Muhammad Ghuri's general Qutb al-Din Aybak, a Mamluk slave from Turkestan, who advanced, taking Delhi, Kanauj, Gwalior, Anhilwara in Gujarat, and Ajmer. By 1199 or 1212, all Bengal was occupied — a defeat not only for Hinduism, but also for Buddhism, which had a greater hold in the eastern region.

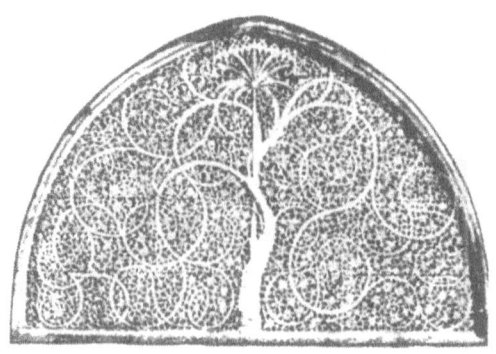

*Stone window ornament from the Sidi Sayyad Mosque at Ahmadabad*

Muhammad Ghuri died in 1206. Adopted as Muhammad Ghuri's son, Qutb al-Din now ascended the throne as sultan, the first sultan in Delhi. He ruled for little more than four years, dying in a polo accident. "Beneficent and victorious...his gifts were bestowed by hundreds of thousands, and his slaughters likewise by hundreds of thousands...." A new age had dawned in India.

## SUCCESSOR STATES OF THE ALMOHADS IN NORTH AFRICA, 1200–1560

After the Battle of Las Navas de Tolosa, the Almohad empire gradually collapsed. In Ifriqiya (modern Tunisia), the Hafsid governor claimed independence in 1228. In 1235 the emir of Tlemcen, Yaghmorasan, proclaimed independence, giving his kingdom the title Zanata Kingdom of the Banu Abd al-Wad. He was of the Ziyanid tribe. In 1248 the Banu Marin, who already held Meknès, seized Fez from the Almohads; in 1269, they conquered Marrakesh. The latter was the final defeat of the Almohads.

These new kingdoms were primarily trading states, with long established connections with western Africa. The Hafsids had the recognition of Christian Mediterranean powers — Venice, Pisa, Genoa, and Sicily — and were in treaty relations with Spain and Egypt. At first, Tlemcen and Fez recognized Tunis as suzerain. Not only the Tunis economy, but also the quality of life was enhanced by immigrants — architects, artists, artisans, and writers — fleeing Christian Spain. The greatest of Islamic historians, Ibn Khaldun, was a descendant of such immigrants.

In the west the Marinids of Fez controlled the outlet of the shortest route to the gold-bearing lands of Mali as well as to supplies of salt and slaves. From Mali a

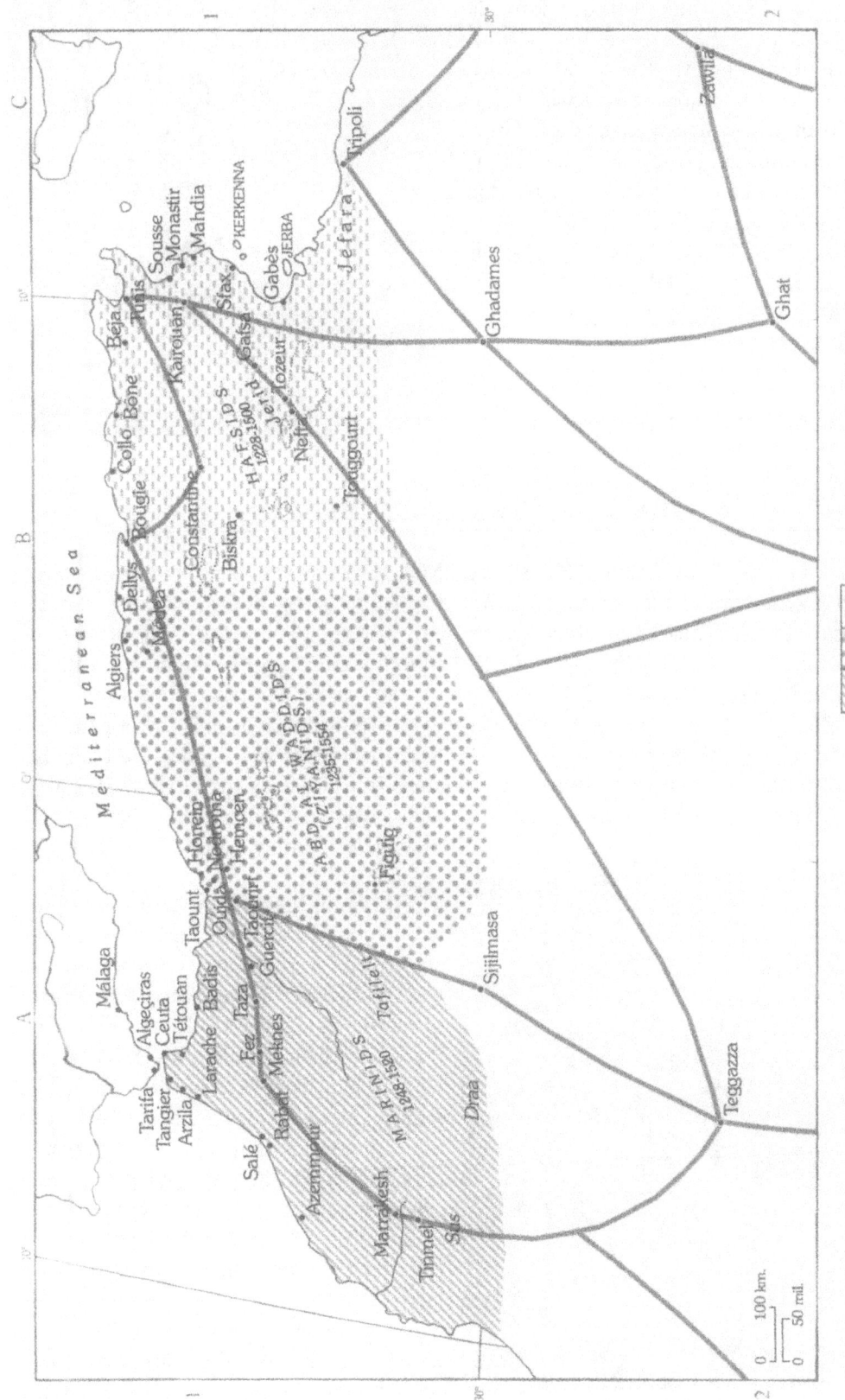

SUCCESSOR STATES OF THE ALMOHADS IN NORTH AFRICA, 1200–1560

fleet of canoes was sent out into the Atlantic in 1310 to ascertain whether there was land to the west. Shortly thereafter, its ruler, the fabled sultan Kankan Mansa Musa, made the pilgrimage to Mecca, with so splendid an entourage and giving so much in alms as to depreciate the value of gold in Cairo. Ibn Battuta's visit to Mali in 1352–1353 on behalf of the Marinid sultan was probably a commercial, diplomatic mission.

*Minaret of the Great Mosque, Rabat, Morocco*

## THE MAMLUKS IN EGYPT, 1250–1517

The Mamluks that Saladin introduced into Egypt were Turks or Greeks. Because they were quartered on Roda, an island in the Nile (Arabic, *Bahr al-Nil*), they were known as Bahri. Their successors after 1382 — known as Burgi because they were quartered in the Citadel (Arabic, *Burg*) — were almost all Circassians from southeast Russia.

*Mausoleum of Qayt Bay, Cairo*

Mamluk means "owned" or "slave," but, far from being a dishonorable status, capture in youth and training as a Mamluk could lead to the highest offices in the state. Strictly, they were not dynasties so much as military oligarchies based on regimental rather than family allegiance. Racially they kept themselves apart from the Egyptians, over whom they were the only dominant force from 1250 to 1517.

The Mamluk system was initiated by a woman, Shajar al-Durr ("tree of pearls"), who ruled for only eighty days before she was murdered. Successive commanders of the Bahri regiment followed, of whom the most distinguished was Baybars I, who ruled from 1260 until 1277. A remarkable general, he cleared Syria of the Mongols and remnants of the Crusaders and broke the power of the Assassins. His generals were sent westward to conquer the Berbers and southward to conquer the Christian kingdoms of Nubia.

Qala'un, a Kipchaq Turk (r. 1279–1290), was the only Bahri Mamluk who succeeded in founding a dynasty. He was succeeded by his second son, al-Nasir

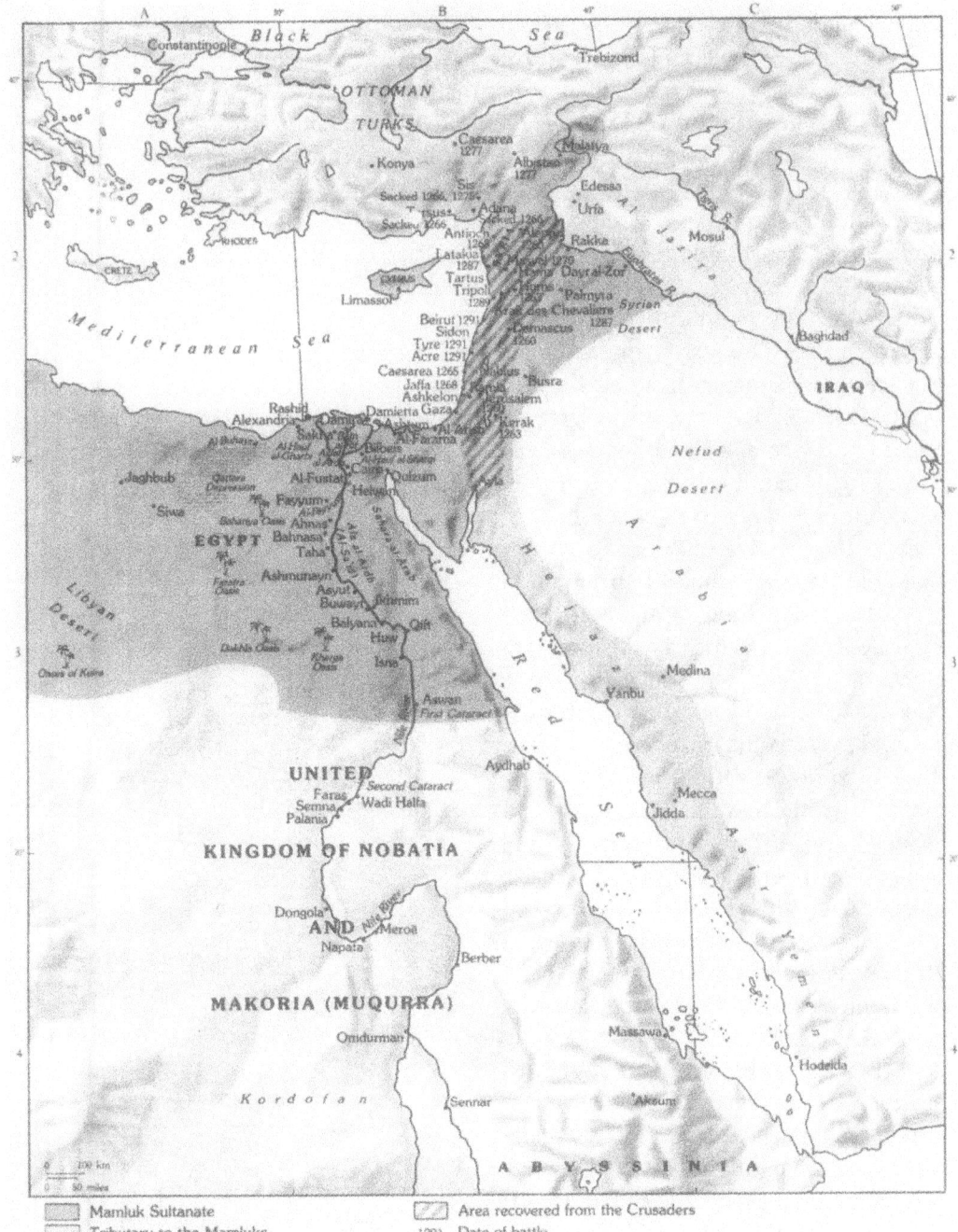

# THE MAMLUKS IN EGYPT, 1250–1517

Muhammad (r. 1293–1294, 1298–1308, 1309–1340), who was succeeded by two sons, eight grandsons, two great-grandsons, and two great-great-grandsons. Al-Nasir is chiefly remembered as the restorer of Cairo after the earthquake of 1303. During this period a special characteristic of Cairene architecture developed — ribbed carved stone domes over mausoleums. He and his successors used building as a form of publicity, endowing mosques, madrasas, dervish convents, hospitals, and public drinking fountains. Al-Nasir's palace set a new trend in *ablaq*, building in alternate courses of red and white stone. The grandest mosque of all, the madrasa and mausoleum of Sultan Hasan (r. 1347–1351, 1354–1361), was built in 1354–1361: the sultan did not live to complete it nor was he buried in it. It provided lodgings for students and professors, up to five hundred persons.

Under the Burgi Mamluks political power lay almost exclusively in the hands of their viziers, a highly unstable form of government. Of twenty-three rulers, six reigned for a total of 103 years out of 134; the remaining seventeen rulers reigned for less than two years each.

Among these rulers one man was outstanding. Of very humble beginnings, Qayt Bay had been bought for the equivalent of fifty dollars. His strength of character took him through all the ranks of the army to commander-in-chief. He was as incorruptible as he was ruthless. He traveled incessantly, visiting Syria, Palestine, and the Hijaz again and again. Wherever he went during his long reign (1468–1496), he left roads, bridges, mosques, fortifications, schools, and other works. His madrasa in Cairo and his mosque and mausoleum in the Northern Cemetery are of incomparable elegance and beauty.

All this elegance and luxury, was achieved by fostering trade at what was the crossroads between China and India on the one hand and the growing prosperity of Europe on the other. It was, however, doomed. On 22 November 1497, Vasco da Gama rounded the Cape of Good Hope; on 7 April 1498, he was at Mombasa; on 20 May he anchored off Calicut in India. Portugal now seized the carrying trade of the Indian Ocean. In 1508 an Egyptian fleet defeated the Portuguese of Chaul, but was annihilated the following year. Qayt Bay had kept a watchful eye on the growing power of the Ottomans. Three years after the defeat of Chaul, Selim I, the Grim (r. 1512–1520), ascended the Ottoman throne. In 1514 the Persians were defeated by Selim at Chaldiran. In 1516 he defeated the Egyptian army at Marj Dabiq in Syria and took Jerusalem. In January 1517 he entered Cairo; for nearly three hundred years, until it revived under Muhammad Ali the Great, Egypt was now a backwater.

*Ornamental Castle dispenser,* Book of Knowledge of Ingenious Mechanical Devices, *Al-Jazari, 1354*

*The Dome of the Rock, Jerusalem*

# THE CITY OF JERUSALEM

The present Jerusalem is a palimpsest of cities, superimposed one over the other, but with buildings from earlier layers protruding into later times. The layout of the Old City is that of the emperor Hadrian's Aelia Capitolina, built in AD 135; the walls were built by the Ottoman sultan Sulayman I, the Magnificent, in 1535–1538.

Occupied by Jebusites until it was taken by David around 1000 BC, the earliest city was located on the ridge south of Mount Moriah, or Temple Mount, known also as the Haram al-Sharif, the Noble Sanctuary. The Tyropoeon valley divides it from the Upper City, Mount Zion and the two northern ridges. It was on Mount Moriah that Solomon built the first Temple, together with his palace and other buildings.

David's Jerusalem (map 1), which covered 10.87 acres, was sacked by Nebuchadnezzar in 587 BC. It was slowly restored after the return of the Jews from captivity in Babylon in 538 (map 2). This was the Jerusalem known to Jesus, together with extensions made under Herod I, the Great, to 140 acres. His grandson Herod Agrippa I, in four years of hectic building activity, increased it to 310 acres (map 2) between AD 40 and 44. This city was totally destroyed, the Temple included, by the future emperor Titus in AD 70. His arch in Rome commemorates the event. Jerusalem lay waste until 135, when the emperor Hadrian laid out the city anew as Aelia Capitolina, named after himself, Aelius. Hadrian's plan was somewhat modified after 326, when the emperor Constantine had the Basilica of the Holy Sepulchre built. Further additions were made by the emperor Justinian I (r. 527–565) in the southern part of the city, when his great church, the Nea, was built (map 4).

Under the Arabs, between 638 and 1099, no substantial changes took place. The caliph Abd al-Malik ibn Marwan (r. 865–705) added greatly to the beauty of the city by building the Dome of the Rock

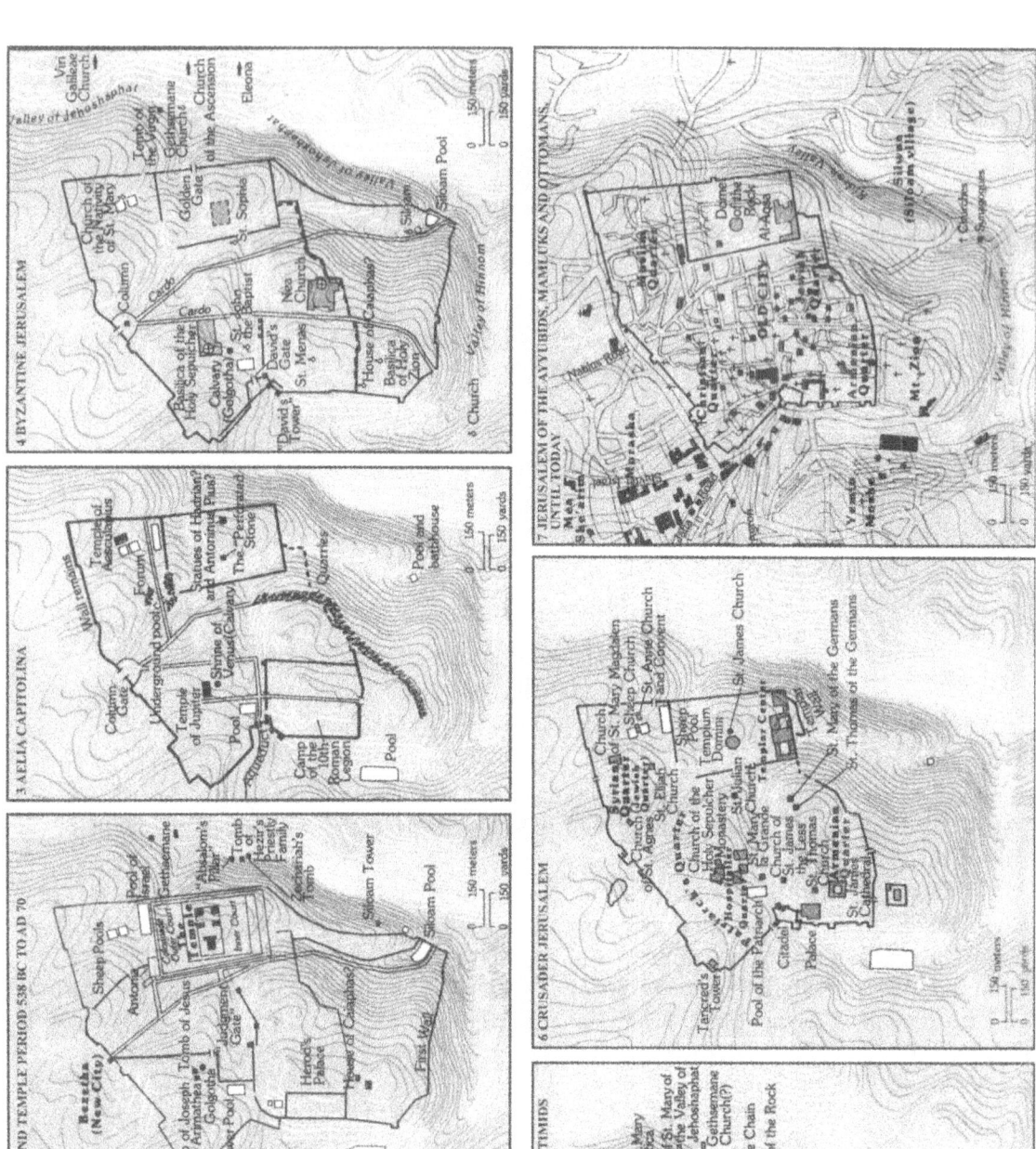

THE CITY OF JERUSALEM

(*al-Qubbat al-Sakhra*), covering the rock from which the Prophet Muhammad is believed to have ascended in his mystical night journey to heaven. At the same time much of the Aqsa Mosque, which has since undergone numerous modifications, was built on the site. It was believed that the caliph Umar I had built the first mosque when he visited Jerusalem in 640. The city had changed little when, in 1009, the mad Fatimid caliph al-Hakim ordered the destruction of all churches and had the Basilica of the Holy Sepulchre largely razed to the ground. By 1048 the Greeks had restored some of it, and under the Crusaders (1099–1187) the existing additions were completed.

Many of the monuments in the Haram al-Sharif and other parts of the city belong to the time when it fell under the Mamluk sultans of Egypt (1260–1517). In 1516 the Ottoman Turks took Syria and in 1517 Egypt. The city now became a backwater, and the area between the Basilica of the Holy Sepulchre and the Damascus Gate was a waste. The revival of the city began in the nineteenth century, partly as a result of Jewish immigration. Continuing up to the present time, the city has far outgrown its sixteenth century walls. Following the British withdrawal in 1947, the city was divided between Israel and Jordan. In 1967, the Old City was captured by Israel. Scientific excavations and restorations have greatly increased knowledge of the history of the Old City. With the support of the late King Hussein of Jordan and the Amir of Kuwait the dome of the Dome of the Rock was entirely renovated and recovered with gold leaf in 1999, at the cost of $8 m., under the supervision of Isam Awwad, an architect from Bethlehem, trained in conservation at the University of York, England.

*Medieval miniature of the city of Jerusalem*

# THE CITY OF MECCA

Islam centers on the "Five Pillars": the profession of faith, prayer five times daily, almsgiving, fasting in Ramadan, and, once in a lifetime, the pilgrimage to Mecca. Some sects add a sixth pillar, *jihad* or holy war. Mecca thus has an unique importance to Muslims. The ceremonies incumbent on the pilgrim culminate with the Id al-Adha, the Festival of Sacrifice, which takes place on the tenth day of the month Dhu-al-Hijjah.

Pilgrimage is an ancient Semitic institution, to which references can be found in the Hebrew scriptures; local shrines likewise attracted pilgrimages. More than six hundred Muslim shrines were recorded in Palestine in 1927. The pilgrimage to Mecca has had the effect of unifying the Islamic world, regardless of race or color, from Morocco and black Africa to Java and China. Of not less unifying effect, the five daily prayers, said only in Arabic, are identical wherever they are said in all the world.

Ancient Mecca was on the caravan route from the southern Arabian ports to both Egypt and Syria. It was already a pilgrimage center before Muhammad. The Kaaba — built, according to Islamic tradition, by Abraham, Hagar, and Isma'il — was the principal shrine. It was this shrine that Muhammad purged of idols, making it the sole temple, or Holy House, of Allah. Although nominally subject to the Umayyad and Abbasid caliphates, Mecca had a somewhat independent existence. From 1269 it was under the Mamluk Egyptian sultans, and after 1517 it came under the Ottoman Turks. Sharifs, descendants of the Prophet Muhammad, ruled as governors. In 1925 it was seized by Ibn Sa'ud and incorporated into Saudi Arabia.

The city centers upon the Haram (Sacred Enclosure) and the holy well of Zamzam. The enclosure has been greatly enlarged by the Saudis, thereby enabling it to accommodate 300,000 worshippers at one time. As many as a million persons attend the pilgrimage.

*The Mosque of Mecca with the Kaaba, from a Persian travel book, 1576*

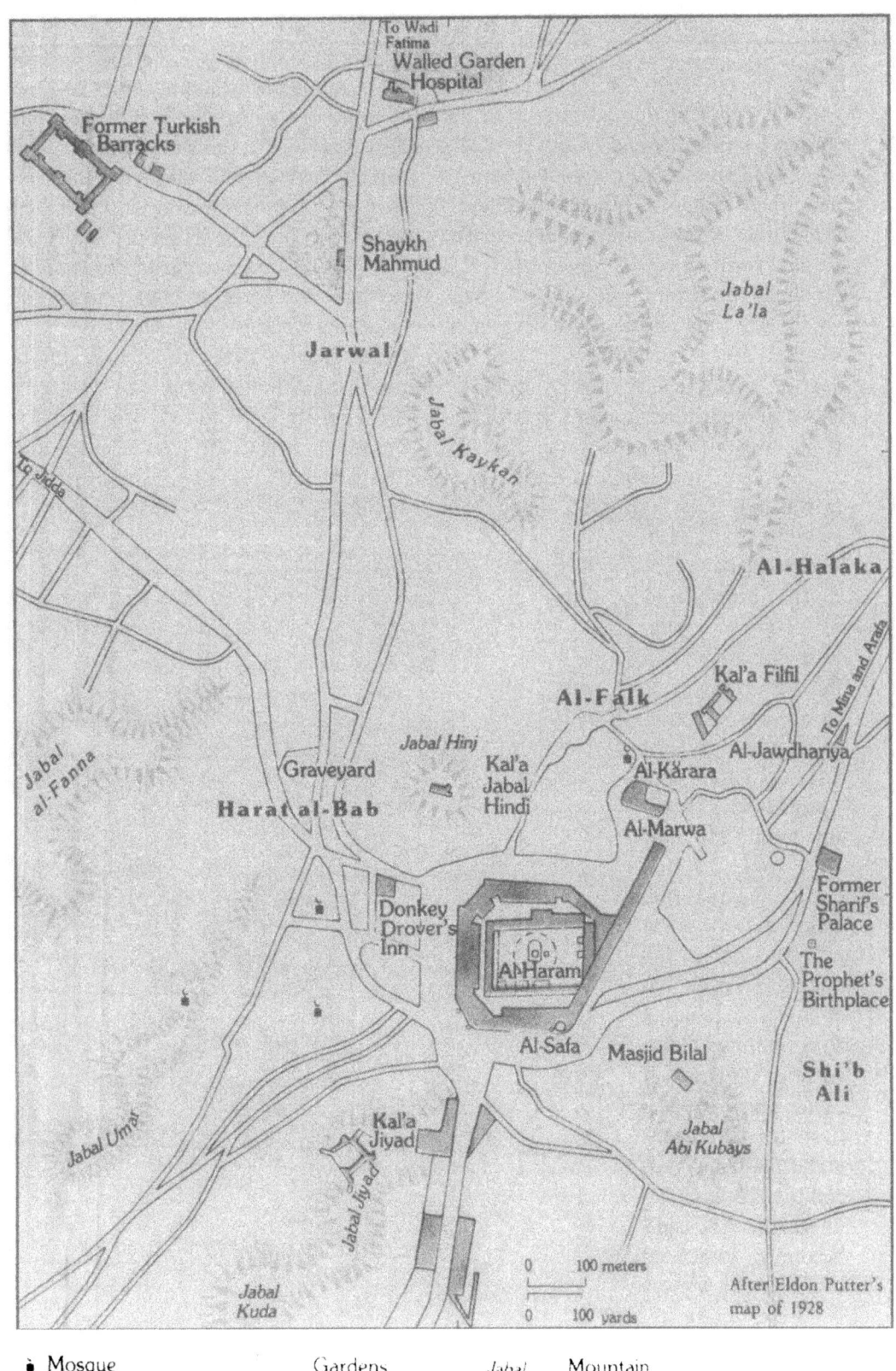

THE CITY OF MECCA

# THE CITY OF MEDINA

In or around 620, some men from Yathrib met Muhammad and were impressed by what he had to say. In 622 a deputation from Yathrib invited him to make it his home — a welcome suggestion in light of the hostility in Mecca. The Prophet's arrival on 24 September 622 is known as the *Hijra* (migration). Yathrib, which was his mother's native city, became known as Medina (Arabic, *Madinat-al-Nabi*, the City of the Prophet).

This marked a turning point in Muhammad's mission. Prior to this migration, he had been simply a religious leader. Now he was not only a prophet, but also a lawgiver, chief judge, commander-in-chief of the army, and civil head of state. After his death in 632, his first four successors — Abu Bakr, Umar I, Uthman ibn Affan, and Ali (632–661) — ruled from Medina. They took the title *khalifa* (caliph, successor and vicar) in all but religious functions. As capital of an ever-expanding Arab empire, Medina was far too off center and gave way first to Damascus under the Umayyads and then to Baghdad under the Abbasids, becoming somewhat of a backwater. Nevertheless, although at no time did a visit to Medina have the prestige of pilgrimage, it ranked second among Muslim holy cities because the tomb of the Prophet is located in the courtyard of the house where he had lived and which had served as the first mosque. Medina became a center of intellectual life, for law, the study of *hadith* (traditional sayings of the Prophet that have the force of law), and of the study and exegesis of the Qur'an.

When the followers of the Wahhabi movement obtained possession of Medina, King Ibn Sa'ud at first forbade pilgrims to visit it. He later relented and enlarged and rebuilt the mosque of Medina.

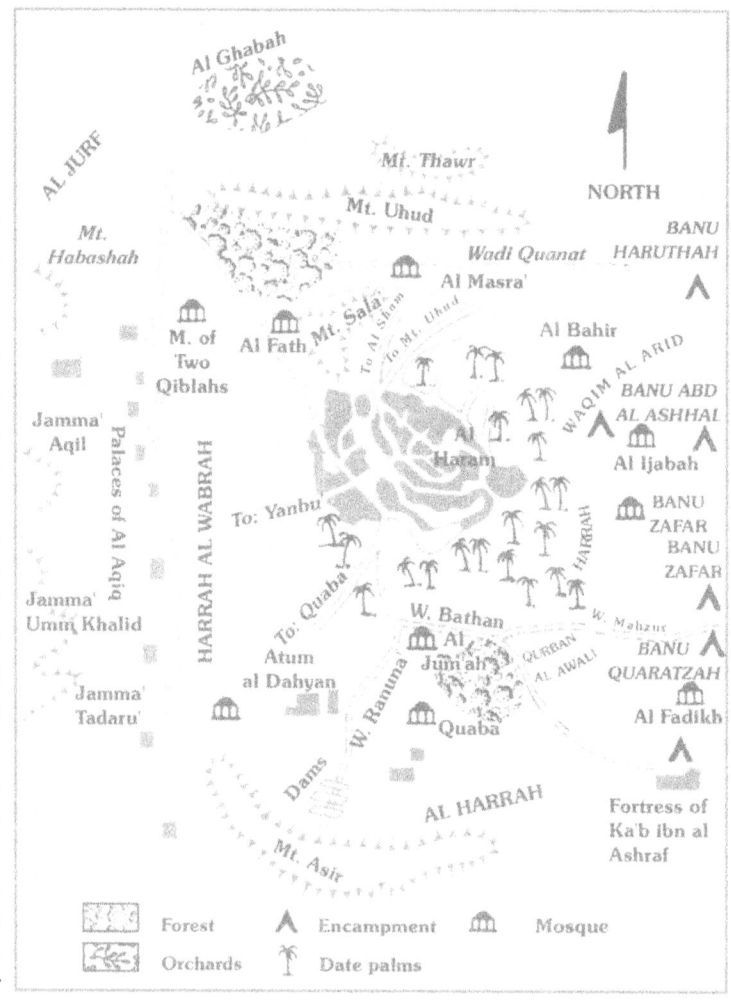

AL-MADINAH AL-MUNAWWARAH AND ITS ENVIRONS

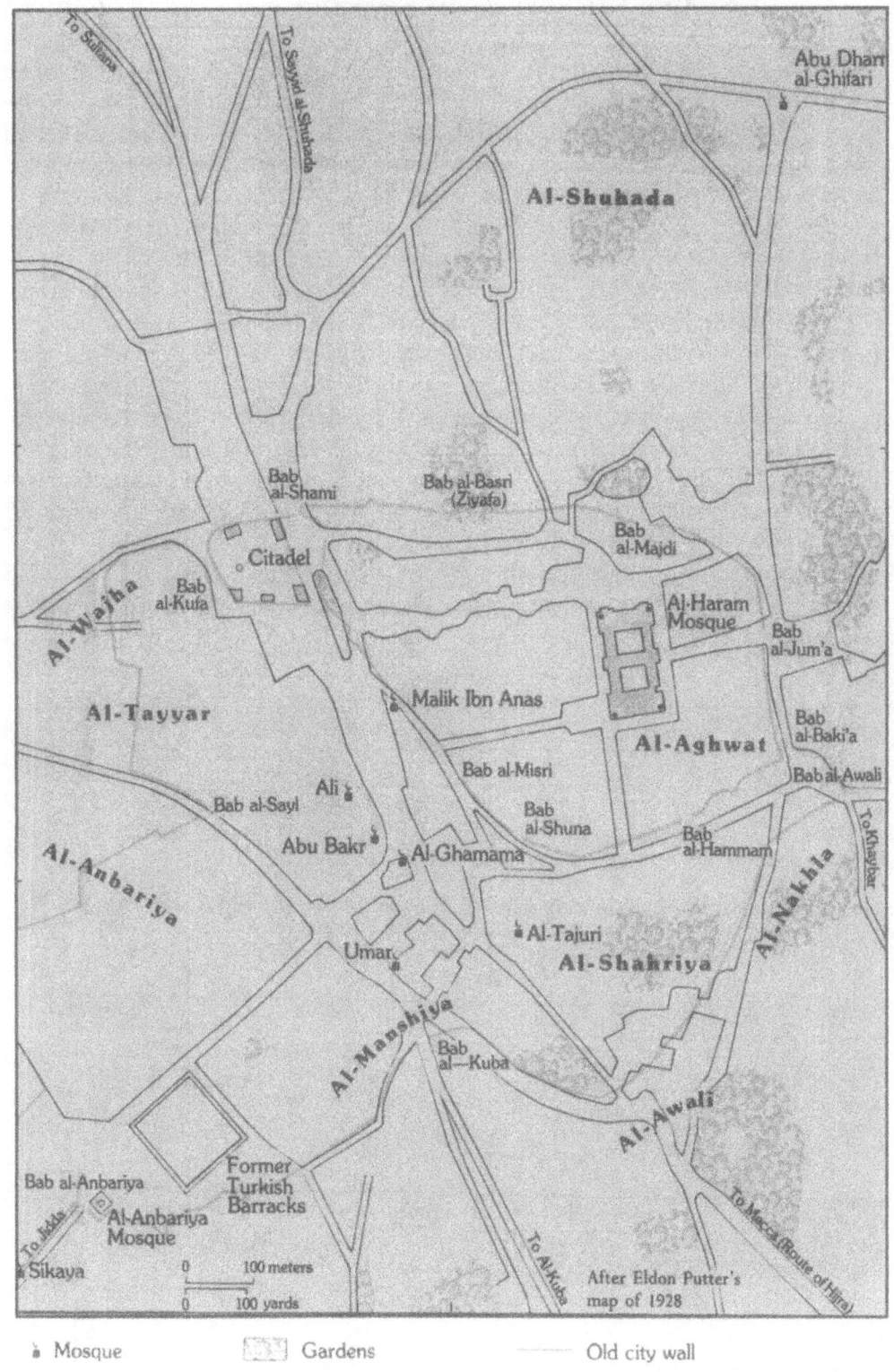

THE CITY OF MEDINA

# THE SPANISH RECONQUISTA, 13TH TO 15TH CENTURIES

The term *reconquista* refers to the recovery of the Iberian Peninsula from the Moors by Spanish Christian kings. This was a slow and drawn out process, partly because the Christian military was weak or merely inactive and slothful, partly because Spanish Christians had adopted Arabic culture and language, yet without changing their religion. Moreover, the finale of Moorish rule in Spain, the small kingdom of Granada (1235-1492), expressed a splendor of material culture, of which the Alhambra and its gardens is a permanent memorial.

Historians date the beginning of the Reconquista from the Christian victory at Covadonga in 718, when the Muslim advance was turned back at the Cantabrian Mountains. It was in fact a mere skirmish, but here the advance of Islam halted and the kingdom of the Asturias was born. By 797 Alfonso II had established a capital at Oviedo and ruled as far west as Galicia and eastward to Santander. During his reign (791-842), a body, believed to be that of the apostle James, was discovered. A national shrine, Santiago de Compostela, was built, to which pilgrims flocked from all Europe. Louis I, the Pious, seized Barcelona in 801, the first territory to be reconquered. Thereafter Barcelona maintained absolute independence; in the Asturias, however, bribes — accepted as tribute — were paid to Muslim kingdoms. Out of the Asturias grew León and Castile, and then Navarre and Aragon. Their progress was marked in 1063 by the papal

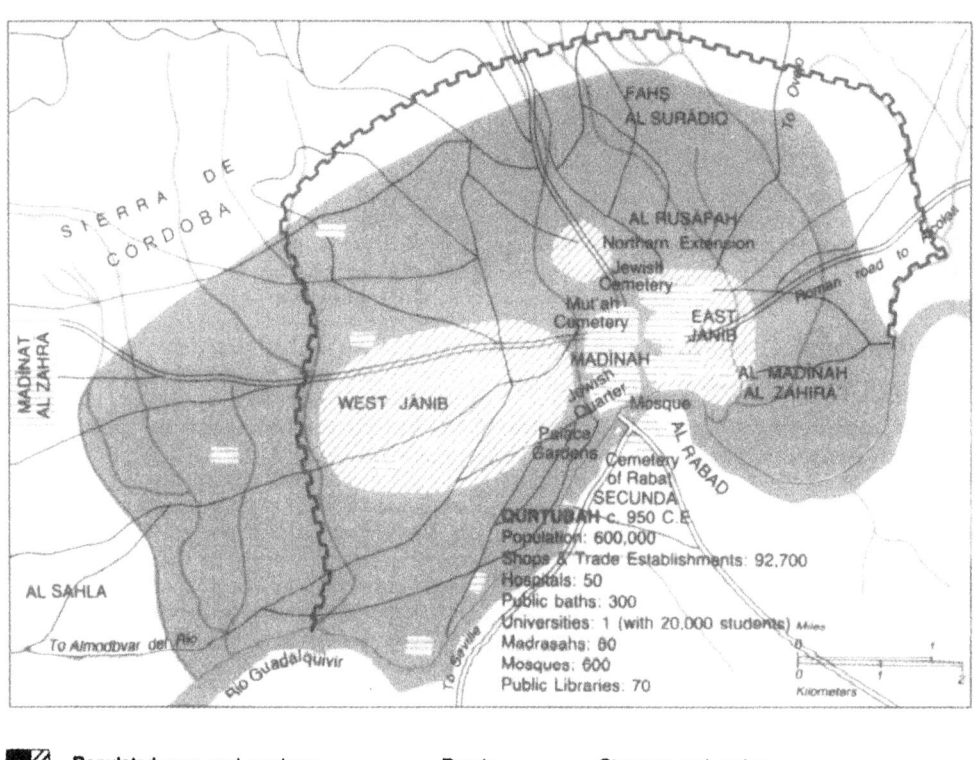

MAP OF CÓRDOBA (QURTUBAH) AS IT WAS IN THE 11TH CENTURY

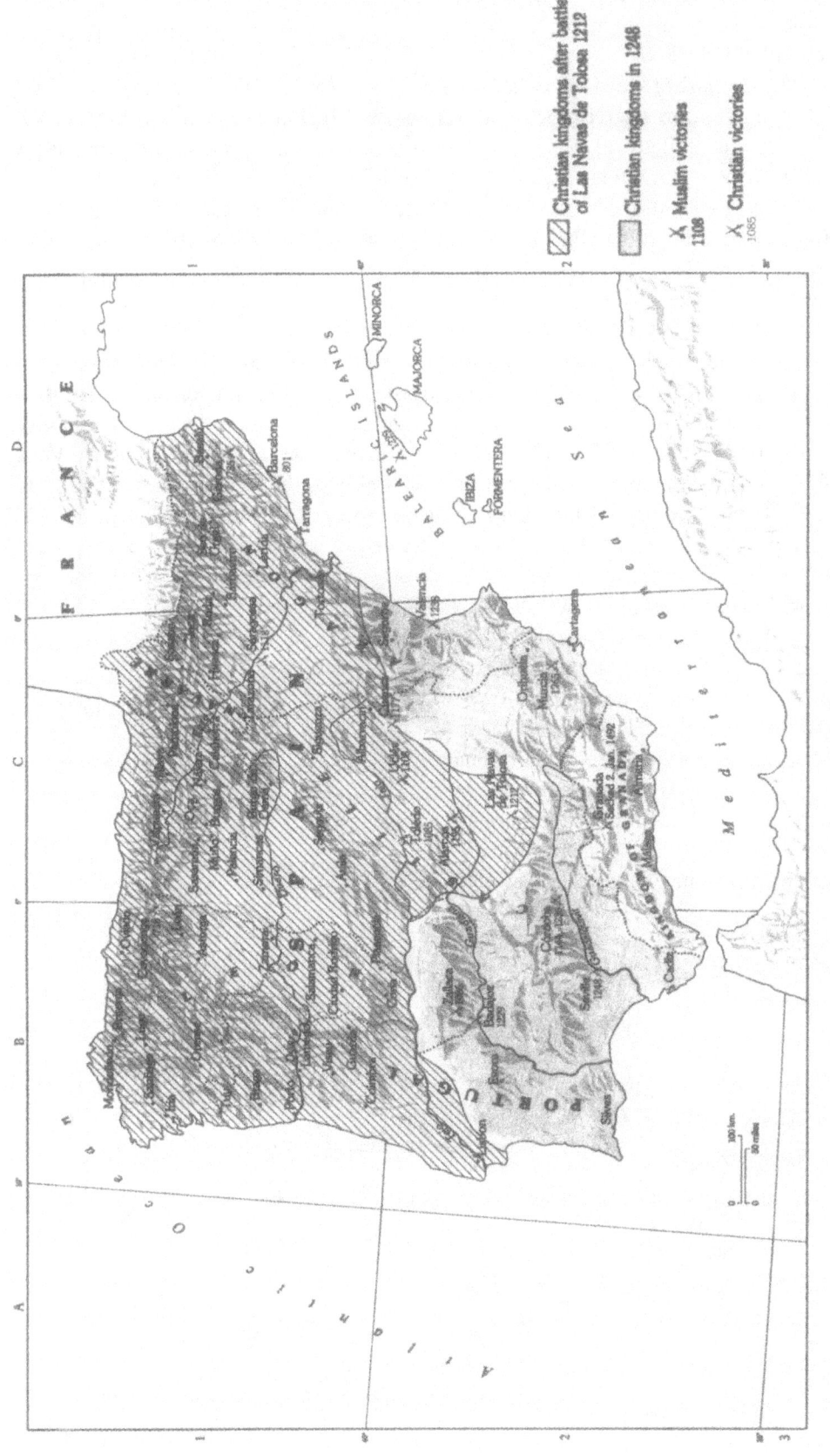

THE SPANISH RECONQUISTA, 13TH–15TH CENTURIES

commendation that the Reconquista was a crusade, the forerunner of those to recover the Holy Land.

When the caliphate of Córdoba collapsed in 1031 the situation altered: al-Andalus (as the Arabs called all Spain) was divided into petty kingdoms. Saragossa, Toledo, Badajoz, and Seville became tributary to Castile. With the death of Ferdinand I in 1065, Castile, León, and Galicia were divided among his three sons, an act that weakened the Christian cause. Nevertheless Alfonso I of León (r. 1065–1109) and Castile (r. 1072–1109), after several raids, succeeded in capturing the ancient Visigothic capital of Toledo in 1085. A further major advance was made in 1143, when Portugal liberated itself, and Lisbon was made its capital with the help of English Crusaders in 1147. By 1179, Castile and Aragon recognized each other's boundaries in the treaty of Cazorla, which divided Spain vertically until the union of the crowns in the fifteenth century. Toledo now became a great cultural center. The masters of Arab, Hebrew, and ancient Greek culture — not simply *belles-lettres*, but also theology, law, science, astronomy, and medicine — were translated into Latin. Students flocked from England, France, and Germany.

In 1212 the united Christian forces defeated the Almohads at Las Navas de Tolosa. Muslim city after Muslim city fell to the Christians. The Great Mosque of Córdoba became a cathedral.

There now remained only Granada. Around 1231 an Arab of Medinese descent, Muhammad I al-Ghalib (r. 1231–1273), carved out a small kingdom around Jaén. In 1235, he made Granada his capital. The Nasrid dynasty encouraged commerce, particularly the silk trade, making Granada the richest city in Europe. The last Nasrid rulers had not the ability of the founder, and the city fell to Castile on 2 January 1492.

It was the end of Arab domination in the West. The eminent historian Stanley Lane-Poole wrote:

> The Moors were banished; for a while Christian Spain shone, like the moon, with a borrowed light; then came the eclipse, and in that darkness Spain has grovelled ever since.

*Fifteenth century Spanish fortress, Castle of Mendozas, at Manzanares el Real*

# V. THE FURTHER SPREAD OF ISLAM
## (I) INDIA

## THE INDIAN SUB-CONTINENT — PHYSICAL

The Indian sub-Continent is presently divided between three republics, Bangladesh, India and Pakistan, together with the two small mountain kingdoms of Bhutan and Nepal. Physically the Himalayas, the highest mountain range in the world, with the Hindu Kush, and the Baluchistan hills, form its northern and western boundaries, with the Arakan hills on the east. The divisions are primarily ones of religion, not of physical geography. Pakistan is 95% Muslim and Bangladesh (formerly East Pakistan, and previously the province of East Bengal) is 80% Muslim; while India is 82% Hindu.

The former state of Kashmir, in the exteme north of India, is, however, majority Muslim, albeit it was ceded to India by its former Hindu ruler. It has been the subject of three major wars and continuing friction.

The Republic of India has three well-defined regions, the Himalayas, the Indo-Gangetic plain, and the southern peninsula. Hindus form 82% of the population, Muslims 11%, Christians 2.32%, Sikhs 1.99%, Buddhists 0.77% and Jains 0.41%. Muslims are thinly spread in this vast region, and are not of primary concern here. In historical times the

*Buddhist carvings in the Ajanta ravine, India*

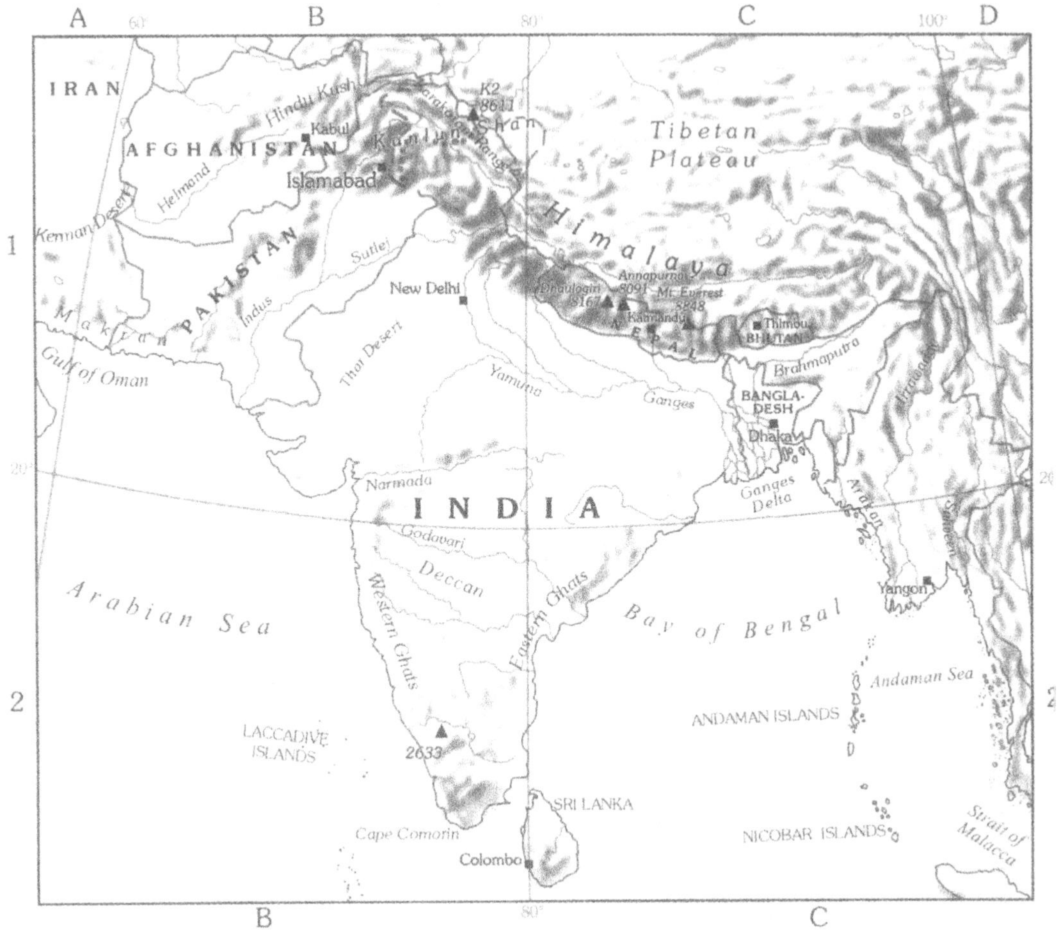

# THE INDIAN SUB-CONTINENT — PHYSICAL

*In a valley of Kashmir, India*

*Gwalior Fort in Mah Singh's Palace, India*

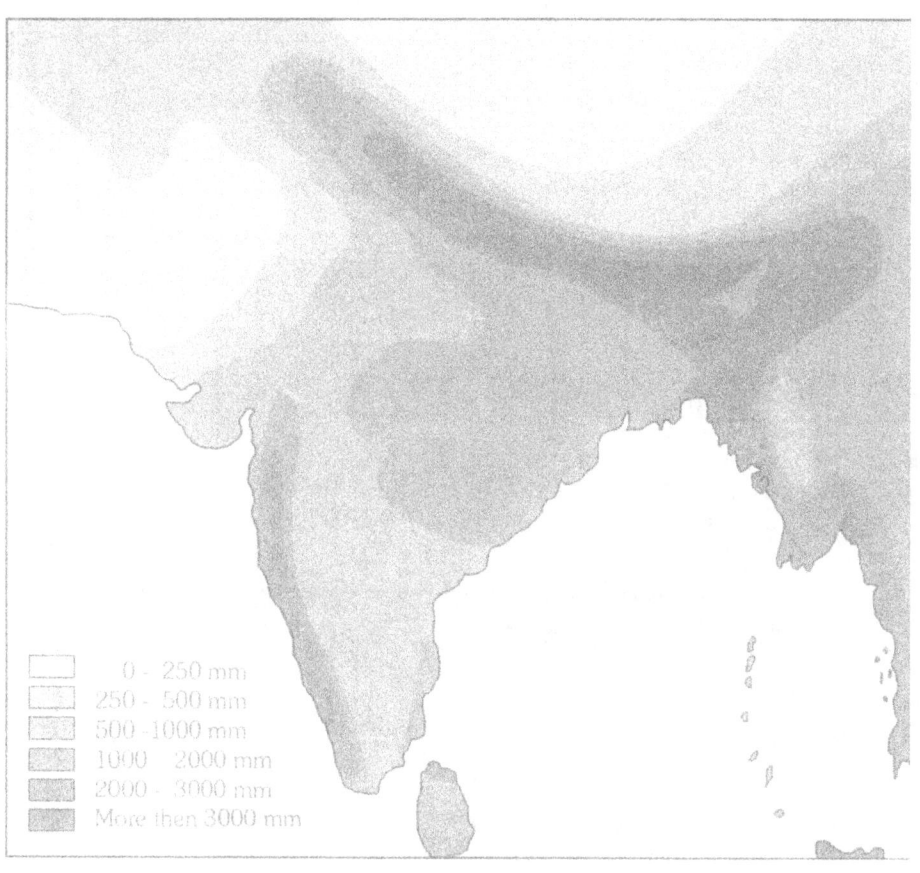

```
   0 - 250 mm
 250 - 500 mm
 500 - 1000 mm
1000 - 2000 mm
2000 - 3000 mm
More than 3000 mm
```

THE INDIAN SUB-CONTINENT — ANNUAL RAINFALL

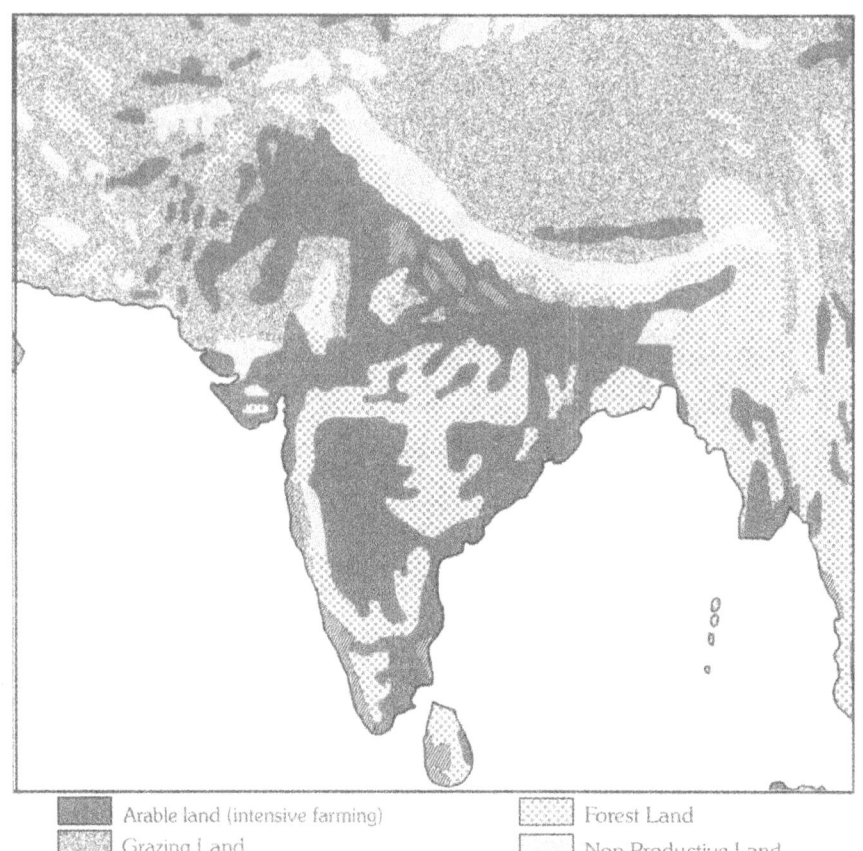

Arable land (intensive farming)　　Forest Land
Grazing Land　　Non-Productive Land
Cultivated Land; Fruit Trees & Vineyards

THE INDIAN SUB-CONTINENT — VEGETATION

*New Delhi, capital city of India*

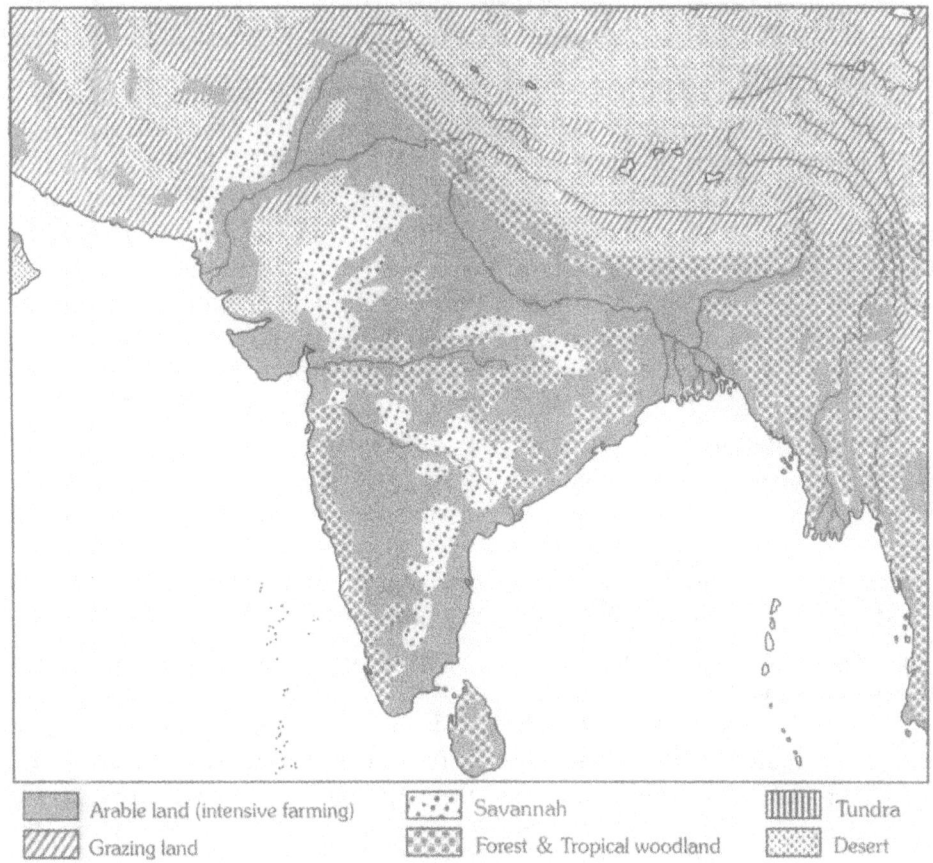

| Arable land (intensive farming) | Savannah | Tundra |
| Grazing land | Forest & Tropical woodland | Desert |

THE INDIAN SUB-CONTINENT — AGRICULTURE AND LIVESTOCK

continuing dessication of central Asia led to successive migrations of different peoples who made their way through the passes of the present Pakistan, among them Persians, Greeks and Afghans. A determined general was not deterred by the mountain ranges, when he was intent on reaching the plains beyond which were fertilised by the great rivers and the monsoons.

Bangladesh is theoretically independent in food production, but this is interrupted from time to time by the horrendous flooding of the Ganges rice-growing area. It also produces jute, cotton, tea, leather, pharmaceuticals, fertilizers, sugar, prawns and natural gas. It is nevertheless one of the poorest countries in the world.

Pakistan is above all the country of five great rivers, the Indus, Jhelum, Chenab, Ravi and Sutlej, with upper reaches in Kashmir, and sources in the Himalayas. Its work force is half absorbed by agriculture, in which cotton, rice, wheat and sugar are the chief crops. It is remarkable for its irrigation areas, the largest in the world, covering 42.5 million acres. It is able to supply most of its material needs, and to export cotton, cloth, carpets, rice, various petroleum products, leather and fish. There are two major seaports and five international airports. There are a number of languages in use, principally Punjabi, with Sindi in that province, and Pushto. The Government, higher education and business use English.

## THE SULTANATE OF DELHI, 13TH CENTURY TO 1525

At the end of the twelfth century Muhammad Ghuri swept across India and established the seeds of Islam from Afghanistan to Bengal. His adopted son, Qutb al-Din Aybak, a Mamluk, founded what is known as the "Slave Dynasty of Delhi" (1206–1290), of which the most eminent was his son-in-law Iltutmish. The inclusion of his domain within the eastern caliphate received formal recognition from Baghdad in 1232.

He was succeeded by his daughter, Rasiyyat al-Din (1236–1240), the first woman ruler recorded in Islam. The nobility deposed her, but the two feeble reigns that followed were no better. Another Mamluk, Ulugh Khan Balban, already vizier, took power and inaugurated a reign of terror (1246–1266). His successors are presented by Indian historians either as religious fanatics or as worthless debauchees. In 1290 the nobility again intervened and enthroned a Khalji Turk, Jalal al-Din Firuz Khalji. In 1292 he repelled a Mongol invasion successfully, only to be murdered by his nephew Ala al-Din (1296–1316). Although Ibn Battuta describes him as "one of the best of sultans," an Indian contemporary speaks of his "crafty cruelty," his vicious conduct, and his lust for blood. His hatred was aimed primarily at Hindus, whose neighboring states were attacked in incessant wars. An infant succeeded him, but was murdered by Qutb al-Din Mubarak (r. 1316–1321), of whom the Indian historian wrote that "he attended to nothing but drinking, listening to music, debauchery, and pleasure, scattering gifts and gratifying his lusts."

In the struggle for power that ensued the ultimate victor was Muhammad ibn Tughluq (r. 1325–1351), to whom Ibn

*Audience hall in the palace of the Moghul Emperor at Delhi*

# THE SULTANATE OF DELHI, 13TH CENTURY TO 1525

Sultanate of Delhi under Iltutmish

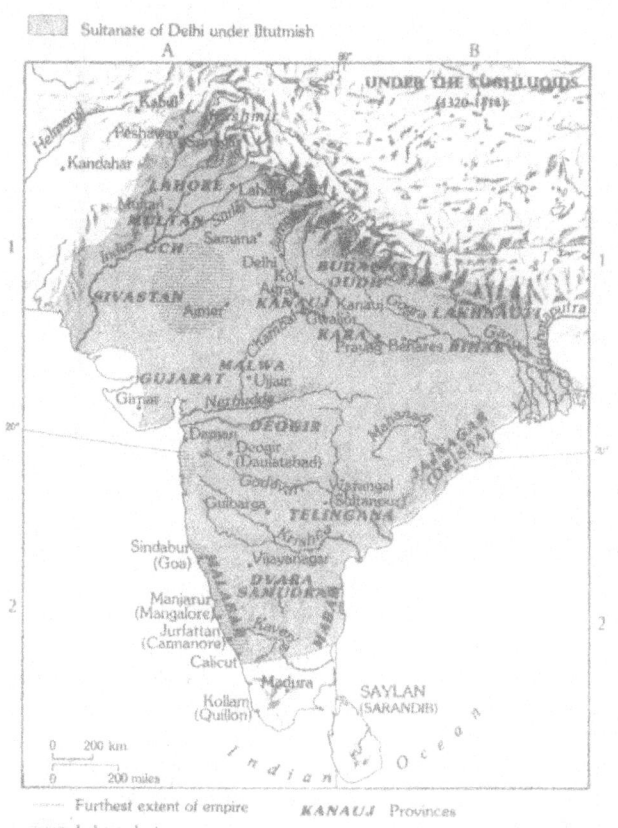

- - - Furthest extent of empire   *KANAUJ* Provinces
Independent area

# THE SULTANATE OF DELHI, 13TH CENTURY TO 1525

Battuta was chief *qadi* (judge) in Delhi for seven years. Both he, a Berber, and al-Biruni, an Indian historian, condemn the sultan's inhuman tyranny, while praising his accomplishments, the elegance of his letters in Arabic and Persian, and his knowledge of logic, philosophy, mathematics, the physical sciences, and medicine. He prayed with regularity, abstained from wine, and was gallant in war. Both believed that absolute power perverted his judgment, and they suspected some degree of insanity. In such circumstances it is not surprising that his conquests were ephemeral. The quickly won empire began to fall apart, and vast territories were lost. The empire was soon conquered by Timur-Leng in 1398.

Timur-Leng had no intention of remaining in India, and until 1450 chaos supervened with shifts of power among local rulers. Finally, in 1451 Buhlul Lodi, an Afghan of the Lodi tribe, was proclaimed sultan. This was the beginning of the Afghan dominance of northern India. He began the task of reunification, which was continued under his son Sikandar Lodi. Jaunpur and Bihar were regained, and his long reign (1489 until 1517) at last ended in a natural death. Hostile to Hinduism, Buhlul Lodi took pains to foster the economy and to keep prices low for those with small means. Like his predecessors he took great interest in architecture and the erection of public buildings, which were greatly damaged by an earthquake in 1505. His son Ibrahim Lodi succeeded him, maintaining his father's economic policies. He was defeated and killed at Panipat by Babur in 1526 — a defeat that signified the end of the Delhi sultanate.

Force had brought a new religion to India and with it a new outlook upon the world. Hindu armies had been shown to be inefficient. The Hindu caste system had been overthrown in vast areas. Not only a new architectural medium, combining Indian with Persian and Arab traditions, but a cosmopolitan culture and knowledge of the world from the Atlas Mountains to Afghanistan had been introduced. The Moroccan Ibn Battuta, chief *qadi* at Delhi, was the most apt example of an irrevocably changed world.

## TRAVELS OF IBN BATTUTA IN SIND, INDIA, THE MALDIVES AND CEYLON, 1340s

Ibn Battuta arrived in Delhi when Muhammad ibn Tughluq was sultan, part of the new Turkish Muslim dominance that was spreading southwards from Afghanistan into former Hindu territory. The sultan decided to send the Muslim *qadi* as his envoy to China in 1342. Ibn Battuta left Delhi traveling via Tilbat (Tilpat), Awu, Hilu, Bayana, and Kuwil (Aligarh), where he became involved in relieving the Hindu siege of al-Jalali. In this region he became separated from his companions, and wandered for several days until he found himself at Tajpur, where he recontacted his party at Kuwil. From Kuwil he went on to Burjpur, Kanauj, Mark (Muah?) Alapur, Gwalior, Parvan (Narwar in Gwalior state?), Amwari, Kajarra (Kujuraho?), Chandiri, Zihar (Dhar) in Malwa, Ujjain, Dawlat Abad, Nandurbar, Songarh, Cambay, Kava, and Gandhar, where he embarked on a ship. The ship called at Bairam (Perim) island, devastated by a Muslim attack, Ququa (Goga), Sandapur (Goa), first captured by the Muslims in 1312, and Hinawr (Honavar), ruled by Sultan Jamal al-Din Muhammad b. Hasan. From there Ibn Battuta traveled by the Malabar coast, ruled by twelve

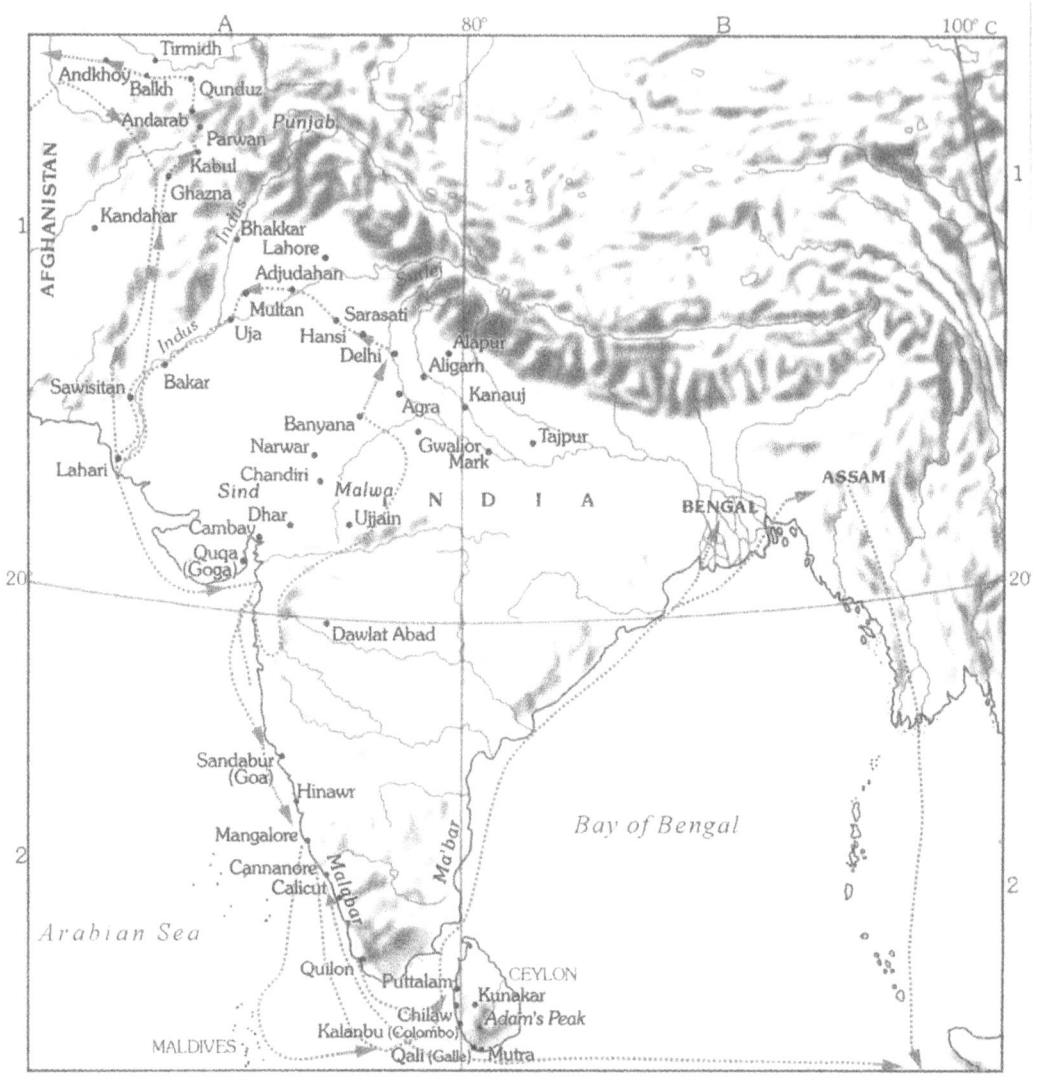

## TRAVELS OF IBN BATTUTA IN SIND, INDIA, MALDIVES AND CEYLON

infidel sultans. He visited Abu Sarur (Barcelore), Fakanur (Bacanor), and Mangalore, ruled by Rama Daw (Ram Deo). There was often trouble between the Muslims here and the local people, but the ruler, anxious to maintain the trade, made peace between them. Next Ibn Battuta sailed to Hili, one of the ports for China, Jurfattan (perhaps Cannanore), Dharmapatam, Pudupattana (now disappeared from the map), Panderani, in which there were many Muslims, and finally Calicut, center for pepper export in Malabar, ruled by its Hindu *zamorin*: in 1414, when Ma Huan came there, it had more than twenty mosques and 30,000 Muslims. Ibn Battuta, who met and recorded many distinguished Muslims throughout his journey, names the Bahraini *shahbandar*, Ibrahim, here.

At Calicut, the sea-going junk he was to

*Arab miniature in an astronomical work. Original in National Library, Paris*

embark on was wrecked, and Ibn Battuta headed by river to Kawlam (Quilon), and then back to Hinawr, where the Muslim ruler gave him lodging. The king launched a *jihad* against the Hindu city of Sandapur (Goa), where the ruler's son had promised to accept Islam if he was assisted in his revolt, and conquered it. Returning by his former route to Calicut again Ibn Battuta received news that his slaves and goods had gone on in another ship to Jawa (Sumatra), where they had been seized by a local ruler. He returned to Hinawr, Goa and finally Calicut again, whence he embarked for Dhibat al-Mahal, the Maldive Islands, Islamised by a Persian in 1153 (or by a Maghribi according to Ibn Battuta).

The Maldivian sultan appointed him as *qadi* there for a while. After considerable adventures, Ibn Battuta traveled on to Sri Lanka, landing at Puttalam and making a pilgrimage via Minneri-Mandel, Chilaw, Kunakar, (Kurunagala or Ratnapura?), to 'the Blessed Footprint', Adam's Peak, returning through a number of villages to Dinawar (Devundara), Qali (Galle), Kalanbu (Colombo), and back to Puttalam, whence he embarked for Ma'bar, the east coast of India. After shipwreck, he was presented to Ghiyath al-Din of Damaghan, of the Muslim dynasty of Madurai, journeying to Fattan and Mutra, and back to Quilon and Calicut again. There he embarked once again for the Maldives, and on to Bengal and Assam. Taking ship eastwards, he went, at last, on to Sumatra.

## THE MUGHUL EMPERORS OF INDIA, 1526–1858

With the break up of Muhammad ibn Tughluq's empire a string of independent Muslim principalities emerged in Bengal, Malwa, Gujarat, Kashmir, the Deccan, Ahmadnagar, Berar, Bijapur, Bidar, Khandesh, and Golconda; in the south

*The Taj Mahal, Agra, India, built by Mughul ruler Shah Jahan for his wife Mumtaz Mahal (17th century)*

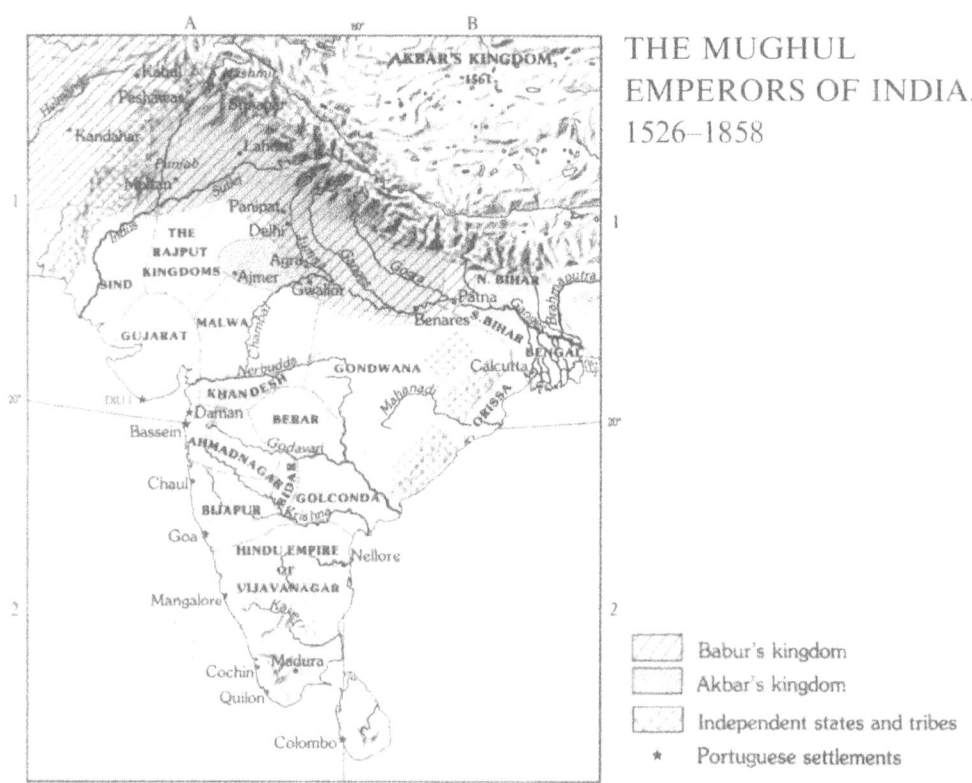

THE MUGHUL EMPERORS OF INDIA, 1526–1858

the Hindu kingdom of Vijayanagar (1336–1640), was established.

In the northwest, Babur (Zahir al-Din Muhammad), ruler of the petty princedom of Farghana, raided India in 1517 and 1519; in 1526 he defeated the sultan Ibrahim Lodi at Panipat and in a battle in which Babur's twelve thousand men overcame the sultan's 100,000 men. By 1530 he had conquered all northern India as far as Bengal.

A period of strife among Babur's sons and grandsons followed, which was ended only by his grandson Akbar, whose career of conquest began in 1564 with the ambition of conquering the whole subcontinent. This goal was only partly achieved when he died in 1605.

*Building Fatepur Sikri*

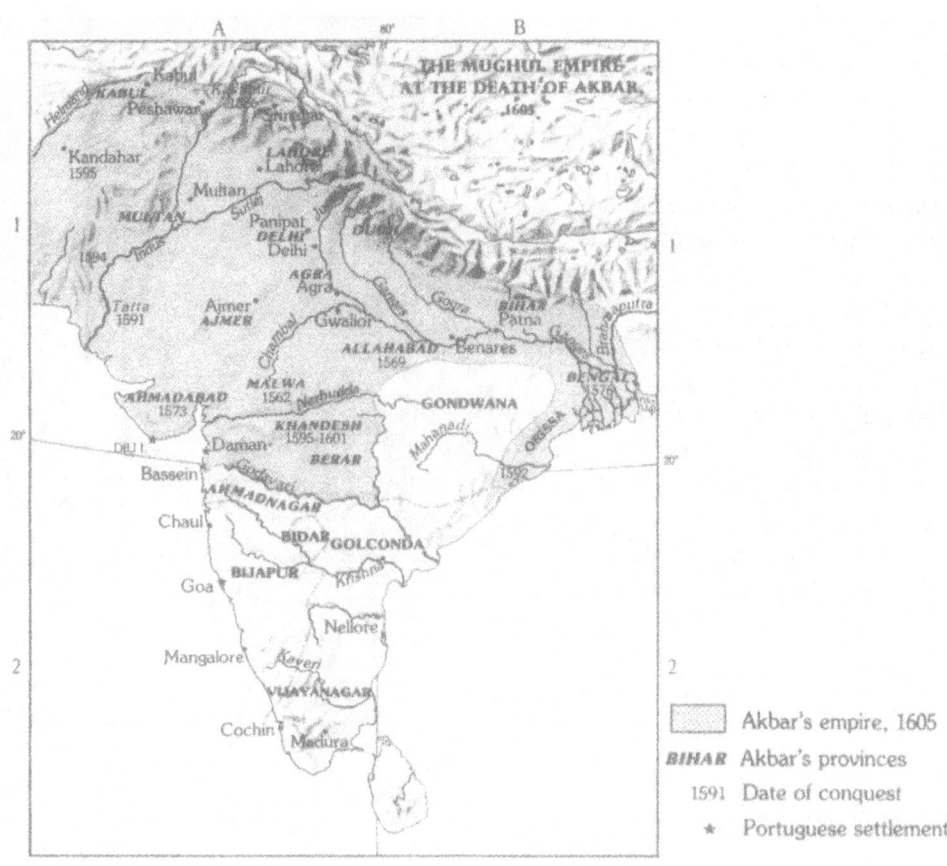

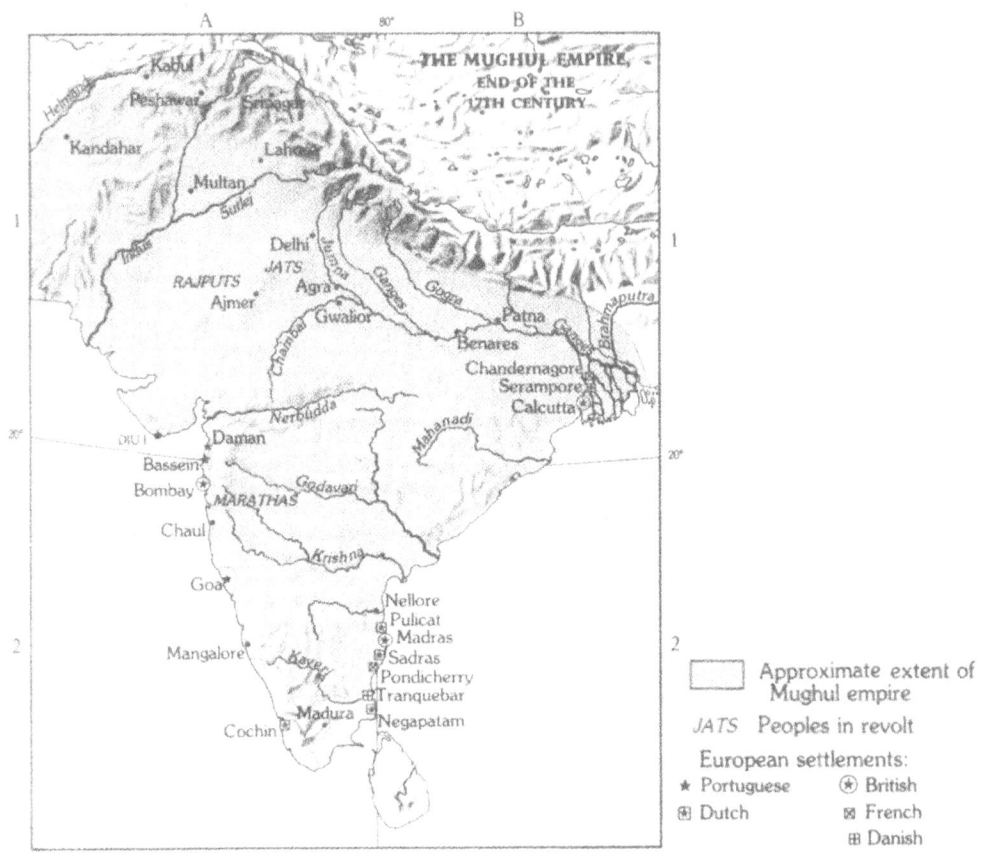

With all the intellectual range of a polymath, Akbar was illiterate. He loved disputation, but he had no systematic learning. He repudiated Islam and attempted to unite Hindus and Muslims in a syncretistic belief that also embraced Christianity. His rule was intensely personal, and it was only the impetus gained in his long reign (1556–1605) that enabled the empire to survive under the weak rule of his successor, Jahangir (r. 1605–1627). Akbar's most important achievement was a reform of the revenue system, which secured the needs of central government while giving security to the peasantry.

*Painting of the Emperor Shah Jahan*

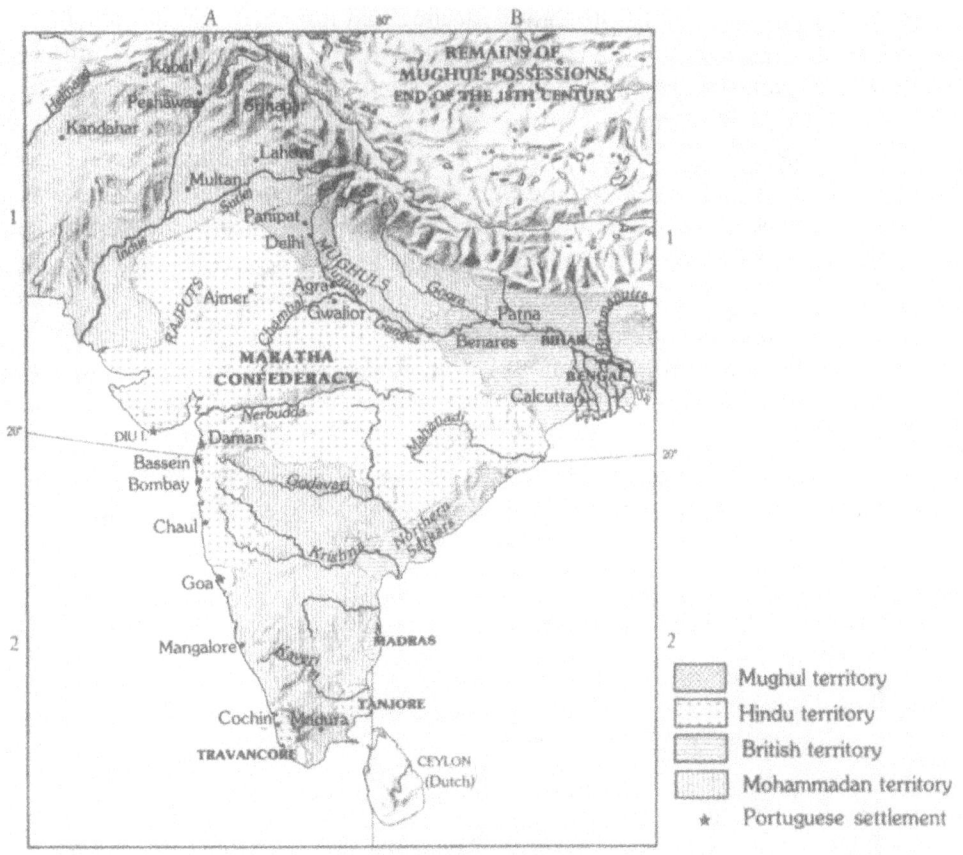

A war of succession followed in which Jahangir's elder son Shah Jahan was enthroned after killing all his male relatives. Between 1628 and 1658 he extended the empire southward, partly by treaties, partly by campaigns ably conducted by his son Aurangzeb (Almagir) as viceroy of the Deccan (r. 1636–1644). Then his attention turned westward, and between 1647 and 1653 Aurangzeb recovered most of the Afghan provinces. In 1656, Golconda was finally annexed. By then Shah Jahan had become incapacitated by age, and in 1658, after a struggle with his

*Mughul Emperor Jahangir, late 16th century*

brothers, Aurangzeb seized absolute power. Another reign of unusual length (1658–1707) began, in which Mughul power in India was at its apogee. However, the conquest of the Deccan, which had a predominantly Hindu population, proved the Achilles' heel of Aurangzeb, who, unlike his predecessors, was bigotedly exclusive in his devotion to Islam. The hated poll tax, which Akbar had abolished, was again revived, and Hindus were actively persecuted. Further, the administration was weak and neglected, and the practice of farming the revenues led inevitably to corruption. The seeds of decline had now been firmly planted.

In the war of succession that followed none of the three claimants was a leader of any consequence. Civil wars dragged on, and slowly the Marathas and others carved out principalities for themselves. By the 1770s the once proud empire had dwindled to the size of a small province around Delhi. New factors in Indian politics contributed to the instability. Commercial rivalry between French and British traders led to wars, often with Indian allied participation, and, under the guise of the East India Company, a British India was growing steadily.

*Pilgrim caravan escorting a high-born lady in a camel litter, from* Maqamat *of Al-Hariri, 1237*

The Mughul Empire was not, however, without a final heir. When, in 1947, the British finally withdrew, the once powerful Mughul state reemerged as Pakistan, a Muslim state that looked westward to Persia and the Middle East rather than to its Hindu neighbor.

## THE BRITISH IN INDIA AND PARTITION, 1947

The British East India Company established trading settlements in India in the seventeenth century, England receiving Bombay as part of the marriage settlement of Charles II's queen, Catherine of Braganza. Trading led to the establishment of a local army, and, following clashes with French settlements and local Indian rulers, the Company was placed under a Board of Control subject to the British Crown in 1784. Gradually control was established over the entire subcontinent and beyond, from Aden and the Gulf as far as Malaysia. Part of the Indian Army mutinied in 1857, following rumours that bullets were greased with pork fat. True or false, it was a demonstration of the bursting of an abscess of discontent with foreign rule and predominance. In 1858 the British Crown appointed Lord Canning as Viceroy, ruling with direct responsibility from Parliament. The final assertion of British power was the proclamation of Queen Victoria as Empress of India on 1 January 1877.

India is the home of origin of two widespread religions, Buddhism and Hinduism. Islam followed with armies in the seventh century, establishing power largely in the north and east. Buddhism grew in strengh in Burma and eastward, and again, to Tibet and other states to the north. It has dwindled in India, leaving Hinduism predominant in the peninsula.

The Indian Empire was brought to an end by the separation of the north-west

*The busy waterfront of Calcutta, the former British Indian capital*

# THE BRITISH IN INDIA

## THE BRITISH IN INDIA, 19TH CENTURY

- British acquisition from Mughuls
- British Indian territory in 1805
- British Indian territory in 1858
- British Indian territory after 1858

*132*

# THE BRITISH IN INDIA AND PARTITION, 1947

and Bengal as Pakistan from peninsular India. The partition was based on the views of the hereditary rulers, and, as it emerged, was largely determined by religion. Two months after partition the Hindu ruler of Kashmir elected to join India, albeit the population was principally Muslim. This has led to wars between India and Pakistan, in 1947-48, 1965, and 1971. A state of low-level hostility persists.

The Eastern province of Pakistan, formerly Bengal, with a population of 120 million, of whom 88% are Muslims, and 10.5% Hindus, seceded from Pakistan as Bangladesh in 1971. It remains one of the poorest countries in the world.

What today is Pakistan is the heir of the great Mughul Empire, with its magnificent buildings, mosques and palaces, artistic and scientific scholarship. It was from the tradition of this area that Arabic acquired the art of numbers, now spread throughout the world.

## PORTUGUESE POSSESSIONS IN INDIA AND THE FAR EAST
### TO THE 20TH CENTURY

In 1498, under Vasco da Gama, the Portuguese had been the first Europeans to penetrate into the Indian Ocean via the Cape, and with their military advantage were able to seize and occupy or destroy many of the great trade centers of India and the Far East. Their first settlement was established at Cochin in 1503. They defeated a Muslim fleet at Diu in 1509, and were able to establish themselves there firmly by 1535 (taking the isle of Sialbet, which they kept until 1739). They also attacked Calicut. From Goa, subject to the Muslim sultanate of Bijapur, taken in 1510, and thenceforward the center of Portugese India, they moved on to Malacca in 1511. From conquered Malacca, emissaries were sent to negotiate trade agreements that permitted them to establish 'factories' in cities under Siamese control, at Pattani, Nakhon Sithammarat, Ayutthaya and Mergui (Tenasserim). Colombo in Sri Lanka also became a Portuguese center, from which to control the cinnamon trade of the kings of Kandy.

Soon the Portuguese were in Ambon, and further north in the Moluccas as allies of the local ruler of Ternate, where they built a fort in 1522. The Spaniards, arriving with Magellan in 1521, supported the rival Tidore, but the

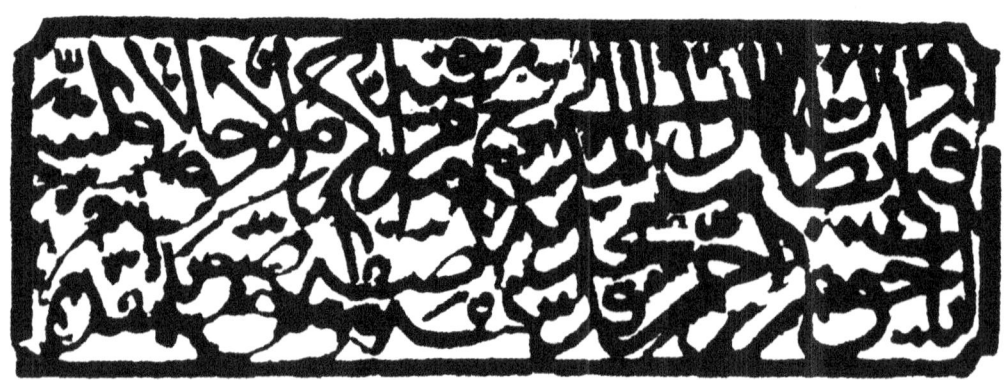

*Arabic calligraphy on wood, Thailand, 19th century*

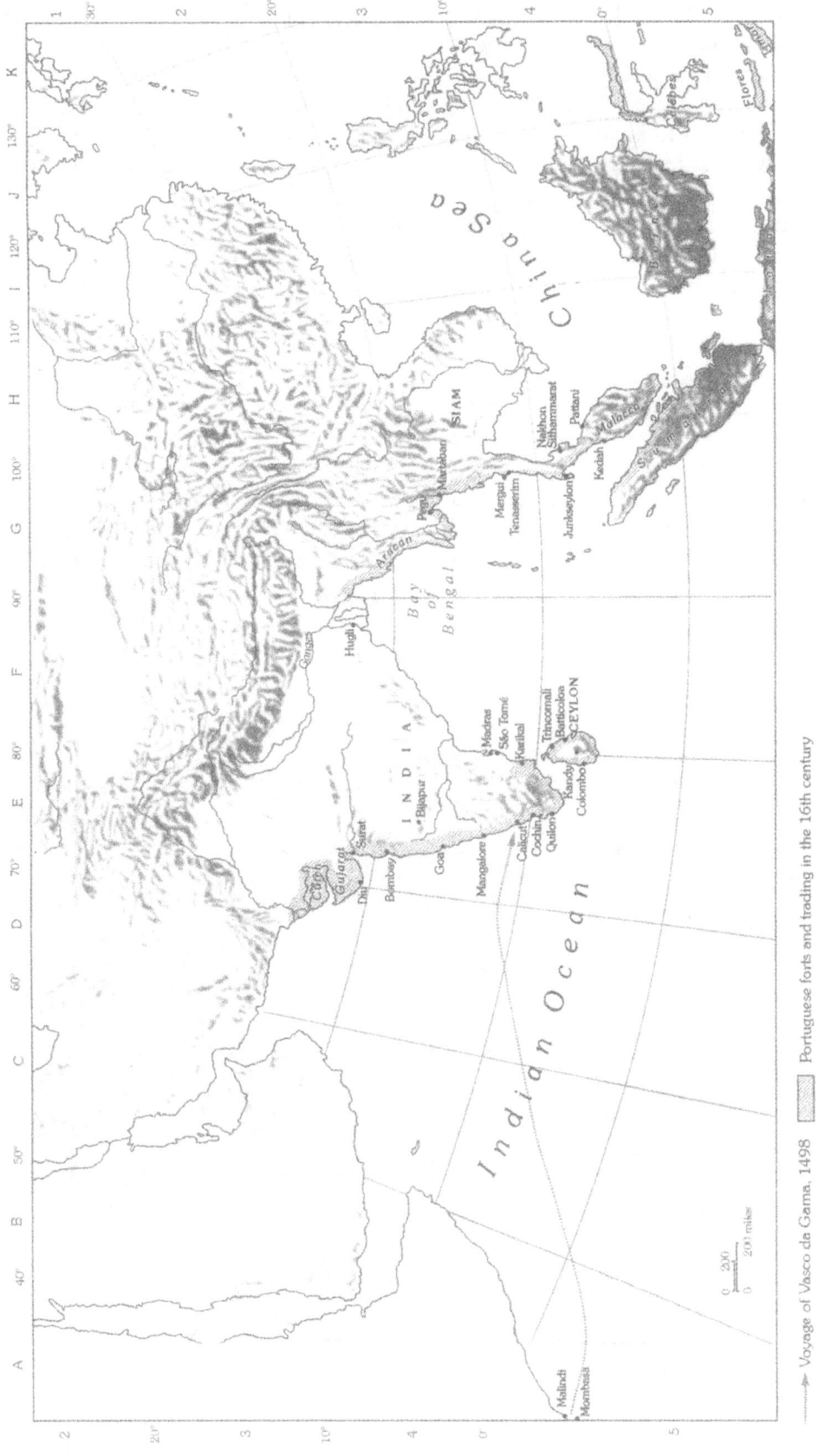

PORTUGUESE POSSESSIONS IN INDIA AND THE FAR EAST TO THE 20TH CENTURY

Portuguese eventually were able to build a fort there in 1578. On Java, the local ruler of Sunda Kalapa, later Jakarta/Batavia, tributary to the Hindu raja of Pajajaran, in 1522 granted the Portuguese permission to build a fort, but the port city was instead conquered by Muslim Bantam. Trade agreements were concluded around 1545 with Bantam, and later with Brunei.

Portugal strengthened its power in the Far East, in India and in Sri Lanka (Ceylon) with forts and monopoly treaties, but the Dutch were to ruin this seaborne imperial control over trade, leaving only some small outposts that remained in Portuguese hands until the 20th century. In 1622 the Dutch attacked the Portuguese settlement at Macao, established in 1557, but were driven off. The vital Portuguese strongpoint of Malacca was lost in 1641, Colombo in Sri Lanka was taken in 1656. By the 1660s, in the face of Dutch rivalry, Portugal was only able to retain Goa, Daman and Diu in India; Bombay came to Britain with Tangier in 1662 as part of Catherine of Braganza's dowry. Like Goa, Daman and Diu, East Timor and Macau in China were retained by Portugal until the twentieth century. The Indian territories were taken by India in 1961, Macau reverted to China on December 31, 1999. East Timor was occupied by Indonesia in 1974. After long resistance elections in August 1999 resulted in an overwhelming vote for independence. The territory, when still not formally independent, was administered by UNTAET (United Nations Transitional Administration on East Timor). Formal independence was achieved in May 2002.

*Lisbon, capital of Portugal, 15th century*

(II) CENTRAL ASIA AND THE MIDDLE EAST

## CENTRAL ASIA — PHYSICAL

Central Asia is a conventional term for the region lying mostly on the east of the Caspian Sea. Its northern border merges into the steppe of Western Siberia, a southern border with the mountain Afghan mountains, and on the east by Mongolia. It includes five republics, of which four are Turkic speaking, namely Kazakhstan, Kyrghyzstan, Turkmenistan and Uzbekistan; Tajikistan, on the southeast of the region close to the Persian border, is Persian speaking. The great majority of the people are Sunni Muslims. The exception, on the west side of the Caspian Sea, is Azerbaijan, where the people are Shi'a Muslims and Turkic speaking. They lie east of Georgia, Armenia and Turkey. In the southern part of the region are the three medieval cities of Samarqand, Bukhara and Khiva, splendid and prosperous in ancient times on the Silk Road, for long the camel-borne trade route between east and west.

*Fabulous birds and beasts, Hariri MS, 1237*

137

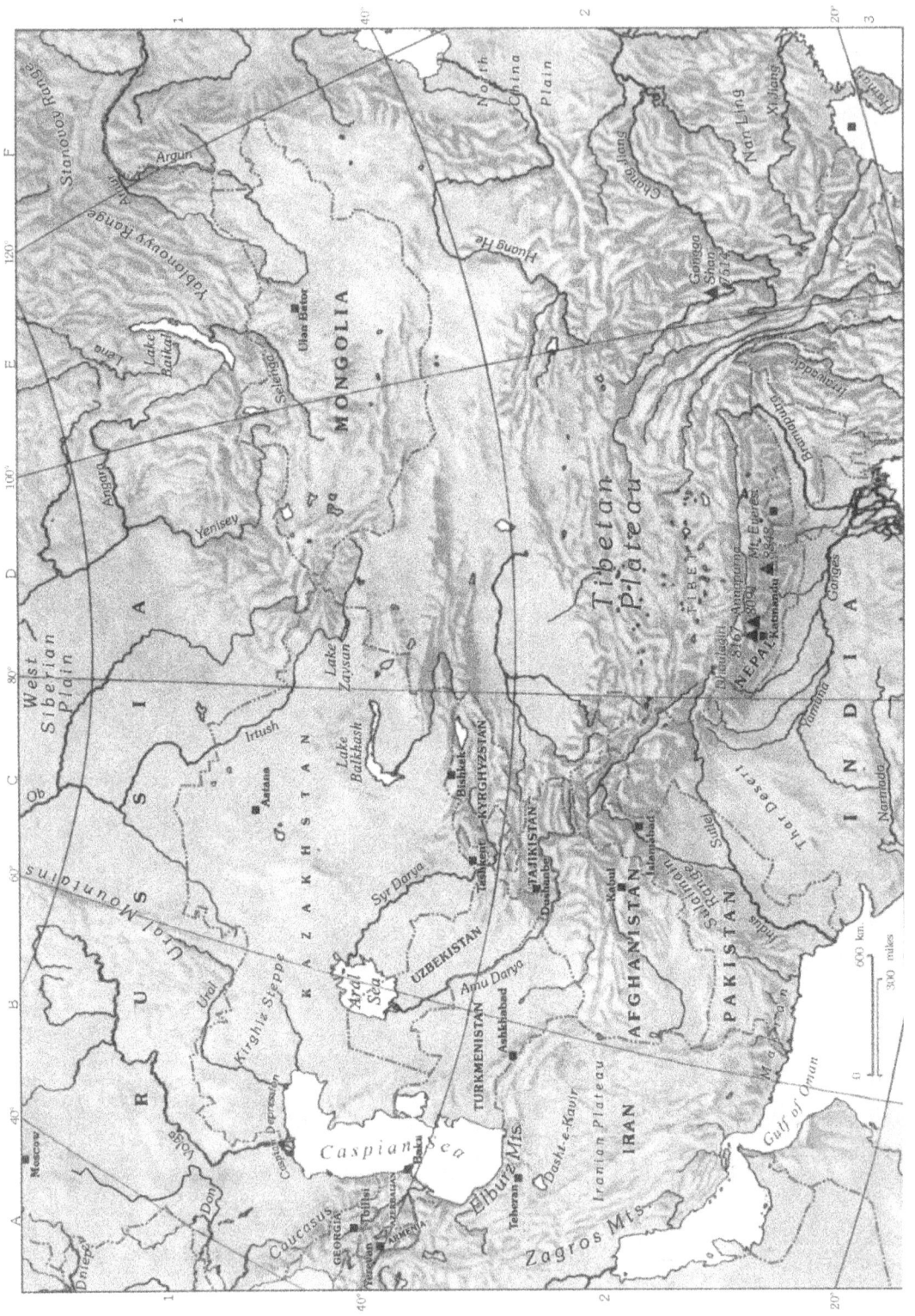

The greatest part of the region is arid and dry. Tajikistan alone enjoys a successful agriculture, growing cotton and rearing cattle, and rich in mercury, lead, zinc, oil, gold and uranium. Industry is specialised in textiles and clothing. But nature has shown extraordinary bounty in the whole region, for the countries bordering the Caspian Sea have the largest scarcely tapped pool of oil and natural gas in the world, with an estimated total of

*Zagros Mountains, Iran*

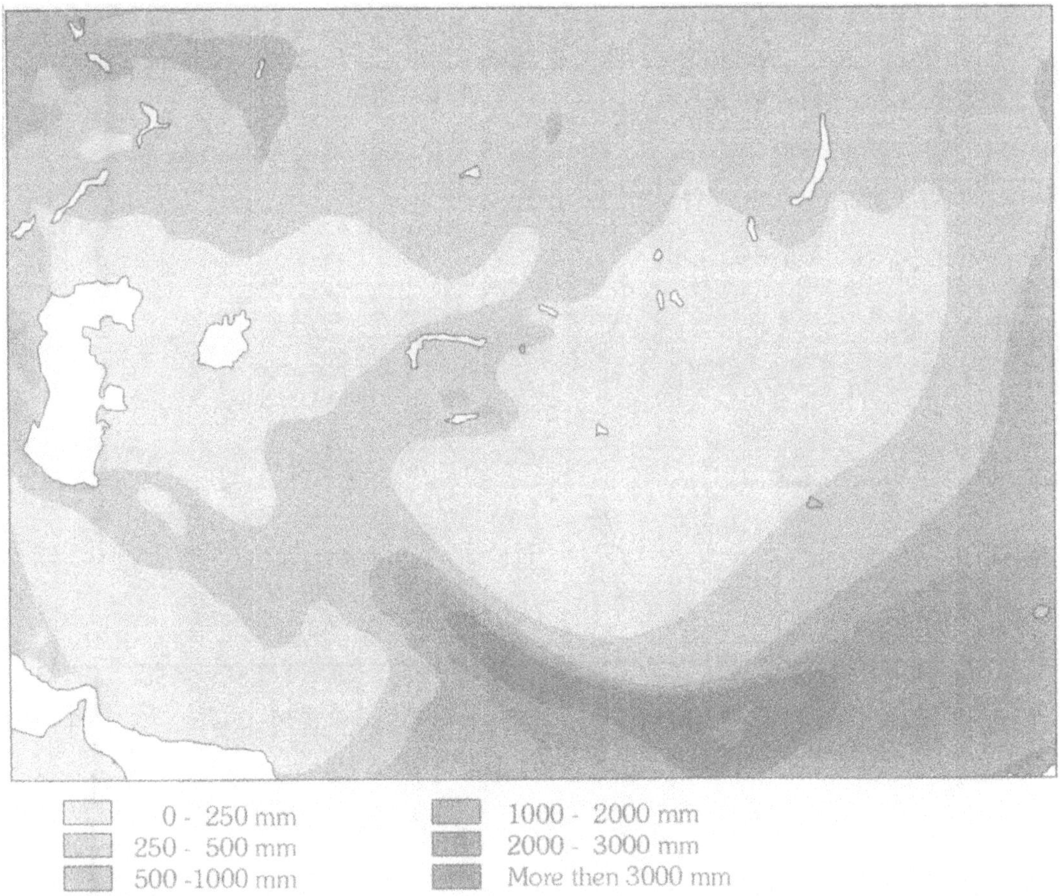

| | |
|---|---|
| 0 - 250 mm | 1000 - 2000 mm |
| 250 - 500 mm | 2000 - 3000 mm |
| 500 - 1000 mm | More then 3000 mm |

CENTRAL ASIA — ANNUAL RAINFALL

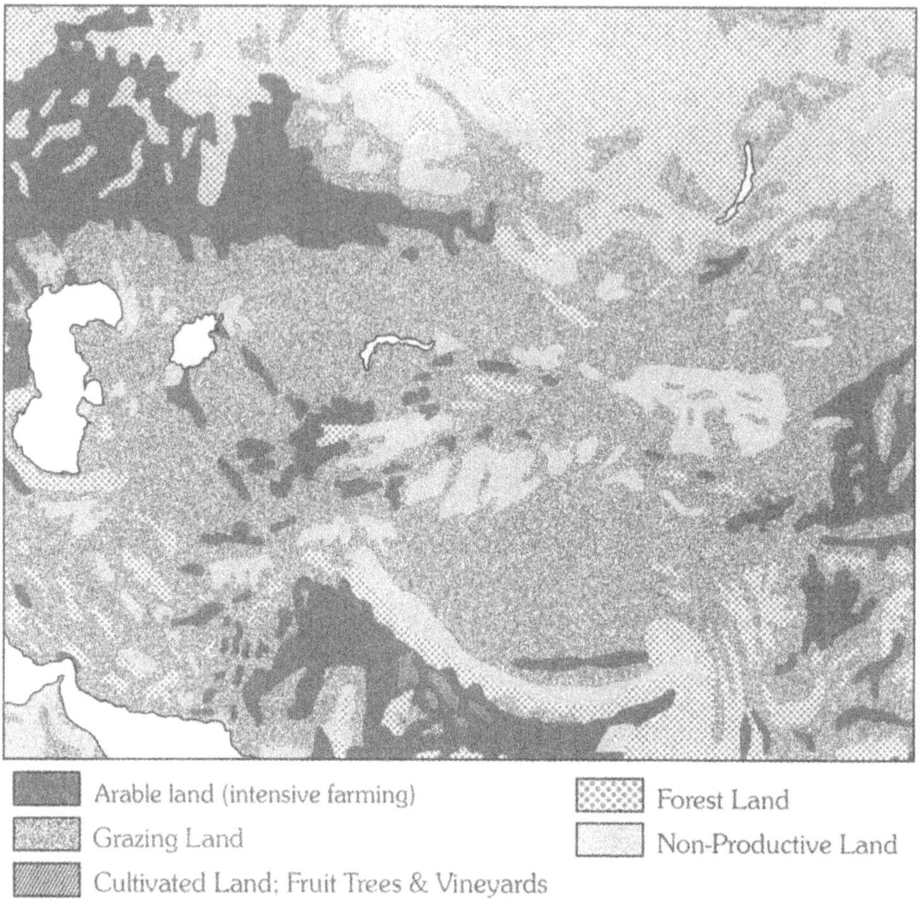

| | |
|---|---|
| ▓ Arable land (intensive farming) | ▨ Forest Land |
| ░ Grazing Land | ▢ Non-Productive Land |
| ▨ Cultivated Land; Fruit Trees & Vineyards | |

CENTRAL ASIA — VEGETATION

*Mount Godwin Austin (K2) in the Karakorum range, northeastern Kashmir*

200 billion barrels. Thus Kazakhstan and Azerbaijan have enormous oil resources; Turkmenistan is the fourth largest natural gas producer in the world and also possesses large oil deposits; Uzbekistan is a world leader in gas production, with oil being progressively discovered. Between the 1880s and 1916 Baku, the capital of Azerbaijan, enjoyed the world's largest oil boom outside the United States – earlier than the discoveries of oil in Persia, Iraq and the Persian Gulf. In Central Asia the earliest pipelines ran northwards through Russia, but now are being developed through Turkey and the Middle East.

*The Rose Garden of Sa'adi, 16th century manuscript*

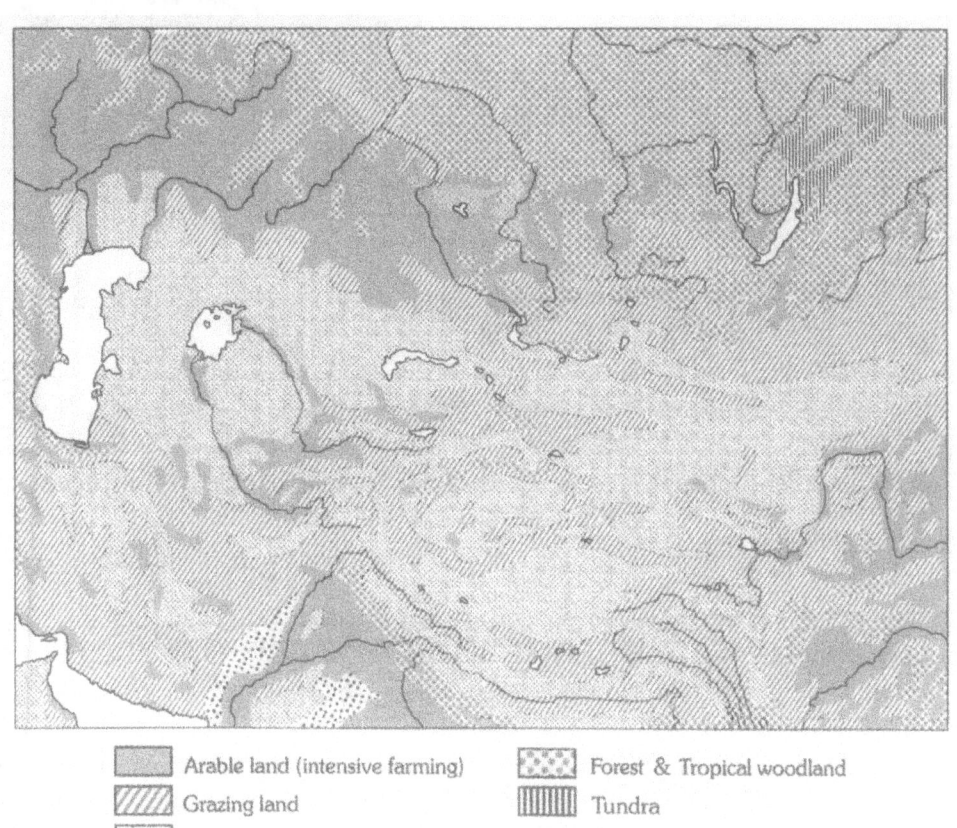

Arable land (intensive farming)
Grazing land
Savannah
Forest & Tropical woodland
Tundra

CENTRAL ASIA — AGRICULTURE AND LIVESTOCK

Apart from this superabundant wealth in oil, there are other sources of natural wealth. Azerbaijan has also iron, copper, lead and salt, a cotton-growing industry and in the breeding of silkworms. Kazakhstan, with its large foreign population, 36% Russians, 5% Ukrainians, 4% Germans, has only 44% Kazakhs. Stock-raising, grain growing, with cotton and wool, make an important contribution to the economy. Kyghyzstan has 52% ethnic Kyrghyz, with 21.5% Russians, and smaller numbers of Europeans and others. It is mainly agricultural. The plains of Turkmenistan are nine-tenths waterless desert, and oil alone makes the country economically viable. There is some cotton cultivation and a long established silk industry. There is some intensive agricultural production, made possible by irrigation. Textiles, silk and leather are also produced. There are valuable mineral deposits, of uranium, oil and gold; in one mine alone 81 tonnes of gold were produced in 1998.

With such economic potential, the emerging importance of the whole region cannot be exaggerated.

*Mount Demavend dominating Teheran, Iran*

## CAMPAIGNS OF HULAGU KHAN AND HIS GENERALS,
### 1253–1260

In the first quarter of the thirteenth century the Mongols, under Chingis Khan, conquered the world from Korea to the Caspian Sea and the Himalayas. The once proud Baghdad caliphate had disintegrated into numerous petty dynasties. The unwieldy empire had had no cohesive administration, and Arabs, non-Arabs, Muslims, non-Muslims, Turks of differing tribes, and Persians inevitably

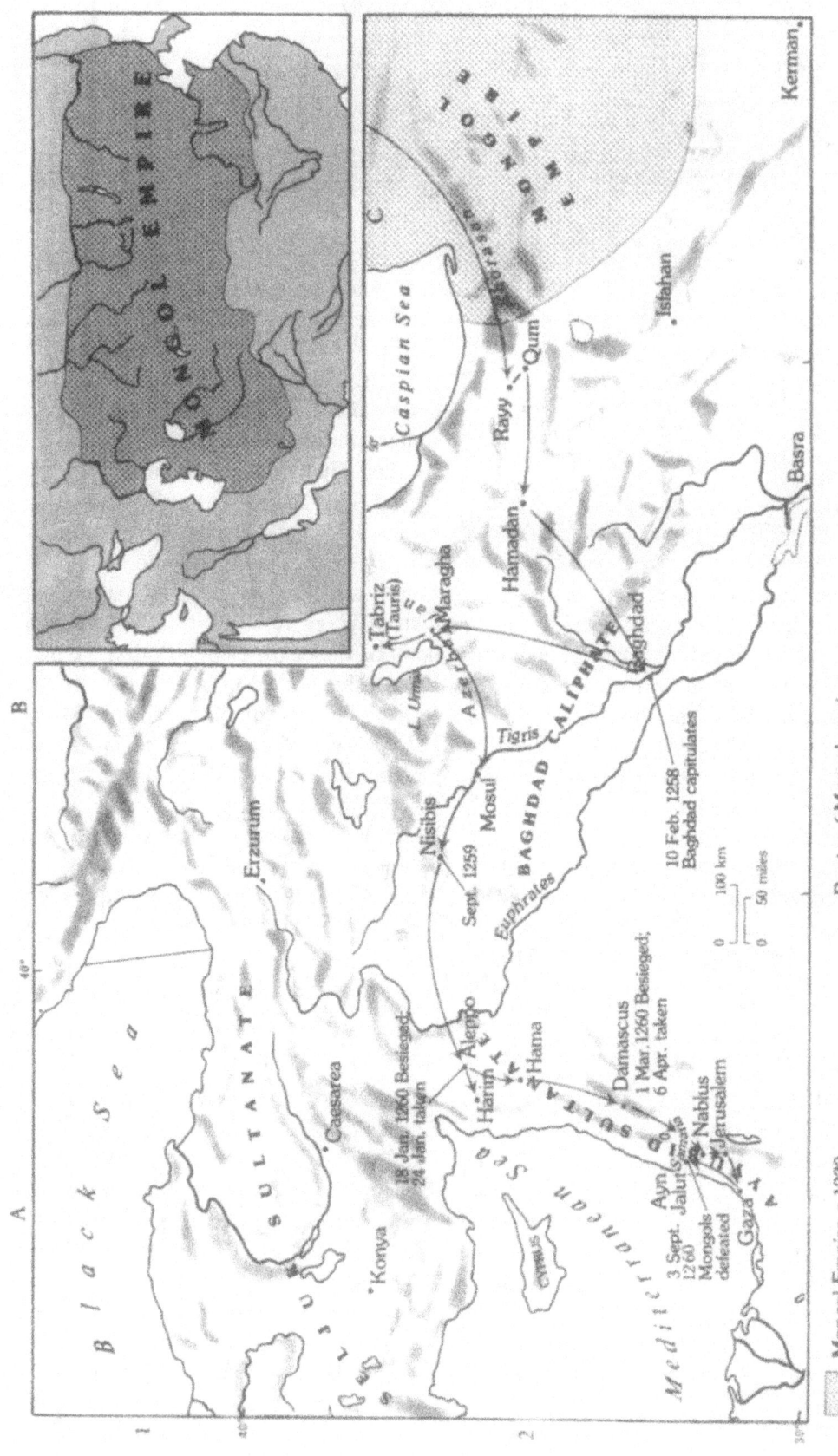

CAMPAIGNS OF HULAGU KHAN AND HIS GENERALS, 1253–1260

*Genghis Khan enthroned with his sons, miniature*

drifted apart. In Islam, too, warring sects added to the degeneration of a society already weakened by slavery, eunuchs, harems, boy and girl slaves, and suffering from epidemics and, in Mesopotamia, disastrous floods.

In 1253, Chingis Khan's grandson, Hulagu, and his army set out from Mongolia with the intention of destroying the Assassins and then the caliphate itself. The caliph ignored Hulagu's request to join him against the Assassins, who by 1256 were largely annihilated. Hulagu then passed through Khorasan to Baghdad, which he invested. On 10 February 1258, he entered the capital. The caliph was put to death with three hundred officials. The city was burned and plundered, and a majority of the population slaughtered without mercy.

In 1260 Hulagu marched into northern Syria, first against Aleppo, and then against Hama and Harim. Fifty thousand persons were killed in Aleppo alone. An army was sent to besiege Damascus, while Hulagu returned to Persia on the news of the death of his brother Mangu Khan. This proved to be a turning point. At Ayn Jalut, near Nazareth, the Mongols were defeated by the Mamluk general Baybars, who was soon to be the Mamluk sultan. Hulagu returned later, but, having failed to make an alliance with the Crusaders to conquer Syria, he again returned to Persia, which was now to become the base of an empire.

## COMMERCE IN THE MIDDLE AGES

Located in the center of the market area of the older part of Cairo is the Khan al-Khalili. It was founded in 1400 by Garkas al-Khalili, master of the horse to the sultan Barquq, and is a maze of lanes among a multitude of little streets. One can only enter it on foot and must beware of passing loaded donkeys. It is a microcosm of medieval markets from the Atlantic to China and from the Hanse towns to Zanzibar. Today one is still assailed by the rich scent of spices, the musk from central Asia, and civet from Ethiopia in the perfumers' booths and by the hammering of the coppersmiths, silversmiths, goldsmiths, and jewelers. Almost every conceivable commodity known to the medieval world can still be found.

Cairo was the trade center of the medieval world, the connecting link between Africa and Asia, of Europe with India and the Far East. Under the Bahri Mamluk sultan al-Nasir (r. 1293–1340,

# COMMERCE IN THE MIDDLE AGES

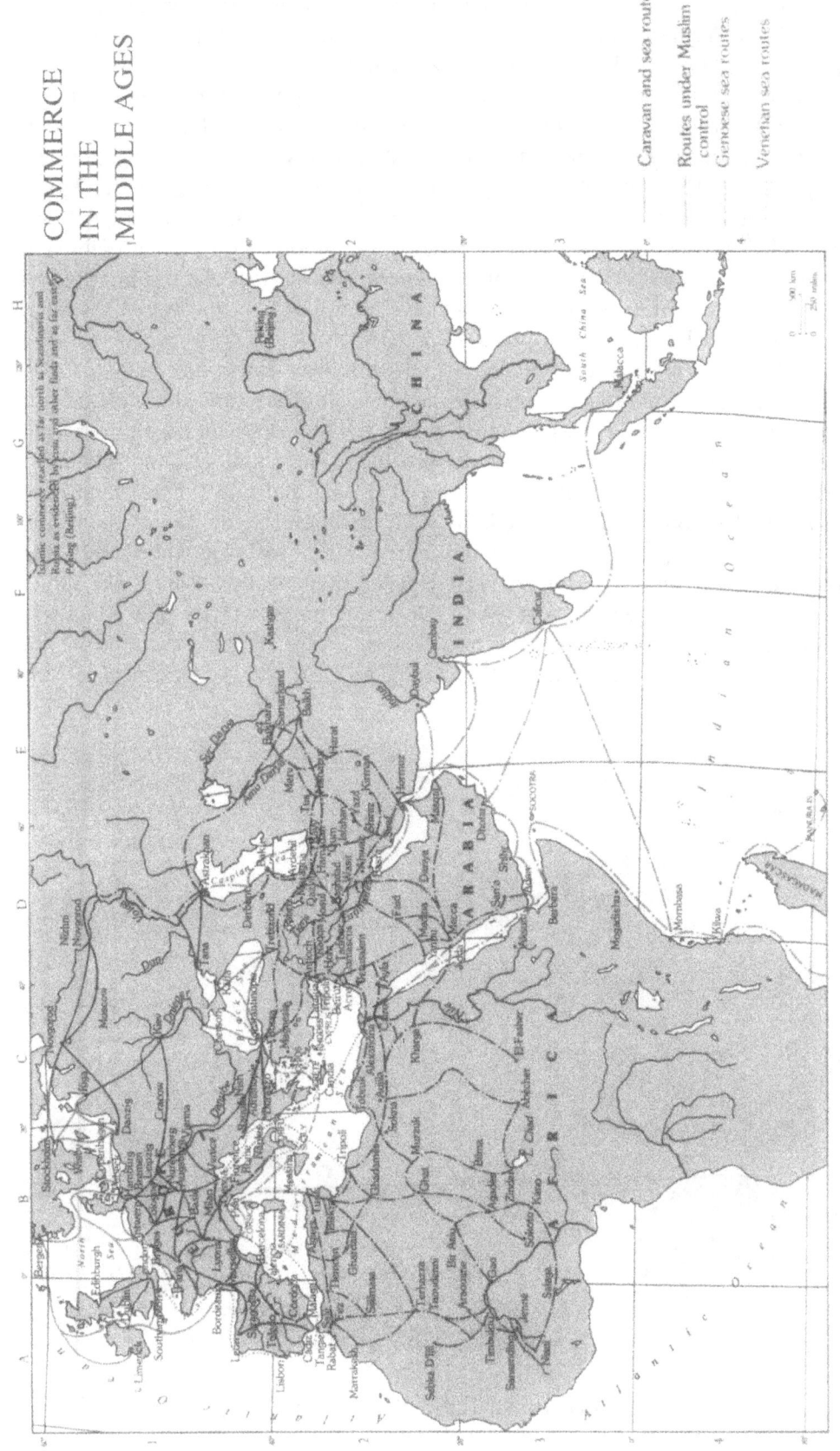

with some intermissions) embassies from Russia, Persia, Yemen, Ethiopia, western Africa, Constantinople, Bulgaria, India, Aragon, and France, and even the Holy See, were established. The goal of all these was commerce. After the disastrous earthquake of 1303, which destroyed most of Cairo, there was a period of unparalleled prosperity. Between 1303 and 1360 no less than forty-three mosques were built, a sure sign of a superfluity of wealth. The fourteenth century witnessed the development of a court culture, and Ibn Battuta remarks on how Mamluk court ceremonial was imitated in Yemen, India, and the petty courts of eastern and western Africa. There and in Malaysia and Indonesia the word sultan was used for the ruler. In the mid-fourteenth century the Chinese admiral Cheng Ho was sent on several voyages in the Indian Ocean, but these voyages appear to have been diplomatic rather than commercial. Trade with China was, however, long established, and even in the tenth century al-Mas'udi complained of the great quantity of ivory that was taken to China, creating a scarcity in Muslim lands. Trade throughout the Indian Ocean was primarily in the hands of Arab seamen, and it is not without significance that coins from Kilwa in eastern Africa with Arabic inscriptions have been found in northwest Australia, possibly from shipwrecks.

All this was only one part of the commerce of Cairo and the Middle East. From the shores of the Levant and from the Black Sea radiated land routes to central Asia and onward to China. The Polo brothers made more than one journey and were acquainted with the whole commercial system of the Great Khan and his tributaries. The Khan was likewise aware of the Levantine world, and on their second journey, at his

*Miniature of an oared vessel, from the* Maqamat, *al-Hariri MS, 1237*

request, the Polo brothers brought him oil from the Holy Sepulchre in Jerusalem. In the aftermath of the first Crusade, consuls were established by Genoa, Pisa, Florence, and Venice in the Levant, Constantinople, Palestine, Syria, and Egypt. In 1251 French consuls were established at Alexandria and Tripoli; after 1268 Barcelona established consuls *in partibus ultramarinis* (in parts beyond the sea). These early consulates were the forerunners of the European consulates in the Ottoman Empire and throughout the Mediterranean. Though other Italian cities, such as Lucca, also participated in the oriental trade, Genoa and Venice were predominant. The object of these consulates was wholly commercial — the promotion of trade contacts and transactions from within their own boundaries, and with the whole commercial system of Europe.

## THE TRAVELS OF IBN BATTUTA, 1324–1348

After al-Idrisi, no Arab geographer of importance emerged. In Granada geographical treatises were replaced by travel literature, among which was Ibn Jubayr's narrative describing his explorations of the East between 1183 and 1217. Ibn Jubayr traveled no further than Egypt, Iraq, and Mecca. Al-Mazini of Granada, however, reached Russia and described the trade of the Bulgars in the Volga region in fossil mammoth ivory, which was exported as far as Khwarizm. Chief among these travel writers was Ibn Battuta, who was born in Tangier in 1304, and died in Marrakesh in 1377. His uncle was *qadi* (religious judge) of Ronda,

*Minaret of the Koutoubya Mosque in Marrakesh, 12th century Almohad dynasty*

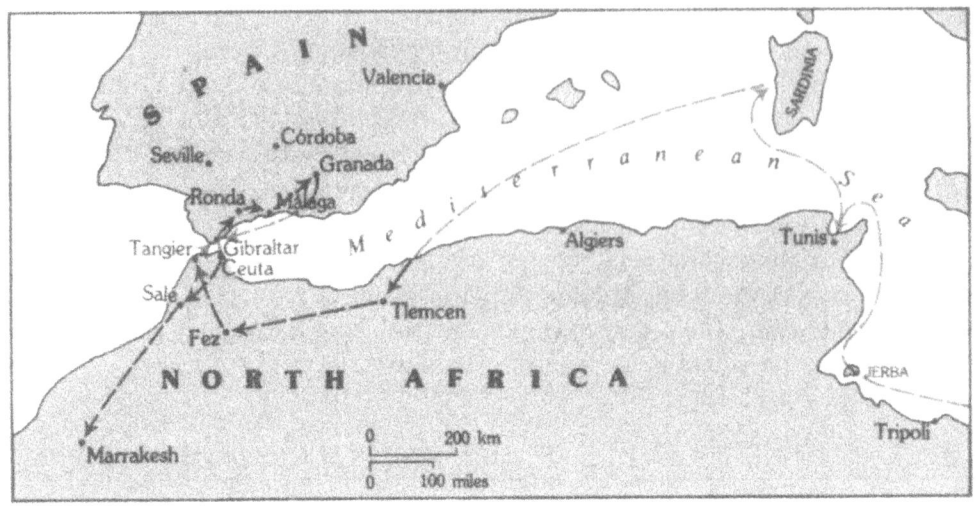

TRAVELS OF IBN BATTUTA IN NORTH AFRICA

near Málaga. Living at a time when it was customary for well-to-do young men to travel as part of their education and to attend lectures in foreign centers of Islamic learning, Ibn Battuta's journeys extended throughout the Islamic world and beyond, into the Black Sea, and, via India, Ceylon, and the Maldives, to Bengal, Assam, Sumatra, and even China. His *Rihla* (travels) thus went far beyond the traditional scope, which was generally confined to journeys to Mecca. As literature his Rihla became popular in Spain and Morocco.

Ibn Battuta's Rihla was transcribed at the command of the Marinid ruler of Fez, Abu Inan. The text was edited by the scholar Ibn Juzayy. Problems regarding the originality of certain passages as well as numerous editorial glosses and

*Madrasa and mausoleum of Sultan Hasan, Cairo: sketch, showing* mihrab, minbar *and* dikka *(raised platform for cantors),* (1356–1362)

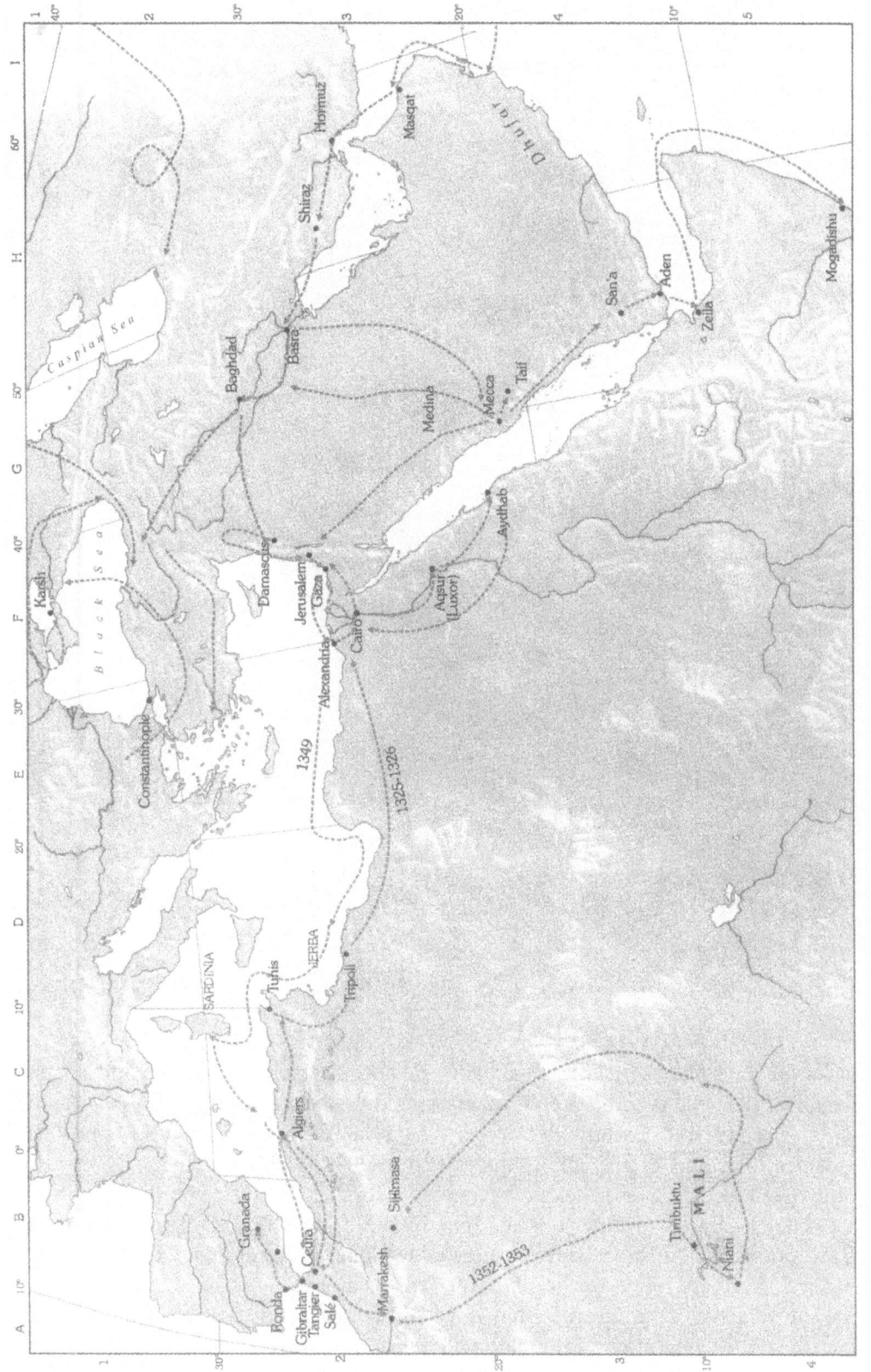

TRAVELS OF IBN BATTUTA 1324–1348

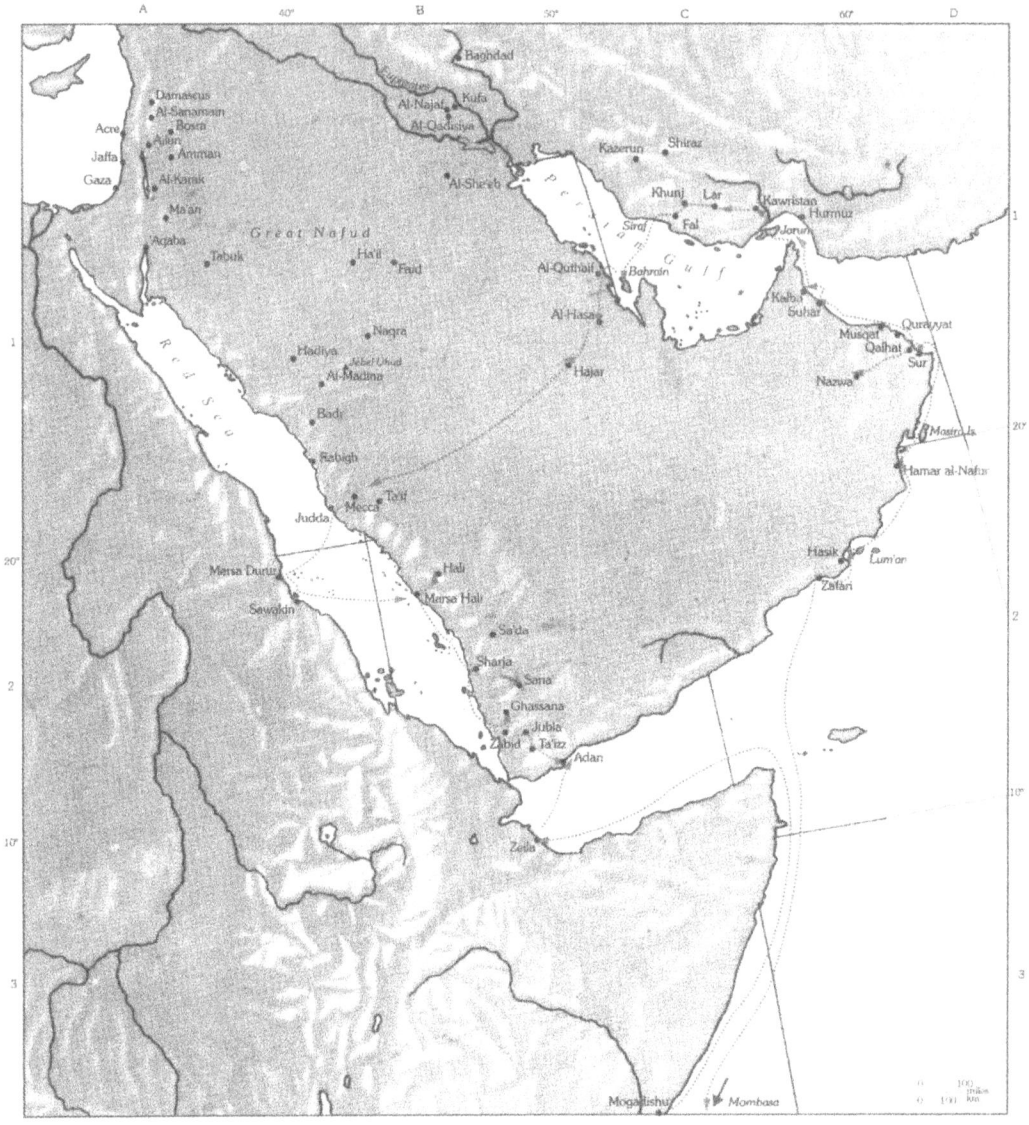

TRAVELS OF IBN BATTUTA IN HEJAZ AND IRAQ

garnishes have plagued scholars. In many instances the style is elaborate, in others it is succinct and irritatingly dry. It includes long and often tedious quotations from poetry. Nevertheless, having set out initially to educate himself, Ibn Battuta seems to have developed a passion for descriptive geography, for the movement of commerce, and for people — their migrations, their national habits, and, above all, their practice of religion. How his journeys were financed is not disclosed. In India and in the Maldives he served as *qadi*, a position he held in Marrakesh when he died. His journey to China was a diplomatic mission, and this would have been financed by Delhi. Despite his interest in commerce, he does not appear to have engaged in it.

Difficulties arise over the details of his journeys and their chronology, but it is possible to arrange them in a less than arbitrary fashion. In 1325 to 1326 he

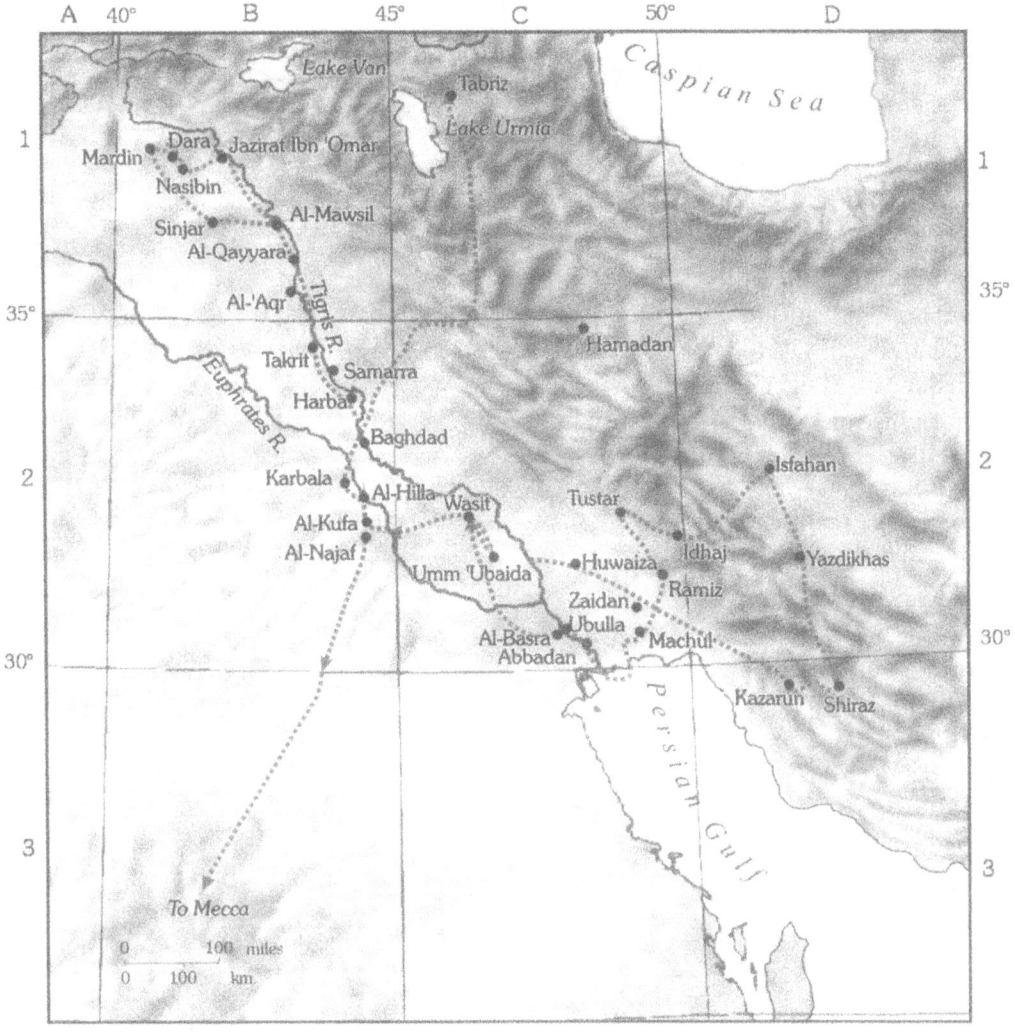

TRAVELS OF IBN BATTUTA IN SOUTHERN PERSIA AND THE GULF

traveled from Tangier along North Africa to Egypt, Upper Egypt, and Syria, leaving Damascus for Mecca in September 1326. In 1326 to 1327 he visited Iraq, Khuzistan, Fars, Jibal, Tabriz, Baghdad, Samarra, and Mosul, before returning to Arabia. He remained in Arabia until 1330, making the Pilgrimage three times. In 1330 he set off for Yemen and traveled by sea to Zeila, Mogadishu, Mombasa, and Kilwa, returning via Oman and the Persian Gulf to make the Pilgrimage once again in 1332. He then traveled in Egypt, Syria, Asia Minor, Constantinople, Transoxiana, and Afghanistan, reaching Delhi in 1333 and remaining there as chief *qadi* until 1342. There followed a year and a half in the Maldives, and then a voyage to Bengal, Assam, and Sumatra, and eventually China. It is disputed whether he actually reached Peking (Beijing). This journey and the return took until 1347, when, after passing up the Persian Gulf and visiting Iraq, Syria, and Egypt, he once again made the Pilgrimage.

Ibn Battuta was twenty-one years old when he set out; he was now forty-five.

He returned home to Fez, via Tunis, Sardinia, and Algeria in 1349, making a visit to Granada and Ronda shortly after, where his uncle was *qadi*. In 1352 to 1353 he made what physically must have been the most difficult journey of all, to the kingdom of Mali, important to the ruler of Fez as a source of gold. His stories, especially of the Turkish lands, India, and China, must have seemed as incredible to his hearers as was James Bruce of Kinnaird's account of Ethiopia to his readers in London in the eighteenth century. Nevertheless, modern scholarship confirms both Bruce and Ibn Battuta.

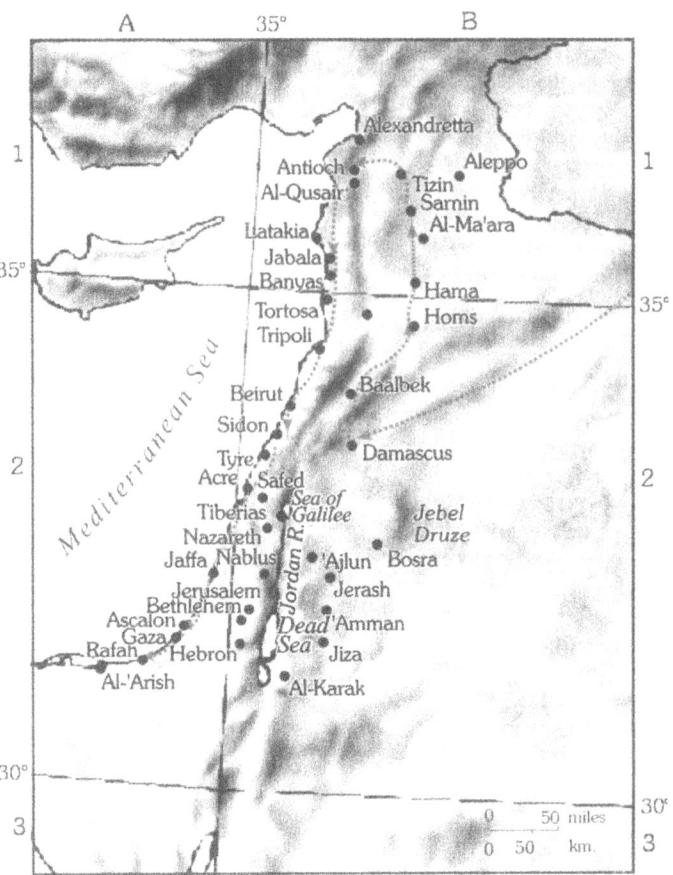

TRAVELS OF IBN BATTUTA IN EGYPT AND SYRIA

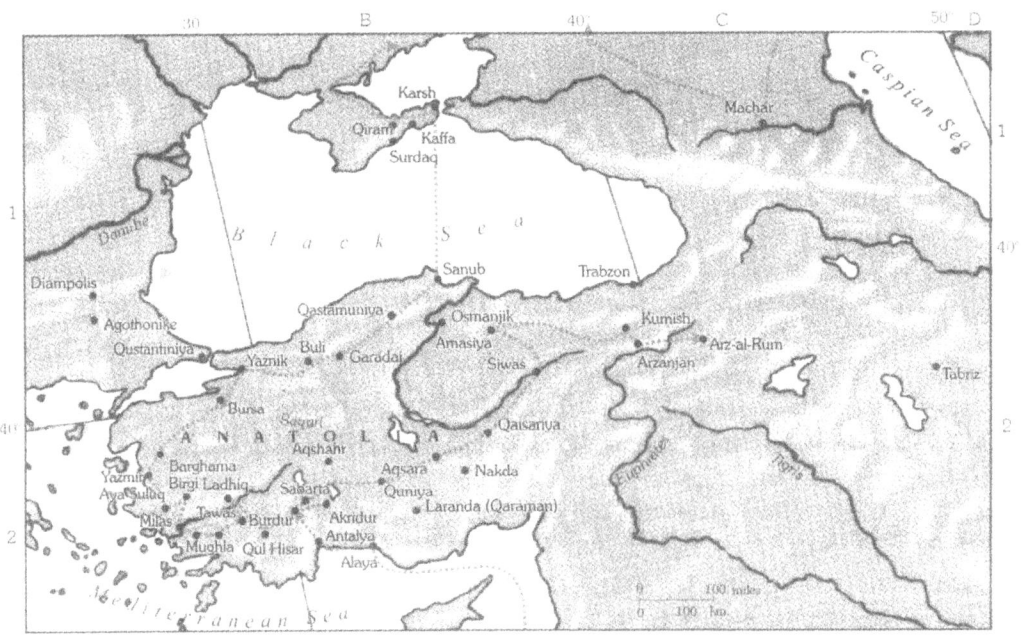

TRAVELS OF IBN BATTUTA IN ANATOLIA, THE BLACK SEA AND CONSTANTINOPLE

# THE SPREAD OF THE BLACK DEATH, 1331–1368

In the mid-fourteenth century a devastating pandemic of plague swept the Middle East and Europe. The historian Ibn Khaldun, who lost his father, mother, and many of his teachers, wrote:

> "Civilization both in the East and the West was visited by a destructive plague which devastated nations and caused populations to vanish. It swallowed up many of the good things of civilization and wiped them out. It overtook dynasties at the time of their senility, when they had reached the limit of their duration. It lessened their power and curtailed their influence. It weakened their authority. Their situation approached the point of annihilation and dissolution. Civilization decreased with the decrease of mankind. Cities and buildings were laid waste, roads and way signs were obliterated, settlements and mansions became empty, dynasties and tribes became weak. The entire inhabited world changed. The East, it seems, was similarly visited, though in accordance with and in proportion to [its more affluent] civilization."

Long before the fourteenth century Middle Eastern people suffered from plague. Arab authors document it fairly well; however, they often do not distinguish the characteristic buboes, or swellings, in the thighs and armpits, so it is not certain whether a given epidemic was typhus, smallpox, cholera, or another contagious disease. From the sixth century on there are records of cases that can be attributed to rat-borne plague in Syria, Ethiopia (possibly Nubia), the Sudan, Egypt, and Asia Minor as far west as Constantinople. In 639 it caused anxiety for the caliph Umar I, who suspended Arab operations in Syria. At the beginning of the Abbasid period, around 750, the plague was rife in Syria and Iraq, recurring in Kufa and Basra as often as every tenth year. It was not less endemic in Europe.

The Black Death of the mid-fourteenth

*Mongols besieging Muslims, c. 1310, as seen by Rashid al-Din (1247–1318). Note that both sides are using Mongol composite bows, the most lethal weapon of the time.*

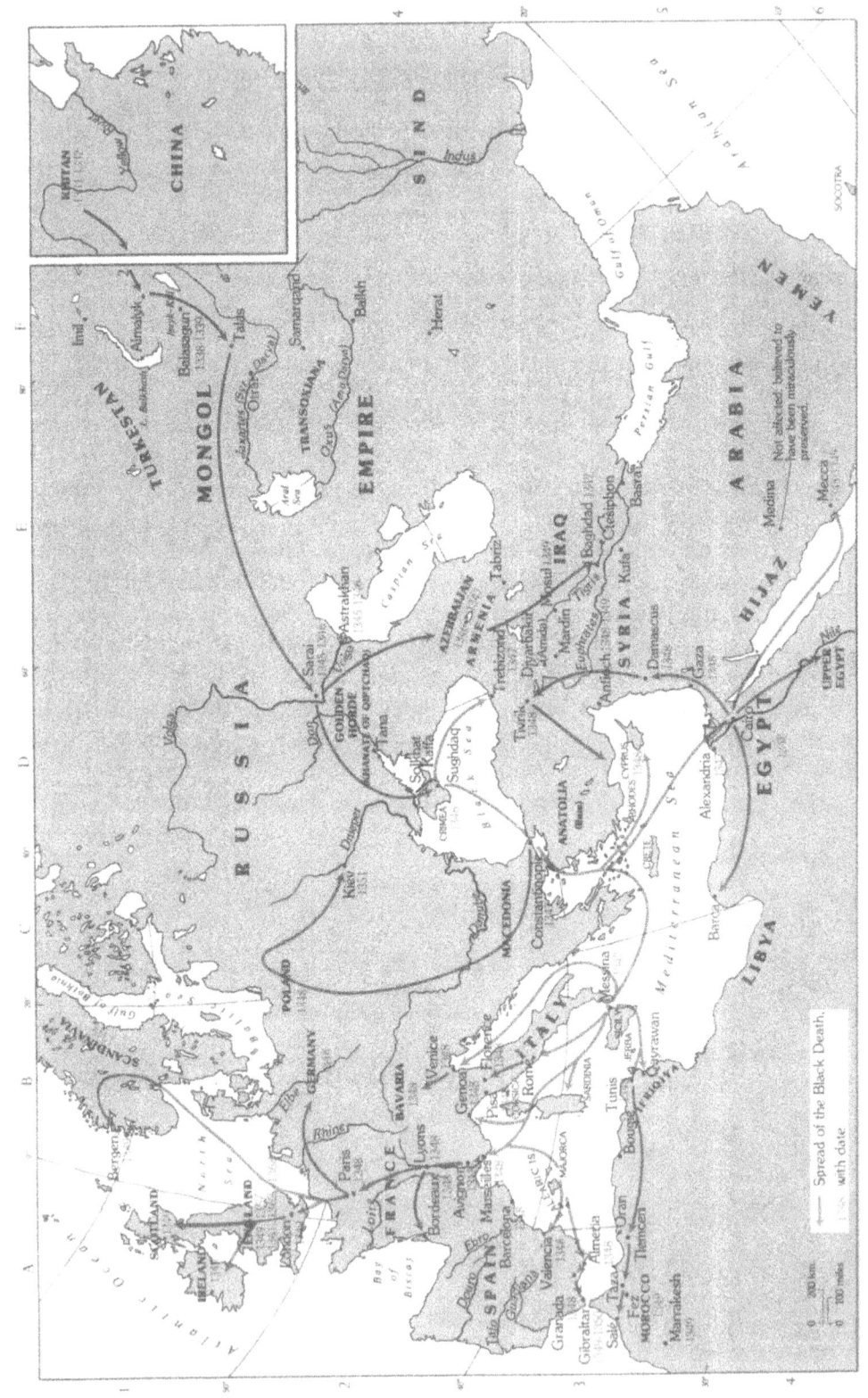

THE SPREAD OF THE BLACK DEATH, 1331–1368

century almost certainly originated in the Asiatic steppes. A second separate source may well have been the island of Tumbatu, off Zanzibar. A permanent reservoir of infection still exists among wild rodents. Sources in both Latin and Arabic agree that the plague was preceded by violent ecological changes, such as earthquakes, flooding, and famines. This conjunction of events is equally clear in the Chinese annals. These disasters destroyed the natural habitats of the wild rodents and drove them into human settlements, where they infected domestic rats, mice, and other animals. The effective agent, however, was not the rodents, but the fleas in their fur. Thus the Black Death was carried into China and India, westward into southeastern Russia, along the trade routes into Syria and Egypt, then into the Mediterranean, and finally into northern Europe. Careful examination of the evidence does not support the older views that it was transmitted solely from China and India along the routes to the Middle East — both by land and sea — or alone by the sea route from China through the Indian Ocean and the Red Sea to Egypt. There is no evidence of the plague in Iraq, Arabia, and Egypt before it had occurred in the Crimea or Mediterranean. When it did occur in Iraq, Arabia, and Egypt, the evidence suggests that it came from the north, for only after it had reached Egypt did it reach Yemen. The most potent source of dissemination appears to have been the Genoese trading agency at Kaffa (Feodosiya) in the Crimea.

It is difficult to estimate the number of deaths, but it is certain that in the towns of Egypt and Syria the population was greatly reduced, with serious economic consequences.

*Timur-Leng and his forces besieging Herat, Persia*

# THE DOMINIONS OF TIMUR-LENG (TAMERLANE),
## 1360–1405

Timur-Leng was born in 1336, allegedly the son of a shepherd. He claimed a common ancestry with Chingis Khan. As a young man he showed distinction in battle, and in 1361 he was appointed vizier of Samarqand. Having defeated various opponents, he made himself ruler of Balkh in 1370; but it took until 1380, and nine expeditions, to make himself master of Jata and Khwarizm. On these expeditions as official protector of Islam, he was accompanied by Naqshbandiya Sufis, holy men, as well as men of letters.

Now he began a far-ranging career of conquest in earnest, either in person or vicariously by his generals. In 1380–1381, Timur sent Toqtomish, the khan of Crimea, against Russia. Moscow was sacked. In 1391 Toqtomish turned against Timur, invading Transoxiana and threatening Samarqand. In 1380-1381 Timur invaded Khorasan, and in 1383 he seized Gurgan, Mazandaran and Seistan; in 1384 the city of Herat rebelled, whereon Timur suppressed its Kart dynasty. In 1384–1385 Mazandaran

*Timur-Leng on his throne, Indian miniature*

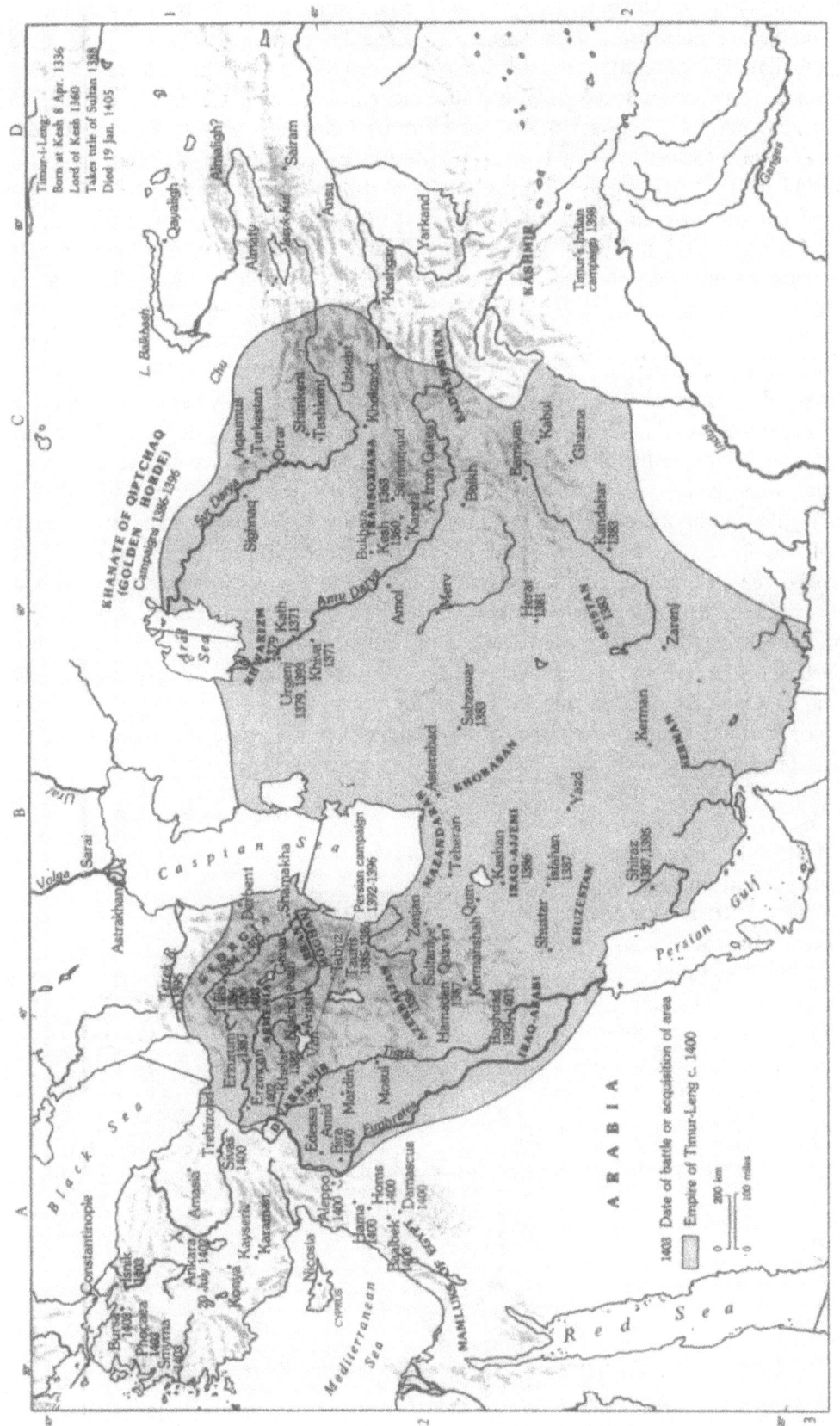

THE DOMINIONS OF TIMUR-LENG (TAMERLANE), 1360–1405

received similar treatment. In 1386–1387 Timur seized Fars, Iraq, Luristan, and Azerbaijan. He wintered at Tabriz, fining Isfahan for rebellion and killing seventy thousand citizens, whose skulls were piled to form towers.

During the next five years he suppressed heretics in the Caspian region, eliminated the Muzaffarid dynasty in Fars, and campaigned in Mesopotamia. In Asia Minor he sacked Edessa, Takrit, Mardin, and Amida. He then conquered Georgia, and finally occupied Moscow, where he remained for a year.

His attention was then drawn in another direction. Contending that the Indian rulers were lax in imposing Islam on their subjects, he attacked India, taking Delhi in 1398. He plundered and destroyed the city, killing eighty thousand citizens. Then he had to hurry westward, for Syria, Iraq, and Azerbaijan were in rebellion. The rebellions repressed, he ravaged Georgia and set out for Asia Minor in 1400, seizing Sivas and Malatya. He proceeded to Syria, taking Aleppo, Hama, Homs, Baalbek, Damascus and Baghdad, where some twenty thousand to forty thousand citizens were massacred. In the following year, 1402, he fought across Asia Minor, through Ankara to Bursa and Smyrna. There he received embassies from Constantinople and Egypt, recognizing his authority. He now retired to Samarqand, where he received further recognition, including that of Castile. Its ambassador left a lively account of the festivities celebrating the marriages of grandsons of Timur.

At the end of 1403 he set out to conquer China. On 17 January 1405, he died. His body was brought back to Samarqand and buried in the Gur-e Amir, a mausoleum that still exists. From 1370 until 1405 this extraordinary and restless character had dominated the Middle East. Yet he had created no permanent empire. He partitioned his vast domain among his sons and grandsons. Grave and serious in demeanor, he was wholly ruthless and without mercy to criminals and to those who displeased him. He had had little education, but he encouraged learning. Public works, administration, commerce, industry, the organization of the army, and, above all, the spread of Islam were his principal concerns.

*Mausoleum of Tamerlane, Samarqand, 15th century*

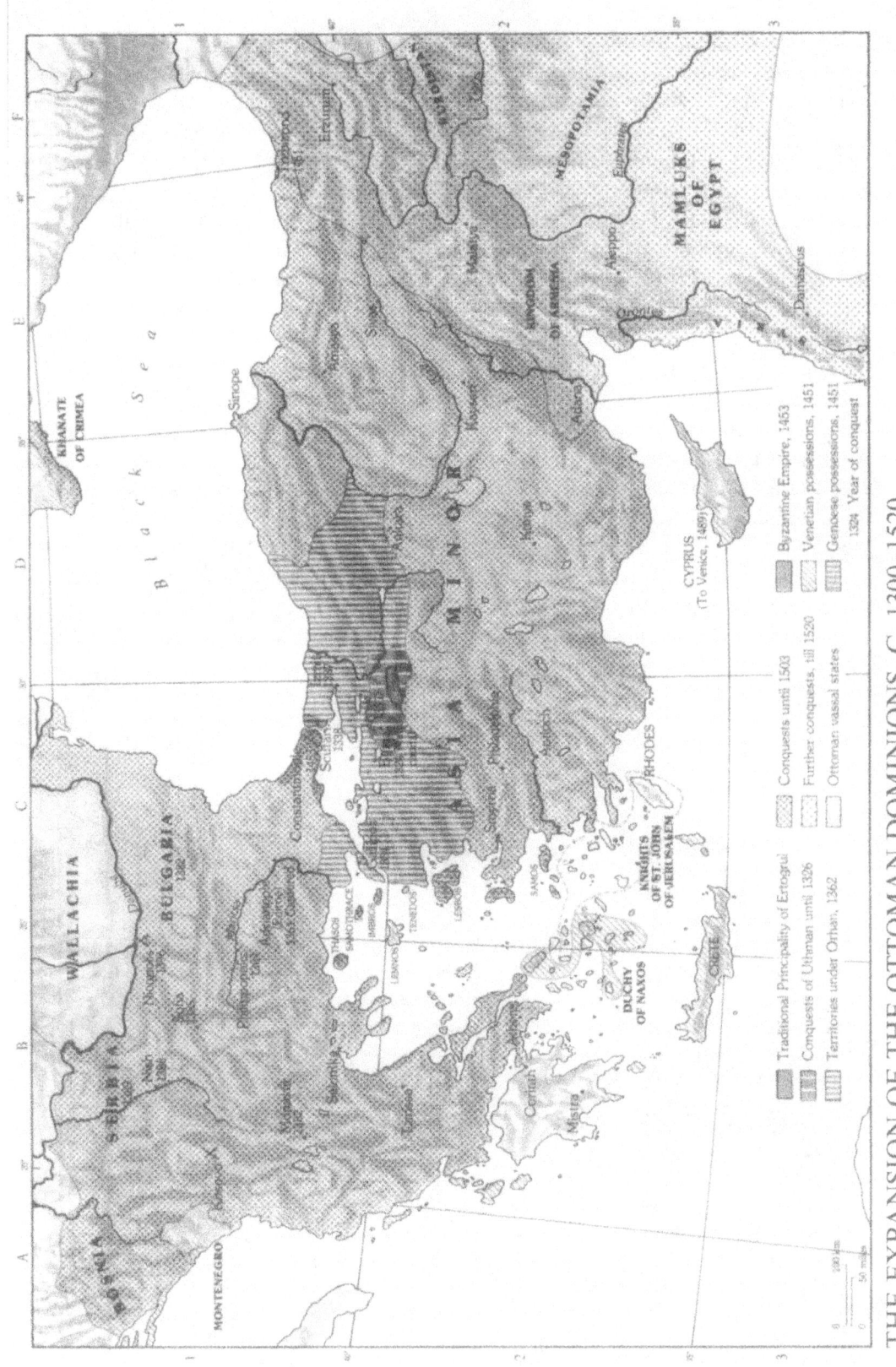

THE EXPANSION OF THE OTTOMAN DOMINIONS, C. 1300–1520

# THE EXPANSION OF THE OTTOMAN DOMINIONS,
## C. 1300–1520

Up to 1517 the history of the Ottoman Turks is characterized by almost continuous territorial expansion. The founder of the dynasty, Uthman I, emerged as a minor chief in northwest Anatolia in 1293 and as leader of a band of *ghazis* (fighters for the faith of Islam), against the Byzantines. By 1517 his descendants held Hungary, the Balkans, the Crimea, Asia Minor, Syria, Palestine, and Egypt. By mid-century North Africa, Mesopotamia, and the holy cities of Mecca and Medina had been added.

After a firm base with Bursa as capital was established in Asia Minor in 1324, the Ottomans by-passed Byzantium and crossed into Europe. The first major conquests in Europe provided a fruitful source of mercenaries. In 1361 Adrianople, the second city of the Byzantine empire, was seized and renamed Edirne, as the Ottoman capital. In 1364 Philippopolis fell. The Ottomans now controlled the principal Byzantine sources of grain and taxation. In 1371 Bulgaria, Hungary, and Serbia allied against the Ottoman advance. In the war that followed most of Bulgaria fell in 1382, Sofia in 1385, Nish in 1386, and all Serbia in 1389. After crushing the allies in a battle at Kosovo the Ottoman conqueror Murad I was killed. His son Bayezid I could not follow up the victory because of a revolt in Anatolia. In a battle at Nicopolis in 1396 Bayezid I finally defeated the allies.

Timur-Leng now felt threatened and campaigned against Bayezid throughout Asia Minor. Bayezid was defeated and taken prisoner at Ankara in 1402. The

*Mosque of Murad II at Bursa, Turkey*

nascent empire was all but extinguished. Quarrels about the succession followed, and only in 1413 did Mehmed I emerge to control all the provinces. Under him and his son, Murad II (r. 1421–1451), the system of indirect rule, which had been earlier Ottoman policy, was restored. In 1422–1423 Murad besieged Byzantium and took huge amounts of gold in ransom. From 1423 to 1430 he challenged Venice's control of the Adriatic Sea. At the same time he freed himself from the jealousy of local Turkish nobles by instituting the Janissary corps — Christians recruited as slaves and instructed and trained as Muslims — the counterpart of the Egyptian Mamluks. This corps, owing allegiance to the sultan alone, enabled the completion of the conquest of the European provinces by 1451.

The proud unconquered city, Constantinople, fell after a brief siege (6 April to 29 May 1453) to Mehmed II (r. 1451–1481). The Ottoman sultan had been transformed into a Byzantine emperor. Only slowly did the civil service become an Ottoman service, and for a long period Greeks, or Greek converts to Islam, remained dominant. While Islam was the state religion, the millet system, which gave each denomination, Christian and Jewish, internal self-government and the power to enforce its own laws, subject to payment of the poll tax, enabled a wide degree of freedom. The Sufi fraternities, and especially the Bektashis, of whose

*Portrait of Sultan Selim I (the Grim)*

order the sultans were members, developed a syncretistic doctrine that was only nominally Sunni.

Under Bayezid II (r. 1481–1512) the empire was further extended with small additions in Europe north of the Danube. His successor, Selim I, the Grim (r. 1512–1520), inherited the aggressive spirit of his ancestors. In 1514 he attacked the Safavids in Persia, routing them at Chaldiran, and took Azerbaijan. No attempt was made to seize their empire. Instead Selim turned south and attacked the Mamluks, all of whose possessions in Syria and Egypt he took without difficulty in 1516–1517.

## THE IL-KHANIDS OF PERSIA, 1236–1353

Between 1218 and 1221, when the Mongols from central Asia advanced to the Middle East, they subjected only part of Khorasan. Around 1251 a further advance was determined. While Mangu Khan was fighting his brother Kubilai in China, their brother Hulagu was sent with 129,000 men to conquer Persia, Mesopotamia, and, if possible, Syria and Egypt. It was this army that the Mamluk general Baybars, later sultan, utterly defeated at Ayn Jalut on 3 September 1260.

Baybars' victory established a final

*161*

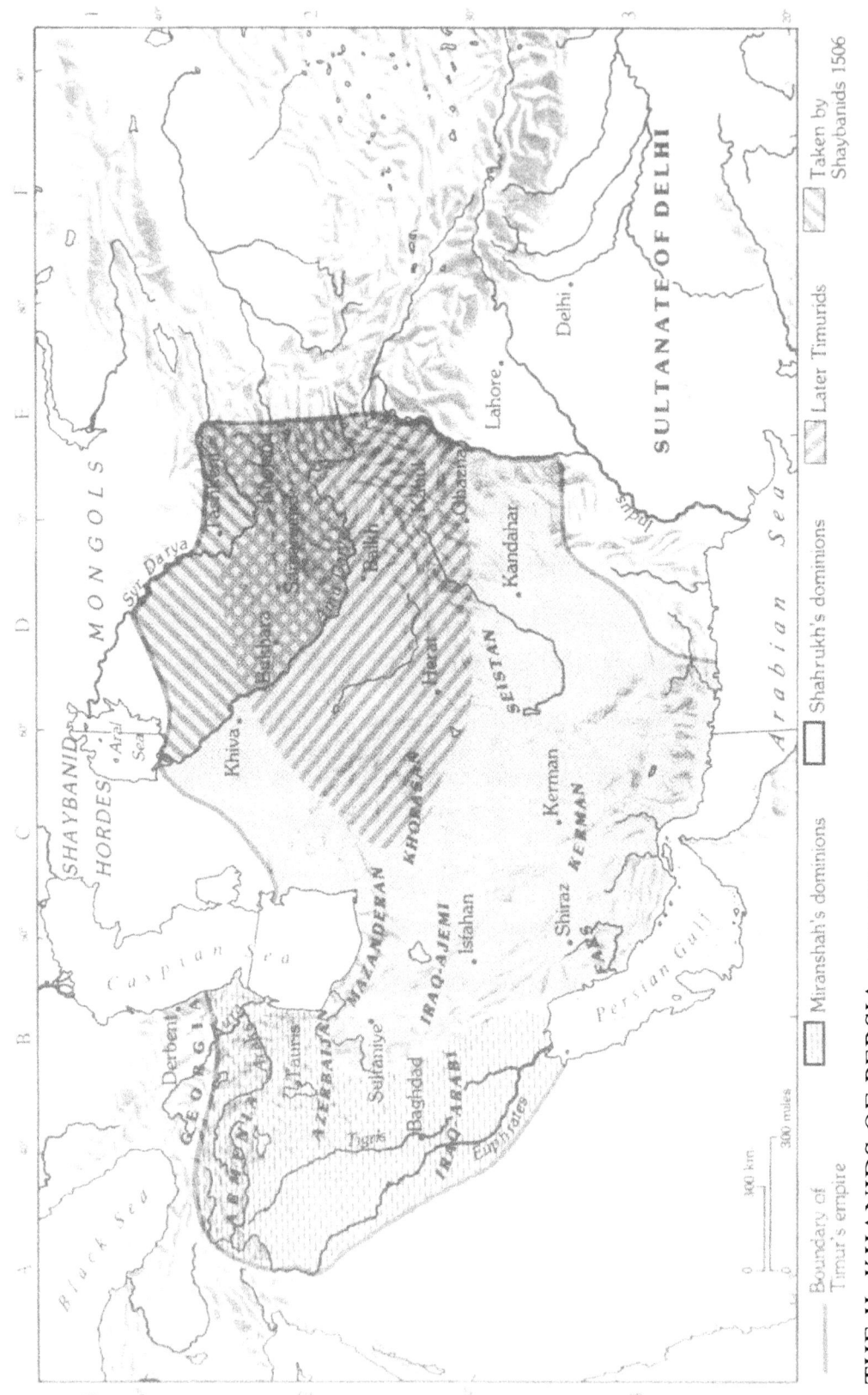

THE IL-KHANIDS OF PERSIA, 1236–1353

boundary for the Mongol advance westward. They now held Armenia and the Seljuq possessions in Asia Minor, Mesopotamia, and much of Persia. They acquired Fars by marriage in 1284. Large parts of Persia were ruled by independent local dynasties. In 1295 the Mongols in Persia adopted Persian culture and the national religion and threw off allegiance to the Great Khan.

Some of the Mongols who invaded Persia were Nestorian Christians, but most were shamanists. When they adopted Islam, they were tolerant toward both Shi'ites and Christians, and politically hostile toward the Sunni Mamluks in Egypt. Abaka (r. 1265–1282), himself a Buddhist, had diplomatic relations with the Holy See and the Crusaders.

Despite its militaristic origin, the Il-Khanid period was one of great artistic activity. Far Eastern influences in textile, ceramics, and miniature painting permeated the Islamic world and, in part, transmuted Seljuq art, whose traditions were continued in the architecture of mosques, madrasas, mausoleums, shrines, khanqas, khans, and other buildings.

*Entrance to the Golden Mosque of Kadhimain, Baghdad*

## THE TIMURIDS, 1369–1506, AND SHAYBANIDS, 1506–1570

The term Timurids can include all Timur-Leng's descendants, but for practical purposes it is limited to those who ruled after him as princes. In the west his son Miranshah inherited Iraq, north Syria, Armenia, and Azerbaijan and, in turn,

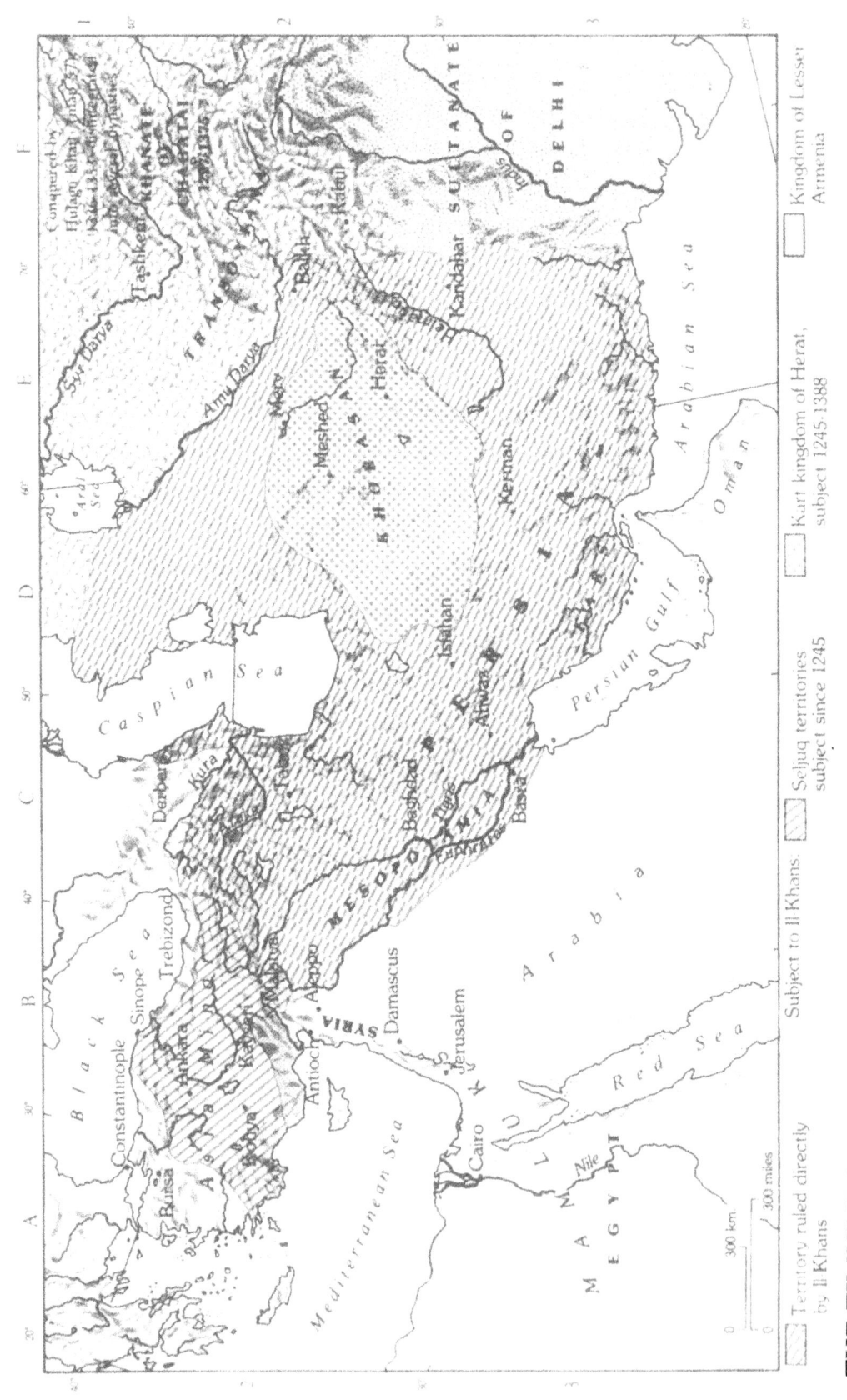

THE TIMURIDS, 1369–1506, AND SHAYBANIDS, 1506–1570

passed it on to his sons. In the east Shahrukh initially ruled only Khorasan. He soon added Transoxiana and eventually controlled most of the area his father had dominated. In contrast with that of his father, his long reign (1405–1447) was one of great tranquillity. At first the emirs had wished to carry war into China, as Timur himself had desired, but this wish was frustrated when they fell out among themselves. Shahrukh's reign thus began with a series of risings, which lasted until 1429. To the last, peaceful period of his reign is owed his great library at Herat.

On the death of Shahrukh decline in the empire began. His sons quarreled among themselves. In Afghanistan the Uzbeks attacked from the north. The princes could not agree to unify, and the empire steadily disintegrated. The period, nevertheless, was remarkable for its culture. Shahrukh himself was devoted to history, and his son Ulugh Beg studied astronomy, poetry, theology, and another son, Baisonghor, calligraphy. Mystical poets, moralists, apologists, geographers, theologians, jurists, mathematicians, and physicians were numerous, and the arts of painting, bookbinding, calligraphy, ceramics, music, and, above all, architecture, flourished.

Of the later descendants, one Babur, established a great empire in India, while in the north Shaybani's descendants ruled beyond the Syr Darya.

*Interior of the Blue Mosque, Isfahan*

## THE SAFAVIDS IN PERSIA, 1501–1737

The Safavids are the most famous of the Persian Islamic dynasties. They left a permanent mark on the country by establishing Shi'ism as the state religion, thus giving the people of Persia what is now known as a sense of national unity, distinct from Arabs, Turks, and other peoples of the north and east.

The family of the founder, Isma'il I, had long been established in Ardabil and were hereditary teachers of religion. Thus backed by religious authority, the future shah Isma'il gradually extended political authority over Shirwan, Azerbaijan, Iraq, and finally the rest of Persia. Shi'ism, which had long been popular in the region, was now a state religion; the Sunni faith was virtually wiped out.

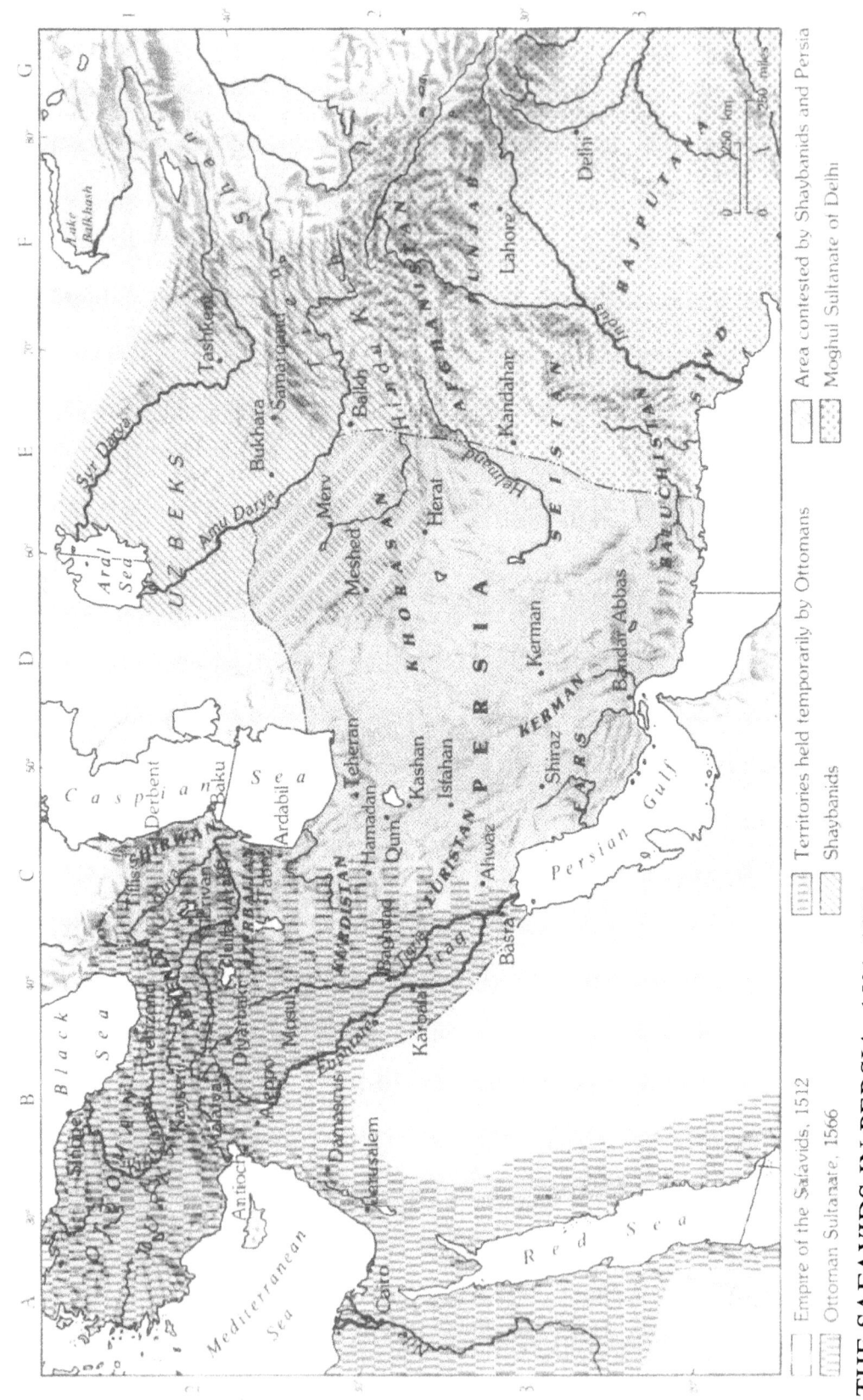

THE SAFAVIDS IN PERSIA, 1501–1737

*Tali Kari Madrasa, Samarqand, 17th century*

Under Tahmasp I (r. 1524–1576), wars against the Uzbeks and the Ottoman Turks gave a further sense of unity, as did the shah's name and title, both derived from pre-Islamic Persia. His successor, Isma'il II (r.1576–1577), was a debauchee. His nephew, Shah Abbas was acclaimed in Nishapur in 989/1581; but only over all Persia at Isfahan in 996/1588. He ruled until 1628. He was the greatest of his line as a warrior against the Uzbeks and Ottomans, an organizer of commerce and international intercourse, and a patron of architecture. Under him Armenians were deported with abominable cruelty in mid-winter from Julfa to New Julfa, near Isfahan, to serve the needs of manufacturing and commerce.

After Abbas's death Kandahar was seized by Babur and Baghdad by the Ottomans. Kandahar was recovered by Abbas II, only to be lost finally in 1709, when a new state emerged in Afghanistan. Shah Sulayman I, also known as Safi IV, ruled Persia from 1666 to 1694 and not only had good relations with the Ottomans but also intercourse with the western powers, including Russia, which was important for the Armenian trade in furs. His son Shah Sultan Husayn was a weak ruler, controlled by the mullahs (doctors of the religious law), whose persecution of the Sunnites had angered the Afghans. The last of the line was Muhammad Shah, who was acclaimed in 1788, and lived in exile until 1794.

*Jahangir's Tomb, Lahore, Pakistan*

## (III) EASTERN AFRICA

## EASTERN AFRICA — PHYSICAL

Eastern Africa, commonly East Africa, consists of the mainland of Kenya, Tanzania and Uganda, with boundaries which were settled in colonial times. In these, Zanzibar and Pemba Islands formed a separate protectorate, which joined with Tanzania as a component of a United Republic in 1964. There is a low-lying seaboard which merges in that of Somalia on the north, and of Mozambique on the south, where the Ruvuma forms a national boundary, and then giving way to a high plateau, rising to 4,000 feet. The great mountain of the Kilimanjaro range is athwart the boundary between Kenya and Tanzania, with a peak covered with permanent snow. To the north lie further mountainous areas in Kenya. Lake Victoria is likewise shared between Kenya and Tanzania. To the west lies Uganda with the Ruwenzori range, and the Great Rift Valley from Lake Albert through Lake Tanganyika to Lake Malawi (or Nyasa). On the north, the area is bounded by Somalia and Ethiopia, and on the west by Rwanda and Burundi, with the Congo, and on the south by Zambia and Malawi. All these external boundaries have been inherited from the colonial period. They ignored, for political reasons, the previously existing economic and political boundaries which served an economic trading system. There are few and small rivers.

The whole area is primarily agricultural, of which maize and millet, with cassava as a famine crop, are the staples. Coconut palms grow on the seaboard and islands, with cloves as a major export from Pemba and Zanzibar. Cattle are reared in areas free from tsetse fly, over large

*The Husuni Palace of the Sultans of Kilwa, isometric reconstruction of the ruins by P.S. Garlake, visited by Ibn Battuta in 1331.*

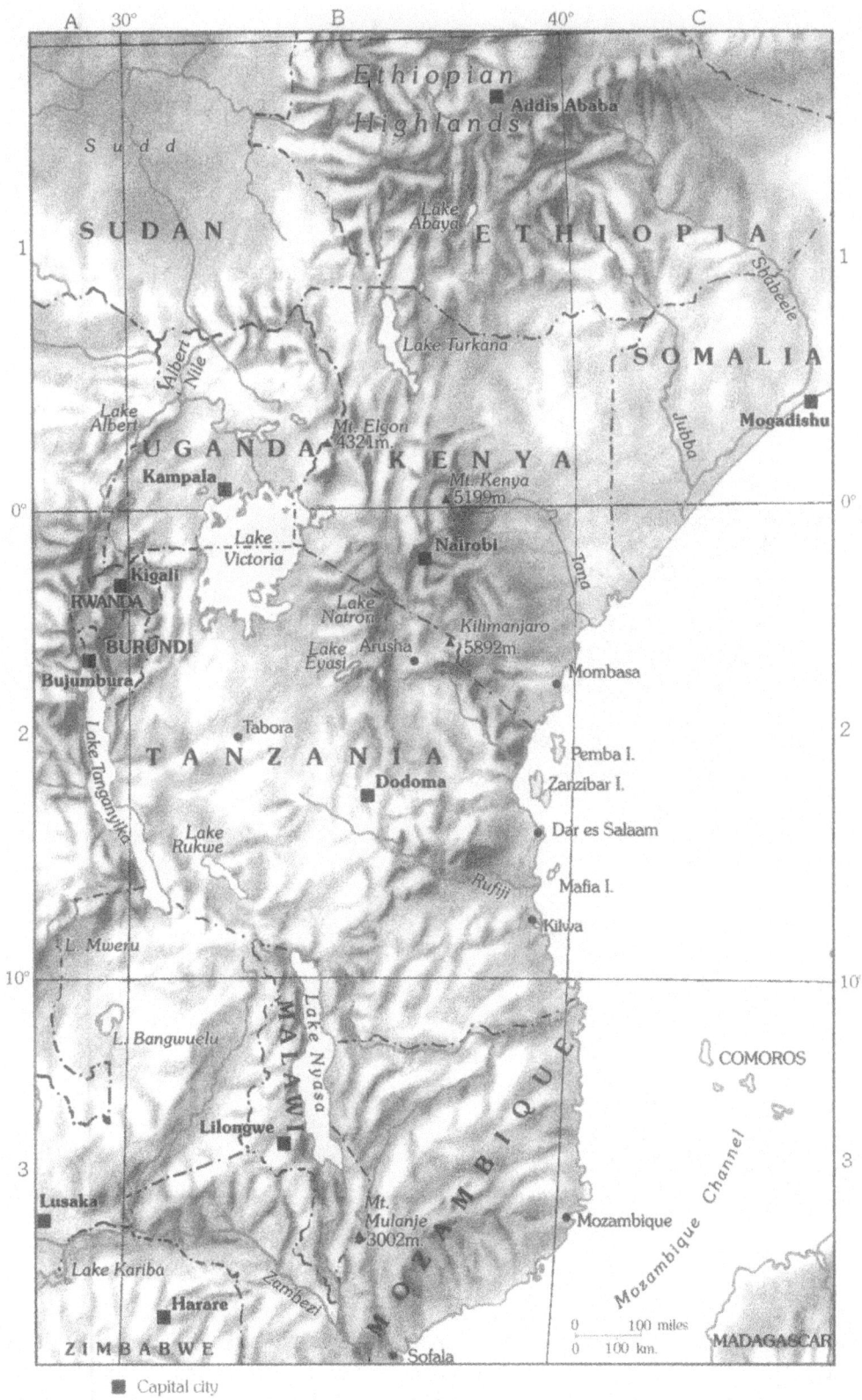

# EASTERN AFRICA — PHYSICAL

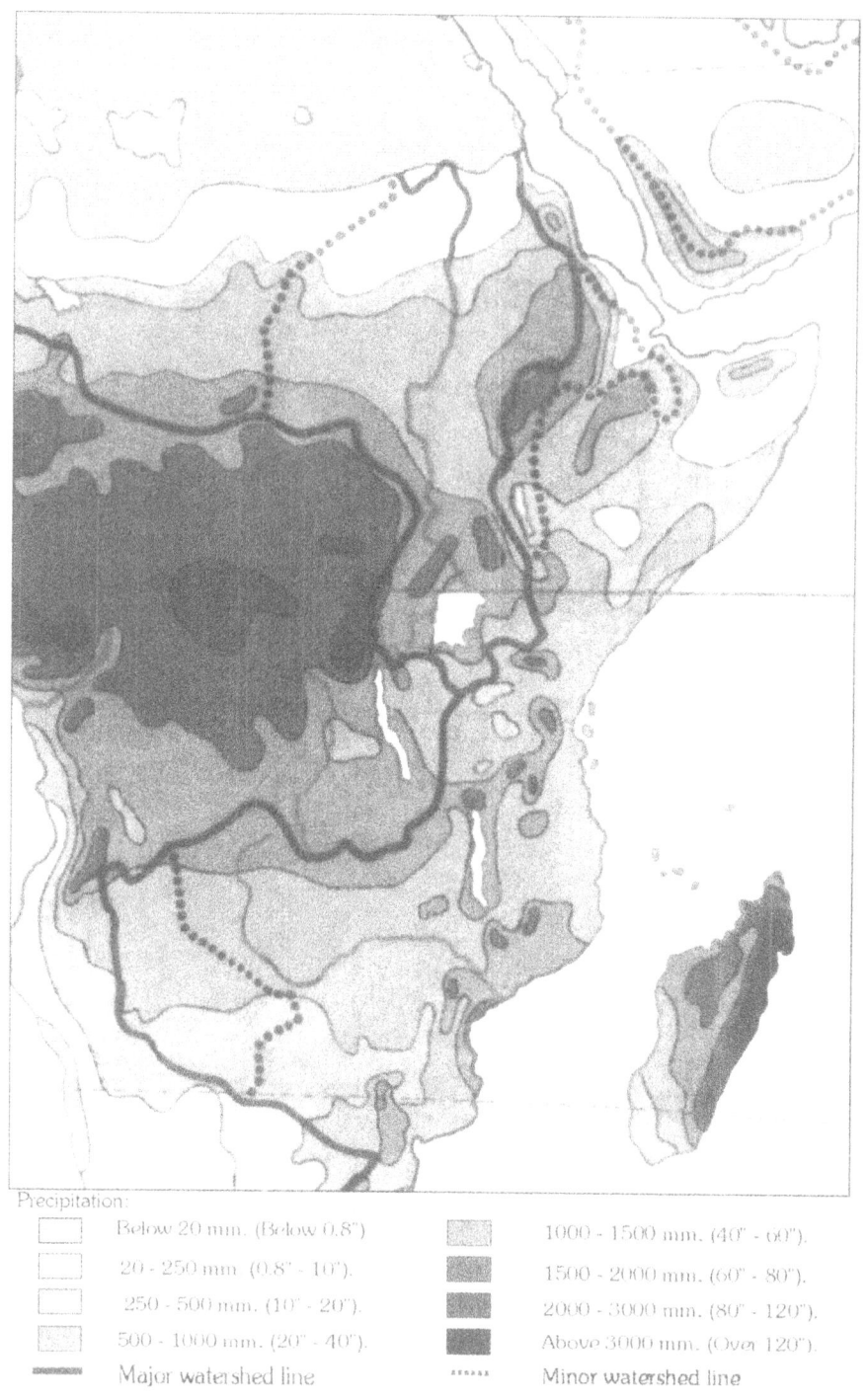

EASTERN AFRICA — ANNUAL RAINFALL

grazing grounds, including those of the Maasai and Kwavi, shared between Kenya and Tanzania, and the Boran in the Northern Frontier District of Kenya. The coast abounds in fish of many varieties; on Lake Victoria *satu*, a kind of *tilapia*, of a related family to those of Lake Tiberias, provide for local peoples. A majority of the peoples belong to the Bantu family of languages, with some

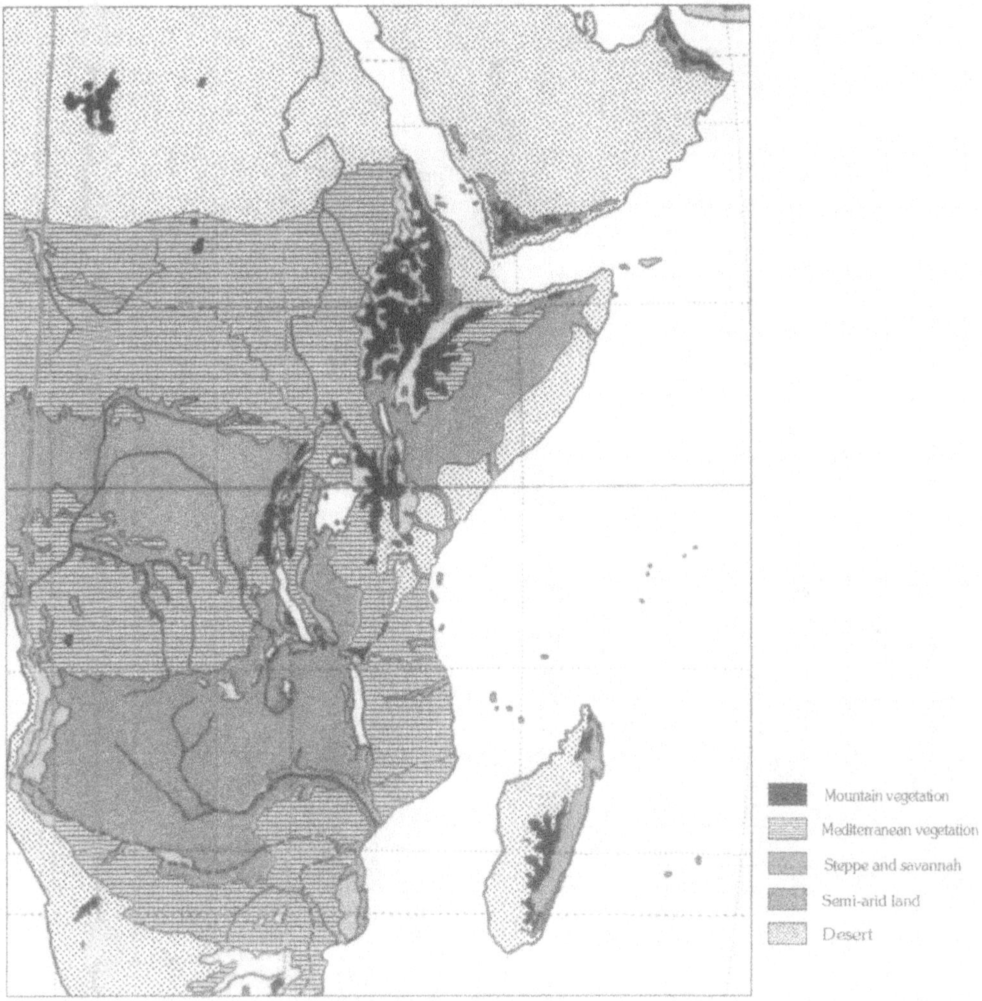

EASTERN AFRICA — VEGETATION

*Fort Jesus, built 1593 to 1596, at Mombasa*

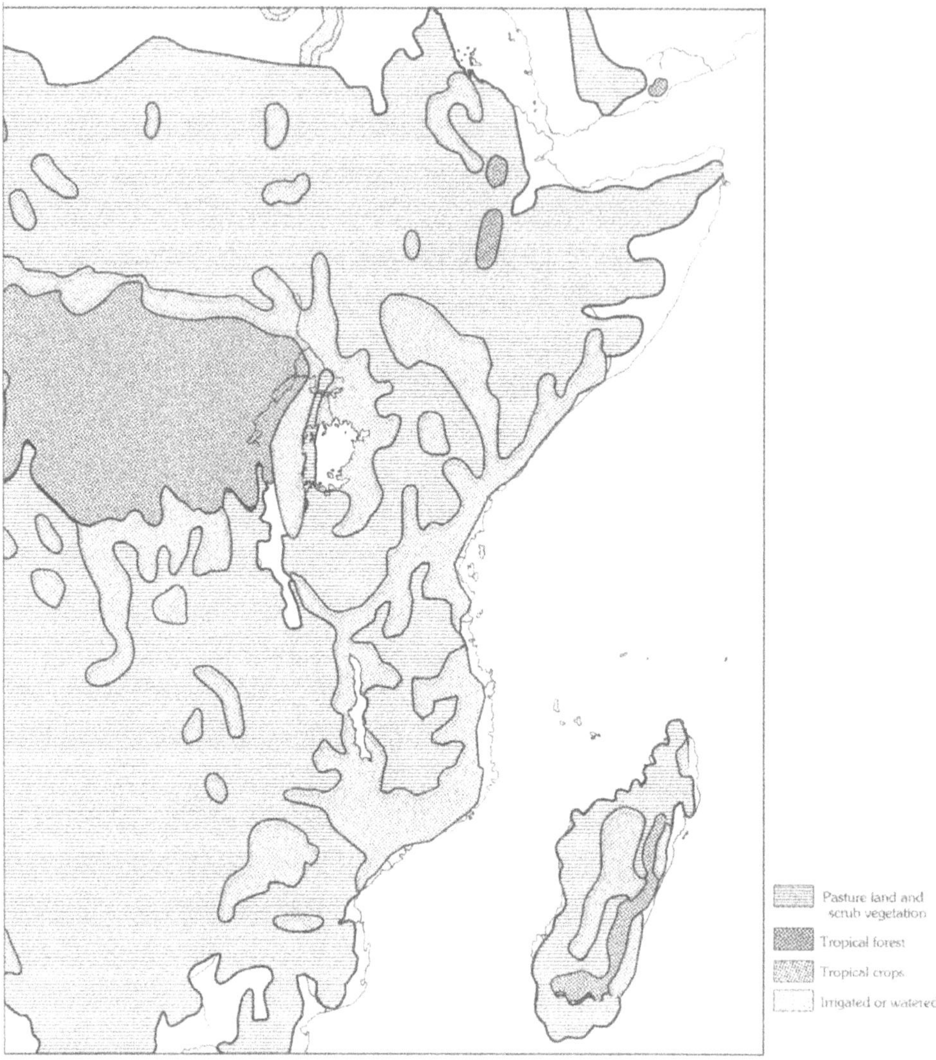

EASTERN AFRICA — AGRICULTURE AND LIVESTOCK

pockets of Nilotic and other languages. Swahili, originally the language of the coast (Arabic, *sahel*), is now understood almost over the whole area, and westwards; already present in the Congo in small areas, it spread as far as the Atlantic during the wars and troubles which followed its independence in 1960.

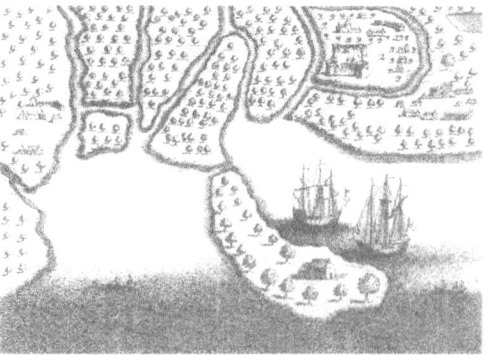

*Madagascar and the East African Coast from "Histoire des Découvertes et Conquestes des Portugais" 1733.*

Animal life of many kinds abounds throughout the whole region, and has provided a tourist industry which attracts visitors from many different nations. Minerals are scarce, but there are deposits of diamonds, mica and gold, which are exploited. In the twentieth century sisal formed a major export.

The climate is moderately tropical, with rainy seasons dependent on the monsoons, in March and November.

*Sisal plantation on the Athi Plains, Kenya*

## NUBIA AND ETHIOPIA, c. 600

Below the First Cataract of the Nile lay three Christian kingdoms, often confused by mediaeval European writers with Ethiopia. Their history is extremely obscure. The northernmost was Nobatia (the kingdom of the Nuba). Beyond the Third Cataract, Makuria or Maqurra (later Dongola) was the heir of the ancient capital of Meroe. From this region, 'Ethiopia' or Meroe, came the eunuch treasurer of Queen Candace who is reported in Acts 8:27-40 to have been baptized by Philip after making a pilgrimage to Jerusalem. The conversion of Nobatia took place around the year 543, when King WRPYWL (Awarfiula) was converted to Monophysite Christianity by missionaries sent by the empress Theodora. Bishop Longinus was sent there shortly afterwards. Makuria was

*Nubian mud-brick buildings*

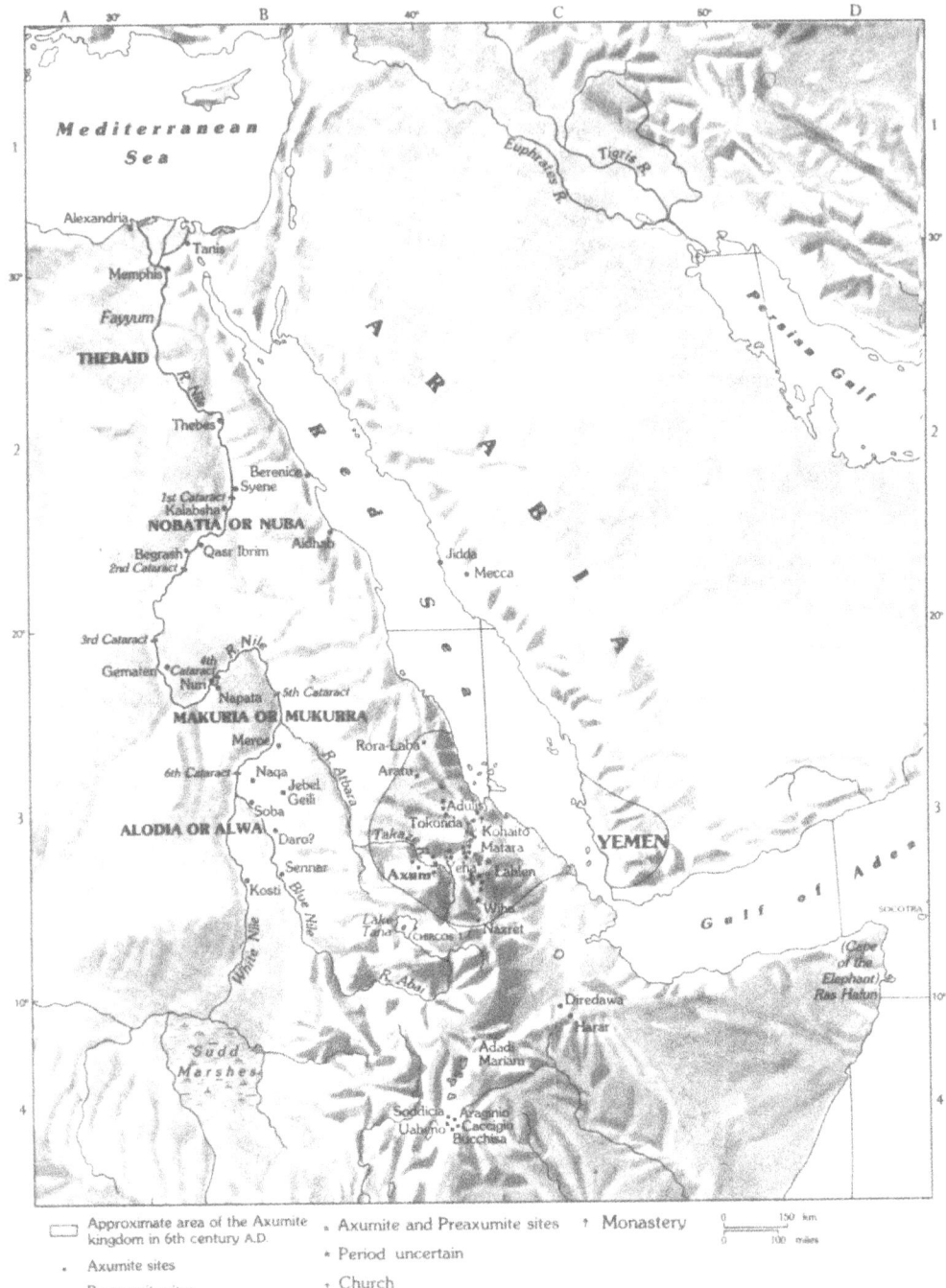

## NUBIA AND ETHIOPIA, C. 600

converted by Orthodox missionaries sent by Justinian around 569. The third kingdom, Alodia or Alwa, with its capital at present-day Soba, was converted to Monophysitism by Longinus. Christianity survived in Makuria from the fourteenth century, and in Soba until the 16th century. Even today women, nominally Muslim, may be seen crossing themselves as they draw water from the Nile, to protect themselves against crocodiles.

The first contact of Nubians with the Muslim conquerors of Egypt was in 651-2, when Abdallah b. Saad invaded the country, only to be stopped by the Nubian forces, especially their famous bowmen. Because of this check, a treaty called the *baqt* was arranged between the Muslims and King Qalidurat of Nubia, and it long remained in force. There has been dispute as to whether the *baqt* was an imposition on Nubia, or more of a mutual arrangement between the two powers. Whatever the case, Nubia was to remain long a Christian state unsubjected to Egypt. The *baqt* did sometimes cause problems, Nubia occasionally failing to send it, and being reminded by the Egyptian authorities. There was some Arab penetration over the centuries into Nubia and the flanking Beja lands, but Nubia remained under Christian rulers until the Mamluk period in Egypt.

*The last extant stone monolith out of some one hundred raised at Aksum in the 1st century AD*

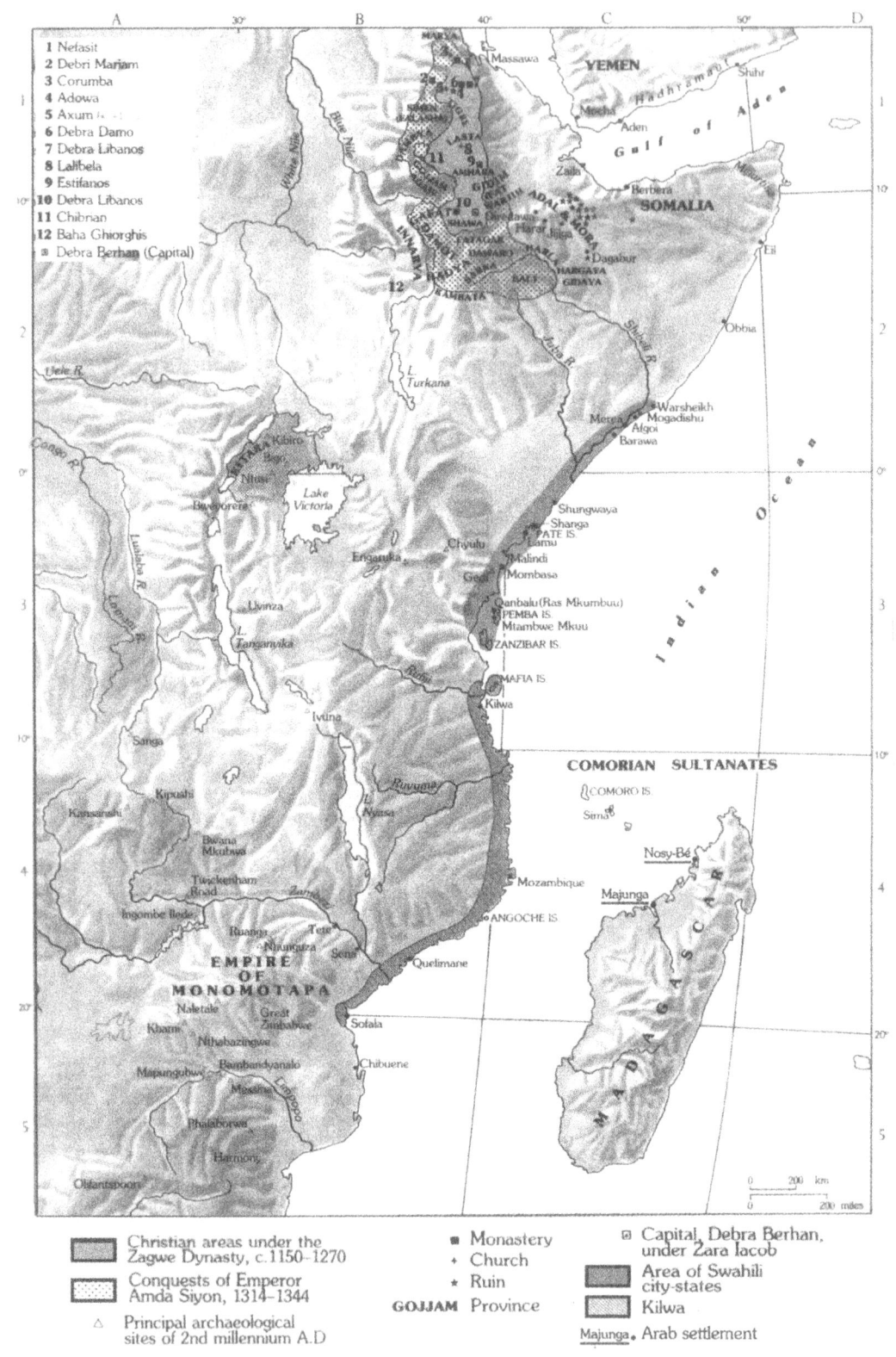

ETHIOPIA AND EASTERN AFRICA, c. 1200–c. 1500

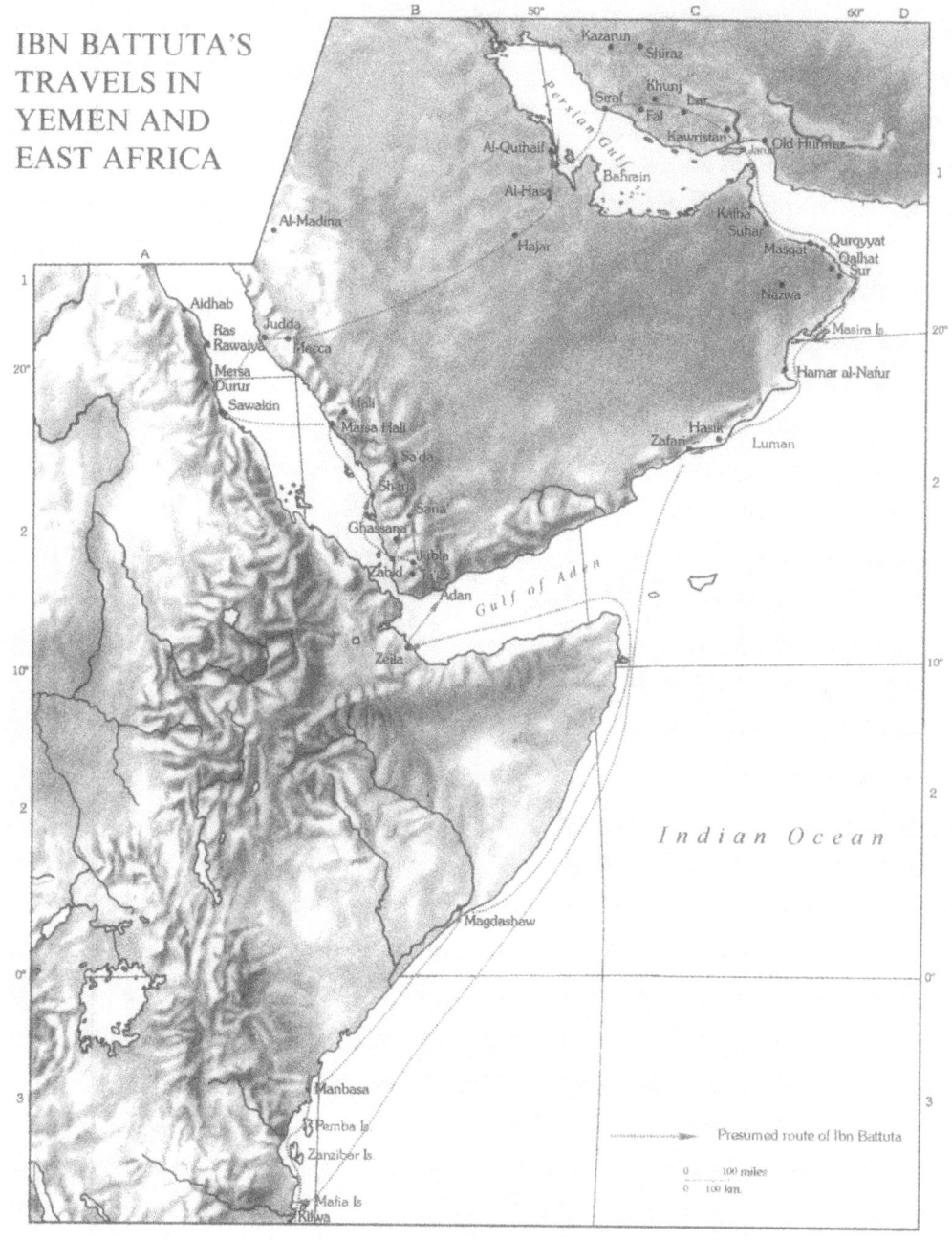

# IBN BATTUTA'S TRAVELS IN YEMEN AND EAST AFRICA

## ETHIOPIA C. 1200–C. 1500

In 1270 the 'Solomonic' line was supposedly restored by Yekuno Amlak (1270-1285), to whom the later 'Solomonid' legends of the Ethiopian royal house attribute descent from Menelik, son of Solomon and the Queen of Saba (Sheba). A succession of largely able and powerful rulers followed until the 16th century. At the same time as the struggle between Yekuno Amlak and the Zagwe was enacted, the Makhzumi sultanate in Shewa was in rapid decline. By 1280 a new dynasty, founded by Ali b. Wali Asma, was reigning in Shewa, destined to

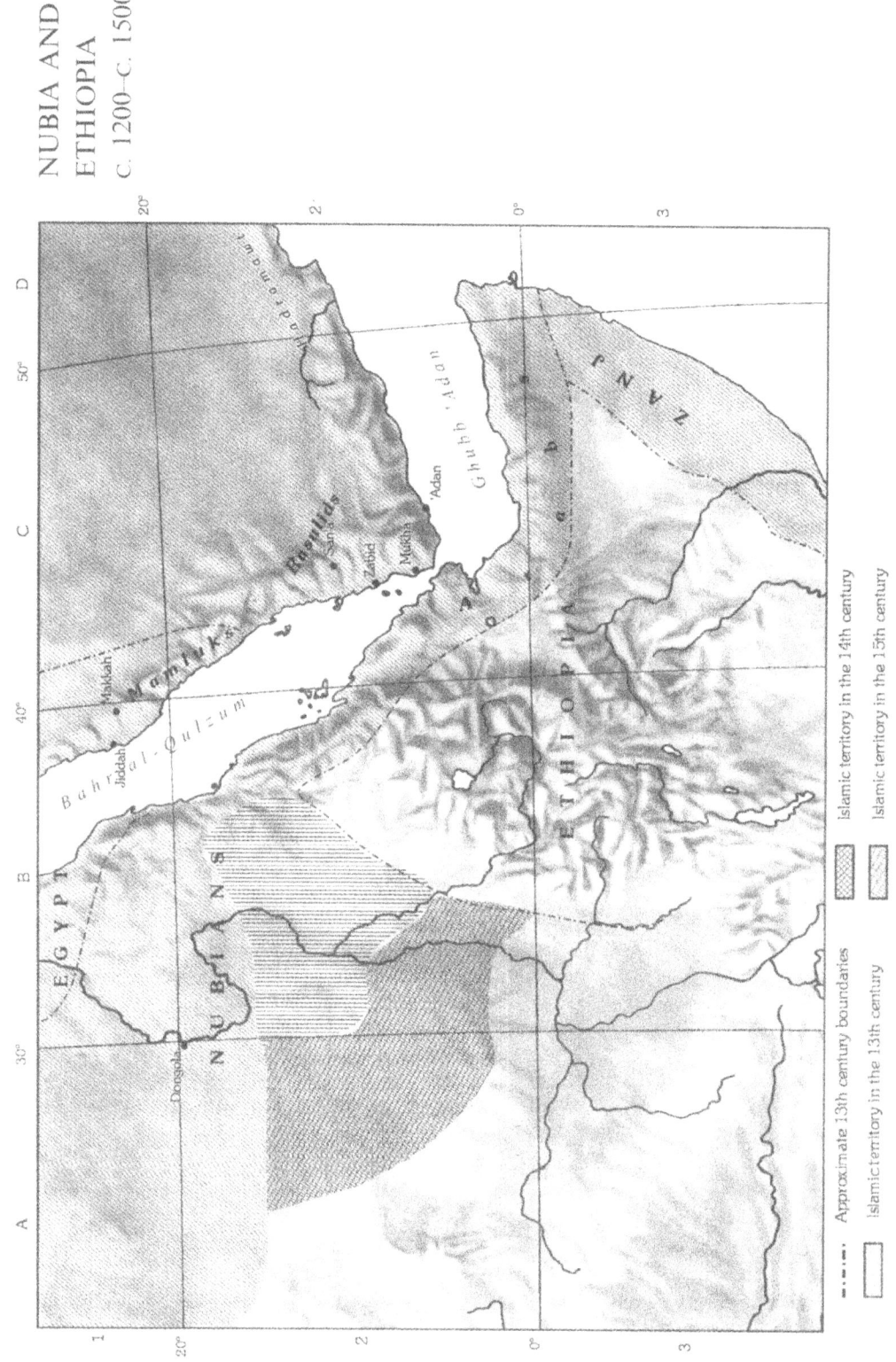

lead the Muslim states of Ifat and Adal (the kingdom of Zeila) in a long struggle against the Christian emperors of Ethiopia. Amda Seyon (1314–1344) in particular is noted for a major struggle against the Muslim states, seven of which are named by al-'Umari as existing in Habasha (Abyssinia): Awfat (Ifat), Dawaru (Dowaro), Arababni, Hadya, Sharkha, Bali, and Dara. Early in his reign Amda Seyon fought Hadya, part of a series of campaigns destined to more than double the empire. Both the designation 'Muslim' for these states, and the notion of Abyssinian 'conquest' need definition. In many cases, Muslim rulers and a small caste of administrators or landowners dominated a Sidama or other population, while after submission to Amda Seyon, the hereditary Muslim rulers continued in office in all but one of the Muslim states, under payment of tribute. Nevertheless, Christian political expansion was accompanied by missionary effort in many areas, no less than by an increase of trade in the area, which brought prosperity even to the neighboring Somali sultanates. Of these there are substantial remains of some twenty cities. In Ethiopia itself some churches and monasteries of this period remain, evidence of surplus wealth to expend on building. Most were to be destroyed by Ahmad Grañ.

Nevertheless, the growing strength of Islam in the plains of Somalia and the coastlands opposite Dahlak, isolating the Christian highland bastion, was a constant source of friction, an obstacle to its access to the sea, even if King Dawit (1380–1412) was able to sack Zeila at one time, and Zara Yaqob personally slew Sultan Badlay of Adal in 1445. All the following kings of Ethiopia, Baeda Maryam, Eskender, Naod and Lebna Dengel fought the Adali Muslims, and in the latter's reign Ethiopia was nearly destroyed by Ahmad Grañ's invasion. Holy War (*jihad*) is commemorated on

*Kassala landscape, Sudan*

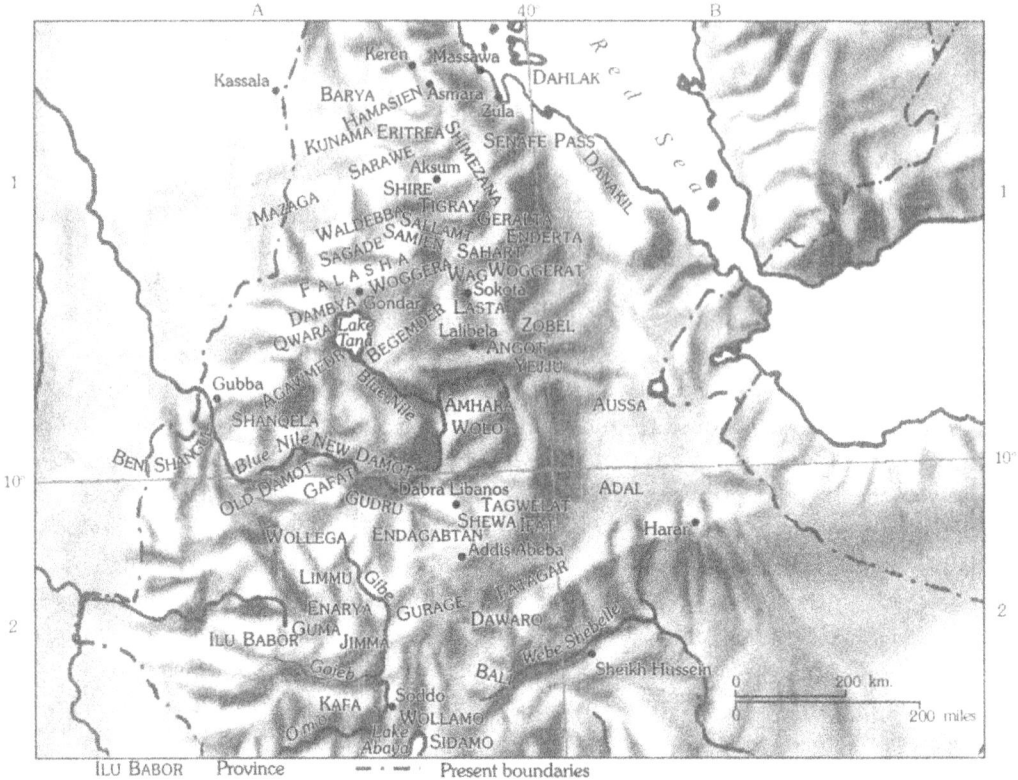

ETHIOPIA, C. 1200 TO C. 1500

many of the coins issued in the Mogadishu region, and would have been profitable as a source of slaves, who were exported chiefly to India in sufficient quantity to be known as '*Habashi*' (Ethiopians). Converted to Islam, they had varying fortunes. Ibn Battuta mentions the respect they engendered as soldiers to protect shipping. In Bengal they even ruled as the Slave Dynasty (1246–1290). The fourteenth and fifteenth centuries in Ethiopia saw a period of great literary output, with translations from Coptic and Arabic.

There were connections yet farther afield: in 1394 Venice sent masons, painters and artisans; an Ethiopian embassy visited Aragon in 1427, and another visited Lisbon in 1452, while Ethiopian monks were present at the Council of Florence in 1441. These contacts established the dream of Ethiopian Christian monarchs (now identified as 'Prester John') concerting with Europeans to crush Islam with a pincer movement that would ultimately destroy Mecca.

*Fort Santiago, Kilwa, Tanzania (rebuilt 1810)*

Nubia — the kingdom of Dongola formed from the joining of Nobatia with Maqurra (little is known about Alwa/Alodia further south) — slowly grew weaker and weaker in the face of the Muslim strength in Egypt. Like Ethiopia, Nubia's church was forced to apply to the Muslims to receive the consecration of its bishops by the patriarch of Alexandria, but native Nubians, sometimes royal sons, were the bishops, not Coptic Egyptians as in Ethiopia

There was an expedition into Nubia by Turan Shah, in 1173, that apparently resulted in a defeat for Nubia. By the 13th century, under the Mamluk rulers Baybars (1260–1277), Qala'un (1279–1290) and al-Nasir Muhammad (three reigns between 1293 and 1341) the Nubian throne was occupied often by rulers imposed with the aid of military force from Egypt. The Dongola dynasty slowly fell into the status of a client monarchy of the powerful Mamluk sultanate at Cairo. King Shakanda, around 1275/76, agreed to pay tribute, and to surrender territory (the provinces of 'the Mountain' and al-'Ali next to Aswan) in the north. The population, given the choice between accepting Islam, death, or the *jizya* (tax on non-Muslims), chose the tax, according to the Muslim historians of the period. Soon King Shamamun succeeded, to be deposed almost immediately by an Egyptian army in 1288, then restored, then deposed again in 1290. The Muslims massacred many people on the expedition to Dongola. But once again Shamamun returned, allowing the Mamluk guard of the new king imposed by Egypt (Budamma) to retire. He reigned until c. 1295.

The interference from Egypt increased. In the end, Sayf al-Din Abdallah, a Nubian prince who had become Muslim, was installed as king of Nubia (1316) in the place of King Karanbas. An inscription survives stating that a mosque was established at Dongola in 1317. Karanbas sent his own nephew Kanz al-Dawla, the son of his sister, and therefore the legal heir, to the sultan, proposing that he become king if the sultan was determined to set a Muslim on the Dongola throne. There was more unrest, more dethronements and enthronements. Kanz al-Dawla was hailed as king of Nubia, but Karanbas appears again as ruler in 1323. Ibn Khaldun says he became a Muslim, but his inscription at Aswan is indubitably Christian. Kanz al-Dawla, chased out by the sultan's armies, returned. In 1349 the Nubians are described by al-Umari as Christians ruled by a king of the family of Kanz al-Dawla.

Arab participation in the general unrest in Dongola is attested later in the century, and evidently Muslim influence was spreading rapidly in the country. Christianity in northern Nubia gradually

*Nubian village*

*Excavations inside the early 11th century mosque, showing the walls of a stone mosque of the 10th century and post holes of earlier timber mosques; the earliest dating to c. 780. Courtesy Mark Horton*

faded before the influence of Islam. In the south, Alwa was overthrown before 1504, according to the Funj chronicle. The legends of the Abdallab of Sudan declare that Abdallah Jamma seized from the Christian rulers of southern Nubia 'the bejeweled crown of the Anaj kings' (Anaj is known as a principality of the region): as at Dongola, Christianity slowly died away before Islam.

A kingdom called Dotawo, of uncertain situation, seems to have separated itself by at least 1144. It was formerly thought that this was a latter-day resurrction of Nobatia, after Dongola became Muslim, but now documents from Ibrim testify to much earlier kings of Dotawo. The seat of the kingdom seems to have been at Jabal Adda. The kingdom of Dotawo is still attested, under a Christian, King Joel, in 1484, long after Muslims were seated on the throne of Dongola.

## EAST AFRICA, 13TH TO 16TH CENTURIES

On the eastern coast of Africa inscriptions attest the stone mosques of Mogadishu as of the 13th century. About 1300 both copper and billon (base silver) currency was issued. Ibn Battuta visited the city around 1330 and formed a favorable impression, after having greatly detested Zeila. Farther south lay a string of small Swahili city-states, of which the Lamu archipelago, Malindi, Mombasa, and Zanzibar were the most important. One of the Lamu islands, Pate, had dynastic links with the Comorian sultanates in the far south.

Between the Rufiji and the Ruvuma rivers, but with possessions far to the south at Mozambique, Angoche, Quelimane, and Sofala, lay the Sultanate of Kilwa. From the Lamu area southward finds of Sassanian-Islamic pottery and coin finds demonstrate commercial activity in continuous sequence from the eighth century. Earlier consecutive evidence is at present lacking. Kilwa became prominent in the twelfth century, when it took possession of the gold trade with the Zambezi hinterland and controlled the series of small ports of the Mozambique coast. Its prosperity, evidenced by a large Friday mosque as well as by sumptuous houses and palaces, was built upon the carrying trade in gold and ivory. Here too, *jihad* was waged against the pagans of the mainland, with profit from slaves taken as prisoners of war. The luxury of the Kilwa sultans and merchants is described by Portuguese writers of the early 16th century.

In 1498, when the Portuguese appeared off Kilwa, local opinion was divided. As one anonymous historian wrote, "some thought that they were good and honest men; but those who knew the truth confirmed that they were corrupt and dishonest persons who had come only to spy out the land in order to seize it."

Both views were extreme. As for seizing the land, the Portuguese were far too few in number to do so. Nevertheless, their possession of firearms was a decisive factor in the taking of Kilwa and Mombasa in 1505, and in their domination of the coast until 1698. In that year the Omani Arabs took the Portuguese Fort Jesus and asserted predominance over all the coast as far as Tungi, just south of the river Ruvuma. It was not wholly effective until about 1827.

In the gold-bearing areas of present-day Zimbabwe great stone fortified kraals were built, with foreign Swahili/Arab settlements at Sena and Tete. Thus wealth was to some extent shared. This was the very southern fringe of the medieval Islamic civilization from which the sons of the sultans of Kilwa were sent abroad to study.

*Arab fort tower, Zanzibar*

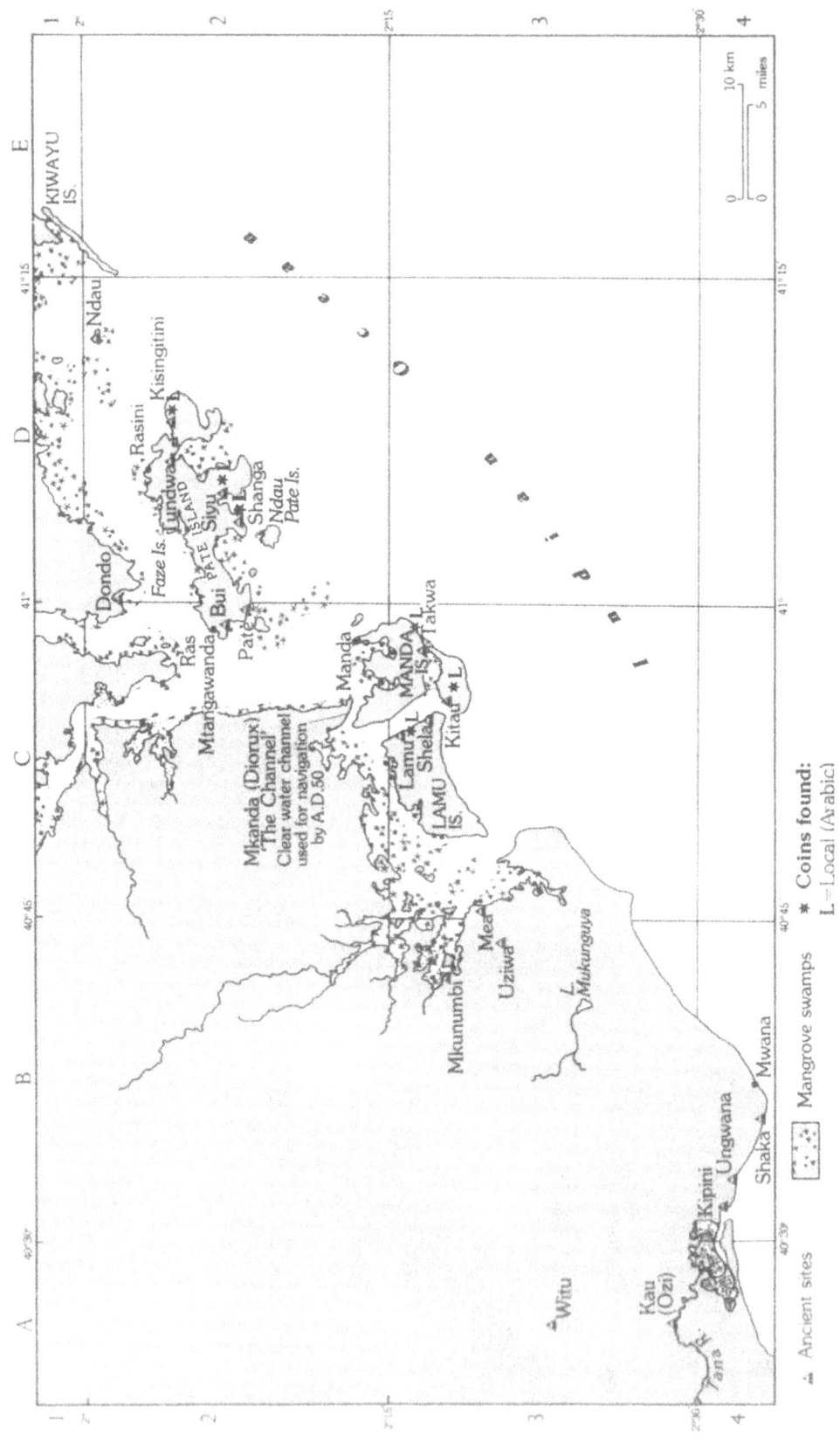

THE LAMU ARCHIPELAGO AND ANCIENT SITES

# THE LAMU ARCHIPELAGO AND ANCIENT SITES

There are no sheltered harbors on the eastern African coast until the islands that form the Lamu archipelago are reached. They are surrounded by a mangrove forest through which a natural channel passes. It is attested already by AD 50 in the *Periplus* of the Erythraean Sea. Flushed twice daily by the tides, this waterway, known as the Mkanda (Swahili) or Diorux (Greek), is the *Channel par excellence* in English. Ivory was the principal export, exchanged for luxury goods, iron ware, and wine; the porters' tracks can still be seen.

From that point until about 750 history is silent. Then twenty-six sites, great and small, attest trade with the Persian Gulf, exchanging ivory and mangrove poles, still the staple trade. At Shanga the ruins of the fifteenth-century Friday mosque rest above the remains of no less than eight successive mosques, the earliest being a simple reed enclosure dating to around 750. This archaeological discovery accords with local traditions that claim trade connections with Damascus and Baghdad at this epoch.

The northernmost island, Pate, claims a dynasty of rulers from about 1200. Its trade connections, from the eighth century at least, later reached India and the Comoro Islands, where its princesses married. Lamu is least known in early history because most of the site was engulfed in sand dunes in the fourteenth century. Numerous mosques, chiefly of the eighteenth and nineteenth centuries, attest its prosperity after the Portuguese departure. Its old-fashioned, elegant Swahili houses are distinctive in design as is its antique furniture of camphorwood and of ebony inlaid with ivory. It is famous for its Swahili poets and literary men, and is also known as a center of pilgrimage for Muslims, who come to venerate a holy man of Arab and Swahili descent, and Comorian birth, in the Mosque College that he founded in 1901.

*The mosque at Ras Mkumbuu, Pemba Island, most likely to be Qanbalu, visited by al-Mas'udi in 916. Courtesy of Mark Horton.*

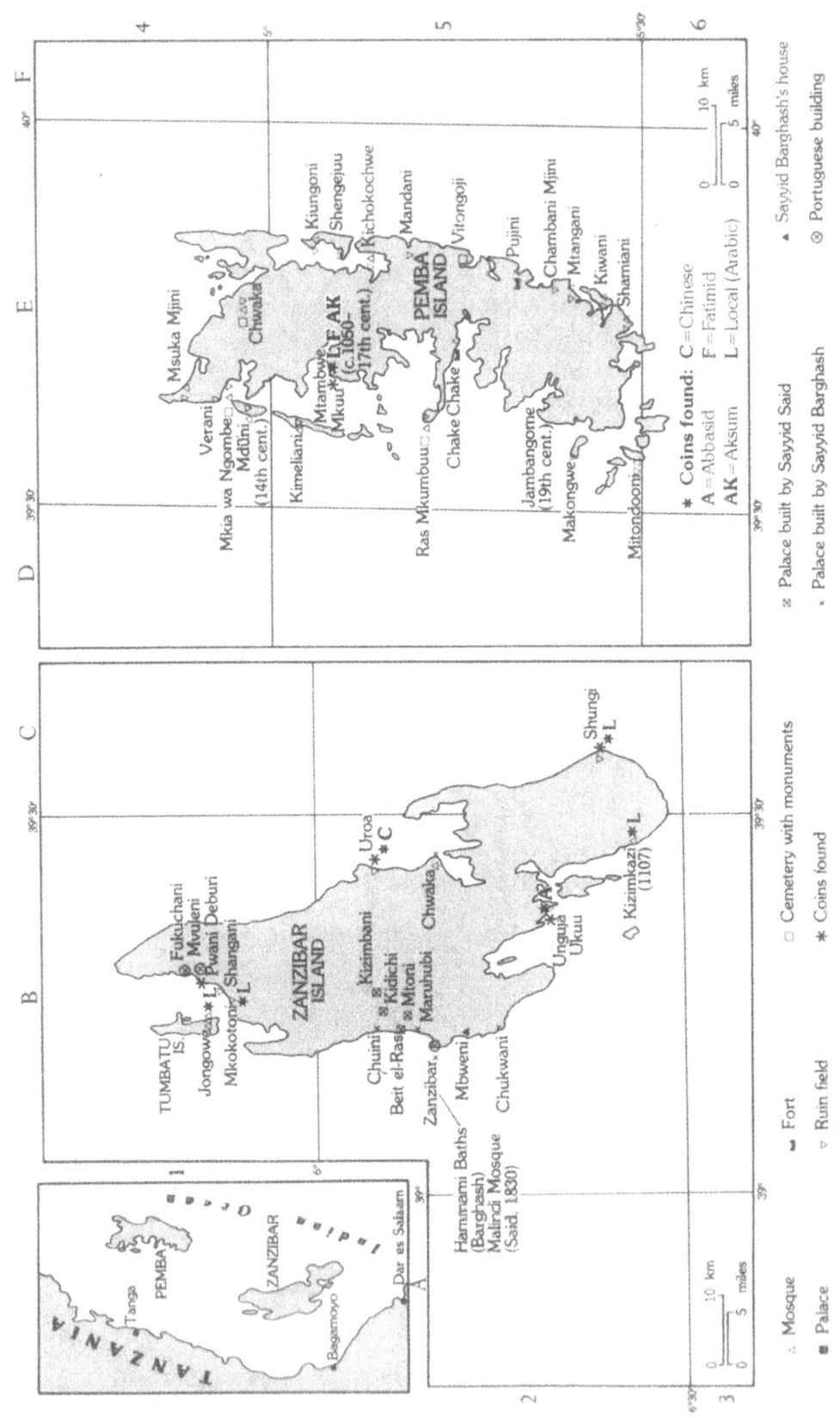

ZANZIBAR AND PEMBA

The history of the islands of Zanzibar and Pemba was not linked until the seventeenth century, when they fell under the suzerainty of Oman. They are part of the area known already by AD 6 as Azania, of which name *Zanzibar* is a mutation. Fishing from dugout canoes, fishing traps made of wicker baskets, and the exporting of tortoiseshell are attested by AD 50. Thereafter, there are occasional references by eighth-century and later Arab writers, and claims that there were local Muslim rulers, there is no solid archaeological evidence before the twelfth century. Stone mosques were built at Kizimkazi on Zanzibar and also on Tumbatu Island with Kufic inscriptions. Their calligraphy was inspired by sculptors at Siraf, in the Persian Gulf, but cut in local stone. Both islands have traditions of different sultans in different parts of the islands.

In the sixteenth century, when the islands became tributary to Portugal, they depended chiefly on agriculture and fishing, while some men took part in the coastal carrying trade in gold, ivory, and other commodities. In or about 1815 the first clove trees were planted, and soon, as a result of the commercial enterprise of Sayyid Said of Muscat and Zanzibar (1804–1856) it had captured the clove trade of the world. Further wealth accrued mid-century and after from slave caravans that reached Lake Malawi and far into the present Zaïre, but it was a commercial rather than a colonial empire. Only on the coast did the ruler exercise any real authority, with local governors and customs posts. A recent

*Astrolabic quadrant used by sailors to locate north-south position*

EASTERN AFRICAN TRADE IN THE INDIAN OCEAN, C. 1500

archaeological survey as a result of the initiative of the Zanzibar government has enabled an historical map to be drawn up. Not least interesting is the long series of coin finds. While those from imperial Rome and from Parthia are somewhat uncertain, local coinage would seem to have been current by the eighth century. There have also been finds of Chinese coins, perhaps connected with the visit of the Chinese admiral Cheng Ho in the fourteenth century.

## EASTERN AFRICAN TRADE IN THE INDIAN OCEAN, C. 1500

We learn of eastern African trade from three vantage points. Ahmad ibn Majid's journals name the ports and give astronomical bearings. Two are Portuguese, Tomé Pires, in Malacca from 1512 to 1515 (before becoming Portuguese ambassador to China), and Duarte Barbosa, in Cannanore on the Malabar coast, around 1517–1518, from whom we learn of the participants and details of their commerce.

Aden was the entrepôt to which merchants from Cairo brought merchandise – chiefly luxury goods – from Italy, Greece, and Syria. From Zeila and Berbera Aden obtained horses as well as Ethiopian slaves who were captured in battle and sent to Asia: none came from farther south. From the Somali ports came local products; gold and ivory came from farther south. The greatest volume of trade from the west and from eastern Africa was directed toward Cambay, India, which in turn was the entrepôt for all the products of Malacca, principally spices. Cambay was a true entrepôt, for the trade with Malacca was conducted by Gujaratis, who brought foreign merchants to Cambay with them, whereupon the latter tended to settle there. These included Cairenes and Ethiopians; men from Kilwa, Malindi, and Mogadishu in East Africa; Persians from various provinces; Greeks from Asia Minor; and Turkomans and Armenians.

The African ports were to some extent specialized. Cambay sent large vessels to Malindi, Mombasa, and Kilwa, selling their goods for gold and then proceeding south as far as Sofala in Mozambique, where trade was carried on with the kingdom of the Monomotapa. Here were collected gold, ivory, and some ambergris, with trade connections reaching out to the far south as far as the Cape. (This much is attested by finds of Chinese porcelain as far south as Port St. John.) Mozambique itself had several smaller ports, which previously had been vassals of the ruler of Kilwa, the chief town of the area. Mombasa too had direct connections with Sofala and Cambay, and it, like its northern neighbor, Malindi, had a rich agriculture. Only Malindi is mentioned as a port having relations with Madagascar, whose many kings, both Moors and heathen, engaged solely in fishing and agriculture and traded with no one. The chief articles taken south were rice, wheat, soap, indigo, butter, lard (ghee?), oils, carnelians, coarse pottery "like that of Seville," and all kinds of cloth. It is perhaps indicative of the wealth of these African cities that they imported food, rice, millet, and some wheat, apart from the obvious imports of luxury textiles.

Excavations in eastern Africa since 1948 have provided a few further details. The quantities of broken Chinese porcelain that litter the beaches and ancient settlements along the eastern African coast are mute evidence of a preference for Chinese porcelain wares. These were not merely used commonly as tableware, but were set into or hung on the walls of houses as decoration and were placed in the more important tombs. Even more prolific are beads, to which it is difficult to assign a provenance; some are certainly from Cambay and Malacca. Finally, an export too commonplace to earn itself mention in literature – the mangrove pole – is nevertheless attested throughout the treeless areas of southern Arabia and in the Persian Gulf by its presence in ancient buildings. The two principal areas from which mangrove poles were harvested were (and still are) the Lamu archipelago and the steamy swamps of the Rufiji delta. Other, smaller areas provided them also.

## ETHIOPIA, 16TH TO 19TH CENTURIES

The early sixteenth century was a turning point for Ethiopia. In 1527 Ahmad Grañ ('left-handed', his nickname), amir of Harar, and virtual ruler of Adal under a puppet sultan, refused tribute to the emperor. Grañ's Danakil and Somali warriors, buoyed up by the amir's desire to launch the *jihad*, but more immediately by the desire for booty, waged war on the Christian empire for thirteen years. By 1541 it was almost lost, and Lebna Dengel had died after fleeing constantly before the Muslim conquest. A small detachment under Cristovão da Gama, grandson of the eminent Vasco, saved the situation together with Emperor Galawdewos, Lebna Dengel's son. Gama was captured, tortured and killed, but the Portuguese artillery won the day. Nevertheless, monasteries and churches had been robbed and looted, and the country reduced to a political and cultural desert.

Harar and the Christian Ethiopian state were to suffer a major blow even as their own conflict continued with amir Nur,

*Amhara two-storey round thatched house, Ethiopia*

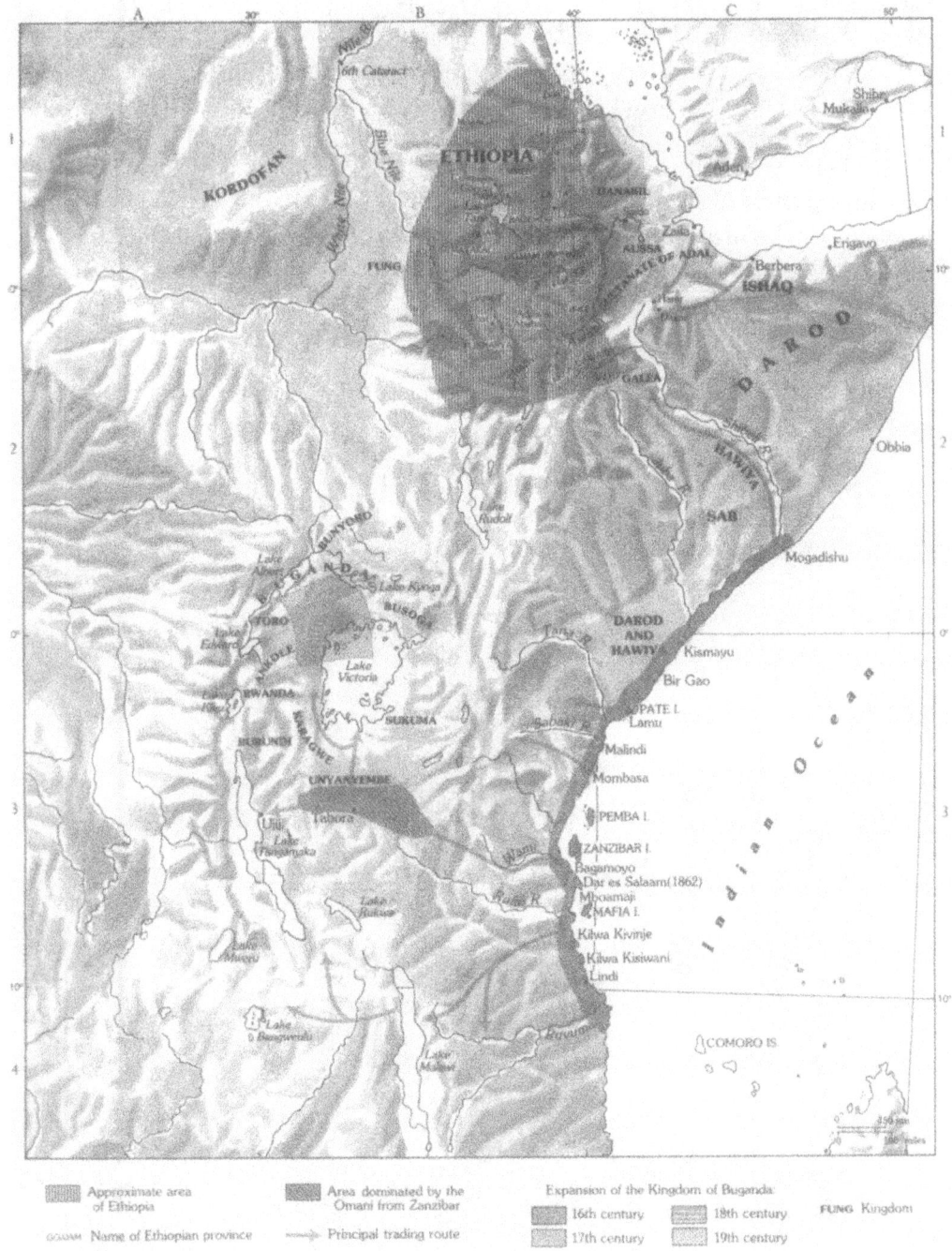

Approximate area of Ethiopia

Area dominated by the Omani from Zanzibar

Expansion of the Kingdom of Buganda:
16th century
17th century
18th century
19th century

GOJAM Name of Ethiopian province

Principal trading route

FUNG Kingdom

# ETHIOPIA AND EASTERN AFRICA, 16TH TO 19TH CENTURIES

Grañ's nephew, in constant war with Emperor Galawdewos (who was killed in the fighting). It was at this time that the Oromo people migrated northwards, destroying all of Harar's territorial influence, and occupying large parts of the Christian highlands as well. As time went on, many of them became Muslim, as they are today. Harar and its offshoot at Aussa survived as independent Muslim sultanates, though Harar's military might was destroyed in battle with Emperor

*191*

Sarsa Dengel of Ethiopia (1563–97). Harar maintained itself by trade, but was seized in the 19th century first by the Egyptians, then, after a very brief restoration, by Menelik of Ethiopia. It is still the chief Muslim town of Ethiopia.

Under Emperor Galawdewos and his successors, a Jesuit mission (1555–1632) failed to comprehend either the theology or the ritual of the Ethiopian church, or to conciliate public opinion and accordingly was expelled on a tide of national feeling. Emperor Fasilidas (1632–1667) founded Gondar, which was to become the fixed capital of the country for some time. It had a special suburb, Islambet or Islamge, in which Emperor Yohannes I (1667–82) decreed that Muslims must live (with another for Jews). The medieval emperors had been peripatetic: the whole court and the senior clergy were organized on a basis of perpetual 'progresses' throughout the empire. It was this that held it together, and the system was not

*Emperor Fasilidas' castle at Gondar, Ethiopia, 16th century*

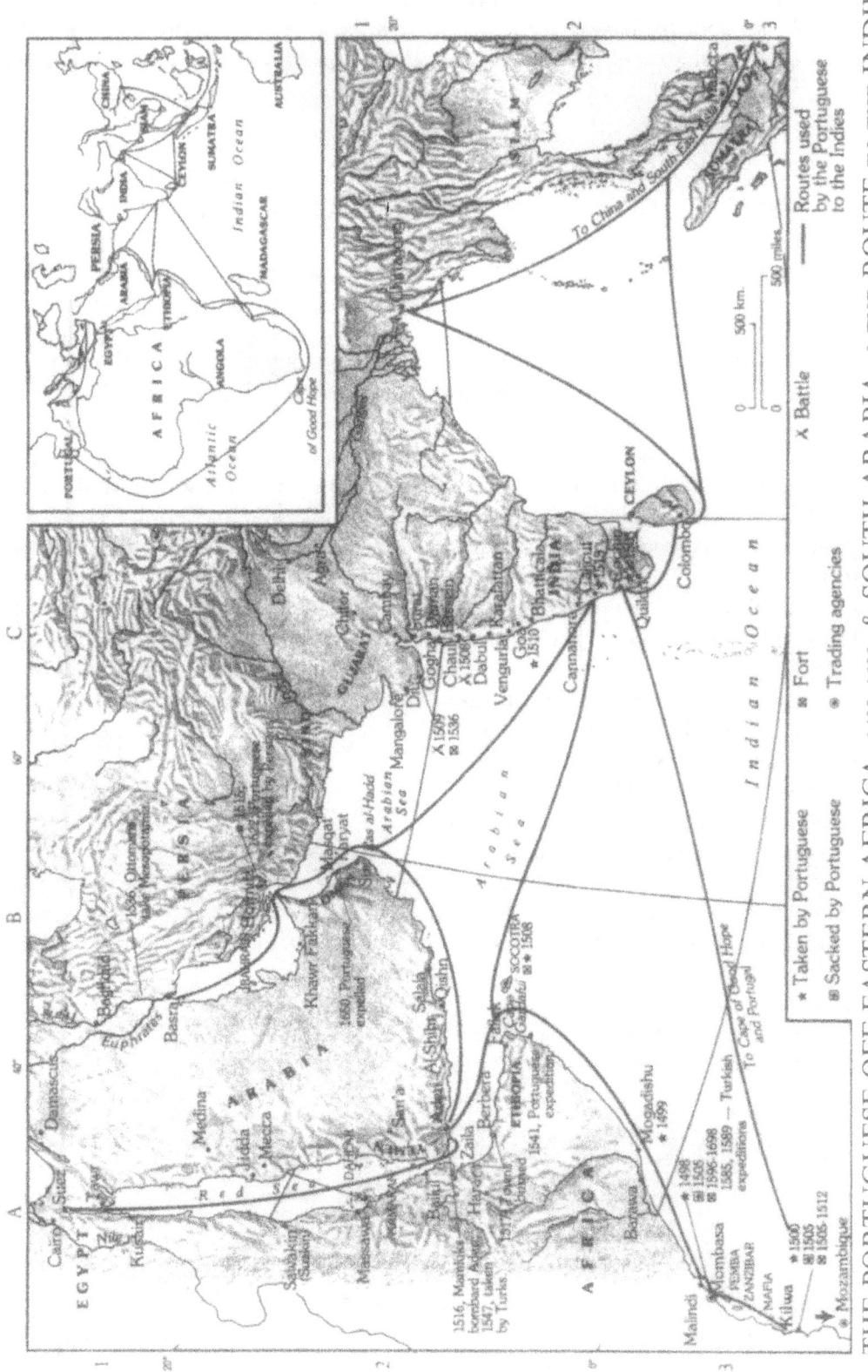

THE PORTUGUESE OFF EASTERN AFRICA, 1498–1698, & SOUTH ARABIA, & THE ROUTE TO THE INDIES

entirely abandoned even if Fasiladas' son Yohannes I, and then Iyasu I, continued to build at Gondar, making it the main rainy season residence of the kings. Iyasu the Great (1680–1704) was the last effective ruler before the emperor Tewodros II (Theodore, 1855–1868): with the isolation of the court from the people, chaos supervened as the empire crumbled amid murders and court intrigues.

## THE PORTUGUESE OFF EASTERN AFRICA, 1498–1698, AND SOUTH ARABIA, AND THE ROUTE TO THE INDIES

Five reasons are said to have prompted the *infante* Henry commonly called Henry the Navigator (although he never went to sea), to promote African discovery: he desired first, to extend geographical knowledge; second, to extend Portuguese trade; third, to discover the real strength of the Moors; fourth, to see whether he might find any Christian prince who could become an ally against them; and finally, "to make increase in the faith of Our Lord Jesus Christ and to bring to him all the souls that should be saved."

His school of cartography, navigation, science, and shipbuilding was established at Sagres in 1415. By the time he died in 1460, Sierra Leone had been reached and a small trade begun. Contact with the Slave Coast of the Bight of Benin belongs to the period 1469–1474, and almost a decade after that the kingdom of Kongo was reached. It was here that the first real attempts at colonial control were made, by conversion to Christianity and the establishment of the kingdom as a vassal of the Portuguese crown. In the Portuguese *feitorias* (factories or trade agencies) commerce began, and, despite papal prohibitions, slaves became the prime object of trade to provide labor for the colony of Brazil.

A second phase, following Bartolemeu Dias's unsuccessful voyage of 1487–1488, was opened by Vasco da Gama's voyage of 1497–1499. After the discovery of the route to India and the establishment of a Portuguese base at Goa, refreshment stations combined with trading posts were established on the eastern African coast. These were never truly profitable, and often barely paid their way. The *infinito ouro* ("infinite gold") that Gama had reported was not there in such quantity or else vanished under the nimble fingers of Swahili and Arab traders. Likewise the Portuguese failed to control the ivory trade so important to India, except when they could ally with one local ruler against a rival, as they did in Pate. Attempts to introduce Christianity were null save in Angola and Mozambique, and successful there largely

*Vasco da Gama*

*The Market at Goa, from* Navigatio in Orientem *1599*

because Portuguese immigrants intermarried and carved out estates. In East Africa missionary effort, begun only in 1596, was ended when the Portuguese Fort Jesus of Mombasa was captured by the rising power of Oman in 1698. The fort still stands, a grim sentinel over Mombasa harbor. The Portuguese were now driven back to Mozambique.

This retreat perhaps meant no great imperial loss, for from Hormuz on the Persian Gulf, bases at Goa and Calicut in India, and at Colombo in Ceylon, trade was maintained that stretched through Malacca to Java, Sulawesi (Celebes), the Moluccas, and as far as Macao. Spices, not gold, were the main source of wealth in the Portuguese eastern empire, and the only serious attempt at conquest or colonization was confined to Brazil. In this the Portuguese were in sharp contrast with the Spanish.

During the seventeenth century the rising star of the Netherlands steadily encroached upon Portuguese interests. By the nineteenth century Cape Verde and Guiné remained, with Angola and Mozambique, in Portugal's sphere of influence. It was only in the 1890s, however, when in the "scramble for Africa" other European powers were seizing African

*Henry the Navigator*

territories, that Portugal began to think in terms of developing their own colonies. They were to become "overseas territories of Portugal," and from them, with the discovery of diamonds in Angola, new wealth began to flow to Lisbon.

## THE DOMINIONS OF OMAN IN EAST AFRICA, 1698–1913

In the mid-seventeenth century Oman chafed under the declining Portuguese hegemony in the Indian Ocean. Around 1650 a delegation was sent from Mombasa to Oman, asking assistance to expel the Portuguese, but no serious response was made until 1696. Superficially, these events might look like the early emergence of nationalism; however, in reality these acts resulted from the ivory trade, in which Mombasa's rival, Pate, had a successful partnership with Masqat.

An Omani fleet was sent to besiege the Portuguese Fort Jesus in 1696 — a long, drawn-out, and inconclusive affair in which Swahilis from Pate played a major part. Disease overcame the defenders, and from 1698 the Omanis had nominal authority from Mogadishu to the Ruvuma River. In practice their control was little more than a series of custom posts, which, needless to say, the locals did all they could to evade. In Mombasa the governorship had become hereditary within the Mazrui family, which had made itself virtually independent. The real author of the new system was Sa'id ibn Sultan (r. 1806–1856), who visited Mombasa in 1827 and brought many eastern African ports under his control. In 1828 he visited Zanzibar, where he introduced clove production on confiscated property. From 1832 until 1840 he alternated residences between Masqat and Zanzibar, moving to Zanzibar in 1840. Zanzibar now became the leading commercial center in eastern Africa, trading in ivory, copal, slaves, hides, and other local products. Coastal cities shared in the growing prosperity, as caravans set out from the coast to the interior, seeking ivory and slaves, and thus reversing the age-old system by which Africans had brought products to the coast. Under Sa'id ibn Sultan's successors the British forced an end to the slave trade and, finally, slavery; and established a protectorate, which was placed under the authority of the British colonial office in 1911.

*Padrão dos descobrimentos—Monument to the Discoveries, built on the 500th anniversary of the death of Prince Henry the Navigator, Lisbon*

# THE DOMINIONS OF OMAN IN EAST AFRICA, 1698–1913

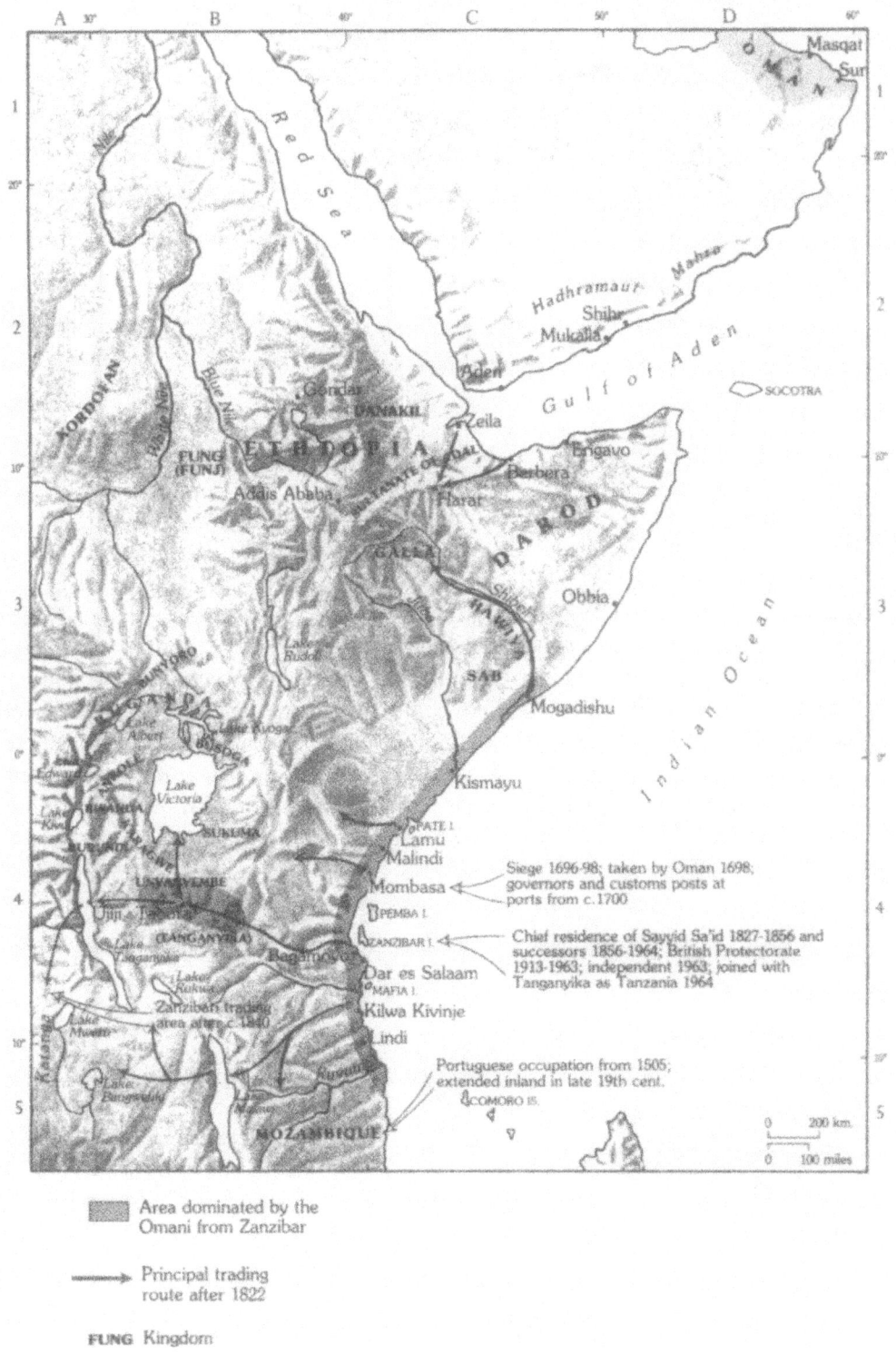

# WESTERN AFRICA — PHYSICAL

*The mud-brick mosque at Jenné, Mali*

By Western Africa is meant an arbitrary area bounded on the north by the Sahara Desert, and on the west and south by the Atlantic Ocean and on the east by the former colonial boundaries with Chad and Cameroun. It includes Senegal, Gambia, Guiné, Guinea, Sierra Leone, Liberia, Côte d'Ivoire, Ghana, Volta, Togo, Benin and Nigeria. It is an area of a multiplicity of peoples and languages: in one of the smallest, Togo, there are four languages in no way comprehensible to each other. The area is watered by four great rivers, the Senegal, the Gambia, and the Niger, together with its tributary the Benue, and the Volta, which arise in mountains in the northern perimeter. These rivers, navigable for small vessels for much of their courses, have long provided a means of communication. Before modern times, paradoxically, the desert was the

*Tuareg tribesmen in the Sahara Desert*

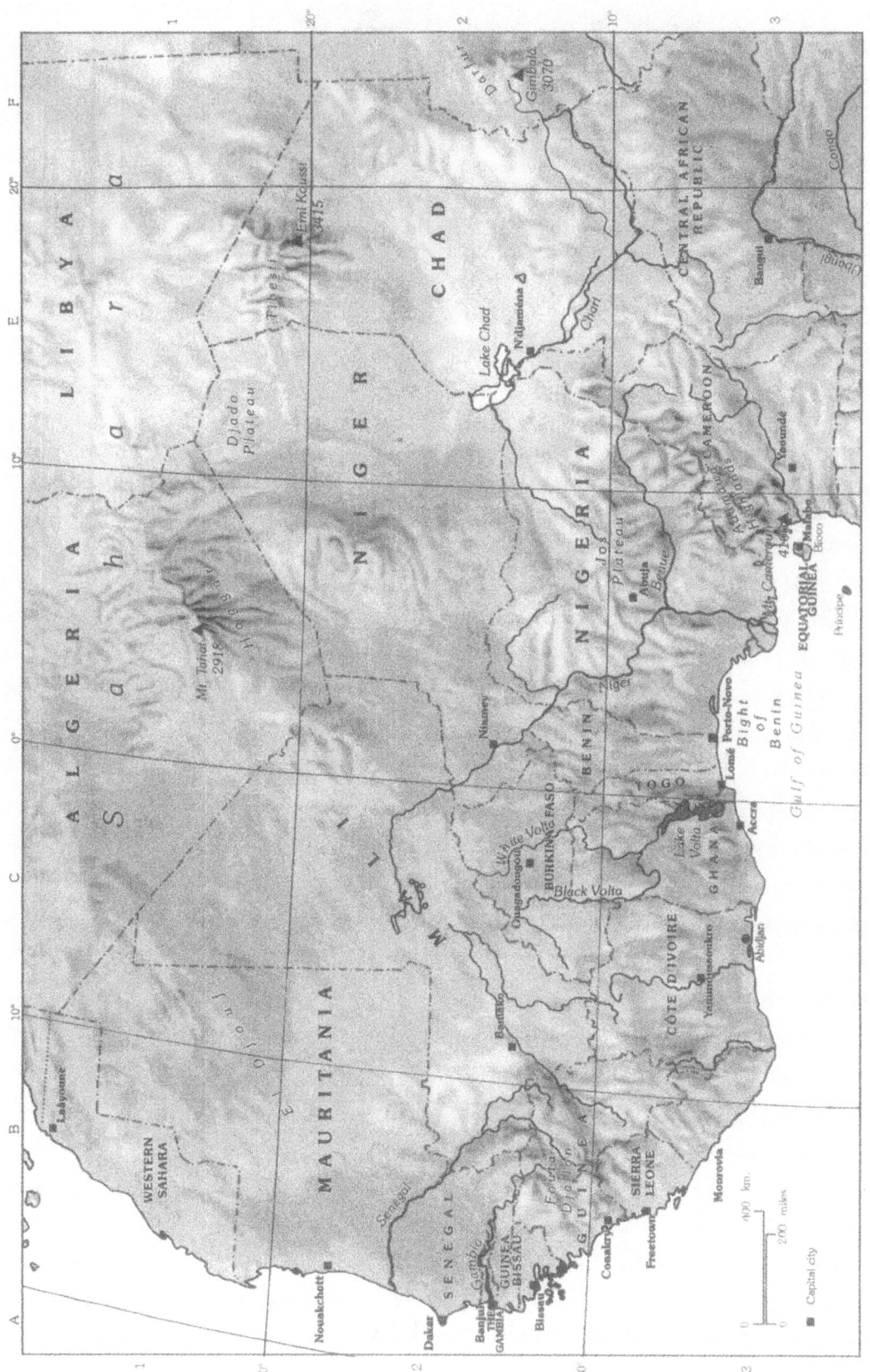

WESTERN AFRICA — PHYSICAL

most important highway; the Tuareg peoples crossed it for salt, gold, gums and slaves. The camel was introduced ca. 46 BC, thus facilitating trade. It was this connection which brought Islam to the area in the eighth century; it is now the dominant religion in most areas.

Broadly speaking, a coastal band extends from the mouths of the Senegal to the Cameroun mountains, and is covered with thick tropical rain forest, behind which is a thicker band of woodland savannah, which slowly gives way to open savannah. Before the desert is reached there is a further band of thorn bush savannah. There are no natural ports other than Dakar, Freetown and Lagos. Elsewhere the sea forms a dangerous barrier with surf, backed by mangrove swamps and sands. The river mouths are blocked by rapids and shallows, especially the mouths of the Niger. Apart from fishermen who do not venture far, there is no tradition of seamanship.

*Dye pits in Kano, Nigeria*

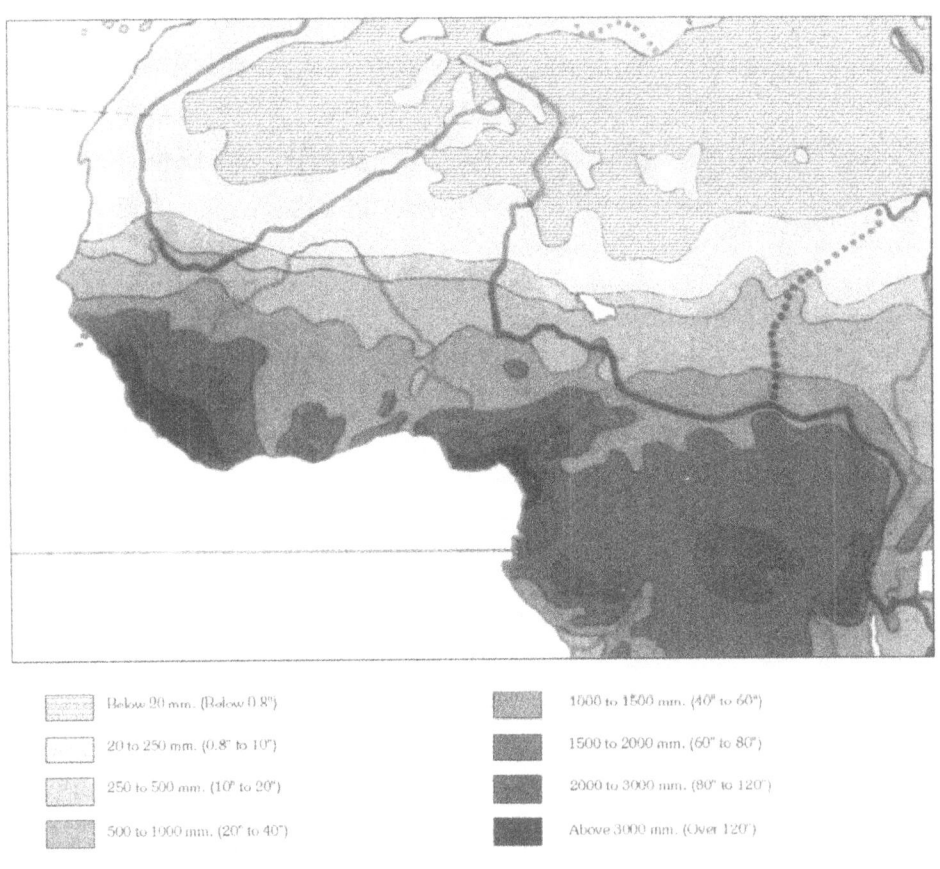

Below 20 mm. (Below 0.8")
20 to 250 mm. (0.8" to 10")
250 to 500 mm. (10" to 20")
500 to 1000 mm. (20" to 40")
1000 to 1500 mm. (40" to 60")
1500 to 2000 mm. (60" to 80")
2000 to 3000 mm. (80" to 120")
Above 3000 mm. (Over 120")

**WESTERN AFRICA — ANNUAL RAINFALL**

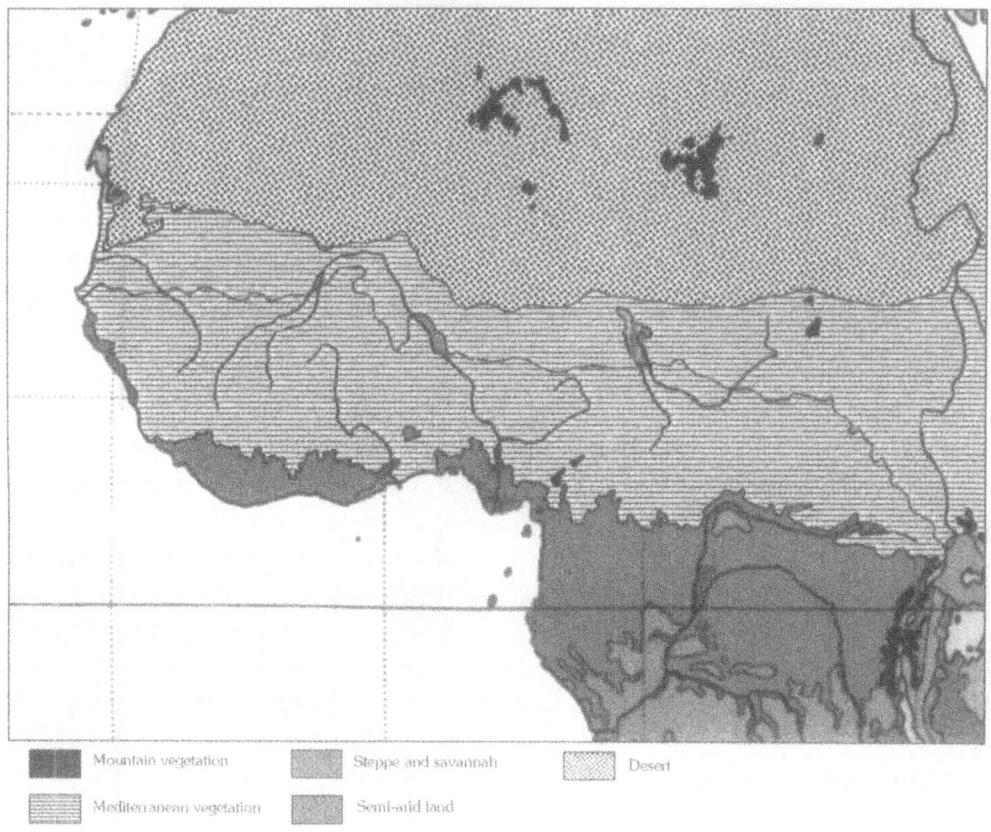

## WESTERN AFRICA — VEGETATION

The magnetic equator crosses the southern coast. The average temperature is 70°F, and rains fall heavily in July and January. Near the coast the climate can be unpleasantly moist. In historical times the main occupations have been agricultural. Gold mining was confined largely to the present Mali, the ancient Ghana. Slaves for export to the north were provided from prisoners taken in inter-tribal wars, apart from the human sacrifices of the ancient kingdom of

*Reed thatched houses built on stilts in river lagoons, Nigeria*

Pasture land and scrub vegetation

Tropical forest

Tropical crops

Irrigated or watered land

## WESTERN AFRICA — AGRICULTURE AND LIVESTOCK

Dahomey, now renamed Benin. Today cultivated cocoa palms provide the principal export of Ghana for the chocolate trade. Anciently pepper was an important export (*malagueta* pepper), but today that of south-east Asia is preferred. In modern times highly profitable and important exports of oil, from Nigeria, and of industrial diamonds from Sierra Leone, have been developed. The forests furnish timber for export, and there are also some exports of other minerals and rubber, the latter chiefly from Liberia.

The heavy rainfall in the tropical rain forest provides a fertile breeding ground for the *anopheles* mosquito, causing malaria, and also for tsetse fly, noxious to humans and to cattle, and various worm-borne diseases.

*Dogon village in Mali*

# THE WESTERN SUDAN IN THE 11TH CENTURY

During the eighth century Berbers and Arabs penetrated the Sahara, by the coastal route from the Wadi Draa, and by northern and western routes from Tripoli and from the Nile, and mingled with the local people. The kingdom of Kanem is claimed to have been founded around 800; in 1085 the tenth ruler became a Muslim. The capital was at Njimi, west of Lake Chad.

Farther west, along the Niger bend, at some time during the seventh century, white nomads established the kingdom of Songhai in the region of Gao. They too intermingled with the local population, and became wholly identified with it. Unlike Kanem, with its Arab founders, these were Berbers of the Lamta and Howara tribes from Tripolitania. They had traveled down the ancient route known to the charioteers of Tassili 'n-Ajjer, the Hoggar and the Tilemsi valley. The capital was at Kukia, some ninety miles south of Gao; its kings, or dias, had authority over the river valley as far as it. Around 1010 Dia Kossoi became a Muslim, reflecting, as later in the century in Kanem, closer commercial links with Fatimid and North African prosperity.

A third kingdom was Ghana. Perhaps even in Carthaginian times it had exported its gold northward. Certainly the trade had begun by the beginning of the Christian era. The mines were in Bambuk, between the rivers Falémé and Senegal, and to the west of Niani. In 734 an Arab caravan brought back gold from the region; in 745 the Arabs established a series of wells along the caravan route as far as the mines, a sure indication of enhanced trade. According to tradition Ghana had forty-four white (Berber) rulers from the fourth century, but nothing is known of them or how their kingdom was organized. In the eighth century they were partly expelled by the Soninke, whose authority stretched over the greater part of the region by the tenth century. Gold was not the sole article of commerce: salt from Teggazza was no less important. In 977 the Arab geographer Ibn Hawqal speaks of the wealth of the trade. Another Arab, al-Bakri of Córdoba, writing in 1077, describes the wealth and gorgeous ceremonial of the court of Ghana, whose kings even had their horse harnesses decorated with gold.

*Pure gold mask from the treasure of an Ashanti king, Ghana*

*Caravan resting, al-Hariri MS, dated 1237*

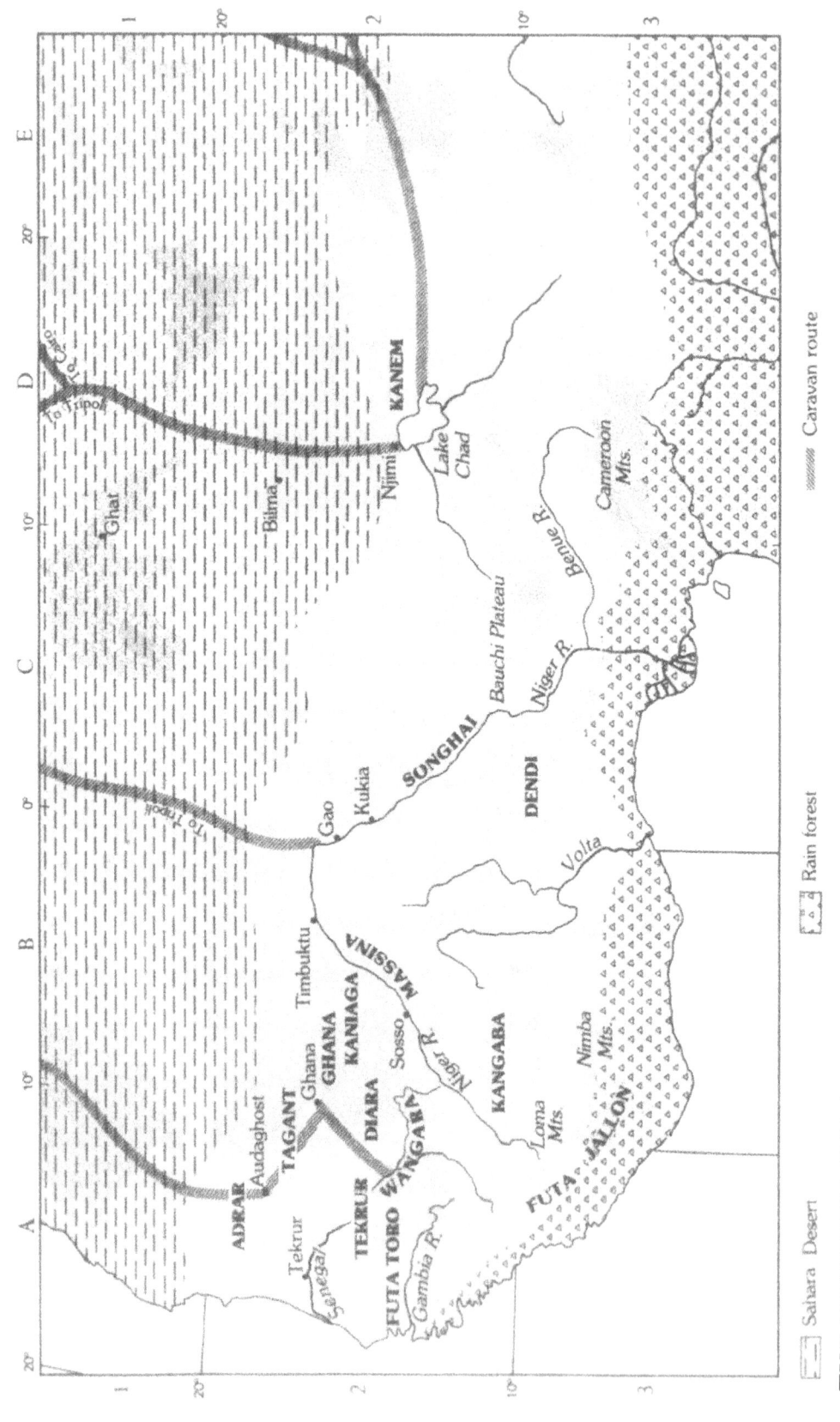

THE WESTERN SUDAN IN THE 11TH CENTURY

# THE WESTERN SUDAN IN THE 12TH TO 14TH CENTURIES

The empire of Ghana broke up at the end of the eleventh century into a number of kingdoms, in some of which the kings and their courts became Muslims. Among the masses the adoption of Islam meant no more than a new syncretism. Sosso took a large part of Ghana, and in 1224 took Walata, an oasis that now became a center of trade and Islamic teaching. Ghana itself became Muslim in the course of the century. In 1235 Sumanguru Kante of Sosso was overcome by Sundiata Keita, the son of a petty Mandingo ruler. He succeeded in establishing Mali as a larger empire than Ghana had ever been, controlling all the gold-bearing regions from Bundu to Mossi (1235–1255). Nominally Muslim, even today sacrifices are made to his name. The apogee of this empire was reached under the fabled Kankan Mansa Musa (1312–1335). His brilliant reign and splendid pilgrimage to Mecca are recorded by Ibn Khaldun, the greatest of the Muslim historians. In Cairo, Kankan Mansa Musa gave so much gold in alms as to depreciate the dinar. With a capital at Timbuktu, his empire stretched from the Atlantic to Gao on the Niger bend. It was visited by Ibn Battuta in 1352–1353.

*Trading fort at Anomabu, Ghana. Many such forts were built to defend European traders to West Africa*

As the century wore on, the empire slowly dissolved, although the dynasty ended only in 1645. To the east, among Hausa-speaking peoples, a number of states had developed in the tenth century. Unfortunately, most of their written records were destroyed in the nineteenth century, except in Kano. One at least paid tribute to Bornu, which as yet was not Islamized. To the south, unknown to the Arab historians, great kingdoms had evolved among the Nupe and the Yoruba in the present Nigeria. The cities of Benin and Ife, and Oyo on the fringe of their forest region, developed cultures of their own which were wholly unaffected by the outside world until the Portuguese made contact with them in the later fifteenth century. The peak of their prosperity was in the thirteenth to fourteenth century.

*Engraving of a fortress-like mosque in the Gonja kingdom, Ghana*

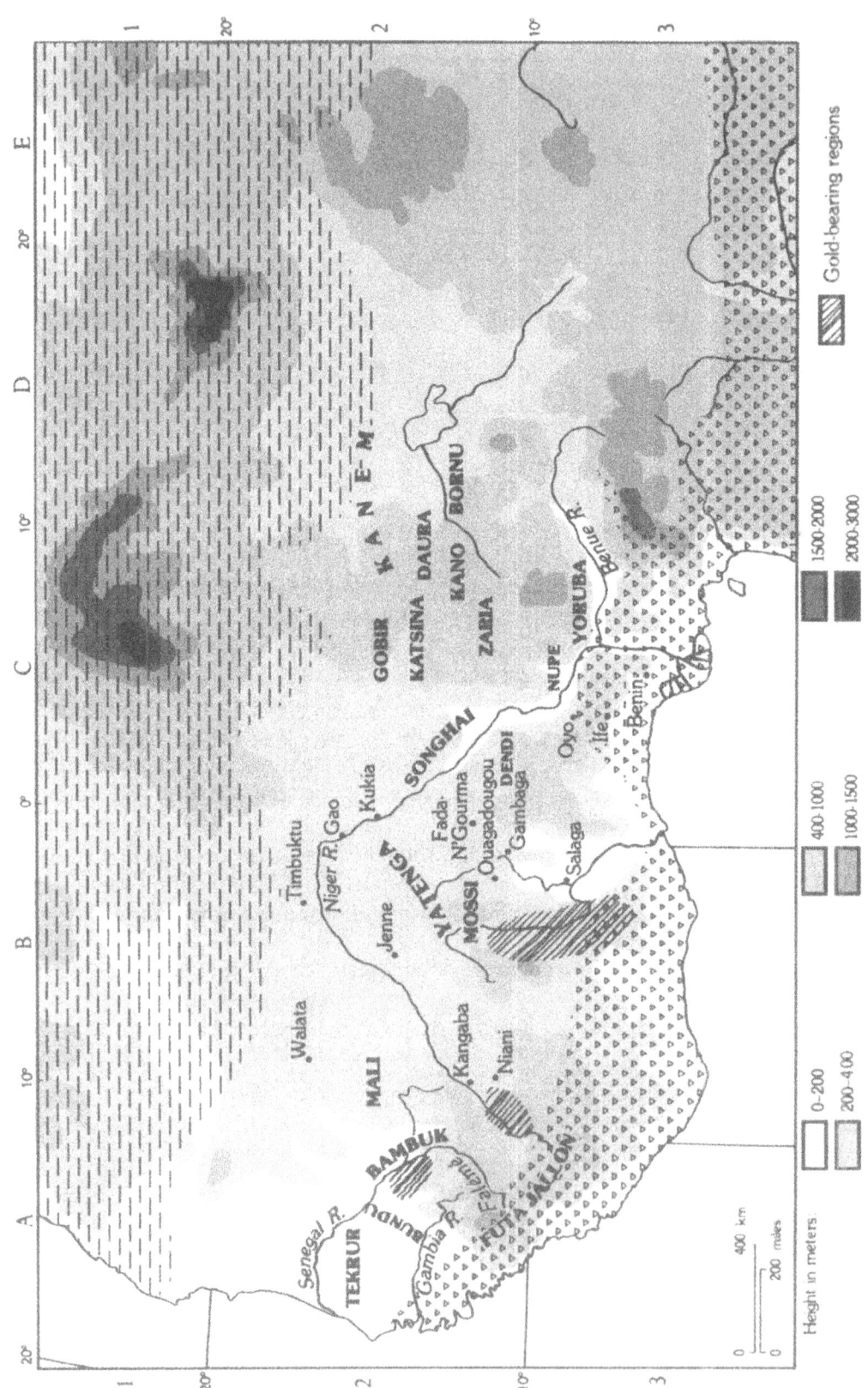

THE WESTERN SUDAN IN THE 12TH TO 14TH CENTURIES

# NORTHERN AFRICAN TRADE WITH THE WESTERN SUDAN, 13TH–14TH CENTURIES.

By the mid-thirteenth century the Almohad empire had disintegrated. It had already ended in Spain in 1212. In 1235 the emir of Tlemcen created the independent Abdulwahid kingdom. In 1236 an independent Hafsid dynasty had been proclaimed. In 1248 the King of León and Castile had taken Seville, leaving only Granada to the Muslims. In the same year the Marinids took much of Morocco, finally seizing Marrakesh in 1269 and killing the last of the Almohads. The new kingdoms were soon in treaty relations with the leading Christian commercial centers – Venice, Pisa, Genoa, and Sicily – and with the new Mamluk sultanate in Egypt and its extension in Syria. Their existence was by no means untroubled, for they were harried in Tunisia and further west by the Banu Sulaim, nomads who had originated in Tripolitania. They attacked the oases that controlled the routes of the southern Sahara, and then Bougie, Bône, and Tunis itself. At Bougie they established the first organized pirate center which made Barbary a byword in later centuries. These cities were only recovered in 1370. At the end of the century the Hafsids held the coast from Tripoli to Biskra, and in 1410 they had extended their reach as far as Algiers. Piracy now spread from Bougie to Tunis and Bizerta. In 1235 Tlemcen had freed itself from the Almohads. It was the entrepôt for the western Sudan as well as an important religious center. From Fez in the fourteenth century the Marinids pursued a career of conquest as far as Tunis, but were repulsed at Kairouan in 1347. The dynasty is especially notable for the glory of their public buildings in Meknès, Salé, Fez el-Jadid, Fez el-Bali, and Marrakesh. These owed much to Moorish refugees from Spain. Of particular importance were the *medersas* (classical, *madrasas*), institutes of advanced religious learning, from which the Qadiriya *tariqa*, or Sufi confraternity, propagated their ideas and devotional practices along the trade routes to south of the Sahara. The conversion to Islam of large tracts of western Africa was to a great extent the work of the Qadiriya. At the same time

*Gate of the city wall of Meknès*

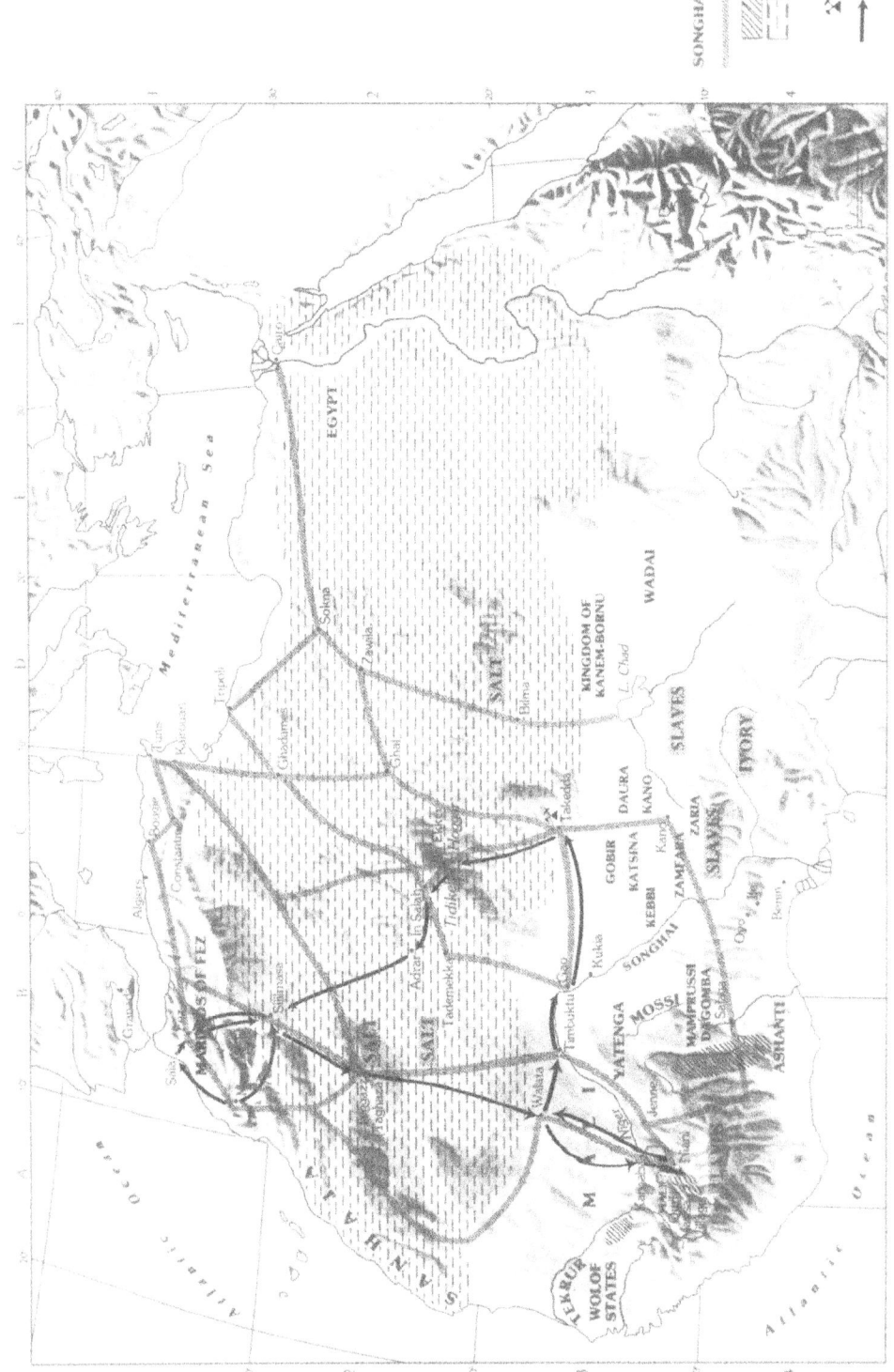

NORTHERN AFRICAN TRADE WITH THE WESTERN SUDAN, 13TH TO 14TH CENTURIES

*The fortress at Monastir, Tunisia*

their toleration of the cult of saints and holy places made possible the absorption and syncretism of earlier religious thought and practice.

Ibn Battuta's journey to Mali and back in 1352–1353 was the last of his adventures which had taken him from Tangier to Cairo and Mecca, the Yemen, East Africa, India, the Maldives and the Far East. Salt, slaves, and gold were the main stock-in-trade that flowed northward, a trade that was long established. Mali had already sent an embassy to Fez when he was in East Africa in 1331. Mali, moreover, looked in another direction, and in 1310 had sent a fleet of canoes into the Atlantic to ascertain whether there might be land westward. It was a total disaster, for only one vessel returned. Kankan Mansa Musa's journey to Mecca with an

*Great Friedrichsburg, the Brandenburg Colony on the Coast of Guinea, 1688*

immense retinue shows how well organized for water supplies were the desert mercantile routes. Gold was the primary source of prosperity, as was commemorated in England by the coin known as the guinea. Of importance, too, were the copper mines of Takedda; copper was exported also to the south. There, on the Bauchi plateau of modern Nigeria, local tin was used as an alloy to make funeral masks by the *cire-perdue* (lost-wax) method. Away to the east, bordering on Lake Chad, the kingdom of Kanem-Bornu had its own routes to Tripoli and to Cairo. Other routes connected it with the Fezzan and with Wadai. Theoretically a Muslim land, it remained obstinately pagan, venerating the king as a god whose face was to be veiled from the eyes of the crowd.

*Sankore Mosque, Timbuktu, 14th–15th centuries*

## THE MOROCCAN CONQUEST OF SONGHAI, 1590–1753

Songhai is remarkable among African states for the continuity of its history and relative stability from about 800 until the Moroccan conquest in 1591. It was founded at Gao by a dynasty which converted to Islam around 1100. The next three hundred years were years of prosperity and expansion. About 1375 Songhai fell under the empire of Mali, and its fortunes were bound up with those of Timbuktu.

This prosperity was based principally on Songhai's control of the gold export of the Akan states in Guinea, and its control of the caravan routes. Along these routes in the Teghazza region not less important were the salt mines, whose product was used not only for consumption but in certain places as currency. Further, the frequent wars in which the Songhai rulers engaged made it a primary source for slaves. (Statistics are difficult to obtain, but it seems that Morocco had 150,000 slaves in the eighteenth century.) These commercial activities were confined to a relatively small merchant class, the mass of the people being agriculturalists.

All these branches of commerce supplied principally Songhai's neighbor Morocco, which had long cast envious eyes on the salt mines and resented the customs dues. During the reign of the *askia* Dawud (1549–1582) Morocco conducted raids on the salt deposits. These continued under his successors, and, finally, under Ishaq II, Sharif Ahmad al-Mansur of Morocco sent Judar Pasha across the desert with four thousand men. Judar himself was a renegade Spaniard, and his army included riffraff from England, France, Italy and Spain. Only fifteen hundred were true Moroccans. Altogether only

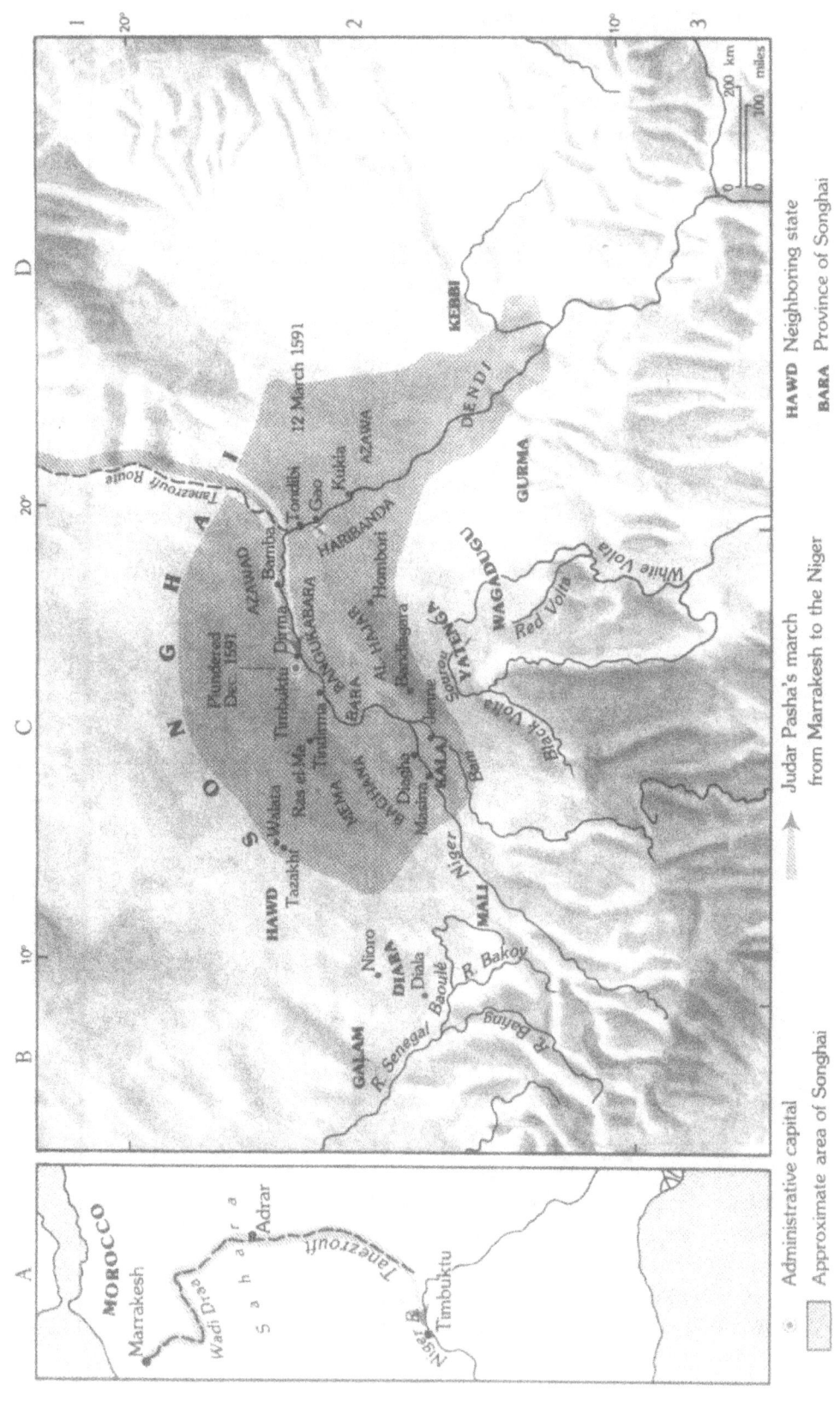

THE MOROCCAN CONQUEST OF SONGHAI, 1590–1753

some one thousand men completed the journey, but their possession of firearms, which Songhai did not have, made conquest inevitable. Talleyrand was later to remark that war is far too important a matter to be left to military men. Here, having conquered and occupied the capital, Judar's troops proved themselves incapable of ruling in peace. Soon the position of pasha was filled by popular acclaim. There followed 150 pashas in the course of 162 years, a period of instability that ruined a hitherto prosperous economy.

## THE WESTERN SUDAN IN THE 16TH AND 17TH CENTURIES

By the sixteenth century, European slave traders, led by the Portuguese, increasingly dominated the coast from the river Senegal as far as Angola. Soon the Bight of Benin would be thick with their forts, as they traded in textiles, liquor, and arms, provoking slave-catching wars and expeditions. Up to 1600 Spain and Portugal were the chief participants in the transatlantic slave trade, aided by the African chiefs of the hinterland. The Portuguese concentrated especially on Angola, a source of silver as well as slaves.

Farther north, Songhai had been seized by a Moroccan army in 1590, which held it nominally until 1753. After the first honeymoon of conquest its progressive

*The renowned trading depot of Timbuktu in the Sahara, Mali*

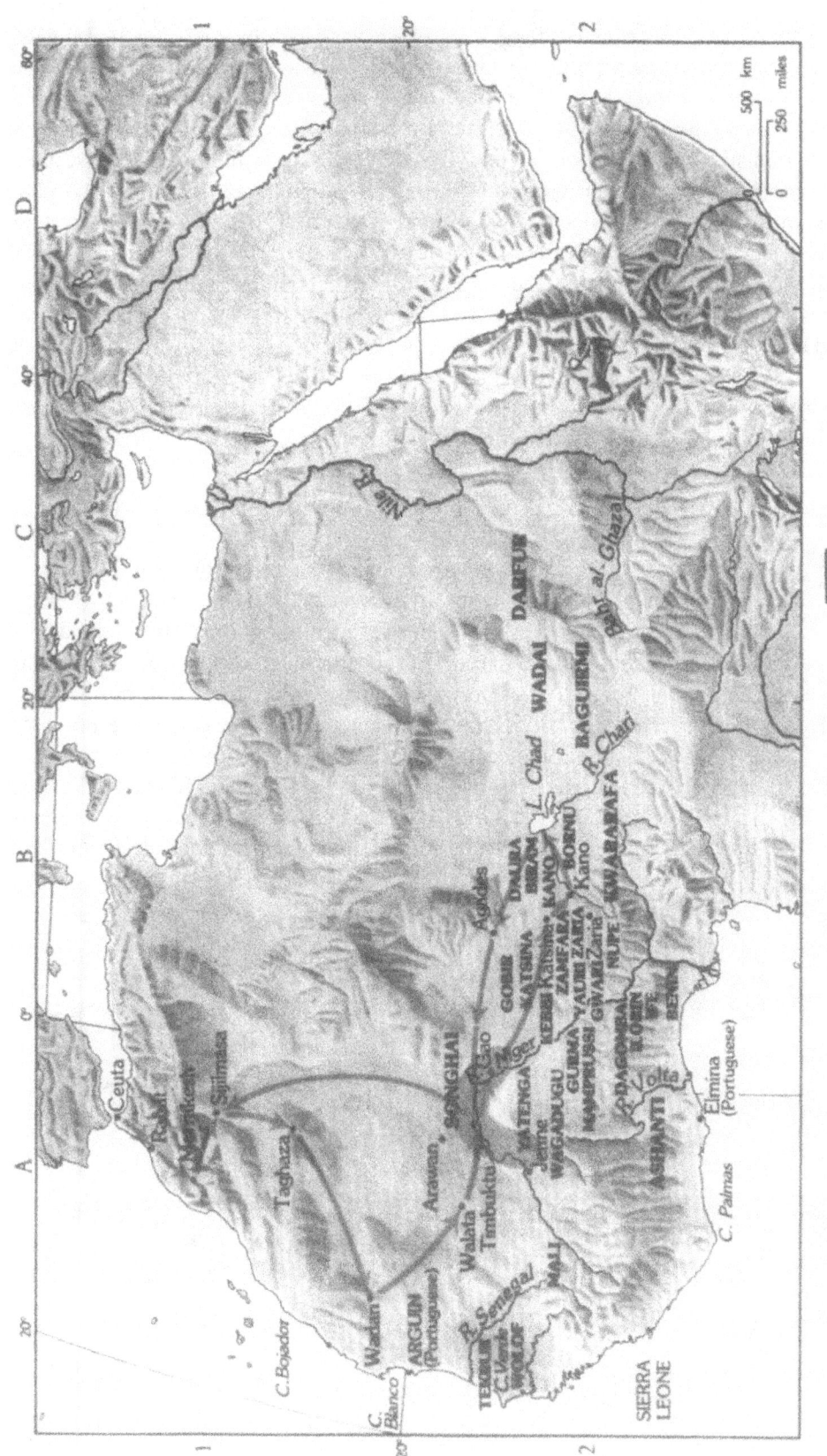

THE WESTERN SUDAN, 16TH AND 17TH CENTURIES

weakness was evident from the instability of its governance. Nevertheless it served Morocco as a recruiting ground in which to catch slaves. For the rest it was a time of disorder, during which the white Tuareg nomads had every opportunity to rob the sedentary black agriculturalists to the south as far as the Niger.

In the east the rulers of Kanem had moved their capital from the northeast of Lake Chad to Bornu, southwest of the lake. Here Mai Idris Alooma (c. 1571 or 1580 to 1603 or 1617) made Bornu a great power in the region. He had trade relations with the Ottomans of Tripoli and Tunis, who provided him with arms. These were employed in well-organized raids to provide quantities of slaves. The ever-aggressive Tuareg later undermined Bornu and brought it to ruin. Farther east three states emerged and gradually grew in importance: Baguirmi, Wadai, and Darfur. They likewise raided and forwarded slaves to the Ottomans. North of the river Benue the city states of what is now northern Nigeria had little stability and fought among themselves as well as against the Tuareg and other nomads. They did not find unity until the nineteenth century.

## THE WESTERN SUDAN IN THE 18TH AND 19TH CENTURIES

In the seventeenth century the Dutch had come to dominate the slave trade, with smaller competitors in Brandenburg, Denmark, and England. During the eighteenth century the English overtook the Dutch and became the dominant force in the area into the nineteenth century and up to the colonial period. This was the peak of the Atlantic slave trade, but now with an ever-increasing number of slaves going to North-American plantations. The trade was fed by the African kingdoms that served the European traders on the coast in what became a symbiotic relationship between African and European to the point of frequent interbreeding. The names of many of the English, Irish, and Portuguese traders are perpetuated in present-day Ghana and elsewhere. In Benin (then

*The town of Kano, at the southern end of the Sahara trade routes*

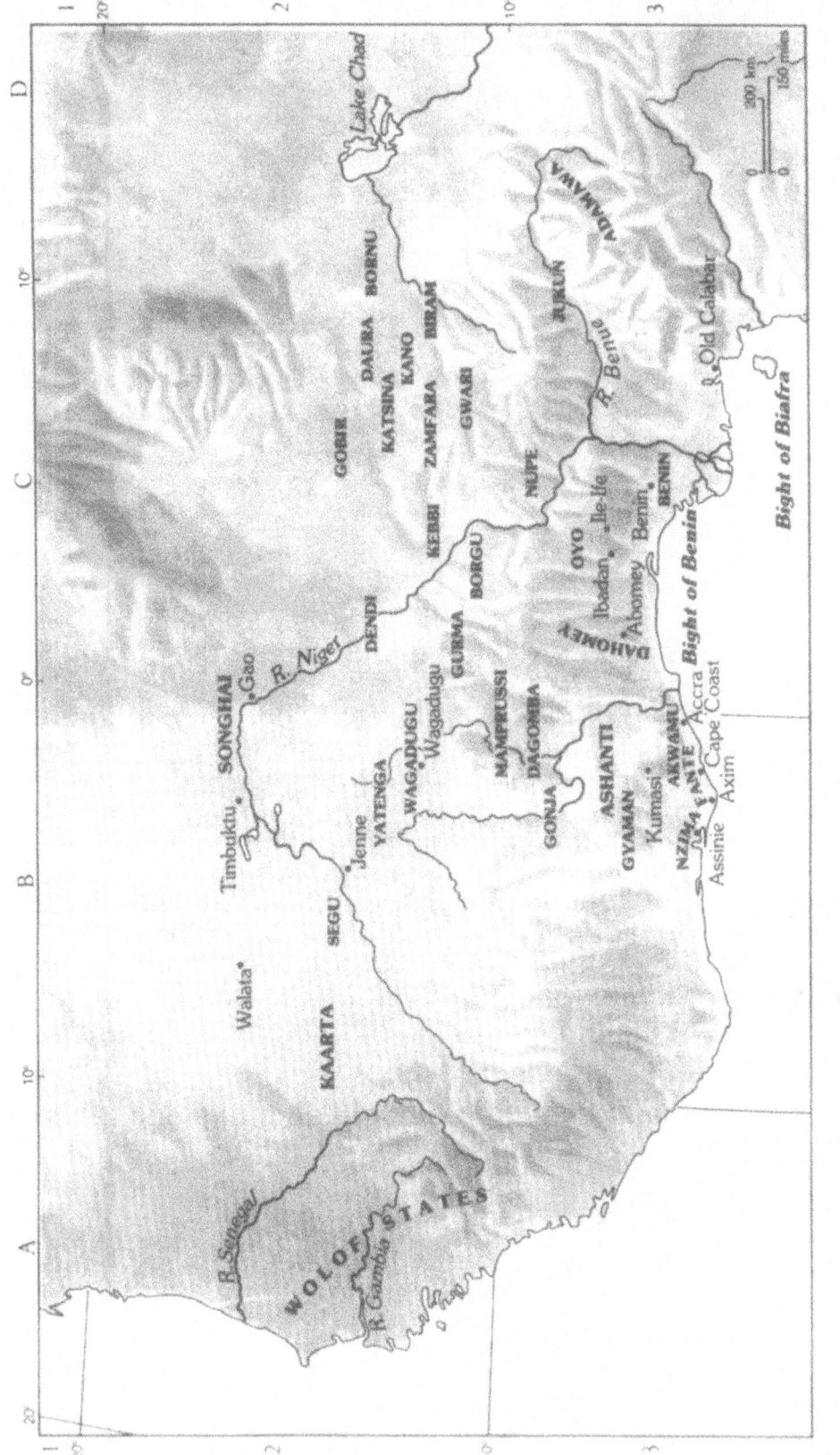

THE WESTERN SUDAN, 18TH AND 19TH CENTURIES

named Dahomey or Abomey) the rulers became a byword for the export and ritual sacrifice of slaves.

The most important development took place in Northern Nigeria, where in the Hausa states Usman dan Fodio established a new Islamic empire with Sokoto as capital. On a military basis it united the whole area as far as Bornu and Adamawa. It was an intellectual and religious movement as well as a military one, and its founder spent the last years of his life solely in religious exercises and pious study.

In Segu in 1818 a similar movement, led by Shehu Ahmadu Lobbo, conquered Jenne and Timbuktu. A puritan and mystic, Shehu Ahmadu rigorously enforced Islamic law. Farther west an adherent of the Tijaniyya dervish confraternity, Omar Sedu Tal, conquered first Bambuk and Kaarta, and then Segu and Macina. He had previously made long stays in Mecca and Cairo, and then spent thirteen years preaching in Futa Jallon. He died in mysterious circumstances in 1864.

In the eastern part of the region near Lake Chad trade was maintained with the north and with Egypt and the Nile Valley.

## (V) SOUTH-EAST ASIA

## SOUTH-EAST ASIA — PHYSICAL

The term South-East Asia includes the modern countries of peninsular 'Indo-China', Myanmar (Burma), Thailand, Laos, Vietnam, Cambodia, and part of Malaysia, together with the archipelago that lies between the Indian Ocean and the Pacific Ocean. This includes other parts of Malaysia (Sabah, Sarawak) and Brunei, the whole of Indonesia, the Philippines and the United Nations' administered territory of East Timor.

Formed by the meeting of the Indian Ocean and Pacific plates, the South East Asian archipelago's outer rim describes a great curve of volcanic activity from Sumatra to Sumbawa, and round to the Philippines. Borneo and Sulawesi occupy the centre of this arc, with peninsular Malaya to the west. The Malay region is joined to the northern mainland by the

*Tropical forest vegetation, Malaysia*

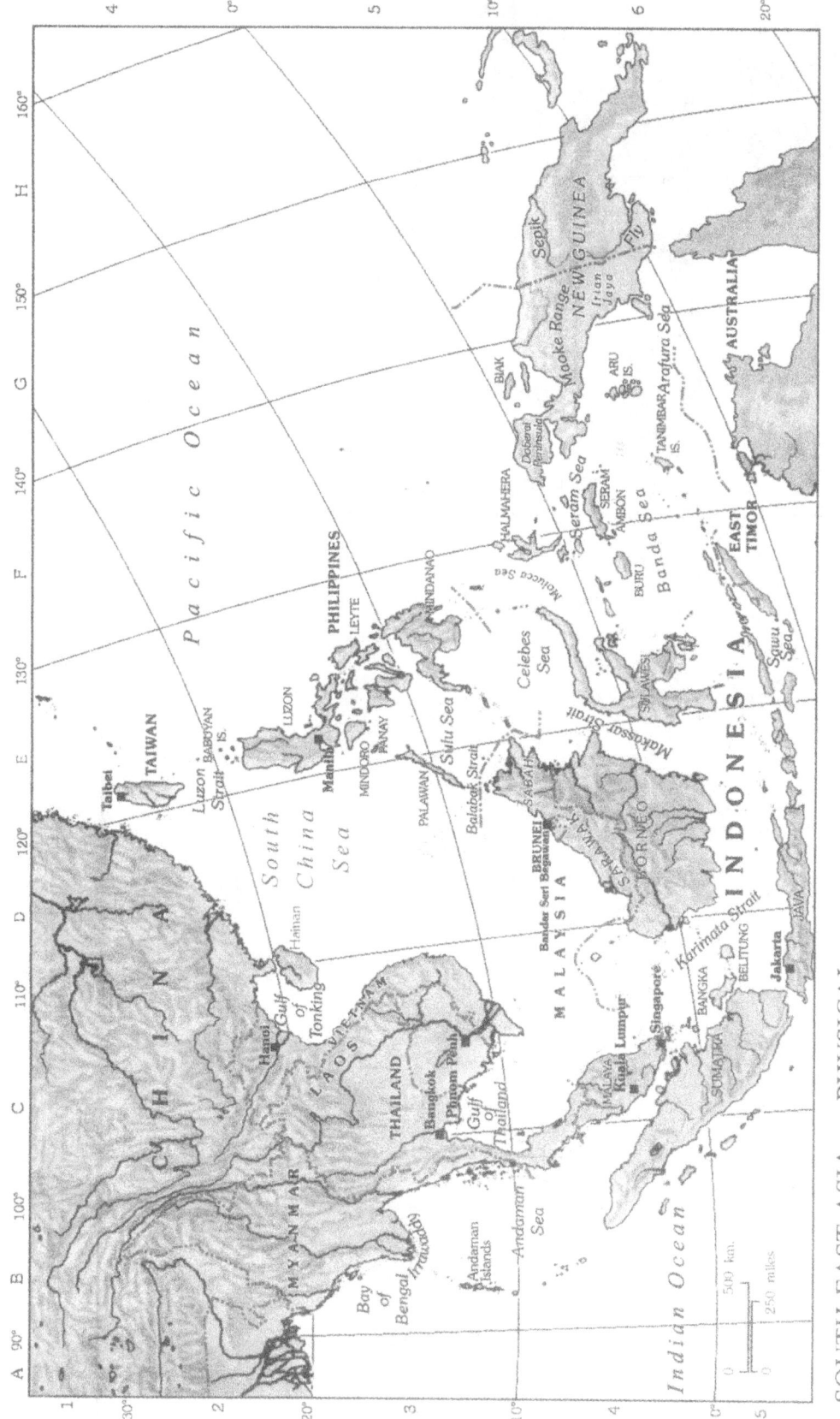

SOUTH-EAST ASIA — PHYSICAL

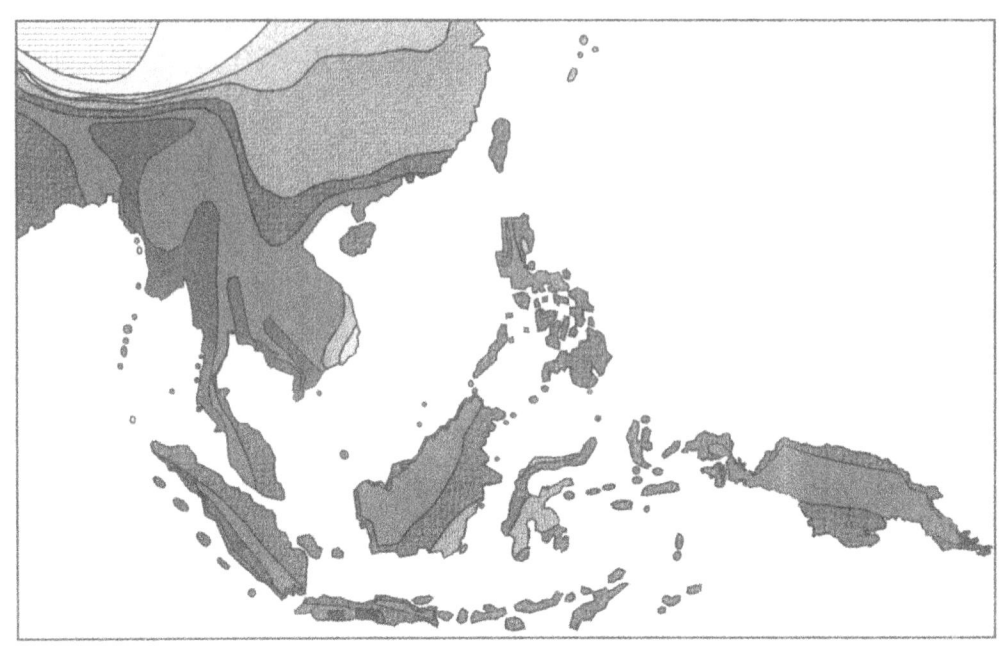

Below 125 mm. (Below 5")
125 to 250 mm. (5" to 10")
250 to 500 mm. (10" to 20")
500 to 750 mm. (20" to 30")
750 to 1000 mm. (30" to 40")
1000 to 1500 mm. (40" to 60")
1500 to 2000 mm. (60" to 80")
Above 2000 mm. (Over 80")

## SOUTH-EAST ASIA — ANNUAL RAINFALL

*Sabah State Mosque, Kota Kinabalu, Malaysia*

*Masjid Kuala Kangsar, Malaysia, 20th century*

slender Thai-Burmese peninsula that separates the Andaman Sea, part of the Indian Ocean or Bay of Bengal, from the Gulf of Thailand. The Strait of Malacca divides Sumatra from Malaya, the Sunda Strait separates Sumatra from Java. The Continental Divide, or Wallace Line, passes south of Mindanao via the Strait of Makasar and between Bali and Lombok; the lands west of this, bordered by the shallow Sunda Shelf, were once part of the mainland.

Within the archipelago, the sea is designated by a variety of names. The Java Sea divides Java from Borneo to the north; the Flores, Banda, Seram and Moluccas Seas occupy the area between the islands from Timor north to the Moluccas. The Celebes (Sulawesi) Sea lies between Sulawesi and the Sulu Archipelago, north of which is the Sulu Sea. In such a setting, a good deal of transport is by water, both externally and along the frequent internal waterways. It

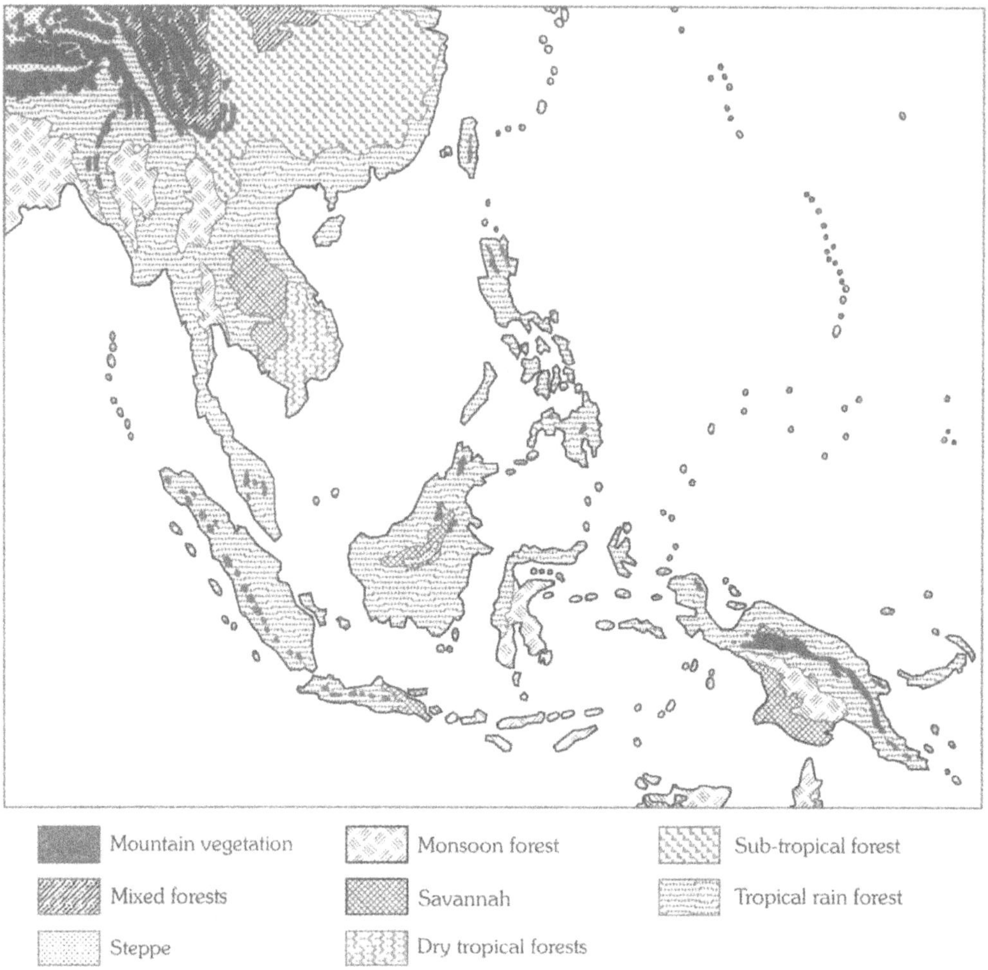

| | | |
|---|---|---|
| ■ Mountain vegetation | ▨ Monsoon forest | ▧ Sub-tropical forest |
| ▨ Mixed forests | ▨ Savannah | ▤ Tropical rain forest |
| ░ Steppe | ▨ Dry tropical forests | |

## SOUTH-EAST ASIA — VEGETATION

*King Faysal Mosque, Marawi City, Philippines*

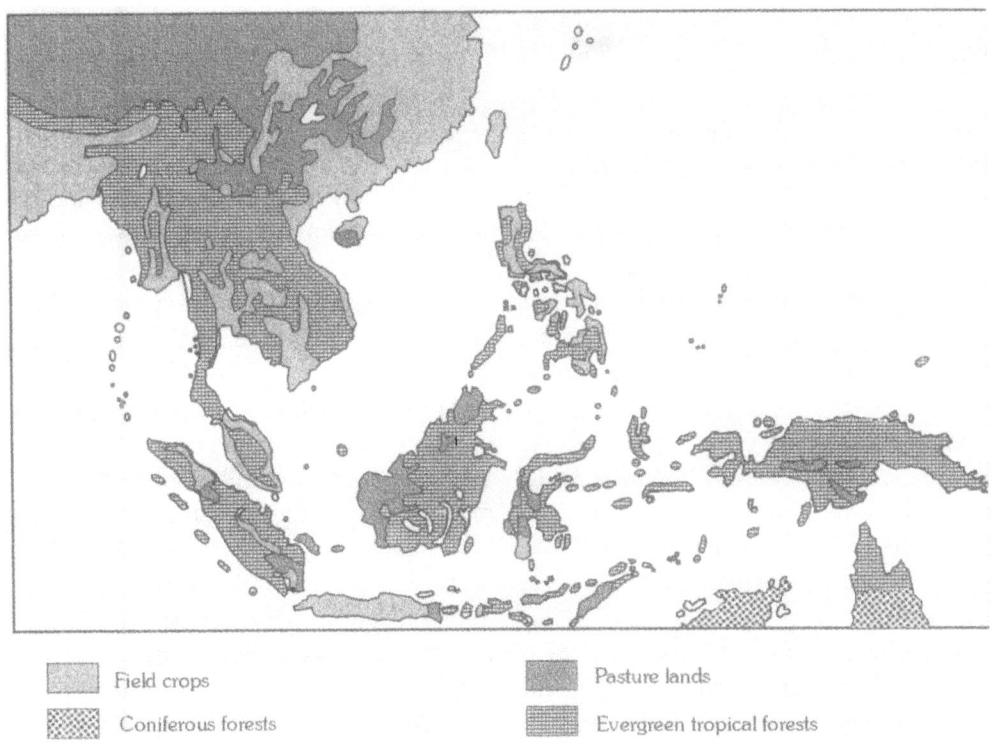

- Field crops
- Coniferous forests
- Pasture lands
- Evergreen tropical forests

# SOUTH-EAST ASIA — AGRICULTURE AND LIVESTOCK

*Mount Kinabalu, Borneo*

was in this way that Hinduism, and then Islam, came to the peninsula and the archipelago, and penetrated, in some places, inland. Mountainous regions are also common enough in this volcanic land. A spine of mountainous terrain runs right through Sumatra from the north and along the west, and in more scattered fashion across central Java, Bali and Lombok, and in Timor. There are mountainous regions in north central Borneo, and in central, southern and northern Sulawesi. These tended not to absorb much influence from outside, being in places more or less impenetrable. The countries of mainland South-East Asia are characterised by the generally north-south flow of the great rivers whose ultimate source in some cases is in the high mountains that make up the chain of the Himalayas, which may be considered South-East Asia's northern demarcation. The Chindwin and Irrawaddy, and the Salween emerge into the Andaman Sea, the Chao Phraya into the Gulf of Siam, the Mekhong, after describing a great curve round northeast Thailand, falls into the South China Sea. North Vietnam and parts of northern Thailand, Laos and Burma are mountainous, with other lesser ranges in Thailand, Cambodia and the Malay Peninsula.

A large part of the area is within the monsoon belt. Temperatures are relatively high, and rainfall is frequent in most areas, though it can be dry in the Isan region of northern Thailand and eastwards, and in the east in the Lesser Sunda Islands. Although soil quality is not generally high, there is, or was, often a rich covering of forest. In cleared areas and river valleys rice cultivation forms a staple.

*The Great Wall of China*

*Railway station in Kuala Lumpur, Malaysia, showing many Islamic features in style*

## EARLY SEABORNE CONTACTS, 7TH TO 15TH CENTURIES

As with Hinduism in earlier centuries, traders on the routes from India that passed the Malay Peninsula and Sumatra towards the Far East, especially China, brought religion in their wake. Arab settlement along the trade routes existed before Islam, it seems, and developed early after the foundation of Islam when the powerful Arab state became an important trading partner. In 878 it is said (Abu Zaid) that Muslim and other merchants in the region of Canton were massacred during the rebellion of Huang Ch'ao, and that many transferred to Kalah (sometimes identified with Kedah) in the Malay peninsula, which then became the major Arab trading center in the East. Some moved on from there to Palembang and other trading cities linked with Kalah. By the Sung period (960-1279), however, Arabs were apparently again the chief foreign traders in Chinese ports. By the late 10th and the 11th century they are noted in Champa (southern Vietnam), where at Phanrang are the earliest surviving Islamic monuments in South-East Asia, inscriptions, one dated equivalent to 1039 AD, the other apparently between 1025–35 AD. These and other traces represent the presence of Islamic traders, not necessarily any beginning of the penetration of Islam among the local people. In 1282 Marco Polo found only one of the eight kingdoms in Sumatra to be Muslim, Ferlec (Perlak), and he states that this was the direct result of trade with Muslim merchants. This religious stimulus must have been active well before — in 1282 the envoys sent by Samudra, further

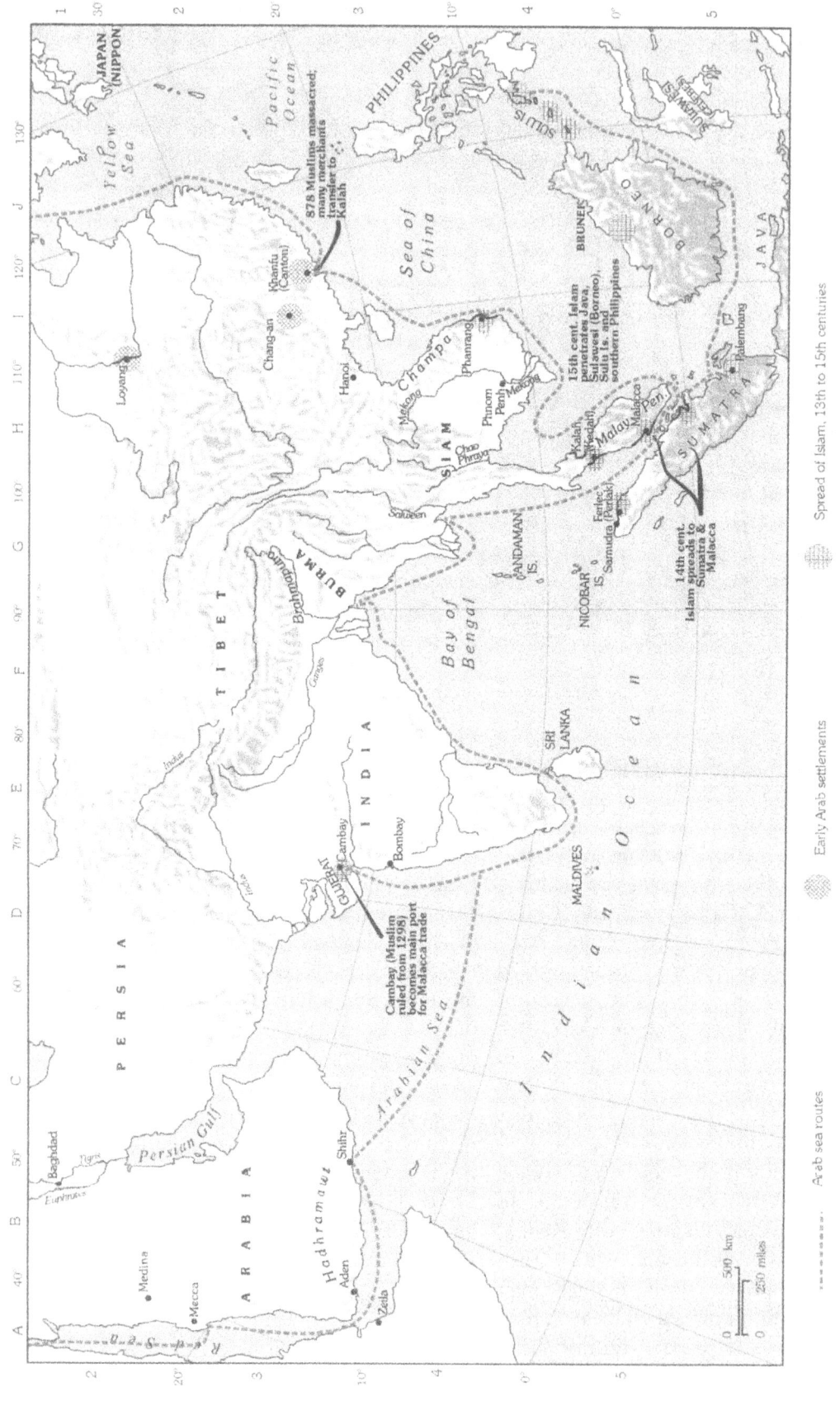

EARLY SEABORNE CONTACTS, 7TH TO 15TH CENTURIES

north on the east coast of Sumatra, to China bore the Muslim names of Husayn and Sulayman. The tomb of the first ruler of Samudra (later Pasai), al-Malik al-Salih, dates to 1297.

When Cambay in Gujarat (NW India) fell to the Muslims in 1298, a port with old trading connections with Indonesia, the Muslim influence inevitably increased. Cambayan merchants began to increase the pace of the spread of the faith in northern Sumatra in the fourteenth century. Frequently, it seems, the port authority of a state would be a foreigner, often a Muslim, and these men, prominent at court and important in the state finances, were able to present the advantages of Islam all the more easily. From Sumatra the faith spread along the trade routes to Malacca (whose ruler converted in the first quarter of the fifteenth century). As a Muslim center, Malacca encouraged the conversion of its Malay dependencies. From Malacca too, Arab and other traders exported Islam to northern Java, and along another trade route to Brunei (in Borneo), the Sulu Islands, and the southern Philippines.

## EARLY ISLAM IN CHINA, 7TH TO 14TH CENTURIES

The coming of an embassy of Arab Muslims, *Ta-shih*, to China in 651 is recorded in the Tang annals. It was sent by *khalifa* Uthman to the Yung-hui emperor, and was followed by many others. Trade in silk and horses developed. By the seventh century, the Arabs were moving into Central Asia, Khwarizm and Samarqand falling in 710–12, Ferghana in 715. China failed to help its tributaries like Tocharistan, and the Arab advance continued. After the overthrow of the Umayyads, in 751, after a temporary success in Ferghana, the Chinese were defeated by the Abbasid forces at Talas (Tashkent). Khanfu (Canton) was plundered by Arabs and Persians in 758 (possibly pirates, since they fled away by sea), and in 760 'several thousand Arab and Persian merchants'

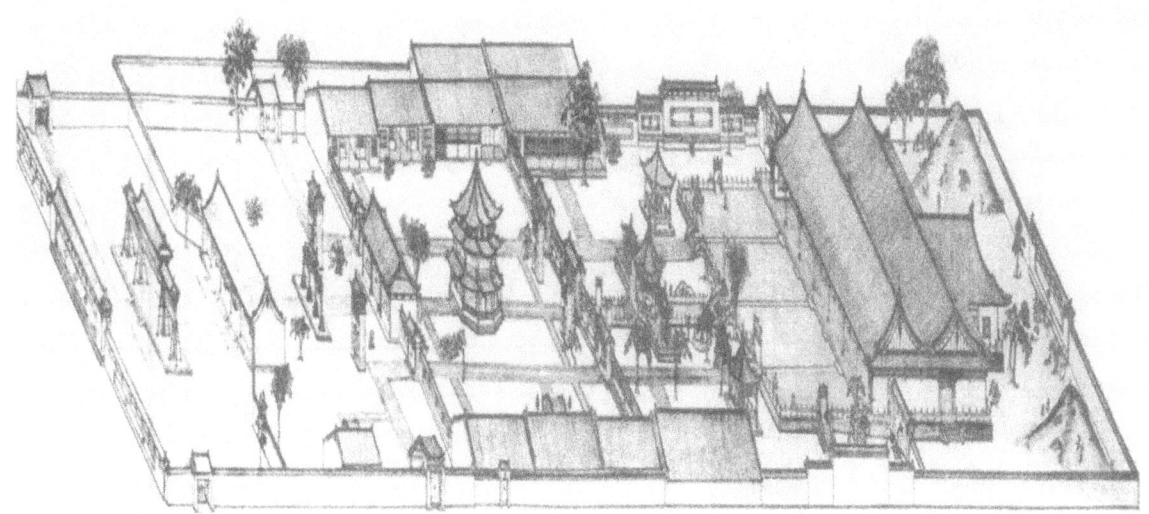

*The Grand Mosque at Xian, China, dating from the 7th century and founded on the Silk Route by Arab traders.*

are said to have been killed at Yangchow, according to the T'ang history. On the other hand, Arab (unofficial?) forces helped the Chinese and their Uighur mercenaries to suppress the An Lu-shan rebellion, their troops assisting in the taking of Ch'ang-an and Loyang in 757. Other Arab soldiers came to Liangchow and Sining in 757. It is traditionally asserted that some later intermarried with Chinese wives and formed an early Arab settlement in China, but Muslim claims for a large immigration into China at this time are regarded as exaggerated. The *Akhbar al-Sind wa'l-Hind*, whose author, Captain Buzurg ibn Shahriyar of Ramhormuz, travelled in China in 851, records that at Khanfu there was a Muslim judge appointed by the emperor over the other Muslims, and that Iraqi merchants came there. Yunnan — centuries later destined to achieve a brief autonomy as a rebellious Muslim state — is said, after the Mongol conquest, to have been given to Sayyid Ajall Shams al-Din 'Umar as governor, who introduced Islam there. His son Nasr al-Din's victory over the king of Mien (Burma, now Myanmar) was recorded by Marco Polo (1277).

In the former Eastern Turkistan, now called Sinkiang, and Dzungaria, the Uighurs were converted to Islam over a long period, between 842 and 1130. The Turkic Kyrghyz and Kazakhs were converted starting from ca. 1400.

Muslims were employed frequently by the Mongol Yuan dynasty (1279–1368) in official and advisory positions, and this was the time of their great expansion there, entering the empire both via Central Asia (originating in places such as Samarqand and Bukhara), and the seaports. Muslim communities and mosques spread quite widely, but mainly in the north, from this time on, though

*Interior of the 10th century mosque at Beijing, China*

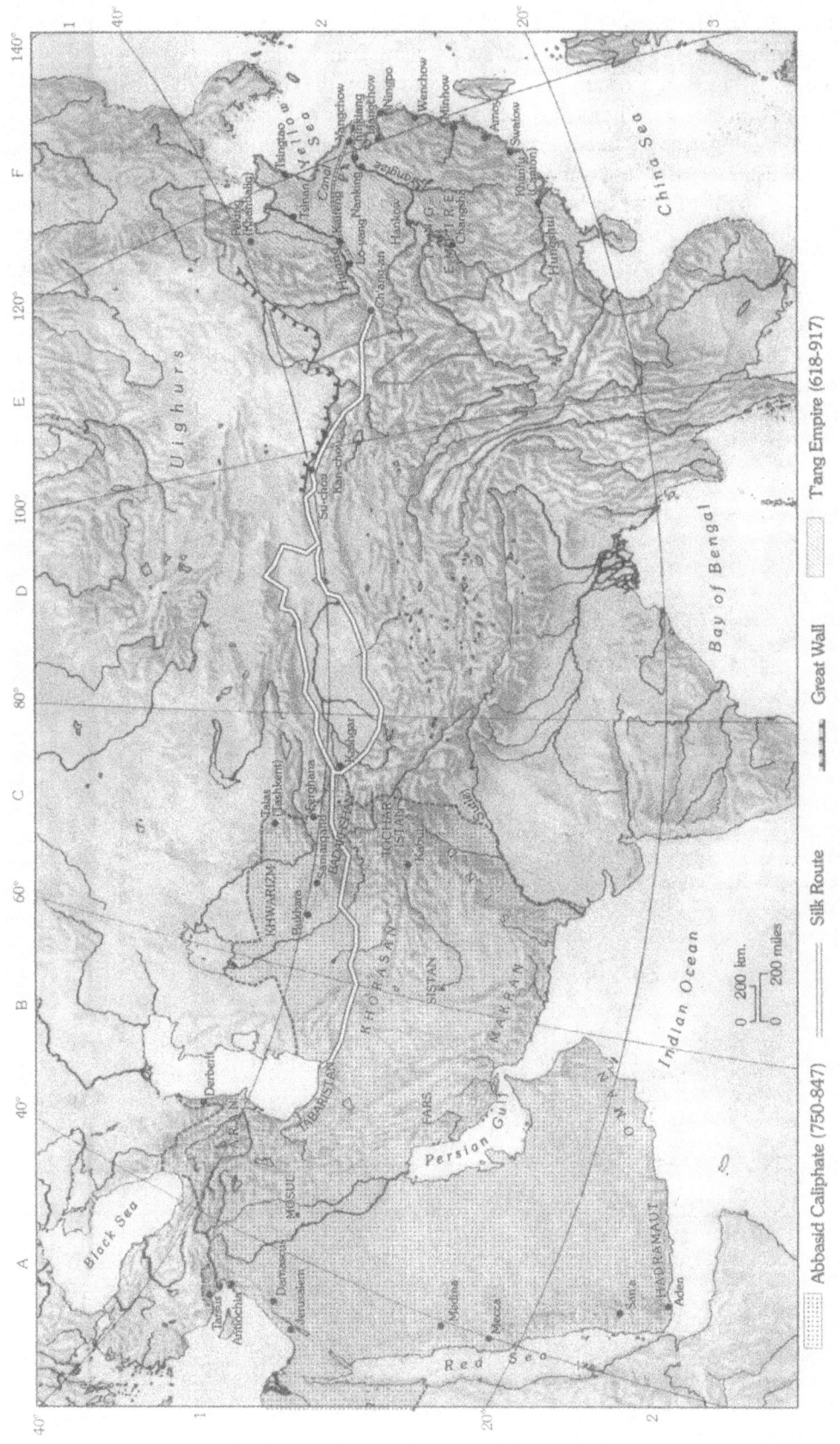

EARLY ISLAM IN CHINA, 7TH TO 14TH CENTURIES

substantial communities remained in Nanking and Hangchow. It was not all plain sailing for the Muslims, however. There was some repression of Muslim customs, and even rebellions at the end of the Mongol period. Marco Polo mentions Muslim centers in Yunnan and the Tangqut area of Kansu and Ningsia 1354. Ibn Battuta mentions the offices of *qadi* and *shaykh al-Islam* in some of the most important places. Canton, Hangchow and Chu'an-chou (Zaytun), with C'hang-an, seem all to have had mosques for their communities of Muslim traders as early as the Sung period (960–1126, 1127–78). Kaifeng, Hainan, Ningpo, Fuchow, and Peking (Beijing) also seem to have had Muslim communities by the Sung period. Claims for the T'ang period remain unsubstantiated, though communities are likely in Canton, Yangchow and Ch'ang-an. Some thirteenth and fourteenth century Arabic epitaphs have been found at Yangchow, Hangchow and Beijing. At Chu'an-chou, some of them specifically refer to 'spreading the faith', and a mosque inscription there alludes to a date equivalent to AD 1009/10 for its foundation, and 1310/11 for its restoration.

*Mosque at Tao-Chou, Kansu Province, China*

# ISLAM IN CHINA, 15TH TO 20TH CENTURIES

With the loss of their privileged position with the arrival of the Ming (1368), a native Chinese dynasty succeeding the foreign Mongols, the Muslims in China tended to become more acculturated to Chinese ways. Integration progressed. Arabic books and inscriptions came to be largely replaced by others in Chinese. By the Ming period there were many millions of *Hui* (Muslims) in China, and

## ISLAM IN CHINA, 15TH TO 20TH CENTURIES

Legend:
- China under the Ming Dynasty (1644)
- HO-NAN  Ming Province
- Extent of Muslim sphere at the beginning of the 20th century
- Mongolian Rule, early 15th century

*The great Ming emperor, Wan-li (r. 1572–1620)*

Islam and individual Muslims could still prosper under certain emperors. Some Muslims still rose to high office, like the Muslim eunuch Cheng Ho, leader of the great Ming fleets that went as far as East Africa and Arabia in the early 1400s. Even if there was some friction late in the dynasty, the Muslims did not support the establishment of the Ching Manchu dynasty in 1644, and even set up a Ming pretender in Kansu in the 1646-48 rebellion there. With assistance from the Central Asian Muslim states, Lanchow, Kanchow, Suchow and other places were captured, but the rebellion was eventually mastered (1649).

In general, however, in the early Ching period, the government regarded the Muslims cautiously, kept them under strict control, but did not provoke them. But as time went on, Muslims rebellions did break out here and there, culminating in major problems in the 1800s.

The period of social unrest, combined with anti-Muslim persecution, in the mid-nineteenth century saw three almost simultaneous Muslim rebellions in China, in Yunnan (where there were Muslim rebellions in 1820-28, 1830, 1846), in Ningsia, Shensi and Kansu (where there had been several previous rebellions and unrest, especially in 1648 and during so-called New Teaching–Old Teaching controversies in 1781) and Eastern Turkistan (where there had been an uprising in 1758).

The Muslim state of P'ing-nan Kuo was established in 1856 in (majority non-Muslim) Yunnan by the *imam* Ma Te-hsin and Tu Wen-hsiu (known as Sultan Sulayman). It lasted until 1873. Many Muslims (Panthays) fled southwestwards to the frontier lands after the failure of the rebellion.

In Kansu and Shensi in the northwest, after the 1781 unrest, a major rebellion broke out in 1862-73, led by Ma Hua-lung. In modern times (from 1958) Muslim predominance has been recognised in the name the Hui Autonomous Region of Ningsia. (Ningsia had been at times part of Kansu, and from 1911 was ruled, like Kansu, by Muslim warlords of the Ma clan, until they were defeated by the Communists).

In Central Asia, Chinese Turkistan (Kashgaria), conquered in 1755, was already in rebellion under its *khojas* in 1757. When the Chinese suppressed the rebellion, local *begs* were installed to govern the Muslims. In 1828 the rebel Jahangir Khoja was captured and killed, but in 1830 the khanate of Khokand attacked Chinese-ruled Kashgaria, followed by several other attacks up to 1862. With the outbreak of the Muslim rebellion in Kansu, which shielded the Uighur lands from Chinese retaliation, an independent Muslim kingdom was founded in Kashgaria by Yakub Beg, from Khokand, between 1862 and 1877. It was after the suppression of this kingdom, recognised at the time by several of the great powers, that the Chinese annexed East Turkistan, administering it from 1884 as the province of Sinkiang (today the Uighur Autonomous Region of Sinkiang (Xinjiang).

The Muslims in China today, known from Mongol times as *Hui-hui*, consist of ethnic Chinese, Mongols in the borderlands with Mongolia and in Kansu, and Turkic peoples in Eastern Turkistan or Sinkiang. All Hui are Sunni; all Turkic Muslims are Sunni (both Hanafi *madhhab*). The few thousand Tajiks in Sinkiang are Ismailis. Religious freedom in terms of worship in mosques, education, and pilgrimage is tolerated, but not separatism as some Turkic nationalists dream of for 'Turan' (former East Turkistan = Sinkiang).

*Yatung village, southern Tibet trading post between Lhasa and Bengal*

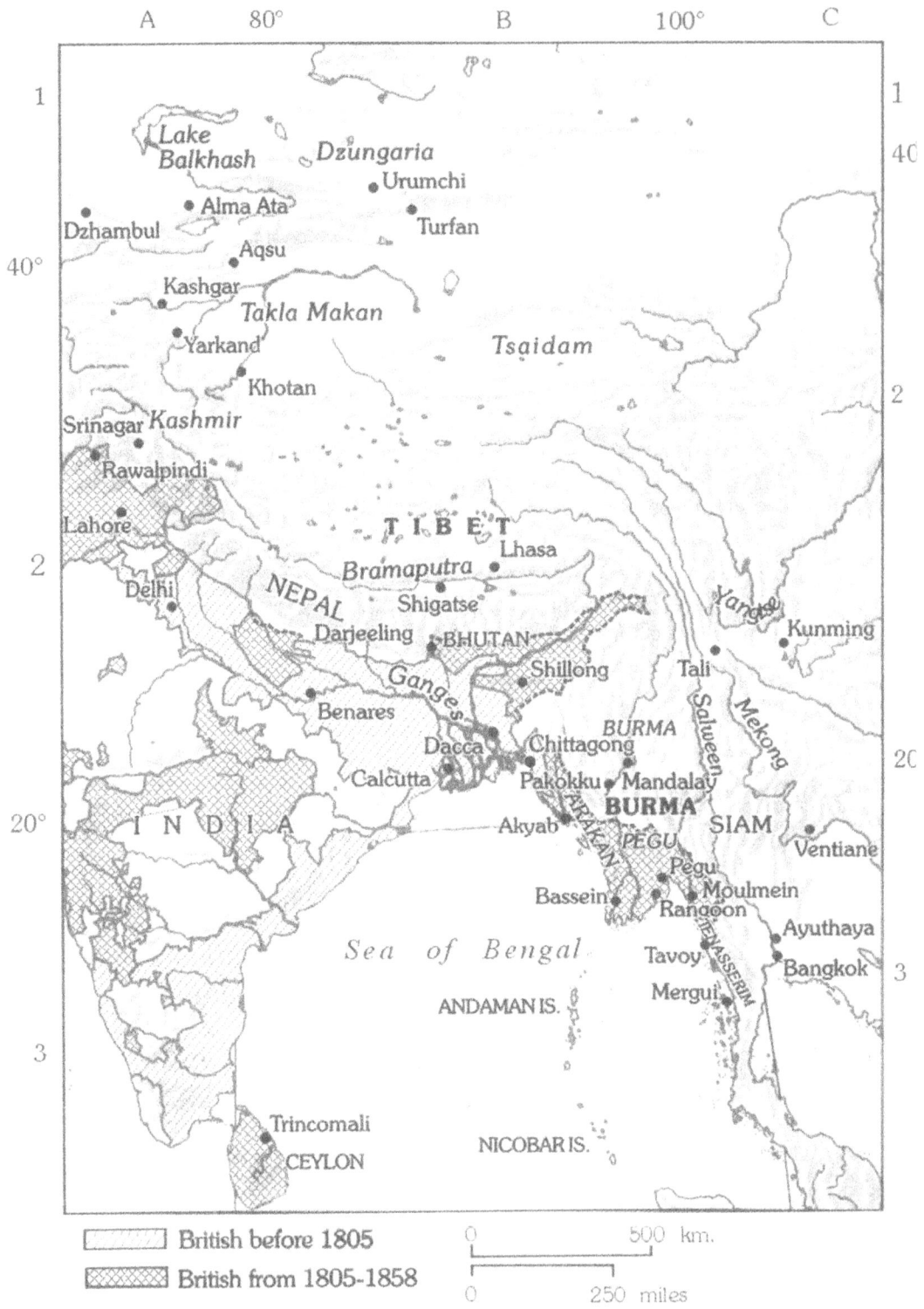

ISLAMIC COMMUNITIES IN ARAKAN, MYANMAR (BURMA) AND TIBET, 9TH–20TH CENTURIES

# ISLAMIC COMMUNITIES IN ARAKAN, MYANMAR (BURMA) AND TIBET, 9TH–20TH CENTURIES

Muslim communities maintained themselves in Burma (Myanmar) and Tibet. In Burma, Persian and Arab traders brought Islam from the ninth and tenth centuries, and in later times Indian Muslim traders or mercenaries began to settle there in considerable numbers. Many Bengali Muslim Indians entered Arakan (later to become part of Burma), becoming very influential there from the fifteenth century, though the Arakan monarchy remained Buddhist. After the British conquest of Burma, beginning from 1824, many Indian Muslims came to Rangoon (Yangon) and other towns as traders and settlers. From Yunnan, the Panthay Muslims also came to trade, many settling after the collapse of Tu Wen-hsiu's state in 1873. (Panthay refers to the trader Muslims of both Yunnan and Upper Burma. They became suppliers of arms to the Yunnan rebels during the rule of 'Sultan Sulayman' there).

Islam first entered Tibet from Kashmir in the fourteenth century, hence the term *Kachee* used for Tibetan Muslims. There are supposed to have been ca. 10,000 Muslims in Lhasa at the beginning of the twentieth century, with other communities in such places as Baltistan, Purig and Leh in Eastern Ladakh. Contact with Chinese Muslims was maintained, and at some trade centers resulted in intermarriage with Chinese Muslims. Tu Wen-hsiu (Sultan Sulayman), in revolt against the Chinese in Yunnan 1856-73, appealed to the Lhasa Muslims to assist him. Today the Muslims in Tibet, especially Lhasa are all Hui. They tend to be seen by Tibetans (and by Beijing) as pro-Chinese settlers.

# ISLAMIC INSCRIPTIONS IN MALAYSIA AND INDONESIA, 11TH TO 15TH CENTURIES

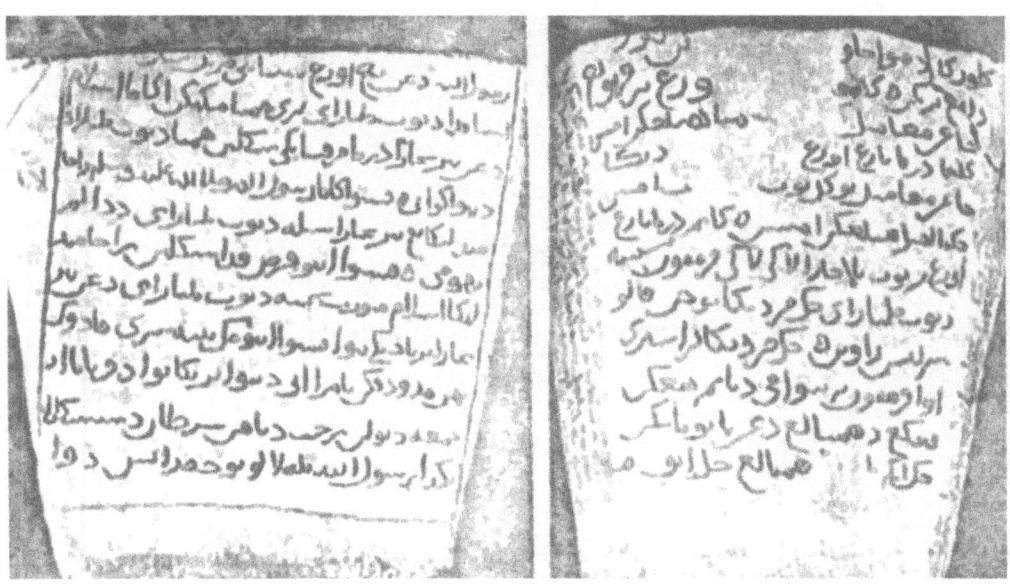

*Trengganu Inscription, dated 4 Rajab 702/Friday 22 February 1303 (description on page 235)*

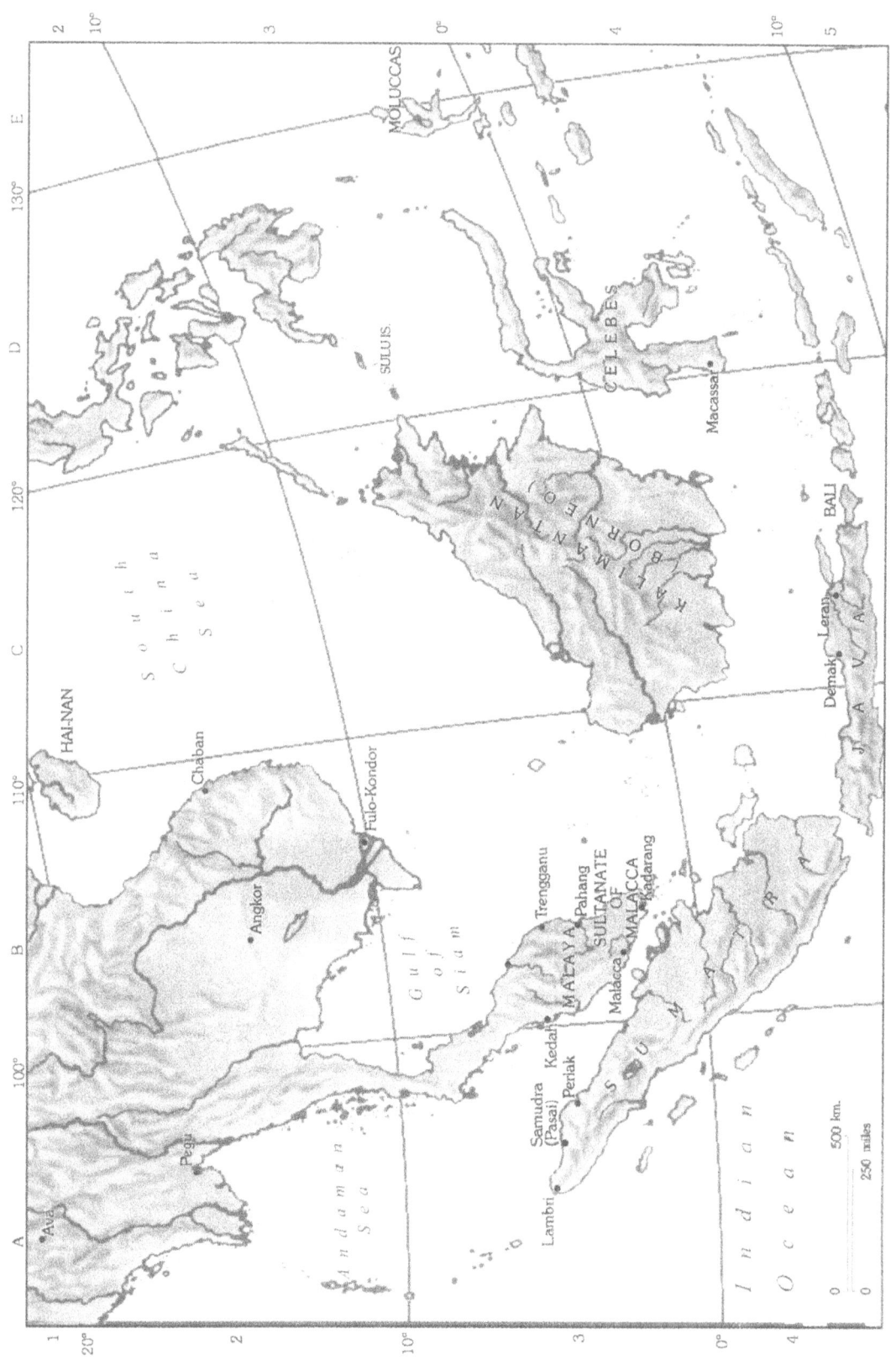

ISLAMIC INSCRIPTIONS IN MALAYSIA AND INDONESIA, 11TH TO 15TH CENTURIES

# ISLAMIC INSCRIPTIONS IN MALAYSIA AND INDONESIA,
## 11TH TO 15TH CENTURIES

The inscription dated to 1082 or 1102 from Leran in Java offers uncertain evidence. It may have been brought in later, but in any event only indicates the presence of a Muslim, and does not attest the installation of the faith so early.

The tombstone of Sultan al-Malik al-Salih, first Muslim ruler of Samudra, is dated 1297. The stone came from Cambay, Gujarat.

A Muslim gravestone dated to 1421 was found on the river bank opposite Samudra (Pasai/Pasé).

At Trengganu a stone inscription, perhaps a boundary marker between Islamic and non-Islamic held territory, dates between 1303 and 1387. Ibn Battuta in 1345–6 found that the ruler of the peninsula (raja of Kedah?) was an infidel, and the Nagarakertagama (1365) cites the region as tributary to the Hindu empire of Majapahit.

An inscription on stone imported from Cambay records the death in 1475 of the ruler of Pahang, son of the Malacca sultan Ala'u'-din.

## MARCO POLO'S SUMATRA, 1292

Marco Polo and his companions passed by Sumatra in 1292 on their return from the Great Khan's land. By good fortune, Marco Polo notes one of the early Muslim kingdoms of Sumatra in what seems to be an early stage of its conversion. Describing the route from China, he mentions Chamba (Champa), then Lokak (Siam/Malay peninsula?) and Bintan. Not far from here was the island kingdom of Malayur, and about 100 miles SE of Bintan one came to Lesser Java island. There were eight kingdoms, each with its own language, possessing

*Marco Polo's ship from: The Book of Marco Polo, c. 1298 ff.*

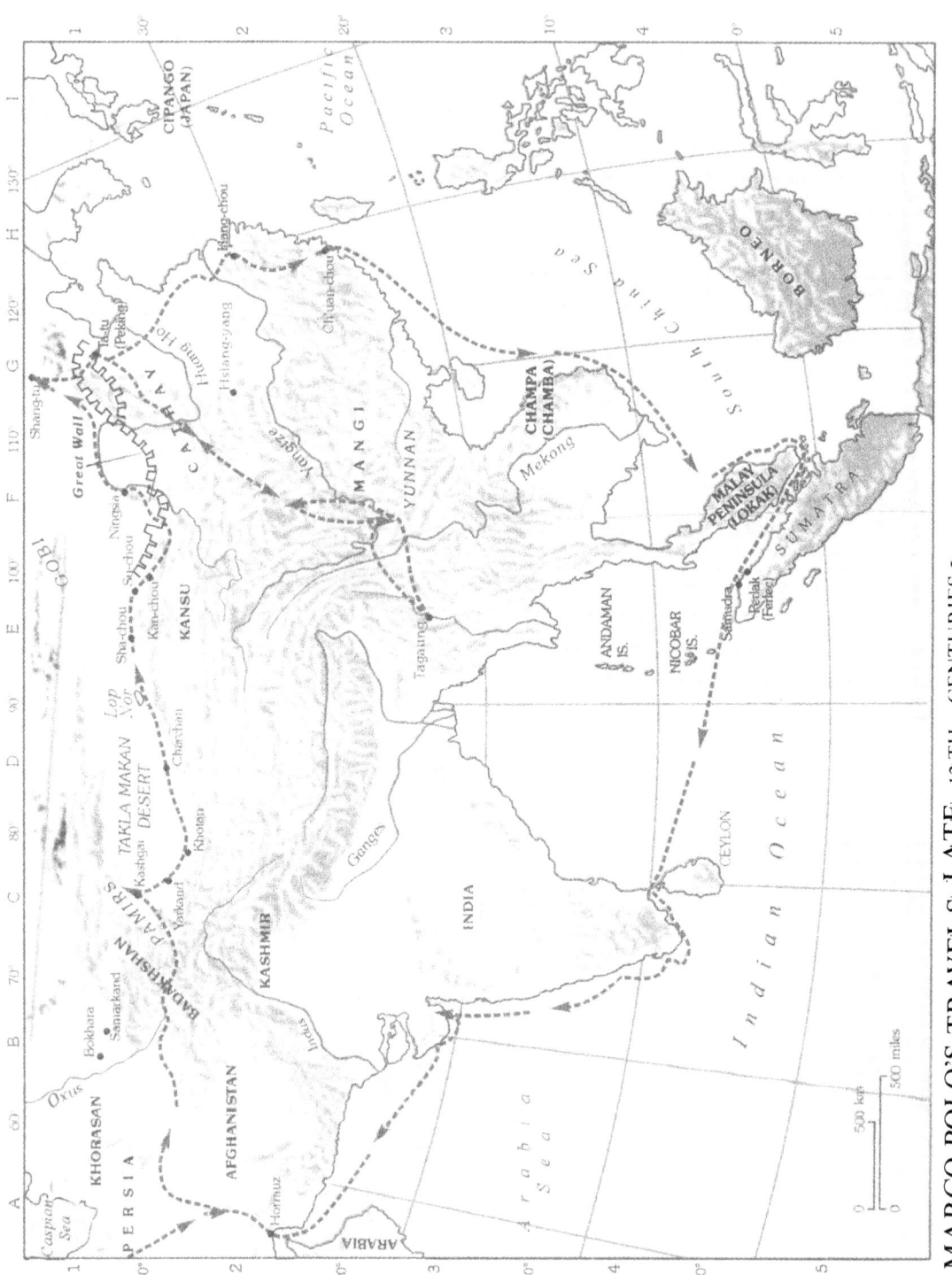

MARCO POLO'S TRAVELS LATE 12TH CENTURIES

rare woods and spices. Marco Polo mentions some details about six of them. He first describes Ferlec (Perlak), just south of Samudra. So great was the trade with Muslims ('Saracen merchants') that many local people, formerly idolaters, had been converted. This applied only to the inhabitants of the city; the inhabitants of the mountains lived 'like beasts'. After Ferlec, Polo describes Basman, Sumatra, Dagroian, Lambri, Fansur, all kingdoms of idolaters. From Lambri it was 150 miles northwards to Nicobar and Andaman.

*Marco Polo, from the titlepage of the first German translation, Nürnberg 1477*

## EARLY ISLAM IN SUMATRA, IBN BATTUTA'S VISIT, 1345–1346

Ibn Battuta visited Samudra or Semudera (hence the name Sumatra for the whole island) twice in 1345–6. Landing at Sarha, a village in the Muslim sultanate of Samudra, he found that the sultan there, al-Malik al-Zahir, followed the Shafi'i rite. The name Ibn Battuta supplies is a title, in this case belonging to Sultan Ahmad (1326–60). Buhruz the vice-admiral received the visitors, and prominent Muslim jurists and officials from Shiraz and Isfahan were sent to bring them to the city of 'Sumutra'. Inland, war against the unbelievers continued, and many had been forced to pay the *jizya* to have peace.

Ibn Battuta and his companions were received by a deputy, and after three days Ibn Battuta met the sultan in the mosque, where he enquired about Sultan Muhammad, Ibn Battuta's master at Delhi, and discussed jurisprudence. The sultan then rode to the audience hall on an elephant, escorted by the rest on horseback, and Ibn Battuta describes how all the different ranks of people greeted their ruler. There were four wazirs, amirs, secretaries of state and army commanders, sharifs and jurists, scholars and poets, pages and mamluks. He also describes how there had been a rebellion by the sultan's nephew, while he was on campaign a month's journey away among the infidels, and as a result the sultan had built the wooden walls and towers that now defended Samudra.

Ibn Battuta stayed fifteen days in al-Jawa, as he called Sumatra, before embarking on a ship prepared by the sultan, destined for Mul Jawa (Java).

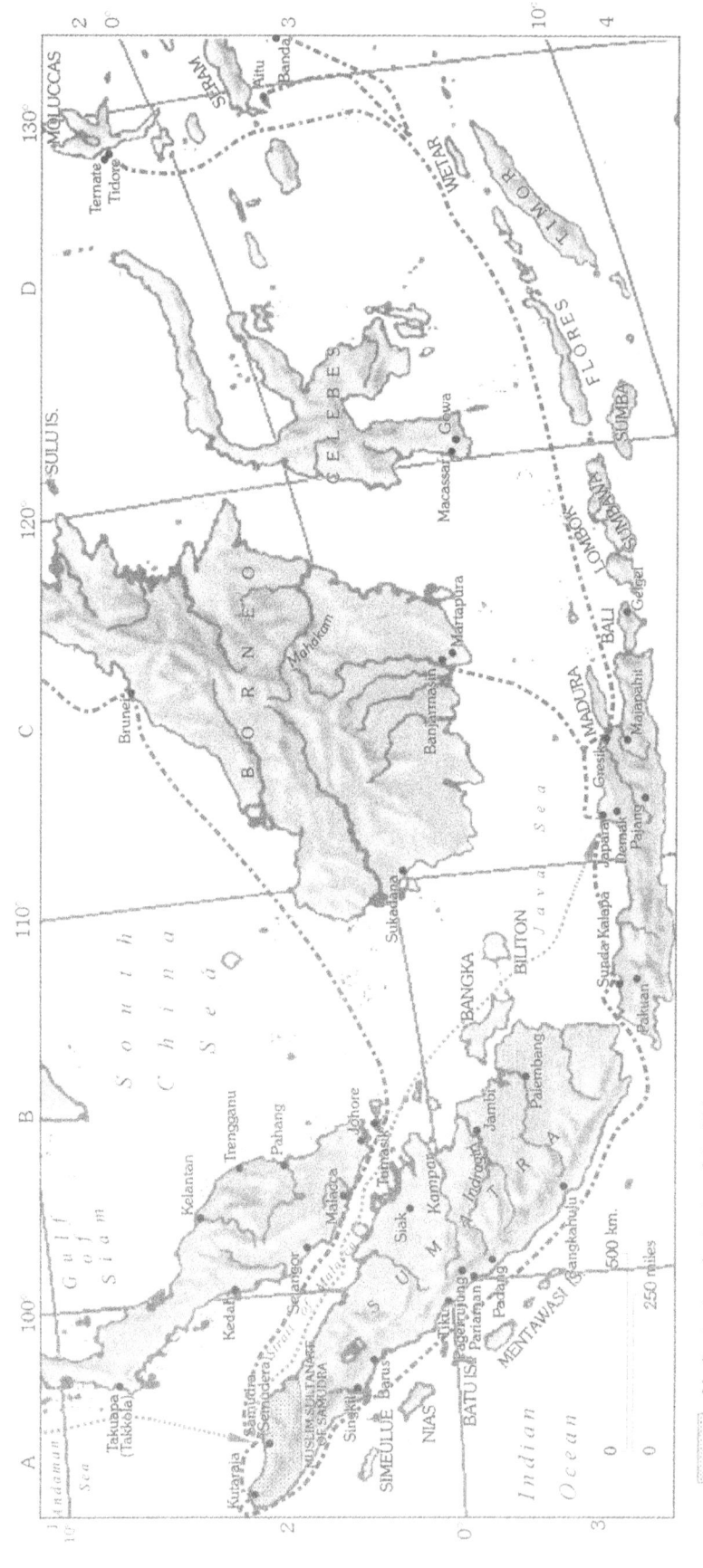

EARLY ISLAM IN SUMATRA, IBN BATTUTA'S VISIT, 1345–1346

*Tuba mountain lake, in the mountains of Sumatra*

## THE MALACCAN SULTANATE AT ITS GREATEST EXTENT,
### 15TH CENTURY TO 1511

Malacca (Melaka), according to Sumatran traditions (recorded by Braz d'Albuquerque, Tomé Pires and João de Barros), was founded by Paramesvara, an exiled prince of Palembang, who had revolted against Javanese domination. He ruled Tumasik (Singapore), then a Siamese vassal, but was expelled in 1398–99. He then took Malacca, c. 1400, sending an embassy to China (c. 1405) to gain imperial recognition. Paramesvara, who became a Muslim at 72 years of age, under the name Megat Iskender Shah, as a result of marriage into the Pasai (Samudra) royal family, recently converted, died apparently in 1424. His successor Muhammad Shah (1424–44) was also called Sri Maharaja, and Raja Ibrahim (1444–45) bore the name Sri Paramesvara Deva Shah, perhaps indicating that Islam was not yet in a position of dominance. Ibrahim was deposed by his brother Raja Kasim, Muzaffar Shah (1445–59) with the aid of Indian Muslims. The Sejarah Melayu records Siamese attempts to take Malacca in the reign of Sultan Muzaffar Shah, and Ma-Huan, a Muslim Chinese writer (1451), adds that the Muslim eunuch Cheng-Ho, passed by Malacca in 1409 and raised it to the status of a kingdom so that the Siamese no longer dared attack it. He describes the reverence of the king and his subjects for Islam, its fasts and penances. In 1459 Raja Abdallah, Mansur Shah, succeeded, followed

*239*

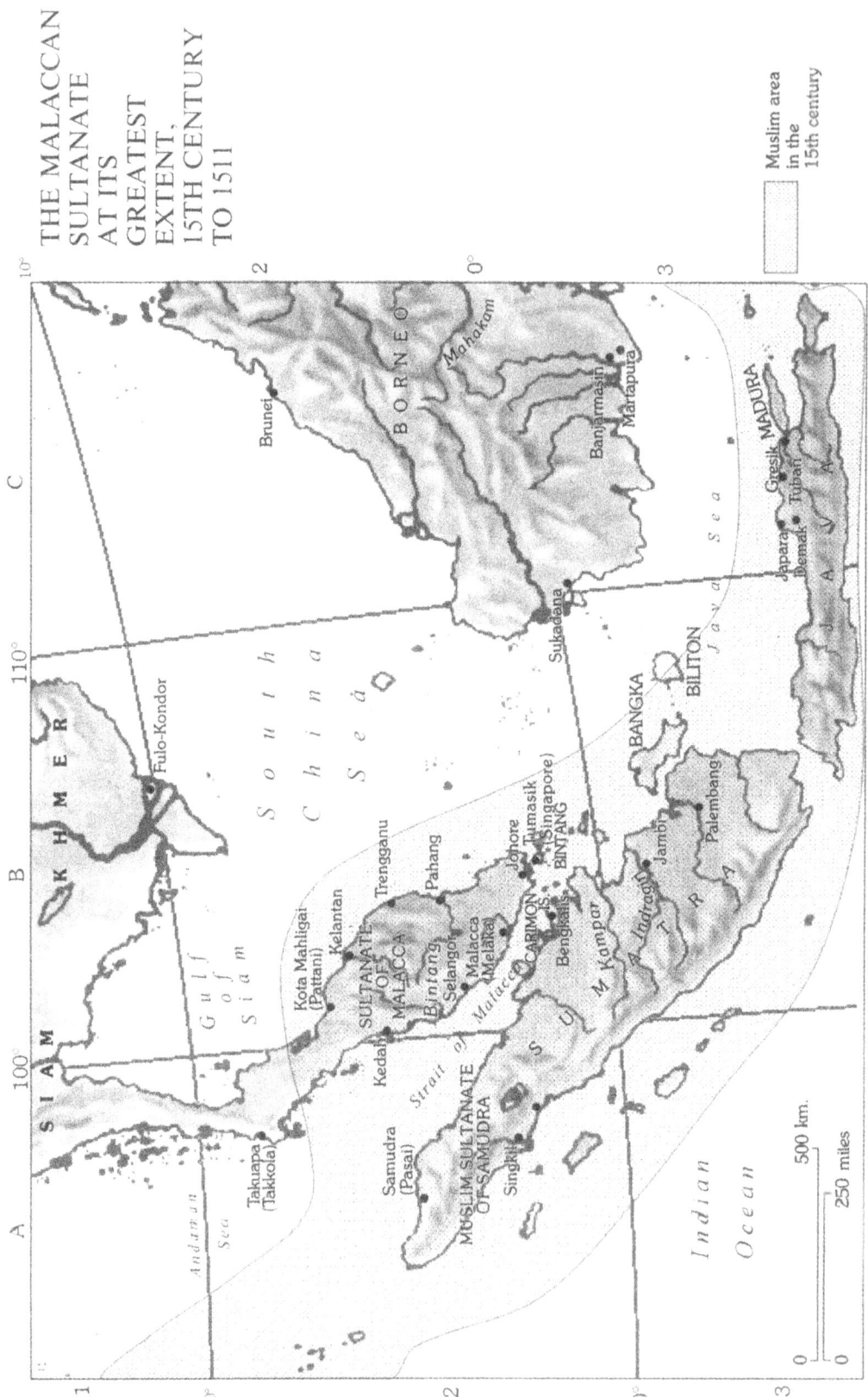

*Ninth century Buddhist temples at Borobudur, Java*

by Sultan Ala'u'-din Riayat Shah (1477–88) and Mahmud (1488–1511), who was driven out by the Portuguese conquest. He and his predecessors enlarged Malacca's sphere to include Pahang, Trengganu, Johore, Jambi, Kampar, Bengkalis, the Carimon Islands and Bintang. Mahmud Shah is said to have received homage, too, from the raja of Kedah, and from a Siamese prince, Chau Sri Bangsa, who seized Kota Mahligai (Pattani). Mahmud confirmed him as ruler under the title Sri Sultan Ahmad Shah. Malaccan power, fed by the Cambay Muslim trade, allowed Malacca to become a center for the propagation of Islam. A son of the sultan became first Muslim ruler of Pahang, Trengganu accepted Islam with vassalage to Malacca, Pattani was converted from Malacca with its vassal Kelantan, and Kedah in 1474 (though local Kelantan stories claim that Islam came to them before Malacca, through traders from Yunnan). In eastern Sumatra, several areas came under Malaccan control, and accepted Islam, and by trade connections from Malacca even parts of Java, Tuban, Gresik, began to move towards Islam.

## THE SPREAD OF ISLAM IN SUMATRA AND JAVA,
### 15TH TO 17TH CENTURIES

Under the influence of Malacca, in eastern Sumatra Rokan became Muslim in the early fifteenth century, followed by Kampar, Indragiri and Siak. In 1509 Diogo Lopes de Sequeira visited Pasai, which was conquered by the Portuguese in 1521. With the fall of Malacca to the Portuguese in 1511, many Muslims migrated to operate from Acheh, which succeeded Pasai and Malacca as the Muslim center of the region. Acheh, with its increasing dominance over several west and east coast principalities, and later (under Iskandar Muda) even over some Malay states (Pahang, 1618; Kedah, 1619; Perak, 1620), were to become centers in which to gather for pilgrimage to Mecca, and great seats of Muslim learning. Acheh seems to have been converted from Pasai by about the mid-14th century. By the early 16th century, with Malacca no longer so attractive, as a

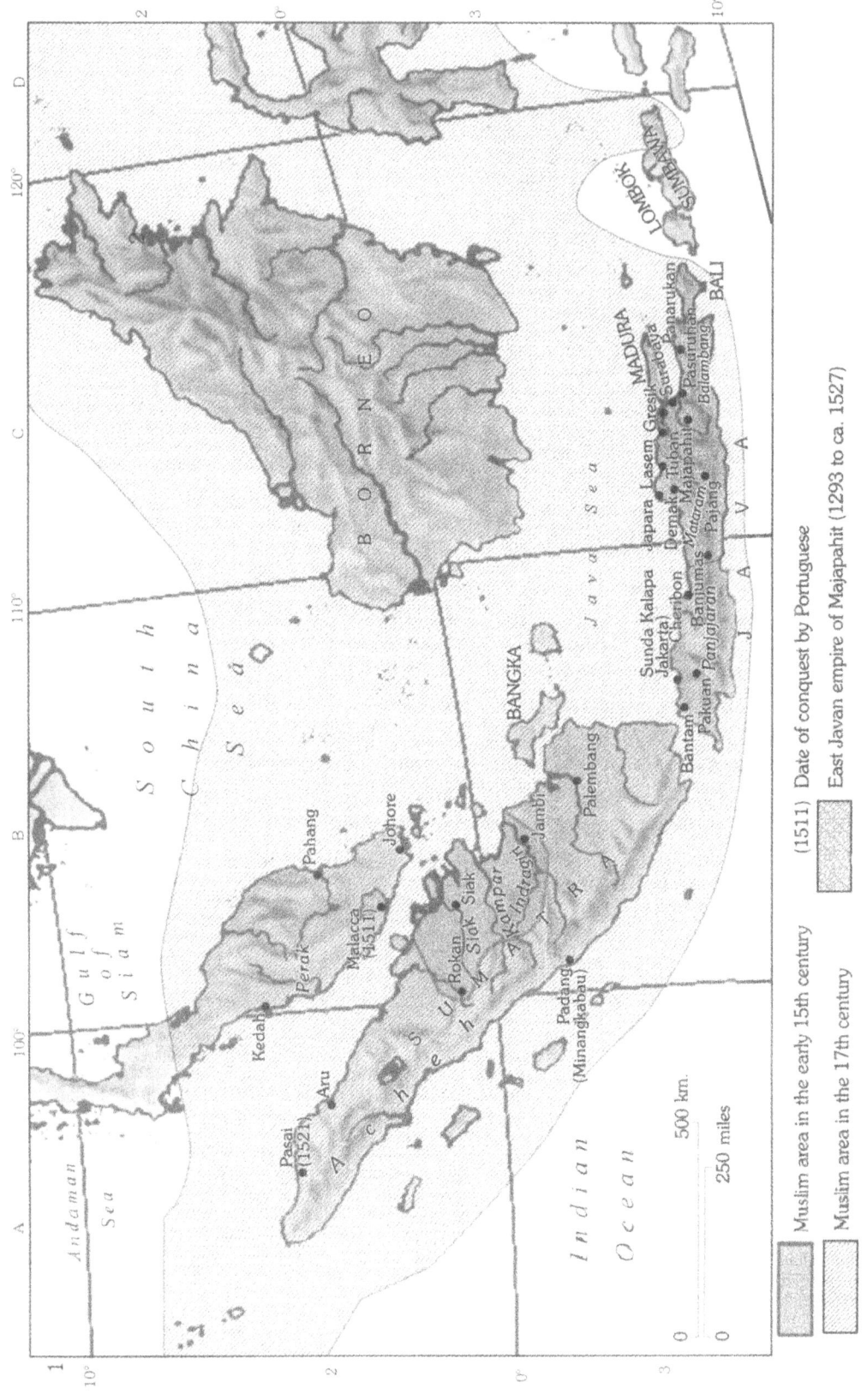

THE SPREAD OF ISLAM IN SUMATRA AND JAVA, 15TH TO 17TH CENTURIES

Portuguese possession, Muslim trade developed greatly at Acheh. Ali Mughayat Shah in 1524 captured Pasai from the Portuguese, and his son 'Ala al-Din added Aru and Johore, even laying siege to Malacca, unsuccessfully. Sultan Iskandar Muda (1608-37) increased Acheh's power along both coasts of Sumatra, until defeated in his attempt to take Malacca in 1629 by the Portuguese. He built a great five storey mosque in Acheh. Islam spread from Acheh into the Gayo and Minangkabau (Padang) regions, though a legend claims that Shaykh Ibrahim of Minangkabau adopted Islam in Java.

The Chinese Muslim Ma Huan noted, between 1415 and 1432, Muslims from the west, and Chinese Muslims, in east Java. Two early attributions for the conversion of Java in traditional stories are *mawlana* Malik Ibrahim or Sunan Gresik, who died at Gresik in 1419, and *raden* Rahmat, who died in 1470. In another version of the conversion of Java is attributed to raden Patah, son of the last king of the Hindu empire of Majapahit and ruler of Demak. He is said to have united several small Muslim states in northern Java, and conquered the country for Islam. Modern studies see the process as more gradual, a slow decay of Majapahit allowing smaller Muslim states to gain independence. There are legends about Muslim officials being appointed by Majapahit kings in the last half of the fifteenth century. Demak, with Japara, conquered and lightly islamised Palembang and Jambi in southern Sumatra, moving on, unsuccessfully, to Malacca in 1512, just after its conquest by the Portuguese. Demak spread its influence in central Java, even to Lombok, which was islamised. From 1521 shaykh Ibn Mawlana of Pasai was active from Demak in the conversion of western Java. Bantam, Muslim by 1525 under shaykh Ibn Mawlana, attacked Pajajaran (capital Pakuan), which lost its port Sunda Kalapa (today Jakarta) in 1526,

*Qabus Mosque, Brunei*

but continued to exist until 1579 when Sultan Panembahan Yusuf (1570–80) of Bantam conquered it. Demak and its Muslim allies ended Majapahit rule around 1527, but had by no means destroyed the Hindu states of the east. Panarukan, attacked in 1546, was not conquered, but Sultan Tranggana of Demak was killed, and Demak's power shattered.

Indian Muslim mystics coming from Sumatra spread the faith in Java, centered on Demak. Even so, much of the interior was not Muslim even by 1597 when the Dutch records begin. The new Mataram sultanate in the south gradually overcame local Hindu-Buddhist resistance: Banjumas (1586), Galuh (1595), Panarukan (1614), Japara and Lasem (1616), Pasuruan (1617), Pajang (1618), Tuban (1619), the island of Madura (1624), Cheribon and Surabaya (1625). Balambang was attacked in 1639 by Sultan Agung (1630–45) of Mataram, but was not finally converted until the late eighteenth century.

To the east, Bali submitted to Islam, despite the efforts of Sultan Agung of Mataram in the 1630s. Instead, it became the repository of the old Hindu culture that was almost wiped out by Islam in Java.

## THE SPREAD OF ISLAM IN BORNEO, SULAWESI AND THE MOLUCCAS, 15TH TO 17TH CENTURIES

Brunei, the first Muslim state in Borneo, was converted around 1500 through Islamic influences which arrived with the Malaccan trade. De Brito, in 1514, reported the presence of Muslim traders, although the ruler was heathen. In 1521, Magellan's companions found a Muslim sultan there, as well as exiled 'Muslims', banished from Brunei, at Cagayan Sulu island, who thought the Spaniards were gods!

At a harbour in Palawan island they captured the Muslim pilots of a junk, who guided them to Labuan and

*Affonso d'Albuquerque, 1453–1515*

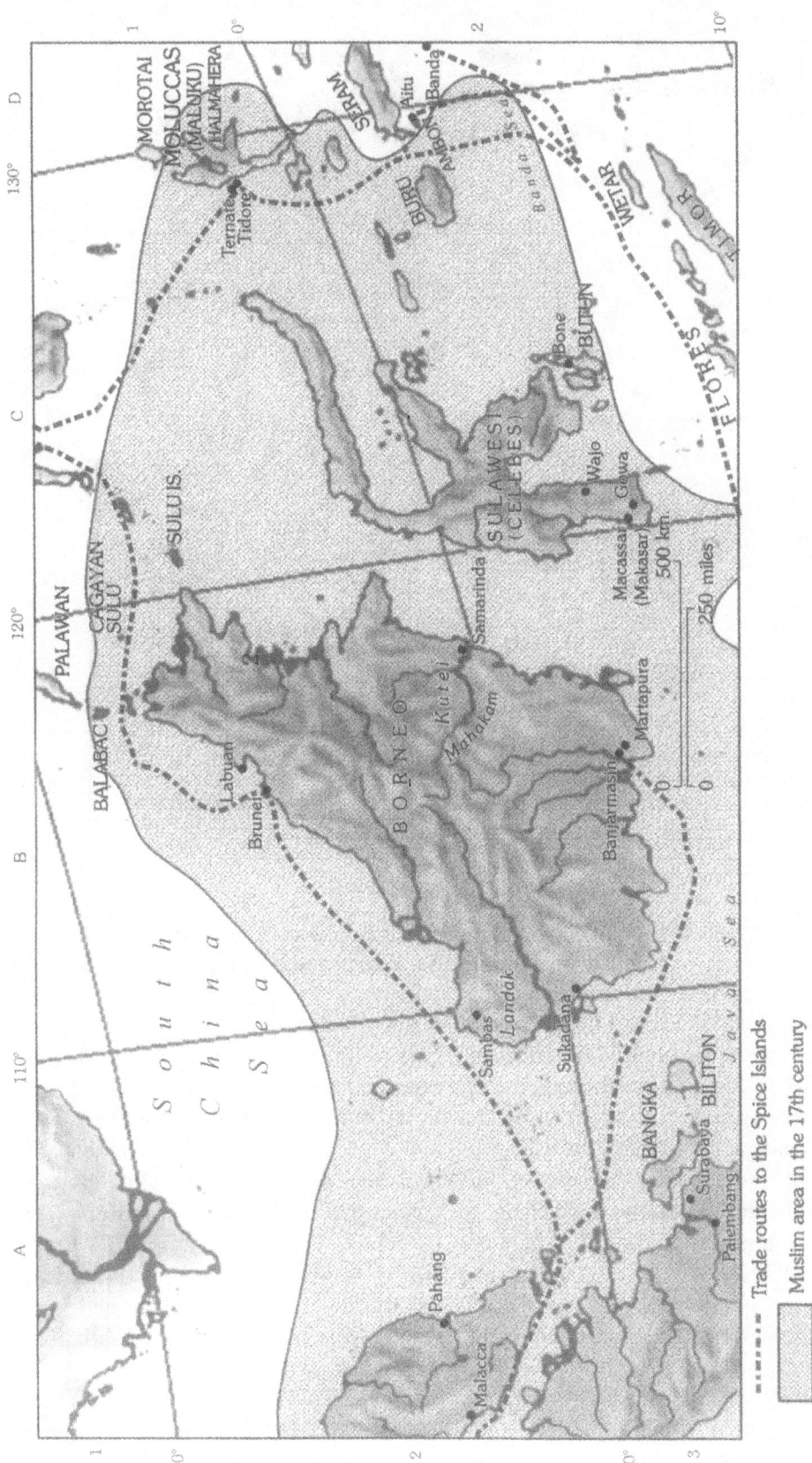

THE SPREAD OF ISLAM IN BORNEO, SULAWESI AND THE MOLUCCAS, 15TH TO 17TH CENTURIES

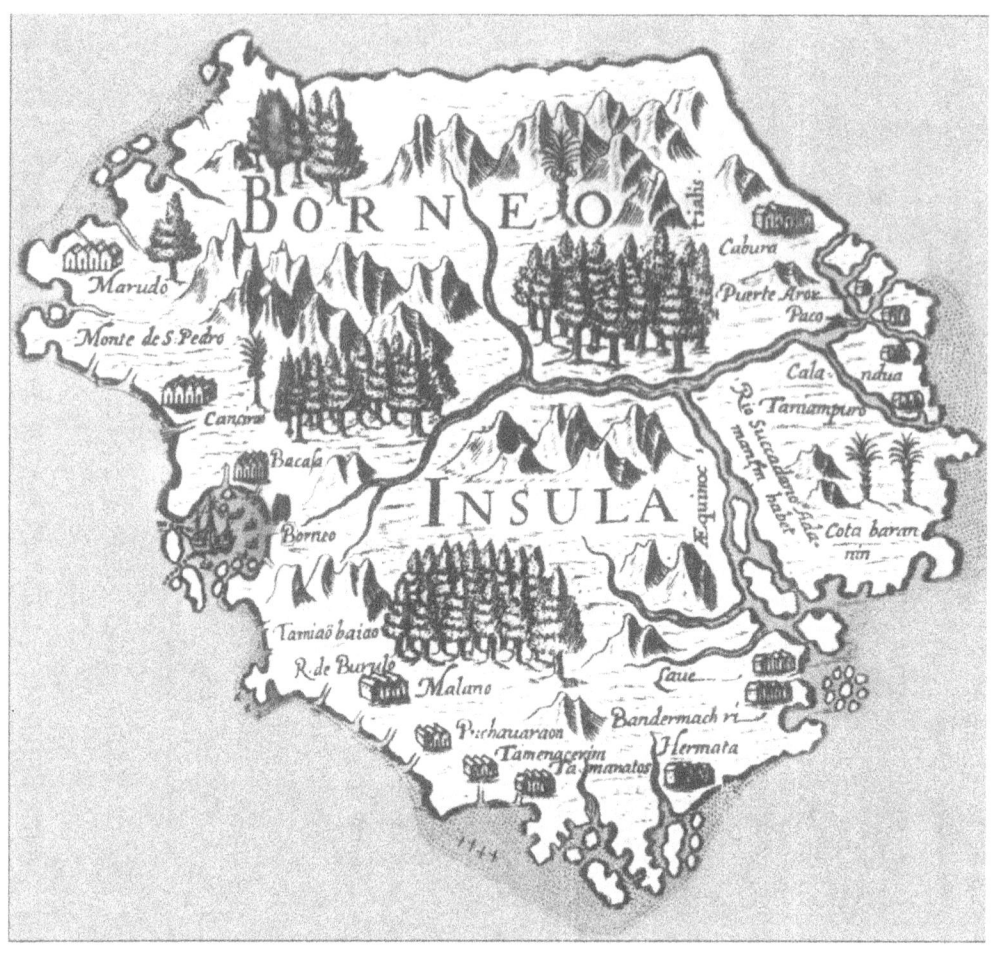

*Borneo, drawn by Olivier van Noort, 1601*

Brunei. They were welcomed by Sultan Siripada, but the visit ended in fighting. Brunei like Acheh had profited from Malacca's fall in 1511. Other Muslim states were subsequently established, Sambas, Sukadana, Landak on the west coast, Banjarmasin further south. The Dutch made some attempt to use these places for trade, in the 18th century, but withdrew, and eventually, from Penang, Britain stepped in, starting with Banjarmasin. After 1813, through Raffles' efforts, the sultan of Sambas and other states recognized British suzerainty; but these states reverted soon to Dutch sovereignty. By 1846, efforts against piracy supported from Brunei led to the British involvement there, and the sultan's recognition of *Rajah* Brooke in Sarawak, and British presence in Labuan.

Islam spread in the years before Portuguese influence expanded in the region (and perhaps as something of a reaction to it), from the ports of northern Java, and Demak, into southern Borneo and into the Moluccas (Maluku) by the second half of the fifteenth century. The ruler of Ternate, Zayn al-'Abidin (1486–1500), was so deeply influenced by Muslim traders (and there had been earlier Muslim influences too), that he went to study in Giri (Gresik) in Java, and returned with the Muslim preacher Tuhubahahul. Ambon is said to have been converted by a qadi called Ibrahim.

Magellan's ships arrived at Tidore late in 1521 (after Magellan's death), and found the ruler to be al-Mansur, while Ternate was ruled by Boleyse (Abdul Hussein).

Sulawesi (Celebes) also had close mercantile contacts with Muslim Indonesia, but the rulers only began to ponder conversion in the late 16th century. In 1605 the prince of Tallo in Makasar officially accepted Islam, influenced by a Giri-trained Minangkabau Muslim, Dato'ri Bandang. The new Muslim ruler then in 1608 launched campaigns successfully to subdue some more northerly principalities, Bone, Soppeng, Wajo'. A large part of the mountainous interior never accepted Islam. The same Muslim preacher, Bandang, and a companion, Tunggang Parangan, are said to have left Makasar to convert Raja Makota of Kutei in eastern Borneo.

Sultan Agung of Mataram in 1622, engaged in the siege of Surabaya, also received the submission of Banjarmasin and Sukedana in southern Borneo. Banjarmasin, easily accessible from Java, is said to have been converted when the ruler Samudra accepted the aid of Demak in Java, on condition of his conversion. As with Sulawesi, the central area, occupied by Dyaks, was never converted.

## SIAM, THE MALAY STATES AND BRITAIN,
### 15TH TO 20TH CENTURIES

The famous and controversial Ramkamhaeng inscription from Sukhothai claims that an unnamed king received submission from '... Sri Dharmaraja, and the seacoast, which is the furthest place'. This has given scope to the imagination for Siamese tributaries as far as Johore and Singapore as early as the 13th century. Thai palace regulations, Kot Montien Ban, claim Ayutthayan suzerainty over the whole Malay peninsula down to Malacca (Melaka) and Ujong

*Thomas Stamford Raffles 1781–1826, one of the founders of Britian's empire in the Far East*

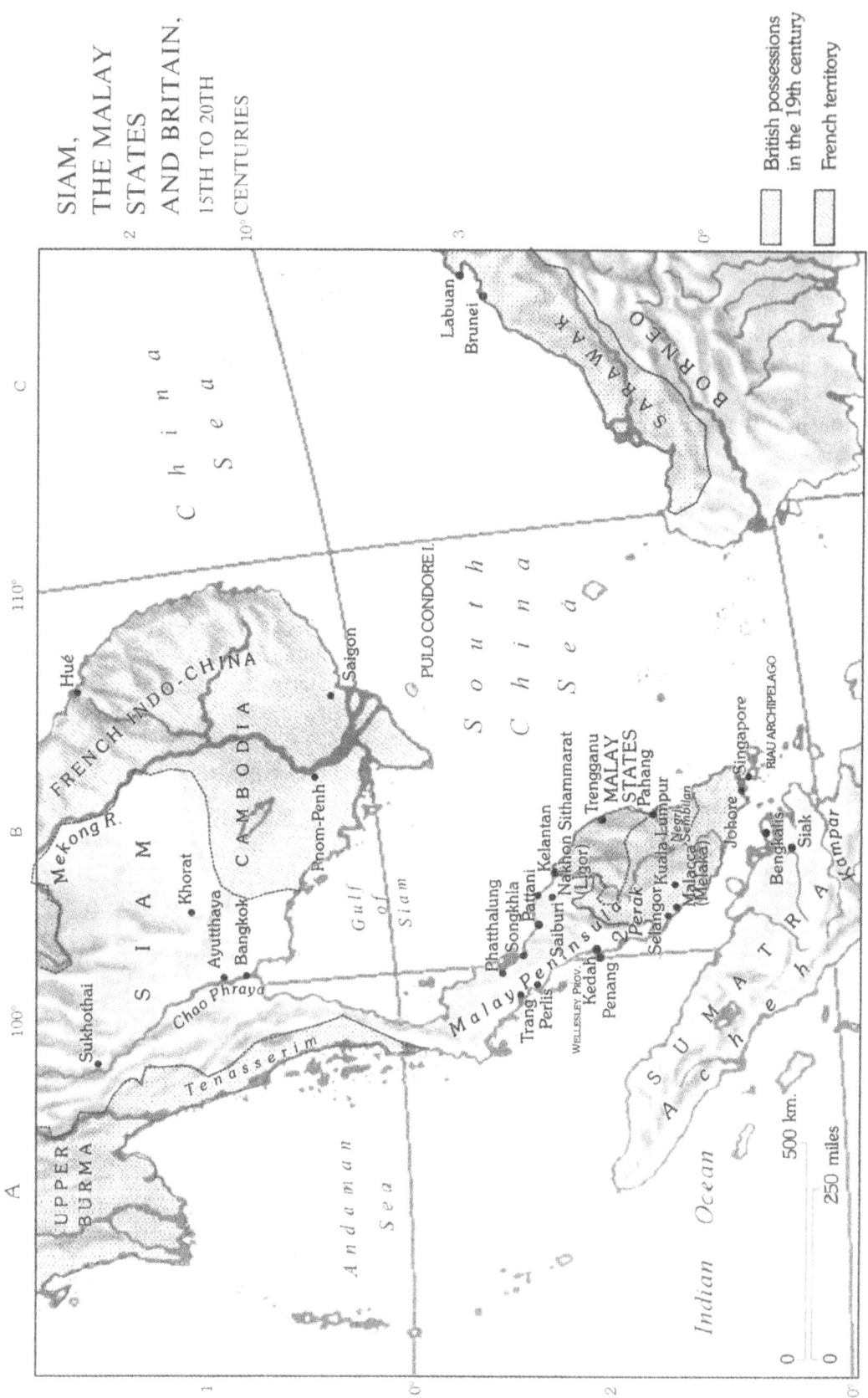

Tanah (Johore/Singapore), and in the 16th century, Portuguese authors include Singapore as among the states under Siamese influence. For a part of the Ayutthaya period (1351–1767) and of the Rattanakosin period (from 1782) many of the northern Muslim Malay states, at least, were tributary to Siam, until they all passed under British colonial rule.

The Malay states were administered from Nakhon Sithammarat (Ligor), where they sent the tributary flowers of gold and silver, the *bunga mas*. From the 17th century Johore did not send any gifts. It became for a time almost an imperial power itself, adding Acheh's former tributary Pahang to its domination of other Malay states, the Riau Archipelago, Bengkalis, and Kampar and Siak in Sumatra. Johore began trade with Britain, as did Kedah, Perak, and Acheh in Sumatra. The Nakhon Chronicles list the states that paid tribute via Nakhon to Siam as Yihon (Narathiwat region), Janatepa (south of Songkhla), Pahang, Pattani, Saiburi, Phattalung, Kedah, Langu (in Trang province), Ace (Acheh), and Phru.

By the nineteenth century, with the British in Penang from 1785, and in Wellesley Province from 1800, questions over the status of the Malay states often arose, with occasional rebellions and treaties that forced Siam to recognise that it had to reckon with the British in its administration of Malay affairs. The *bunga mas* were still sent by the Malay *rajahs* from Kelantan, Trengganu, Pattani (divided since its rebellion in 1790 into seven parts, the others being Saiburi, Yiring, Raman, Yala, Rangae, and Nongchik), Kedah, Perlis and Satun. By a treaty of 1909, Siam transferred its rights of suzerainty over Kelantan, Trengganu, Kedah and Perlis to Britain. These states and Johore did not join, however, the federation, whose administration settled at Kuala Lumpur.

In the south, the Straits Settlements governors observed the advancing chaos in the Malay states, with rebellions of Chinese in the tin mines, piracy, and disorder. A new spirit of advance was outlined by the Sumatra treaty, 1871, that left the Dutch free to start their war against Acheh, and the British to abandon non-intervention in Malaya. From 1874 British Residents were installed in the 'protected states', Perak, Selangor, and Sungei Ujong in what was to become Negri Sembilan (a congeries of Minangkabau settlements). They reported to the governor of the Straits Settlements. In 1888 Pahang was added, then in 1895 Negri Sembilan. Kuala Lumpur became the administrative center.

TRAVELS OF IBN BATTUTA
IN CHINA, ASSAM
AND SOUTH-EAST ASIA

Journeys of Ibn Battuta: ——— Earlier   – – – Later

*Mosque of Turfan, Xinjiang Province, China, 17th century*

## TOMÉ PIRES' ACCOUNT OF TRADE, C. 1515

Tomé Pires, ex-apothecary to Prince Afonso of Portugal, was in India as 'factor of drugs' and later in Malacca (Melaka), just after its capture by the Portuguese in 1511. He wrote between 1512 and 1515 about the region in his *Suma Orientale*. Pires, as supervisor of the spice trade at Malacca, was well placed to obtain information. He discusses Arabia Felix (Yemen) with its vigorous trade in captured Abyssinian slaves, its merchants and merchandise from Cambay, Aden, Ormuz, Zeila, Berbera, Kilwa, Malindi, Brava, Mogadishu, and Mombasa. The merchants of Aden collected in Cambay the merchandise of Malacca, cloves, nutmeg, mace, sandalwood, brazil wood, silk, pearls, musk, porcelain, which they could then distribute in the Middle Eastern region. Malacca conducted a vigorous trade with Cambay, based on the Gujarati merchants who traded particularly in cloth of different kinds, seeds (nigella, cumin, aloes, fenugreek), roots like rampion, lac, storax and so on. In return they received the merchandise of the Moluccas, Banda, and China. In addition to the places mentioned above, Pires notes that merchants at Cambay included men from Abyssinia, Persians, Turkomans, Armenians, Guilans, Khorasanis, and Shirazis. There were many of these, too, in Malacca, and many merchants of the Deccan, also, set up companies in Cambay.

## ISLAM IN SOUTHERN THAILAND,
### 17TH TO 19TH CENTURIES

In the 16th and 17th centuries, Muslim *shahbandars*, or port authorities, and other trading agencies, were employed by the rulers of Siam – we find one at Cebu in the Philippines recorded during Magellan's voyage. These were part of the trading diaspora, Persians and others, and had no religious influence of importance in this Buddhist land.

Part of the tradition of Nakhon Sithammarat in S. Thailand is the list the twelve 'naksat' cities (cycle of twelve animal years, each one representing a city or country supposedly under Nakhon's control): Muslim areas included are Saiburi (in Naratiwat province), Pattani, Kelantan, Pahang and Kedah. This seems to reflect mid-Ayutthayan period claims to suzerainty over the Malay regions of the south. Nakhon itself, with Songkhla and Phuket, were generally regarded by visitors as being largely Malay in population, though largely Buddhist in religion. Pattani, for much of the seventeenth

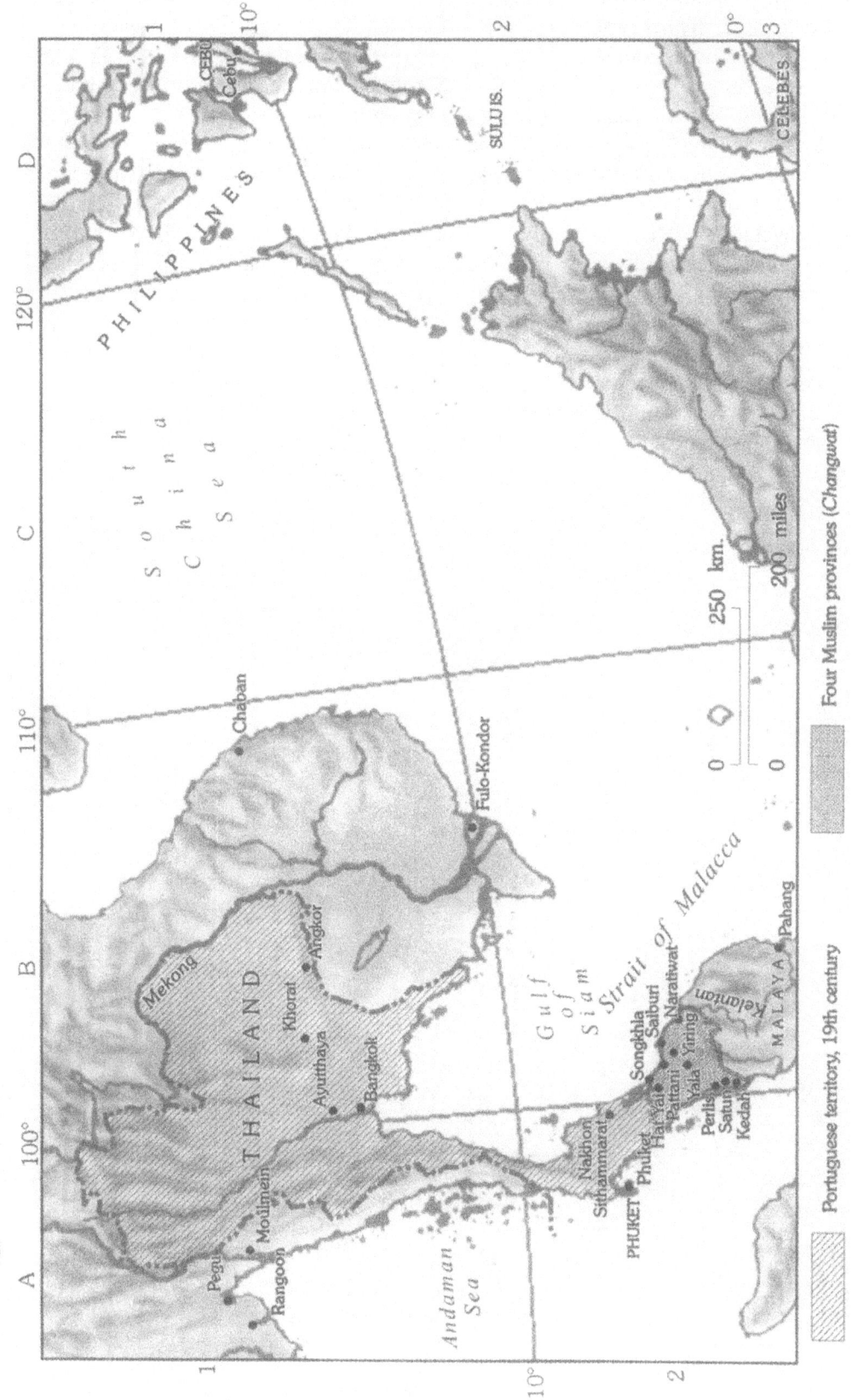

ISLAM IN SOUTHERN THAILAND, 17TH TO 19TH CENTURIES

century ruled by queens, and trading with the Portuguese, British and the Dutch, several times caused trouble by revolting from Ayutthaya, and was as often compelled to submit again. After its rebellion in 1790, Pattani was divided into seven parts, Pattani itself, with Saiburi, Yiring, Raman, Yala, Rangae, and Nongchik. Kedah, also in rebellion, was in 1839 pacified by replacing the Siamese governor with Malays, and by dividing the state into three parts, Kedah, Polit (Perlis) and Kabangpasu, each with its own sultan. Satun, too, was given its own sultan, and temporarily removed from Nakhon's jurisdiction into that of Songkhla (Singora).

In Thailand today there are four Muslim and largely Malay ethnic *changwat* or provinces: Pattani, Naratiwat, Yala and Satun. All the rest of the former southern tributaries now belong, after a period under British control, to Malaysia. Muslims in Thailand today represent about 2% of the population. Apart from the southern province Muslims, Pakistanis in the cities, some ethnic Thai, Chinese Haw Muslims in the north, a number of Chams and other small foreign Muslim groups, make up the rest, mainly Sunni with some Shi'a. There are mosques in about half the *changwat* of Thailand catering for these groups.

Muslim separatist movements in the

*Jami Mosque, Brunei, Borneo*

southern provinces, including Songkhla, still occasionally manifest themselves, though it has much reduced since the end of the fighting against Communist groups in the area. In April 2001 a bomb was planted at Hat Yai in Songkhla province, attributed by the police to the Bersatu (Unity) separatist group, formed around 1994. Among the disparate groups associated with Bersatu is the Pattani United Liberation Organisation (Pulo). These groups are said to be small and relatively insignificant.

## ISLAM IN CAMBODIA AND AMONG THE CHAMS,
### 17TH TO 20TH CENTURIES

Islam met with a well rooted religious tradition in Buddhist Cambodia, but there was a brief episode in 1642 when the third son of King Chay Chetta II, called Chan, seized the throne with the assistance of Cham and Malay mercenaries, prominent in Cambodian politics by then for some time already. It was important for Chan to keep the support of the Muslim Chams and Malays, and he had a Malay wife himself, so he announced his conversion to Islam as King Ibrahim. The Muslim traders in the country persuaded the king to reverse his favour towards Dutch merchants at Phnom Penh. In 1643 there was a massacre, and Dutch ships were destroyed. The Muslim Chams and Malays revolted after Chan's defeat and capture in 1658, but were defeated. Many fled to Siam with Chan's sons, but others remained and were to feature during periods of unrest in succeeding reigns.

In Cambodia nowadays, the Chams are exclusively Muslim. There are settlements of Chams, and a number of mosques, on the Tonle Sap river, some kilometers north of Phnom Penh. In Vietnam those in the Mekong Delta tend to be Muslim, whilst those along the central coast tend to be Hindu. What happened to convert the Cham remnant or diaspora to Islam is largely speculation, but probably the Cham ruling classes remained Hindu while the lower castes converted to Islam. Their Islam is fairly heterodox, fasting only one day a week in Ramadan, drinking alcohol at will, and the like.

*The famous 12th century Buddhist Temple at Angkor Wat, Cambodia*

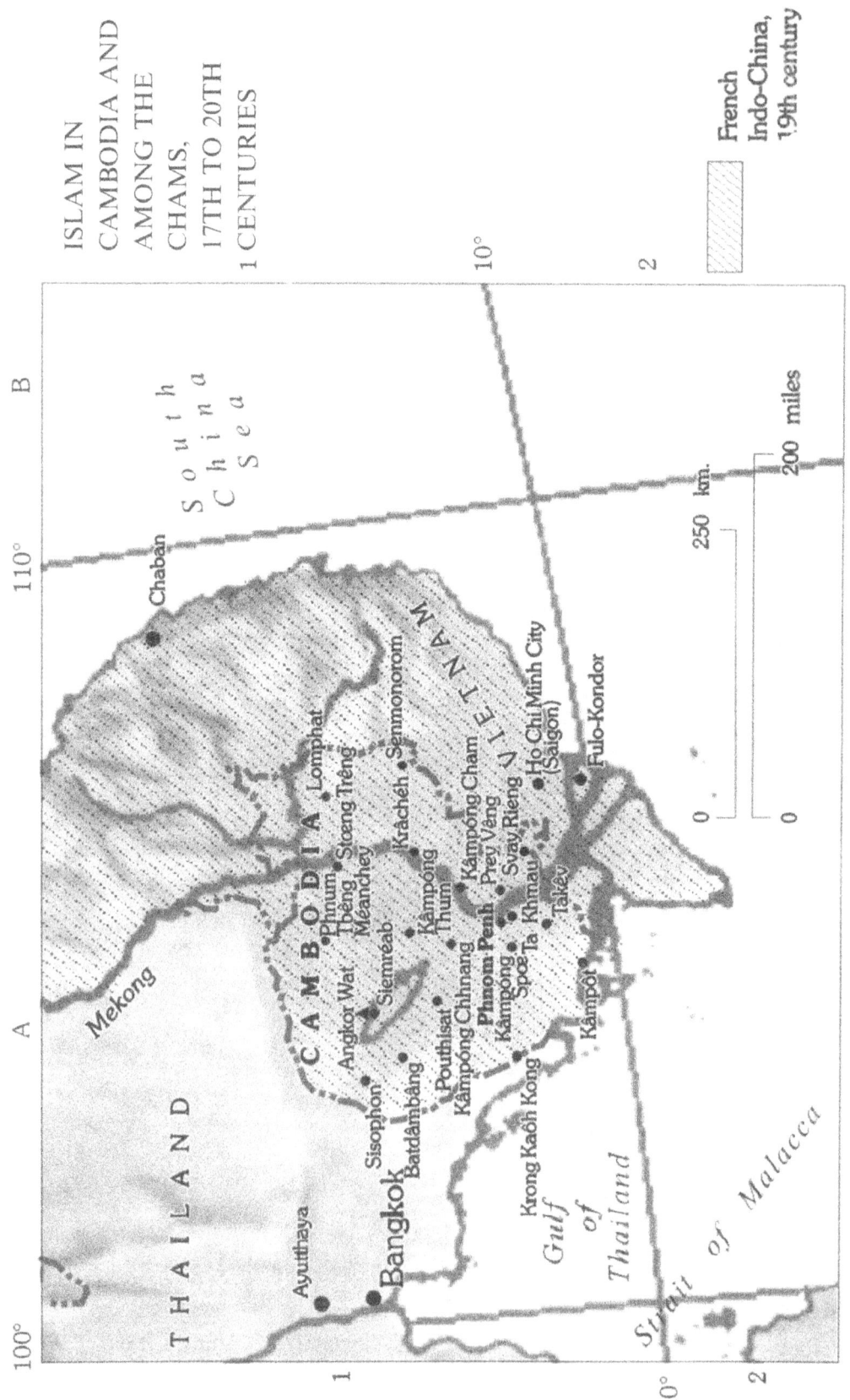

# SOUTH-EAST ASIA AND BRITAIN,
## 17TH TO 20TH CENTURIES

British seventeenth century relations with the Muslim states of South-East Asia gradually exchanged trade for political dominance. The British set up and abandoned several factories in Muslim areas, the first being the Pattani factory (founded in 1612) in 1623. The factory founded in 1669 for tin export at Kedah, too, was abandoned. Bantam, under Dutch pressure, was abandoned in 1682 and replaced by Bencoolen in W. Sumatra, and the Balambangan (Sulu) concession of 1762 was wiped out by pirates in 1775. It was replaced by Labuan (Brunei) in the same year, but abandoned soon after. The use of Dutch Batavia being fraught with difficulties, it was next suggested that Bintan, south of Singapore, might serve. After that, Phuket (Junk Ceylon) was considered. Then, largely for naval reasons concerning Indian security in the French wars, Penang became a British settlement in 1785.

But the final discovery of the perfect place for the British in face of the current situation in the east had to wait until Raffles came upon Singapore. This place was under a Malay chief, but it was necessary to ratify any agreement with the sultan of Johore: Raffles therefore installed a new one in 1819, from among the claimants to that formerly important Malay state. With the possession of Penang and Singapore, the British were ready to enter into internal Malay affairs. This led to a number of things. Interference with Siamese claims over Kedah and other northern Malay states, in the end came to Siam's final surrender of

*Singapore refounded in 1819 by the English*

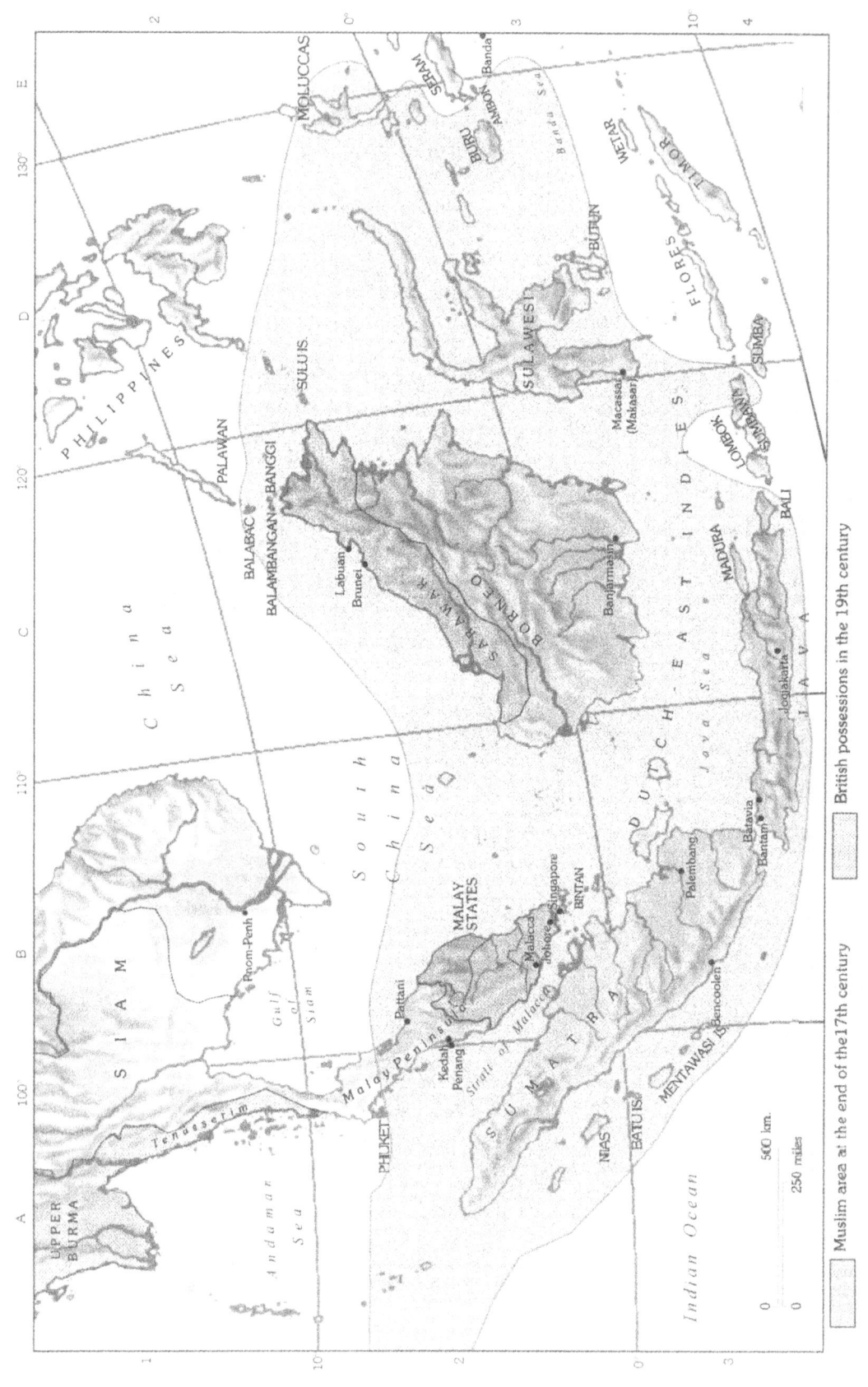

SOUTH-EAST ASIA AND BRITAIN, 17TH TO 20TH CENTURIES

*Sir James Brooke (1803–1868), the 'White Rajah' of Sarawak*

these claims to Britain in 1909. Malacca and Singapore were placed under Penang's control as the Straits Settlements in 1826; then Singapore took the lead in 1832.

In 1795, after the expulsion of William IV of Orange and the declaration of the Batavian Republic under French protection, many of the Dutch possessions in the east, on the west coast of Sumatra, Malacca, Amboina and the Bandas, were taken over by the British. They were restored by the Peace of Amiens in 1802, but mostly reconquered in 1803 when war broke out again with Napoleon, whose brother Louis became king of Holland. The Dutch governor-general in Java, Daendels, alienated the sultans of Bantam and Jogjakarta, and reduced or removed the garrisons of Banjarmasin in Borneo, Palembang in Sumatra and Makasar in Sulawesi, though he strengthened Amboina in the highly profitable Moluccas. In 1810–11 Amboina, Batavia, the rest of Java, Palembang, Timor, Makasar were surrendered to the British, and Stamford Raffles became lieutenant-governor of Java, Madura, Palembang, Bali, Banjarmasin (W. Borneo) and Makasar. All this, however, went back to Holland after the final defeat of Napoleon in 1815

## ISLAM IN THE PHILIPPINES, 15TH TO 20TH CENTURIES

Preachers of Islam seem to have followed Brunei's trade routes to the Sulu archipelago, if we accept the *tarsila* or chain of ancestry of the Sulu sultanate. One of them, Karim al-Makhdum, founded Islam in Sulu. He was followed by the arrival of the Muslim *raja*, Bauguinda of Sumatra, and his courtiers, then by one Abu Bakr, a *sayyid* coming supposedly coming via Palembang and Brunei to

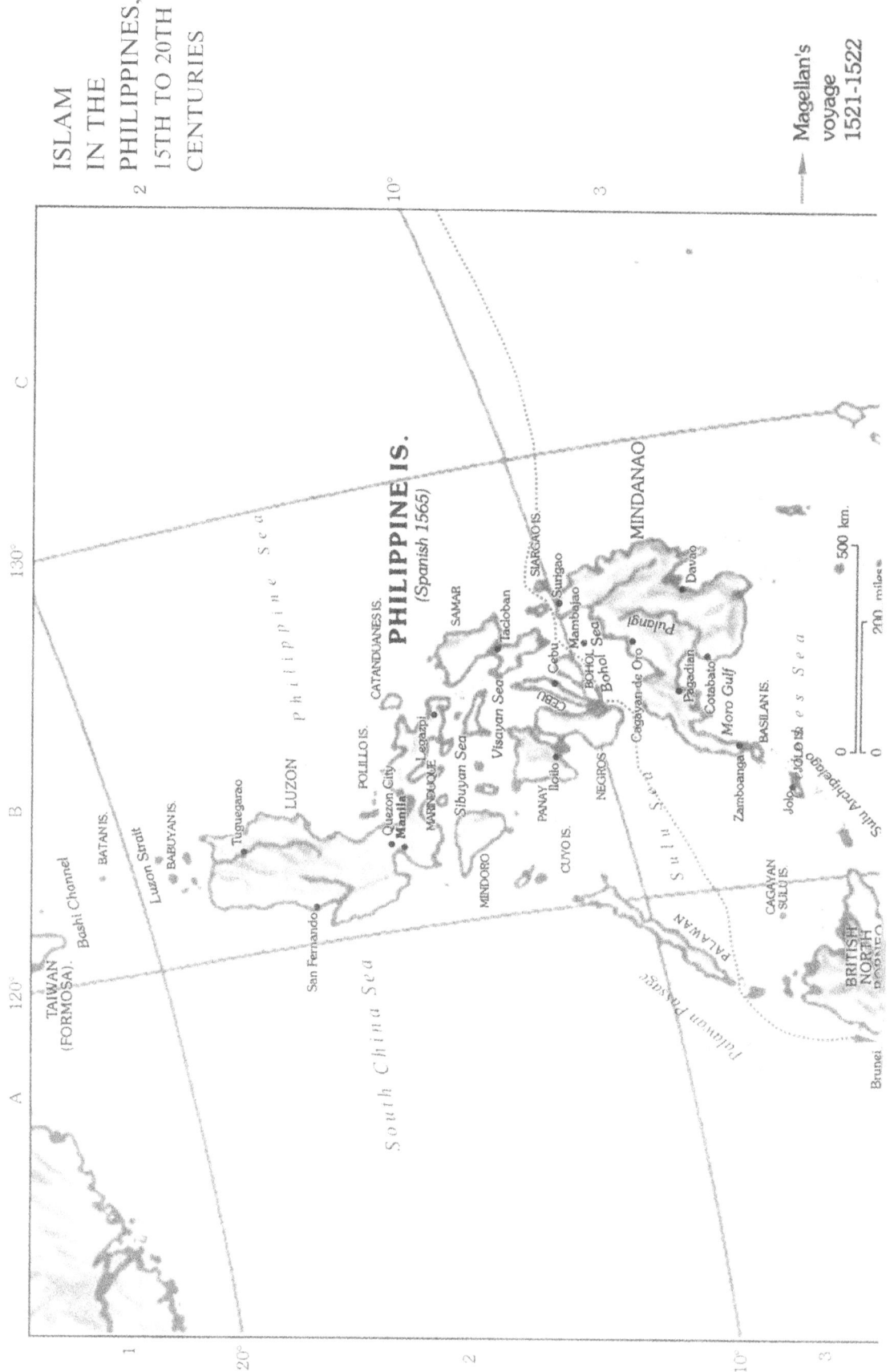

ISLAM IN THE PHILIPPINES, 15TH TO 20TH CENTURIES

→ Magellan's voyage 1521-1522

marry into the family of the raja, and become sultan himself under the title Sultan Sharif al-Hashim (c. 1450–80).
Islam reached the Pulangi valley in Mindanao, to both the Maguindanao and Buayan dynasties, it is said, through sharif Muhammad Kabungsuwan. He came from Johore, son of an Arab claiming descent from Muhammad. He is said to have married a local woman, and many of the people converted. A Buayan raja is said to have married a daughter of the sharif, while the Maguindanao dynasty claimed direct descent through the sharif's son. The two dynasties both quarrelled and intermarried, and by the mid-seventeenth century the Maguindanao dynasty had achieved supremacy. But by the end of the century their own power was weakening in face of the Spaniards, who occupied the lower Pulangi valley and the Iranun coastal territories, the traditional seat of the power of the sultans. Buayan power was resuscitated during the conflict with the Spaniards, and many smaller sultanates sprang up as Maguindanao decayed.

In 1521, when Magellan's fleet reached Cebu, north of Mindanao, the chief Humabon was advised by a Muslim who seems to have been an agent for Siamese trading. Islam was unable to penetrate to the Manila region to any significant degree, though the ruling family was supposedly Muslim in 1565 (Legazpi), because of the coming of the Spaniards, with whom there was to be continual war with the Muslim south.

Islam has continued its progress in the southern Philippines, culminating recently in the 1990s and early this century with considerable unrest. Jolo and Basilan have been the scene of kidnappings, beheadings and other extremist manifestations, with demands by the Abu Sayyad group for the independence as a Muslim state of the southern third of the Philippines.

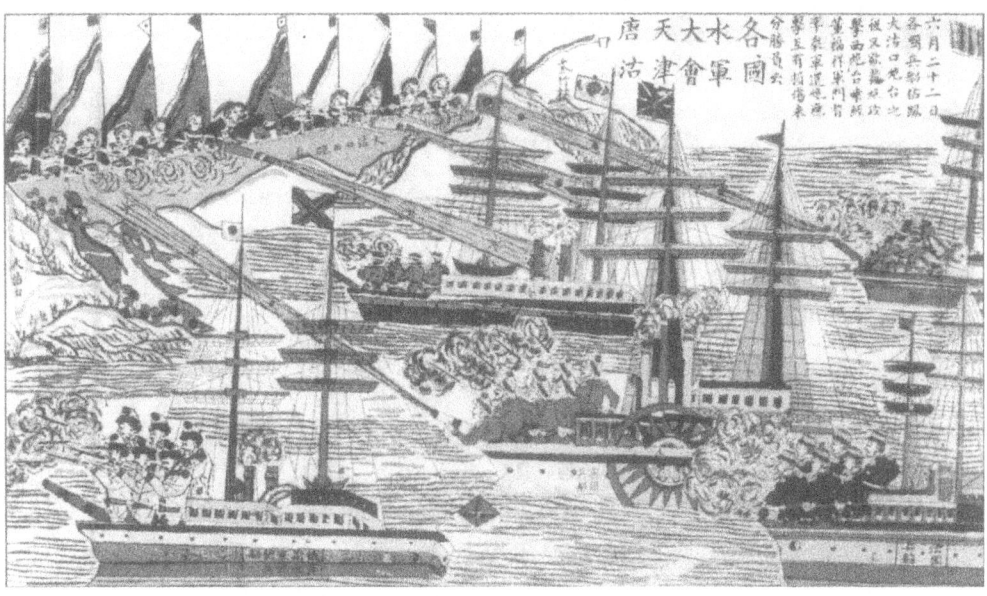

*Western forces attack Boxer rebels, in the Boxer Rebellion, 1900. Chinese ink drawing.*

# VI. THE OTTOMAN WORLD AND EUROPEAN IMPERIALISM

## THE OTTOMAN EMPIRE AT ITS GREATEST EXTENT,
### 16TH TO 17TH CENTURIES

When Selim I the Grim succeeded, he killed his brothers, seven of their sons, and four of his own sons. He left only Sulayman (r. 1520–1566), the ablest son. With the acquisition of Egypt he captured the commercial and intellectual

*Ottomans capture Rhodes, 1522*

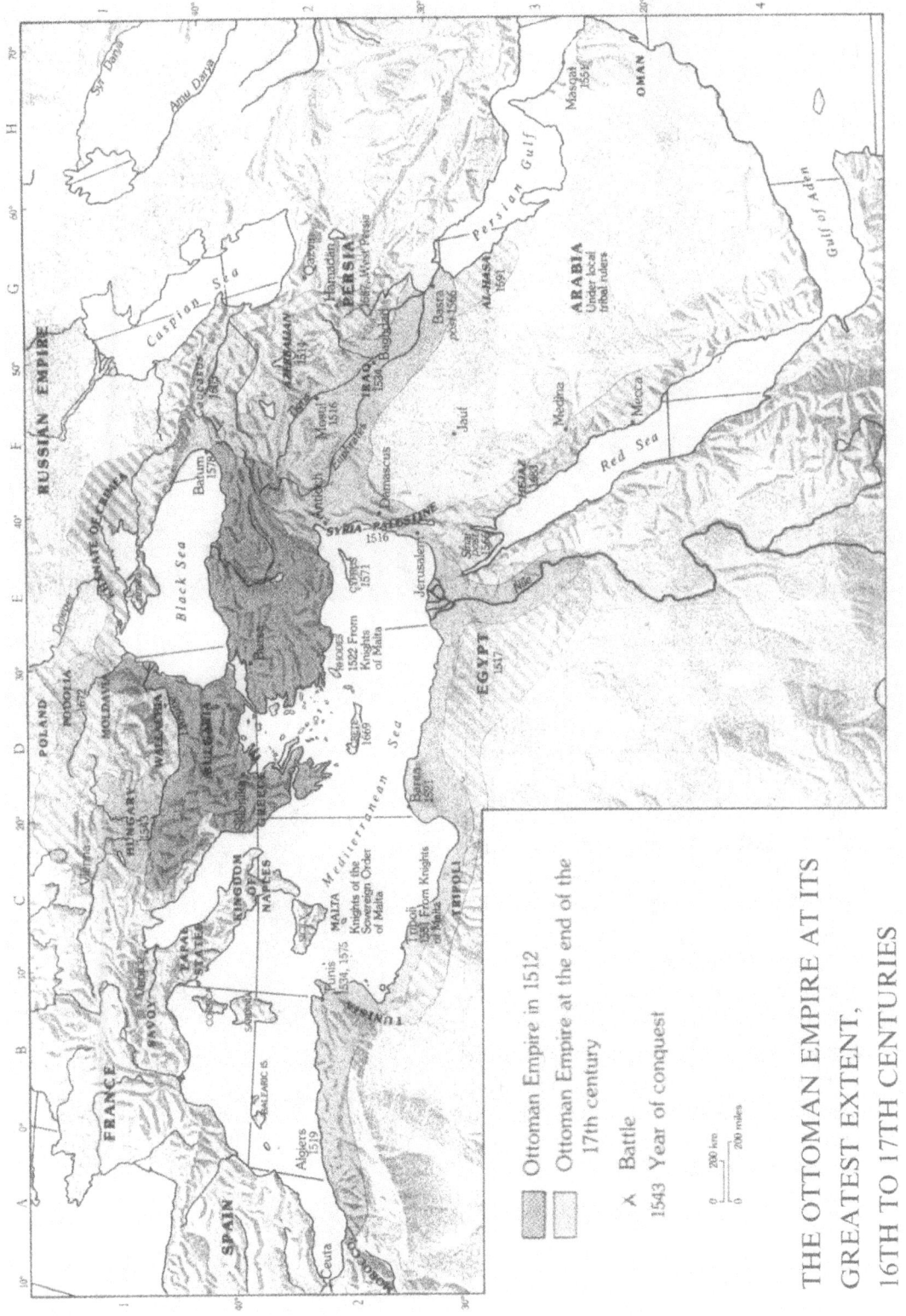

THE OTTOMAN EMPIRE AT ITS GREATEST EXTENT, 16TH TO 17TH CENTURIES

*Tophane Mosque, Istanbul*

capital of Islam. Though the Portuguese had command of the sea trade with the East, Selim I still commanded the land routes of Egypt, Arabia, Syria, and Asia Minor. Eastern Europe, too, was firmly part of the Middle East. Under Sulayman the Magnificent, as Europeans called him, or the Lawgiver, as Turks called him, the empire fought the Habsburgs in a Europe weakened by Protestant dissidence. In spite of this fighting, in 1536, France was able to establish strong commercial ties with Istanbul. The favorable trade conditions granted by the Sublime Porte are known as the Capitulations. They gave France predominance in the Levant, with long-term effects that are still apparent.

*Sultan Qansawh al-Ghawri of Cairo, 1501–1516*

During Sulayman's reign northern Africa was added to the empire. He and his father were the first Ottoman sultans to pay attention to the Indian Ocean, and naval bases were built at Suez in 1517 and Basra in 1538. The Portuguese were not powerful enough to dominate the Indian Ocean completely, and to some extent the trading positions of Syria and the Middle East recovered from the shock of their initial incursion. Sulayman's reign marks the apogee of Ottoman power; under his successors decline set in. Selim II, the Sot (r. 1566–1574) and Murad III (r. 1574–1575) were weak, and the period between 1570 and 1578 is known as the "sultanate of women" because of the excessive influence of the harem on appointments. Thereafter, until 1625, power passed into the hands of the Janissaries.

In spite of the naval disaster at Lepanto (1570), the Ottomans retained command of the Mediterranean throughout most of the seventeenth century. Tunis was conquered by the Turks in 1574; Fez was seized from Portugal in 1578, and Crete from Venice in 1669. The military spirit of the original conquerors had declined, and the camp gave way to the boudoir. This decline was clear to all Europe during the Habsburg war (1593–1606). In the East the shah of Persia, Abbas I, was able to retake the Caucasus and Azerbaijan in 1603 and Iraq in 1624, though he lost Iraq again to Murad IV in 1638. Although victorious, the long sea war with Venice (1645–1669) was commercially debilitating for the Ottomans, who failed to destroy Venice.

The tide turned in 1683. From 14 July to 12 September, the Turks besieged Vienna, but at Kahlenberg, Parkau, and finally Stettin the Ottomans were routed. Although war continued with Austria, Poland, and Venice until 1698 — during

*The Turkish camp before the walls of Vienna*

*Painting of the Battle of Lepanto 1571, in which the Turks were defeated*

**OTTOMAN TERRITORIES IN EUROPE,** 16TH TO 17TH CENTURIES.

which time their "Holy League" of 1684 was joined in 1686 by Russia — the Ottomans were never able to threaten Europe again. Nevertheless, between 1683 and 1792 there were forty-one years of war in which the Ottomans fought the Holy League. During the next century they fought Russia in 1710–1711; Austria and Venice in 1714–1718; and Russia and Austria together in 1734–1739, 1768–1774, and 1787–1792. The Ottomans lost Hungary, the Crimea, Croatia, Slavonia, and Transylvania.

These wars, which had begun with a Polish cavalry action of the greatest bravery at the siege of Vienna, were the beginning of a new era in eastern Europe. It not only brought Russia into the concert of Europe; it made Russia a participant in Middle Eastern affairs. It was also the beginning of the collapse of the inchoate, cumbrous Ottoman system, which was not completed until the end of World War I.

*Salimiyyah Mosque, mid-sixteenth century, Edirne, Turkey*

## THE FILALI SHARIFS OF MOROCCO, FROM 1631

When the last Hasani sharif was assassinated in 1653 the succession was disputed. One of the least conspicuous claimants was Muhammad al-Sharif, head of the Filali lineage of sharifs, who claimed descent from the Prophet's grandson Hasan. He had been expelled from the sultanate of Sijilmasa in 1646. By 1664 his son, Moulay al-Rashid, had laid the foundation for a monarchy that endures to this day. He took Fez in 1666 and Marrakesh in 1668 by creating an army of negroes, who were either bought or the descendants of slaves. Placed into the army at the age of eighteen; married to negro wives who had been trained in the royal palaces; given training for three years as muleteers and housebuilders and then for five years in archery, musketry, and fieldcraft; these men formed an army of 150,000 by 1686, dependent on the sultan alone. A new and splendid capital was built at Meknès.

The formidable army controlled the *blad*

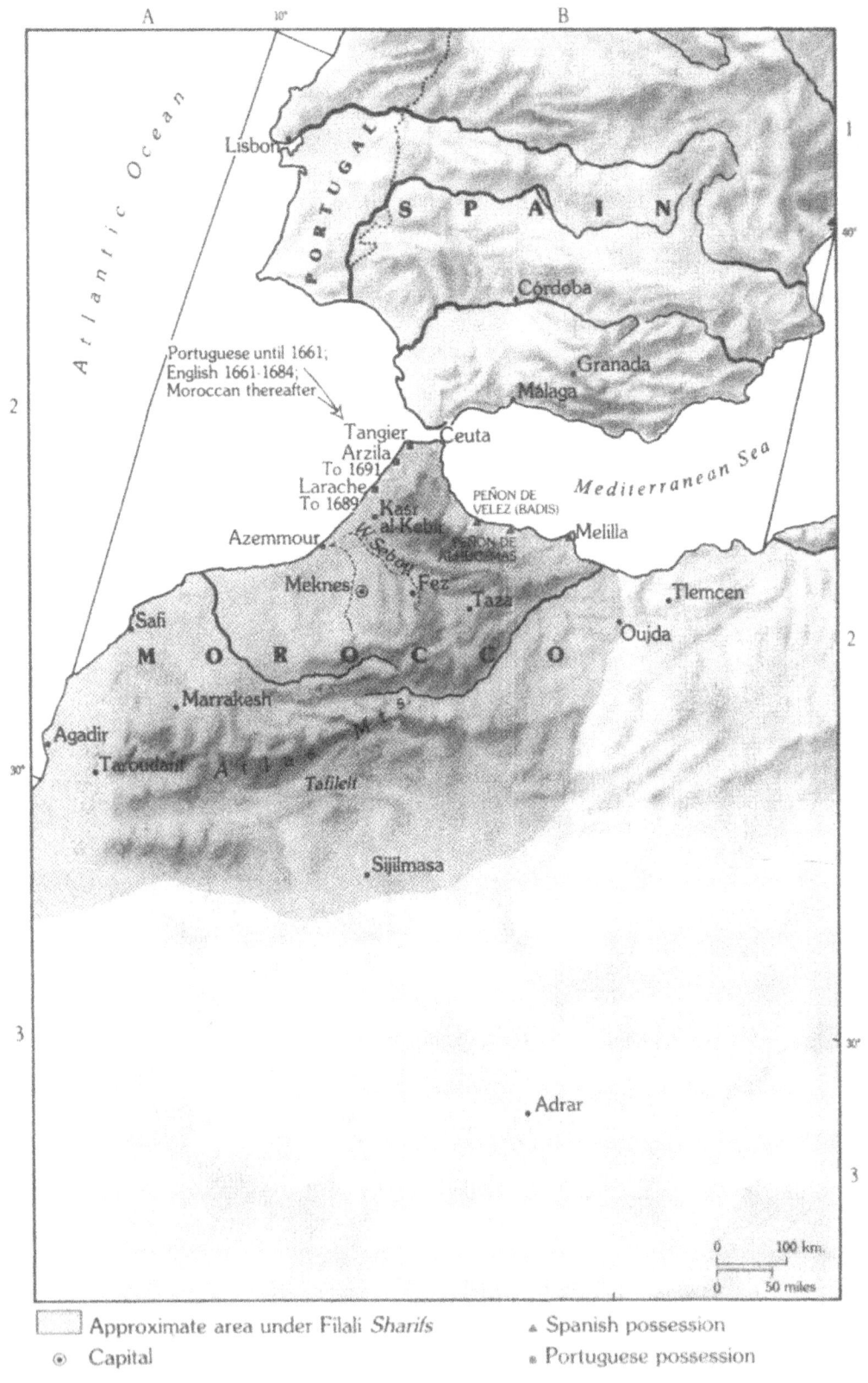

THE FILALI SHARIFS OF MOROCCO, FROM 1631

*The Cherarda Gate, Fez, Morocco*

*al-makhzan* (the lands of the government) and the *blad al-siba* (lands of no authority, in which the sultanic writ did not run). Until a French protectorate was installed in 1912, these areas varied according to the ability and strength of the individual rulers. Among these rulers Moulay Ismail (r. 1672–1727) was the most remarkable. Under him the *blad al-siba* was virtually nonexistent. Of him and his successors Voltaire remarked that Moroccan veins contain vitriol, not blood. His passion for war was equaled only by his passion for women; the harem of Meknès contained five hundred women; subsidiary harems were located at Fez and Marrakesh.

In the late nineteenth century Abd al-Aziz (r. 1894–1908) was too young, too impetuous, and too weak to carry out a consistent policy. This failure and that of his usurper and brother, Moulay Abd al-Hafid to maintain order, gave the French the opportunity to seize control. The French ruled it as a protectorate until 1956, when the monarchy was restored.

## THE OTTOMAN EMPIRE IN DECLINE, 1699–1913

Except for the years 1710–1711, when some territory was recovered from Russia, the period between the Treaty of Carlowitz (1699) and the Treaty of Jassy (1792) were years of successive military disasters for the Ottoman Turks. To Russia they lost all their possessions north of the Black Sea — the Caucasus, Bessarabia, Podolia, and the Crimea — from which they had recruited a large proportion of their best fighting men. In

*Medallion of Sultan Abd al-Majid of the Hagia Sophia mosque, Istanbul*

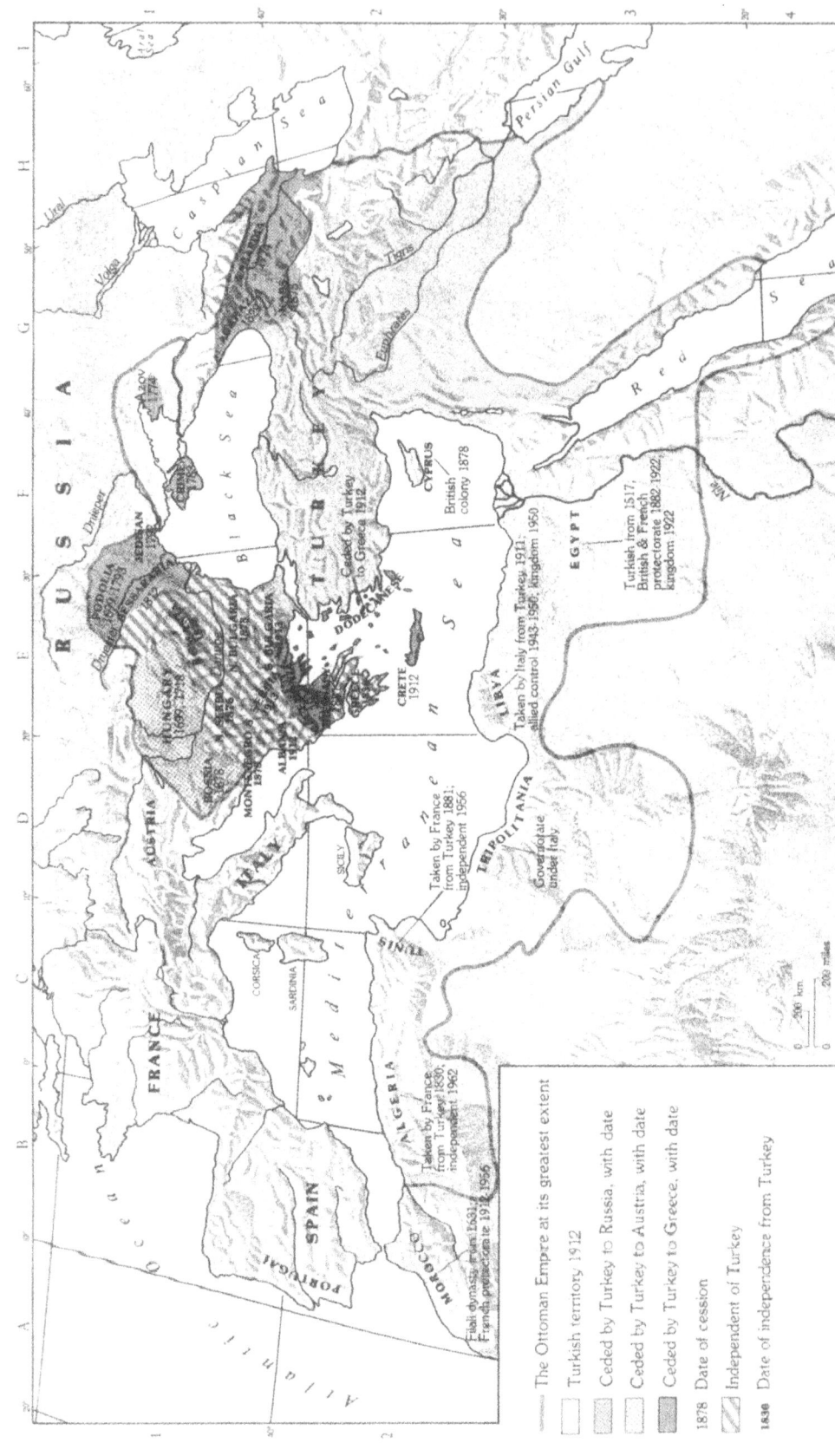

THE OTTOMAN EMPIRE IN DECLINE, 1699–1913

the west they lost Hungary, Transylvania, Bukovina and the Banat of Temisvar causing them to retire to the frontier of 1512 on the Danube. In addition Austria and Russia intervened more and more in the affairs of the Christian subjects of the Porte, exercising an influence that reached a climax in the Crimean War.

In Anatolia, the Balkans, and Lebanon, local rulers established themselves in virtual independence, collecting their own taxes and making remissions to the treasury whose masters were too weak to restore a strong central government. Officialdom was wholly corrupt, from top to bottom. Thus in 1808, when, following a fire, restoration work was needed in the Holy Sepulchre in Jerusalem, a total expenditure of funds raised in Russia of 2.5 million roubles included no less than 1.5 million in bribes. Ottoman society was not only corrupt, it was supine. The Muslim population had no part in the industrial or commercial life of the empire, and took little interest in science or technology. These they left to Jews, Christians, Greeks, and Armenians, peoples they regarded as inferior, together with a small proportion of European merchants, many of them Italian. Having isolated itself, the Muslim population had little or no contact with the West. No books were printed in Turkish before 1727. The Tulip period (1717–1730) was exceptional in its posi-

*Medallion of Sultan Muhammad II on horseback*

tive passion for Westernization, expressed in the growing of tulips.

The most damaging characteristic within Ottoman Turkey in this period was the inertia of the army and the navy, which was wholly destroyed by the Russians at Cesme in 1770. Most obstructive to change was the Janissary corps, once the finest military cadre in existence. Nevertheless, it was impossible to prevent the spread of ideas, and shock waves spread throughout the Ottoman system when Napoleon Bonaparte invaded Egypt. Shortly thereafter the Ottoman viceroy, Muhammad Ali Pasha, made Egypt an independent power in all but name; in central Arabia the Wahhabi movement under Ibn Saud was wholly independent, as were the small sheikhdoms on the shores of the Persian Gulf;

*The Deir Mar Musa Monastery perched on a clifftop in Syria*

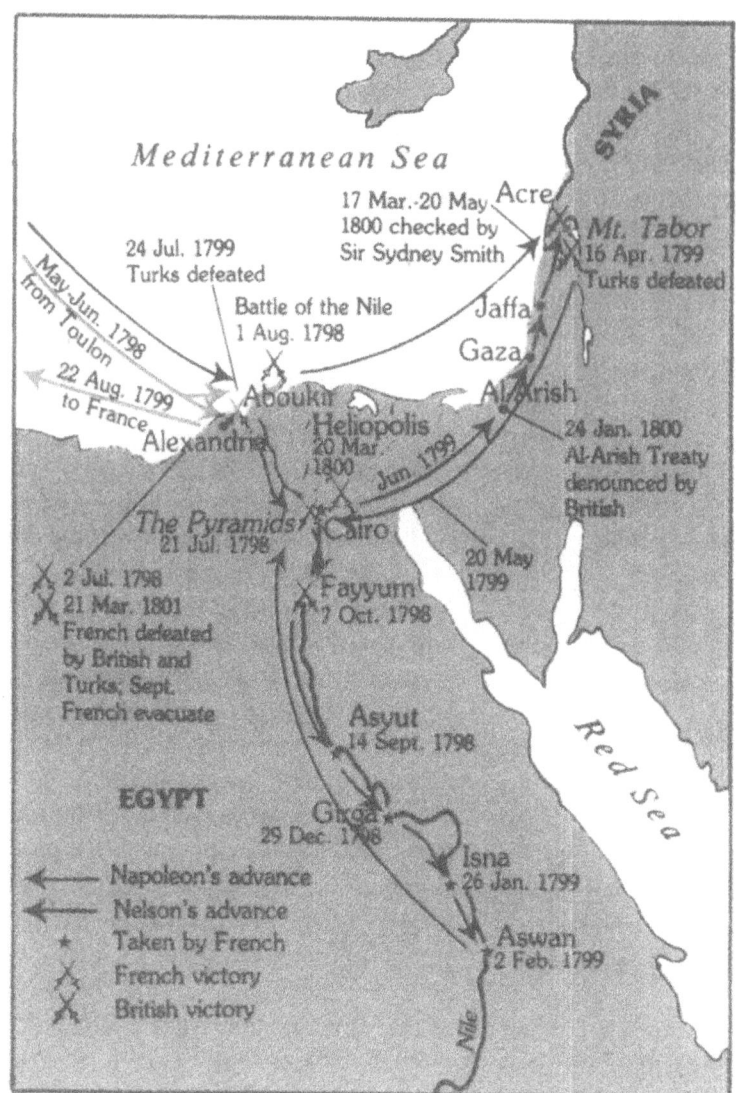

THE FRENCH IN EGYPT AND SYRIA, 1798–1804

and Oman, long independent, was carving out a commercial empire in eastern and central Africa. In Europe the Balkan provinces dropped like ripe pears throughout the latter half of the nineteenth century and into the twentieth.

In the early nineteenth century a number of educational reforms were instituted, and in 1846 a plan for state education was drawn up. By 1914 there were 36,000 Ottoman schools. Less numerous, though not less important, were Greek and Armenian schools, as well as schools run by British, French, and United States missionary bodies. Among these, Robert College (1863) in Istanbul and the Syrian and Jesuit colleges in Beirut developed into universities. In these institutions pro-Western and antitraditionalist attitudes inevitably developed, with demands for reform. It was a tottering state that entered World War I allied to imperial Germany, because it was too weak to reform itself: the war brought its final doom.

*View of the city of Cairo, 19th century*

## THE BARBARY STATES, 17TH AND 18TH CENTURIES

The Ottoman Turks had no more interest in the development or prosperity of their North African provinces, so easily acquired, than they had in any of the others. They had come by sea, and, so long as taxes were paid, were content to look seaward. The seventeenth century was the golden age of piracy in the Mediterranean. Spain made several attempts to take Algiers, but it was not until after 1750 that English and French naval forces began to overcome piracy. It is estimated that in 1650 there were 35,000 Christian captives in Algiers and considerable numbers in Tripoli and Tunis. After 1750 the decline of Algiers was hastened by plague and famine.

*Napoleon Buonaparte as a young man*

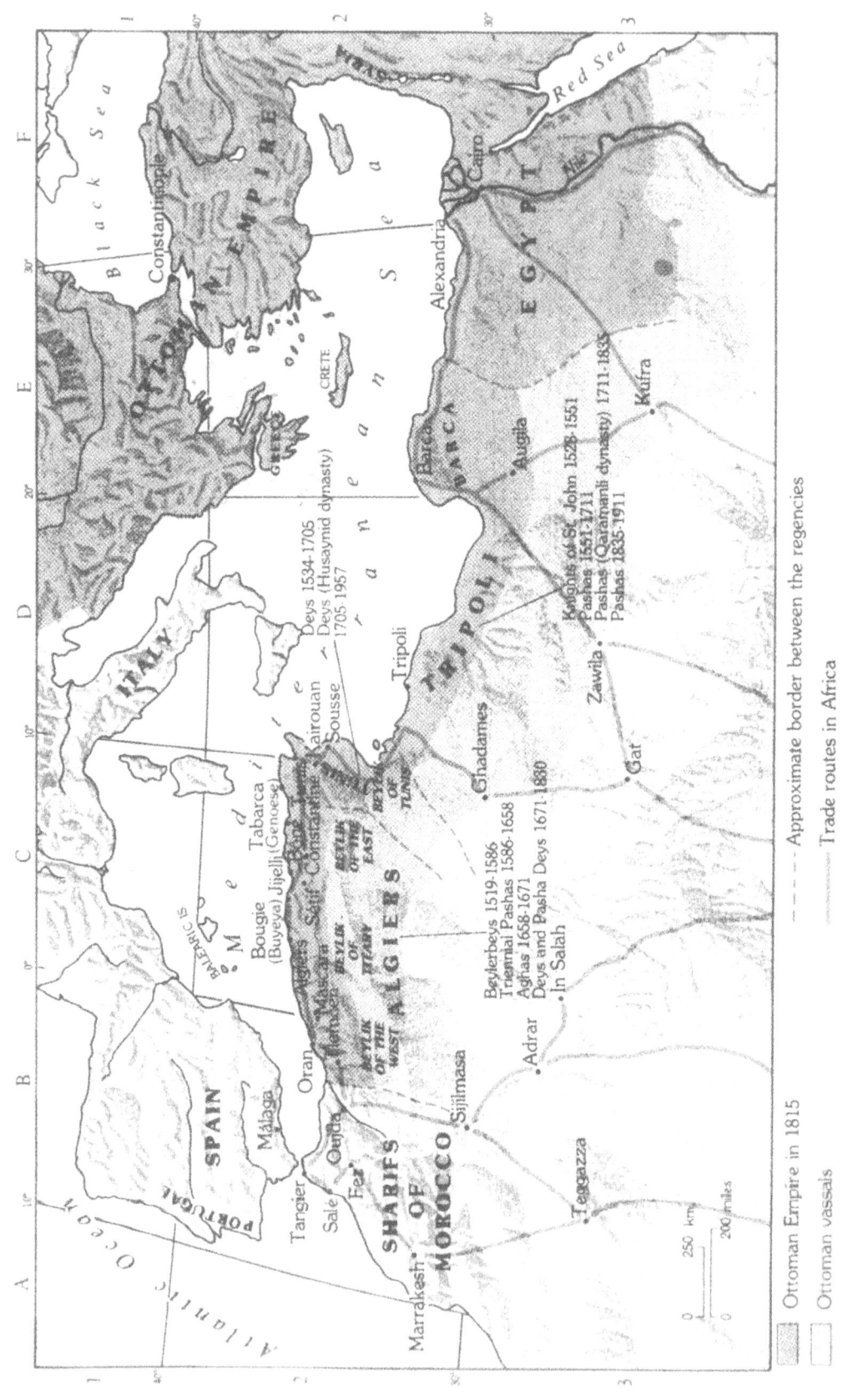

THE BARBARY STATES, 17TH AND 18TH CENTURIES

In Tunis the family of a Corsican renegade, Murad, became hereditary beys from 1631 to 1702. Husayn ibn Ali, the son of a Cretan renegade, was an agha of Janissaries and treasurer to the bey. Proclaimed bey by the military he established a Husaynid dynasty, which ruled until 1957. In Tripoli the Qaramanli family ruled as hereditary pashas from 1714 until 1835, when the Ottomans imposed direct rule.

Piracy was not effectively suppressed until 1819. Following the Congress of Vienna, at which the suppression of piracy was a major concern, a combined Anglo-Dutch fleet attacked Algiers in 1816. The city, however, was so run down that only 1,200 Christian captives were found. In Tripoli the practice of paying tribute in return for freedom from piracy led to war between Tripoli and the United States.

France established a protectorate over the Algerian coastline in 1830, but the occupation of the hinterland continued into the later nineteenth century. Taking advantage of national bankruptcy, a protectorate over Tunisia was added in 1881. Following war between Italy and Turkey, Italy acquired Tripoli and all Libya in 1911.

*Turkish head tax receipt for a Christian subject*

*View of Tangier*

# THE UNITED STATES WAR WITH TRIPOLI, 1801–1815

Tripoli has a commanding position in the Gulf of Sidra, in the central Mediterranean. Under the caliphate it was generally subject to whomever was ruling Tunisia. In 1146 the Normans pillaged the city; from 1321 until 1401 it was ruled by the independent dynasty of Bani Ammar, with a short interval under Bani Makki from 1354 until 1369. It then returned to Tunisian suzerainty, until between 1528 and 1553 it was held by the Knights of St. John of Rhodes. Then it was incorporated into the Ottoman Empire. The Turkish corsair Dragut is buried in one of the mosques.

In 1714 Ahmed Pasha Qaramanli, the Turkish governor, achieved virtual independence as an hereditary regent. Thereafter the regency sent "presents" to Istanbul, which were accepted as tribute. Its strategical position made it an admirable center for piracy, and during the eighteenth century payments were made by European nations to the regency for protection of their commerce.

Among these was the United States, which paid protection money from 1796. In 1801 the pasha demanded from the United States an increase in the tribute of $83,000. This was refused, and a naval force was sent to blockade Tripoli. During four inconclusive years the Americans lost the frigate *Philadelphia*, and the commander and crew were taken prisoners. A theatrical incident was provided by William Eaton, who marched five hundred men across the desert from Alexandria in order to place the brother of the reigning pasha on the throne. With the aid of American vessels he succeeded in taking the small port of Derna. Shortly afterward the pasha relinquished his demands, but he obtained $60,000 as ransom for the prisoners.

Further outrages took place in 1815, and American vessels again blockaded Tripoli and forced the pasha to desist. The Ottomans reasserted their authority in 1835.

*The city of Tangier, Morocco, 1803, at the time of the United States' war with Tripoli*

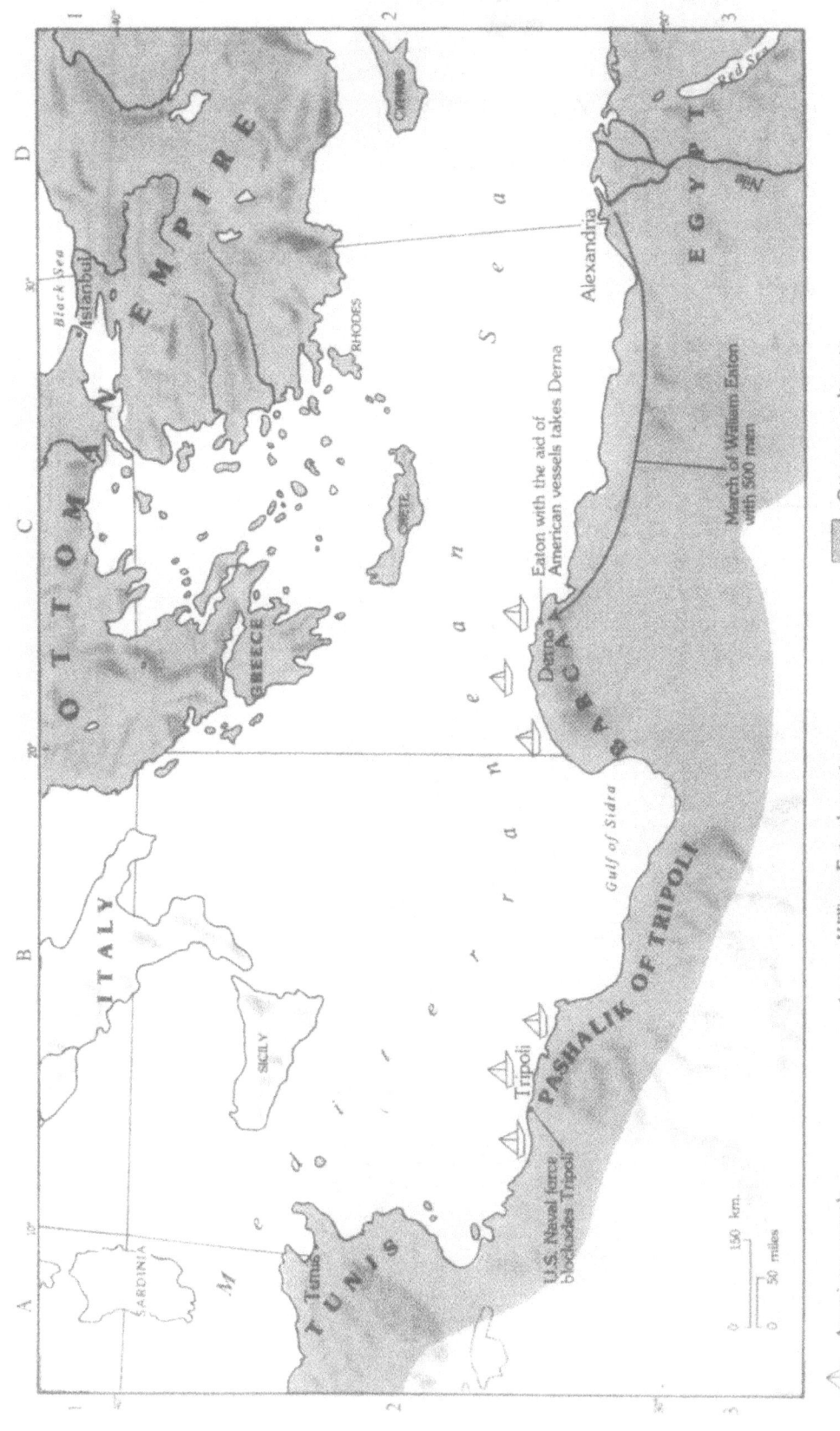

THE UNITED STATES WAR WITH TRIPOLI, 1801–1815

# THE EGYPTIAN CAMPAIGN IN THE HEJAZ, 1812–1818

When the Muslim reformer Muhammad ibn Abd al-Wahhab died in 1792, his extreme puritanical doctrines, warmly supported by the chieftain Ibn Saud, had been established in most of Arabia. In 1801 Ibn Saud's son, Abd al-Aziz, seized Mecca, and, in 1804, Medina. After 1806 for many years it was not possible for a non-Wahhabi to make the pilgrimage to Mecca.

From the point of view of the Ottoman Empire these events were a gross religious insult and an economic disaster that interrupted the normal channels of trade. To Muhammad Ali Pasha of Egypt, seeking to establish himself, these events presented an opportunity to achieve recognition and to rid himself of certain elements in his army. Muhammad Ali's first attempt to retake the holy cities, which was led by his son Tusun, ended in a disaster; however, in 1812, with fresh troops, Yanbu and then the holy cities were taken. In 1813 Muhammad Ali made the pilgrimage in person. In the interior the Wahhabi rebels remained all-powerful. In 1815 Muhammad Ali mounted expeditions against Yemen and against the Wahhabi in Nejd. Tusun was succeeded by his brother, Ibrahim Pasha, and the war took on a more aggressive character. In 1818, with an army of eleven thousand men, Ibrahim laid siege to the Wahhabi villages and finally took their capital, Dariya. The successor to Abd al-Aziz, Abdullah, was sent to Istanbul, where he was executed in front of Hagia Sophia. Ibrahim ravaged the Wahhabi rebel's territory at leisure and then evacuated his army to Egypt.

*Muhammad Ali*

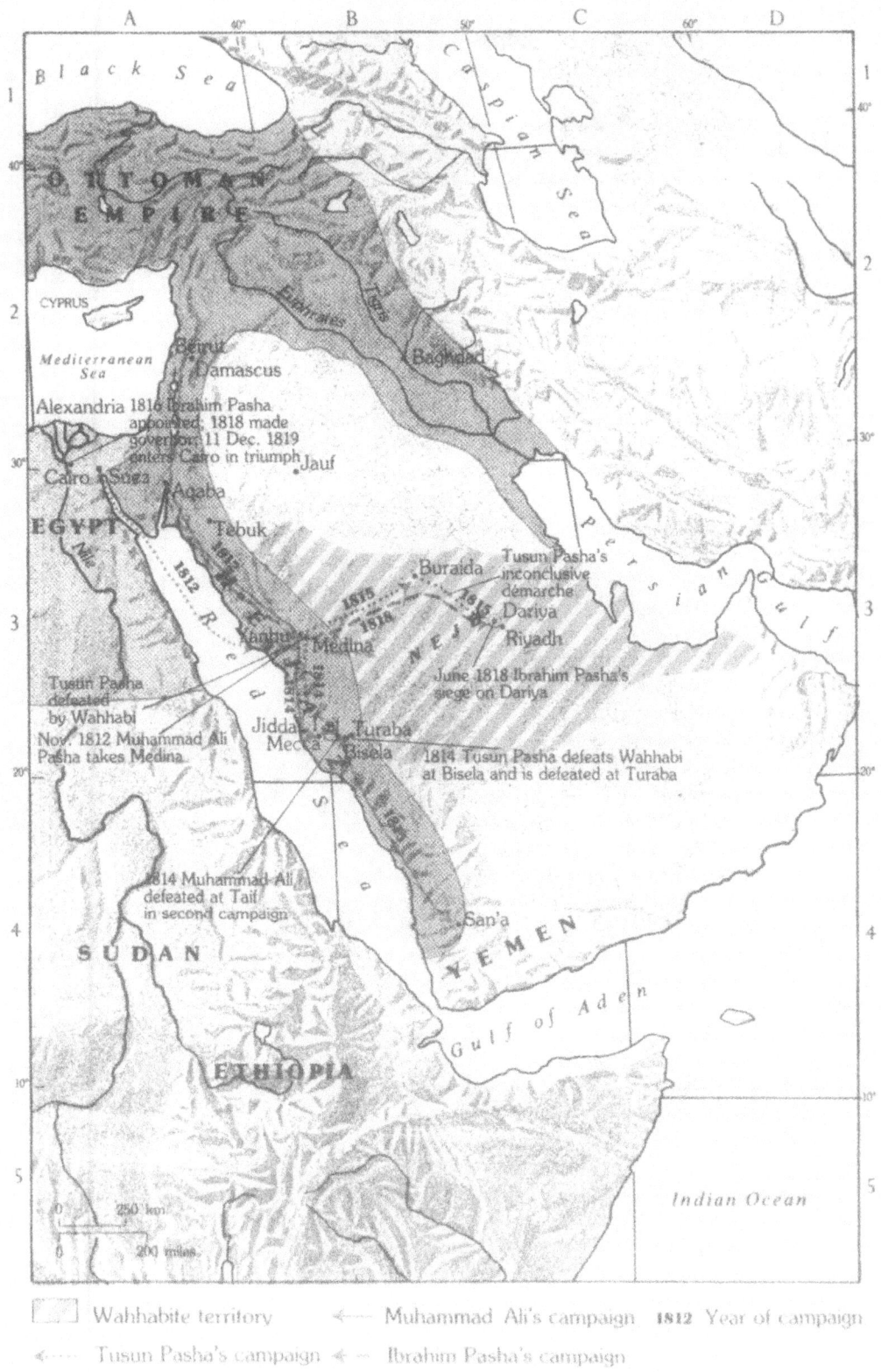

**THE EGYPTIAN CAMPAIGN IN THE HEJAZ, 1812–1818**

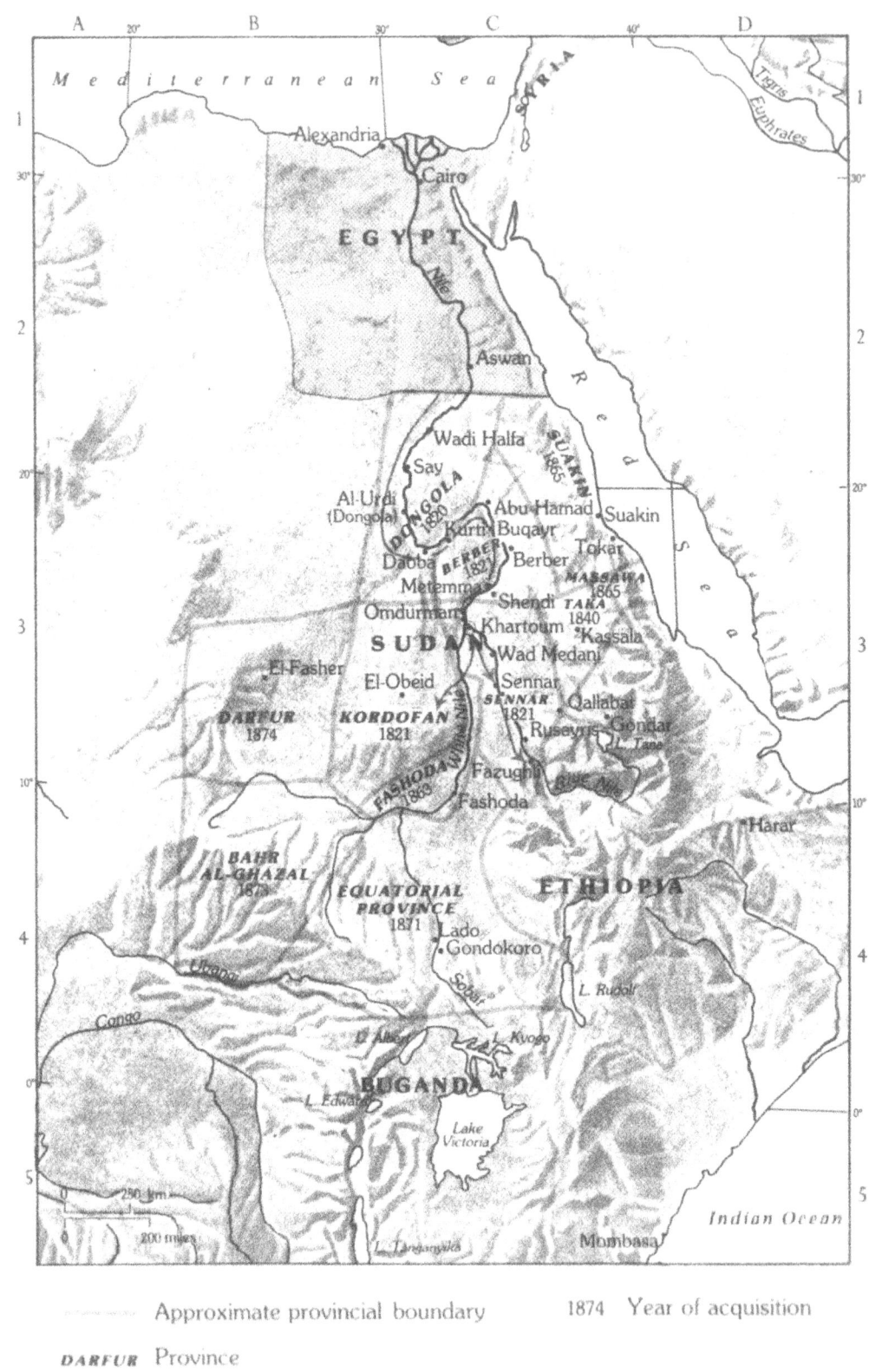

THE EGYPTIAN CAMPAIGN IN THE SUDAN, 1820–1880

# THE EGYPTIAN CAMPAIGN IN THE SUDAN, 1820–1880

By 1820 Muhammad Ali was autonomous viceroy of Egypt, paying tribute only to the Porte. In 1811 he broke the power of the Mamluks in Egypt, but a remnant established itself in the petty Funj state of Dongola. Here they built a walled town, recruited slaves, and began to extend their power in the region. In 1812 Muhammad Ali sent an embassy to order the Funj ruler to expel the Mamluks, but the ruler lacked authority to do so. Two other factors weighed heavily with Muhammad Ali: Dongola was the center of a prosperous slave trade and, by repute, was rich in gold mines.

A further factor was unrest among Muhammad Ali's Albanian troops. In 1820 his third son, Isma'il Kamil Pasha, led six thousand men on what was nominally an Ottoman expedition, but what in fact was a private venture of the viceroy. By 4 November the Shayqiyya were defeated at Kurti near Dongola, and thereafter there was no serious military resistance. In February 1821 Isma'il pressed southward, and by 13 June he had taken Sennar. Shortly thereafter the Kordofan province surrendered. At the end of 1821 Ibrahim Pasha took command, and occupied the gold-bearing region of Fazughli. A rebellion in his rear, protesting against high taxation, was speedily suppressed.

Egyptian authority was now established over the Sudan, and a period of conciliation followed. Khartoum was founded as the capital, and commerce was encouraged by the protection of trade routes. Petty wars continued until 1838, when Egyptian borders reached Ethiopia. A long period of feeble and capricious rule followed, during which European traders penetrated the country. Under the khedive Isma'il Pasha (r. 1863–1879), Egyptian territories were considerably expanded. Under European pressure, a struggle began against the slave trade, which culminated in the Mahdist rebellion.

*Midshat Pasha*

*The Mahdi's Tomb, Omdurman*

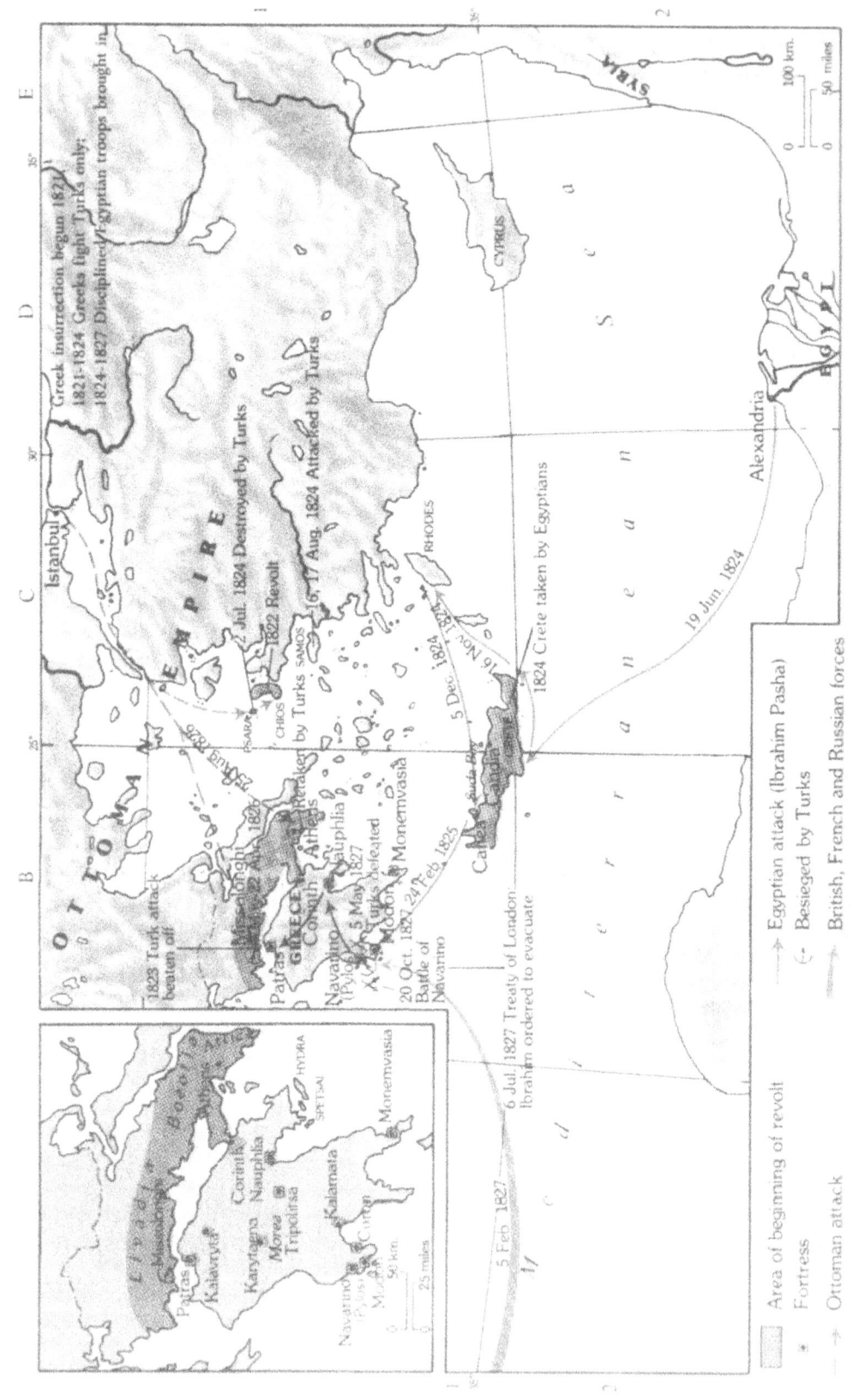

IBRAHIM PASHA'S CAMPAIGN IN GREECE, 1824–1833

# IBRAHIM PASHA'S CAMPAIGN IN GREECE, 1824–1833

When Ibrahim Pasha withdrew from the Sudan in 1822 a new opportunity arose for Muhammad Ali. On 13 January 1822 Greece proclaimed its independence of Turkey. Christian Europe, in which the governing classes had a classical tradition in education, expressed immediate sympathy for Greece. The sultan thus looked to Muhammad Ali as an ally rather than as a vassal.

In April 1823 an Egyptian army put down the rebellion in Crete. As a reward Muhammad Ali was created Pasha of Acre, with instructions to reconquer Greece. After an unsuccessful start in 1823, Ibrahim Pasha, in command of a force of Albanians and Egyptians, disembarked in 1824. In 1825 the greater part of Morea was taken, and the city of Tripolitsa entered. Ibrahim continued to Nauphlia, where an English squadron was stationed. In 1826 his army attacked Missolonghi, where the remainder of the insurrectionaries had assembled. Assaults of 24 February and 6 April failed, but famine forced the heroic defenders to surrender. They were massacred without pity.

From 26 August until 2 June 1827, Ibrahim besieged Athens. An attempt by the British naval commander, Thomas Cochrane, to set fire to the Egyptian fleet in Alexandria was foiled, and Muhammad Ali pursued him as far as Rhodes. By now all Europe was moved by Greek losses, and Britain, France, and Russia combined to attack the Turco-Egyptian fleet at Navarino. On 26 October 1827, the Turco-Egyptian fleet was destroyed.

In Morea Ibrahim continued to resist, but his army had tired of war. The Egyptian troops were restless, and 2,700 Albanians deserted en bloc. In September 1828 a French expedition forced Ibrahim to surrender, and in the following year Greek independence was recognized by the Treaty of Adrianople.

*Castelfranco, Venetian Castle on Crete*

# THE EGYPTIAN CAMPAIGN IN SYRIA, 1831–1841

Between 1828 and 1829 Turkey was at war with Russia, and Ibrahim Pasha was ordered to take the fleet to the Dardanelles and to enter Syria with 28,000 men. So slow was Muhammad Ali in carrying out the order that the sultan showed his displeasure by nominating Ibrahim Pasha to be prince of Mecca, a rank higher than his father.

In 1830 Ibrahim besieged Acre with 35,000 men. Though the garrison of 25,000 defied Ibrahim for six months, Acre was taken on 27 May 1832. Ibrahim then marched north and took Damascus without resistance. The pasha of Aleppo unsuccessfully tried to stop his advance into Syria. On 26 July Ibrahim took Aleppo and cut off the Turkish forces.

Ibrahim now turned against the Ottomans, who raised an army of Albanians and Bosnians against him. He defeated them near Konya on 22 December 1832. He was received with enthusiasm in Asia Minor; on 28 February 1833, the port city of Smyrna opened its gates to a single officer with four men. Ibrahim by then had reached Kutaya and threatened Bursa. Nothing stood between him and Istanbul.

*Interior of the Church of the Nativity, Bethlehem*

The integrity of the tottering Ottoman Empire had long been a dogma of European foreign policy, and there was a general fear that it might collapse. The French ambassador intervened. Ibrahim was offered the land of ancient Palestine, which he refused, demanding all Syria,

*View of Aleppo, Syria, 19th century*

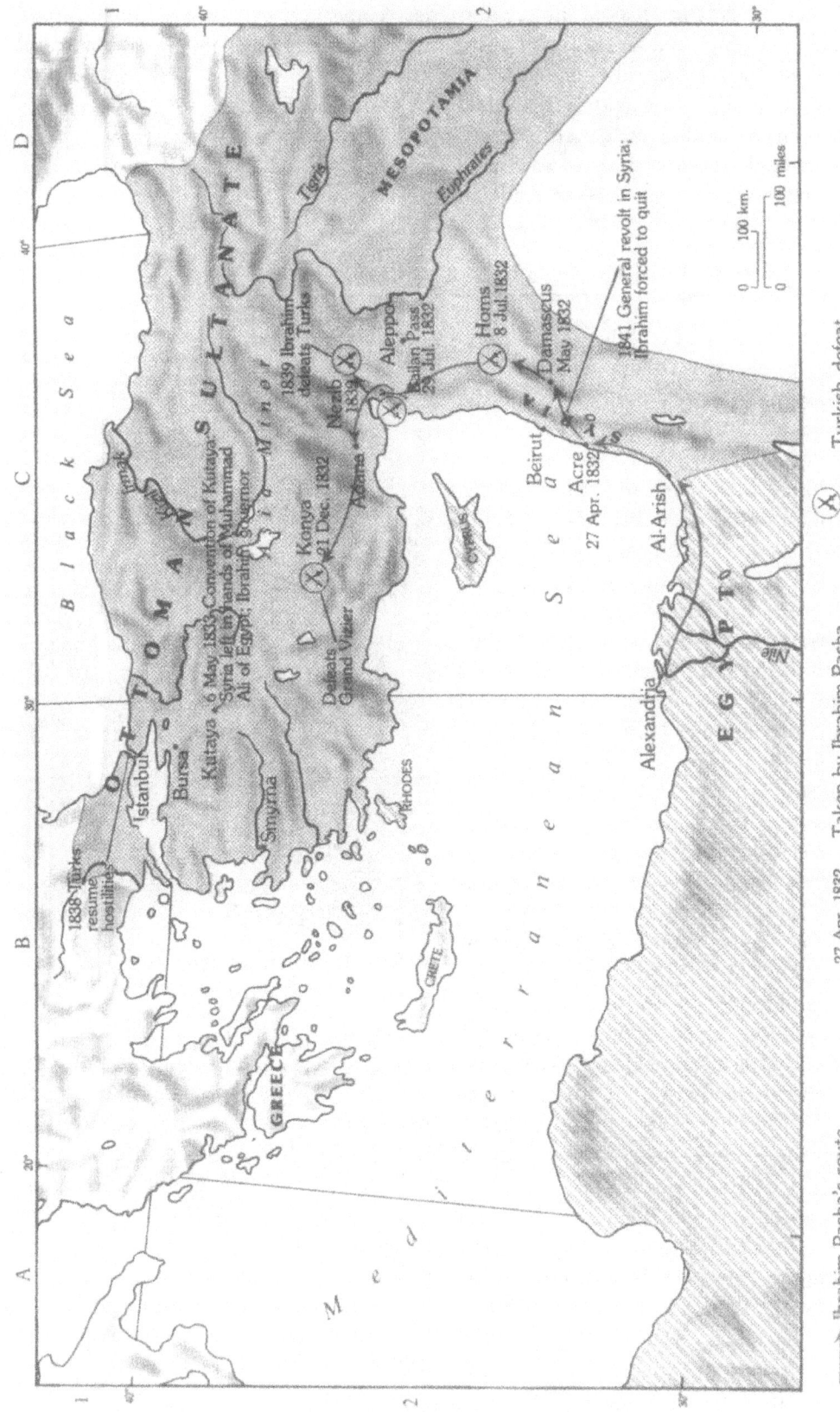

THE EGYPTIAN CAMPAIGN IN SYRIA, 1831–1841

part of Mesopotamia, and the Turkish province of Adana. Russia now intervened, and a squadron and twelve thousand men effectively changed the situation. In 1833 a *hatti-sherif* (decree) ceded all Syria and Adana district to Muhammad Ali, while the secret treaty of Unkiar-Skelessi provided a Russian guarantee of the Ottoman domains. This decree marked the apogee of Egyptian expansion. It now held Syria, the holy cities, and the Sudan. There was, however, an Achilles' heel, for in November 1837 Britain took possession of the colony of Aden.

## THE SUEZ CANAL, 1869, AND WORLD TRADE

Only a narrow neck of land, 125 miles long, divides Africa from Asia, and the Mediterranean from the waters of the Red Sea. Trade eastward from the Mediterranean originally passed up the Nile and then overland to southern Egyptian ports. An inscription of Seti I at Karnak records a canal dated equivalent to 1380 BC that connected the Nile with the Great Bitter Lake. Its course is still traceable. In the sixth century BC, Pharaoh Necho II chose a different route, which was completed in 520 BC by the Persian ruler Darius I. In 285 BC, Ptolemy Philadelphus connected it to the Red Sea, but by 31 BC it had become unusable. The Roman emperor Trajan (r. 98–117) is said to have repaired and enlarged this canal in AD 98, joining it to the Nile at Babilyun, now Old Cairo, but some writers attribute this enlargement to Amr ibn al-As. The canal was closed deliberately by the caliph al-Mansur in 770, when he feared attacks from pirates in the Red Sea. Nevertheless parts of it remained open until 1861, when it was used by French engineers to construct the fresh-water canal from Cairo to Suez between 1861 and 1863.

The caliph Harun al-Rashid (r. 786–809) is credited with a scheme to pierce the Isthmus of Suez. He abandoned it for fear the Byzantines might use it to attack him. The scheme was not raised again until after 1500, when the Venetians wished to construct a canal to outflank

*Ferdinand-Marie de Lesseps*

the Portuguese who had captured the spice trade by sailing round the Cape of Good Hope. The Ottoman conquest of Egypt put a stop to the project in 1517. Louis XIV of France toyed with the idea of an expedition to Egypt to build a canal in 1671, but nothing came of it, nor of the proposal of Ali Bey, Mamluk governor of Egypt, to do so in 1770. In 1798 Napoleon Bonaparte ordered a survey of the isthmus with a view to constructing a canal, but nothing more than debate took place until 1854, when the French

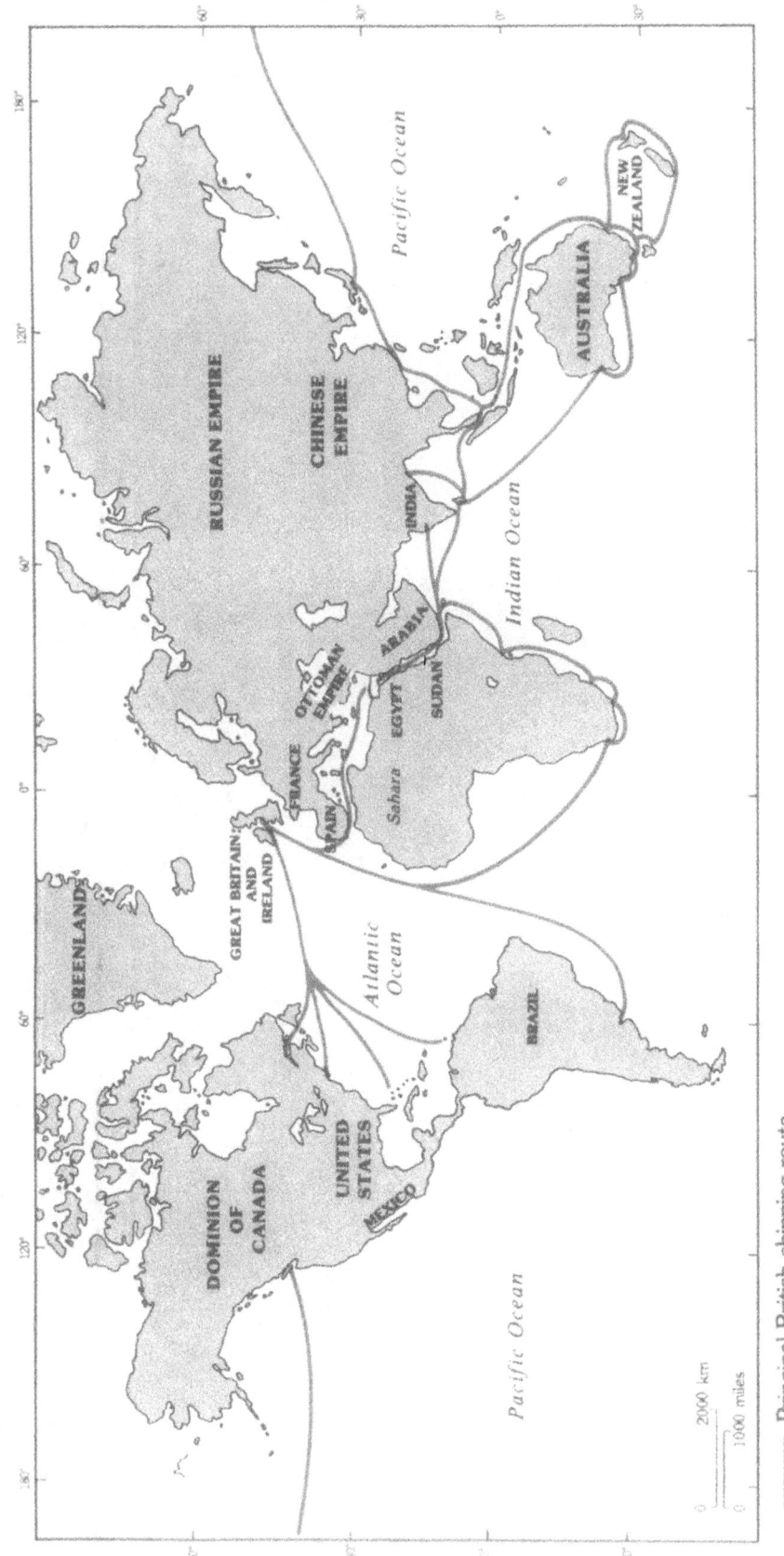

THE SUEZ CANAL, 1869, AND WORLD TRADE

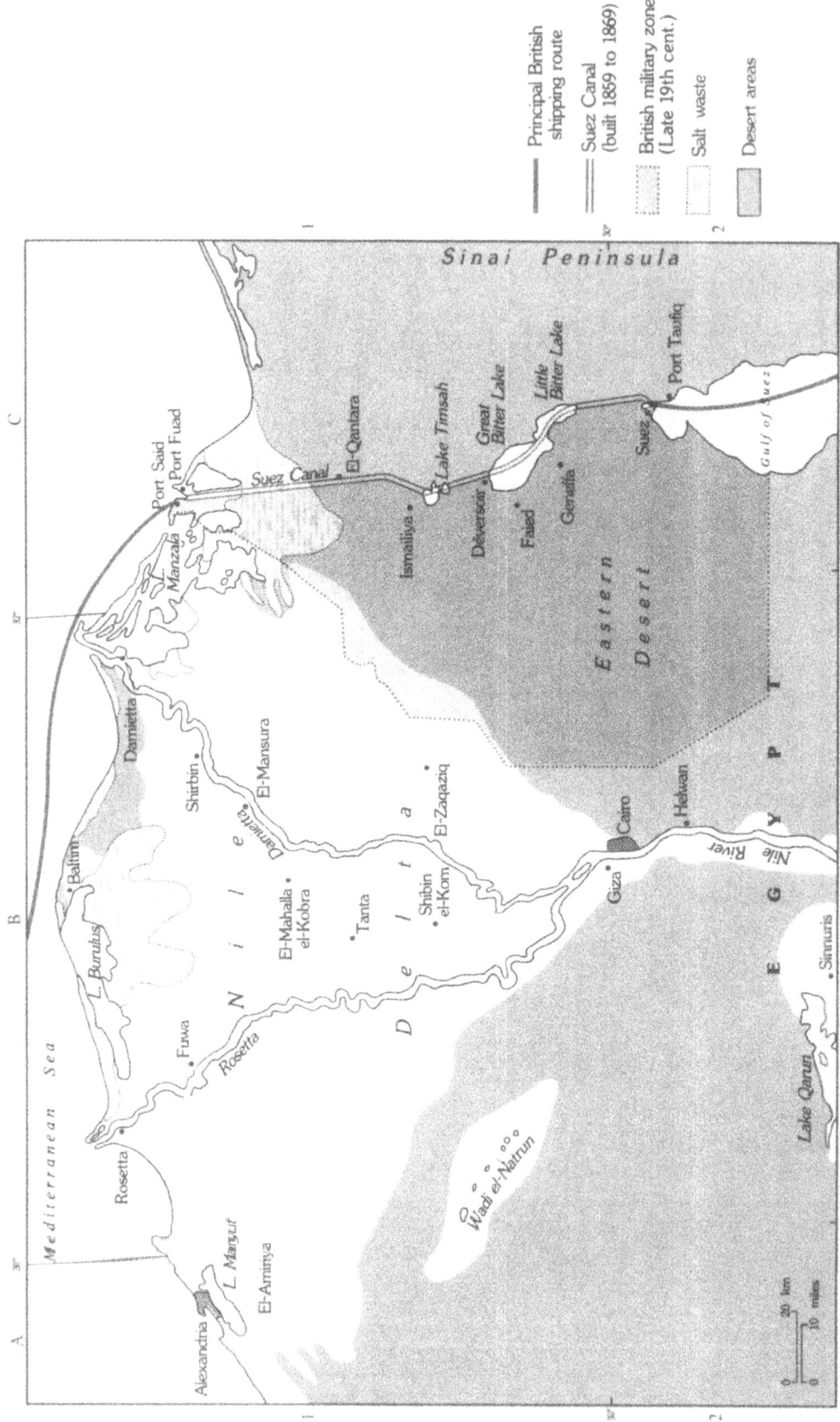

THE SUEZ CANAL, 1869

*The Suez Canal*

engineer Ferdinand-Marie de Lesseps formed the Compagnie Universelle du Canal Maritime de Suez and subsequently obtained a concession from the khedive Said Pasha, granting a ninety-nine-year lease from 1856. Diplomatic opposition followed from England; other countries, including Russia and the United States, held aloof. England feared for her maritime interests. Despite difficulties regarding labor, finance, hot weather, and disease, the completion of the canal was celebrated in November 1869, when the empress Eugénie of France led a convoy of sixty-six vessels down the canal, leaving Port Said on 17 November and reaching Suez on 20 November.

From 1869 to 1870, there were 486 transits; by 1966–1967 the number recorded had reached 20,000. Following the beginning of commercial exploitation of Persian oil in 1907, the canal became the main artery of the oil trade. In 1913, 291,000 tons were carried through the canal; by 1966, the volume had reached 166 million tons.

At first, 52 percent of the shares of the canal company were held by France and 44 percent by the khedive. His extravagant habits forced him to sell his shares, which Benjamin Disraeli acquired for Britain. This acquisition secured the strategic route to India and led to British domination in Egypt until 1956. In that year, following British refusal to finance an additional dam above Aswan, Gamal Abdel Nasser nationalized the canal. France and Britain went to war, but were halted by U.S. financial intervention. Following war with Israel in 1967, the canal remained closed until 1975. Its importance has declined because of the growth of air transport, the virtual disappearance of the sea passenger trade, and the development of oil supertankers, which, when they are laden, the canal is only just able to accommodate.

# ISLAM IN AFRICA, 7TH TO 20TH CENTURIES

Although the African coastal territories of the Mediterranean were Islamized in the seventh and eighth centuries, Islam does not seem to have penetrated south of the Sahara much before the eleventh century. The coast of eastern Africa, however, is an exception. The earliest evidence of Islam in Africa, recently excavated at Shanga, off the Kenyan island of Lamu, is a mosque that was rebuilt nine times between around 750 and 1450, the first construction being a simple enclosure of reeds. Possibly, Islam reached Madagascar during the early part of the period. In the Ethiopian lowlands inhabited by Somali herdsmen it is difficult to measure its progress, but by the thirteenth century there were stone-built mosques in trading towns along the coast to the south and the islands of Pemba, Zanzibar, and Mafia. Except in the Horn of Africa there is no evidence of the penetration of Islam inland before the nineteenth century.

In the west Islam seems to have reached southern Morocco and Mauritania in the eleventh century, but rulers of Mali were not converted until the thirteenth century. Though the first to make the pilgrimage to Mecca was Sakura in 1293–1294, that of his successor, Mansa Musa, in 1324 was rare enough to be sensational. Perhaps the most significant of his acts was his return with the architect Ishaq al-Saheli, who built the mosques of Gao and Timbuktu, from which learned men eagerly disseminated Islam. In spite of its proximity to Egypt, Nubia was not completely Islamized until the sixteenth century.

From the late twelfth century the intellectual hegemony of the university mosque of al-Azhar drew students from as far afield as western Africa and Indonesia. Among its dependencies were hostels for students from the Sudan, by which was meant the whole of Muslim "black Africa," as well as from Malaysia and beyond. *Awqaf* (charitable bequests) provided them with food, lodging, clothing, and pocket money. Returning home literate and with a knowledge of law, they were assured of a career.

At the beginning of the nineteenth

*Sultan's Palace at the harbor in Zanzibar*

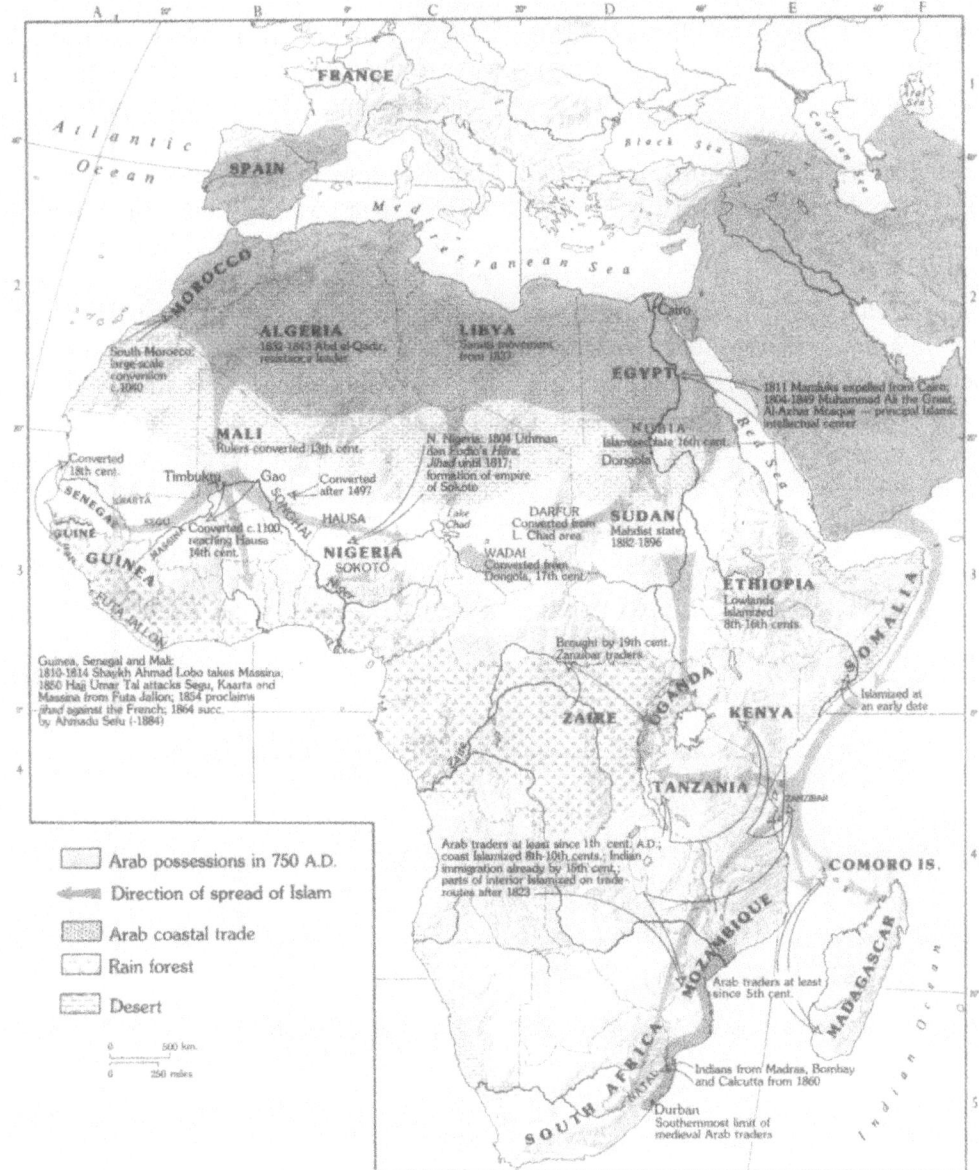

# ISLAM IN AFRICA, 7TH TO 20TH CENTURIES

century and up to midcentury a number of remarkable men appeared in Africa. In Egypt, following Napoleon Buonaparte's incursion, Muhammad Ali Pasha (r. 1806–1849) brought Egypt into the modern world as a power in its own right within the world community. Islam now penetrated equatorial Africa from Egypt. In the west this achievement was matched by Usman dan Fodio, a religious reformer whose *jihad*, or holy war, was both military and spiritual. This was the basis of the empire of Sokoto in northern Nigeria, which embraced a number of earlier states, and it gave a Muslim character to the region that has become permanent. Similar movements arose under Ahmad Lobo in Massina and later in the century under al-Hajj Umar Tal in Segu, Kaarta, and Massina. In these movements the spiritual basis stemmed from Sufi religious fraternities, especially the Tijaniyya, thus linking them with the outside world.

In the east the replacement of the Portuguese by the Arabs of Oman after the fall of Mombasa in 1698 had no immediate effect. The first ruler of Oman to take a personal interest in eastern Africa was Sa'id ibn Sultan (r. 1806–1856), who first visited these Omani dominions in 1827. He finally moved to Zanzibar in 1840. Up to 1823 African traders brought their products to the coast. By 1844 this process was wholly reversed, and Arab and Zanzibari Swahili traders traveled inland, reaching the Congo by the end of the century. In their wake followed members of Sufi fraternities, who received ready acceptance in Uganda as well as Zaïre. Similarly the Mahdist state in the eastern Sudan of 1882 to 1896 and the Sanusi movement, which began in eastern Libya in 1837, derived initially from Sufis. These movements adapted to African ideas, and on the eastern African coast they established the "Mosque College" of Lamu in 1901, the principal center of Swahili culture and a center of popular pilgrimage even at the present time.

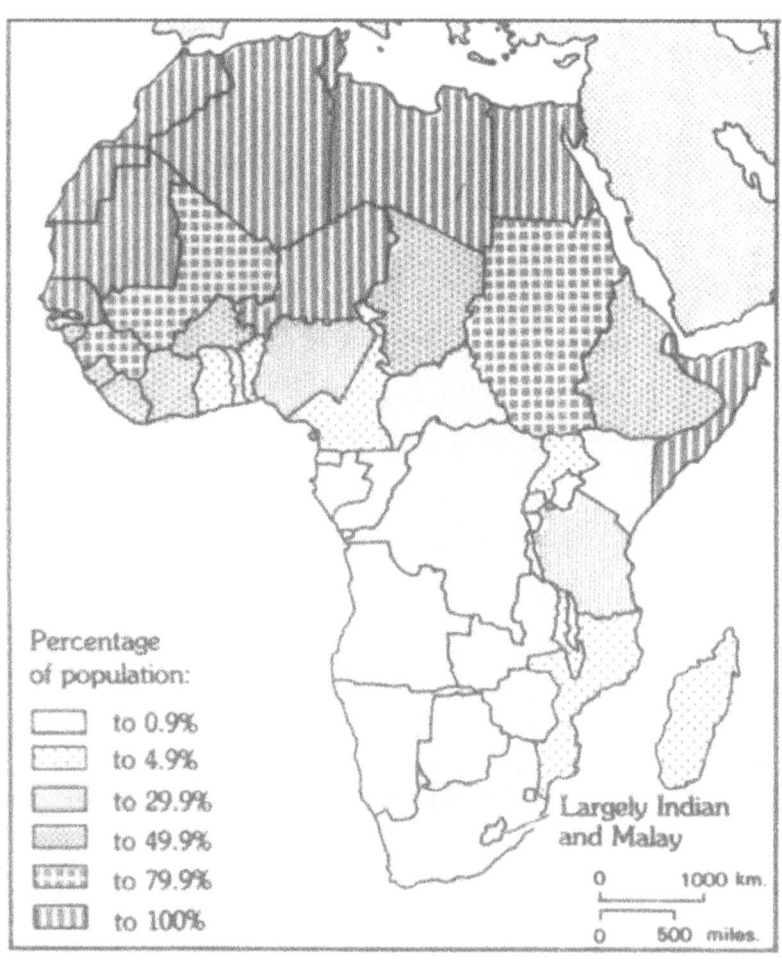

PRESENT DISTRIBUTION OF ISLAM

# NOTABLE EUROPEAN TRAVELERS IN THE EAST,
## 14TH TO 16TH CENTURIES

European Travelers in the East following the Polos offered very varied material to their readers. Odoric of Pordenone, traveling between 1316 and 1330, journeyed from the Coromandel Coast of India to Sumatra (where he mentions three kingdoms, including Lamori and Sumolchra), Java, ruled by a great king with seven other rulers under him, Borneo (where he mentions unidentifiable places called Patem and Talamasin) and Champa, where the king was polygamous and possessed 14,000 elephants. He then voyaged on to Canton in China. He claims to have visited the Nicobar Islands, too, but his description bears little resemblance to reality.

Jordain de Sévérac, who was in India in 1330, describes the trade in spices, and adds some more or less tall tales about Java (Sumatra) and Champa, while John Marignolli of Florence, who travelled to China in 1342, and returned in 1346, describes 'Saba' (Java or Sumatra), with its queens descended from Semiramis and other similar stories. Nicolo de' Conti's long stay in the East, starting from Damascus in the early 1400s, also resulted in a report about the exotic lands of the East, as he related to Poggio Bracciolini. He described journeys through Persia and the Malabar Coast and other regions of India, including Bizenegalia (Vijayanagara, the great Hindu capital ca. 150 miles inland from Goa), and the port of Calicut, Sri Lanka, Taprobana (not Sri Lanka, but 'Sciamuthera', Sumatra), Java, and Tenasserim, Arakan, Ava and Panconia (Pegu) — all in modern Myanmar — and Bengal, as well as, perhaps, traveling on to China. Hieronimo de Santo Stefano in 1496 also reported on Pegu, then at war with Ava. He had travelled from the Coromandel Coast in India. In Sumatra, he was plundered of his goods by a Muslim ruler when his ship was blown off course on its journey to Malacca. He was discouraged by this, and returned to Cambay. A few years later in 1502 Ludovico de Varthema set out on a journey through Egypt, Syria, Arabia, Persia and India. Like Nicolo de' Conti, he converted, in theory at least, to Islam, and as such was able to report on the Holy Places of Islam. In South East Asia he describes Ternassari (Tenasserim) and its junk trade with Malacca, Pegu, still at war with Ava, the great spice and silk emporium of Malacca, Pedir near Acheh, rich in pepper, silk, benzoin, Banda with its nutmeg and mace, the Moluccas, Borneo, and Java, where a great king ruled over many subject kingdoms. Thence he returned to Malacca, and to 'Cioromandel', perhaps Negapatam.

*Gian Francesco Poggio Bracciolini, from an illuminated manuscript, c. 1475*

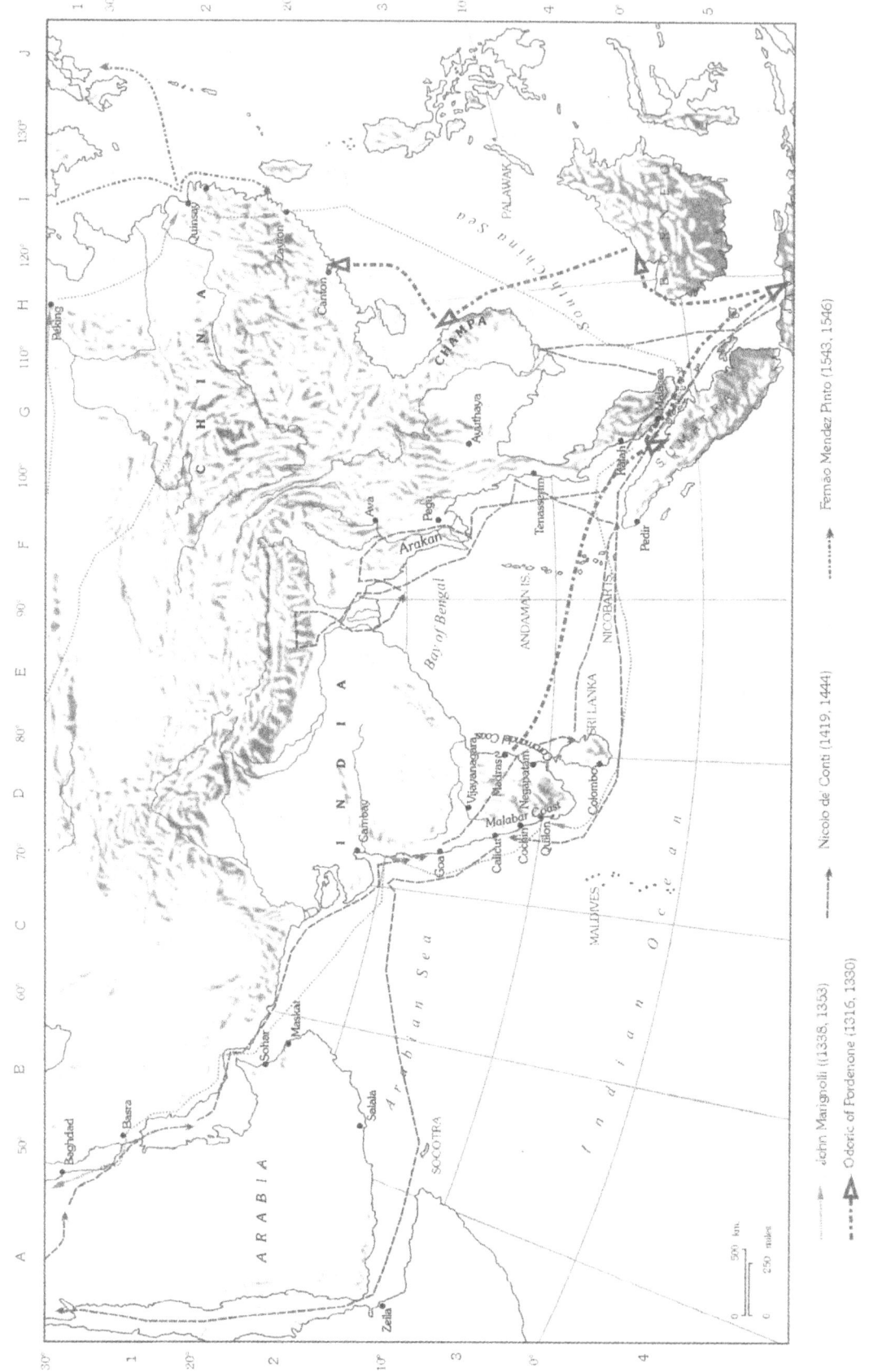

NOTABLE EUROPEAN TRAVELERS IN THE EAST

Tomé Pires, who was in Malacca just after the Portuguese conquest, wrote his *Suma Orientale* between 1512-15. (See Tomé Pires' account of trade, c. 1515). Not long after, his compatriot Fernão Mendez Pinto traveled in the East for twenty one years until 1558. The resulting book, *Peregrinão*, published posthumously in 1614, has often been considered unreliable. In the 1540s, Pinto passed by 'Sanchão' and 'Lampacau' in China. He lived in Siam (Sornau) for a while in the 1540s, trading at Pattani and Lugor (Nakhon Sithammarat).

*François-Auguste-René-de Châteaubriand (1768–1848)*

# NOTABLE EUROPEAN TRAVELERS IN THE MIDDLE EAST,
## 18TH TO 20TH CENTURIES

Apart from rare contacts with the Mongols, before the sixteenth century European contacts with the Middle East were confined almost entirely to Egypt and the Holy Land. Venice and other Italian cities had an almost exclusive trade with them. Pero da Covilhã, sent at the expense of the Portuguese Crown in 1487 to locate the coasts of Arabia, India, and East Africa, was an exception. The sixteenth century opened with the remarkable journey of Ludovico de Varthema, who was urged by the desire "to behold the various kingdoms of the world" and was the first known European to reach Mecca. Those whose object was largely curiosity were succeeded in the seventeenth century by men whose object was trade with India, China, and, occasionally, Persia, leaving Asia Minor, Syria, and Arabia virtually a complete blank.

It was not until 1766 that a Dane, Carsten Niebuhr, became the first scientific explorer to describe the Levant and Arabian coast, returning overland via Persepolis and Baghdad to Aleppo and Istanbul. Shortly thereafter war between Persia and Russia led to a complete exploration of Caucasia. Hydrographers and consular agents now joined journeys

*Johann Ludwig Burckhardt, ("Ibrahim Ibn Abd Allah") (1784–1817)*

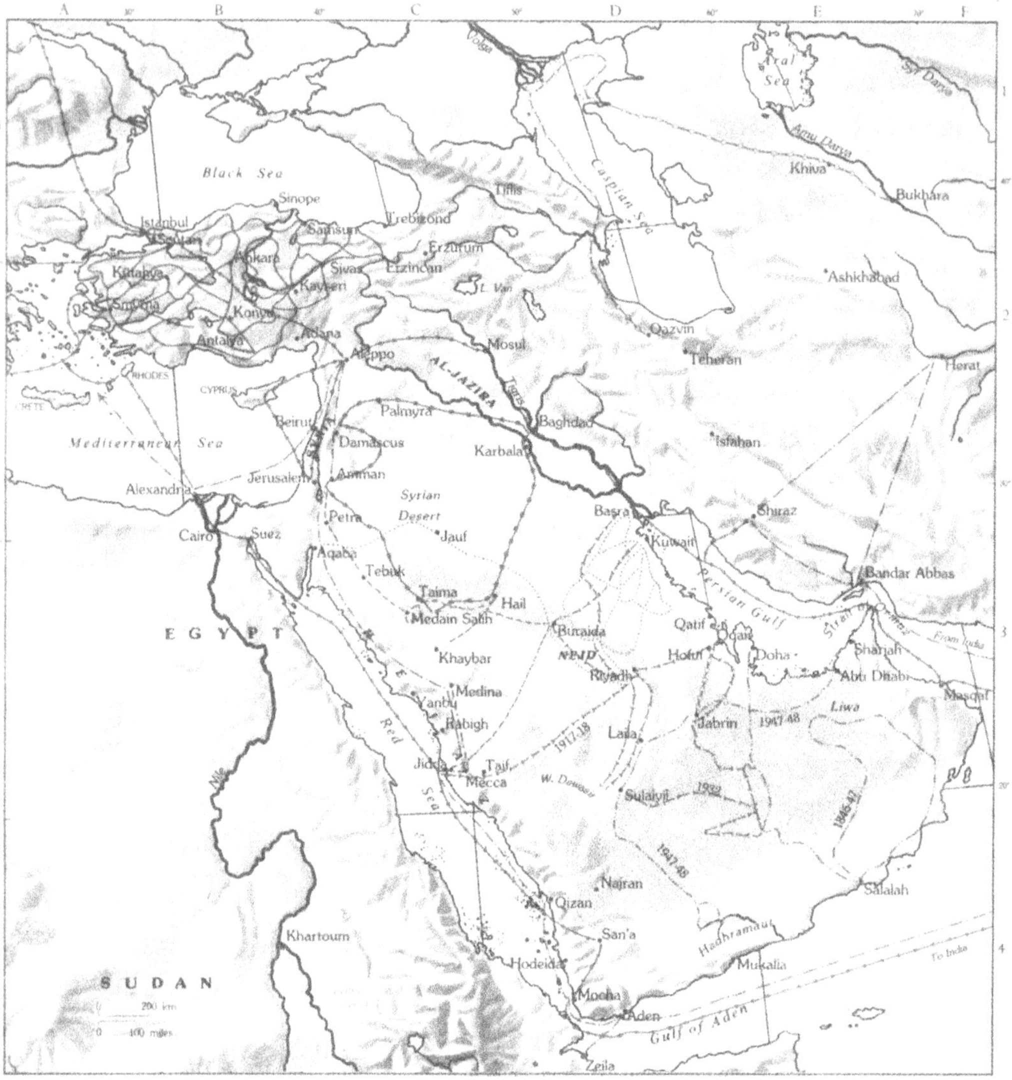

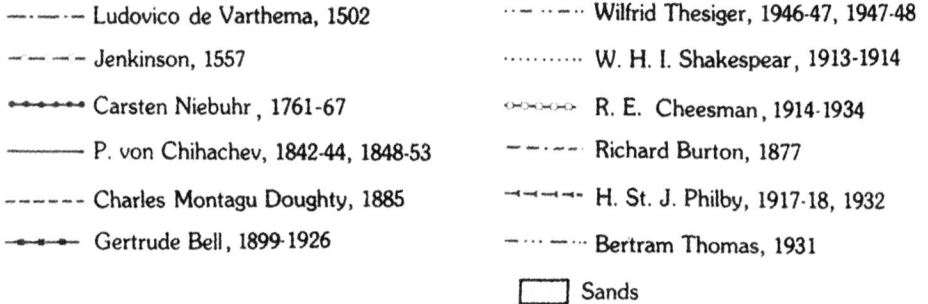

—··—··— Ludovico de Varthema, 1502
— — — Jenkinson, 1557
•—•—• Carsten Niebuhr, 1761-67
———— P. von Chihachev, 1842-44, 1848-53
- - - - - - Charles Montagu Doughty, 1885
—■—■— Gertrude Bell, 1899-1926
··—··—·· Wilfrid Thesiger, 1946-47, 1947-48
············ W. H. I. Shakespear, 1913-1914
◇—◇—◇ R. E. Cheesman, 1914-1934
—·—·— Richard Burton, 1877
—⊢—⊢— H. St. J. Philby, 1917-18, 1932
—··—··— Bertram Thomas, 1931
☐ Sands

## NOTABLE EUROPEAN TRAVELERS IN THE MIDDLE EAST, 18TH TO 20TH CENTURIES

from Britain, Russia, and Germany, the most spectacular of which were the journeys of the Russian diplomat P. von Chihachev between 1842 and 1853.

The vast research on the Holy Land now became scientific. In 1798 to 1801 Palestine was mapped by Napoleon's surveyors who had recorded the Nile Delta, but the results were a state secret until 1817. By then U. I. Seetzen in 1805, François-Auguste-René de Chateaubriand in 1806, and Johann Ludwig Burckhardt in 1812 had traveled there. In the same year Lady Hester Lucy Stanhope became the first individual to conduct an excavation at Ascalon, in the hope of finding buried treasure. The true father of Palestinian exploration was the American scholar, Edward Robinson, who determined he could not teach biblical literature without visiting the country. His *Biblical Researches in Palestine, Mount Sinai, and Arabia Petraea* (1841) constitutes a real landmark. A number of small expeditions added to the stock of topographical knowledge, until in 1864 a party of Royal Engineers was sent at the expense of Baroness Angela Georgina Burdett-Coutts to provide a water supply for Jerusalem. This led to the foundation of the Palestine Exploration Fund in 1865, and the Surveys of Western Palestine (1871–1877) and Eastern Palestine (1871–1882).

In the rest of Syria and in Mesopotamia things moved more slowly. Northern Syria was surveyed in the first half of the nineteenth century, but the real father of Syrian studies was Henry Creswicke Rawlinson. British political agent in Baghdad from 1843 until 1855, he made himself the foremost authority on the region in geography, history, and politics. During this time the English archaeologist Austen Henry Layard and French archaeologists were opening new win-

*"Robinson's Arch," Jerusalem, named for Edward Robinson. From Charles Wilson's* Picturesque Palestine, Sinai And Egypt, *c. 1880*

dows into the history of Assyria and Babylon. Arabia now began to be explored, following the Egyptian expedition of 1812. Burckhardt reached Mecca in disguise in 1814 and gave a precise and scholarly description of the city. Oman was explored by James Wellsted in 1836. Richard Burton made the pilgrimage to Mecca disguised as an Afghan in 1877, and in 1885 the Dutch scholar Christiaan Snouck Hurgronje gave a detailed account of the social life of the city. Toward the end of the century Charles Montagu Doughty traveled in northern Arabia: his *Travels in Arabia Deserta* (1888) still stands as the greatest classic on Arabian travel and Bedouin life.

Doughty's work laid the foundation for works that arose as a result of World

War I, among which were those by Gertrude Bell (written just before the war), W. H. I. Shakespear, Harry St. John Bridger Philby, R. E. Cheesman, and T. E. Lawrence, known commonly as Lawrence of Arabia. Later in the twentieth century Philby carried out further journeys, chiefly in Najd and Saudi Arabia. The last part of Arabia to be explored, the "empty quarter" in southeastern Arabia, was crossed finally, using different routes, by H. St. J. Philby, Bertram Thomas, and Wilfrid Thesiger.

*Abd al-Kadir, Emir of Maskara, 1803–1883*

## RUSSIAN EXPANSION INTO CENTRAL ASIA

Russia proper is a huge plain, broken by no natural boundaries except for the Ural Mountains. The nucleus of the future state was owed to the enterprise of Norse adventurers, whose principal settlement was Kiev. From 1238 until 1462 Russia was dominated by the Mongols of the Golden Horde, commonly known as Tatars. In 1380 a coalition of princes led by the Tsar or Prince of Moscow defeated the Tatars at Kulikovo; its work was not completed until the reign of Ivan IV (The Terrible) in 1584.

Only at the end of his reign were the first forts built to contain incursions across the Urals, a policy continued under his son Féodor and his successors. In the seventeenth century merchant settlements spread across Siberia into pagan lands. In the Urals, in the reigns of Anna (1730–1740) and Elizabeth (1741–1762) two further forts were built, on the Kyrghyz Steppe in 1734, and at Orenburg in 1743. The object of their policy was wholly defensive against nomadic incursions; there was no question of empire-building or anything comparable to the "scramble for Africa."

*Ivan the Terrible, Tsar: 1533–1584*

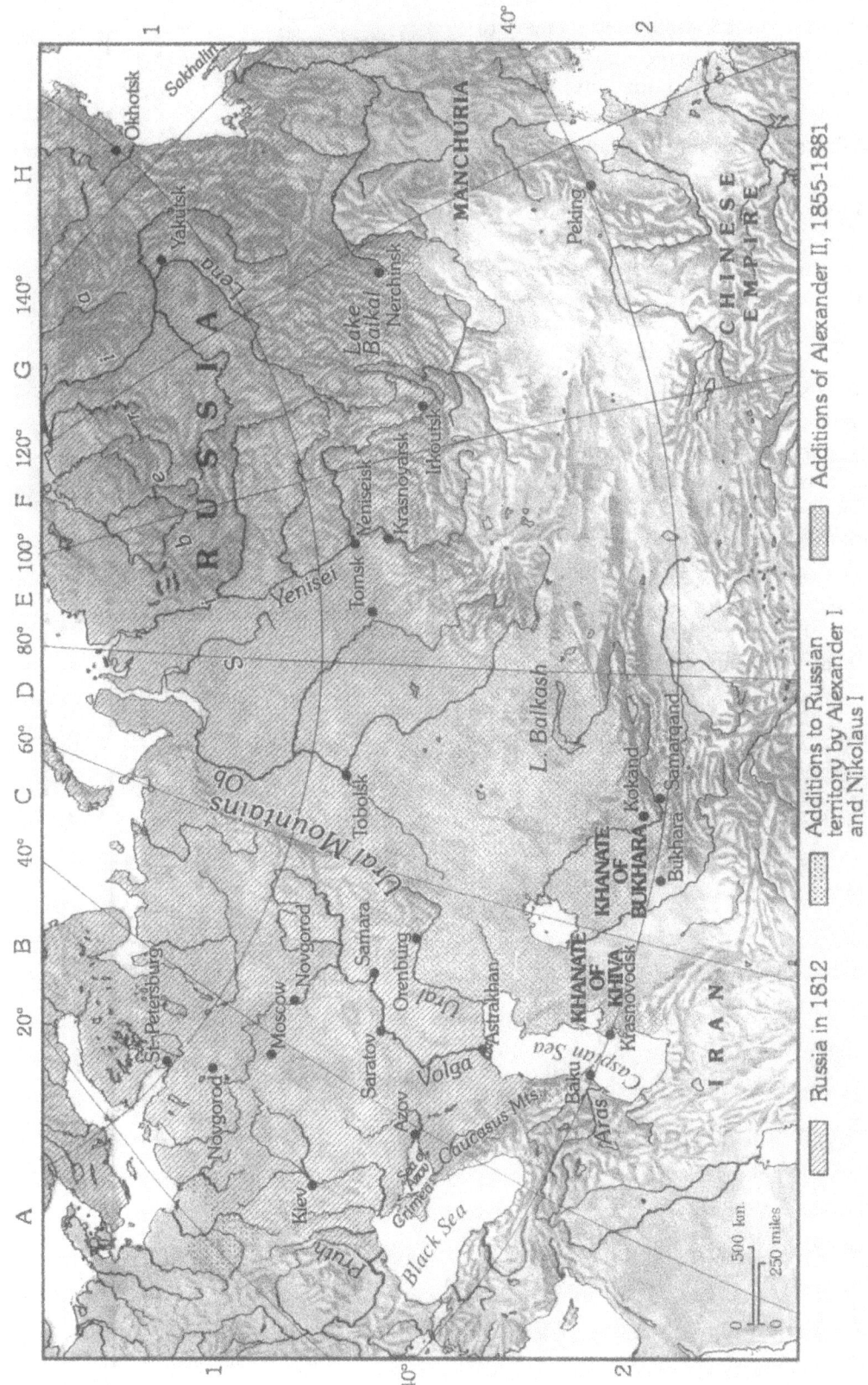

RUSSIAN EXPANSION INTO CENTRAL ASIA

Almost all the expansion of Russia into Asia was accomplished in the reign of Alexander II (1855–1881). The Treaty of Aigun with China gave him Amur and Sakhalin Island without any military operations in 1858. The object was to provide an outlet for Siberian trade into the Pacific.

It was only from 1864 until shortly after his assassination in 1881 that Central Asia was added to the Russian dominions. The once-proud Khanates of Bokhara and Khiva became the vassals of the White Tsar, while retaining the externals of their former sovereignty. As to religion, while the Orthodox Church was paramount as the state religion, Islam was not violated. A state of stagnation simply persisted. It was not until the turn of the century that pogroms against the Jews were initiated. Russians moved to these territories mainly for trade; there was no attempt at what later came to be called colonial-

*Alexander II; Tsar: 1818–1881*

ism. Divided into provinces, it was this that the Communists were to take over in after 1917.

*Saint Vassily Church, Red Square, Moscow, built in the 1550s to commemorate Russia's victory over the Tatars*

## EUROPEAN PENETRATION OF AFRICA, UP TO 1830

In French history Napoleon's Egyptian expedition (1798–1801) is accounted as a series of military and naval disasters, yet the late president Gamal Abdel Nasser's *Philosophy of the Revolution* acclaims it as having "broken the chains of the past." Europe had in fact intruded not only into Egypt but into the crumbling Ottoman Empire. Napoleon's Institute of Egypt, the group of scholars who accompanied his expedition, had reopened doors that had been closed since 1517. It now remained, under the khedive Muhammad Ali Pasha (r.1806–1849), for Egypt to rejuvenate itself. The reforms that he set on foot, if they did little for the peasantry, were accomplished by officers initially recruited from Europe, but now strictly under his control. Thus at this stage, ideas percolated but without colonial intervention.

Farther west, Algeria had a nominal allegiance to Turkey, as did Tripolitania and Tunisia. Although tribute was paid to Turkey, the great nomadic tribes were independent in all but name. When France attempted to seize the country in 1830, they took nothing but the seaboard, and it was not until after 1841 that real conquest began. Resistance, led by Abd el-Kader, lasted until 1847, but in Algeria the Kabyle held out until 1857, Aurès until 1849, and the southern oases until 1852–1854.

In West Africa France had a trading toehold in Senegal. Portugal had what were denominated colonies in Guinea, the Cape Verde Islands, St. Tomé and

*Napoleon I Buonaparte in 1798, painted by David*

*Napoleon Buonaparte surveying troops*

299

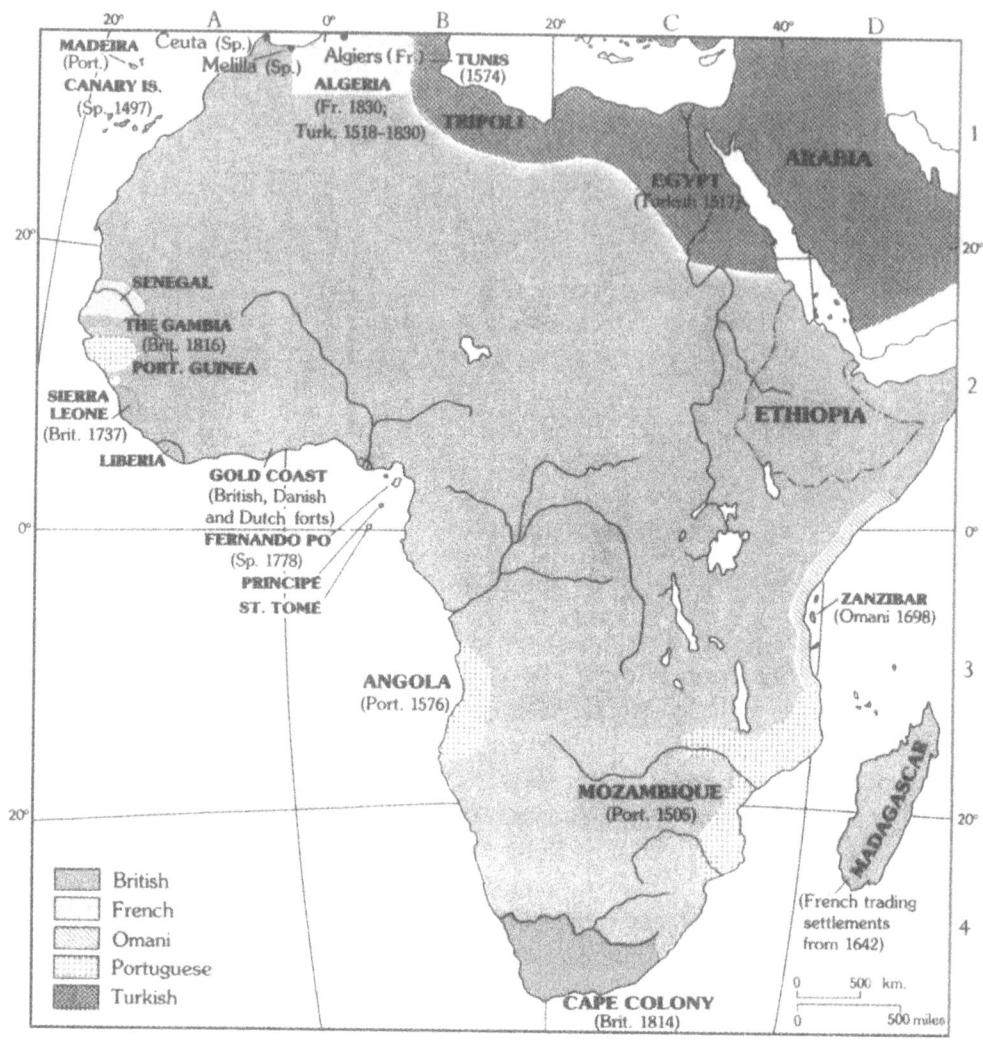

# EUROPEAN PENETRATION OF AFRICA, UP TO 1830

Principé, Angola and Mozambique. Here the Portuguese had intermarried freely, and their progeny enjoyed a quasi-feudal existence. Liberia was a colony for freed slaves, shortly to be enfranchised as a republic by the United States. Apart from the small colonies of The Gambia and Sierra Leone, Britain had acquired Cape Colony at the end of the Napoleonic Wars. Except as a refreshment station on the sea route to India, it was of no particular interest or importance. On the eastern side of Africa France maintained small trading settlements in Madagascar, as she had done since 1642. Farther north, along a thin stretch of coast, the red flag of Zanzibar had flown since the fall of Fort Jesus of Mombasa in 1698. The rulers of Zanzibar appointed customs officials; direct intervention, in the person of the ruler, Sayyid Said, did not take place until 1827, and it was 1843 or 1844 before the first trading caravans penetrated the African interior. His ventures were encouraged by American, British, French, and, later, German consuls.

# EUROPEAN PENETRATION OF AFRICA, UP TO 1890

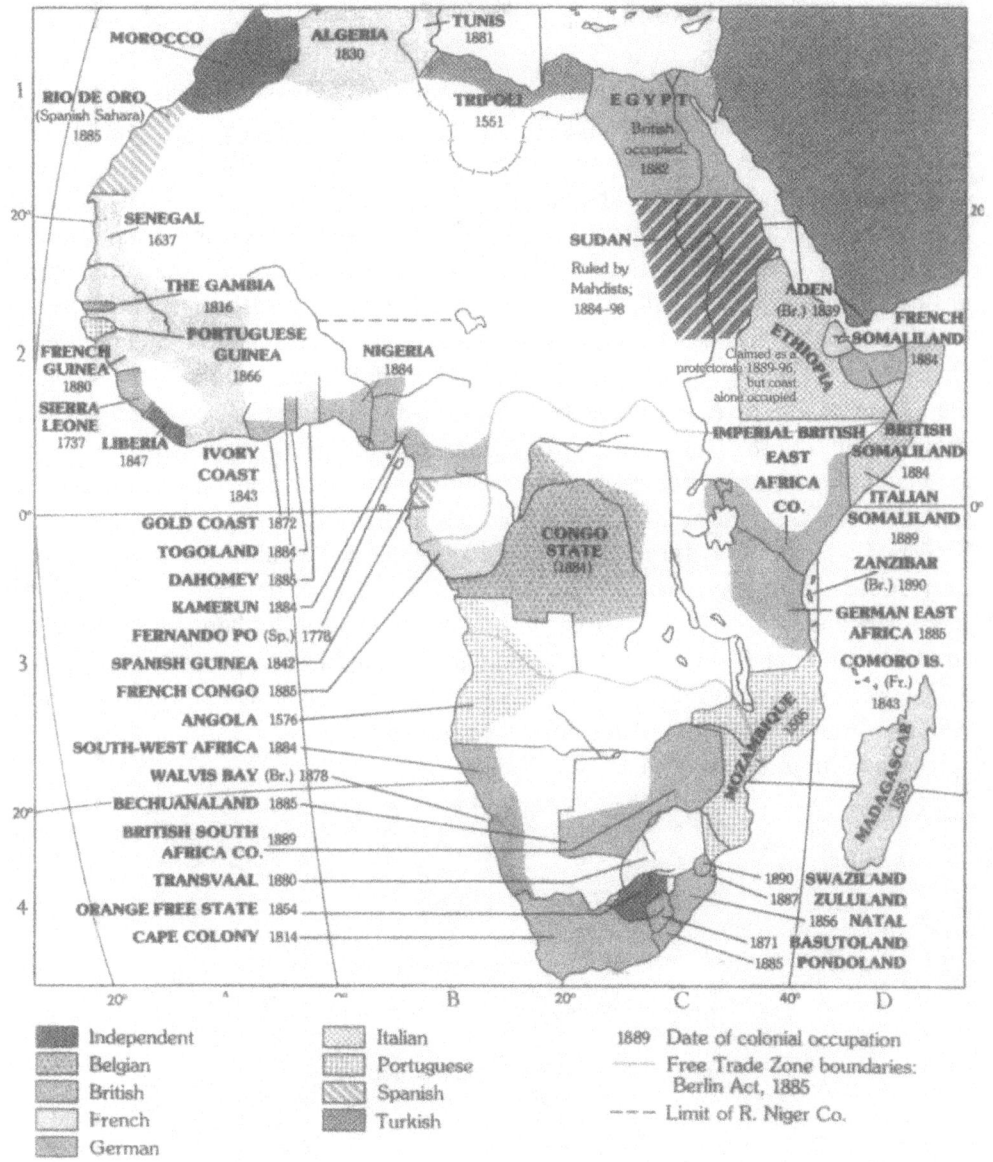

## EUROPEAN PENETRATION OF AFRICA, UP TO 1890

By 1890 the whole map of Africa had altered. To the previous imperial powers had been added Germany, Italy, and Spain. It was true that in the center of the continent the Sahara and other large tracts lay unconquered, but hardly one foot of coastland remained that was not under European control, save the seaboard of Ethiopia. This area was under dispute with Italy which had proclaimed a protectorate of Eritrea. The dispute led to the battle of Adowa and a decisive defeat for Italy, which was forced to withdraw this claim on 26 October 1896. They had recovered it by 1914.

Some fundamental changes should be

noted. Ottoman Turkey had now virtually disappeared from the northern seaboard save in Egypt, where the khedive ruled as viceroy for the Ottoman sultan. Morocco under its sultan, Liberia under a president, and then Orange Free State under a Boer president were the only truly independent states. The Sudan, free under the khalifa (successor) of the Mahdi, was technically in rebellion against Egypt, and his rule was to be terminated shortly by the battle of Omdurman (1896). The dominions of the Sultan of Zanzibar became a British protectorate in 1890. On the African mainland the Sultan's possessions were split between German East Africa (later Tanganyika) and the Imperial British East Africa Company, which paid the sultan an annual rent for control of a coastal strip (later Kenya). Portugal had gained nothing, but had consolidated her hold on the interior of Mozambique, agreeing on boundaries with Britain and Germany. The greatest beneficiaries of the scramble were Britain and France, to which the Berlin Act (1885) would give formal recognition.

At this stage it is difficult to assess how much difference the new masters had made to the lives of ordinary people. Everywhere, save in the long-established Cape Colony, administrators were few and far between. Only the rudiments of public services had been introduced, and these but little outside the capital cities. What had been interrupted, however, were the long-established lines of commerce. In the new dispensation economic boundaries had been wholly ignored and had to be rebuilt. A point no less serious, and one that would lead to great trouble for the imperial powers, was the fact that ethnic boundaries had also been disregarded, and in many cases were no more than lines arbitrarily drawn upon inaccurate maps.

*General Charles George Gordon firing on Mahdi's forces on the outskirts of Khartoum, 1885*

## DUTCH POSSESSIONS IN INDONESIA, 17TH CENTURY

The Dutch, after the Portuguese monopoly of the Cape route was broken at the end of the sixteenth century, carved themselves out a very substantial eastern empire. Based at first on a few trade centers, the Dutch later either occupied

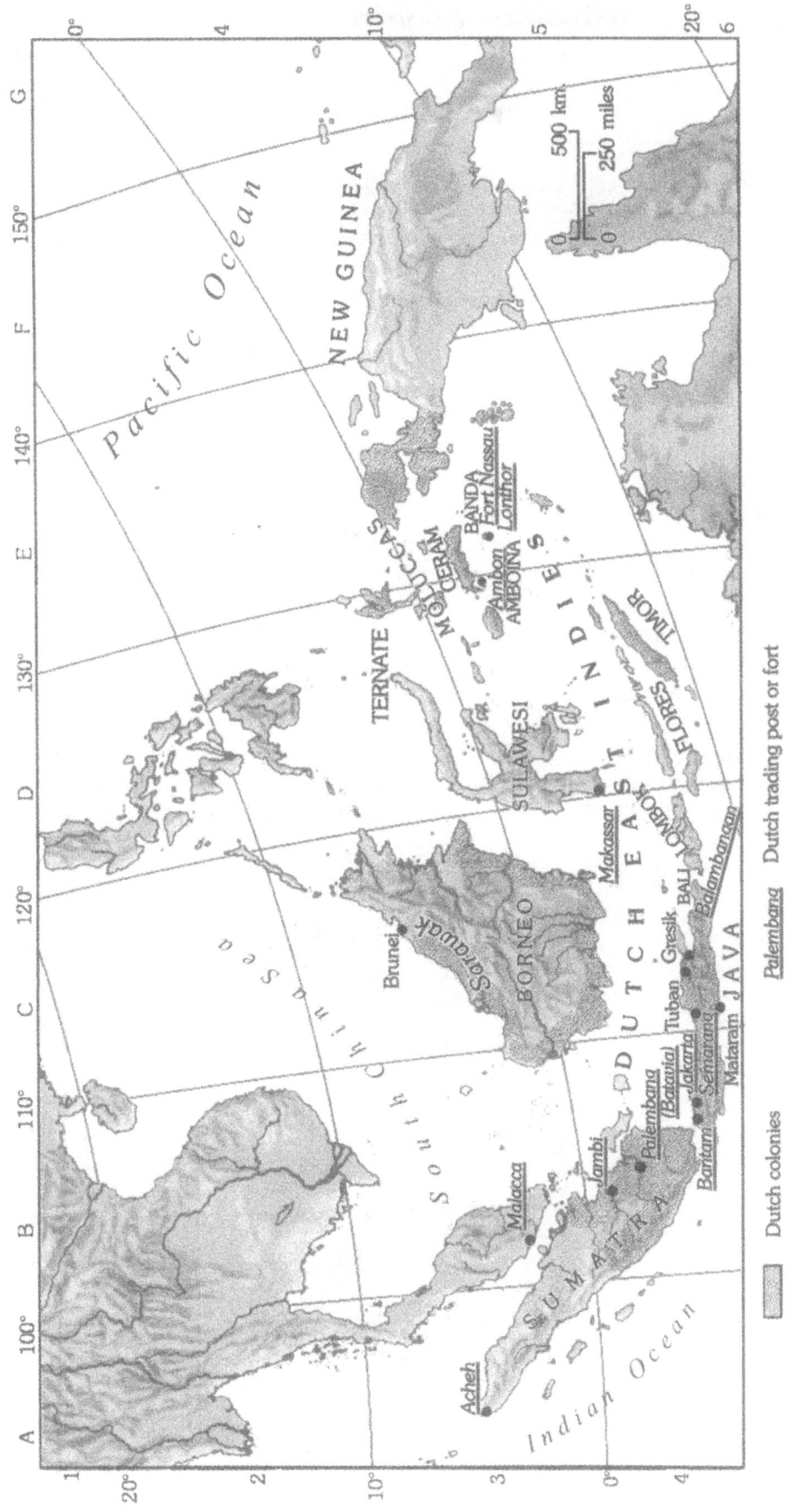

DUTCH POSSESSIONS IN INDONESIA, 17TH CENTURY

strategic centers, secured by forts, or by military force bound local rulers to treaties guaranteeing monopolies, thus opening the way to eventual political dominance. In the end, the Dutch East Indies stretched from Sumatra to western New Guinea, from Borneo (excluding British North Borneo, Brunei and Sarawak), Sulawesi, the Moluccas and other islands to Java, Bali, Lombok, Flores and western Timor.

The first Dutch expeditions visited Bantam, Jakarta, Tuban, and Gresik in Java, Sumatra, Borneo, as well as Ternate in the Moluccas and Lonthor in the Banda Islands, where a factory was established in 1599. In 1600 an agreement was made with a chief of Ambon (Amboina), where, as in many other places, the Dutch became allies of the local rulers against the Portuguese. In 1605 the Portuguese fortress there came under Dutch control, and between then and 1609 the Dutch consolidated their position in the Moluccas. They occupied the island of Banda Neira, building Fort Nassau.

The Dutch devoted great efforts to building forts, supplying garrisons, and providing plenty of shipping. In 1619 Jakarta was seized, to become, under the name Batavia, the center of operations of the VOC, the Dutch East India Company that took over from previous trading companies. The Muslim sultan Agung of Mataram, who had united most of Java except Bantam (Banten) in the west and Balambangan in the east (which eventually fell in 1639) under his suzerainty, failed to take Batavia in 1628–29 (Bantam had already tried in 1627).

The expansion of Dutch influence in Java and the islands increased. At this period rivalry between the Dutch and the English, also eager for a share in the spice trade, often generated support by local peoples as a foil to Dutch power. The Banda Islands, Lonthor, Run, were taken in 1621 by Governor-General Coen, securing nutmeg supplies, Ambon and Ceram were forced to submit and Ternate was taken from the Portuguese, securing cloves. A treaty of 1638 with Makasar's sultan recognized Dutch

*Dutch colonial buildings at Malacca (Meleka), Malaysia*

rights in the Moluccas. Portuguese Malacca fell in 1641.

Resistance to Dutch commercial monopoly in Makassar, in the Muslim center of Hitu in Ambon, and in Hoamoal, was suppressed by 1656. Palembang was destroyed in 1659. In 1662 the Minangkabau came under Dutch protection, and the next year, with the departure of the Spanish, the Dutch alone were left in the Moluccas. The influence of Acheh in Sumatra was reduced in 1666, and between 1667–69, Hassan Udin's Makassar at last fell under Dutch rule. In 1677 a new sultan of Makaram, Amangkurat II, was compelled to agree to strict trade rules, and the surrender of Semarang and other northern coastal areas, in return for Dutch support. The important pepper port of Bantam, ruled by Sultan Agung, came under Dutch control during the civil war of 1683. Both Mataram and Bantam became Dutch dependents in some sort, and the old system of maintaining a network of strong forts together with a few islands like Ambon and Banda began to give way to a Dutch territorial empire in Indonesia. Jambi was seized in 1687.

## DUTCH POSSESSIONS IN INDONESIA
### FROM THE 18TH CENTURY

As the 18th century progressed, Mataram suffered several wars of succession, losing territory and influence to the VOC. In 1743 Paku Buwono II ceded the whole northern coast of Java, and Madura, and in 1749, on his death bed, he recognised VOC sovereignty. In 1755 internal disputes divided Mataram into two states, ruled from Surakarta and Jogjakarta, and well into the nineteenth century these functioned with minimal Dutch interference. The new sultan of Bantam, too, in 1752, ceded his sovereignty to the VOC. In Sumatra, Acheh remained independent, and the Bugis in Sulawesi and others developed pirate 'states' that caused much trouble to the Dutch well on into the nineteenth century. A major if temporary change came with the foundation of the Batavian Republic under

*Bandung Technological Institute, Java.*

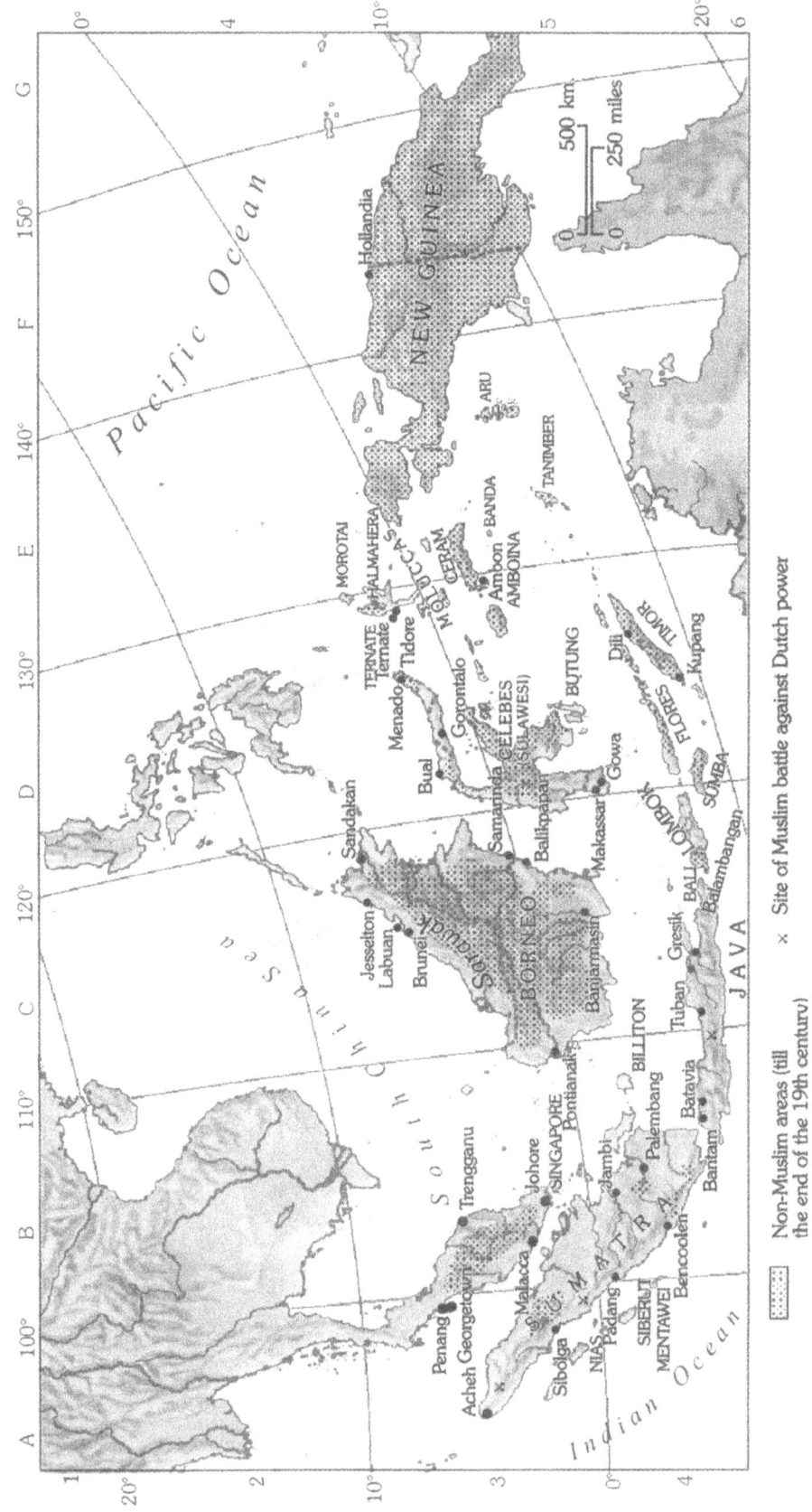

DUTCH POSSESSIONS IN INDONESIA, FROM THE 18TH CENTURY

French influence in 1795, when, until 1815, much of what Holland possessed in Indonesia came under British control. Southeast Asia and Britain, seventeenth to twentieth centuries). Restored after Napoleon's defeat, the Dutch reorganised their colonial empire, concentrating heavily on Java. They fought the Java War against the strongly Muslim prince Dipo Negoro of Jogjakarta from 1825-30, and much new territory, Banjumas, Bagelen, Madiun and Kediri, fell under direct Dutch rule.

British acquisition of Labuan and north Borneo, the presence of *Rajah* Brooke in Sarawak, and the discovery of useful mineral deposits encouraged the Dutch to strengthen control over the whole archipelago for fear of outside interference. Banjarmasin was annexed (1859–1863), and Sambas and Pontianak pacified. Billiton was occupied in 1851. Bali was partly annexed, and partly reduced to Dutch suzerainty between 1846-49. The Bugis of Boni in Sulawesi were temporarily subdued in 1858-59. In Sumatra, where piracy was rife, Dutch military efforts prevailed. In 1856 the Lampongs districts, in 1858 the Batak districts, in 1868 Bencoolen, were all subdued. Palembang, though brought under Dutch control in 1825, still required pacifying. Siak, with its dependencies, came under Dutch sovereignty in 1858. Muslim resurgents in Minangkabau were defeated. In Acheh, a major war broke out with the Dutch in 1873, and although Dutch governors were appointed, unrest continued under claimants to the throne, with strong Muslim support, until the early 1900s. In 1898 the system of recognising a local ruler who agreed to Batavian supremacy was introduced in Acheh, and spread soon to Bali and many other places. Some 300 small states accepted this arrangement, and came under Dutch control.

The Dutch East Indies were occupied by the Japanese during the Second World War, and the greater part became the largely Muslim state of Indonesia in 1949.

*Sir James Brooke (1803–1868)*
Rajah *Brooke*

# PORTUGUESE POSSESSIONS IN AFRICA, 20TH CENTURY

Of the three former Portuguese possessions in Africa, in Guinea-Bissau neither Christianity nor Islam have made much progress, the people being greatly attached to ancestor-worship, while in Angola the people were largely converted to Christianity from the sixteenth century onwards.

Following Vasco da Gama's voyages to India, in 1505 King Manuel I of Portugal ordered forts to be built at Mozambique and at Sofala.

The object was to control the gold and ivory trade of the interior, where trading centers were set up at Sena and Tete. An attempt to acquire territory in 1570 ended in total disaster, and effectively Portugal exercised little or no control over the coast. The interior was controlled by pagan chiefs. In 1750 the Sofala garrison numbered only thirty. Primarily interested in trade, the Portuguese were dependent on bribing the coastal chiefs. In 1752 a visitor made an administrative survey; there was not much evidence of religion; *nipa,* a brandy was brewed from wild palms. The chief of Inhamarungo 'follows the Muslim religion, but gives no indication beyond not eating pork.' At Angoche on the coast a powerful chief, 'dressed in silken robes, with a gold fringed headdress,' received the traveler. He spoke passable Portuguese, and excellent Arabic. He had schools where the Qur'an was taught and mosques used daily.

Inland, Islam was not noted until 1771, with an increase after 1839. Sufi from the Comoro Islands were active missionaries. A migration of 'learned men' to Angoche from the Comoros took place, to teach Arabic and Islamic law. By 1906 Islam had reached the northern shores of Lake Malawi, within Mozambique. (A conversion of Yao within Malawi is recorded between 1870 and 1910, but it is not known which Sufi fraternity was responsible.)

The present state of the country does not enable an accurate assessment of the situation.

*Bridge over the Save River, Mozambique*

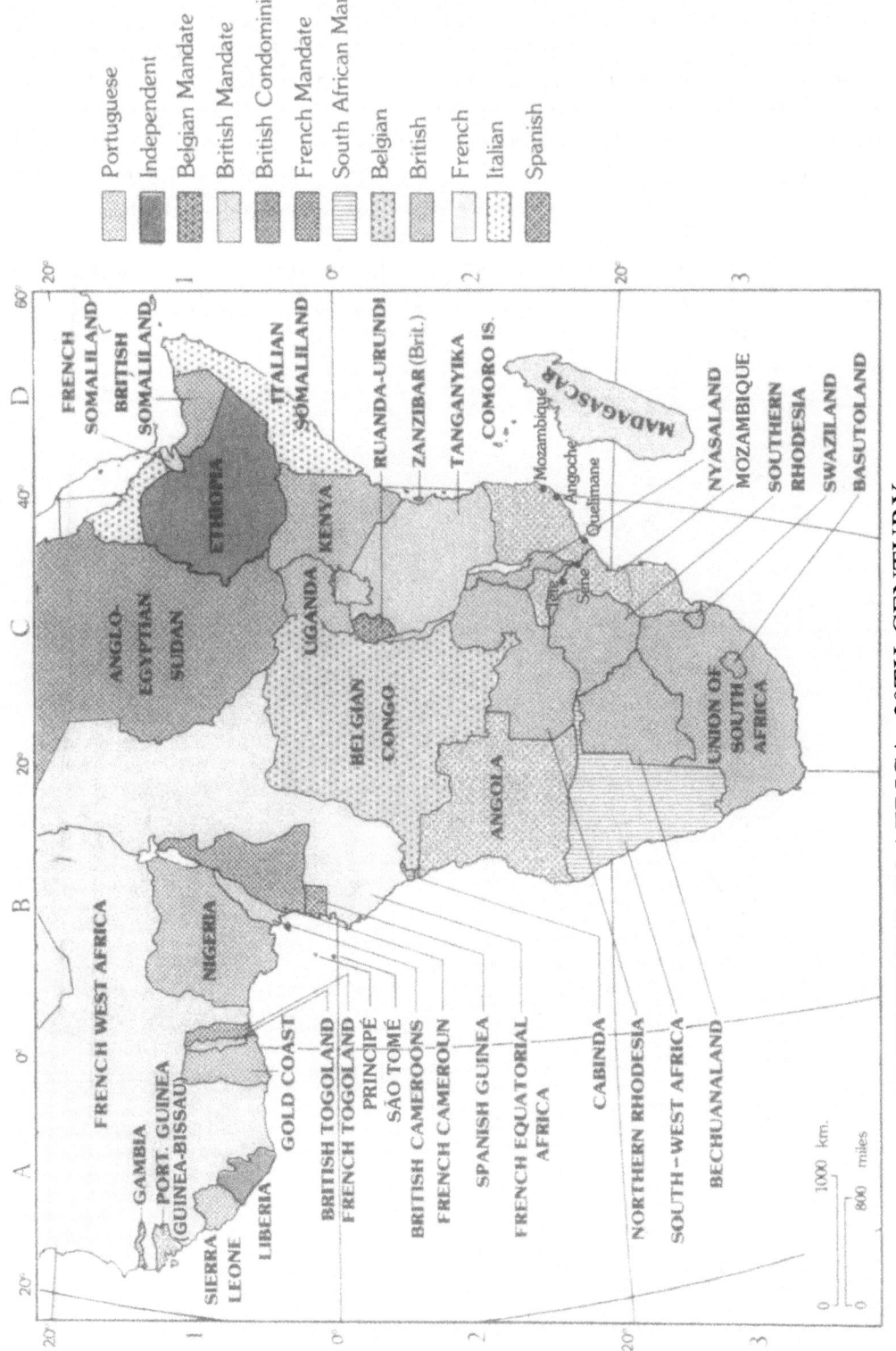

PORTUGUESE POSSESSIONS IN AFRICA, 20TH CENTURY

# FORMER SPANISH POSSESSIONS IN WEST AFRICA

Spanish interest in western Africa was initiated in the thirteenth century because of its proximity to the Canary Islands. A fort was established on the mainland for trading, at a site today unidentified, in 1472. Spain did not take formal possession of the coast between Capes Blanco and Bogador until 1885. It was administered from the Canary Islands.

The Muslim inhabitants are primarily cattle breeders. Included in the Río de Oro were a number of offshore islands. Spain withdrew in 1975, sharing the country between Morocco and Mauritania, and Western Sahara became independent as the Sahrani Arab Democratic Republic, with a government which today (2002) is still in exile. Over seventy states have recognised the legitimacy of the Polisario Front Government, and likewise the Organisation of African Unity. Nevertheless, Mauritania renounced its claim to its share of the territory in 1979, which was added to the share of Morocco. In 1988, Morocco agreed with the Polisario Front to a referendum to determine the future of the whole area, but this has not yet taken place. It is expected in 2002.

# FORMER SPANISH POSSESSIONS IN WEST AFRICA

## EGYPT AND OTHER POWERS, 20TH CENTURY

By 1876 the extravagance and incompetence of Ismail Pasha, Khedive (Viceroy) of Egypt subject to the Ottoman Sultan, compelled his principal creditors, Britain and France, to take control of Egyptian state finances. It began a process which resulted in what was known as Dual Control, imposed in 1876, suspended in 1878, and reimposed in 1879. An Egyptian rebellion led to a joint bombardment of Alexandria in 1882, with resulting subjugation of the country. Britain agreed by a Convention in 1887 to withdraw within three years; it was never honored.

In spite of financial recovery in 1889,

*Al-Azhar University, Cairo*

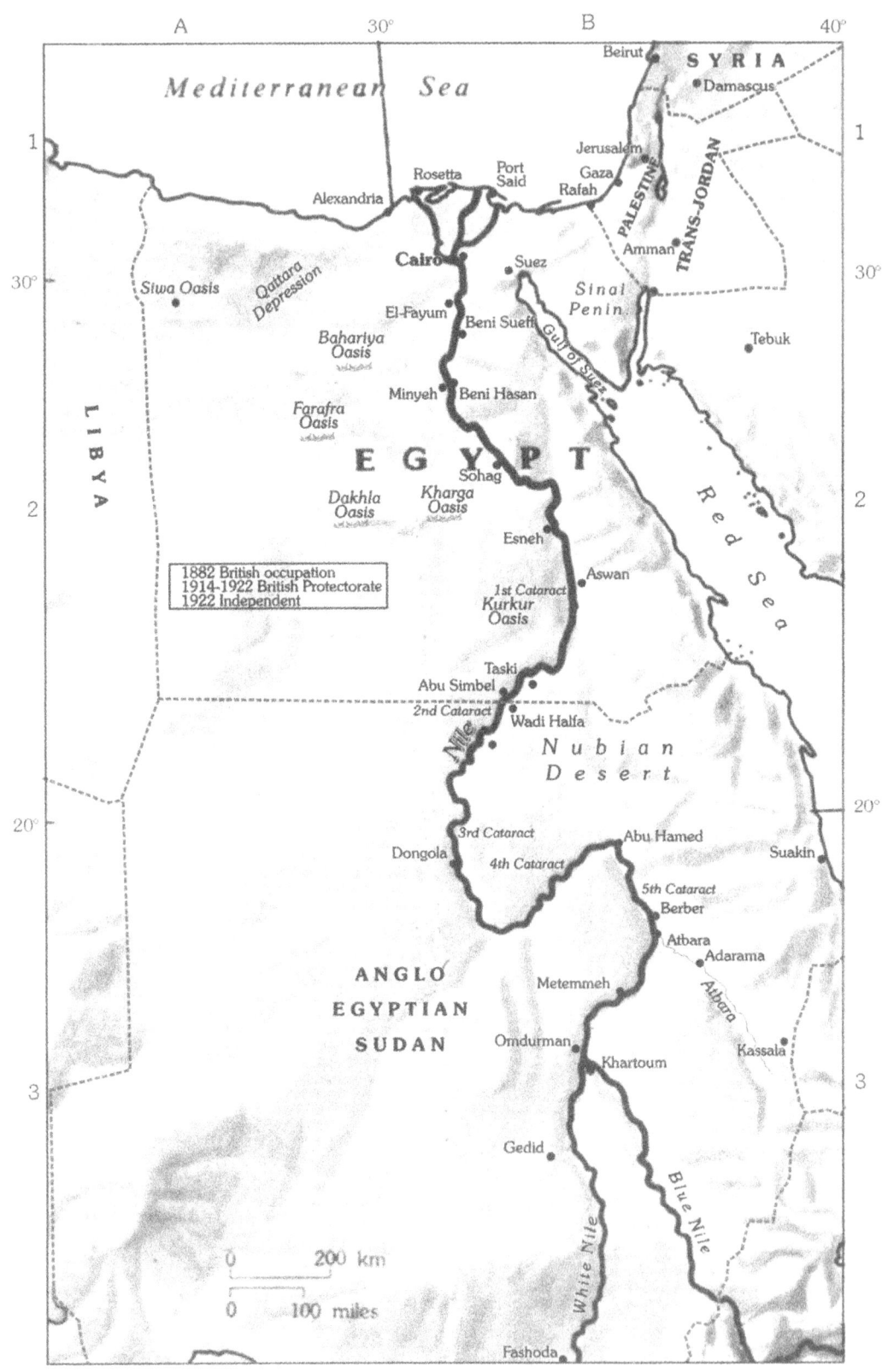

EGYPT AND OTHER POWERS, 20TH CENTURY

with a budget surplus, and a form of constitutional government, Britain remained the effective paramount power until 1957. Various factors contributed, not least the adroit diplomacy of Sir Evelyn Baring (later Lord Cromer), Consul-General 1883–1907, and the weakness of successive Egyptian governments. Not until 1906–10 did an Egyptian statesman of the first rank emerge, Saad Zaghul.

When war broke out in 1914, in order to protect the Suez Canal, British paramouncy was formalised in 1914 by the proclamation of a British Protectorate and the occupation of Egypt by British troops, holding the Canal in the two World Wars. Saad Zaghul demanded independence in 1918. He was deported as an agitator in 1919, and then released to attend the Conference of Paris.

The British Protectorate was formally ended in 1922, and Egypt recognised as an independent kingdom. King Fuad I, nevertheless, had little more than a nominal sovereignty. It was the misfortune for Egypt that his heir, Faruq (1936–52) was a dissolute hedonist. This, and the likelihood of a general war, enabled an Anglo-Egyptian Twenty Year Treaty, allowing Britain to station 10,000 troops in the Canal Zone and Cairo. Egypt was admitted to the League of Nations in 1937. The growing tide of nationalism precipitated the rise of Gamal 'Abd al-Nasr (Abdel Nasser) and the abdication of the monarch, and finally for the nationalisation of the Canal in 1956. War ensued, but common sense prevailed within a month of the arrival of a joint Anglo-French landing. Egypt occupies a unique position in the Islamic world, in the al-Azhar University, a potent intellectual force serving all Islamic nations, in which endowments provide instruction in Islamic theological subjects as well as modern studies.

## THE SUDAN, 19TH TO 20TH CENTURY

The Egyptian campaign of 1820 led by Ibrahim Pasha began the unification of an area containing peoples of different origins hitherto never united. In the north and center were Arabs and Nubians; in the south Nilotic and other African peoples. Islam is the state religion, although in the south the Nilotic peoples are generally pagans or Christians. In the nineteenth century Egyptian control extended to the Muslim province of Harar, now in Ethiopia. Egyptian rule lasted from 1820 until 1880, exploiting African products and principally enslaving the population, so reducing the people –

*Lord Kitchener of Khartoum (1850–1916)*

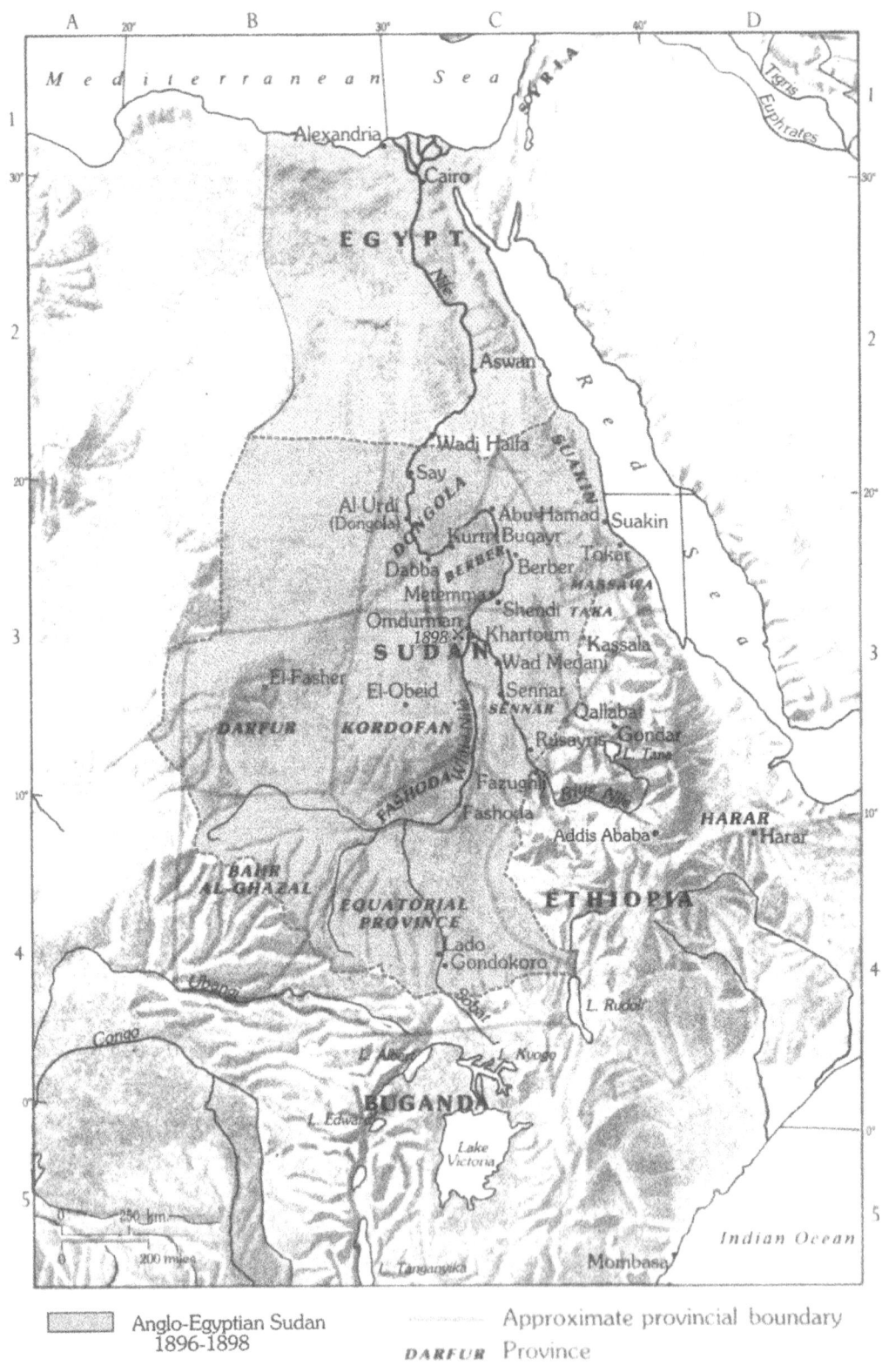

THE SUDAN, 19TH AND 20TH CENTURIES

who had nothing to lose but their rags – that one Muhammad Ahmad was inspired to declare himself Mahdi, the Rightly Guided One who was to appear before the last days of the earth. He welded together the northern peoples in rebellion, and by 1882 he had annihilated an Egyptian army.

At this moment Britain had occupied Egypt, and ordered the evacuation of Egyptians from the Sudan. By 1884 General Charles George Gordon had died at the hands of a dervish force which controlled almost all the north. In 1889 the *Khalifa* (Caliph, successor of the Mahdi) made an abortive attack on Egypt. Fighting continued, and in 1896 Egyptian and British troops retaliated under General H.H. Kitchener (later Earl Kitchener of Khartoum). On 2 September 1898 he fought a decisive battle at Omdurman, which enabled the combined force to take Khartoum.

From 1897 until 1957 the Sudan was ruled as a joint condominium under Britain and Egypt, with Britain as very much the dominant partner. Slavery and slaving were abolished, and corruption suppressed; legitimate trade in cotton and other local products was encouraged to give the country a solid economic basis.

The south was given formal status of autonomy within the Sudan in 1972, but in 1983 insurrection erupted, which left some 1.4 million dead, including some 300,000 who died of famine in 1988. Thousands more died of famine in 1994. It is estimated that three million refugees have fled to nearby states. An accord was reached in 1999 for a four-year period, followed by a referendum on a choice between federation within the Sudan or complete indedpendence.

It is not noticeable that Islam has been able to progress in the south.

*Al-Mahdi's (Muhammad Ahmad's) tomb, Omdurman, Sudan*

# VII. THE TWENTIETH CENTURY

## THE EXPANSION OF SAUDI ARABIA, 20TH CENTURY

The Saudi family ruled Dariya in Wadi Hanifa, in the province of Nejd in central Arabia, in the fifteenth century. It came to prominence in the eighteenth century when it accepted the puritanical Islamic revivalism of Muhammad Abd al-Wahhab, whose teachings were based on those of the jurist Ahmad ibn Hanbal (780–855). Under this inspiration, the Saudi family raided the Hejaz, Iraq, and Syria and captured Mecca in 1806. Because it caused a loss of revenue, these acts angered the Ottomans. They sent armies under Ibrahim Pasha from Egypt in a series of campaigns (1812–1818).

Although the family still possessed considerable territory, it fell into eclipse after 1865, when, after a civil war, the al-Rashid family displaced them.

Abd al-Aziz Ibn Saud was born in Kuwait around 1880. He was determined to regain his patrimony. With only fifteen men, he seized Riyadh in 1902, killing the Rashidi governor. In 1913 he took al-Hasa on the Persian Gulf, and Asir in 1920–1926; Hail was taken in 1921 and the Hejaz, including the cities of Mecca and Medina, in 1924–1925. These territories formed what was proclaimed a kingdom in 1932.

Though it began as a poor kingdom, an oil concession awarded in 1933 and the first export of oil in 1938 brought riches. Even during 1990 new reserves of oil were identified in central Arabia, with the result that Saudi Arabia is not only the possessor of the greatest oil reserves in the world, but the richest of oil states. Nevertheless, although there have been certain concessions to modernity, Saudi Arabia remains the most puritanical of Arab states, forbidding the consumption of alcohol even to foreigners and making it illegal for women to drive cars or appear unveiled in public. A major problem is presented by the number of royal family members — in all more than seven hundred persons — who enjoy every possible state preferment, privilege, and luxury, as opposed to the relative poverty of the majority of the people.

*A busy market town in Southern Arabia*

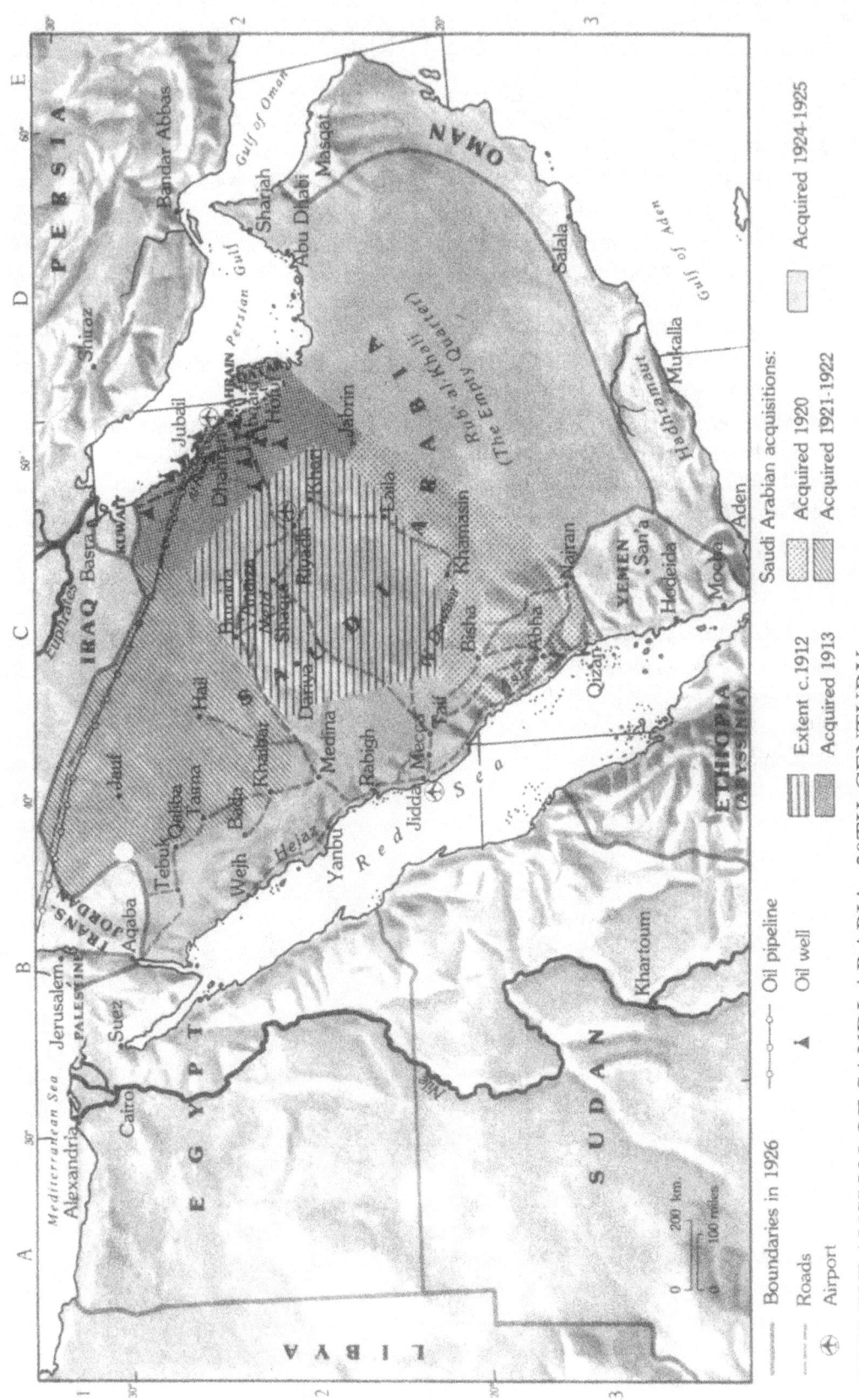

THE EXPANSION OF SAUDI ARABIA, 20TH CENTURY

# WORLD WAR I: THE TURKISH FRONTS IN THE CAUCASUS, SYRIA, MESOPOTAMIA AND ARABIA

When war broke out in 1914 Bulgaria, Greece, Montenegro, and Serbia united against Turkey, where imperial Germany had long prepared a toe hold in the case of war. In November 1914 Britain and France declared war on Turkey. Their objective was twofold: to preserve vital British communication through Egypt with India as well as French interests in the Suez Canal and to relieve Russia from Turkish pressure in the Caucasus.

The Ottoman sultan proclaimed a *jihad* against the Allies, but, with the aid of British gold, this was declared invalid by the sharif of Mecca. At the end of 1914 a Turkish army from Syria attempted to cut the Suez Canal, but it was stopped on the canal's banks. Although ill-equipped, the Russians attacked Erzerum and repulsed the Turks at Kars and Ardahan in January 1915. A Russian offensive in 1916 took Erzerum, Trebizond, and Erzincan, but all these efforts were rendered vain by the collapse of Russia in 1917.

In 1915 the British and French had attacked Turkey in the Dardanelles, with the goal of taking Istanbul. In spite of their failure, the flower of the Ottoman army was destroyed. The Turks at this time organized massacres of Armenians in Anatolia and especially in Istanbul, in which some 750,000 Armenians perished out of a total population of some two million. Many Armenians fled to Syria and Mesopotamia.

In Mesopotamia an expeditionary force, largely from India, took Basra in 1914, but it was not able to reach Baghdad until 1917. With British encouragement, and under the inspired leadership of T. E. Lawrence, the Arabs of Hejaz revolted in

*Turkish flags flying on the Citadel of the Old City of Jerusalem*

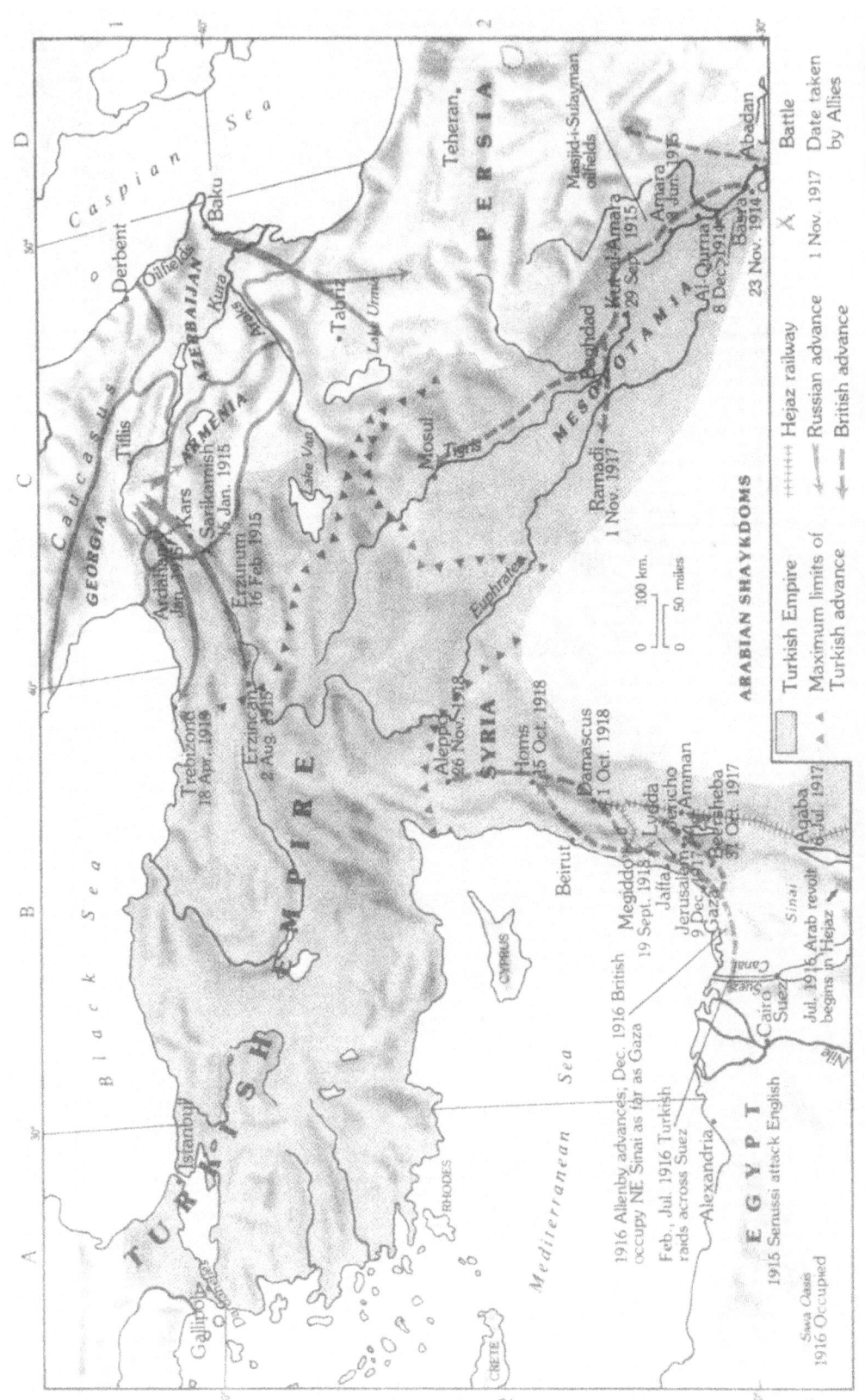

WORLD WAR I: THE TURKISH FRONTS IN THE CAUCASUS, SYRIA, MESOPOTAMIA AND ARABIA

*Turkish cavalry crossing the Jordan River, escaping from British troops in the First World War*

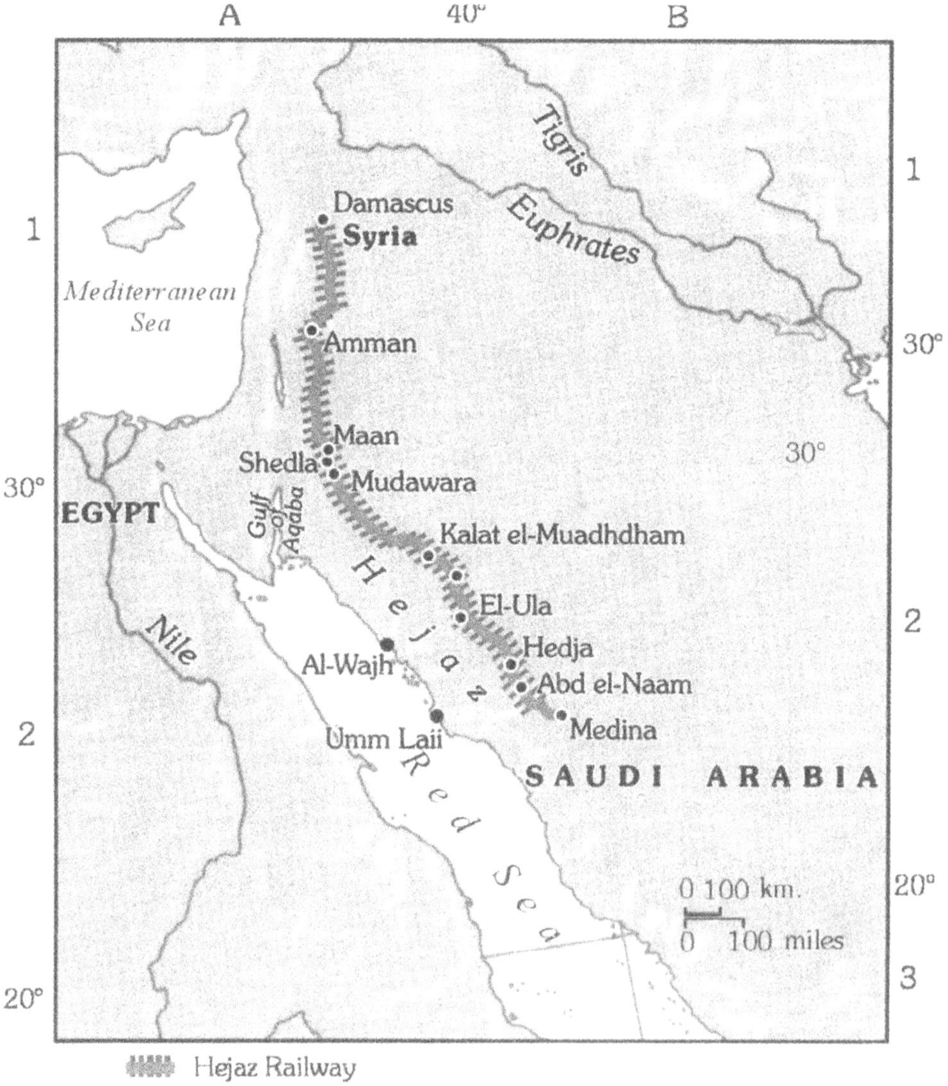

**THE HEJAZ RAILWAY**

July 1916. They served the Allied cause by harassing the Turks along the line of the Hejaz railway, during the advances in Mesopotamia and Syria. Baghdad fell to the Allies in March 1917, costing 92,500 casualties. From Egypt the British general Edmund Henry Hynman Allenby mounted an attack on Syria in 1917. Jaffa was taken on 17 November 1917, and Jerusalem on 9 December. Allenby

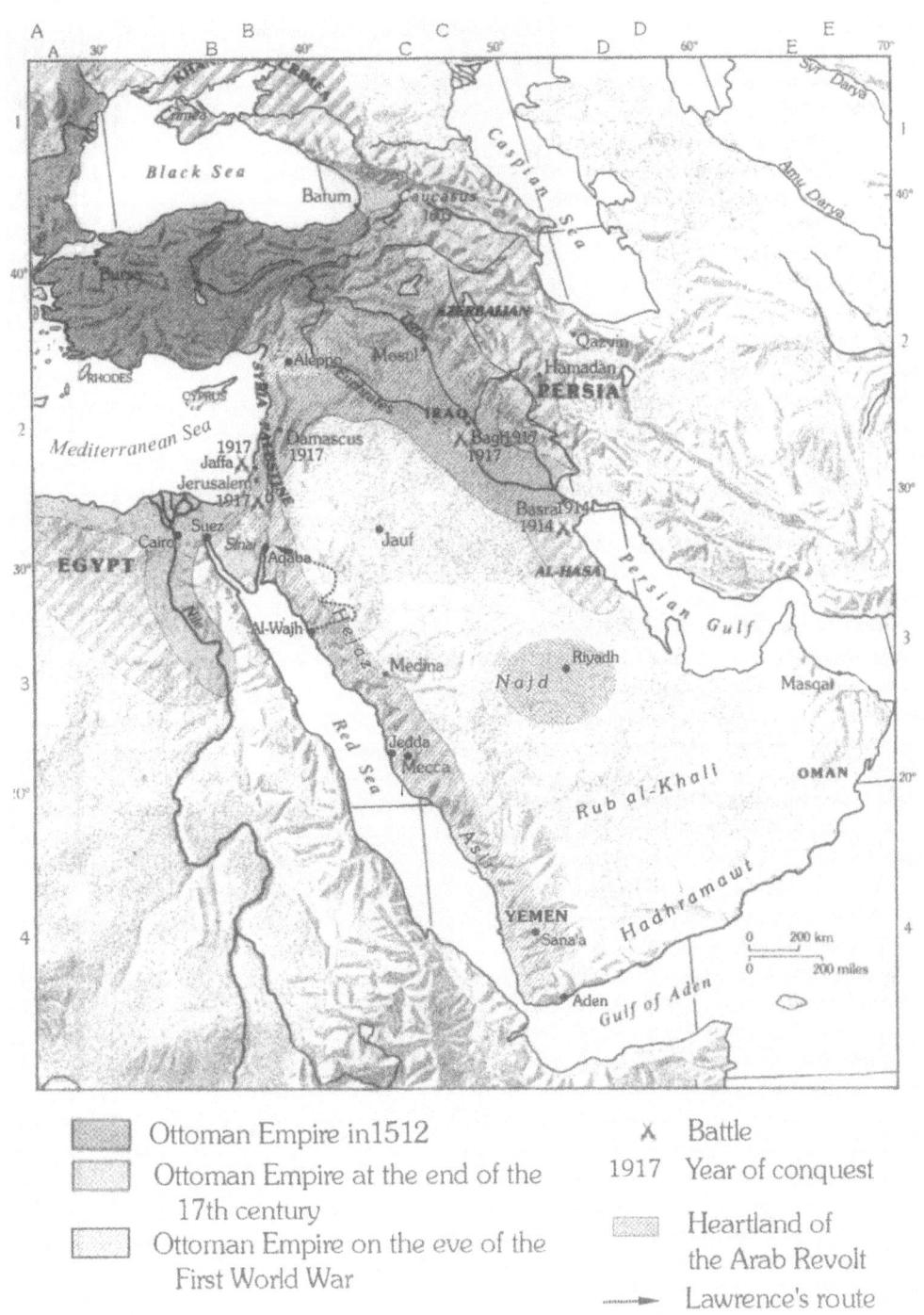

## THE ARAB REVOLT

*Thomas Edward Lawrence (1888–1935) "Lawrence of Arabia"*

continued northward through Damascus, where the Arabs took part in the victorious entry, to Aleppo. The Turkish army finally surrendered on 30 October 1918.

*Troops landing at Gallipoli*

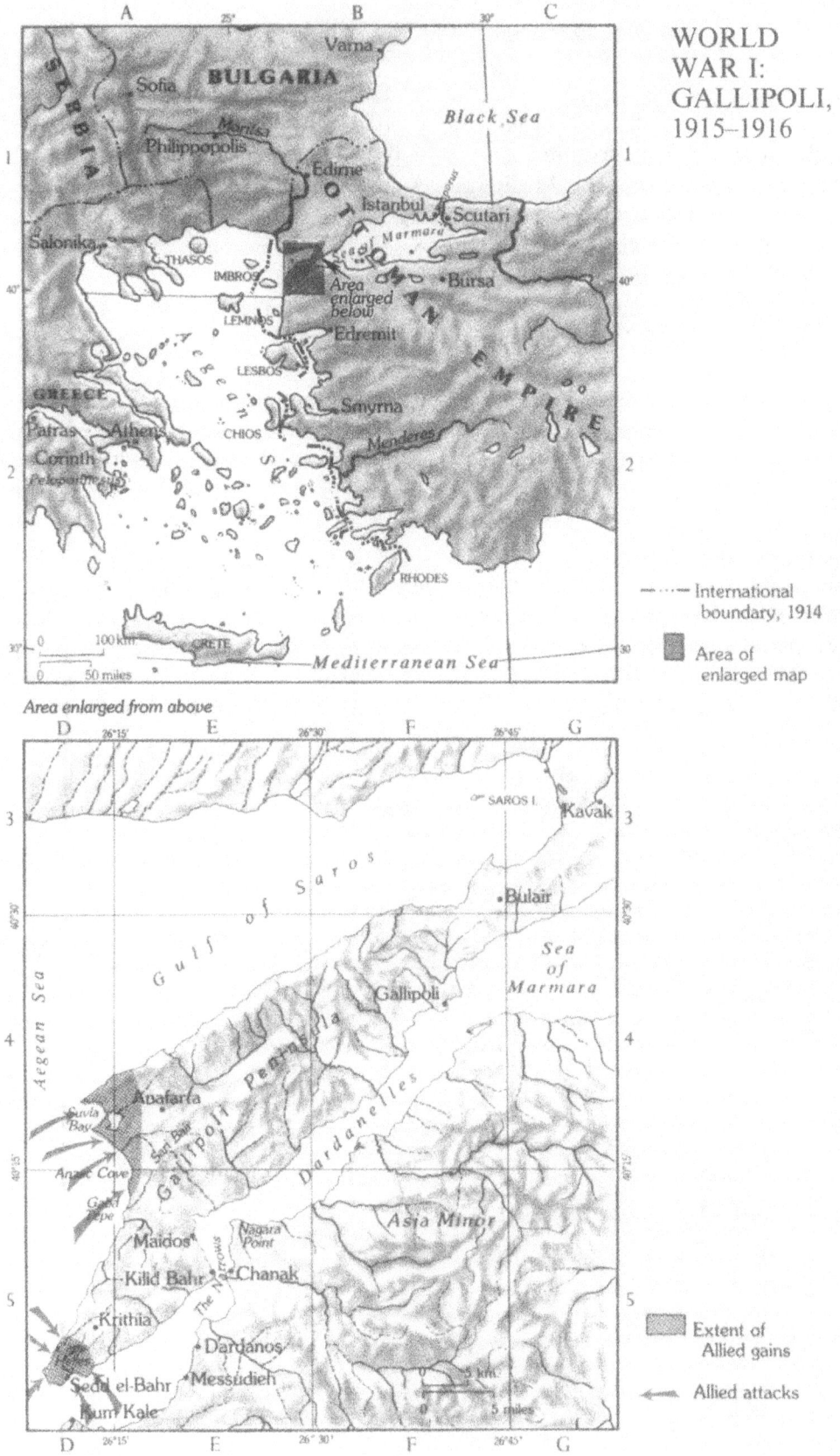

# WORLD WAR I: GALLIPOLI, 1915–1916

The purpose of the campaign in the Dardanelles was to take Istanbul and thereby secure communications for the Allies with Russia from the Mediterranean to the Black Sea. The entry of the Turks into the war had, in fact, cut Russia off from sea communications for most of the year. In addition, the Germans had closed the Baltic to the Russian navy.

A joint British and French fleet was assembled, but a series of naval bombardments proved ineffective. Accordingly a heterogeneous army was assembled, and French and British troops, including those from Australia, New Zealand and the United Kingdom landed on 25 April and several following days. By mid year the Allies had gained very little ground. On 6 August an offensive began, with heavy losses on both sides and little or no progress being made. The Allies, moreover, suffered greatly from heat, for which they were unprepared, and from disease. By 15 August the British commander was asking for 95,000 reinforcements, a figure based on an estimate of the Turkish force.

By mid-September the French government regarded the campaign as futile. From an Ottoman point of view, the troops were holding down Allied divisions that could have been employed against them elsewhere, and they were content to offer no more than a passive defense. Moreover, they occupied the higher ground. Slower to reach a conclusion than the French, the British eventually determined on evacuation, which began on 19 December, the Allies having had 130,000 men killed, wounded, and missing. It had been an ill thought-out exercise of utter futility.

*A small mosque near Edirne, Turkey*

*Abdallah, Amir, later King, of Transjordan, who took part in the Arab Revolt against Turkish rule during World War I*

# THE MIDDLE EAST FOLLOWING THE TREATY OF VERSAILLES, 1919

When the Conference of Paris met in 1919 the principal problem in the Middle East was the dismemberment of the Ottoman Empire. Britain and France were already bound to one another by the Sykes-Picot Agreement of 1916. It provided for French control of coastal Syria, Lebanon, Cilicia in Asia Minor, and northern Iraq and for British control in central Iraq and Basra and northern Palestine. Southern Palestine was to be placed under international administration, with Arab states to be recognized in the remaining Arab territories. Britain was further committed to the Zionist movement by the Balfour Declaration of 1917 to further the establishment of a "Jewish national home" in Palestine. The precise meaning of this expression, however, was never clearly defined in terms of institutions or territorial boundaries.

After some argument and adjustment, Britain obtained League of Nations mandates over Palestine, Transjordan, and Iraq; France obtained mandates over Lebanon and Syria. Egypt, under British occupation since 1882, became a kingdom in 1922 and had the former Ottoman province of Sinai attached to it.

*Abdul Hamid II, Ottoman Sultan*

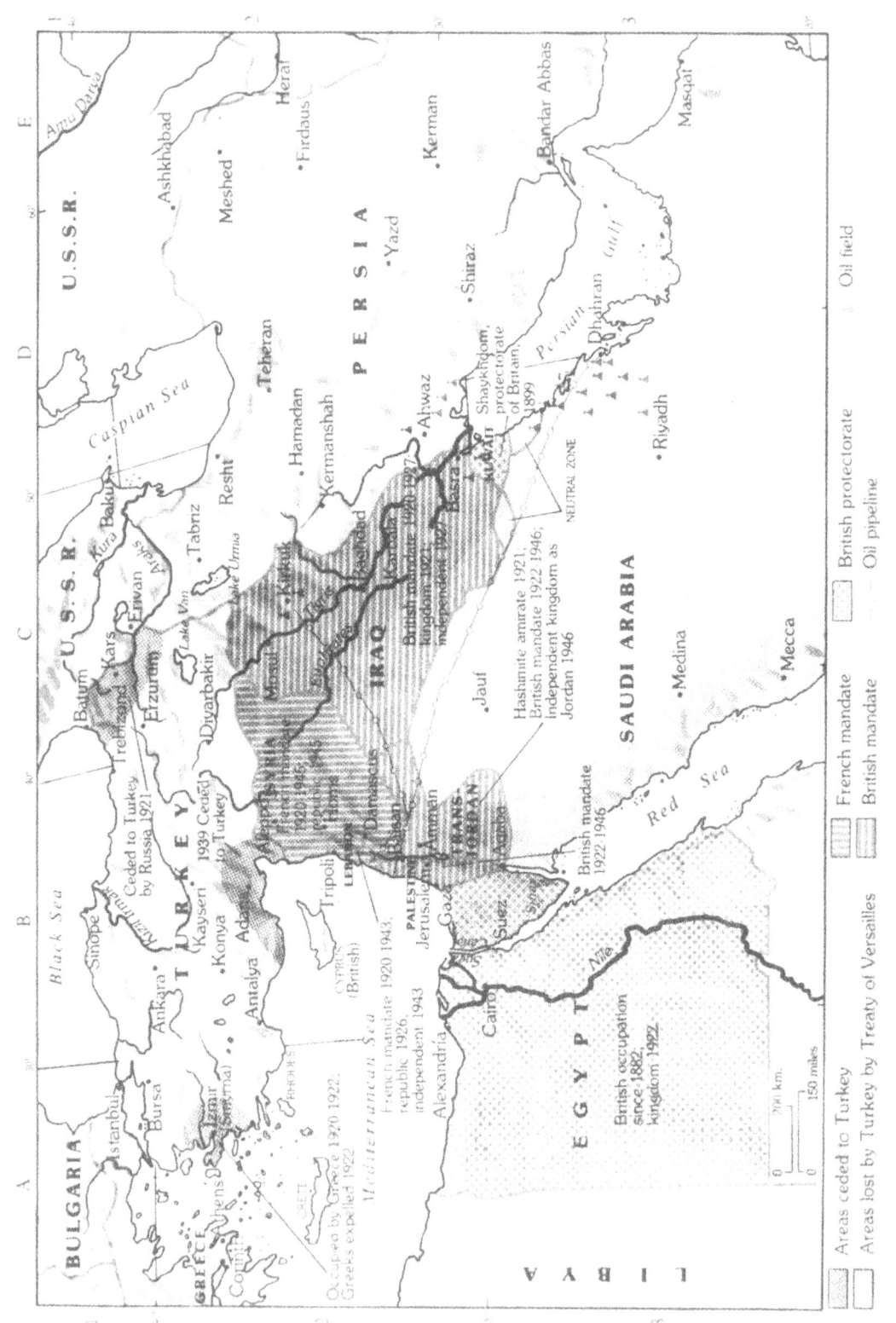

THE MIDDLE EAST FOLLOWING THE TREATY OF VERSAILLES 1919

Some adjustments followed. Remembering that Asia Minor, Syria, Palestine, and Egypt had once been Byzantine provinces, Greece tried to establish itself in Smyrna and its environs in 1920. The Turks drove the Greeks out in 1922. Cyprus, ethnically Greek and Turkish, remained in British possession.

The mandated territories in the Middle East, Africa, and the Far East were committed to the mandatory powers for administration, welfare, and local development until the local population was deemed ready for self-government. The French mandates were terminated in 1943; the British mandate over Iraq was terminated in 1927, Jordan in 1946, and the remainder of Palestine in 1948.

## THE JEWISH DIASPORA, 1920S–1930S

In 1650 Jews numbered about one million and were concentrated chiefly in eastern Europe and the Ottoman Empire. Toward the end of the nineteenth century there were some 7.5 million Jews in eastern Europe, or 70 to 75 percent of the world's Jewish population. This number was due primarily to a natural increase, which Jews shared with others in Europe. During the nineteenth century Jews in western Europe, except for Spain, enjoyed almost full civil liberty. In Russia, however, massacres occurred between 1886 and 1906. Pogroms accelerated an existing migratory movement after the 1870s, establishing new Jewish communities in the U.S.A., Canada, Argentina and other Latin American countries, South Africa and many western European countries. This movement was also part of a general movement throughout Europe from the Old World to the New World, or to establish colonies in Africa and Australia.

The modern Zionist movement, first organized in the 1880s, eventuated in the creation of the State of Israel in 1948. From AD 70 the Diaspora had never lost

*The Second Zionist Congress, Basle 1898*

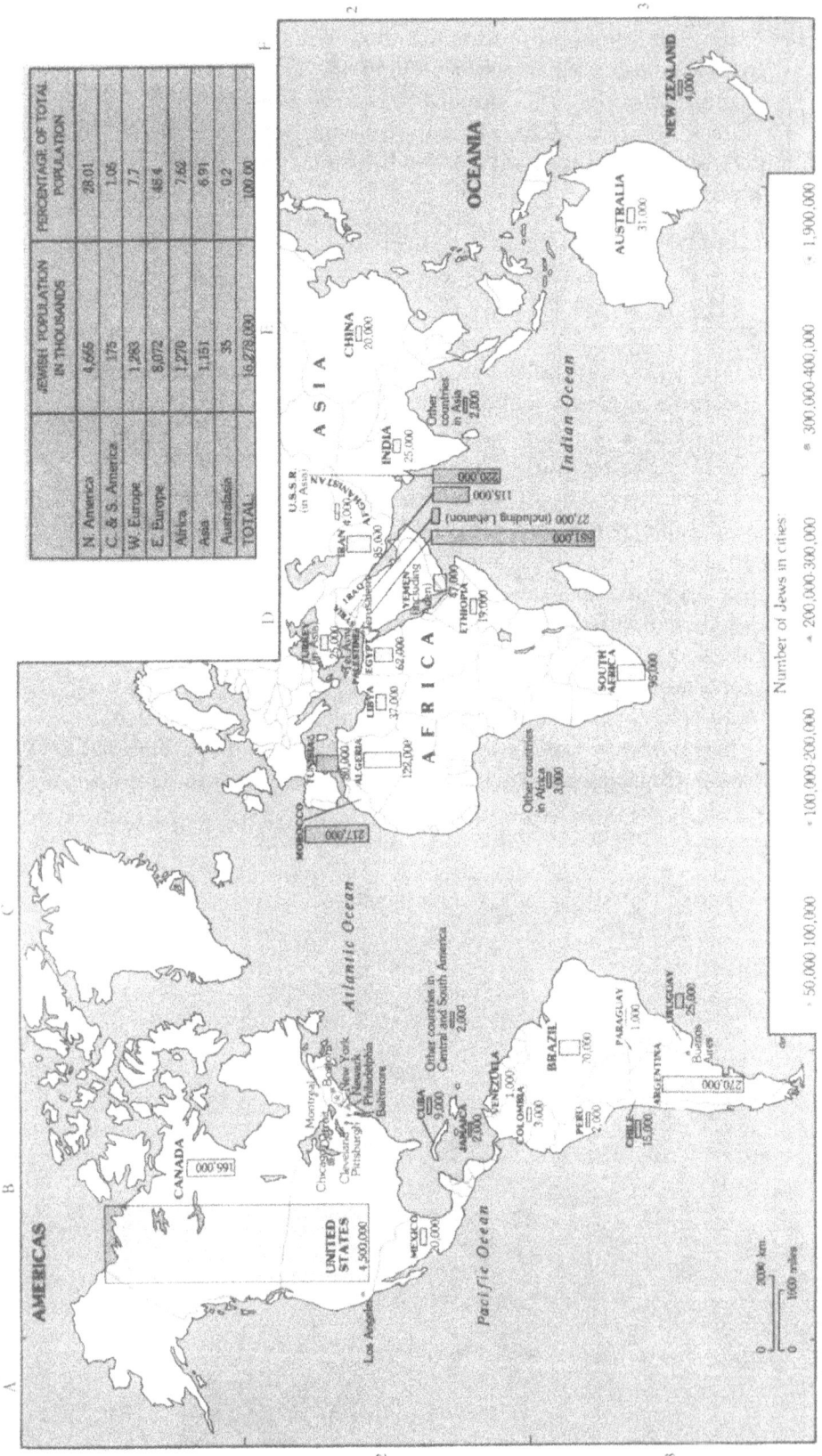

THE JEWISH DIASPORA, 1920S–1930S

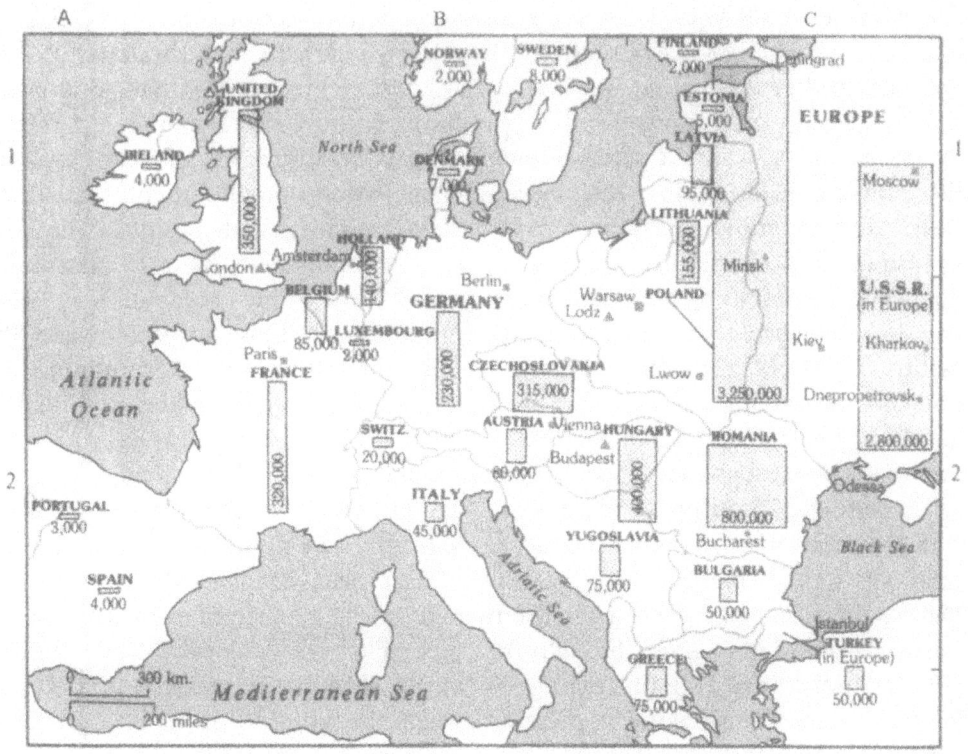

THE JEWISH DIASPORA — EUROPE

its sense of nationhood nor its historical link with Palestine. Anti-Semitism, as narrowly defined not to include other Semites, fostered this sense. The idea of a continued Jewish existence among non-Jewish societies was rejected by some Jewish groups. Theodor Herzl's *The Jewish State* (1896) crystallized these ideas, as did the First Zionist Congress he convened in Basle in 1897. After 1901 the congress met biennially.

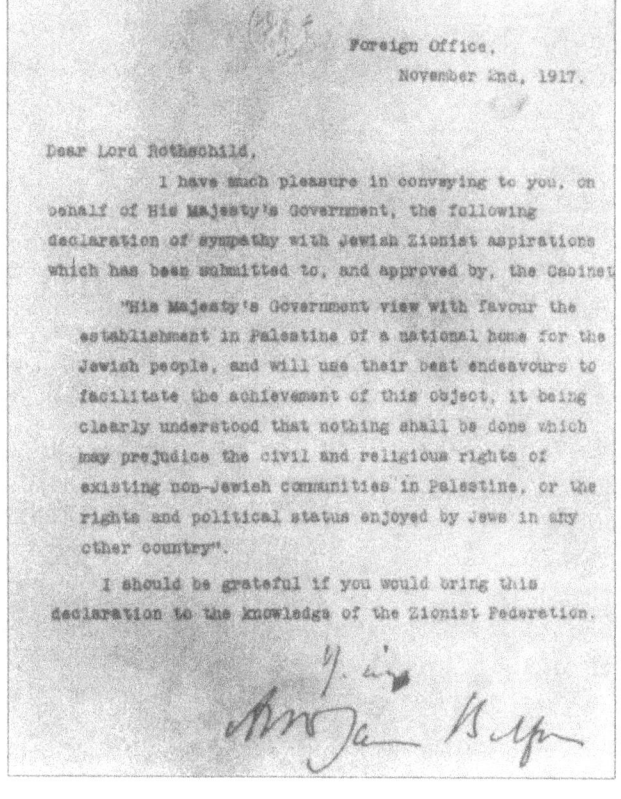

*The Balfour Declaration 1917*

The return of the Jews to Palestine began only as a trickle. When Britain took Palestine in 1917 the Balfour Declaration (2 Nov. 1917) promised the Jews a "national home," without defining what the term should or could mean. Nevertheless the declaration provided an impetus in an atmosphere rendered politically favorable by the mandate of Palestine, conferred by the League of Nations in July 1922. The Jewish population was now about 85,000, or approximately 11 percent of a total population of some 750,000 persons, chiefly Arabs. The Arabs were excluded from the discussion, with the result that friction ensued from what was a valid complaint.

During the 1920s and 1930s a small but steady stream of immigrants brought the Jewish population of Palestine to 581,000 in 1939, as the Jewish world population reached its demographic high point of 16,651,000. Of these 56% lived in Europe, 29% in North America, 1.05% in central and South America, 7.6% in Africa, and 0.2% in Australasia.

A unique feature of Jewish migration was the extent to which Jews were urbanized. Nearly one-third of all Jews lived in twenty-two communities of more than 100,000 Jewish inhabitants. The two largest communities were in New York and Warsaw, but even so they were minorities in those cities. Outside the U.S. community of 4.5 million, the largest Jewish communities were in Poland (3.5 m.) and Russia (2.8 m.). Though prominent in public life, the actual number of Jews was so small as scarcely to be noticeable in the majority of European countries. This partly explains why reports of persecution as a preamble to the Holocaust were regarded in Britain with scepticism. It was only when the number of refugees reached considerable proportions that the real facts began to be believed.

*Members of the Royal Commission on Palestine, 1937, chaired by Earl Peel*

# PALESTINE, FROM THE PEEL COMMISSION TO THE WAR OF INDEPENDENCE

Although President Woodrow Wilson's principle of the right to political self-determination was accepted at the Peace Conference in 1919, it was applied unevenly in the Middle East. The claims of Armenians and Kurds were disregarded, and Arab lands were partitioned between Britain and France. The mandate over Palestine disregarded the views of Zionists and of Palestinian Arabs.

In 1921 Britain enabled Abdallah, brother of the King of Iraq, to become Amir of what is now Jordan. Although included in the mandate over Palestine, it was governed separately from Jordan.

Winston Churchill's Memorandum of June 1922, while reaffirming the Balfour Declaration, nevertheless recognized a "double obligation" to Arab and to Jew. The concept of a simple unitary or of a federal state was acceptable to neither party and was rejected. During the 1920s the British temporized, but in 1929 Arab and Jewish nationalisms boiled over into riots. A commission of inquiry found that the main cause of the violence was Arab antagonism to a Jewish "national home"; another report concluded that further Jewish immigration was unacceptable. In 1930 a white paper reinforced views unfavorable to Jewish hopes, but it was modified in 1931.

In January 1933 following the establishment of Nazi Germany, Jews in Europe faced a major crisis. Jewish immigration at once increased. Many of the immigrants were educated, giving a new character to a largely agricultural society. Almost immediately a "national home" became a concern for survival.

The influx of Jews, even though it might mean greater prosperity for Arabs, was regarded by Arabs as an obstacle to national independence. The Arabs had a high rate of natural increase, far outweighing any possibility that the Jews might reach equality of numbers. A manifesto of the Arab Executive Committee in March 1933 declared that "the general tendency of the Jews to take possession of the lands of this holy country and their streaming into it by hundreds and thousands through legal and illegal means had terrified the country." The document regarded the Jewish immigrants "as the true enemy whom they must get rid of through every legal means." In 1936, and lasting until 1939, violence erupted.

In these circumstances Earl Peel reported the belief of the Palestine Royal Commission that partition was the only possible solution. A United Nations decision of 29 November 1947 recommended partition on lines similar to the Peel Report.

*Thomas Woodrow Wilson (1856–1924), president of the USA (1913–1921)*

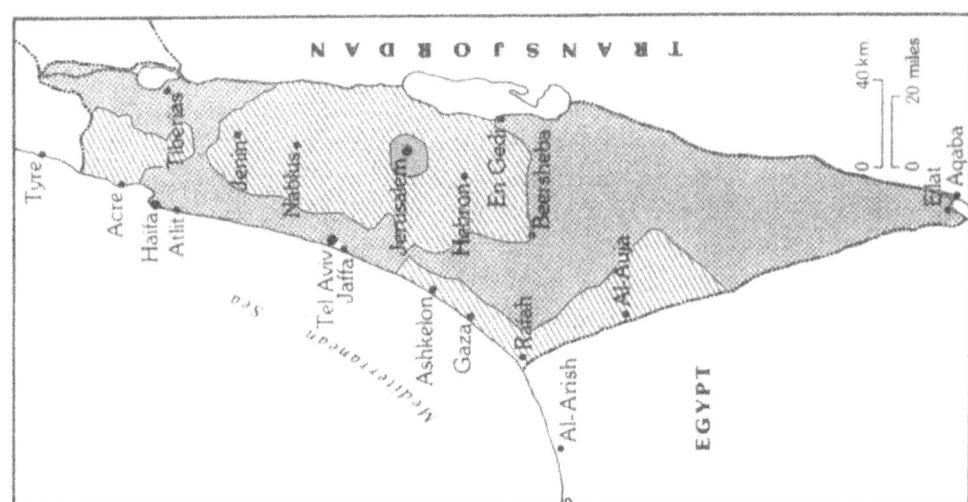

U.N. PARTITION PLAN, 29 NOV. 1947

Mandate line
Jewish state
Arab state
Internationalized area

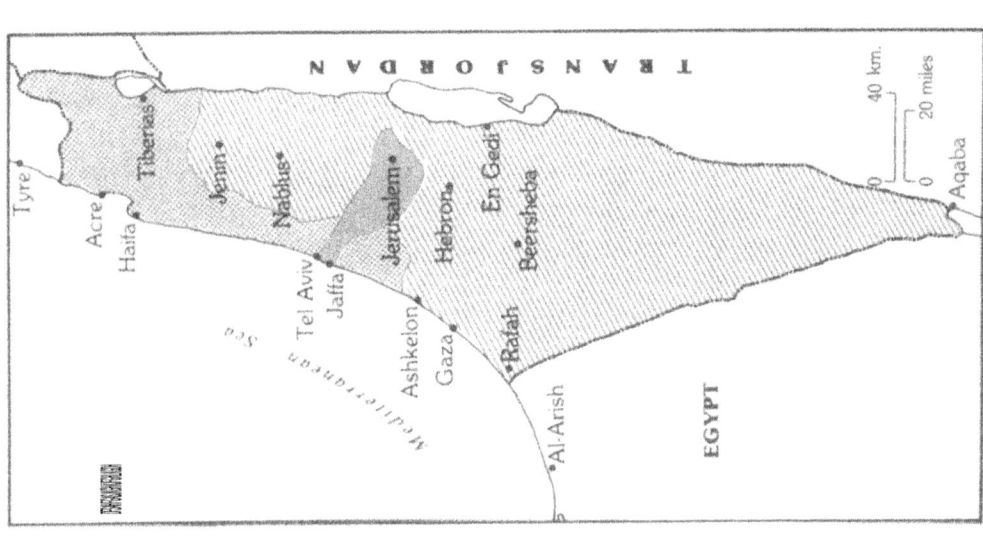

PEEL COMMISSION PROPOSAL, 1937

Mandate line
Jewish state
Arab state
British Mandate area

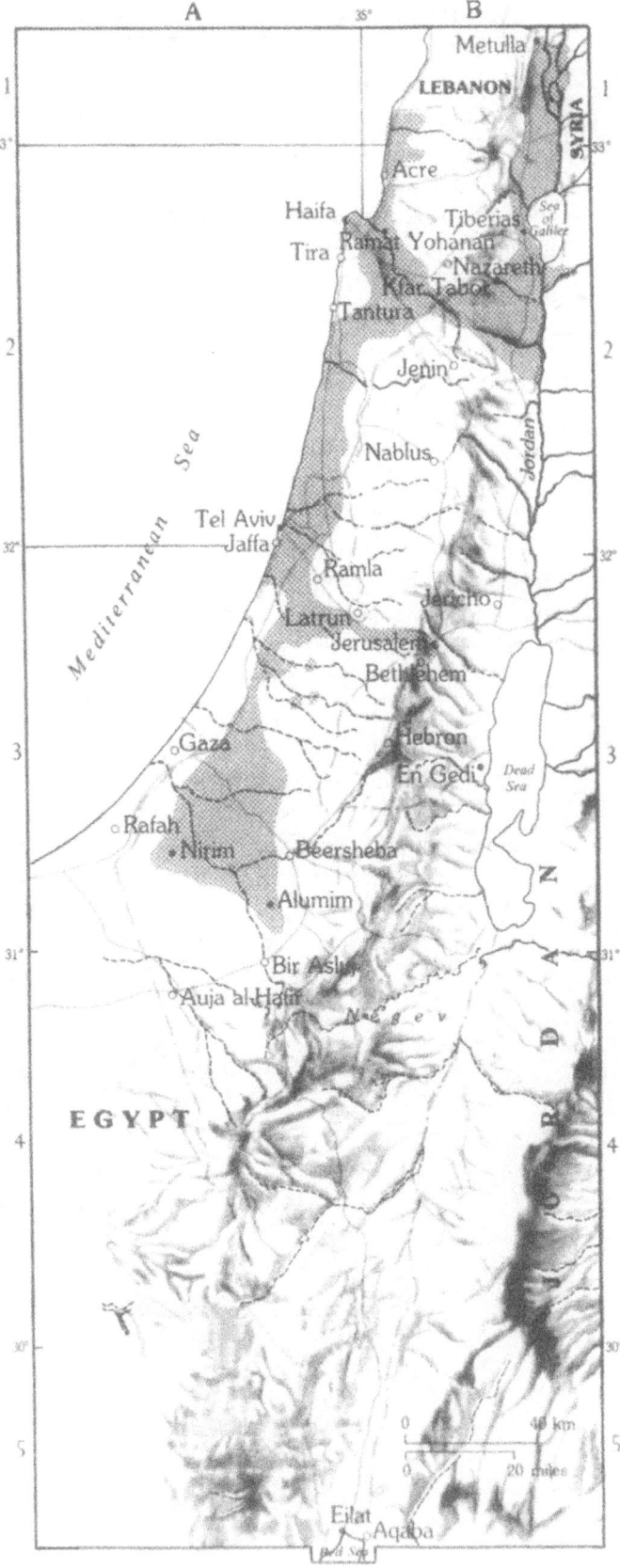

THE WAR OF INDEPENDENCE, 1948–1949

# WORLD WAR II: EGYPT AND NORTH AFRICA, 1940–1941

The jackal Mussolini, as Churchill called him, declared war on the Allies on 3 June 1940, following the British retreat at Dunkirk. He took Nice and Savoy; on 4 July he invaded the Sudan from Ethiopia; in August he took British Somaliland. Now before his eyes arose the glittering prospect of an Italian empire stretching from Tripolitania to Egypt and Iraq, and south through the Sudan to Uganda and Kenya. The whole of this vast area, including Cyprus and Greece, was within the area of the British Middle East command based in Cairo. Through its center passed the Suez Canal and the Red Sea, the life line of communication with India and the East. No less important was the Persian Gulf, which was to become the life line to Russia.

By 7 February 1941, the British had driven the Italians out of Cyrenaica. While Mussolini's eyes were set on territorial aggrandizement, the Italian people had no stomach for war, nor had they regarded the British with hostility. Two British divisions destroyed ten Italian divisions, and took 130,000 prisoners.

*Benito Mussolini (1883–1945)*

The German high command saw things differently and sent Erwin Rommel to take command of German forces in Africa on 12 February 1941. On 31 March he attacked over fifteen hundred miles of desert. A highly confused battle followed throughout the year, which exhausted both sides. Rommel could not follow up his limited success and retreated. This was fortunate for the British, for British and Australian units had been withdrawn to face the Japanese in the Far East, while other British units were committed in Kenya and the Sudan. As things were, it was a stalemate.

*Erwin Rommel (1891–1944)*

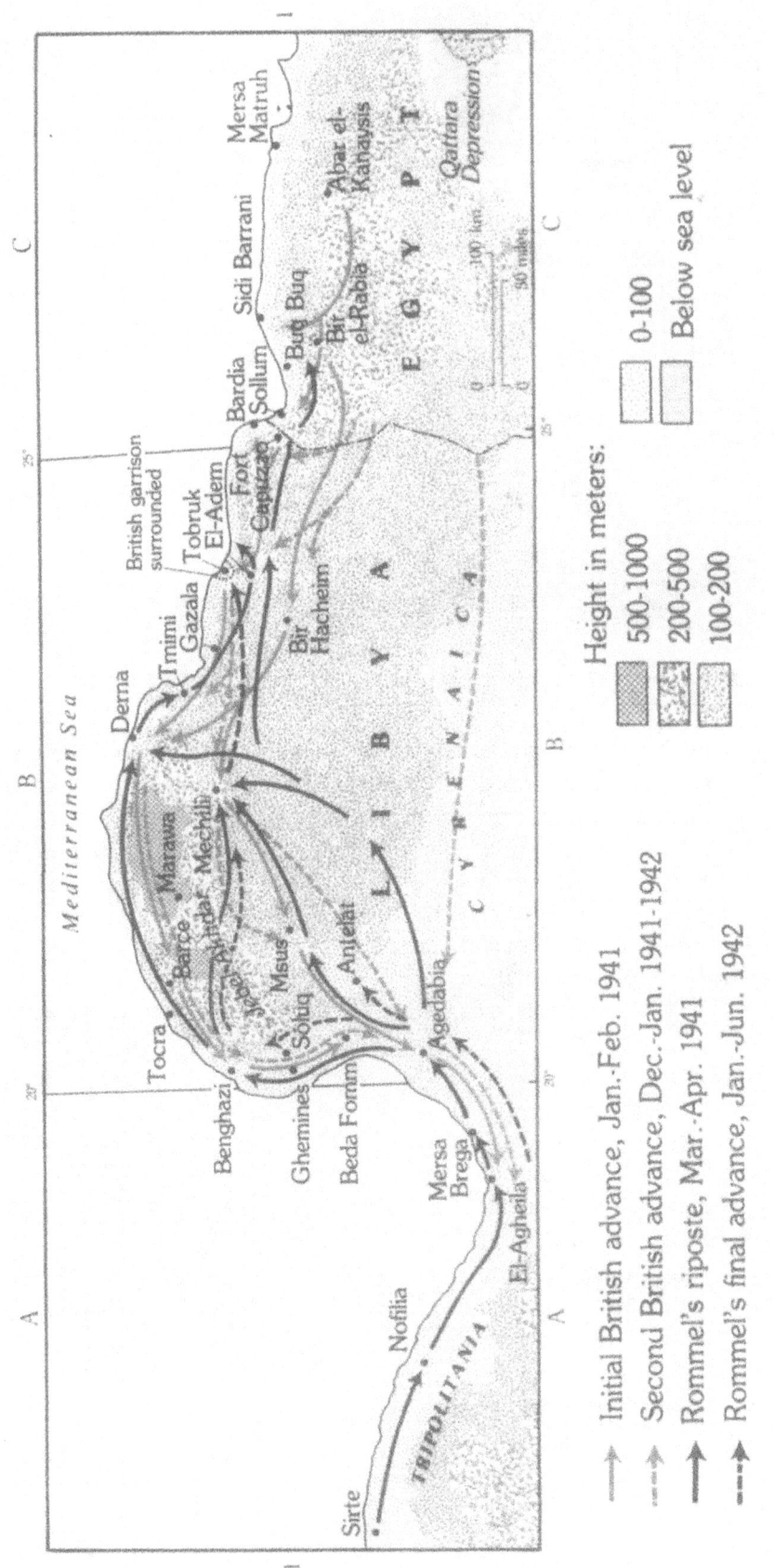

WORLD WAR II: EGYPT AND NORTH AFRICA, 1940–1941

*German Panzer tank enters a Libyan town*

## WORLD WAR II: SUDAN, ETHIOPIA AND SOMALIA, 1941

Following Italy's entry into the war in 1940, Italian forces in Ethiopia seized Kassala from the British and overran British and French Somaliland. These territories were of strategic importance to Middle Eastern command in Cairo because from these locations one could control the Red Sea, the passage to the Far East, and the French naval installation at Djibouti.

In 1940 the British already had a working partnership with Ethiopian guerillas. An offensive was mounted on 19 January 1941, which drove the Italians out of Kassala. This column, under General Platt, was held up at Keren until 1 April, when the Italian forces collapsed. The British were able to enter Asmara on the following day.

Supported by Ethiopian guerillas, the unit known as the Gideon Force, under Major Orde Wingate, and eight hundred Sudanese troops, entered Ethiopia south of Gallabat. Frequent raids, rather than a frontal attack, gave the Italians the illusion that they were being attacked by a vastly superior force. The Ethiopian emperor Haile Selassie accompanied the Allies. On 16 May General Platt encircled

*Haile Selassie I*

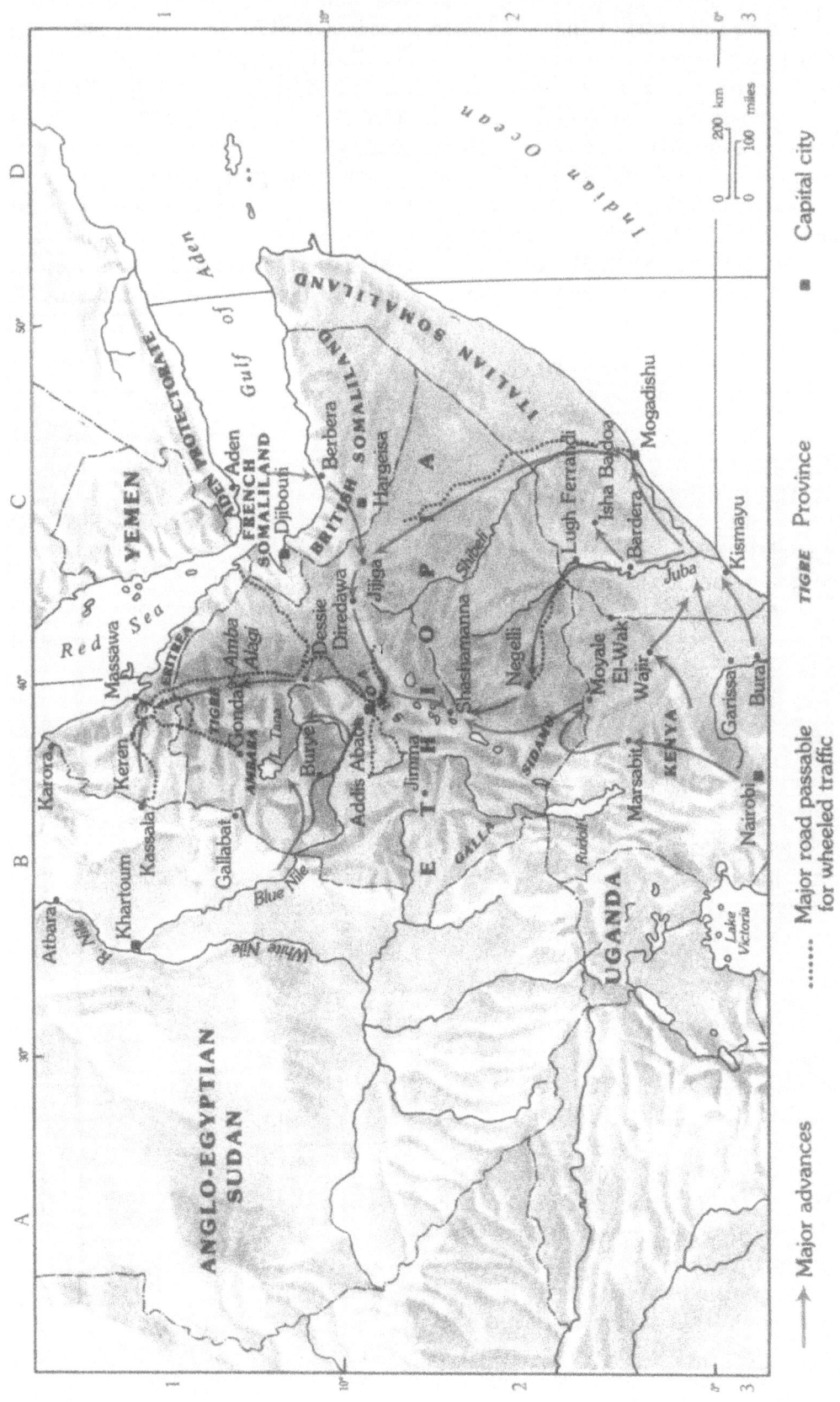

WORLD WAR II: SUDAN, ETHIOPIA AND SOMALIA, 1941

the Italian forces at Amba Alagi, and with their surrender, Italian resistance collapsed.

In British Somaliland, with the support of the South African air force, Nigerian and South African brigades took Mogadishu on 25 February. After a brilliant march across the Ogaden desert they took Jijiga on 17 March, Diredawa on 29 March, and reached Addis Ababa on 6 April. The success of all three columns was assured by the Royal Air Force, based in the Sudan and Aden, which attacked the Italian air force and protected Red Sea convoys, while the South African air force supported the southern column.

At the Ethiopian emperor's personal request British advisers now assisted the restoration of orderly government. The recovery of Ethiopia and Somaliland had effectively taken no more than ten weeks.

## WORLD WAR II: IRAQ AND IRAN, 1941

Following World War I the League of Nations made Iraq a mandated territory under Great Britain. After local consultations with a council of state in 1920, Faysal I, second son of the sharif of Mecca, was made king as a constitutional monarch. The country was considered stable enough to govern itself in 1930 and was recognized as fully independent.

This proved optimistic. After Faysal I's death in 1933, he was succeeded by the boy king Ghazi I. A series of coups, none of them successful, followed. Anti-British, nationalist feeling and unrest, fermented by Axis powers and hatred of British policy in Palestine, resulted in the emergence of a pro-Nazi party. It was led by Rashid Ali al-Ghaylani, who seized power in May 1941. This gave the Axis a toe hold in the Middle East and cut off Iran, now essential to the Allies as a supply route to Russia. Crossing the desert in August 1941, the British-led Arab Legion took Baghdad supported by British armored cars, deposed Rashid Ali, and restored constitutional rule.

In 1921 Reza Khan, commander of a Cossack brigade, overthrew the Qajar dynasty in Iran and made himself shah in 1925. His rule was essentially military, and, from 1932, following the rise of Hitler, he leaned more and more toward Nazi Germany. His army consumed one third of the budget. By 1941 a German fifth column was firmly established in Iran, and in 1941 Britain and Russia presented a joint ultimatum demanding the immediate expulsion of German technicians, cultural officials, and tourists. Reza Shah refused. On 25 August Britain and the U.S.S.R. jointly invaded Iran. On 16 September Reza Shah abdicated. He was succeeded by his son Muhammad Reza, whose compliance insured a line of communications for Allied supplies to beleagured Russia.

*Reza I, Shah of Iran, 1925–1941*

338

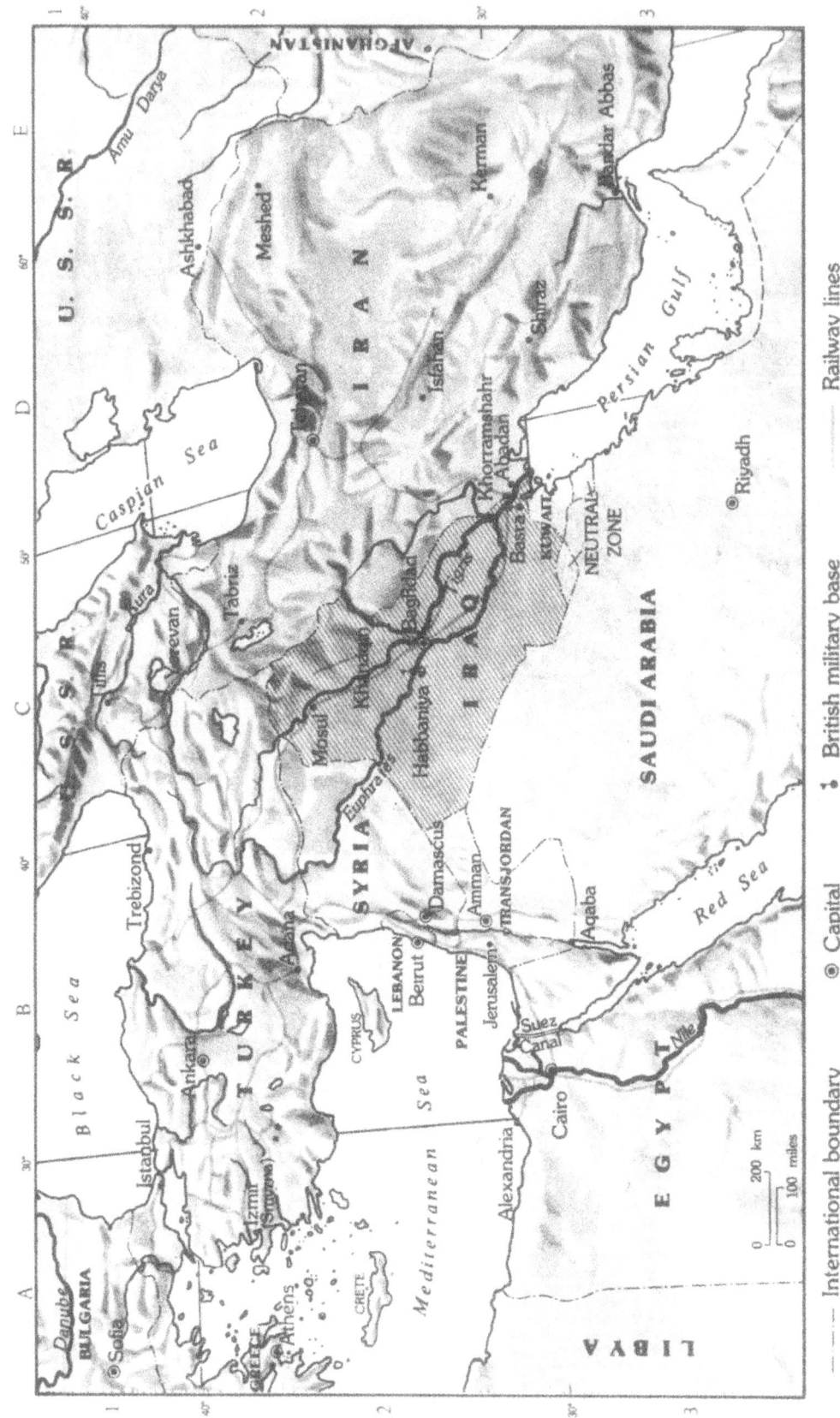

WORLD WAR II: IRAQ AND IRAN, 1941

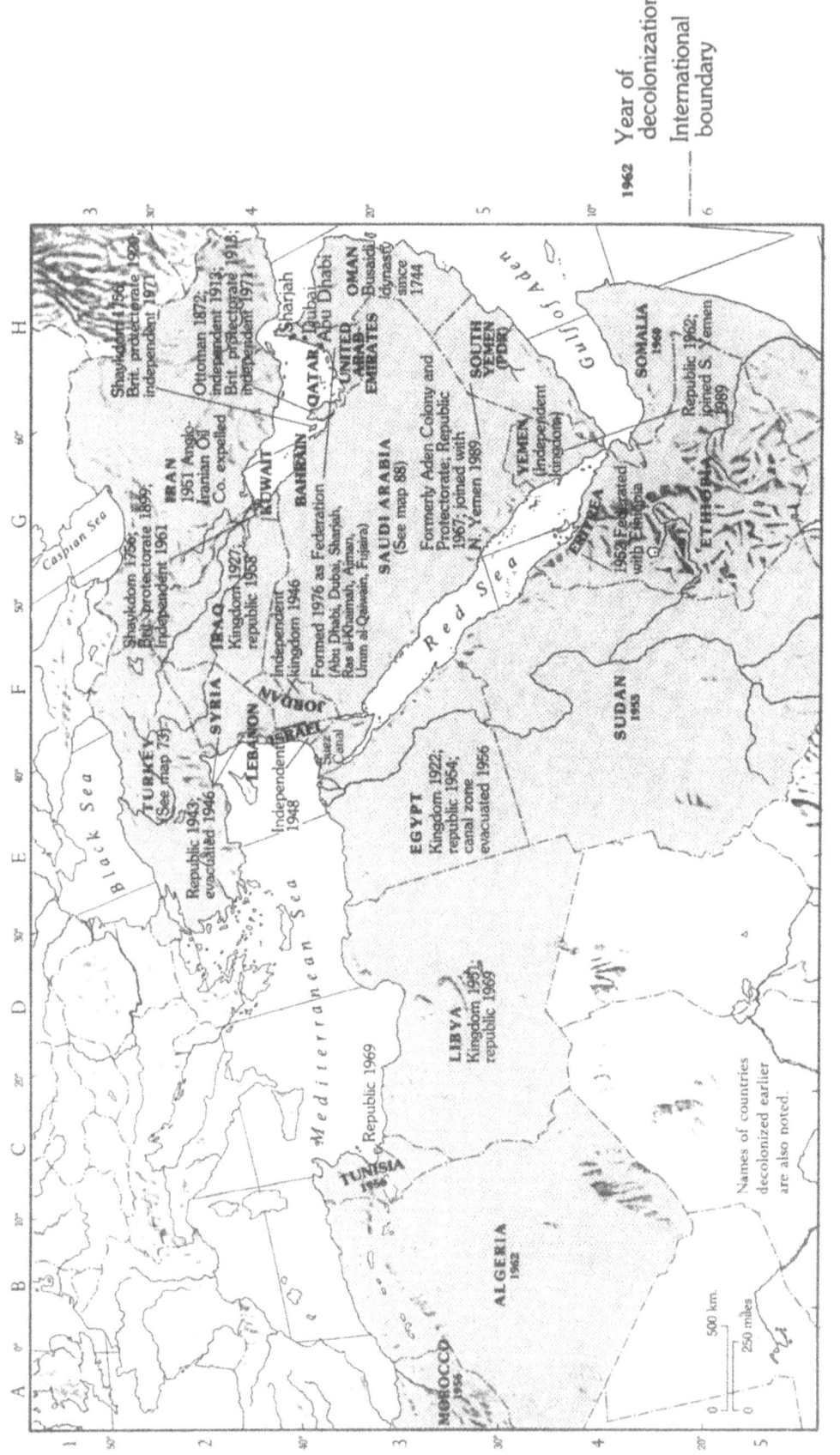

DECOLONIZATION OF THE MIDDLE EAST, 1946-1967

# DECOLONIZATION OF THE MIDDLE EAST, 1946–1967

At the end of World War II Allied troops controlled the area from Morocco to the borders of Iran. The Americans held Morocco, Algeria, and Tunisia; the British held all the rest. Egypt had a nominal independence, which was nullified in practice by the presence of British troops in the Delta and on the Suez Canal; Iraq had been recognized as a kingdom in 1927; Lebanon and Syria had had their mandates terminated in 1943 and were declared independent republics; Saudi Arabia, Yemen, and Turkey had never acknowledged dependence.

In Morocco, Algeria, and Tunisia large French populations, together with Spaniards and Italians, presented problems. In Algeria local French resistance continued until independence was granted in 1962; the others became independent in 1956. In Libya the emir was recognized as King Idris I in 1951, but for a time continued to have British advisers. In order to forestall Egyptian demands, the Sudan became independent in 1956. In spite of tension, the British stayed in the Canal Zone, regarding it as a safeguard of free passage to India. The weakness of this policy was shown when President Nasser nationalized the canal in 1956, and compelled evacuation.

Farther east, the emir of Transjordan was recognized as King Abdallah of Jordan in 1946. The British remained in Palestine until 1948, failing to make arrangements for successor government when they repudiated the mandate. Israel was thus born with an empty treasury and under attack from Lebanon, Syria, Iraq, Jordan, and Egypt. The Persian Gulf states, which had been protectorates, declared independence during the 1960s and 1970s; Aden, after a bloody civil war between opposing would-be successor factions, became an independent republic in 1968. If it was the end of one era, it was the beginning of another, with many problems as yet unresolved.

*French troops patrolling the sidewalks in Algiers' European neighborhood, March 1962*

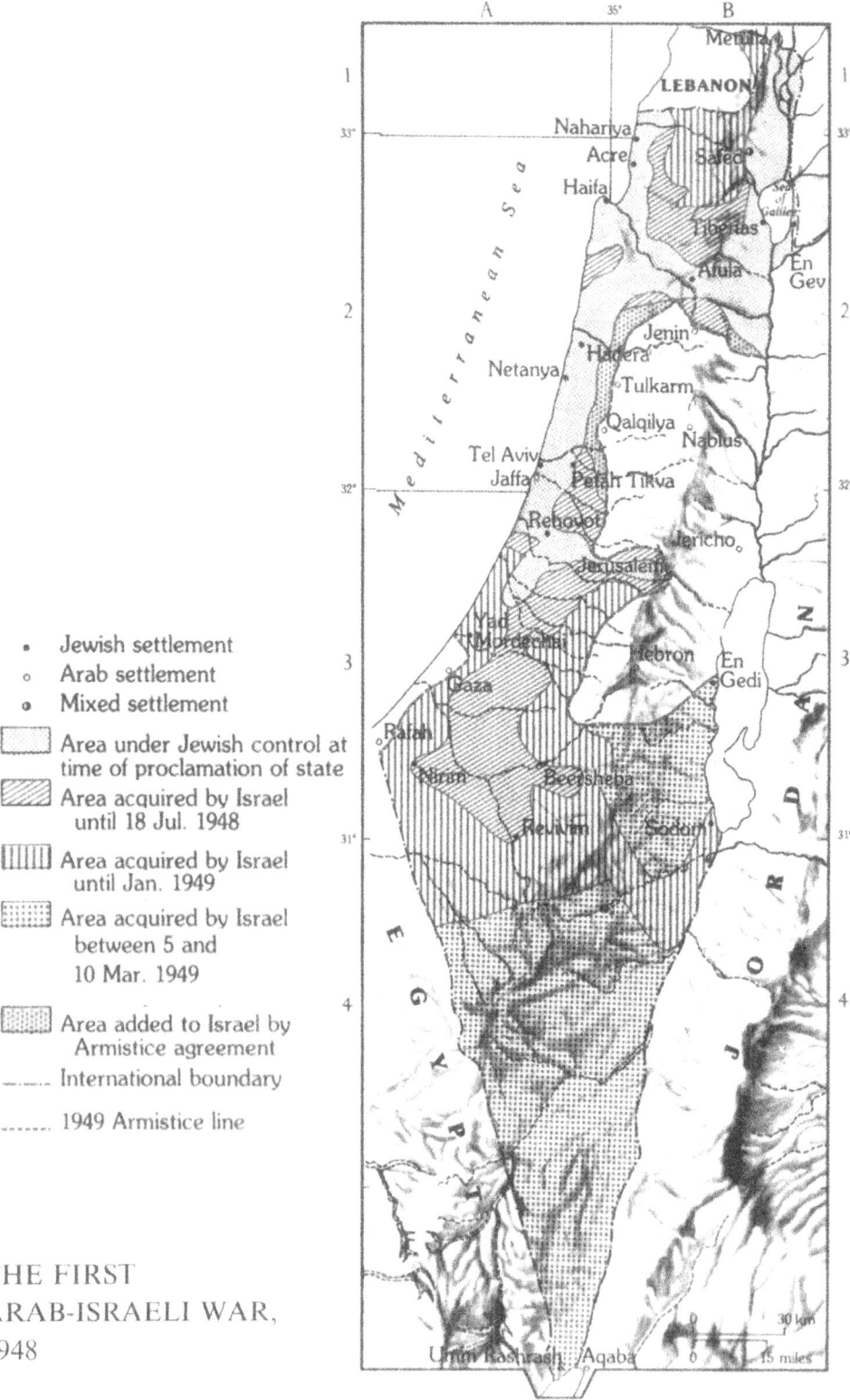

THE FIRST ARAB-ISRAELI WAR, 1948

# THE FIRST ARAB-ISRAELI WAR, 1948

*Map which appeared in the Arabic press, showing the encirlement plan of attack of Arab forces on Israel*

War between Israel, its Arab neighbors, and other Arab states both far and near — whether as open warfare, armed truce, or a state of war without active hostilities — has continued since 1948. During a period of over fifty years Israel has consolidated its position and even expanded its boundaries. In addition, since 1967, it has occupied and administered the West Bank, formerly Jordanian territory, and the Gaza strip, which was part of Palestine and held by Egypt from 1948 until 1967. The succession of events, and the consequent boundary changes, are traced on maps which follow. Juridically Jordan has relinquished all claim to the West Bank, but since it has not been annexed by Israel — other than East Jerusalem and the Old City — it has the suspended status of occupied territory under international law. The annexation of parts of Jerusalem has not been accorded international recognition. On 15 May 1948, at midnight, David Ben-Gurion proclaimed the establishment of the State of Israel. The following morning the armies of Egypt, Jordan, Lebanon, and Syria invaded the former Palestine, but soon lost impetus. They had neither common command nor cohesion, in spite of overwhelming superiority in men, arms, tanks, and aircraft. An Israeli army was assembled from organizations that had carried on underground warfare against the British, but which had acted hitherto without coordination. The Israeli army, with massive American financial support and with arms gathered from many sources, was able to establish itself, and, in spite of its weakness, to bring about a military stalemate. Although the very irregular boundaries and the displacement of some one million Palestinian Arabs pleased no one, an armistice was signed in February 1949.

*David Ben Gurion, first prime minister of the State of Israel*

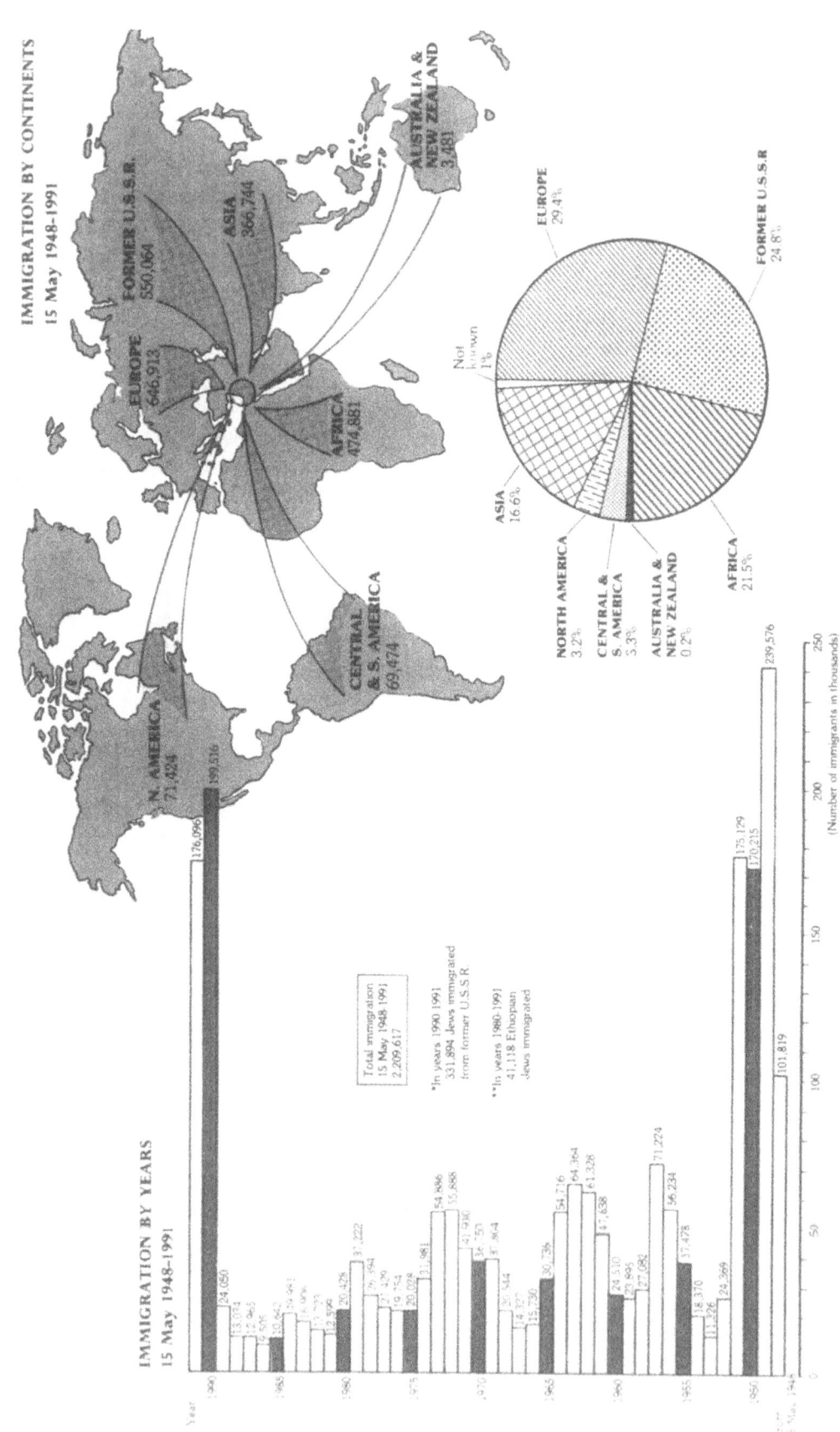

IMMIGRATION TO ISRAEL, FROM 15 MAY 1948

# IMMIGRATION TO ISRAEL, FROM 15 MAY 1948

There have been four major *aliyot* (immigrations) to Israel. Under Abraham and then under Moses, the whole people moved. When the exiles returned from Babylon in 538 BC only part of the community moved; the remainder stayed in Iraq until 1948. The final return had already gathered momentum when the modern Zionist movement was inaugurated and increased only slowly between the two world wars.

In 1947 few people in Britain, the seat of the mandatory power, had much understanding of what was to unfold. A vague goodwill toward Arabs and Jews alike held that, once the mandatory power had departed, they would settle down together in some manner.

The British departure on 14 May 1948 unloosed Pandora's box. Both Jordan and Egypt seized Palestinian territory. A rump was left to Israel, which immediately had to defend itself against its neighbors. It was not only a military war of survival. Under Britain a rigorous quota system was maintained. "Illegal" immigrants were denied entry; either they were returned whence they came or interned in Cyprus.

What took place is unparalleled in human history. Between 15 May 1948 and the end of the year 101,819 immigrants were admitted; 239,576 entered in the following year. In each of the two following years more than 170,000 people were admitted. No other state has more than doubled its population within four years or absorbed, housed, and provided for heterogeneous immigrants from forty-four different countries, and divided by as many languages, from Europe, Asia, and northern Africa. It was an extraordinary feat of national construction, accomplished without serious bloodshed, but resulting in some 1.5 million Arab refugees for whom, after more than fifty years, no resolution is yet in sight.

Exodus *carrying immigrants, in Haifa port, 1947*

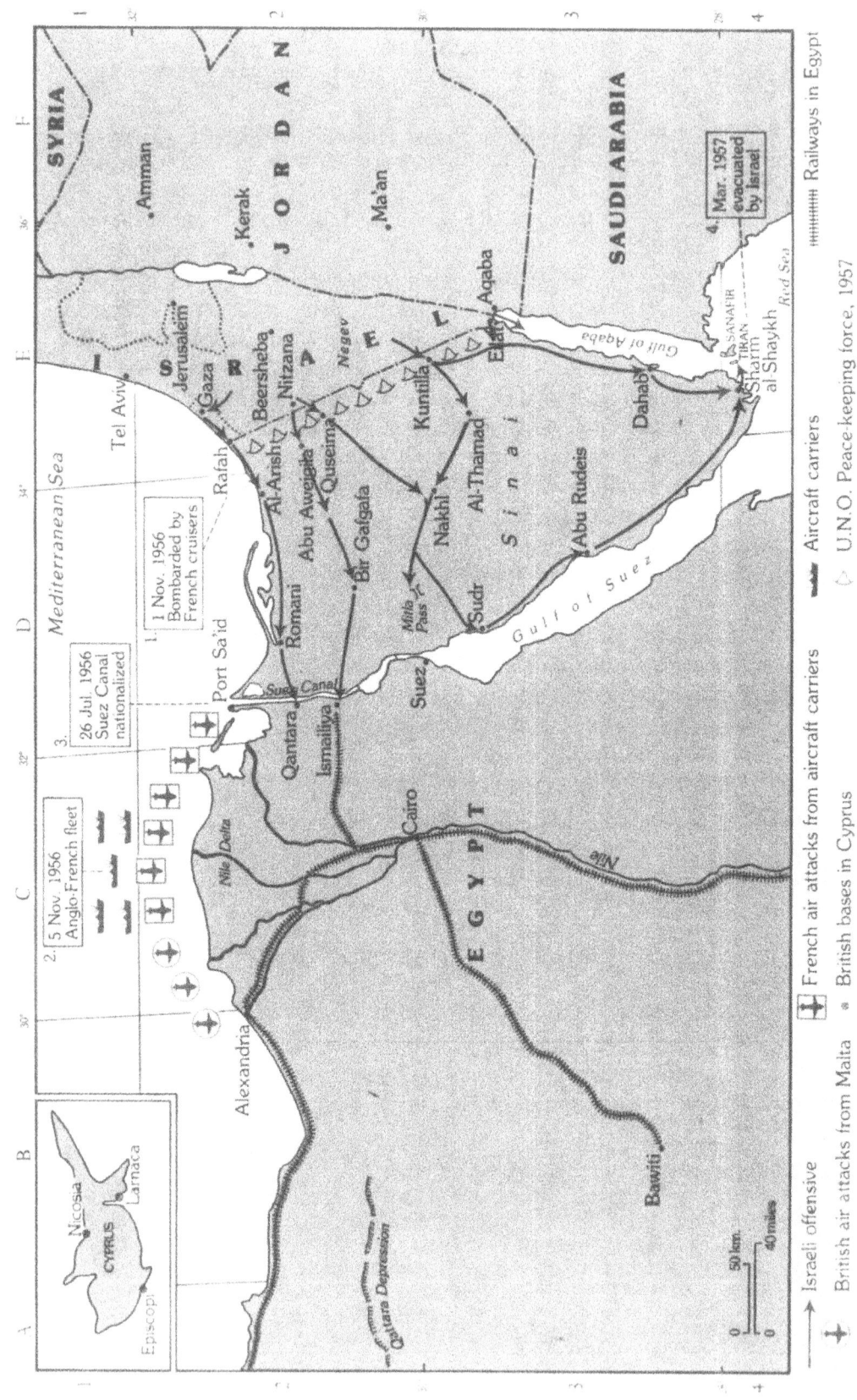

THE SUEZ WAR, 1956

# THE SUEZ WAR, 1956

The Suez War — between Britain, France, and Israel on the one hand, and Egypt on the other — was short in duration and failed to lead to any lasting solution of the problems addressed. On 18 June 1956, Britain had withdrawn from the Suez Canal Zone, leaving Egypt free after a period of eighty-four years of foreign occupation. President Gamal Abdel Nasser had been elected on 3 June, and on a tide of external military support from the U.S.S.R. Because of this support, on 19-20 July, Britain and the United States informed Egypt that they would not finance the Aswan High Dam. Nasser promptly countered by nationalizing the Suez Canal and seizing all foreign assets owned by the Canal Company. Nasser's actions were clearly contrary to existing agreements with Britain and France, the principal participants in the company. Acting in concert with Israel, war began on 29 October with the Israeli occupation of Sinai, and, on 31 October, with the Anglo-French bombardment of Egyptian military installations. On 5 November British troops landed in Egypt and would have had no difficulty overcoming the Egyptian forces. Acting on an initiative by the United States, the United Nations compelled an Anglo-French cease-fire on 7 November and sent a UN emergency force on 15 November. The compelling factor had been the American threat to withdraw support for the pound sterling. Several unsatisfactory results followed. Stationing UN peace-keeping forces between Israel and Egypt solved nothing. The British and French lost all control of the canal, and both lost power and prestige vis-à-vis the Arab nations. American intervention enabled President Nasser, in spite of his military disaster, to claim a moral victory, which was confirmed by his overwhelming reelection. The U.S.S.R. thereby gained, for the time being, a preponderance in the Middle East to the detriment of all the other concerned powers.

*Gamal Abdel Nasser*

*Israeli frigate runs the Egyptian blockade on the Tiran Straits*

# THE SECOND ARAB-ISRAELI WAR, 1967

This war is known by such names as the "Lightning War" and the "Six-Day War" because of its short duration, from 5 to 10 June 1967. It was a moment of high tension in the Middle East, for the persistent propaganda of President Nasser had precipitated violent riots against the British in Aden, and service families had been withdrawn. Nasser took the opportunity to demand the withdrawal of the UN peace-keeping force in Sinai. When the secretary-general of the UN temporized, Nasser replied by closing the Strait of Tiran and the Gulf of Aqaba to Israel. The effect was to deny oil supplies to Israel.

The Israeli government regarded this as an act of war. On 5 June air attacks were mounted against Egypt, Jordan, and Syria, and, within six days, the whole of the Sinai peninsula, with its oil deposits, had been occupied. The Jordanian West Bank was seized and occupied, and the Golan Heights, which overlooked the upper reaches of the Jordan River, were occupied. At the same time the Old City of Jerusalem was taken and declared to be annexed to the capital of Israel. These acts, which have not received international recognition, and the creation of some 1.5 million Palestinian refugees, constitute issues of bitter contention between Israel and its Arab neighbors.

*King Hussein of Jordan*

The Six-Day War was not only a demonstration of Israeli military strength and capability. It destabilized the Nasser regime in Egypt, and by so doing it ultimately prepared the ground for agreement between Egypt and Israel. It also provoked the emergence of the Palestine Liberation Organization, which Israel would have to take into account.

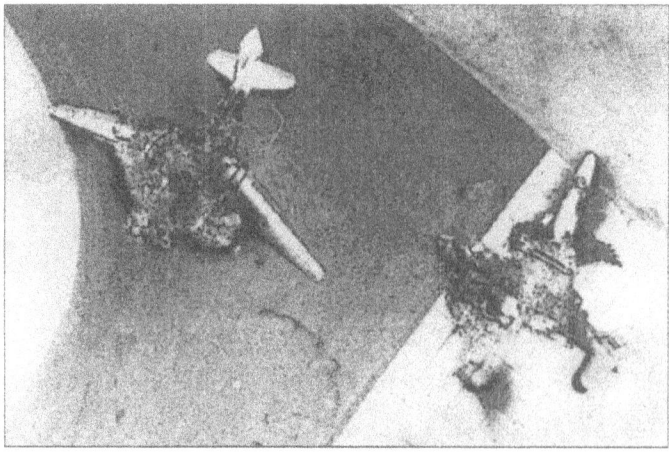

*Egyptian fighter aircraft bombed on the tarmac, Egypt, June, 1967*

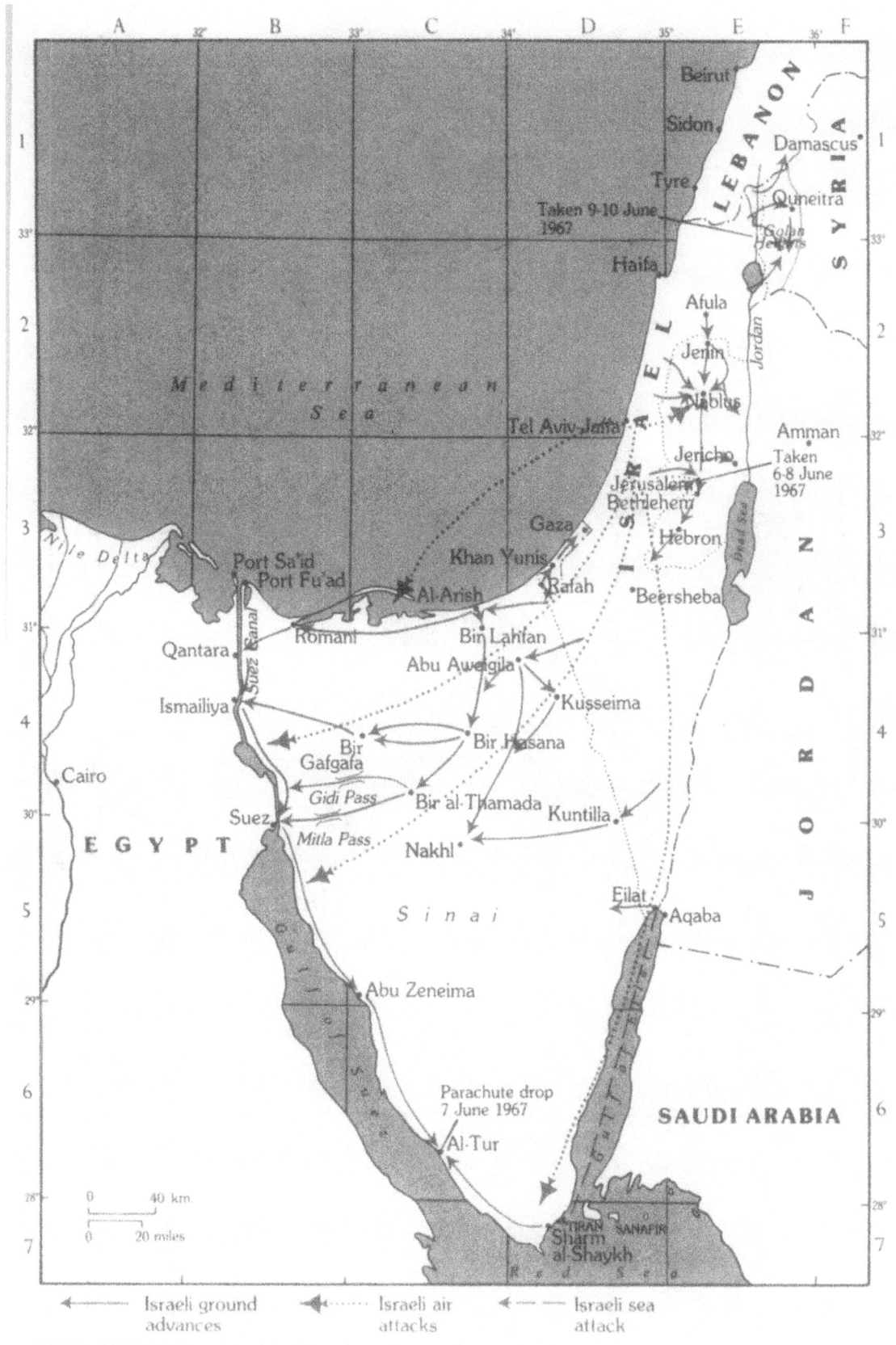

THE SECOND ARAB-ISRAELI WAR, 1967

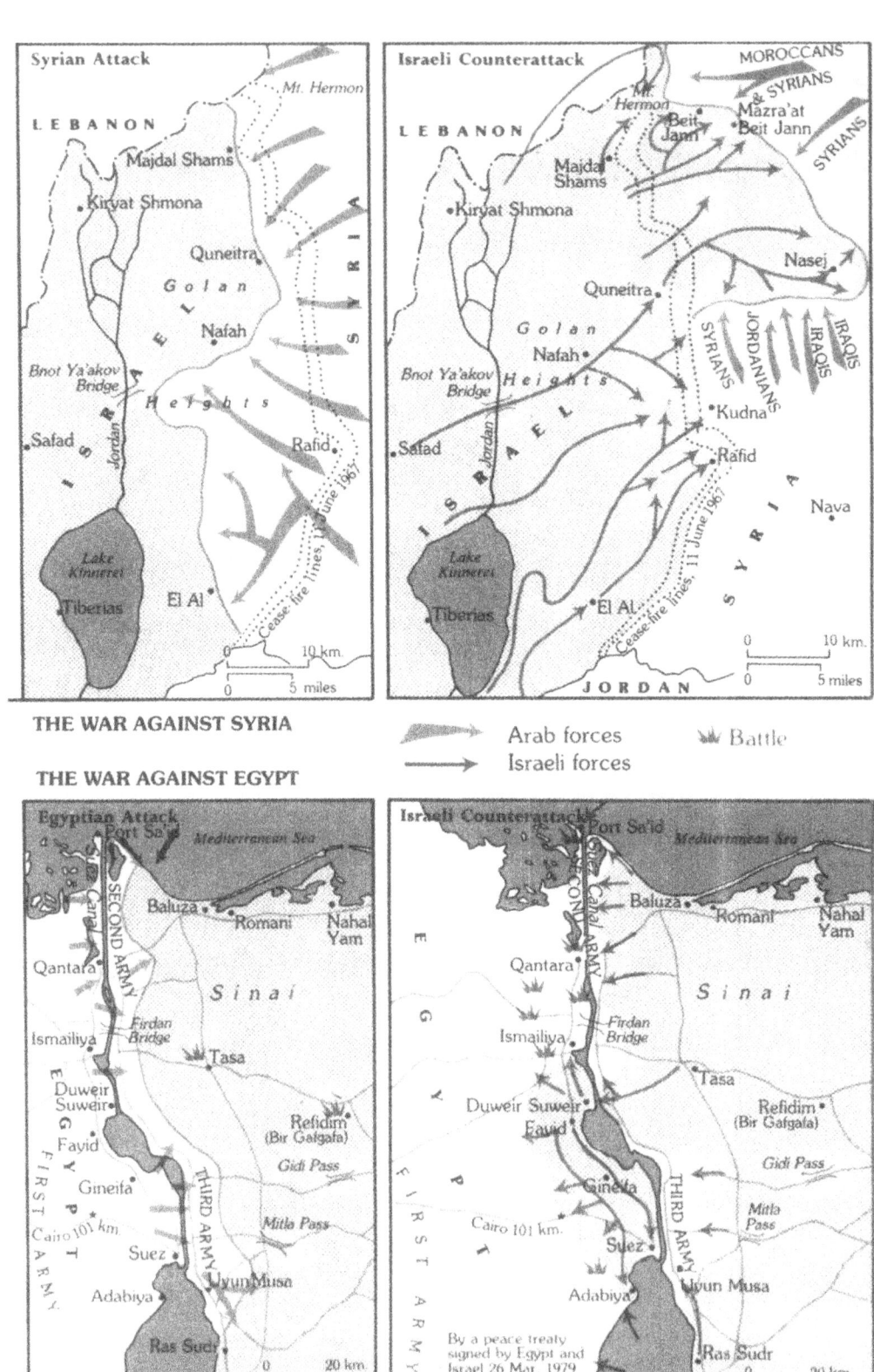

THE THIRD ARAB-ISRAELI WAR, 1967

# THE THIRD ARAB-ISRAELI WAR, 1973

The Six-Day War was felt as a deep humiliation not only by the three nations that had been defeated — Egypt, Jordan, and Syria — but by the entire Islamic world. Arabs, preponderant in population, wealth, and arms, had been defeated by, as they saw it, a puny and illegitimate nation. Bitterness, which went back to the times of the British mandate, now overflowed.

On 22 November 1967, the United Nations passed Resolution 242, recognizing the Arab territories occupied by Israel to be truly Arab possessions, but demanding that the Arab powers recognize the State of Israel. This they would not do.

Nasser died in 1970. His successor, Anwar al-Sadat, sought to restore Egyptian self-confidence, particularly that of his army. In 1972 he expelled eighteen thousand Russian military advisers and broke off diplomatic relations with the U.S.S.R.

On 6 October 1973, on the Day of Atonement (*Yom Kippur*), when every devout Jew was fasting in repentance, Egypt and Syria attacked Israel in Sinai and on the Golan Heights. Their combined forces had a tremendous superiority in tanks — 3,000 against 1,700. The effect of the surprise attack and this superiority gave the Egyptians a series of victories. After the expulsion of the Russians from Egypt, the power vacuum had been filled by the United States — a position that was contrary to U.S. policies and interests. Secret negotiations brought the hostilities to a close on 22 October and led ultimately to talks between Egypt and Israel, which eventuated in the Camp David Agreement of 1979.

*Moshe Dayan*

*Anwar al-Sadat*

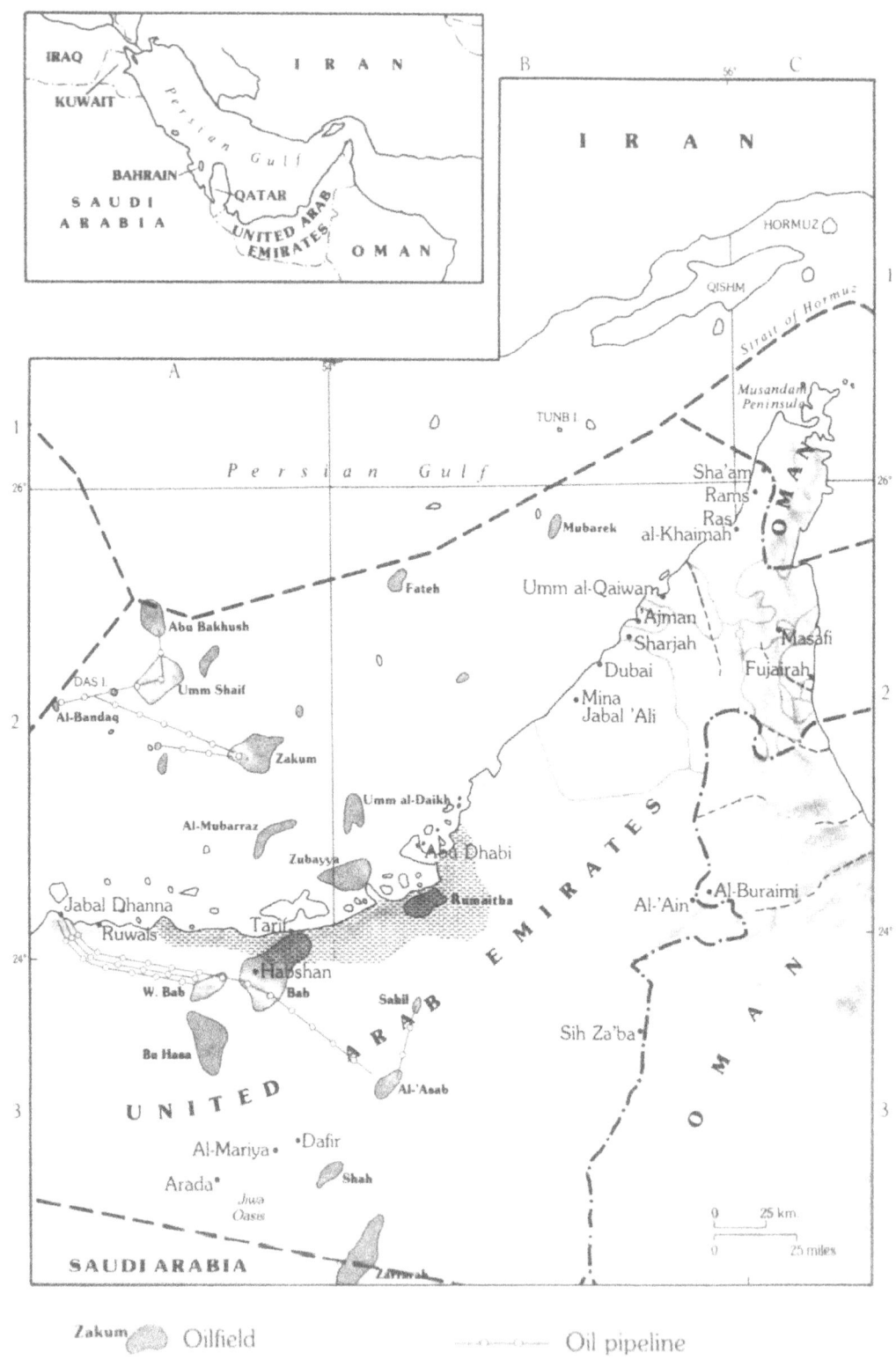

**THE UNITED ARAB EMIRATES AND THE GULF STATES**

# THE UNITED ARAB EMIRATES AND THE GULF STATES

The states of the Persian Gulf include Oman, Kuwait, Bahrain, and Qatar, together with the United Arab Emirates — a federation of states that was formed by treaty in 1971, consisting of Abu Dhabi, Dubai, Sharjah, Ajman, Umm al-Qaiwan, and Fujairah, to which Ras al-Khaimah was added in 1972. Their importance, which is disproportionate to their population or size, stems from both their ownership of a great proportion of the world's oil reserves and their strategic position.

Oman had a separate history from quite early times, but the remaining states were formed during the eighteenth century in response to the growth in East-West trade and the weakening power of the Ottoman Empire. In the nineteenth century they were taken under British protection in a series of treaties, partly because of their need for assistance against Wahhabi expansion in what is now Saudi Arabia. All these states are located on the western side of the Gulf; the strategical crux is Hormuz Island on the Iranian side; from here the Portuguese controlled the Gulf from 1518 until Dutch, English, and French East Indies Companies set up nearby in the seventeenth century. In 1650 the Omanis freed the seaport of Masqat, their best port, from Portuguese control, and by 1698 they had established a seaborne empire down the eastern African coast from Mogadishu to the border of Mozambique.

The shaykhdoms and emirates of the inner gulf had no part in these events. Some derived riches from pearl fisheries; others derived a meagre living from fishing, and, in some places, agriculture. By 1800 wood was being imported from India to service a boatbuilding industry. It was but a short step from building vessels for commercial purposes to using them for piracy, the seaborne counterpart of the Bedouin *ghazzu* (raids in search of booty). It was because of this that on 8 January 1800 Britain compelled the acceptance of a general treaty of peace.

*Mosque in Kuwait; one storey mud-brick structure*

# ISRAEL, LEBANON AND SYRIA

From 1516 until 1917 Lebanon formed part of the Ottoman Empire. After the Treaty of Versailles in 1919, it became a League of Nations mandate, entrusted to France. In 1926 it became a republic, but in 1941 it was occupied by Free French forces. It regained a nominal independence in 1943 and actual independence in 1946.

Made up of the rich Bekaa valley lying between two mountain ranges — the Lebanon and the Anti-Lebanon — and a fertile coastal belt, this country is a museum of Christian and Muslim sects. Among the latter, apart from Sunni Orthodox, there are Ismaili, the survivors of Assassins; the Alawi (Nusayri); and the Druse, warlike mountaineers who practise graduated secret rites. The greatest number of Christians is found in the region north of Beirut, Sunnis occupy the south, with Shi'ites of different sects in the Bekaa valley and the mountains on the east.

Hostility among the different groups led to protracted civil war and intervention by Syria in 1976. The Palestine Liberation Organization took advantage of the situation to establish a base from which to attack Israel. This led to full-scale Israeli intervention in 1978 and the occupation of the southern part of the country as a *cordon sanitaire*. Israel again intervened in 1982 and expelled the Palestine Liberation Organization. A UN peace-keeping force has been virtually powerless. Syria again intervened in 1987, with an army of 37,000 men and assisted by Iranian troops.

In the earlier stages of the conflict Syria was backed by the U.S.S.R., which opposed American support for Israel. President Assad of Syria, who had seized power in a miltary coup in 1970, died in June 2000, when he was succeeded by his son. The Israeli *cordon sanitaire* has now been withdrawn from Lebanon, a sign that immediate anxieties have been to some extent allayed.

*The main square,"Place des Martyrs", Beirut, Lebanon*

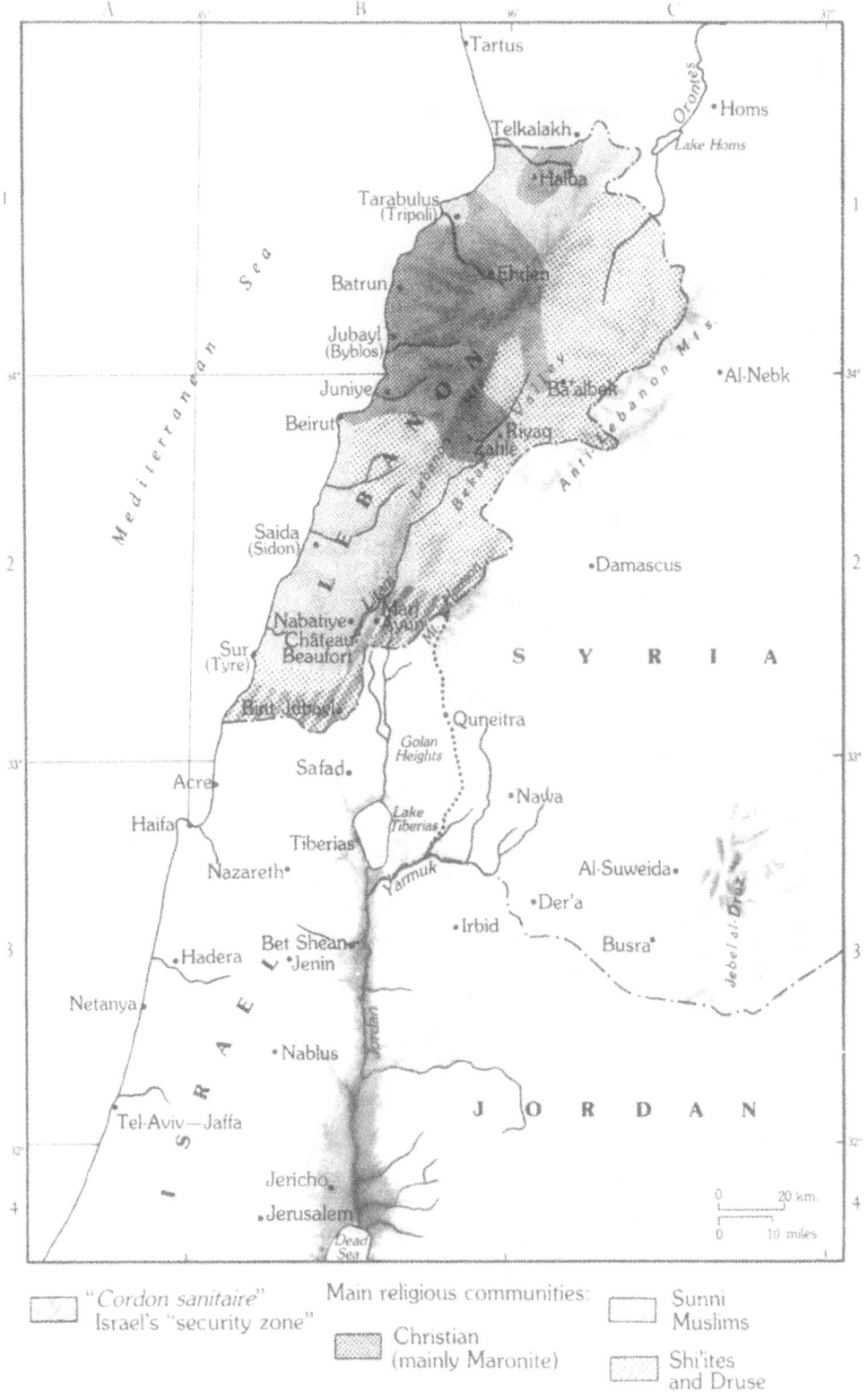

ISRAEL, LEBANON AND SYRIA

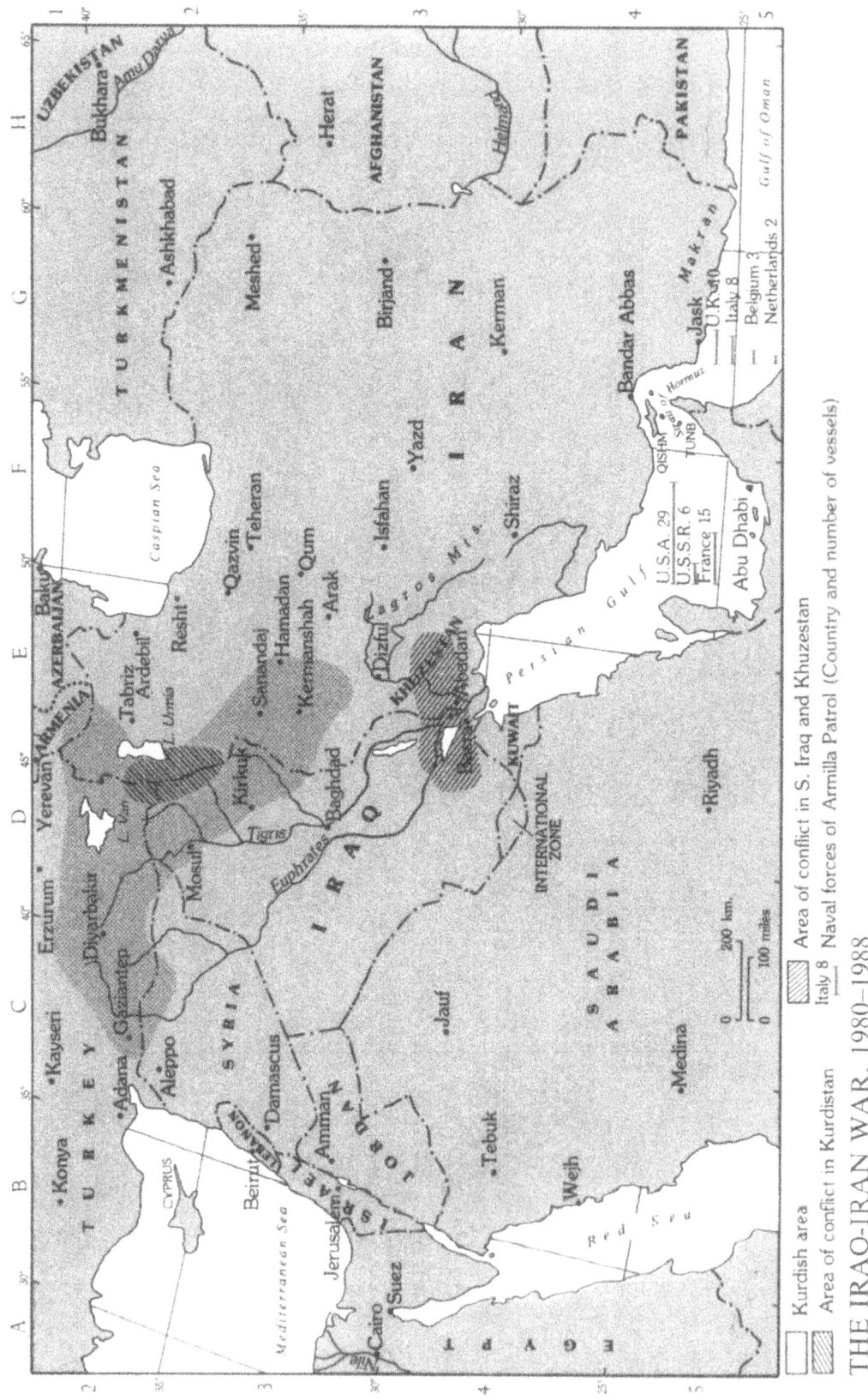

THE IRAQ-IRAN WAR, 1980–1988

# THE IRAQ-IRAN WAR, 1980–1988

At the end of World War I, with the dissolution of the Ottoman Empire and the creation of the new state of Iraq in 1921, certain boundary questions with neighboring Persia (Iran) were left unresolved. These questions involved the confluence of the Tigris and Euphrates rivers below Basra, which is known as the Shatt-al-Arab, and the three Tunb Islands in the Strait of Hormuz. The former thus controls access to Iraq's only port, Basra. Through the latter, and the Gulf, forty percent of the world's oil trade passes, not only from Iran and Iraq, but also from the Gulf States.

In 1979 the return of the Shi'ite leader Ayatollah Khomeini to Iran led to anxiety in Baghdad, for the southern two-thirds of Iraq were controlled by Shi'ites, whereas the north and the government were Sunni Muslims. In 1980 the Iraqi president, Saddam Hussein, abrogated the 1973 agreement with Iran, which had granted to Iran some 518 square kilometers (200 square miles) north of the Shatt-al-Arab, and demanded the return of the Tunb Islands. Hussein's actions led to border skirmishes on the part of Iraq, and finally to wholesale war, in which the Iraqis had some initial success. Iraq had superior air power (600 to 100 aircraft) and ground power (3,500 to 1,000 tanks), although a much smaller population (16 million as compared to Iran's 45 million). A war of attrition followed, with the bombing of oil installations and cities and with an estimated 1.5 million casualties. In the northeast of Iraq, where the majority of the population are Kurds by race and Sunnis by faith, rebellions erupted among the Kurds that were put down by the Iraqi government with napalm and poison gases in a manner so cruel as to be unsurpassed since Chinggis Khan.

In order to secure the free passage of oil supplies to the West an international naval force of seventy-five vessels controlled the waters on both sides of the Strait of Hormuz — United States, U.S.S.R., and France on the west side, and Great Britain, Italy, Belgium, and the Netherlands on the east, with seventy-five vessels in all. A peace was patched up in 1988.

*Saddam Hussein*

# THE RUSSO-AFGHAN WAR, 1979-1988

In the nineteenth and twentieth centuries Afghanistan had been a focus of conflicting British and Russian political interests. The Treaty of Gandamak gave Britain control of the Khyber Pass, a principal commercial route between India and Soviet Central Asia, and of Afghan foreign policy. This treaty was effective until 1948. In 1953 General Mohammed Daoud Khan seized power and a parliamentary democracy was instituted. Economic and military assistance was obtained from the U.S.S.R. A military coup overthrew the monarchy in 1973, and installed Daoud as president. In 1977 he made Afghanistan a one-party state. Shortly thereafter he was assassinated, and a democratic republic with a Communist constitution was proclaimed. The Afghans do not form a single people. They are divided ethnically among Pashtuns, Baluchis, Tajiks, Nuristanis, Hazaras, Turkmen, Uzbeks, and Kyrghyz; they are divided by religion between Sunni and Shi'ite Muslims. Eleven separate resistance movements erupted, with opposing religious characteristics, from Islamic fundamentalism, traditionalism, and Wahhabism to moderates, royalists, and, among the Hazaras, pro-Iranian unionists. It was in the face of this chaos that on 27 December 1979 the Soviet Army entered Afghanistan at the request of a government that was no longer able to maintain order. As in the nineteenth century, when the British Indian forces had been baffled by the skill and resource of Afghan guerillas, so now Soviet forces with tanks, aircraft, and vastly superior equipment were able to cause devastation without succeeding in conquest. The devastation was so vast that three million persons fled to Iran and Pakistan. The last Soviet soldier did not leave the

*The British envoy, Sir Alexander Burnes, assassinated in Kabul, November 1841*

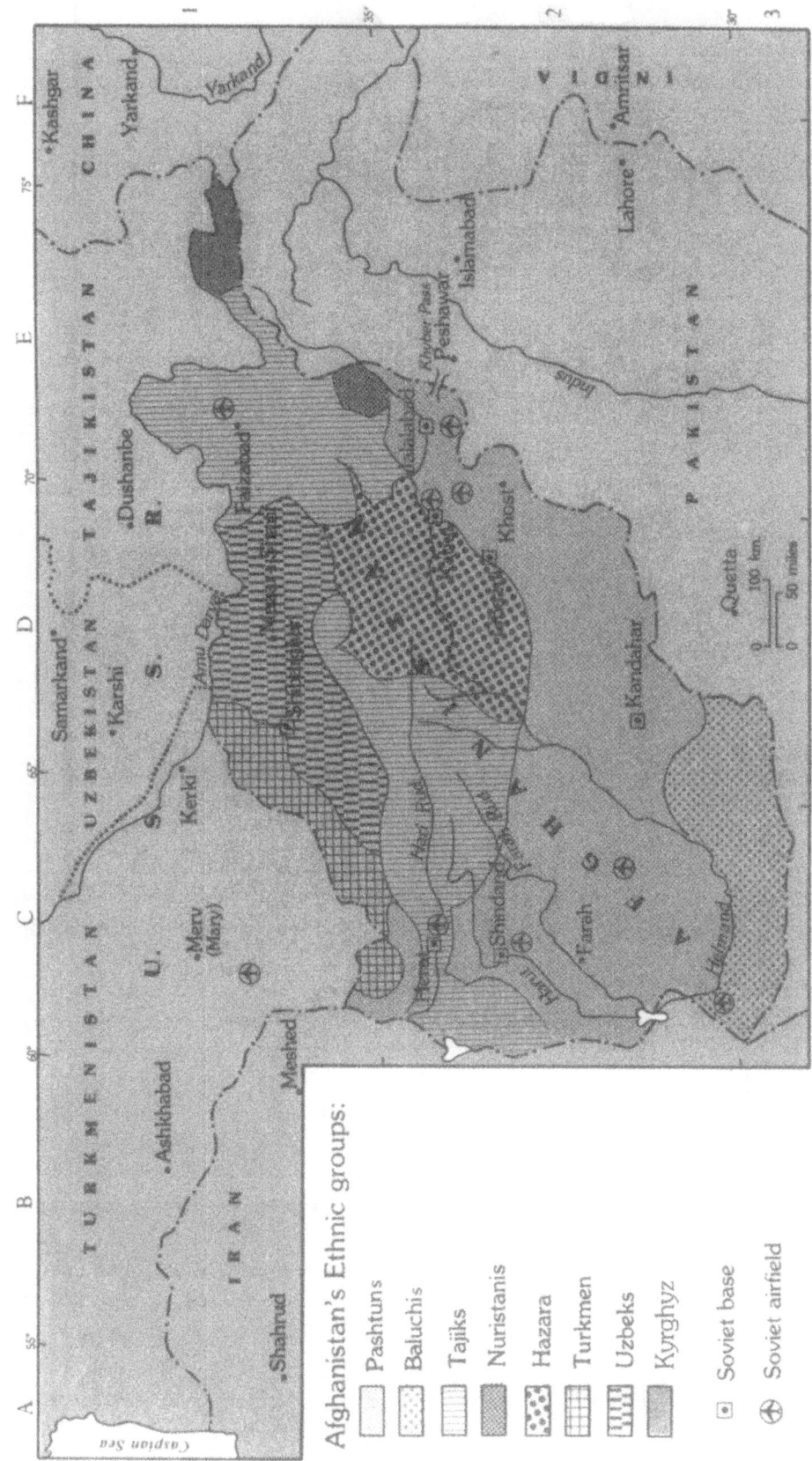

THE RUSSO-AFGHAN WAR, 1979–1988

country until 1988.

*Mujahidin* (Fighters of Holy War) were largely responsible. These resistance groups ultimately over-ran Kabul, and were by no means united. They fought amongst themselves, and in 1994-95 their divided armies were defeated by *Taliban* (Movement of armed Islamic students). Till 2001 Taliban occupied most but not all of the country.

Taliban is a fundamentalist Islamic group, preaching the strictest adherence to Islamic law. It makes no concessions to changes in social custom, such as obtain in other Islamic countries. In 1999 the United Nations imposed limited sanctions on Afghanistan for refusing to hand over an Islamic terrorist, Osama bin Laden, to the United States authorities for crimes committed against United States nationals.

| Ethnic group & Islamic sect | Party |
|---|---|
| Pashtun (Sunni) | Hezb-e-Islami<br>Jamiat-e-Islami<br>Harakat-e-Enquelab-e-Islami<br>Majaz-e-Islami<br>Jabha-e-Nijat Milli |
| Tajik (Sunni) | Jamiat-e-Islami |
| Tajik (Shi'ite) | La Shura |
| Hazara (Shi'ite) | Harakat-i-Islami<br>Nasr<br>Sepah-i-Pasdaran |
| Turkmen (Sunni) | Jamiat-e-Islami |
| Uzbek (Sunni) | Jamiat-e-Islami<br>Harakat-e-Enquelab-e-Islami |
| Any (Wahhabi) | Ittihad-e-Islami |

# FORMER RUSSIAN ISLAMIC COUNTRIES IN ASIA,
## FROM THE 20TH CENTURY

A number of the former Soviet Central Asian provinces declared independence following the retreat of Communist power from total control under the presidency of Mikhail Gorbachov, known as *peristroika* (complete restructuring) in 1985. On 26 December 1991 the U.S.S.R. formerly ceased to exist, and a new Russian Federal Treaty was signed on 11 March 1992. It gave a species of independence.

Tatarstan declined to sign, but eventually compromised, as did Bashkortosan. In Azerbaijan fighting between pro-Soviet forces and ethnic Armenians had begun in the region of Nagorny-Karabakh, an Armenian populated region. The matter is unresolved, with a population which is majority Muslim.

Kazakhstan, in the north, the largest in area, was under White Russian control between 1919 and 1920. Under Stalin's Five Year Plans the previous nomadic culture with its small towns was made to disappear by 'purges.' The merchant and learned religious classes were either murdered or starved on collective farms. Their place was taken by forcefully deported Tatars and Germans. They were able to declare independence in 1995.

Kyrghyzstan declared itself independent on 31 August 1991. It is a Turkic speaking people merged with indigenous peoples, as well as with Russians and Uzbeks. Outside the towns the people are still partly nomadic. There is tension between them and the Russian townsmen and the wealthy Uzbeks, business men, and the majority in the town of Osh.

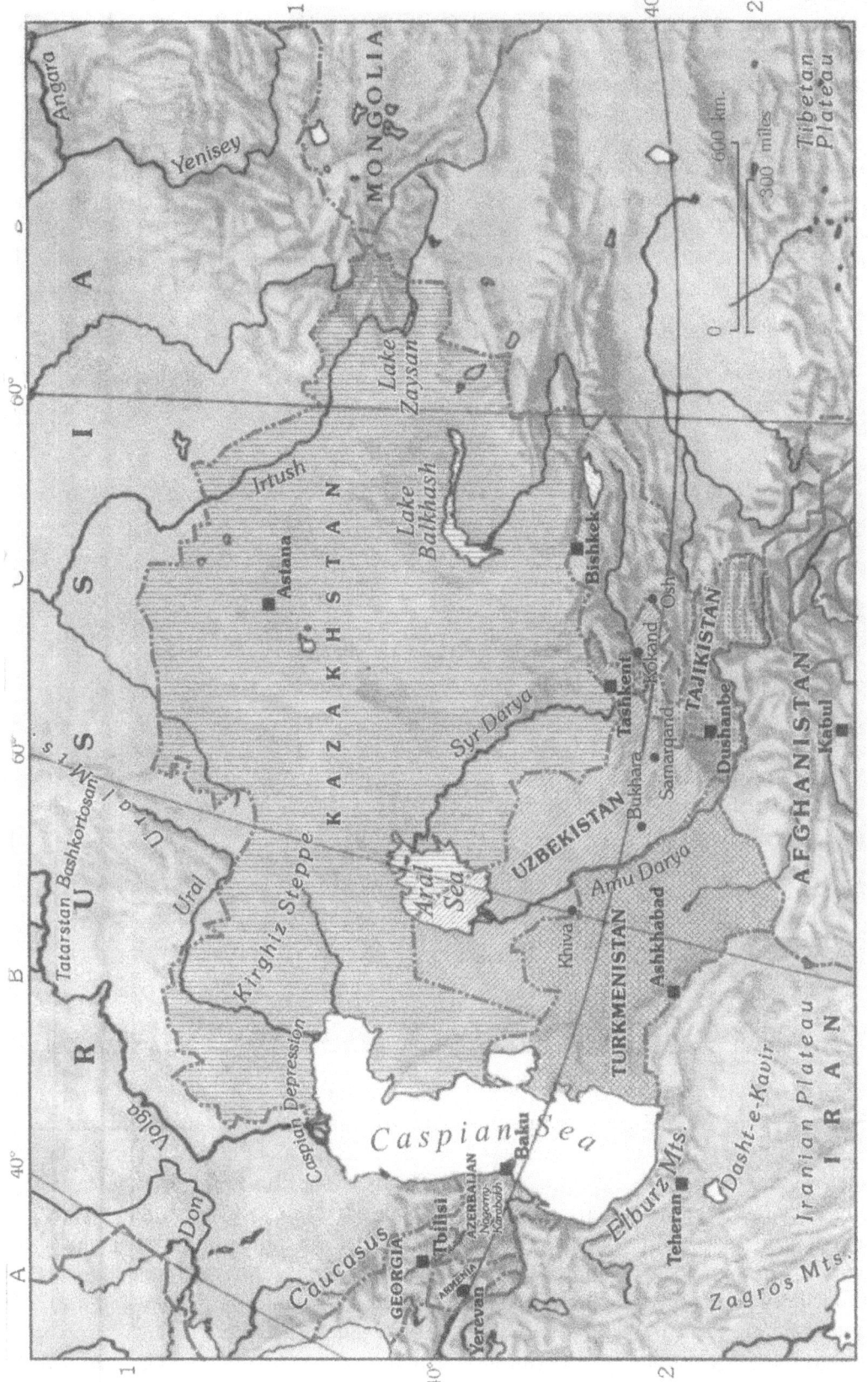

FORMER RUSSIAN ISLAMIC COUNTRIES IN ASIA, FROM THE 20TH CENTURY

Tajikistan fell under Soviet power in 1918, and the emirate of Bukhara was conquered in 1920. In the middle ages Bukhara and Samarqand had been amongst the most important cultural and religious centers in the Islamic world. The people are predominantly Sunni. Tajikistan became an autonomous republic within the U.S.S.R. in 1929, and independent in 1991.

Turkmenistan similarly became autonomous in 1925: the Communist Party, renamed the Democratic Party, remains in power. It has become prosperous from the export of natural gas and of petroleum. Uzbekistan is the political heir of the former Khanates of Khiva, Kokand and Bukhara. Under the Soviet regime a massive irrigation program made it a major producer of cotton. It has also valuable mineral deposits, especially gold.

*Memorial with statue of Lenin, in the Turkmenistan capital, Ashkhabad*

## THE UNION OF NORTH AND SOUTH YEMEN, 1990

Yemen, known to the Romans as Arabia Felix, ("Happy Arabia"), is a prosperous agricultural area in the mountains of southwest Arabia with an arid lower zone. There the best of the frankincense and myrrh used in the temples of the ancient world grew naturally.

It included a number of ancient kingdoms, among them the legendary Saba, whose rulers are attested by inscriptions from c. 850 BC until the sixth century AD. Recent excavations at Marib attest its existence as a cultic center already in 1500 BC. The rulers of the Sabaean capital are recorded from the eighth century BC. A number of ports, of which Aden was the chief, served as entrepôts for trade between India, Africa, and with Yemen and the Far East.

Converted to Islam in the seventh

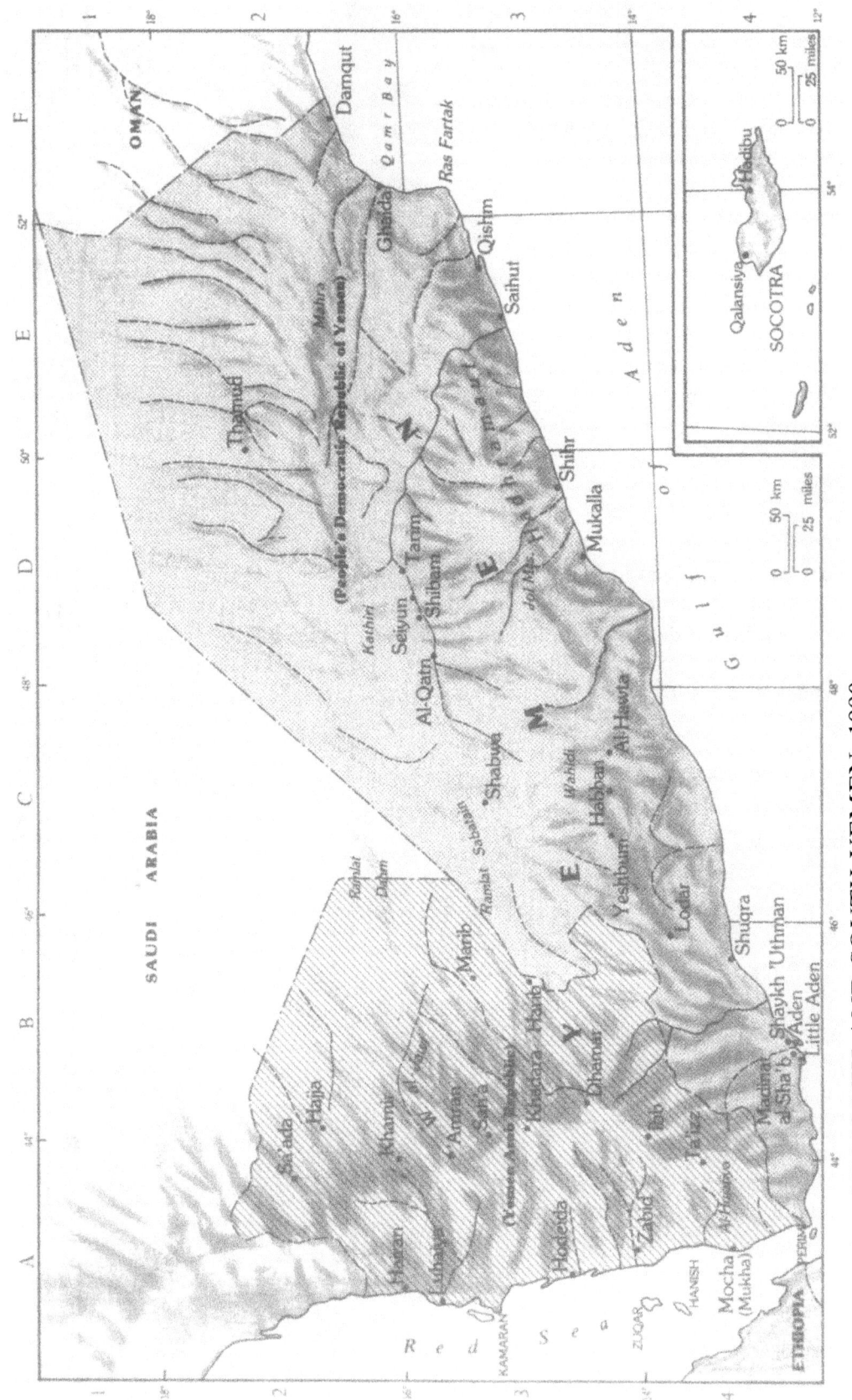

THE UNION OF NORTH AND SOUTH YEMEN, 1990

century, and nominally subject to the caliphate, local dynasties of sultans sprang up in both the highland and lowland areas. Under the Ottoman Empire a tenuous allegiance was honored as much in the breach as in the observance; in the highland area the Imam regained independence in 1918.

Between 1839 and 1962 Britain, in a series of advisory treaties, converted the southern area into the Aden Protectorate. Until the 1960s life in both areas continued much as it had been in the Middle Ages, except in the port of Aden. Backed by Egyptian troops, a revolution took place in northern Yemen in 1962. Under British pressure, a federation (Arabic, *al-Ittihad*) of all the southern sultanates was formed in the southern area in 1962. From 1962 to 1967 a civil war, largely confined to Aden, contested which party should succeed to power after the British departure, promised for 1967. A Marxist party gained the upper hand, making Aden a Russian naval base in 1967.

Of the two areas the northern was the more stable. A catalyst was the discovery of oil and gas in the Marib/Wadi al-Jawf area in the north and in much greater quantities near Shabwa in the south. Export began in 1987, taking advantage of a refinery in Little Aden built in British times. The south is greatly dependent on the agriculture of the north, and the unification on 22 May 1990 was to the advantage and prosperity of both areas.

*The old port city at Aden*

## MINORITIES IN THE MIDDLE EAST

The Middle East is a kaleidoscope of races and religions, in the center of which Arabs predominate. Ottoman Turkish law gave each *millet* (religious community) the right to its own domestic law. Within this framework rigidly separate communities evolved, their boundaries seldom crossed in marriage. Thus, in spite of Turkish overlordship and Arab predominance, Armenians, Assyrians,

*Nebi Shu'eib — the holiest shrine of the Druse*

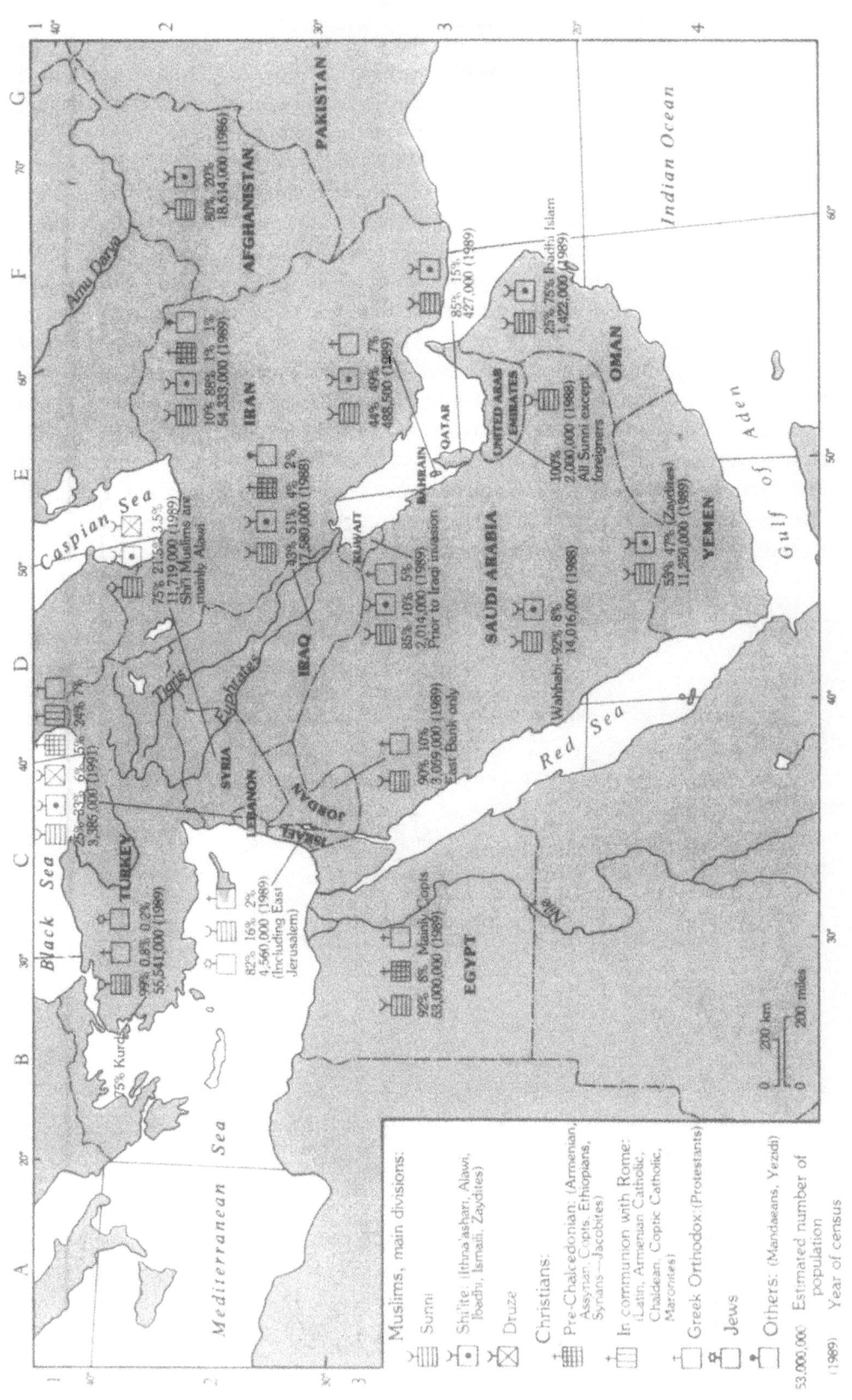

MINORITIES IN THE MIDDLE EAST

365

Circassians, Georgians, Greeks, Jews, Kurds, Mandaeans (Sabeans), Syrians, Turkmen, and others formed obvious divisions. Among Christians Pre-Chalcedonians (Armenians, Assyrians, Copts, Ethiopians and Syrians), and Greek Orthodox all have Catholic counterparts, or Uniate bodies, under the wing of the Latins and united in their obedience to the Pope in Rome. In the nineteenth century a number of Protestant denominations added their missionaries, under the protection of their respective consuls, but they did not form recognized *millets*. Among Jews exclusive national synagogues catered to differing national origins, with subdivisions that ranged from ultraorthodox to liberal. Ladino was spoken by Sephardim, Yiddish by Ashkenazim, each a *lingua franca* apart from the Hebrew of liturgy. Further divisions formed a kaleidoscope of their own, the extreme being proclaimed even today by a wall graffito in ultraorthodox Mea Shearim: "Judaism and Zionism are diametrically opposed."

While the great majority of Muslims are Sunni (orthodox), Shi'ites (sectarians) are divided into many sects. Ithna'asharis predominate over Alawis (Nusayris), Ibadhis, Ismailis, and Zaydites, with further fractions such as the Druses. Mandaeans and Yezidis (Manichaeans) are esoteric syncretistic sects. In Iran Zoroastrians are a relic of what was once the national religion.

The problem of the Kurdish minority in Iran, Iraq, Russia, Syria, and Turkey is considered elsewhere. No consistent statistics for this group are available.

*A wall graffito in the ultraorthodox Mea Shearim Quarter in Jerusalem*

*Miniature of a bearded holy man (dervish), 17th century, Isfahan, Iran*

## KUWAIT, 1991

At the end of the seventeenth century a group of Arabs expelled from Iraq by the Ottoman government for brigandage and piracy settled in Kuwait. Led by the Al-Sabah family, by 1758 they numbered ten thousand, owned eight hundred vessels and engaged in trade, fishing, and pearling. The Ottomans exercised no effective control over them. In 1898 the British government learned that Russia wished to construct a coaling station there. Acting promptly, the British made a treaty in 1899 in which Kuwait agreed not to dispose of any territory to a foreign power without British consent. This treaty effectively introduced British protection, which terminated only on 2 June 1961, when a new treaty gave Kuwait independence.

When oil was discovered in Kuwait in the 1930s, Iraq immediately laid claim to it. This claim was renewed by armed force in July 1961, when General Kassim proclaimed Kuwait "an integral part"

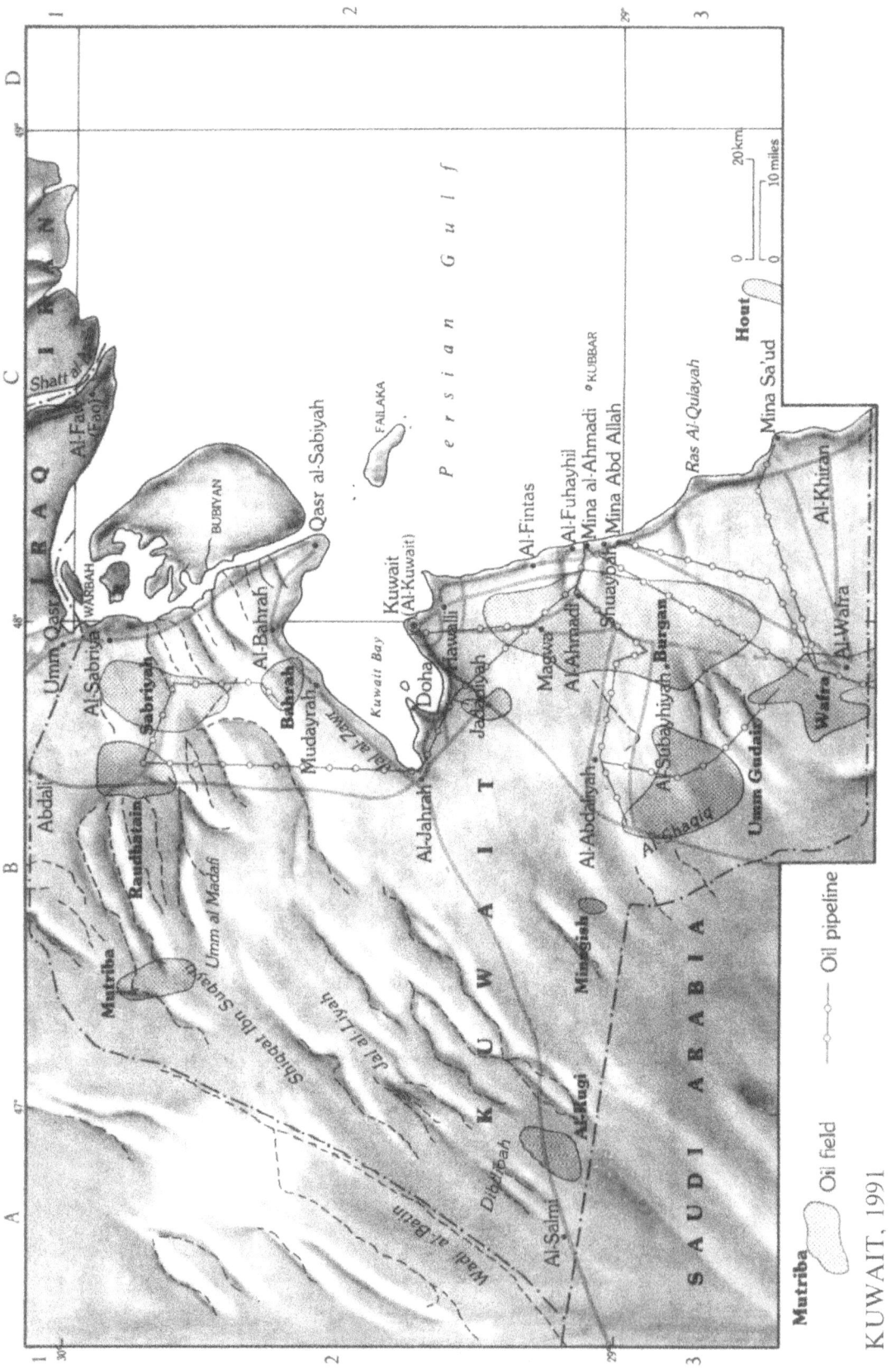

KUWAIT, 1991

of Iraq. British troops were sent in accordance with the treaty, and the claim was disallowed by the United Nations.

Following the war between Iraq and Iran, President Saddam Hussein of Iraq was left with an immense quantity of arms, including biological, neurological, and nuclear weapons, and the largest air force in the Middle East. When he attacked and seized Kuwait in August 1990, contrary to UN warnings, it appeared that nothing could stop his advance to seize all the Gulf States, and even Saudi Arabia and thus possess the greatest part of the oil production and reserves of the world. King Faysal of Saudi Arabia appealed to the UN for aid, and a UN force, the largest contingent of which was from the United States, was speedily assembled and sent to Saudi territory. An overwhelming and swift campaign compelled a cease-fire after five days of fighting (24–28 February 1991).

The core of the Iraqi army escaped, but a UN mission is still in existence in 2002 to destroy biological and nuclear devices as agreed at the time of the cease-fire. The Iraqi government that initiated the attack survives in office.

*Kuwaiti national oil company building in Kuwait City*

# VIII. ISLAM IN 2002

## POLITICAL AND POPULATION

The map includes all members of the Arab League, together with Israel and the six Islamic republics that were part of the U.S.S.R. The population figures shown are chiefly United Nations estimates. The figures for Kuwait, recorded on 1 August 1990 include foreign nationals, many of whom were longstanding Kuwaiti residents with children born in Kuwait. A similar distortion of population figures is probably true of other oil-producing states. Following the Gulf War many foreign nationals were repatriated from Kuwait, and the population figures estimated by UN for Kuwait also reflect the indiscriminate murders that took place on a large scale during the Iraqi occupation. In spite of possible distortions, many of the percentages represent genuine trends of population growth. In 1917, Egypt had a population of 12,750,918; by 1997 it had passed sixty two million. In 1912, Syria had a population of 2,626,160 as against some fifteen million in 1997. Ottoman Palestine numbered only about 700,000 persons. The population of Israel has, of course, been greatly increased by Jewish immigration, principally since 1948, and reached, in 2001, about 6.5 million. During the same period Palestinian Arabs have emigrated to many different countries, especially to the oil-producing countries of the Gulf.

The boundaries of a majority of these countries can be regarded as stable, although that of Kuwait is still disputed by Iraq. The boundaries of Israel contain former Jordanian territories, which were acquired in 1967 and are administered as

*Muslims praying in the Al Aqsa Mosque, Jerusalem*

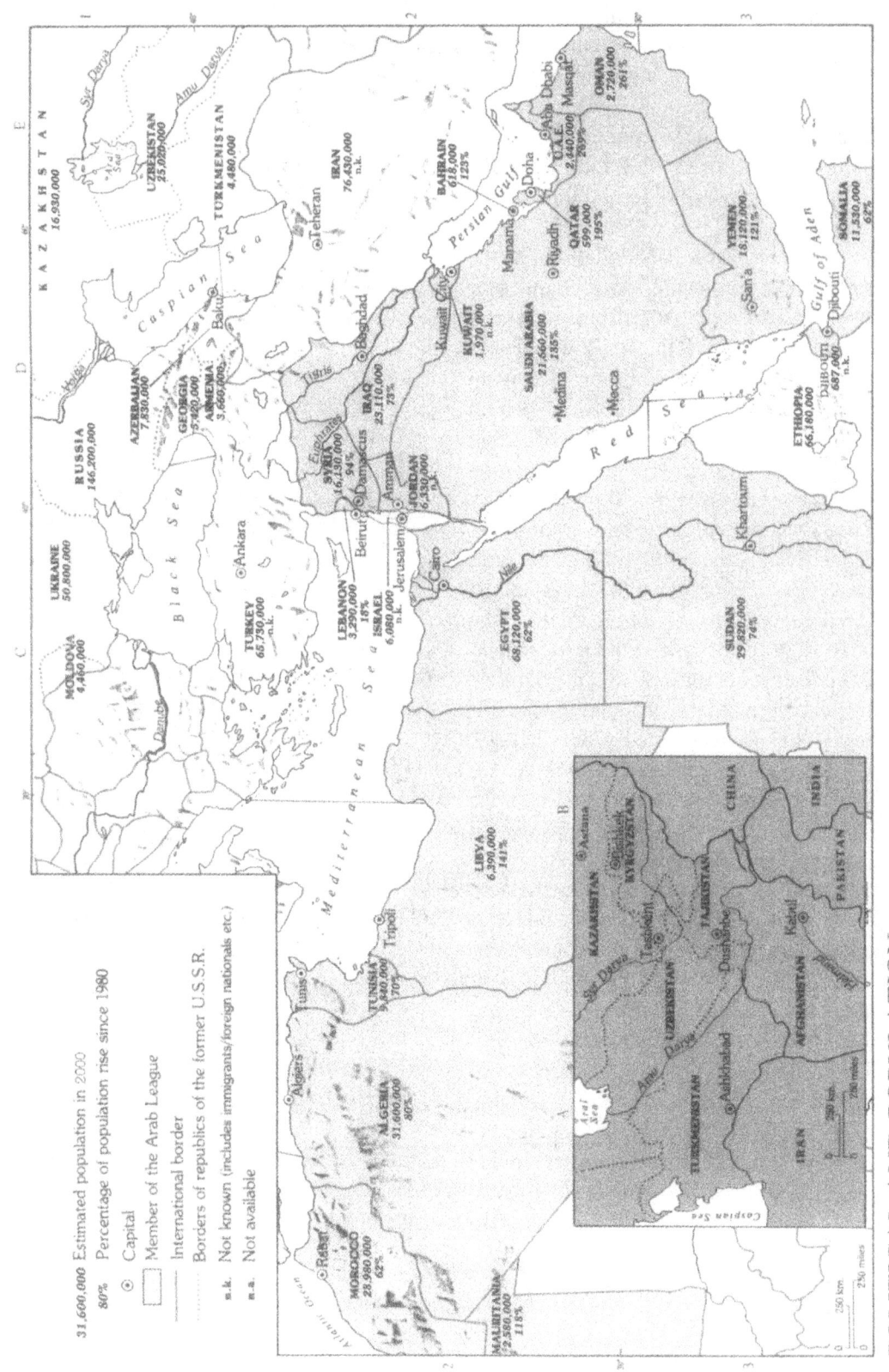

POLITICAL AND POPULATION

occupied territory in accordance with international and Jordanian law. The Golan Heights and the Old City of Jerusalem have been annexed by Israel, but these claims have not been accorded formal international recognition. In these occupied territories Palestinian Arabs form a majority estimated at about three millions.

At the Conference of Paris, 1919, the participants professed policies of self-determination for small nations, but these policies were unevenly applied in the Middle East. The former Ottoman provinces were carved up between Britain and France, and the claims of small nations disregarded. A short-lived Armenian republic was swallowed up by Russia, and Kurds found themselves divided between Iran, Iraq, Syria and Turkey, and what in 1923 became the U.S.S.R. Migrations of Kurds in the early 1990s from Iraq, following genocidal persecution, into Iran and Turkey, are too recent to be brought to account here. The newly created Iraq of 1919, containing the oil-bearing wilayet of Mosul, was one-third Kurdish, one-third Sunni (being the former wilayet of Baghdad) and one-third Shi'ite (the former wilayet of Basra). The settlement reflected British imperial oil interests rather than any genuine political realities. Indeed, so unreal was this creation that until 1957 cabinet meetings were conducted in the Turkish language.

The crumbling of the U.S.S.R. into twelve independent republics during 1991 brought into being no less than six Muslim republics whose ancestry made them heirs of the caliphate at its greatest expansion. These six republics have small populations compared with those to the south and west of them, but all possess nuclear facilities. In Kazakhstan one-tenth of the whole nuclear armament of the former U.S.S.R. is to be found. Thus these nations can have a military potential out of all proportion to their population figures. In them too the growth of Islamic fundamentalism, hostile to western European countries, further complicates the complex political situation that exists from Pakistan and Iran to Libya and Algeria. Fifty years ago Islamic countries as a whole had little or no economic strength. The wealth that oil production has brought and the development of education and professional expertise in its wake, have transformed the Middle East as a whole into a most potent factor in global politics.

*Kemal Atatürk, architect of modern Turkey*

## NATURAL RESOURCES

Since 1907, when oil was first exported from southwest Persia, the exploitation of oil resources has come more and more to dominate the economy of the Middle

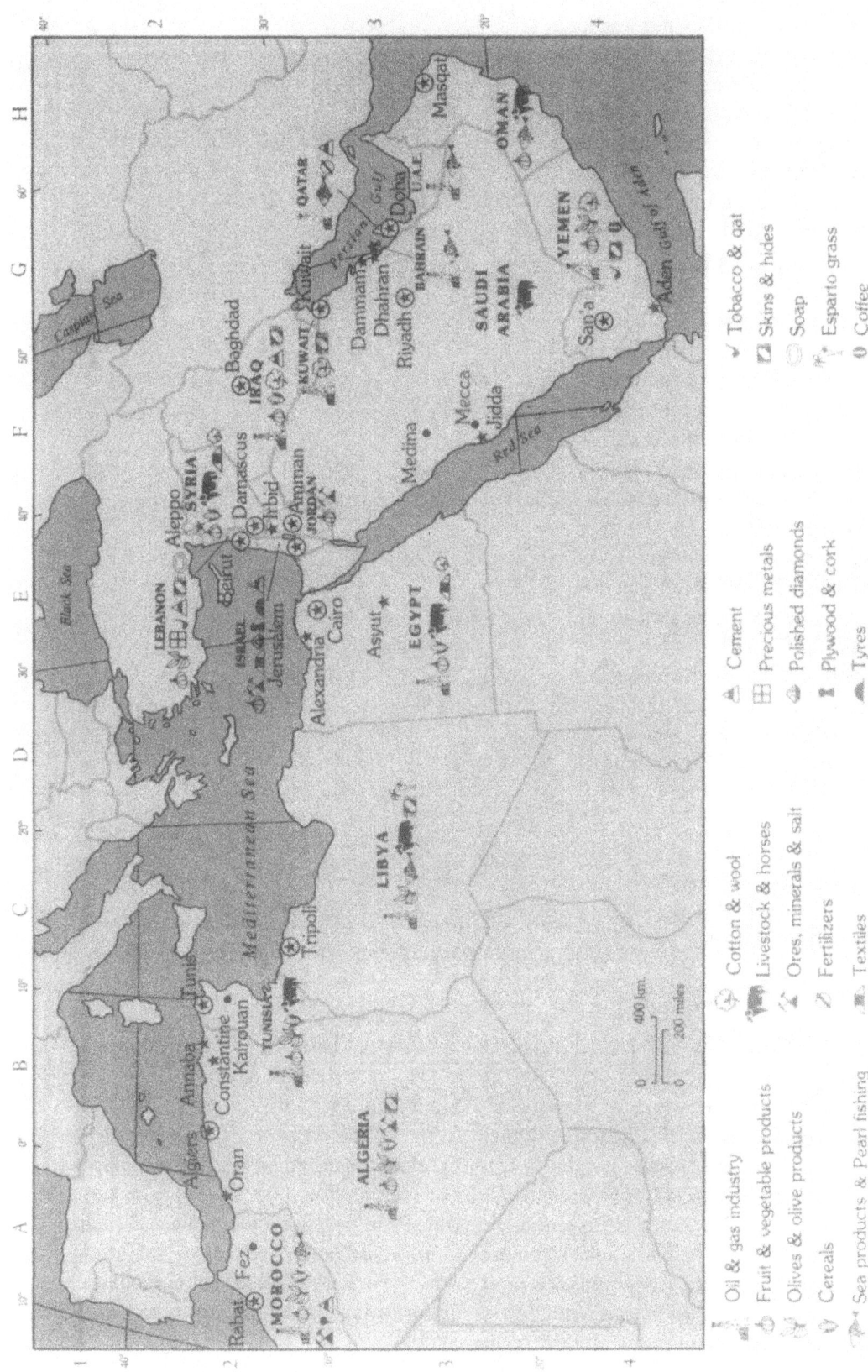

NATURAL RESOURCES

East. The discovery of fresh resources is perhaps not yet at an end, given the discovery of oil in the Marib and Shabwa areas of Yemen in 1987 and in central Saudi Arabia in 1991. The Gulf has long been the predominant oil-producing region, with 40 percent of the world's oil produced in Iraq and Kuwait. So rich is the world in oil resources that the stoppage of these two sources in 1990 had only a temporary effect upon world economy.

In other respects the distribution of natural resources is very uneven, varying from the relative richness of Morocco and Algeria to the sparsity of the Gulf region, where petroleum is by far the largest source in natural wealth.

Much of the development in this respect has been the work of American and British oil companies, and French companies in northern Africa.

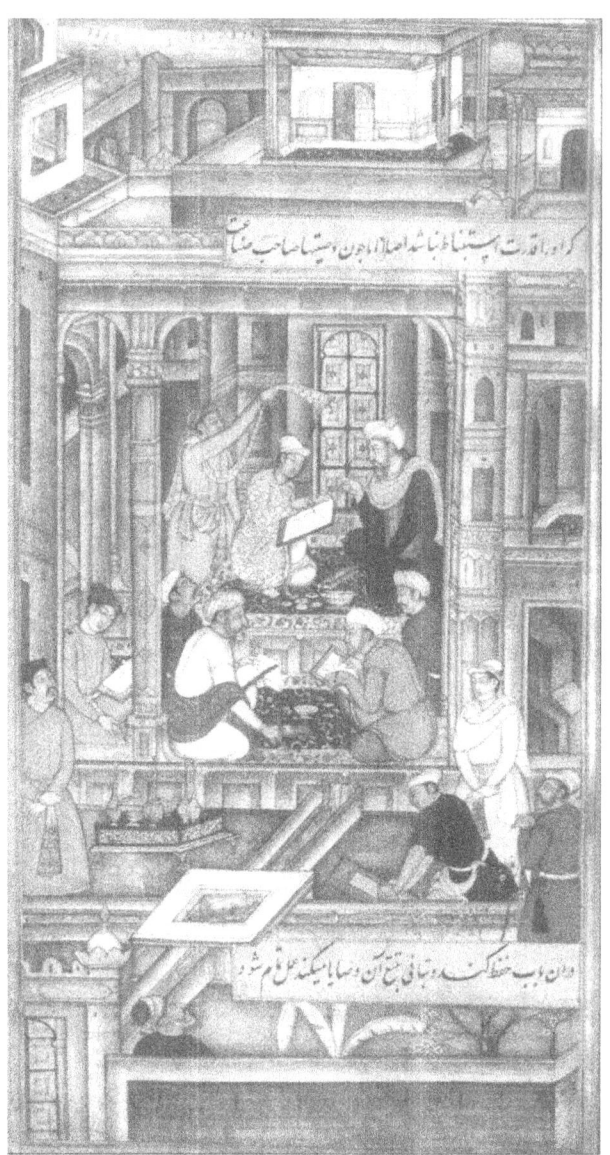

*Manuscript showing the royal atelier, Mughal, late 16th century, India*

## HIGHER AND RELIGIOUS EDUCATION, LITERACY

In Egypt and Lebanon, and more recently Israel, secular institutes of higher learning have long provided an infrastructure. In very recent times universities have developed in Saudi Arabia and the Gulf, where much of the infrastructure has been maintained by the migration of Palestinian Arabs. In Kuwait until very recently these immigrants greatly outnumbered the native-born populations, by at least two to one. The growth in numbers of a highly educated native-born population must now be expected to transform the character of the region and to produce new problems. This, among other causes, has led to considerable emigration, especially to the United States.

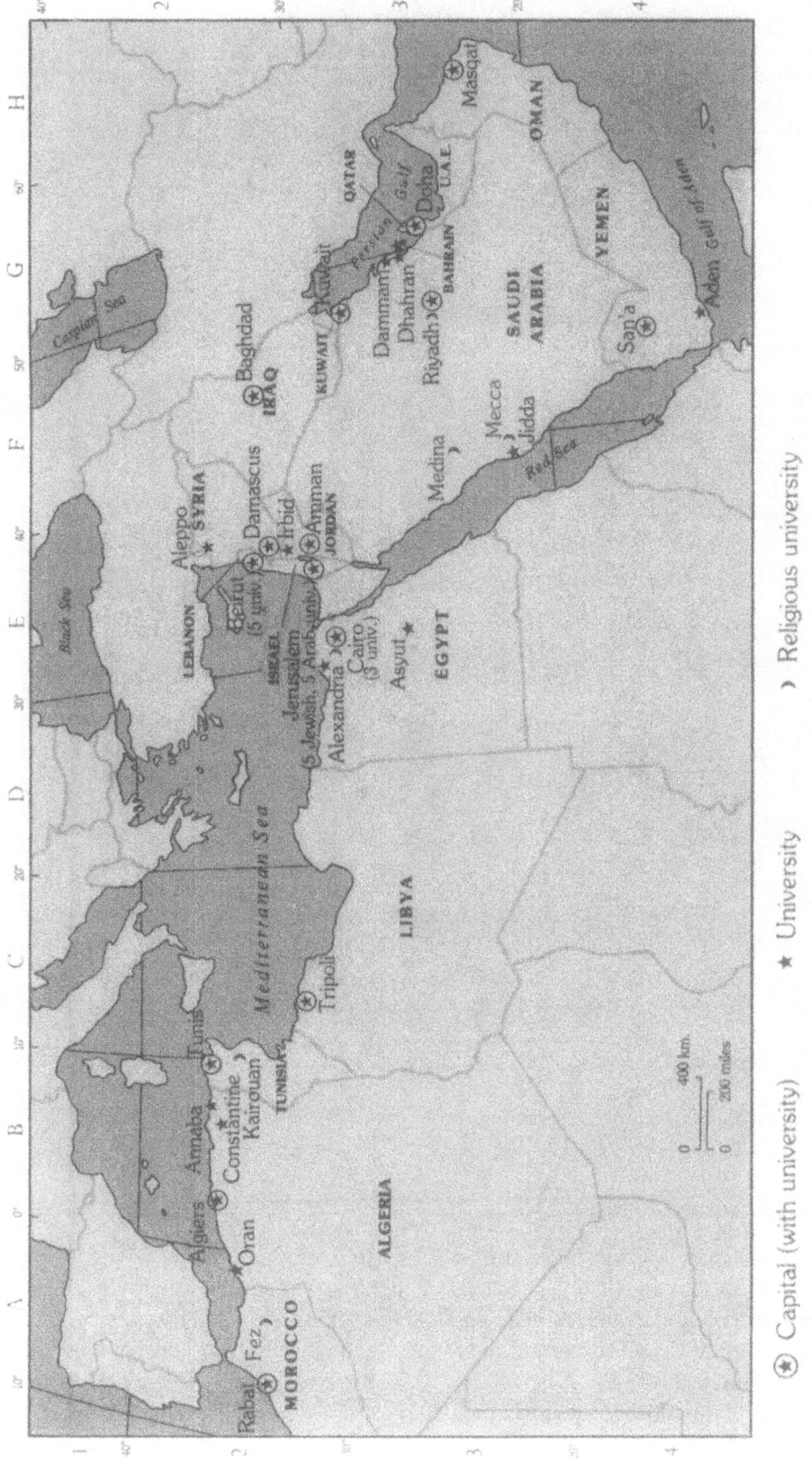

HIGHER AND RELIGIOUS EDUCATION, LITERACY

*Tint drawing of a young man receiving instruction from Muslim teachers, 17th century*

## ISLAM IN THE BALKANS

After the death of the Communist dictator Josef Tito in 1980 Yugoslavia disintegrated. Croatia, Macedonia, and Bosnia-Hercegovina all declared independence; the remainder, Serbia and Montenegro, announced the formation of a new federation as the Federal Republic of Yugoslavia. Within this Federation, in southern Serbia, the province of Kosovo, which was 90% Albanian and Muslim, was autonomous until this status was revoked by Slobodan Milosevic, then leader of the League of Communists of Yugoslavia, in 1992.

Bitter fighting between Serbs and ethnic Albanians followed, which led to open war.

Intervention by NATO and Russia took place; 800,000 persons fled or were forced to leave their homes. In May 1999 Milosevic and others were indicted by the UN War Crimes Tribunal at The Hague for crimes against humanity. A UN Interim Administration Mission was installed, and the refugees began to return to what was left of their homes.

The area of Kosovo, together with Albania, itself 70% Muslim, was the last limit of Ottoman European possessions from 1468. Yugoslavia is 18% Albanian, with a further 8% Muslim Slavs, and thus forms a significant minority in a country where the majority religion is Serbian Orthodox with a small Roman Catholic minority.

*Ferhadija Mosque, Banja Luka, Yugoslavia*

*The Sahat Kulla (clock tower) and Ethem Bey's Mosque, Tirana, Albania*

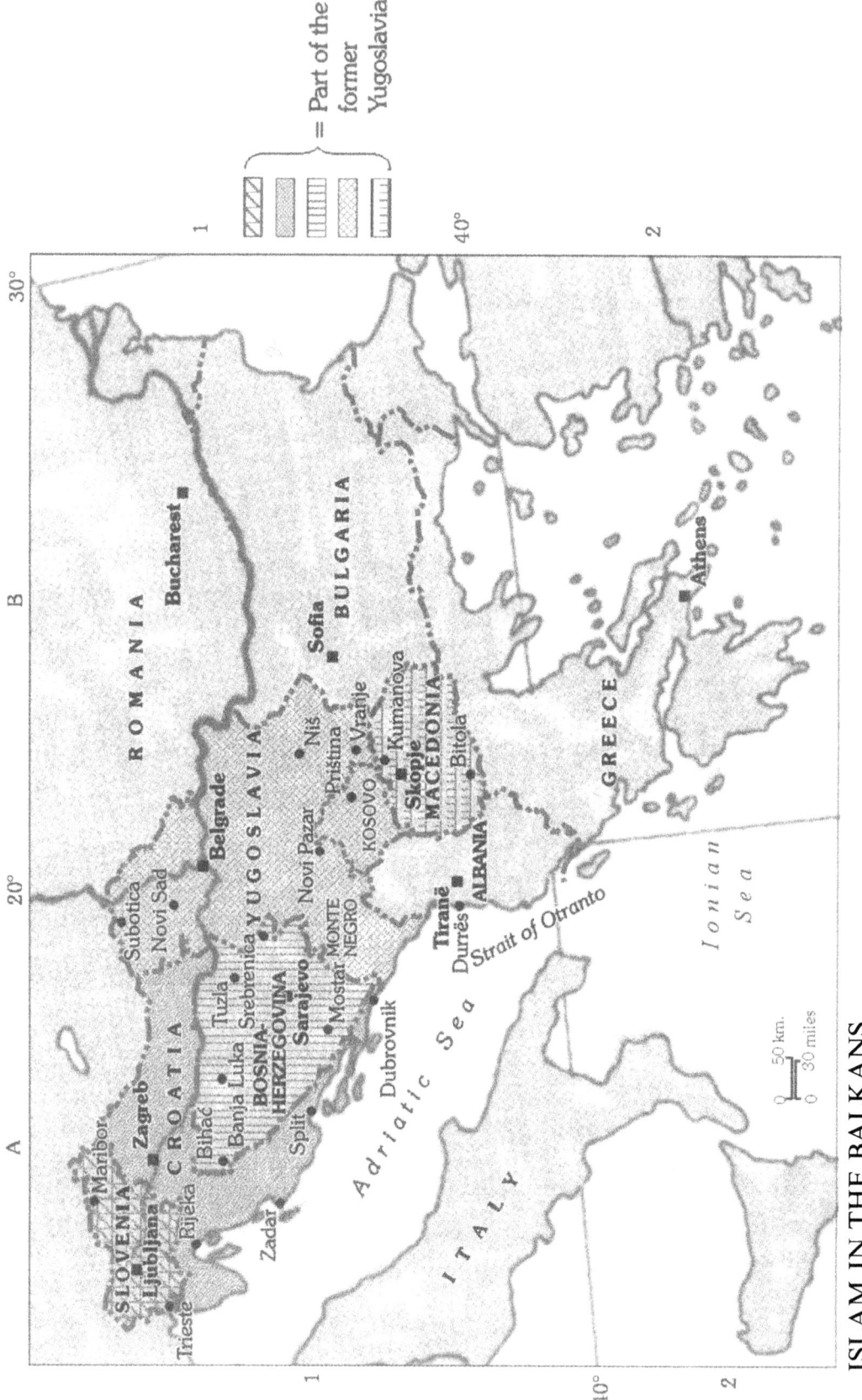

ISLAM IN THE BALKANS

# THE PALESTINIAN DIASPORA

There are so numerous differing estimates of the numbers of Palestinians who have left their homeland since 1948 that it is difficult to rely upon any one set of figures. Howard Adelman, in R. Cohen, *Cambridge University Survey of World Emigration,* gave as what probably is as close an estimate as can be achieved, in 1995. No recent figures are available of religious affiliation since the end of the British Mandate, when Palestinian Christians formed approximately 10% of the population. As recent estimates based on archaeology confirm, the Arab armies that invaded in 634 were small in number, and were by no means the sole progenitors of Palestinian Arabs as a whole; these, rather, were the descendants of all the different ethnic elements who had reached the western horn of the Fertile Crescent from time to time, and who had come to speak Arabic.

Migration runs like a thread through human history, and even pre-history. The Jewish migration into Israel was on so massive a scale that it could never have been predicted. The Provisional Israel government of 1947 never declared an intention to expel 1.3 million Arabs from their homeland. Yet, by the end of 1948 there were some 260,000 refugees from the fighting on the West Bank. The 'Gaza Strip', under Egypt until 1967, doubled its population to 431,000 by natural increase. Others had fled from the fighting, others had left for economic reasons. There was a spontaneous apprehension, not dissimilar to the current (2001) emigration from Afghanistan - before a single shot had been fired. Kuwait was a principal recipient; shortly, out of a total of 0.8 million, half the population was Palestinian. More recently, following the Iraq war on Kuwait, four-fifths of these were forced to migrate again, chiefly to Jordan, having shown overt sympathy with Iraq when it attacked.

An acute observer has noted among the refugees in Jordan, in the camp near es-Salt, what he describes as a refugee mentality. Having reached a place of safety, overcrowded and squalid as it –

*Palestinian refugees fleeing*

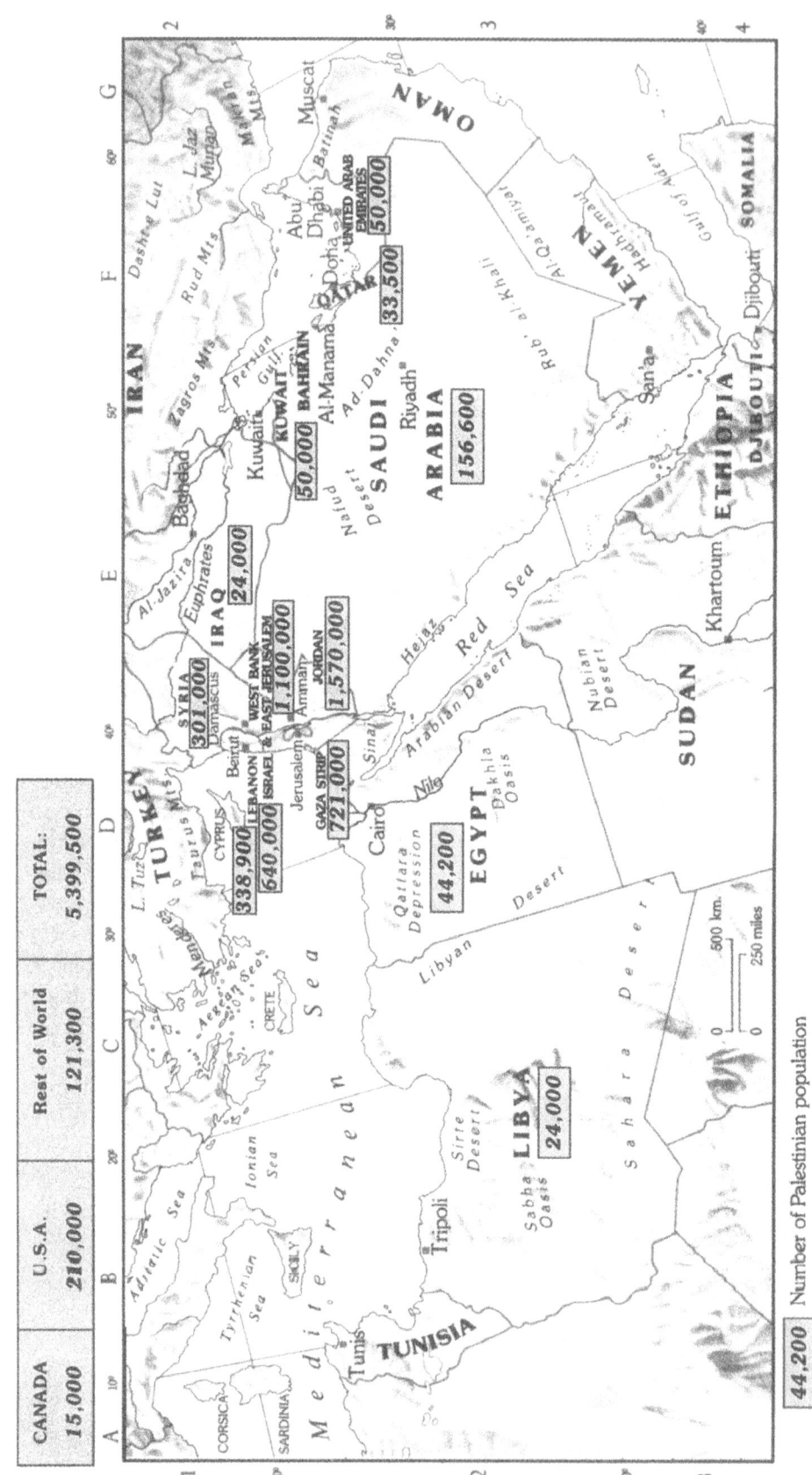

THE PALESTINIAN DIASPORA

and indeed the Gaza Strip – is, there is little disposition to move on or any ordinary ambition. Others, like the Circassians in the nineteenth century, have settled in Jordan and prospered in business. It is questionable whether there is any general desire to return. What is common to all is a general sense of affronted pride and incomprehension.

Its counterpart was a remark of a former Sultan in Yemen when its entire Jewish population emigrated in 1948: 'Whatever shall we do without our Jews?' Palestinian Christians are said to have double the emigration rate of Muslims. It is not that they have suffered any worse indignities than any others. It is because they have had a better education, making it easier to emigrate and to find work abroad. In this, as in Lebanon and Jordan, Christian missions of different denominations had played a major role.

## ISRAEL AND PALESTINIAN AREAS AND SETTLEMENTS

The area under the direct authority of the State of Israel is approximately that of the former Mandated Territory of Palestine. It includes, however, self-governing areas devolved by Israel to the Palestine National Authority (PNA): the 'Gaza Strip', the 'West Bank', and the enclave of Jericho, and also includes a number of scattered settlements, of which seventeen are in the region of Hebron. Towns included are Bethlehem, Nablus, Ramallah, Jericho, Khan Yunis and Rafah, with Gaza City (Ghazzah). All these were formerly administered as Occupied Territories within International Law. Against this, in 1987, a campaign of

*Jewish West Bank settlement of Talmon in the foreground, with an Arab village in the background*

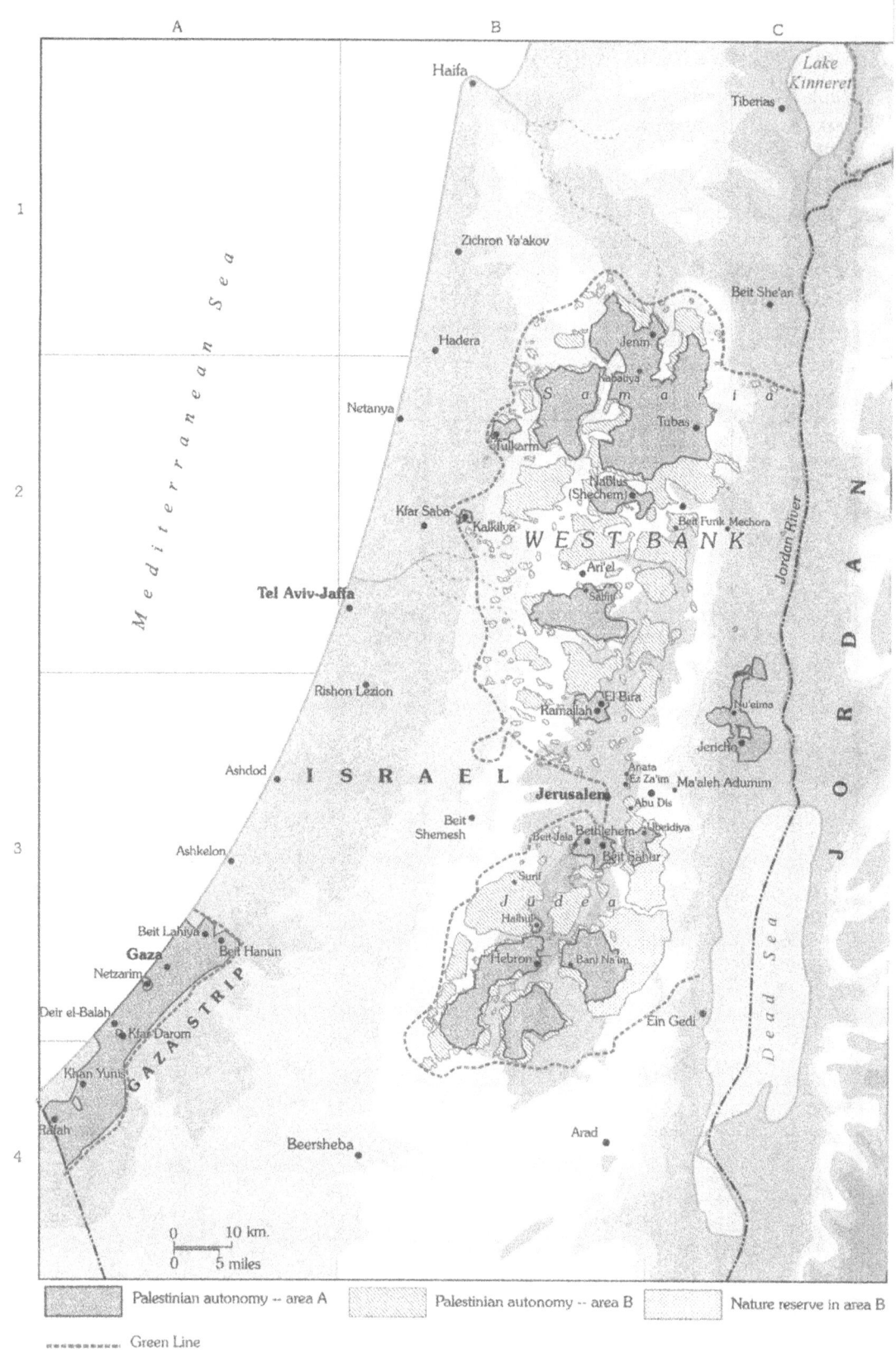

ISRAEL AND PALESTINIAN AREAS AND SETTLEMENTS

unrest, *intifada*, was unleashed by the Palestine Liberation Organization (PLO). In 1991 a peace process was initiated, which led to a 'Declaration of Principles on Interim Self-Government Arrangements' on 13 September 1993. The PLO renounced terrorism, recognised Israel as a state with the right to secure borders; Israel recognised the PLO as the legitimate representative of the Palestinian people. Further agreement was reached in 1995: Israel now recognised PNA authority over culture, direct taxation, education, social welfare and tourism; agreement on the future of East Jerusalem, claimed by both parties as capital, was reserved. At elections in 1996 Yassir Arafat won 88.1% of the vote as Leader *(Rais)* of the PNA. Little progress was made at intermittent talks during 1996 and 1997; it had been Arafat's intention to declare an independent state on 4 May 1999, but the talks foundered.

The 15 May 2000, the anniversary of the founding of the State of Israel, which Arabs call *al-Nakba* (the Catastrophe), was the occasion of violent protests and exchanges of fire between the Israeli army and the Palestinian police. An attempt by Bill Clinton, then President of the United States, to negotiate a comprehensive settlement between Ehud Barak, then Prime Minister of Israel, and Yasser Arafat, Chairman of the Palestine Authority, failed miserably. Violence has since increased considerably. Following the suicidal attacks by aircraft on New York by 'fundamental Islamic' terrorists on 11 September 2001, the issues between Israel and the Palestinian Arabs have become part of the urgent need for a general settlement within the whole orbit of the Middle East, together with Afghanistan and the states of Central Asia. In any case, terrorism, though encouraged by some religious leaders, is contrary to the teaching of the Qur'an, and condemned by almost all nations.

*Signing ceremony of the Sharm el-Sheikh agreement between Ehud Barak and Yassir Arafat. Courtesy of the Israel Government Press Office.*

# THE PILGRIMAGE TO MECCA

Islam has no church, no hierarchy, and no formal organisation. It is thus that it is the more remarkable that each year the 'Id al-Adha, which commemorates the Patriarch Abraham's readiness to sacrifice his son Isaac in obedience to Divine injunction, draws pilgrims from almost every country in the world after some 1400 years. This is the Pilgrimage to Mecca, the *Hajj* par excellence. There have been many accounts of this in different languages since Richard Burton's day, but his account of the ceremonies is amongst the most moving.

It is one of the Five Pillars of the Faith that every Muslim, if able, should make the journey to Mecca once in a lifetime. Originally the pilgrimage was performed naked, but the Prophet ordained that, on entering the Holy Territory of Mecca, two white sheets should be worn, one covering the body and the shoulders, the other over the head, leaving the face bare and the top of the head. This is known as the *ihram*. Likewise, pilgrims were forbidden to cut their hair or nails, and to refrain from sexual intercourse until after their sacrifice at Mina.

In Mecca pilgrims circumambulate the Ka'aba seven times. Some kiss it or the Black Stone, said by some to have been Abraham's pillow. They then run between the hills of Safa and Maswa nearby, and gather at the hill of Arafat. Returning to Mecca, they sacrifice sheep or camels at Mina, and stone the Devil (Iblis) ceremonially.

The duty of pilgrimage (Qur'an 2.192 ff.) is often completed, either coming to or returning from Mecca, by a visit to Medina (*al-Madina al-Munawarrah* the City of Light), the first city to embrace Islam, and where the Prophet Muhammad was buried.

*Arabic devotional manuscript showing the holy cities of Mecca and Medina*

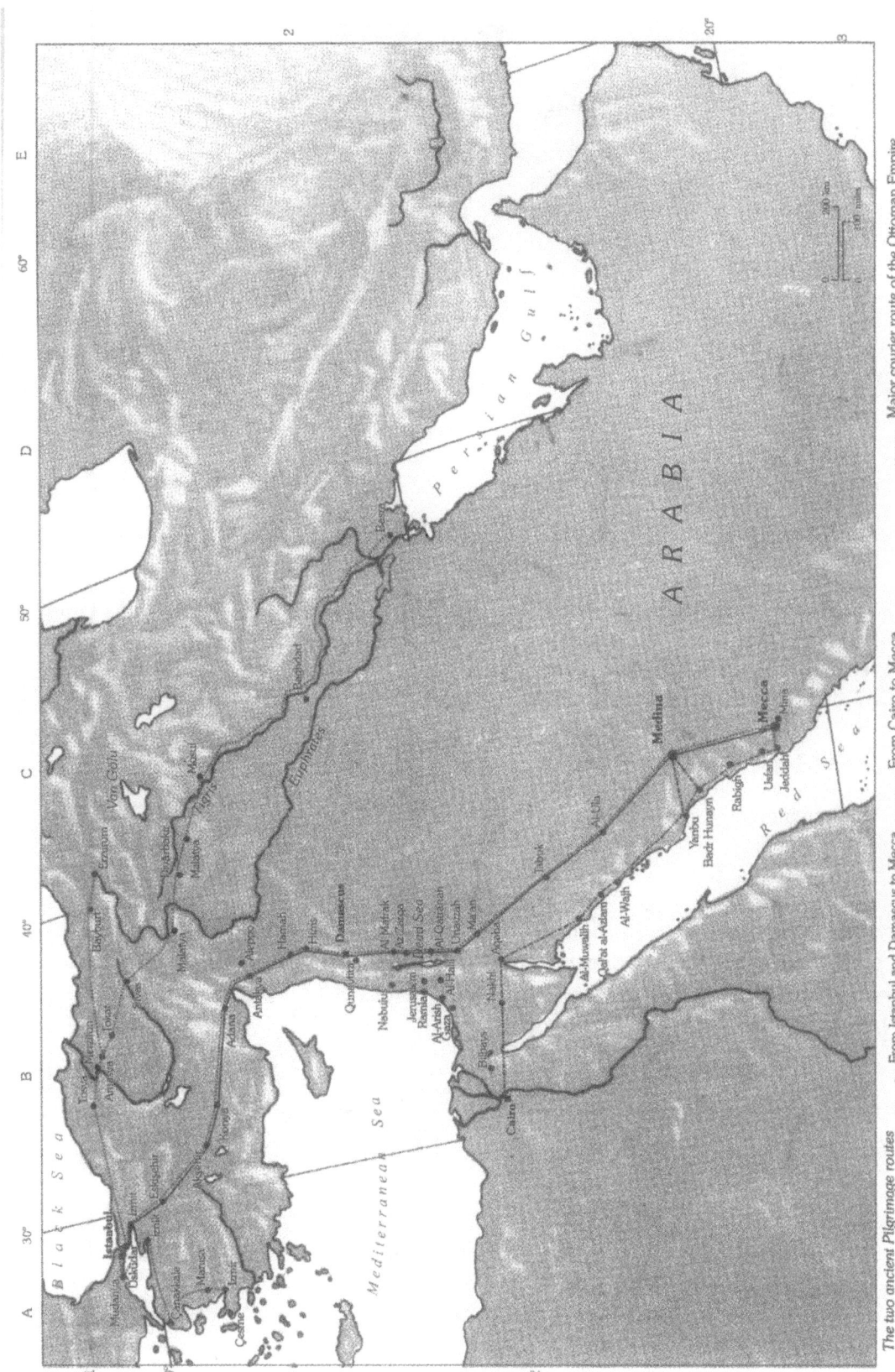

The two ancient Pilgrimage routes ——— From Istanbul and Damascus to Mecca ········ Major courier route of the Ottoman Empire
to Mecca and Medina: ——— From Cairo to Mecca

## THE PILGRIMAGE TO MECCA

*Muslims at prayer at the* Ka'aba *in Mecca during the* Hajj

These ceremonies have not varied for some 1400 years. While today the majority of the pilgrims travel by air, some still do so on foot. In the 1960s poor pilgrims from Pakistan could be seen traveling on foot with their wives and children along the coasts of southern Yemen; some travelled as beggars round the shores of the Persian Gulf. In all, in 2001, some 1.86 million persons, a figure which included 500,000 Saudis, according to official records, are estimated to have made the Pilgrimage.

*A holy pilgrim from a page in a royal album inscribed as the work of Nadir al-Zaman, early 17th century, Mughal Indian*

# AFGHANISTAN IN 2002

Afghanistan in 2002 is a medley of different peoples, all Muslims, though with different religious and political aims, surrounding the Hindu Kush massif. The majority people are the Pashtuns, some 6.5 million of whom, about half the population of the country, live south and east of the Hindu Kush, in the region of the cities of Kabul, Jalalabad, Khost and Kandahar. Like most of the rest of the population, including the ousted Taliban, they are Sunni Hanafi Muslims. The ex-king, Mohammed Zahir Shah, offered as a possible leader of national unity at the moment, is a Pashtun, as is Mullah Omar and other Taliban leaders. The rest of the population is represented by three main groups, mainly Sunni but with Shiites as well. The 3.5 million Tajik who live in the northeast of Afghanistan, chiefly in Badakshan, are Sunni Hanafi Muslims, except for the minority Ismaili Mountain Tajik group in the Pamirs. Tajiks like Burhanuddin Rabbani, leader of the *Jamiat-e-Islami* party, are prominent in the anti-Taliban Northern Alliance that is currently conquering Afghanistan with American help. A million or so Sunni Hanafi Uzbeks, too, live in Aghanistan, west of the Tajik

*The statue of Buddha at Bamian, Afghanistan, blown up by the Taliban; before and after*

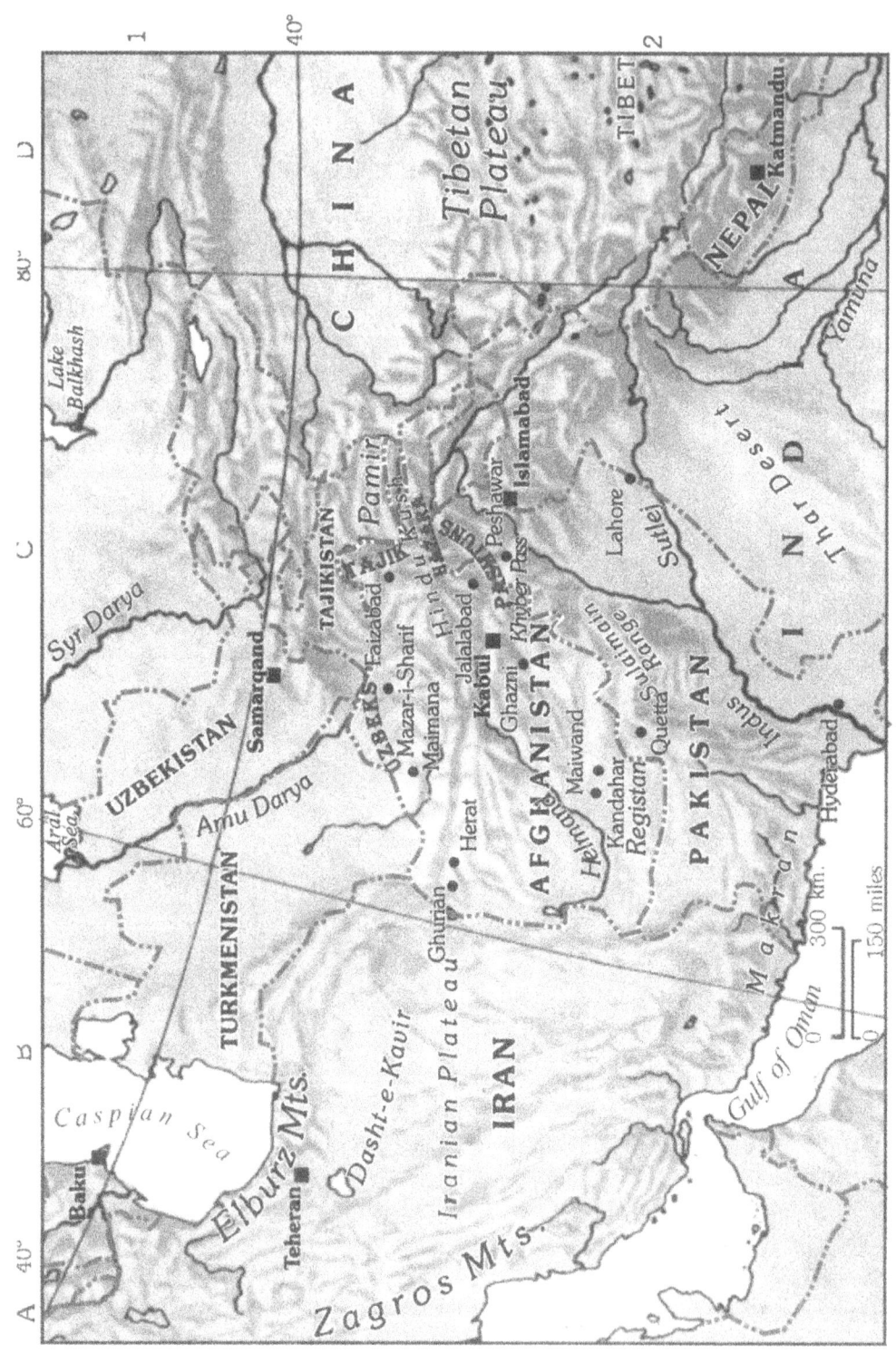

**PASHTUNS** Peoples

AFGHANISTAN IN 2001

*Osama Bin Laden in a television broadcast on Al-Jazeera Television after September 11th, 2001*

region around Mazar-i-Sharif.

Among the leaders is another powerful figure in the Northern Alliance, Abdul Rashid Dostum, who heads the largely Uzbek National Islamic Party (*Jombesh-e-Melli Islami*).

A fourth significant group is the Mongol Hazara people, also represented in the Northern Alliance. There are some 900,000 of them living in the central Hindu Kush, with a center at Chakcharan. They are chiefly Shiite Muslims, who share some support from their co-religionists in Iran. As for the other main ethnic groups, Pashtuns live over the border in Pakistan in similar numbers to those in Afghanistan, and Uzbeks and Tajiks have their own national states just over the borders.

## ISLAM IN THE WORLD TODAY

While Islam continues to have its spiritual roots in the holy cities of Mecca, Medina, and Jerusalem and its intellectual roots in the al-Azhar university mosque in Cairo, its greatest numerical strength is in Indonesia (80% of a population of 149,451,000), Pakistan (97% of a population of 84,501,000), India (12% only out of a population of 684,000,000), Bangladesh (85% of a population of 90,660,000), and the Russian Federation, (44,236,000 Muslims, or 16.87 percent of a total population of 262,084,654 according to the 1979 census). Religious statistics, however, are notoriously misleading, for they can state only a declared religious allegiance.

Revivalist movements have arisen from time to time among, for example, the Wahhabis and, in earlier times, the

Ibadhis of Oman and Tunisia. The Senussi movement appeared in the nineteenth century in Libya; the Muslim Brotherhood formed in Egypt; and what is known as Muslim fundamentalism has become widespread during the present time.

A unique feature of the growth of Islam has been the work of the Sufi brotherhoods since the twelfth century. Originating among Persian mystics in Baghdad, the Sufi teachings spread Islam to the courts of Malaysia and Indonesia in the twelfth century. With a succession of sultans who were themselves Sufis, they provided the religious impulse for the Ottoman Empire. Shortly after the beginning of the nineteenth century, the Sufis spread Islam among the ordinary people in western and eastern Africa. Membership in these fraternities, as indeed in Islam itself, gave adherents a sense of

*Al-Azhar University, Cairo, Egypt*

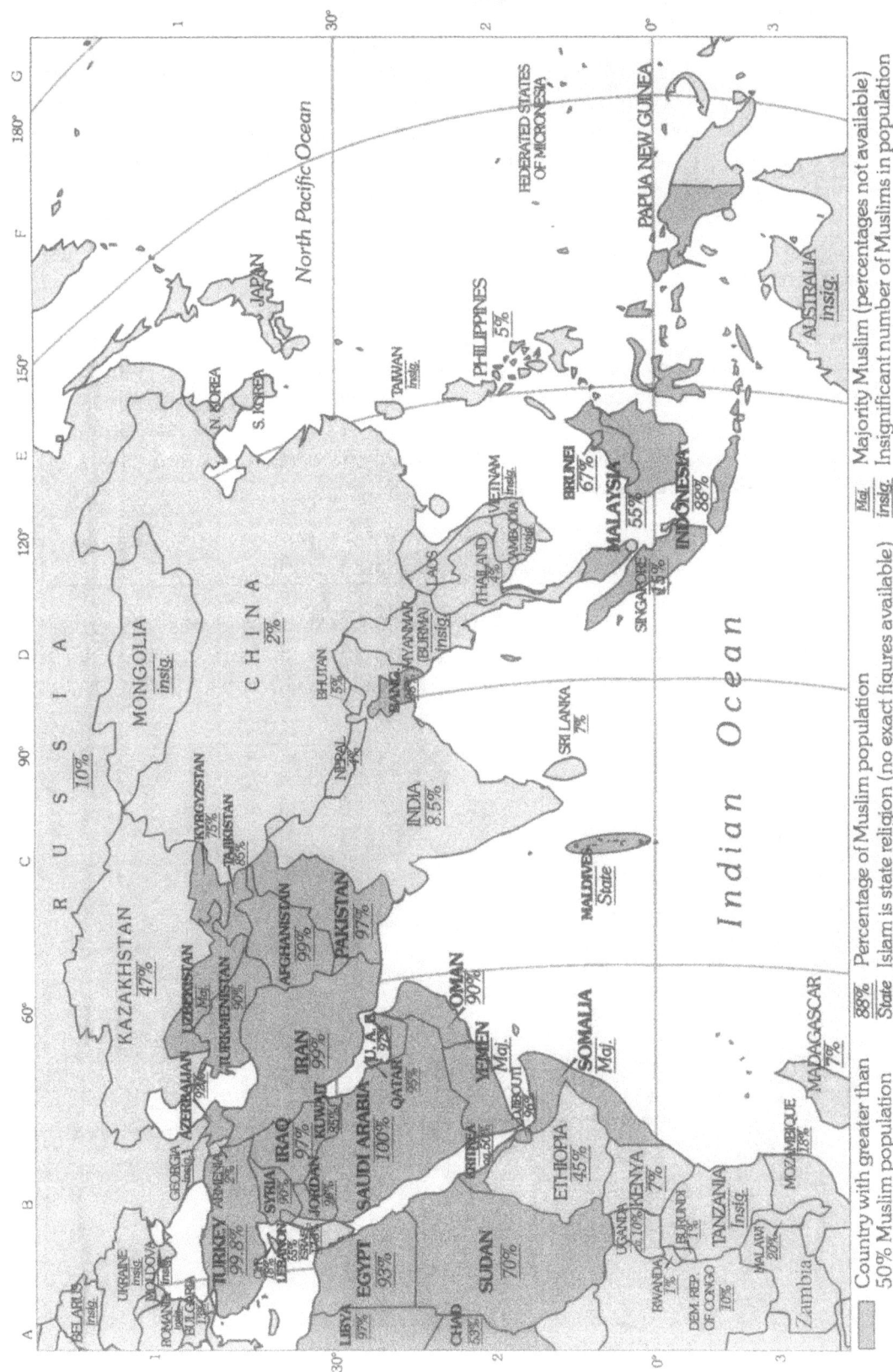

ISLAM IN THE WORLD TODAY (See also page 394.)

belonging to an international fellowship, preserving cherished values in spite of war and colonization. With or without Sufi membership, that sense is very much alive today, especially when the community as a whole appears to be threatened. Strictly defined, Islam has no organized church or hierarchy. Each Muslim is a priest for himself. Nevertheless, there is a "learned clergy" (*ulama*); their function is to interpret and declare the religious law, for in Islam all law derives from the Qur'an and the *hadith* (the traditional sayings or decisions of the Prophet Muhammad). This absence of formal structure is by no means necessarily a weakness, for the interpretations of the lawyers adhere strictly to precedent enabling a decision given in Cairo to be the same as one given in Canada, Bangladesh, or Indonesia. This uniformity and solidarity of law, never actively opposed atheistic communism in Soviet Russia; Muslims simply ignored its proponents in their practical and spiritual lives. Among Muslims, there are, however, wide variations in contemporary attitudes and practices. In al-Azhar women are admitted as pupils, and in many parts of the Muslim world they practise as teachers, whether of religion or of secular subjects in schools and universities. While this adaptation has not kept pace with social changes in other parts of the world, it is reaching its goals in its own fashion.

## ISLAM AND THE WEST, 2002

Islam is deeply implanted in the West, with important minorities in many countries. In Britain, for example, Pakistani Muslims are conspicuous in certain, mainly urban, areas; in France, North Africans; in Germany, Turks; in the

*The fort at Hyderabad, Sind Province, Pakistan (named after the Prophet Muhammad's son-in-law)*

United States, Black Muslim Brotherhoods and many other groups. There have been many minor conflicts, riots in Bradford, England, and similar troubles in both Germany and France. However, the chief lines of conflict seem to have been, and still are, drawn on ethnic grounds, not over the status of Islam the World Trade Center twin towers in New York, and the Pentagon in Washington, followed by the United States raids on Afghanistan to attempt to extradite the leader of the al-Qaida group, Osama bin Laden, a new element seems to have entered the arena. The American president, George W. Bush,

*The Twin Towers pierced by aircraft, New York City, 11th September 2001*

itself. Where elements of Islam are concerned, they are over relatively minor matters. Recent examples are the protest of a very small minority Muslim group in Italy over an ancient fresco that depicts Muhammad in a humiliating posture, or difficulties over such matters as veils for girls in classrooms in England and France.

With the attacks in September 2001 on may have made a diplomatic gaffe in referring to a 'crusade', but Islam in western countries has certainly come under much closer scrutiny.

Warnings from responsible elements, in Islam as well as outside it, continue to emphasize that neither Islam as a religion, nor Muslims as followers of that religion, are in question here, but groups outside what many Muslims, including

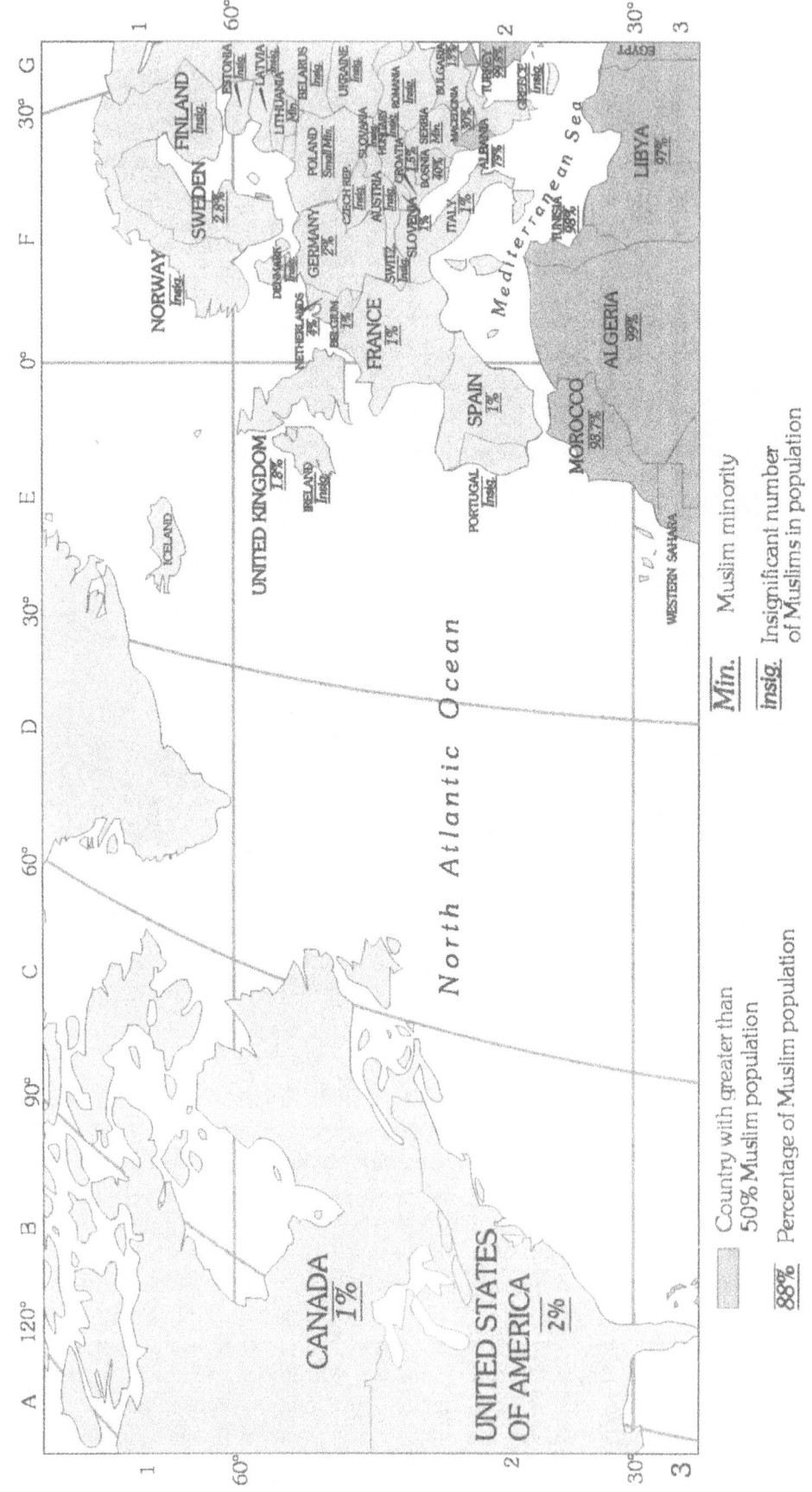

ISLAM AND THE WEST, 2002 (See also page 391.)

the great authorities from such centers as al-Azhar in Egypt, accept as constituting Islam. It was Muslim as well as Christian rulers and officials that the *Hashashun*, the Assassins, killed in an earlier rather similar situation. Nevertheless, in a press unleashed after the spectacular events in the United States, we often read of fears that a 'clash of civilizations', the world of Islam against the world represented by western values, might occur as extreme Muslim groups whip up fervor on one side, and indignation against attacks mounts on the other. Ongoing conflicts in which a western-Islamic opposition can be seen, such as the Israel-Palestine clashes, offer a political rationale for extremist rhetoric.

The concept of the *jihad* is endlessly discussed, what it means, what the precise responsibilities of a Muslim are; but the definitions do not usually countenance suicide bombings and the like. The exact affiliations of terrorists (who, of course, do not regard themselves in that light, but as fighters for Islam) are also often discussed. It is frequently pointed out that although the radically Muslim Taliban have sheltered al-Qaida in Afghanistan, the active elements in terrorist attacks tend to be dissident Saudi, Egyptian, or Gulf State citizens, often of the 'purist' Wahhabi-style persuasion that is taught and propagated by the Saudi government itself. They are not (usually) Afghans, Iranians, Sudanis, Iraqis, Libyans or Syrians whose states are accused of fomenting terrorism. The same Wahhabi-style inclination is true of Algerian Muslim fundamentalists, or the hard-line Muslim guerillas of Kashmir. It is from the oil states of Islam, too, generally allies of the west, that the money that fuels some of the radical Muslim groups derives. The question is not, then, a matter of any clearly divided lines between the states of Islam, and the West.

At the moment, fears of polarization between western and Islamic-oriented civilizations seem much exaggerated. With the large Muslim minorities in the first group, and the non-fundamentalist stance of much of the second, the disparity is not as great as some writers have sought to claim. Nor do the Taliban or Osama bin Laden seem to speak for anything beyond a minority of Muslims. There is indeed uncertainty about the direction of some aspects of Islam, and its relations with the rest of the world in the fourteenth century of its existence, but we cannot sensibly predict the outcome.

*Islamic calligraphy depicted in the shape of a boat. The English translation is: "I believe in God, and His angels, and His books, and His prophets, and the Day of Judgment and in His providence with what it includes of fortune and misfortune, and the resurrection after death."*

# INDEX

## A

Abaka ......................... 163
Abbas I ....................... 263
Abbas II ...................... 167
Abbasid caliphate . 44, 51, 57, 59, 67, 71, 73, 80, 153, 225
Abbasid Dynasty ............. 42
Abbasids ............. 48, 61, 73
Abd al-Aziz ........... 267, 276
Abd al-Aziz Ibn Saud ..... 316
Abd al-Kadir, Emir of Maskara 296
Abd Allah ...................... 67
Abd al-Majid ................. 267
Abd al-Malik ibn Marwan 40, 105
Abd al-Mumin ibn Ali 91, 93
Abd al-Rahman .............. 67
Abd al-Rahman al-Ghafiqi 48
Abd al-Rahman I ............ 48
Abd al-Rahman III al-Nasir ... 67
Abd el-Kader ................. 299
Abdallab of Sudan ......... 182
Abdallah b. Saad ............ 174
Abdallah Jamma ............ 182
Abdallah, Raja ............... 239
Abdul Hussein ............... 247
Abdul Rashid Dostum .... 389
Abdullah, brother of Amr ibn al-As ........................ 39
Abdullah, Successor of Abd al-Aziz ......................... 276
Abdullah, King of Jordan ...... 331, 341
Abdulwahid .................. 207
Ablaq ........................... 104
Abomey ....................... 216
Abraham ...... 14, 35, 108, 384
Abu al-Abbas ................. 42
Abu al-Misk Kufur .......... 59
Abu Bakr ..... 25, 28, 110, 257
Abu Dhabi .................... 353
Abu Hamid al-Ghazzali .... 63
Abu Inan ...................... 148
Abu Sarur (Barcelore) ..... 124
Abu Sayyad .................. 259
Abu Ubaydah ibn Jarrah .. 32
Abu Yusuf Ya'qub al-Mansur 93
Abu Zaid ...................... 223
Abu Zayd al-Balki ........... 66
Abyssinia ..................... 250
Ace .............................. 249
Achaemenid ................... 51
Acheh 241, 243, 249, 291, 305, 307
Acre .. 59, 87, 88, 94, 281, 282
Adal ..................... 179, 190
Adamawa ..................... 216
Adam's Peak ................. 125
Adana .......................... 284
Addis Ababa ................. 338
Aden .. 21, 131, 189, 250, 284, 338, 341, 348, 362, 364
Adowa .......................... 301
Adrianople ................... 160
Adud al-Dawlah .............. 51
Aegean Islands ............... 44
Aelia Capitolina ............. 105
Afghanistan ... 17, 61, 74, 120, 123, 137, 151, 167, 358, 379, 387, 393
Afghan(s) .. 119, 123, 295, 395
Afonso of Portugal, Prince .... 250
Africa ......................... 146
Africa, eastern ............... 71
Africa, western .............. 71
Agha ........................... 273
Agha Khan .................... 63
Aghlabids ........ 44, 56, 57, 71
Agung of Mataram, Sultan .... 244, 247, 304, 305
Ahmad, Sultan ............... 237
Ahmadnagar ................. 126
Ahmed Pasha Qaramanli . 274
Ajman ......................... 353
Ajmer .......................... 100
Ajnadain ....................... 32
Akan states .................. 210
Akbar ................... 127, 128
Akhbar al-Sind wa'l-Hind 226
Akhenaton .................... 10
Akkadian .................. 7, 30
Aksumites ................ 25, 26
Ala al-din ............. 120, 243
Ala al-din Husayn .......... 98
Al-Abbas ...................... 42
Alamut ......................... 63
Al-Andalus .............. 67, 114
Alapur, Mark ................ 123
Alarcos ......................... 93
Al-Arish ....................... 35
Al-Askar ....................... 96
Ala'u'-din Riayat Shah .... 241
Ala'u'din, Sultan ............ 235
Alawi (Nusayri) ...... 354, 366
Al-Azhar 69, 71, 97, 288, 313, 389, 392, 395
Al-Aziz ......................... 71
Albania ....................... 376
Albanian troops, army ... 279, 282
Al-Biruni ................ 74, 123
Aleppo . 81, 90, 144, 158, 282, 293
Alexander II, Pope .......... 83
Alexander II, Tsar .......... 298
Alexander the Great  4, 10, 16, 17, 35, 40
Alexandria .. 4, 19, 23, 35, 37, 71, 83, 94, 147, 274
Alexandria, bombardment of .. 311
Alexius I Comnenus, Emperor 84
Al-Farama (Pelusium) ...... 35
Alfonso I of León .......... 114
Alfonso II .................... 112
Alfonso VI ..................... 80
Alfonso VIII of Castile ..... 93
Al-Fustat ............. 59, 71, 96
Algeria . 56, 93, 152, 299, 341, 372, 374
Algerian Muslim fundamentalists ........... 395
Al-Ghazzali ................... 53

Algiers ....... 73, 207, 271, 273
Al-Hajj Umar Tal .......... 289
Al-Hakim ................. 71, 107
Alhambra ................ 80, 112
Al-Hamdani .................. 67
Al-Hariri .................... 4, 146
Al-Hasa ....................... 316
Al-Hashim, Sharif, Sultan 259
Al-Hira ......................... 32
Ali ........ 32, 40, 56, 71, 110
Ali b. Wali Asma .......... 177
Ali Bey ........................ 284
Ali Ibn Yusuf ................. 71
Ali Mughayat Shah ....... 243
Al-Idrisi ......................... 94
Al-Ikhshid, Muhammad ... 59
Al-Ittihad .................... 364
Aliyot ......................... 345
Al-Jahiliyah .................. 27
Al-Jalali ...................... 123
Al-Khalili, Garkas .......... 144
Allah ............................ 28
Allenby, General Edmund 35, 321
Al-Mahdi ...................... 52
Al-Mahdi (Muhammad Ahmad) .................... 315
Al-Mahdiya ................... 73
Al-Malik al-Salih, Sultan 225, 235
Al-Malik al-Zahir ........... 237
Al-Malwiyeh .................. 54
Al-Ma'mun .................... 63
Al-Mansur ... 51, 73, 247, 284
Almanzor ...................... 76
Al-Mahdia ..................... 71
Al-Maqdisi .................... 66
Al-Mas'udi ............... 65, 146
Al-Mazini .................... 147
Almohad ...... 91, 93, 100, 207
Almoravid ....... 71, 73, 78, 80
Al-Mu'izz .................. 71, 73
Al-Muktafi .................... 53
Al-Mu'minim, Amir ......... 80
Al-Muqaddasi ................. 66
Al-Muqtadir ................... 53
Al-Murabitun see Almoravd
Al-Mutamid ................... 52
Al-Mutasim ................... 52
Al-Muta-wakkil .............. 49
Al-Nakba (Catastrophe) .. 383

Al-Nasir Muhammad ..... 102, 103, 144, 181
Alodia see Alwa
Alp Arslan ................ 81, 88
Alphabet, Early Arabic .... 30
Alphabet, Early Aramaic .. 30
Alphabet, Early European 30
Alphabet, Early Phoenician 30
Alphabet, Early Syriac ..... 30
Alptigin ........................ 74
Al-Qahira 96, 97 see also Cairo
Al-Qaida ............... 393, 395
Al-Qa'im ...................... 51
Al-Qata'i ....................... 96
Al-Qubbat al-Sakhra ....... 107
Al-Rahman .................... 69
Al-Rayy ........................ 61
Al-Ruha (Edessa) ........... 84
Al-Sabah ..................... 367
Al-Sadat, Anwar ........... 351
Al-Saffar ...................... 61
Al-Umari .............. 179, 181
Al-Utbi ......................... 74
Alwa (Alodia) ......... 174, 181
Al-Zahra ....................... 67
Amangkurat II .............. 305
Amba Alagi ................. 338
Amboina ............... 257, 304
Ambon ..... 134, 246, 304, 305
Amda Seyon ................ 179
American consul ........... 300
American financial support .... 343
Amharic ........................ 30
Amida ......................... 158
Amir al-umara ............... 51
Amir of Kuwait ............ 107
Amr ibn al-As . 32, 35, 37, 39, 57, 96, 284
Amur .......................... 298
Amwari ....................... 123
An Lu-shan .................. 226
Anaj ........................... 182
Anatolia ..... 84, 160, 269, 318
Andaman ......... 219, 222, 237
Anglo-Dutch ................ 273
Anglo-Egyptian Twenty Year Treaty ....................... 313
Angoche .............. 183, 308
Angola 194, 195, 212, 300, 308
Anhilwara ................... 100

Ani ............................. 88
Ankara ................ 158, 160
Anna .......................... 296
Anopheles ................... 202
Anti-Lebanon ............... 354
Antioch ............... 83, 84, 94
Anti-Semitism .............. 329
Anti-Taliban Northern Alliance 387
Antony of Egypt ............ 23
Apulia .......................... 84
Aqsa Mosque ............... 107
Arab 28, 52, 123, 142, 225, 233, 313
Arab Chancery ............. 40
Arab conquest ............... 32
Arab currency ............... 40
Arab Executive Committee .... 331
Arab Judiciary .............. 40
Arab Legion ................ 338
Arab traders ................ 194
Arababni ..................... 179
Arabia 19, 27, 30, 66, 151, 262, 293, 316
Arabia Felix (Yemen) 250, 362
Arabic .................. 40, 308
Arafat, Yassir ........ 383, 384
Aragon 67, 93, 112, 114, 146, 180
Arakan .......... 115, 233, 291
Aramaean origins ........... 28
Aramaic .................. 16, 30
Ardabil ....................... 165
Ardahan ..................... 318
Argentina ................... 327
Armenia . 1, 16, 19, 66, 87, 88, 137,
Armenian royalty .......... 87
Armenian schools .......... 270
Armenians ... 81, 88, 189, 250, 269, 318, 331, 364, 366
Aru ............................ 243
Aryan ........................... 8
Ascalon ...................... 295
Ashanti ....................... 203
Asia Minor 153, 160, 262, 325, 327
Asir ........................... 316
Askia Dawud ............... 210
Asmara ....................... 336
Assad, President of Syria . 354

398

Assam .......... 125, 148, 151
Assassins (Neo-Ismailis) 63, 71, 81, 84, 87, 94, 144, 354, 395
Assyria .................... 12, 16
Assyrians ............... 364, 366
Astrologers ............... 96, 97
Asturias .................. 67, 112
Aswan .................. 181, 287
Aswan High Dam .......... 347
Atabegs of Damascus ....... 87
Athens ....................... 281
Atlas Mountains ....... 40, 123
Atziz ............................ 81
Augustus .................. 19, 21
Aurangzeb (Almagir) 129, 130
Aurès ......................... 299
Aurès Mountains ............ 73
Aussa ......................... 191
Australia, northwest ....... 146
Austria ............. 17, 263, 265
Ava ........................... 291
Awfat (Ifat) .................. 179
Awqf ......................... 288
Awu .......................... 123
Aylah .......................... 32
Ayn Jalut ............... 144, 161
Ayn Shams (Heliopolis) .... 35
Ayutthaya ....... 134, 249, 252
Ayutthayan .................. 247
Ayyub .......................... 94
Ayyubid ....................... 94
Azania ....................... 187
Azerbaijan . 16, 137, 141, 142, 158, 161, 263, 360

# B

Baalbek ...................... 158
Babilyun (Babylon) 35, 96, 284
Babur (Zahir al-Din Muhammad) . 123, 127, 165, 167
Babylon ... 8, 14, 16, 105, 345
Badajoz ...................... 114
Badakshan .................. 387
Badhan ........................ 26
Badis .......................... 73
Badlay, Sultan ............... 179
Badr al-Jamali ................ 98
Baeda Maryam ............. 179
Bagelen ...................... 307
Baghdad 42, 44, 49, 51, 52, 53, 54, 57, 59, 61, 65, 69, 71, 73, 81, 88, 142, 144, 151, 158, 293, 295, 321, 338, 357, 390
Baguirmi ..................... 214
Bahr al-Nil ................... 102
Bahrain ....................... 353
Bahri Mamluk ........ 102, 144
Bairam ....................... 123
Baisonghor .................. 165
Baku .......................... 141
Balambang .................. 244
Balambangan (Sulu)  255, 304
Baldwin I ..................... 84
Baldwin II .................... 84
Balearic Islands .............. 71
Balfour Declaration   325, 329, 330, 331
Bali .. 179, 219, 222, 244, 257, 304
Balkans .................. 160, 269
Balkh ............... 61, 74, 156
Baltistan ..................... 233
Baluchis ..................... 358
Baluchistan .................. 115
Bambuk ................ 203, 216
Banat of Temisvar ......... 269
Banda ....... 219, 250, 291, 305
Banda Islands ............... 304
Banda Neira ................. 304
Bandang, Dato'ri ........... 247
Bandas ....................... 257
Bangladesh 115, 119, 134, 389, 392
Bani Ammar ................. 274
Bani Makki .................. 274
Banjarmasin 246, 247, 257, 307
Banjumas ............... 244, 307
Bantam (Banten) .... 136, 243, 244, 255, 257, 304, 305
Bantu family of languages  170
Banu Abd al-Wad ......... 100
Banu Hilal .................... 73
Banu Marin ............ 93, 100
Banu Sulaim ............ 73, 207
Baqt .......................... 175
Barak, Ehud ................. 383
Barbarossa (Frederick I) ... 87
Barbary ...................... 207
Barbosa, Duarte ............ 189
Barca ........ 96 see also Barqa
Barcelona ............... 112, 147
Baring, Sir Evelyn (later Lord Cromer) .................... 313
Barqa (Barca) ................ 39
Barquq ....................... 144
Bartolemeu Dias ............ 194
Bashkortosan ................ 360
Basilan ....................... 259
Basle ......................... 329
Basman ....................... 237
Basra 51, 66, 153, 263, 325, 357
Batak ......................... 307
Batavia ..... 136, 255, 304, 307
Batavian Republic ... 257, 305
Battle of Poitiers ............ 54
Bauchi plateau .............. 210
Bauguinda of Sumatra .... 257
Bayana ....................... 123
Baybars I 54, 87, 102, 144, 161, 181
Bayezid I ..................... 160
Bayezid II .................... 161
Begs .......................... 231
Beijing .................. 228, 233
Beirut ............... 84, 270, 354
Beja .......................... 175
Bekaa ........................ 354
Bektashis .................... 161
Belgium ...................... 357
Bell, Gertrude .............. 296
Ben Maimon, Mosheh see Ibn Maymun, Musa
Bencoolen ............. 255, 307
Bengal 100, 120, 126, 134, 148, 151, 180, 291
Bengal, Bay of .............. 219
Bengali Muslim Indians ... 233
Bengkalis ............... 241, 249
Ben-Gurion, David ........ 343
Benin ......... 194, 198, 202, 205
Benue .................. 198, 214
Berar ......................... 126
Berbera ................. 189, 250
Berber(s) ... 39, 48, 49, 71, 80, 102, 123, 203
Berlin Act (1885) ........... 302
Bersatu (Unity) Group .... 253
Bethlehem .............. 84, 381
Beys .......................... 273
Bhutan ....................... 115
Bidar ......................... 126
Bight of Benin .............. 212

Bihar .............................. 123
Bijapur ................... 126, 134
Billiton ........................... 307
Bimaristan al-Adudi ......... 51
Bin Laden, Osama ... 360, 393
Bintan ..................... 235, 255
Bintang ......................... 241
Biskra ........................... 207
Bizenegalia .................... 291
Bizerta .......................... 207
Black Death ........... 153, 155
Black Muslim Brotherhoods ... 393
Black Sea  19, 66, 146, 148, 324
Black Stone ..................... 28
Blad al-makhzan ............. 265
Blad al-siba ................... 267
Board of Control ............ 131
Boer ............................. 302
Bogador ........................ 310
Bohemond I .................... 84
Bokhara ........................ 298
Boleyse ......................... 247
Bombay .................. 131, 136
Bône ............................. 207
Bone ............................. 247
Boran ........................... 170
Bordeaux ........................ 48
Borneo  216, 219, 222, 225, 244, 247, 257, 291, 304, 307
Bornu ................ 205, 214, 216
Bosnia-Herzegovina ........ 376
Bosnians ....................... 282
Bougie .......................... 207
Bracciolini, Gian Francesco Poggio ........................... 291
Bradford, England .......... 393
Brava ............................ 250
Britain (British) .... 1, 246, 249, 252, 287, 318, 367, 372, 392
British conquest of Burma  233
British Consul ................ 300
British East India Company ... 131
British North Borneo ...... 304
British policy in Palestine  338
British Protectorate ......... 313
British Residents ............ 249
British retreat at Dunkirk  334
British Somaliland .. 334, 336, 338

Brittany ........................... 84
Brooke, Sir James, Rajah Brooke ........ 246, 257, 307
Brunei  136, 216, 225, 244, 246, 255, 257, 304
Buayan .......................... 259
Budamma ...................... 181
Buddha ......................... 387
Buddhism ............... 100, 131
Buddhist .................. 115, 163
Bugis of Boni .......... 305, 307
Buhlul Lodi ................... 123
Buhruz .......................... 237
Bukhara  51, 61, 137, 226, 362
Bukovina ...................... 269
Bulgaria ................. 146, 318
Bulgars ......................... 147
Bulugin ibn Zairi ............. 73
Bundu ........................... 205
Bunga mas .................... 249
Burckhardt, Johann Ludwig ... 293, 295
Burdett-Coutts ............... 295
Burg see Citadel
Burgi ...................... 102, 104
Burhanuddin Rabbani ..... 387
Burjpur ......................... 123
Burma  131, 216, 222, 226, 233, 291
Bursa .............. 158, 160, 282
Burton, Richard ...... 295, 384
Burundi ........................ 168
Bush, George W.............. 393
Buto ................................. 8
Buwayhids ...................... 51
Byzantine province of Africa .. 39
Byzantine(s) ......... 37, 66, 160
Byzantium ...................... 25

# C

Caesarea ................... 32, 87
Caesarea Maritima .......... 23
Cagayan Sulu ................. 244
Cairo  8, 35, 42, 51, 54, 66, 69, 71, 73, 87, 88, 94, 96, 98, 102, 103, 104, 144, 146, 189, 205, 209, 210, 216, 271, 284, 313, 334, 336, 389, 392
Calicut  104, 124, 125, 134, 195, 291

Cambay ... 123, 189, 190, 225, 233, 241, 250, 291
Cambodia ....... 216, 222, 253
Cambyses II ......... 10, 16, 35
Cameroun ..................... 198
Cameroun mountains ...... 200
Camp David Agreement of 1979 ........................... 351
Canaanites ............... 10, 28
Canada ................... 327, 392
Canal Company ............. 347
Canal Zone ........... 313, 341
Canary Islands ............... 310
Candace, Queen ............. 173
Cannanore ............. 124, 189
Canning, Lord, Viceroy ... 131
Canton ..... 223, 225, 228, 291
Cape Colony .................. 300
Cape of Good Hope  104, 134
Cape route .................... 302
Cape Verde .................... 195
Cape Verde Islands ......... 299
Capes Blanco ................. 310
Capitulations ................. 262
Carchemish ..................... 14
Carimon Islands ............. 241
Carthage .............. 12, 30, 39
Carthaginian-Phoenician ... 12
Carthaginian(s)  10, 12, 203 see also Phoenicians
Caspian Sea ... 16, 51, 66, 137, 139, 142
Castelfranco .................. 281
Castile . 93, 112, 114, 158, 207
Catechetical School .......... 23
Catherine of Braganza ..... 131
Catholic counterparts see Uniate bodies
Caucasia ....................... 293
Caucasus ................. 263, 318
Cazorla ......................... 114
Cebu ...................... 250, 259
Celebes .................. 219, 247
Central Asia ............. 17, 225
Ceram .......................... 304
Cesme .......................... 269
Ceylon .. 66, 123, 148, 195 and see Sri Lanka
Chad ............................ 198
Chakcharan ................... 389
Chaldaea ........................ 14

Chaldiran .............. 104, 161
Cham .................... 252, 253
Chamba ...... 223, 235 *see also* Champa
Champa .......... 225, 235, 291
Chan ......................... 253
Chandiri ..................... 123
Ch'ang-an .............. 226, 228
Changwat ..................... 252
Chao Phraya ................. 222
Charlemagne ....... 17, 44, 81
Charles II ................... 131
Châteaubriand, François Auguste-René de .. 293, 295
Chau Sri Bangsa ............ 241
Chaul ........................ 104
Chay Chetta II, King ...... 253
Cheesman, R.E. .............. 296
Chenab River ................ 119
Cheng Ho . 146, 189, 230, 239
Cheribon ..................... 244
Chilaw ....................... 125
China 21, 40, 63, 66, 123, 124, 146, 148, 161, 222, 225, 235, 239, 250, 291, 293
Chindwin ..................... 222
Chinese .......... 28, 233, 249
Chinese coins ................ 189
Ching Manchu dynasty ... 230
Chinghis Khan . 142, 144, 156, 357
Christ, baptism ............. 66
Christian shrines ........... 66
Christianity ....... 23, 128, 308
Christians .. 28, 49, 61, 65, 80, 81, 115, 269, 366
Chu'an-chou ................. 228
Churchill, Winston .. 331, 334
Cilicia ................... 84, 325
Cioromandel .................. 291
Circassians ....... 98, 102, 366
Cire perdue (lost-wax) method 210
Citadel (in Cairo) . 94, 98, 102
Clement III ................... 83
Clermont ...................... 83
Clinton, Bill ................. 383
Cloves .................. 168, 304
Cochin ........................ 134
Cochrane, Thomas ......... 281
Coen, Jan Pieterszoon, Governor-General ....... 304

Coin finds .................... 189
Coinage ........................ 80
Colombo 125, 134, 195 *see also* Kalanbu
Communists .................. 231
Comorian Sultanates ....... 182
Comoro Islands ...... 185, 308
Compagnie Universelle du Canal Maritime de Suez 287
Congo ......................... 168
Conrad III ..................... 87
Constantine the Great 23, 105
Constantinople 83, 84, 87, 146, 147, 151, 153, 158, 161
Continental Divide ......... 219
Copper mines ................ 210
Coptic ................. 37, 66, 81
Coptic Egyptians ............ 181
Copts .................... 81, 366
Córdoba .. 48, 67, 73, 76, 112, 114
Cornwall ....................... 12
Coromandel Coast .......... 291
Corsica .................. 71, 273
Côte d'Ivoire ................ 198
Crete ........ 44, 263, 273, 281
Crimea ............ 155, 160, 265
Croatia ....................... 376
Crusade, Second ............. 87
Crusade, Third ............... 87
Crusade, Fourth ............. 87
Crusade, Fifth ............... 87
Crusade, Sixth ............... 87
Crusade, Seventh ............ 87
Crusades, Crusaders .... 42, 102
Currency ..................... 182
Cyprus ............ 12, 37, 327, 334
Cyrenaica ................ 39, 334
Cyrus II .............. 16, 30, 35

# D

Da Covilhã, Pero ............ 293
Da Gama, Cristovão ....... 190
Da Gama, Vasco .... 104, 134, 190, 194
Daendels, Herman Willem 257
Dagroian ..................... 237
Dahlak ....................... 179
Dahomey .... 202, 216 *see also* Benin
Dakar ......................... 200
D'Albuquerque, Affonso . 244

D'Albuquerque, Braz ...... 239
Damaghan .................... 125
Daman ........................ 136
Damascus 8, 32, 39, 40, 46, 48, 81, 84, 87, 94, 110, 144, 151, 158, 185, 282, 291
Damascus Gate ............. 107
Danakil ....................... 190
Dane .......................... 293
Danube River ............... 269
Dara ..................... 25, 179
Dardanelles ..... 282, 318, 324
Darfur ........................ 214
Darius I ...................... 284
Dariya .................. 276, 316
David, King ............. 14, 105
Dawaru (Dowaro) .......... 179
Dawit ......................... 179
Dawlat Abad ................ 123
Dayr al-Bahri .................. 8
Days of Ignorance ........... 27
De Barros, João ............. 239
De Brito ...................... 244
De Compostela, Santiago 76, 112
De' Conti, Nicolo .......... 291
De Lesseps, Ferdinand-Marie . 284, 287
De Lusignan, Guy ........... 87
De Santo Stefano, Hieronimo 291
De Sévérac, Jordain ........ 291
De Sequeira, Diogo Lopes 241
De Varthema, Ludovico . 291, 293
Deccan ..... 126, 129, 130, 250
Declaration of Principles on Interim Self-Government .... 383
Delhi .. 74, 100, 123, 130, 151, 158, 237
Delta, Nile ............... 71, 341
Demak ...... 243, 244, 246, 247
Derna ......................... 274
Devundara *see* Dinawar
Dhar *see* Zihar
Dharmapatam ............... 124
Dhibat al-Mahal ............ 125
Dia Kossoi ................... 203
Diamonds .................... 202
Dias (Kings) ................. 203
Diaspora ..................... 327

*401*

Dinawar .......................... 125
Diorux .......................... 185
Dipo Negoro, Prince ....... 307
Diredawa ...................... 338
Disraeli, Benjamin .......... 287
Diu ...................... 134, 136
Djibouti ........................ 336
Dome of the Rock, Jerusalem 40, 81, 105
Dongola  39, 173, 181, 182, 279
Dorylaeum ..................... 84
Dotawo ......................... 182
Doughty, Charles Montagu .... 295
Dragut .......................... 274
Druse ... 63, 81, 354, 364, 366
Dual Control ................. 311
Dubai ........................... 353
Dutch  246, 249, 252, 255, 302, 304
Dutch East India Company ... 304
Dutch East Indies ........... 307
Dutch merchants ............ 253
Dutch records ................ 244
Dyaks ........................... 247
Dzungaria ..................... 226

# E

Earthquake of 1303 ........ 146
East Africa .................... 209
East Bengal ................... 115
East India Company ....... 130
East Indies Companies .... 353
East Jerusalem ............... 343
East Pakistan ................. 115
East Timor ............. 136, 216
East Turkistan ........ 230, 231
Eastern Ladakh .............. 233
Eaton, William .............. 274
Ecbatana (Hamadan) ....... 16
Edessa ................. 87, 88, 158
Edessa, County of .......... 84
Edirne .................. 160, 324
Edomites ....................... 30
Egypt   1, 4, 10, 14, 16, 35, 66, 73, 87, 93, 94, 100, 107, 147, 151, 153, 158, 160, 161, 216, 260, 262, 284, 293, 318, 327, 341, 345, 351
Egypt, armies ................ 343
Egypt, population ........... 370

Egyptian fleet ................ 104
Egyptian Hieroglyphic ...... 30
Egyptians ....................... 37
El Cid ........................... 78
Elamites ........................ 28
Elizabeth, Empress of Russia . 296
England  114, 210, 304 see also Britain
English ......................... 119
English Crusaders ........... 114
Epiphany ....................... 66
Erzerum ........................ 318
Eskender ...................... 179
Ethiopia 30, 144, 146, 152-153, 173, 279, 288, 313, 334, 336
Ethiopian guerillas .......... 336
Ethiopians ................ 81, 366
Etruscan ........................ 30
Eudoxus of Cyzicus ......... 21
Eugenie, Empress ........... 287
Euphrates River ......... 12, 96
Eusebius Pamphili .......... 23

# F

Fakanur (Bacanor) ......... 124
Falémé River ................ 203
Fansur .......................... 237
Far East ........................ 209
Farghana ............. 40, 57, 59
Fars ......... 16, 151, 158, 163
Faruq ........................... 313
Fas ............................... 56
Fasilidas, Emperor ......... 192
Fatima .................... 40, 71
Fatimid  51, 57, 59, 63, 67, 73, 84, 203
Fatimid Caliphate ............ 69
Fatimid Shi'ism ............... 94
Fattan .......................... 125
Faysal, King of Saudi Arabia . 331, 338, 369
Fazughli ....................... 279
Feitorias (factories) ........ 194
Ferdinand I ................... 114
Feodosiya see Kaffa
Ferghana ...................... 225
Ferlec (Perlak) ........ 223, 237
Fez 54, 100, 148, 152, 207, 209, 263, 265, 267
Fez el-Bali .................... 207
Fez el-Jadid .................. 207

Fezzan ......................... 210
Filali ............................ 265
Firdawsi ........................ 74
First Cataract ................ 173
First Zionist Congress ..... 329
Five Pillars of the Faith .. 384
Flanders ........................ 84
Florence ....................... 147
Florence, Council of ....... 180
Flores .................... 219, 304
Fodio, Usman dan .. 216, 289
Fort Jesus of Mombasa .. 183, 195, 196, 300
Fort Nassau .................. 304
France . 48, 83, 114, 146, 210, 318, 325, 357, 392, 393
Frankincense .................. 10
Frederick II .................... 87
Free French Forces ......... 354
Freetown ...................... 200
French .................. 257, 267
French consul ................ 300
French influence ............ 307
French Somaliland ......... 336
Fuad I, King ................. 313
Fuchow ........................ 228
Fujairah ........................ 353
Funj ............................. 279
Fustat ........................... 35
Futa Jallon ................... 216

# G

Gabes ............................ 73
Gabriel .......................... 28
Gades (Cadiz) ................ 12
Galawdewos, Emperor ... 190, 191
Galicia ................... 112, 114
Gallabat ....................... 336
Galle ............... 125 see Qali
Galuh ........................... 244
Gambia ................. 198, 300
Gandamak .................... 358
Gandhar ....................... 123
Ganges River ......... 100, 119
Gao ......... 203, 205, 210, 288
Gaugamela ..................... 17
Gaul ............................. 12
Gayo ............................ 243
Gaza City (Ghazzah) ...... 381
Gaza Strip ....... 343, 379, 381
Ge'ez ............................ 30

Genghis Khan ................ 144
Genoa ....... 87, 100, 147, 207
Geography (Claudius
   Ptolemy's) .................... 27
Georgia ................. 137, 158
Georgians ................. 81, 366
German Consul ............. 300
German East Africa ....... 302
Germans ..................... 142
Germany ... 83, 114, 301, 302,
   318, 392, 393
Ghana ....... 73, 198, 203, 205
Ghana, Ancient ............. 201
Ghassan ..................... 19, 27
Ghazi (title) ................... 74
Ghazi I ......................... 338
Ghazna (Ghazni) ......... 74, 98
Ghaznavids ............... 61, 76
Ghazzu ........................ 353
Ghiyath al-Din ............. 125
Ghuri see Muhammad Ghuri
Ghurids ................... 98, 100
Ghuzz Turkmans ............. 98
Gibraltar ..................... 17, 39
Gideon Force ................ 336
Giralda Tower ................ 93
Giri (Gresik) ............ 246, 247
Giza ............................. 96
Goa .. 125, 134, 136, 194, 195,
   291
Godfrey de Bouillon ........ 84
Golan Heights . 348, 351, 372
Golconda ..................... 126
Gold ....... 73, 200, 205, 210
Golden Horde ................ 296
Goloconda ................... 129
Gondar ........................ 194
Gorbachov, Mikhail ....... 360
Gordon, Charles George   214,
   302, 315
Goths ........................... 49
Grañ, Ahmad ......... 179, 190
Granada  78, 112, 114, 147, 152
Great Britain ..... 357 see also
   Britain
Great Khan ............. 146, 163
Great Mosque of Córdoba  49,
   69, 114
Great Mosque of Kairouan  56
Great Mosque of Tlemcen   71
Great Rift Valley ........... 168

Greece . 4, 189, 281, 318, 327,
   334
Greek Alphabet ............... 30
Greek Orthodox ............ 366
Greek schools ............... 270
Greeks . 81, 119, 189, 269, 366
Gregory X ...................... 88
Gresik . 241, 243, 304 see also
   Giri
Guilans ........................ 250
Guiné .................... 195, 198
Guinea ........... 198, 210, 299
Guinea-Bissau ............... 308
Gujarat ..... 100, 126, 225, 235
Gujarati merchants ........ 250
Gujaratis ..................... 189
Gulf of Aqaba ............... 348
Gulf of Guinea ............... 12
Gulf of Sidra ................ 274
Gulf of Thailand ........... 219
Gums .......................... 200
Gur-e Amir .................. 158
Gurgan ........................ 156
Gwalior ................. 100, 123

# H

Habasha ...................... 179
Habashi ...................... 180
Habsburg ............... 262, 263
Hadhramawt ................. 66
Hadith (traditional saying) .....
   110
Hadrian ....................... 105
Hadya ......................... 179
Hafsid(s) ............... 100, 207
Hagar ................... 27, 108
Hagia Sophia ......... 267, 276
Haifa ............................ 87
Hail ............................ 316
Haile Selassie I ............. 336
Hainan ........................ 228
Hajj ............................ 384
Hakam II ...................... 69
Hama .................... 144, 158
Hamdan Qarmat .............. 63
Hammad ....................... 73
Hammadid ..................... 73
Hammurabi ..................... 8
Hanafi madhhab ........... 231
Hangchow ................... 228
Hanno .......................... 12
Hanse towns ................ 144

Haram (Sacred Enclosure) 108
Haram al-Sharif ........ 81, 105
Harar ............ 190, 191, 313
Harim .......................... 144
Harun al-Rashid .. 42, 44, 56,
   284
Hasan, Sultan .... 32, 104, 265
Hashashun .................... 395
Hassan ibn al-Numan al-
   Ghassani .................... 39
Hassan Udin ................. 305
Hat Yai ........................ 253
Hatshepsut ...................... 8
Hatti-sherif ................... 284
Hausa .......................... 205
Haw Muslims ............... 252
Hazaras ................. 358, 389
Hebrew ............... 16, 30, 366
Hebron ................... 14, 381
Hejaz .............. 27, 59, 316
Hejaz railway ............... 321
Hellenic cultural empire .... 17
Hellenism ....................... 4
Henry the Navigator  194, 195
Heraclius ....................... 32
Herat ................... 156, 165
Herod Agrippa I ....... 96, 105
Herod I, the Great ......... 105
Herodotus ....................... 4
Herzl, Theodor ............. 329
Hierakonpolis .................. 8
Hijra (migration) ....... 32, 110
Hili ............................. 124
Hilu ............................ 123
Himalayas ........ 115, 119, 142
Himyar .......................... 27
Himyaritic ..................... 30
Hinawr (Honavar) ... 123, 125
Hindu  100, 115, 123, 128, 130,
   253
Hindu-Buddhist ............. 244
Hindu caste system ........ 123
Hindu culture ............... 244
Hindu Kush  17, 115, 387, 389
Hindu raja ................... 136
Hindu temples ................ 74
Hindu territory ............. 123
Hindu zamorin .............. 124
Hinduism . 100, 123, 131, 222,
   223
Hisham II ...................... 76

Hispano-Arabs ................ 49
Hitler, Adolf .................. 338
Hittin ........................... 88
Hittites ........................... 8
Hitu ............................ 305
Hoamoal ...................... 305
Hoggar ........................ 203
Holland ................. 257, 307
Holocaust ..................... 330
Holy Family ............. 35, 96
Holy Land ................... 293
Holy League of 1684 ....... 265
Holy Places of Islam ....... 291
Holy See ...................... 146
Holy Sepulchre 81, 83, 84, 105, 107, 269
Holy Sepulchre, Basilica of .... 107
Holy War .. 179 *see also* Jihad
Homs ........................... 158
Hormuz Island ........ 195, 353
Horns of Hittin ............... 94
Howara ........................ 203
Huang Ch'ao ................. 223
Hui .............................. 228
Hui Autonomous Region of Ningsia 231 *see also* Ningsia
Hui-hui ........................ 231
Hulagu Khan 54, 142, 144, 161
Humabon ..................... 259
Hungary ............ 160, 265, 269
Hurgronje, Christiaan Snouck 295
Husayn (descendant of Muhammad) ................ 32
Husayn (envoy of Samudra) .... 225
Husayn ibn Ali .............. 273
Husaynid dynasty ........... 273
Hussein, King of Jordan .. 107
Hussein, Saddam ..... 357, 369
Hyksos .......................... 10

# I

Ibadhis ................. 366, 390
Iberian alphabet ............... 30
Iberian Peninsula ....... 46, 112
Iblis ............................ 384
Ibn Abd al-Wahhab, Muhammad ................ 276
Ibn Abi-Amir, Muhammad 76
Ibn Abu-Sufyan ............... 32

Ibn Affan, Uthman ......... 110
Ibn al-Husayn, Tahir ....... 59
Ibn al-Idhari ................... 76
Ibn Battuta 102, 120, 123-125, 146-148, 150, 180, 205, 209, 228, 235, 237
Ibn Hanbal, Ahmad ........ 316
Ibn Hawqal ............... 65, 66
Ibn Juzayy ................... 148
Ibn Khaldun 96, 100, 153, 181, 205
Ibn Majid, Ahmad ......... 189
Ibn Mawlana of Pasai ..... 243
Ibn Maymun, Musa ......... 94
Ibn Nafi, Uqbah ............. 39
Ibn Nusayr, Musa ............ 39
Ibn Saud (Wahhabi chieftain) . 269, 276
Ibn Sa'ud, King ...... 108, 110
Ibn Sina ........................ 61
Ibn Tashfin, Yusuf .......... 80
Ibn Tughluq, Muhammad ...... 123, 126
Ibn Tulun, Ahmad 57, 59, 96
Ibn Tumart, Muhammad .. 91
Ibn Ziyad, Tariq ............. 39
Ibrahim (Bahraini Shahbandar) 124
Ibrahim (qadi) ............... 246
Ibrahim ibn al-Aghlab . 44, 56
Ibrahim ibn Muhammad al-Istakri ....................... 96
Ibrahim Lodi .......... 123, 127
Ibrahim of Minangkabau, Shaykh ..................... 243
Ibrahim Pasha . 276, 281, 282, 313, 316
Ibrahim, King ................ 253
Ibrahim, Raja ................ 239
Id al-Adha ............. 108, 384
Idris I, King ................. 341
Idris ibn Abdallah ........... 56
Ifat .............................. 179
Ife .............................. 205
Ifriqiya ................... 44, 100
Ihram ........................... 384
Ikhshidids ................. 57, 59
Il-Khanids .................... 161
Iltumish ....................... 120
Imperial British East Africa Company ................... 302
Imperial Rome .............. 189

Imperial Russia ............... 17
India . 17, 21, 40, 61, 66, 104, 115, 123, 134, 146, 148, 185, 209, 291, 318, 334, 358, 389
Indian Army .................. 131
Indian Muslim mystics .... 244
Indian Ocean 21, 134, 146, 219
Indo-China ................... 216
Indo-Gangetic Plain ......... 115
Indonesia . 136, 146, 216, 225, 247, 288, 302, 305, 307, 389, 389, 390, 392
Indragiri ....................... 241
Indus River .......... 1, 40, 119
Inhamarungo ................. 308
Institute of Egypt ........... 299
Intifada ....................... 383
Iran .......... 16, 357, 366, 372
Iranians ................. 354, 395
Iranun ......................... 259
Iraq 32, 51, 74, 141, 147, 151, 153, 158, 263, 316, 325, 341, 345, 357, 366, 369, 372, 379
Iraq, British Mandate ..... 327
Iraqi .............. 226, 369, 395
Iraq-Iran War ............... 357
Irrawaddy .................... 222
Isam Awwad ................ 107
Isfahan .. 51, 74, 90, 158, 167, 237
Ishaq al-Saheli ............... 288
Ishaq II, Sharif Ahmad al-Mansur of Morocco ..... 210
Ishmael .................... 27, 28
Iskandar Muda, Sultan .. 241, 243
Islam 23, 26, 65, 128, 131, 308, 384
Islambet (Islamge) ........... 192
Isma'il ....... 61, 108, 165, 167
Isma'il Kamil Pasha ........ 279
Ismail Pasha, Khedive (Viceroy) ................... 311
Ismaili ......................... 354
Ismaili Mountain Tajik ... 387
Ismailis ... 63, 71, 81, 231, 366
Israel ................... 347, 383
Israel government, 1947 ... 379
Israelites ................. 14, 61
Istanbul ... 274, 282, 293, 318, 324

404

Italy  46, 73, 210, 273, 301, 357, 393
Ithna'asharis .................. 366
Ivan IV (the Terrible), Tsar .... 296
Iyasu I, the Great ........... 194
Iznik (Nicaea) ................. 90

# J

Jabal al-Tariq ................. 39
Jaen ........................... 114
Jaffa ........................... 87
Jahangir ................. 128, 129
Jahangir Khoja ............... 231
Jakarta ................. 243, 304
Jakarta/Batavia ............... 136
Jalal al-Din Firuz Khalji .. 120
Jalalabad ...................... 387
Jamal al-Din Muhammad b. Hasan ........................ 123
Jambi ............. 241, 243, 305
James, Apostle ............... 112
Jamiat-e-Islami ............... 387
Janatepa ...................... 249
Janissaries ..................... 273
Janissary corps ............... 269
Japanese ................. 307, 334
Japara ................. 243, 244
Jata ........................... 156
Jaunpur ....................... 123
Java  136, 195, 219, 222, 225, 233, 237, 241, 243, 246, 247, 257, 291, 304, 305
Java Sea ...................... 219
Java War ...................... 307
Javanese ...................... 239
Jawa (Sumatra) .. 125, 237 *see also* Sumatra
Jebusites ...................... 105
Jenné ................... 198, 216
Jericho ........................ 381
Jerusalem  19, 32, 57, 66, 81, 83, 84, 87, 94, 104, 105, 389
Jerusalem, Walls ............. 105
Jesuit colleges ................ 270
Jesuit mission ................ 192
Jesus .......................... 105
Jewish community (in Alexandria) ................. 19
Jewish national home ..... 325
Jewish quarter (in Babilyun) ... 96

Jewish scholarship (in Tiberias) 66
Jewish settlements ............ 28
Jewish Square Hebrew Alphabet ..................... 30
Jewish State .................. 329
Jews  16, 65, 81, 84, 269, 327, 329, 330, 366, 370
Jhelum River ................. 119
Jibal ........................... 151
Jihad ........ 190, 289, 318, 395
Jizya .......................... 181
Joel, King .................... 182
Jogjakarta ....... 257, 305, 307
John II, Pope ................. 46
Johore  241, 243, 247, 249, 255, 259
Jolo ........................... 259
Jordan  327, 341, 343, 345, 348, 351, 379, 381,
Jordan River ................. 348
Jordan, armies ............... 343
Jubayr ........................ 147
Judaea ......................... 19
Judah ........................... 14
Judaism .................. 23, 366
Judar Pasha .................. 210
Judges ......................... 14
Julfa .......................... 167
Junk Ceylon *see* Phuket
Jurfattan ..................... 124
Jurjan ......................... 61
Justin II, Emperor ........... 25
Justinian I ............. 105, 174

# K

Ka'aba ............. 28, 108, 384
Kaarta ................. 216, 289
Kabangpasu .................. 252
Kabul ......................... 387
Kachee ........................ 233
Kadmos, son of Agenor ... 28
Kaffa (Feodosiya) ........... 155
Kahinah (prophetess) ....... 39
Kahlenberg ................... 263
Kaifeng ....................... 228
Kairouan  37, 39, 48, 56, 57, 71, 207
Kajarra ....................... 123
Kalah ......................... 223
Kalanbu (Colombo) ........ 125
Kampar ................. 241, 249

Kanauj ................. 100, 123
Kanchow ..................... 230
Kandahar ............... 167, 387
Kandy ........................ 134
Kanem ................. 203, 214
Kanem-Bornu ............... 210
Kankan Mansa Musa .... 102, 205, 209, 288
Kansu ............. 228, 230, 231
Kanz al-Dawla .............. 181
Karanbas ..................... 181
Karatay Madrasa ............ 94
Karim al-Makhdum ........ 257
Karnak ....................... 284
Kars .......................... 318
Kart dynasty ................. 156
Karwan ........................ 39
Kashgaria  231 *and see* Turistan
Kashmir ... 115, 119, 126, 134, 233, 395
Kasim, Raja .................. 239
Kassala ....................... 336
Kassim ....................... 367
Kava .......................... 123
Kawlam ....................... 125
Kayble ........................ 299
Kazakhs ................. 142, 226
Kazakhstan  137, 141, 142, 360, 372
Kedah  223, 235, 241, 249, 250, 252, 255
Kediri ........................ 307
Kelantan ......... 241, 249, 250
Kenya ....... 168, 288, 302, 334
Keren ......................... 336
Kerman ........................ 61
Khalid ibn al-Walid .... 32, 35
Khalifa (caliph)  110, 302, 315
Khalji Turk .................. 120
Khan al-Khalili .............. 144
Khan Yunis .................. 381
Khanates of Khiva ......... 362
Khandesh .................... 126
Khanfu (Canton) ............ 225
Kharijite ...................... 40
Khatib al-Baghdadi ......... 51
Khedive Isma'il Pasha ..... 279
Khiva ................... 137, 298
Khokand ..................... 231
Khomeini, Ayatollah ....... 357

*405*

Khorasan .. 40, 42, 51, 61, 74, 144, 156, 161, 165
Khorasanis .................... 250
Khost ........................... 387
Khumarawayh ................ 59
Khuzistan ..................... 151
Khwarizm .. 40, 147, 156, 225
Khwarizmian Turks ......... 87
Khwarizmians ................. 52
Khyber Pass ................... 358
Kiev .............................. 296
Kilimanjaro .................... 168
Kilwa   146, 151, 183, 189, 250
King of Judaea see Herod
Kipchaq ......................... 102
Kipling, Rudyard .............. 1
Kitchener, H.H. (Earl Kitchener of Khartoum) .... 313, 315
Kizimkazi ...................... 187
Knights Hospitaler ..... 87, 88
Knights of St. John of Rhodes 274
Knights Templar ........ 87, 88
Kokand ......................... 362
Kongo ........................... 194
Konya .................. 90, 94, 282
Koran ......... 42, 59, 61, 308
Kordofan ...................... 279
Korea ............................ 142
Kosovo .................. 160, 376
Kot Montien Ban .......... 247
Kota Mahligai (Pattani) .. 241
Kuala Lumpur ........ 222, 249
Kubilai ......................... 161
Kufa ............................. 153
Kufic inscriptions ........... 187
Kulikovo ....................... 296
Kunakar ....................... 125
Kurdish ............ 71, 366, 372
Kurds ....... 331, 357, 366, 372
Kurti ............................ 279
Kurunagala ................... 125
Kutaya ......................... 282
Kutei ............................ 247
Kutub Mosque ................ 74
Kuwait 316, 353, 367, 369, 370
Kuwait City .................. 369
Kuwil (Aligarh) .............. 123
Kwavi ........................... 170
Kyrghyz .................. 226, 358

Kyrghyz Steppe ..... 1, 51, 296
Kyrghyzstan ........... 137, 360

## L

La Mezquita .................. 49
Labuan ..... 244, 246, 255, 307
Ladino .......................... 366
Lagos ........................... 200
Lake Chad   203, 210, 214, 216
Lake Malawi ................. 308
Lakhm ........................... 27
Lalibela ........................ 175
Lamau .......................... 185
Lambri .......................... 237
Lamori .......................... 291
Lampacau ..................... 293
Lampongs ..................... 307
Lamta ........................... 203
Lamu .............. 182, 190, 288
Lanchow ....................... 230
Landak ......................... 246
Lane-Poole, Stanley ........ 114
Langu ........................... 249
Laos ..................... 216, 222
Las Navas de Tolosa   93, 100, 114
Lasem ........................... 244
Later Aramaic Alphabet ... 30
Later Phoenician Alphabet   30
Later Syriac Alphabet ...... 30
Latin Alphabet ............... 30
Latin America ................ 327
Latin Kingdoms .............. 81
Latins ........................... 366
Lawgiver .......... 262 see also Sulayman I, the Magnificent
Lawrence, T.E................ 296
Layard, Austen Henry ..... 295
League of Nations .. 313, 330, 338, 354
Learned clergy (ulama) .... 392
Lebanon .. 12, 63, 71, 81, 269, 325, 341, 354
Lebanon, armies ............. 343
Lebna Dengel ........ 179, 190
Legazpi ......................... 259
Leh ............................... 233
León .... 67, 93, 112, 114, 207
Leran ............................ 233
Levant .. 12, 81, 146, 147, 293
Lhasa ........................... 233
Liangchow .................... 226

Liberia ...... 198, 202, 300, 302
Libya 1, 96, 273, 341, 372, 390
Libyan Alphabet .............. 30
Libyan Pentapolis ............ 37
Libyans ........................ 395
Lightning War ............... 348
Ligor ............................ 249
Lisbon .................. 114, 180
Little Aden .................... 364
Lobo, Ahmad ................. 289
Lodi ............................. 123
Lokak ........................... 235
Lombok .... 219, 222, 243, 304
Longinus ...................... 173
Lonthor ........................ 304
Lorraine ........................ 84
Louis, King of Holland ... 257
Louis I, the Pious ........... 112
Louis VII ....................... 87
Louis IX ........................ 87
Louis XIV .................... 284
Loyang ......................... 226
Lucca ........................... 147
Lucullus ........................ 19
Lugor ........................... 293
Luristan ........................ 158
Lydians .......................... 28
Lyons ............................ 23

## M

Ma Hua-lung ................. 231
Ma Huan ....... 124, 239, 243
Ma Te-hsin, Imam .......... 230
Maasai .......................... 170
Ma'bar .......................... 125
Macao .................. 136, 195
Macedonia .................... 376
Macina ......................... 216
Madagascar ..... 189, 288, 300
Madinat-al-Nabi see Medina
Madiun ........................ 307
Madrasas ...................... 207
Madura      244, 257, 305
Madurai dynasty ............ 125
Mafia ........................... 288
Magellan, Ferdinand 134, 244, 247, 259
Maghrib ......................... 94
Maghribi ....................... 125
Magi .............................. 66
Maguindanao dynasty ..... 259

406

Mahdi ............. 91, 302, 315
Mahdi's Tomb ............... 279
Mahdist rebellion .......... 279
Mahmud ...................... 241
Mahmud of Ghazna ... 74, 98
Ma-Huan ...................... 239
Mai Idris Alooma .......... 214
Maimonides *see* Ibn Maymun, Musa
Majapahit ....... 235, 243, 244
Makaram ...................... 305
Makasar ........ 247, 257, 304
Makhzumi .................... 177
Makota, Raja ................ 247
Makuria ................ 173, 174
Malabar ................ 124, 189
Malabar Coast ........ 123, 291
Malacca ... 134, 136, 189, 190, 195, 225, 235, 239, 241, 247, 250, 257, 291, 293, 305
Malaccan trade .............. 244
Malaga ......................... 148
Malagueta pepper .......... 202
Malaria ......................... 202
Malatya ........................ 158
Malawi ......................... 168
Malay mercenaries ......... 253
Malay Peninsula ............ 223
Malay states ................. 249
Malaya ................. 216, 219
Malaysia 63, 131, 146, 216, 390
Malayur ....................... 235
Maldives (Maldive Islands) .... 123, 125, 148, 151, 209
Maldivian ..................... 125
Mali . 100, 102, 152, 201, 205, 209, 210, 288
Malik Ibrahim ............... 243
Malik-shah ..................... 88
Malindi .......... 182, 189, 250
Malta .............. 46, 56, 71
Maluku *see* Moluccas
Malwa .................. 123, 126
Mamluk(s) 98, 107, 108, 146, 161, 207, 279, 284
Mandaeans (Sabeans) ...... 366
Mandaic ......................... 30
Mandated Territory of Palestine .................... 381
Mandingo ..................... 205
Mangalore .................... 124
Mangrove ..................... 185

Mangu Khan .......... 144, 161
Manichaeans ....... 65 *and see* Yezidis
Manila .......................... 259
Mansur Shah .................. 239
Mansura ......................... 73
Maqurra ........................ 173
Marathas ....................... 130
Mardin ......................... 158
Mari ................................ 7
Marib ....... 27, 362, 364, 374
Marignolli, John, of Florence . 291
Marinid(s) ....... 102, 148, 207
Marinids of Fez ............. 100
Marj Dabiq ................... 104
Mark (in India) .............. 123
Mark Antony .................. 19
Mark the Evangelist ......... 96
Maronites ....................... 81
Marrakesh . 93, 147, 207, 265, 267
Marsalia (Marseilles) ........ 12
Marw (Merv) .................. 61
Marxist ........................ 364
Masada .......................... 19
Masqat ................. 196, 353
Massina ........................ 289
Maswa .......................... 384
Mataram ................ 244, 305
Mauritania ............. 288, 310
Mazandaran .................. 156
Mazir-I-Sharif ................ 389
Mazrui .......................... 196
Mea Shearim ................. 366
Mecca .. 27, 28, 57, 59, 66, 71, 90, 108, 110, 147, 148, 151, 160, 180, 209, 216, 241, 276, 288, 293, 295, 316, 384, 389
Medersas ...................... 207
Medes ............................ 16
Media ............................ 17
Medina 27, 28, 57, 59, 71, 90, 96, 110, 160, 276, 316, 389
Mediterranean Sea ..... 37, 324
Megat Iskender Shah . 239 *see also* Paramesvara
Megiddo ........................ 94
Mehmed I .................... 161
Mehmed II ................... 161
Mekhong ...................... 222
Meknès ..... 100, 207, 265, 267

Mekong Delta ................ 253
Melaka *see* Malacca
Memphis .................... 8, 96
Menelik ................. 177, 192
Menes .............................. 8
Mergui ......................... 134
Meroe .......................... 173
Mesopotamia . 1, 16, 144, 318, 321
Middle Kingdom ............. 10
Midrarite ....................... 54
Mien ............................ 226
Millet ................... 364, 366
Milosevic, Slobodan ........ 376
Mina ............................ 384
Minangkabau (Padang) .. 243, 247, 249, 305, 307
Mindanao ..................... 259
Ming .................... 228, 230
Minneri-Mandel ............. 125
Miranshah .................... 163
Missolonghi .................. 281
Mithradates .................... 19
Mkanda ........................ 185
Moabites ........................ 30
Modern Arabic Alphabet .. 30
Modern European Alphabets . 30
Modern Hebrew Alphabet  30
Modern Persian Alphabet . 30
Mogadishu 151, 182, 189, 196, 250, 338
Mohammed Daoud Khan  358
Mohammed Zahir Shah .. 387
Moluccas . 134, 195, 219, 246, 250, 257, 291, 304, 305
Mombasa .. 66, 104, 151, 181, 182, 183, 189, 196, 250
Mongol army .................. 54
Mongol composite bows .. 153
Mongol conquest ............ 226
Mongol Hazara .............. 389
Mongol Yuan dynasty ..... 226
Mongolia ......... 137, 144, 231
Mongols 51, 102, 142, 161, 293
Monomotapa ................. 189
Monophysitism .............. 174
Montenegro ........... 318, 376
Morea .......................... 281
Morocco 73, 91, 123, 210, 288, 302, 310, 341, 374
Mosaic concept ................. 1

Moscow .................. 158, 298
Moses ........................... 345
Mosque College ............. 185
Mossi ........................... 205
Mosul ............... 94, 151, 372
Moulay Abd al-Hafid ..... 267
Moulay al-Rashid ........... 265
Mount Moriah ............... 105
Mount Zion ................... 105
Mozambique .... 168, 183, 194, 195, 300, 302, 308
Mu'awiyah .................... 40
Mughul ........... 130, 131, 134
Muhammad, Prophet . 25, 28, 32, 40, 61, 65, 107, 110, 393
Muhammad Abd al-Wahhab .. 316
Muhammad Ahmad ........ 315
Muhammad Al-Sharif ..... 265
Muhammad Ali Pasha ... 269, 279, 281, 282, 284, 289, 299, 276
Muhammad Ali the Great  104
Muhammad Ghuri .. 100, 120
Muhammad I al-Ghalib ... 114
Muhammad II, Sultan ..... 269
Muhammad Kabungsuwan .... 259
Muhammad Reza ........... 338
Muhammad Shah .... 167, 239
Mujahidin ..................... 360
Mul Jawa ... 237 see also Java
Mullah Omar ................. 387
Multan ......................... 74
Murad (Corsican renegade) .... 273
Murad II ....................... 161
Murad III ..................... 263
Murad IV ..................... 263
Muslim Brotherhood ....... 390
Muslim fleet .................. 37
Muslim shrines .............. 108
Muslims   66, 84, 115, 230, 253
Muslims in Thailand ....... 252
Mussolini, Benito ........... 334
Mu'tazilite .................... 61
Mutra .......................... 125
Muzaffar Shah ............... 239
Muzaffarid dynasty ......... 158
Myanmar see Burma

# N

Nabataea ................. 19, 27
Nabataean Alphabet ....... 30
Nablus ........................ 381
Nagarakertagama .......... 235
Nagorny-Karabakh ........ 360
Najd ........................... 73
Nakhon Chronicles ........ 249
Nakhon Sithammarat ..... 134, 249, 250, 293
Naksat ........................ 250
Naksh-e Rostam ............ 63
Nandurbar ................... 123
Nanking ...................... 228
Naod .......................... 179
Naphtha-throwers ......... 42
Naples ........................ 46
Napoleon Bonaparte (Buonaparte) . 35, 257, 269, 271, 284, 295, 307
Napoleonic Wars ........... 300
Napoleon's Egyptian expedition ................. 299
Naqshbandiya Sufis ....... 156
Naratiwat .................... 250
Narbonne ................ 46, 48
Narwar ....................... 123
Nasr ........................... 61
Nasr II ........................ 61
Nasr al-Din .................. 226
Nasrid ........................ 114
Nasser, Gamal Abdel, ('Abd al-Nasr) .... 287, 299, 313, 341, 347-348, 351
National Home (Jewish) .. 330
Nauphlia ..................... 281
Navarre ............... 67, 93, 112
Naysabur (Nishapur) ....... 61
Nazareth ............ 66, 87, 144
Nazi Germany .............. 331
Nea Church ................. 105
Nebi Shu'eib ................ 364
Nebuchadnezzar ........... 105
Negapatam .................. 291
Negri Sembilan ............. 249
Nejd ............... 27, 276, 316
Neo-Ismailis ........ 63 see also Assassins
Neo-Punic Alphabet ....... 30
Neo-Sinaitic Alphabet ..... 30
Nepal .......................... 115

Nestorian Christians ....... 163
Netherlands ....... 357 see also Holland
New Guinea ................. 304
New Julfa .................... 167
New Teaching-Old Teaching controversies 1n 1781 ... 230
New York City ............. 330
New Zealand ................ 324
Niani .......................... 203
Nicaea ........................ 84
Nice ........................... 334
Nicobar Islands ....... 237, 291
Nicopolis ..................... 160
Niebuhr, Carsten ........... 293
Niger ............. 198, 200, 203
Nigeria ..... 198, 202, 210, 214
Nigerian army ............... 338
Nikiu .......................... 35
Nile River  8, 35, 37, 102, 203
Nilotic language ...... 171, 313
Ningpo ....................... 228
Ningsia .................. 228, 230
Nish ........................... 160
Nizam al-Mulk .............. 91
Nizamiyah .......... 63, 69, 91
Njimi .......................... 203
Nobatia ................. 173, 182
Nongchik ............... 249, 252
Nora ........................... 12
Normandy .................... 84
Normans ................. 73, 274
Norse (Norsemen) .......... 296
North Africans .............. 392
North Vietnam .............. 222
Northern Alliance .......... 389
Nuba .......................... 173
Nubia (Sudan) ................. 1
Nubia . 94, 102, 153, 181, 182, 288
Nubian(s) .......... 39, 174, 313
Numidians .................... 49
Nupe .......................... 205
Nur al-Din ................... 94
Nuristanis .................... 358
Nusayris ...................... 81

# O

Occupied Territories within International Law ........ 381
Octavian ...................... 19
Odoric of Pordenone ....... 291

Ogaden .......................... 338
Oil .......... 202, 316, 357, 367
Oil from the Holy Sepulchre .. 147
Oil interests ................... 372
Oil-bearing wilayet ......... 372
Old Cairo ............ 35, 96, 284
Old City of Jerusalem .... 105, 343, 348, 372
Old Hebrew Alphabet ...... 30
Old Kingdom ................... 8
Oman . 66, 151, 187, 195, 196, 269, 295, 353, 390
Omar Sedu Tal ............. 216
Omdurman ...... 279, 302, 315
One Thousand Nights and a Night (title of book) ...... 42
Orange Free State ......... 302
Orenburg ...................... 296
Organisation of African Unity 310
Origen ........................... 23
Ormuz ......................... 250
Oromo .......................... 191
Osh .............................. 360
Ostia ............................. 46
Ottoman ............ 76, 96, 105
Ottoman Empire  260, 353, 364
Ottoman Palestine .......... 370
Ottoman schools ............ 270
Ottoman Turks . 98, 107, 108, 160, 167
Oviedo ......................... 112
Oyo .............................. 205

# P

Pachomius ...................... 23
Padang see Minangkabau
Pahang ..... 235, 241, 249, 250
Pajajaran ................ 136, 243
Pajang ......................... 244
Pakistan  1, 115, 119, 131, 134, 372, 386, 389
Pakistani(s) ............ 252, 392
Paku Buwono II ............. 305
Pakuan ........................ 243
Palawan ....................... 244
Palembang  223, 239, 243, 257, 305, 307
Palestine  12, 94, 108, 147, 160, 325, 327, 330, 341

Palestine Exploration Fund .... 295
Palestine Liberation Organisation (PLO) .... 354, 383
Palestine National Authority (PNA) ....................... 381
Palestine Royal Commission .. 331
Palestinian Arabs ........... 331
Palestinian Christians ...... 379
Palestinian territory (seized) .... 345
Palestinians ................... 379
Palmyra ......................... 27
Palmyrene Alphabet ......... 30
Pamirs .......................... 387
Panarukan ..................... 244
Panconia (Pegu) ............. 291
Panderani ..................... 124
Panembahan Yusuf, Sultan .... 244
Panipat ................. 123, 127,
Panthay Muslims ........... 233
Pantheon ....................... 19
Paramesvara ................. 239
Paris ............................. 87
Paris, Conference of   313, 325, 372
Parkau ......................... 263
Parliament (British) ........ 131
Parthia ........................ 189
Party Kings .................... 78
Parvan ......................... 123
Pasai ............. 225, 239, 241
Pasargadae .................... 16
Pasha of Acre see Muhammad Ali ........................... 281
Pashtuns ................ 358, 387
Pasuruan ...................... 244
Patah ........................... 243
Pate ......... 182, 185, 194, 196
Patem .......................... 291
Patriarch of Alexandria ... 83, 181
Patriarch of Antioch ........ 83
Patriarch of Jerusalem ...... 83
Pattani  134, 241, 250, 252, 255, 293
Pattani United Liberation Organisation (Pulo) ..... 253
Peace Conference, 1919 ... 331

Peace of Amiens ............. 257
Pedir ........................... 291
Peel Report ................... 331
Peel, Earl ...................... 331
Pegu ............................ 291
Peking (Beijing) ...... 151, 228
Pemba Island .... 66, 168, 185, 187, 288
Penang .......... 246, 249, 255
Pentagon (U.S.)............... 393
Perak ..................... 241, 249
Peregrinão ..................... 293
Perim ........................... 123
Periplus of the Erythraean Sea  21, 185
Peristroika ..................... 360
Perlak see Ferlec
Perlis ........................... 249
Persepolis ................ 16, 293
Persia (Iran)   1, 17, 25, 35, 66, 71, 123, 137, 141, 144, 146, 263, 293, 357
Persian Alphabet ............. 30
Persian Gulf .. 16, 21, 63, 131, 141, 190, 269, 316, 334, 341, 374
Persian Ismaili Assassin .... 91
Persian mystics ............... 390
Persian oil ..................... 287
Persian rulers .................. 54
Persian settlement ........... 51
Persian traders .............. 233
Persians . 42, 52, 61, 119, 142, 189, 225, 250
Peshawar ....................... 74
Peter ............................. 96
Peter I of Aragon ............ 80
Petra ............................. 27
Phanrang ...................... 223
Pharaoh Necho II ........... 284
Pharaonic canal .............. 37
Phattalung .................... 249
Philadelphia .................. 274
Philby, Harry St. John Bridger 296
Philip .......................... 173
Philip Augustus ............... 87
Philippines . 216, 225, 250, 259
Philippopolis ................. 160
Philo of Alexandria ......... 23
Phnom Penh ................. 253
Phoenicia ...................... 28

409

Phoenicians .............. 1, 10, 12
Phru ........................... 249
Phuket ................. 250, 255
Piacenza ....................... 83
Pictographic writing ........ 28
Pilgrimage .................... 66
Pilgrims ..................... 386
P'ing-nan Kuo ............. 230
Pinto, Fernão Mendez .... 293
Piracy ................. 271, 353
Pires, Tomé 189, 239, 250, 293
Pisa . 84, 87, 94, 100, 147, 207
Platt, General .............. 336
Poland ................. 263, 330
Polisario Front Government ..
 310
Polit (Perlis) ................ 252
Poll Tax ..................... 130
Polo brothers ................. 88
Polo, Marco .... 146-147, 223,
 228, 235, 237
Pontianak ................... 307
Pontus .......................... 19
Pope (obedience to) ........ 366
Port St. John ............... 189
Porte .......................... 279
Portugal ... 104, 114, 212, 299,
 302
Portuguese 134, 136, 243, 246,
 252, 262, 263, 284, 304, 308
Portuguese authors ......... 249
Postal service, Arab ........ 40
Pre-Chalcedonians .......... 366
Prester John ................. 180
Prince of Mecca ............ 282
Principé ..................... 300
Pro-Nazi ..................... 338
Proto-Sinaitic/Canaanite ... 30
Provence ...................... 84
Ptolemies ..................... 17
Ptolemy, Claudius ...... 26, 27
Ptolemy Philadelphus ...... 284
Pudupattana ................. 124
Pulangi ....................... 259
Punic Alphabet .............. 30
Punic Wars ................... 12
Punjab ............... 17, 74, 100
Punjabi (language) ......... 119
Punt ........................... 21
Purig .......................... 233
Pushto ....................... 119

Puttalum ..................... 125
PWNT ........................... 8
Pygmalion .................... 12
Pyramids ..................... 96
Pyrenees ...................... 40

# Q

Qadi .......................... 246
Qadiriya tariqa ............. 207
Qajar dynasty ............... 338
Qal'a Beni Hammad ........ 73
Qala'un ................. 102, 181
Qali .......................... 125
Qalidurat of Nubia, King 175
Qanbalu ....................... 66
Qansawh al-Ghawri ........ 262
Qaramanli ................... 273
Qarmatian ................ 61, 63
Qasba .......................... 73
Qatar ......................... 353
Qayrawan ..................... 39
Qayt Bay ................ 98, 104
Queen of Saba (Sheba) .... 177
Quelimane ................... 183
Quilon ........................ 125
Quqa (Goga) ................ 123
Qur'an ..... 383 *and see* Koran
Qurtabah, see Córdoba
Qutb al-din Aybak .. 100, 120
Qutb al-Din Mubarak ..... 120
Qutb Mosque ............... 165

# R

Rabat ................ 73, 93, 102
Raffles, Stamford ... 246, 255,
 257
Rahmat ....................... 243
Rai Pithaura ................ 100
Rama Daw (Ram Deo) ... 124
Ramallah ..................... 381
Raman ................. 249, 252
Ramkamhaeng ............... 247
Ramla .......................... 84
Rangae ................. 249, 252
Rangoon ..................... 233
Ras al-Khaimah ............ 353
Ras Mkumbu ................ 185
Rashid Ali al-Ghaylani ... 338
Rashidi ...................... 316
Rasiyyat al-Din ............. 120
Rattanakosin ................ 249
Ravi River .................. 119

Rawlinson, Henry Creswicke ..
 295
Raymond I .................... 84
Raymond IV .................. 84
Rayy ........................... 74
Reconquisita ................ 114
Red Sea 37, 98, 284, 334, 336
Revolution, Northern Yemen,
 1962 ....................... 364
Reza Khan ................... 338
Reza Shah ................... 338
Rhodes ................. 260, 281
Riau Archipelago .......... 249
Ribat ..................... 53, 80
Richard I of England ....... 87
Rihla ......................... 148
Río de Oro .................. 310
Robert College ............. 270
Robinson, Edward .......... 295
Roda .......................... 102
Roderick ...................... 39
Rokan ........................ 241
Romanus IV Diogenes ..... 88
Rome . 12, 23, 46, 83, 96, 105
Rommel, Erwin ............. 334
Ronda ............... 91, 147, 152
Royal Air Force ............ 338
Rubber ....................... 202
Rufiji River ................. 182
Rufiji delta .................. 190
Ruiyadh ...................... 316
Rukn al-Dawlah .............. 51
Rum (Rome) .................. 90
Run ........................... 304
Russia . 66, 102, 141, 146-147,
 265, 282, 284, 293, 296, 318,
 327, 330, 366
Russian Federal Treaty ... 360
Russian Federation ......... 389
Russian military advisers . 351
Russians ..................... 142
Rustamids .................... 54
Ruvuma River . 168, 182, 183,
 196
Ruwenzori ................... 168
Rwanda ...................... 168

# S

Saad Zaghul ................. 313
Sa'adi ........................ 141
Saba (Java or Sumatra) ... 27,
 291, 362

Sabaean .............. 30, 65, 362
Sabah .................. 216
Sadat, Anwar *see* Al-Sadat, Anwar
Safa .................. 384
Safayids ............. 161, 165
Saffarids .............. 59, 61
Safi IV .................. 167
Sagres .................. 194
Sahara ......... 4, 57, 73, 203
Sahara, desiccation of ....... 8
Sahrani Arab Democratic Republic ............. 310
Saiburi ......... 249, 250, 252
Sa'id ibn Sultan ............ 196
Said Pasha .............. 287
St. Paul's outside the Walls 46
St. Peter .................. 46
St. Tomé .................. 299
Saint Vassily Church ....... 298
Sakhalin Island ........... 298
Sakura .................. 288
Saladin (Salah al-Din Yusuf) .. 71, 87, 94, 97
Salé .................. 207
Salt .................. 73, 200
Salween .................. 222
Saman .................. 61
Samanids ............. 59, 61
Samaritan .................. 30
Samarqand 61, 137, 156, 158, 225-226, 362
Samarra ........ 44, 52, 54, 151
Sambas .............. 246, 307
Samudra ... 223, 233, 237, 247
Sanchão .................. 293
Sandapur (Goa) ...... 123, 125
Sanhaja Berber .............. 73
Sankore Mosque .......... 210
Santander .................. 112
Saqqara .................. 96
Saragossa .................. 114
Sarawak .... 216, 246, 304, 307
Sardinia ........ 12, 46, 71, 152
Sarha .................. 237
Sarsa Dengel ............. 192
Sassanian-Islamic coin finds ... 183
Sassanian-Islamic pottery . 183
Satrap system ............. 16
Satun .............. 249, 252

Saudi Arabia ... 108, 316, 341, 374
Saudi family ............... 316
Savoy .................. 334
Sayf al-Din Abdallah ...... 181
Sayyid Ajall Shams al-Din 'Umar .............. 226
Sayyid Said of Muscat and Zanzibar ......... 187, 300
Sciamuthera ............. 291
Sea Peoples ............... 10
Secure borders ............ 383
Seetzen, U.I. .............. 295
Segu .................. 216
Sejarah Melayu ............ 239
Selangor .................. 249
Seleucids .................. 17
Selim I the Grim .... 104, 161, 260, 262
Selim II, the Sot ............ 263
Seljuq (Seljuk) Turks .. 51, 76, 81
Seljuq dynasty of Syria ..... 90
Seljuq Tughril Beg .......... 51
Seljuq Tughril Beg ...... 51, 88
Seljuqs ......... 73, 84, 87, 90
Semarang .................. 305
Semiramis .............. 291
Semitic origin .................. 7
Semitic Languages ...... 28, 30
Sena .............. 183, 308
Senegal ......... 80, 198, 299
Senegal River ... 200, 203, 212
Sennar .................. 279
Senussi .................. 390
September 11th 2001 ....... 393
Seram .................. 219
Serbia .............. 160, 318, 376
Seti I .................. 284
Seville ......... 48, 93, 114, 189
Shabwa .................. 374
Shafi'i rite .................. 237
Shah Abbas ............. 167
Shah Jahan ........... 128, 129
Shah Sulayman I ........... 167
Shah Sultan Husayn ....... 167
Shahanshah ............. 51
Shahbandars .............. 250
Shahrukh .................. 165
Shajar al-Durr ............. 102
Shakanda, King ............ 181

Shakespear, W.H.I. .......... 296
Shamamun .............. 181
Shamanists .............. 163
Shanga .............. 185, 288
Sharif of Mecca ............ 318
Sharifs .............. 108, 265
Sharjah .................. 353
Sharkha .................. 179
Shatt-al-Arab .............. 357
Shaybani .................. 165
Shayqiyya .............. 279
Shehu Ahmadu Lobbo .... 216
Shem .................. 28
Shensi .................. 230
Shewa .................. 177
Shi'a *see* Shi'ite
Shi'ism .................. 165
Shi'ite Buwayhid ............ 74
Shi'ite caliphate .............. 69
Shi'ite dynasty .......... 51, 61
Shi'ite Fatimid .............. 81
Shi'ite (Shi'a) Muslims 65, 69, 71, 87, 137, 252, 354, 357, 358, 366, 372
Shiraz .............. 49, 237
Shirazis .................. 250
Siak .............. 241, 249, 307
Sialbet .................. 134
Siam .. 222, 249, 253, 255, 293
Siamese ......... 134, 239, 247
Sicily . 46, 56, 71, 73, 100, 207
Sidama .................. 179
Sidi Oqba .................. 37
Sidon .............. 84, 87
Sidonians .................. 10
Sierra Leone 194, 198, 202, 300
Sijilmasa .................. 54
Sijistan .................. 61, 74
Sikandar Lodi ............. 123
Sikhs .................. 115
Silk Road (Route) .......... 137
Silk Route (Road) .......... 222
Silver .................. 212
Sinai .......... 325, 347, 348, 351
Sind .......... 40, 74, 100, 123
Sindi .................. 119
Singapore . 239, 247, 249, 255, 257
Singora .................. 250
Sining .................. 226
Sinkiang .............. 226, 231

*411*

Siraf .................. 66, 187
Siripada, Sultan ............ 246
Sivas ..................... 158
Six-Day War ......... 348, 351
Slave Dynasty of Delhi .... 120
Slavery .................... 315
Slaves ................ 67, 200
Slavonia .................. 265
Slavs ...................... 67
Smyrna ............... 158, 327
Soba ..................... 174
Socotra ................... 30
Sofala ........... 183, 189, 308
Sofia ..................... 160
Sokoto .............. 216, 289
Solomon .............. 14, 105
Solomonic line ............ 177
Solomon's Israel ........... 12
Solomon's Temple ......... 14
Somali ......... 179, 190, 288
Somalia ....... 10, 12, 21, 168
Songarh .................. 123
Songhai ............ 203, 210
Songkhla ... 249, 250, 252, 253
Soppeng .................. 247
Sornau .................... 293
Sosso ..................... 205
Sousse .................... 73
South African Air Force .. 338
South Arabian Alphabet
  (Southern Semitic) ........ 30
South-East Asia ............ 216
Southern Arabia ............ 190
Southern Palestine ......... 325
Soviet Army ............... 358
Soviet Central Asia .. 358, 360
Soviet Russia .............. 392
Spain 1, 12, 39, 42, 66, 67, 71,
  73, 93, 100, 210, 212, 301, 327
Spaniards ........ 134, 259, 305
Spanish Reconquisita ...... 112
Spanish Umayyad ...... 46, 48
Sphinx ..................... 96
Sri Dharmaraja ............ 247
Sri Lanka (Ceylon) . 125, 134,
  136, 291
Sri Maharaja .............. 239
Sri Paramesvara Deva Shah ...
  239
Sri Sultan Ahmad Shah ... 241

Stanhope, Lady Hester Lucy ..
  295
State of Israel ......... 327, 381
Stephen V, Pope ............ 46
Stettin .................... 263
Strabo ..................... 21
Strait of Hormuz ........... 357
Strait of Malacca ........... 219
Strait of Tiran .............. 348
Straits Settlements ... 249, 257
Subh (Dawn) ................ 76
Subuktigin .................. 74
Suchow .................... 230
Sudan 153, 284, 302, 334, 338
Sudan-Eritrean coasts ... 8, 21
Sudanese ................... 71
Sudanis ................... 395
Suez ................. 263, 284
Suez Canal 284-287, 313, 318,
  334, 341
Suez Canal Zone ........... 347
Suez War .................. 347
Sufi ..... 53, 161, 207, 308, 390
Sufi brotherhoods .......... 390
Sufism ..................... 63
Sughd (Sogdiana) ........... 40
Suhar ...................... 66
Sukadana .............. 246, 247
Sukhothai .................. 247
Sulawesi (Celebes) .. 195, 216,
  247, 257, 304, 305, 307
Sulayman I, the Magnificent ..
  105, 225, 260, 262, 263
Sulayman ibn Qutlumish .. 88
Sulayman, Sultan .... 230, 233
Sulu archipelago ........... 257
Sulu Islands ............... 225
Sulu Sea .................. 219
Suma Orientale ....... 250, 293
Sumanguru Kante .......... 205
Sumatra ... 125, 148, 151, 216,
  219, 223, 225, 235, 237, 243-
  244, 249, 255, 257, 291, 304-
  305, 307 *and see* Java
Sumbawa .................. 216
Sumerian .................... 7
Sumero-Akkadian Cuneiform .
  30
Sumolchra ................. 291
Sunan Gresik .............. 243
Sunda Islands ............. 222
Sunda Kalapa ......... 136, 243

Sunda Shelf ............... 219
Sunda Strait .............. 219
Sundiata Kante ............ 205
Sung period ............... 228
Sungei Ujong .............. 249
Sunni Hanafi Muslims .... 387
Sunni Hanafi Uzbeks ...... 387
Sunni Islam ............ 71, 94
Sunni Muslims .... 61, 69, 231,
  252, 354, 357, 358, 366, 372
Surabaya .............. 244, 247
Surakarta ................. 305
Surveys of Eastern & Western
  Palestine ................. 295
Susa ....................... 16
Sutlej River ............... 119
Swahili city-states .......... 182
Swahili language .......... 172
Swahili poets ............. 185
Swahili traders ............ 194
Sykes-Picot Agreement .... 325
Syr Darya ................. 165
Syria 35, 48, 59, 63, 66, 71, 73,
  80, 94, 96, 102, 144, 147, 151,
  153, 158, 160-161, 189, 262,
  282, 284, 316, 318, 321, 325,
  327, 341, 351, 354, 366, 372
Syriac liturgy ............... 81
Syrian colleges ............. 270
Syrians ...... 49, 366, 370, 395

# T

Tabaristan ................. 61
Tabriz ................ 151, 158
Tadmor (Palmyra) .......... 27
Taghaza .................... 73
Tahert .................... 54
Tahirids ................... 59
Tahmasp I ................ 167
Tajikistan ........ 137, 139, 362
Tajiks ....... 231, 358, 387, 389
Tajpur .................... 123
Takedda .................. 210
Takrit .................... 158
Talamasin ................. 291
Talas .................... 225
Taliban ......... 360, 387, 395
Talleyrand ................ 212
Tallo, Prince of ........... 247
Talmudic School of Córdoba
  80
Tamachek ................. 30

Tancred .......................... 84
T'ang ...................... 226, 228
Tang annals .................... 225
Tanganyika ..................... 302
Tangier 136, 147, 151, 209, 274
Tangqut ........................ 228
Tanzania ....................... 168
Taprobana ..................... 291
Tarain .......................... 100
Tarsila ......................... 257
Ta-shih ........................ 225
Tashkent ...................... 225
Tassili 'n-Ajjer ............... 203
Tatars ......................... 296
Tatarstan ...................... 360
Tebaldi, Nicholas ........... 88
Teghazza ...................... 210
Templars from Portugal ... 93
Temple Mount (Jerusalem) .... 105
Tenasserim ............. 134, 291
Ternassari ..................... 291
Ternate ..... 134, 246, 247, 304
Tete ..................... 183, 308
Teutonic knights ............. 88
Tewodros II ................... 194
Thai palace regulations .... 247
Thai-Burmese peninsula ... 219
Thailand ................ 216, 222
Thebes .......................... 10
Thesiger, Wilfrid ............. 296
Thomas, Bertram ........... 296
Tiberias ......................... 66
Tibet ..................... 131, 233
Tibetan Muslims ............ 233
Tidore ................... 134, 247
Tigre ............................. 30
Tigrinya ......................... 30
Tigris River .......... 12, 51, 52
Tijaniyya ...................... 216
Tilapia ......................... 170
Tilbat (Tilpat) ................ 123
Tilemsi valley................. 203
Timbuktu .. 205, 210, 216, 288
Timor ....... 219, 222, 257, 304
Timur .......................... 158
Timurids ...................... 163
Timur-Leng 123, 155, 156, 160, 163
Tito, Josef ..................... 376
Titus ............................ 105

Tlemcen ............ 80, 100, 207
Tocharistan .................... 225
Togo ............................ 198
Toledo .................... 78, 114
Tonle Sap ..................... 253
Toqtomish ..................... 156
Toulouse .................. 46, 84
Tours ............................ 48
Tower of David ............. 81
Trajan .......................... 284
Trang ........................... 249
Tranggana ..................... 244
Transjordan ................... 325
Transoxiana .. 59, 61, 74, 151, 156, 165
Trans-Saharan trade ........ 12
Transylvania .......... 265, 269
Treaty of Adrianople ...... 281
Treaty of Aigun ............. 298
Treaty of Versailles, 1919 . 354
Treaty of 1899 (Kuwait/Britain) 367
Trebizond ..................... 318
Trengganu ......... 233, 241, 249
Tripoli (in Syria) ............. 84
Tripoli ... 73, 87, 93, 147, 203, 210, 271, 273
Tripolitania 73, 203, 207, 299, 334
Tripolitsa ...................... 281
Tu Wen-hsiu ........... 230, 233
Tuareg .................. 200, 214
Tuban ............. 241, 244, 304
Tuhubahahul ................. 246
Tukharistan .................... 74
Tulip Period .................. 269
Tulunids ........................ 57
Tumasik ....................... 239
Tumbatu Island ...... 155, 187
Tunb Islands ................. 357
Tunggang Parangan ........ 247
Tungi ........................... 183
Tunis .. 73, 100, 152, 207, 263, 271
Tunisia 37, 44, 56, 63, 73, 93, 100, 207, 273, 299, 341, 390
Tunisian ........................ 57
Turan ........................... 231
Turan Shah ................... 181
Turkestan ........... 40, 51, 100
Turkey 137, 141, 281, 282, 318, 341, 366, 372

Turkic language .............. 360
Turkish ............... 30, 76, 98
Turkish mercenary guards . 67
Turkish Muslim ............. 123
Turkistan (Kashgaria) .... 226, 230, 231
Turkmen ......... 358, 360, 366
Turkmenistan .. 137, 141, 142, 362
Turkoman rulers ............. 54
Turkomans ............. 189, 250
Turks .......... 44, 71, 142, 392
Tusun .......................... 276
Tutush ........................... 90
Tyre ........................ 12, 84

# U

Ubayd Allah al-Mahdi ..... 71
Uganda ................. 168, 334
Uighur Autonomous Region of Sinkiang (Xinjiang) 226, 231
Uighurs ........................ 228
Ujjain .......................... 123
Ujong Tanah ................. 247
Ukranians ..................... 142
Ulugh Beg ..................... 165
Ulugh Khan Balban ........ 120
Umar I ...... 35, 107, 110, 153
Umar Khayyam .............. 91
Umayyad ...... 32, 40, 48, 225
Umm al-Qaiwan ............. 353
Uniate bodies ................ 366
United Arab Emirates ..... 353
United Kingdom ............ 324
U.N. Resolution 242 ....... 351
UNTAET (United Nations Transitional Administration on East Timor) .......... 136
U.N. War Crimes Tribunal, the Hague ....................... 376
U.S.S.R..... 338, 351, 354, 357, 358, 370, 372
United States ... 327, 351, 357, 393
United States, war with Tripoli 274
Universities (in Middle East)... 374
Unkiar-Skelessi .............. 284
Upper Burma ................ 233
Upper Egypt ............ 73, 151
Ur .......................... 8, 14

*413*

Ural Mountains ............. 296
Urartu ........................... 1
Urban II, Pope .......... 83, 84
Ur-Semitic ...................... 30
Uthman, khalifa ............. 225
Uthman I ...................... 160
Utica ............................. 12
Uzbek National Islamic Party (Jombesh-e-Melli Islami) ..... 389
Uzbekistan ...... 137, 141, 362
Uzbeks 165, 167, 358, 360, 389

# V

Vaktil Mosque ................ 49
Valencia ......................... 78
Venetian ....................... 284
Venetians ....................... 87
Venice ... 84, 87, 94, 100, 147, 180, 207, 263, 265, 293
Viceroy of Egypt ............ 279
Victoria, Queen, Empress of India ........................ 131
Vienna, siege of ....... 263, 265
Vietnam ................ 216, 253
Vijayanagar ............ 127, 291
Visigothic ....................... 39
VOC, the Dutch East India Company ............ 304, 305
Volga .................... 147, 198
Voltaire ....................... 267
Von Chihachev, P............ 295
Von Schlozer, August Ludwig 28

# W

Wadai .................. 210, 214
Wadi al-Jawf ................. 364
Wadi Draa .................... 203
Wadi Hanifa .................. 316
Wahhabi .. 110, 269, 276, 353, 395
Wahhabis ..................... 389
Wahhabism ................... 358
Wajo' .......................... 247
Walata ........................ 205
Wallace Line ................. 219
War between Tripoli and the United States .............. 273
Wars (India, Pakistan) ..... 134
Warsaw ........................ 330
Weapons, biological, neurological, nuclear .... 369
Wellesley Province .......... 249
Wellsted, James .............. 295
West Bank ............. 348, 381
Western Africa ... 57, 198, 288
Western Arabia ................ 94
Western Arabic (alphabet) . 30
Western Sahara .............. 310
Western Semitic (Byblos) Syllabic Alphabet ......... 30
Western Siberia .............. 137
Western Timor ............... 304
White Russian ............... 360
Wilayet of Baghdad ........ 372
Wilayet of Basra ............ 372
William IV of Orange ..... 257
Wilson, Thomas Woodrow .... 331
Wingate, Orde, Major ..... 336
World Trade Center ........ 393
WRPYWL (Awarfiula) .... 173

# X

Xian ............................ 222
Xinjiang ....................... 231

# Y

Yaghmorasan ................ 100
Yakub Beg .................... 231
Yala ..................... 249, 252
Yanbu ......................... 276
Yangchow .............. 226, 228
Yangon ........................ 233
Yao ............................. 308
Ya'qub ibn al-Layth al Saffar . 61
Yaqut ........................... 67
Yarmuk ......................... 32
Yathrib ........................ 110
Yazid I ibn Abi-Sufyan ..... 32
Yazid II ......................... 42
Year of the Elephant ....... 25
Yekuno Amlak .............. 177
Yemen . 12, 25, 30, 48, 63, 66, 80, 146, 151, 209, 250, 341, 362, 374, 386
Yezidis (Manichaeans) .... 366
Yiddish ........................ 366
Yihon (Narathiwat) ........ 249
Yiring .................... 249, 252
Yohannes I ............. 192, 194
Yom Kippur .................. 351
York ............................ 107
Yoruba ........................ 205
Yuan dynasty see Mongol Yuan dynasty
Yung-hui ...................... 225
Yunnan 226, 228, 230, 233, 241

# Z

Zagros Mountains ............. 1
Zagwe .......................... 177
Zaïre ........................... 187
Zallaca .......................... 80
Zambezi ....................... 183
Zambia ........................ 168
Zamzam ................. 27, 108
Zanata .................... 73, 100
Zangi ............................ 94
Zanzibar .. 144, 155, 168, 182, 187, 288, 300, 302
Zara Yaqob ................... 179
Zarathustra (Zoroaster) ...... 1
Zaydites .................. 63, 366
Zayn al-'Abidin .............. 246
Zaytun ........................ 228
Zeila ........ 151, 179, 189, 250
Ziggurat .......................... 7
Zihar (Dhar) .................. 123
Zimbabwe .................... 183
Zionism ....................... 366
Zionist movement .... 327, 345
Zionists ....................... 331
Zirid ............................. 73
Ziyadat-Allah I ............... 46
Ziyanid ........................ 100
Zoroastrian ... 61, 65, 66, 366

www.ingramcontent.com/pod-product-compliance
Lightning Source LLC
Chambersburg PA
CBHW082022300426
44117CB00015B/2316